National Intelligencer Newspaper Abstracts 1859

Joan M. Dixon

HERITAGE BOOKS
2009

HERITAGE BOOKS
AN IMPRINT OF HERITAGE BOOKS, INC.

Books, CDs, and more—Worldwide

For our listing of thousands of titles see our website at
www.HeritageBooks.com

Published 2009 by
HERITAGE BOOKS, INC.
Publishing Division
100 Railroad Ave. #104
Westminster, Maryland 21157

Copyright © 2009 Joan M. Dixon

All rights reserved. No part of this book may be reproduced or transmitted in any form or by any means, electronic or mechanical, including photocopying, recording or by any information storage and retrieval system without written permission from the author, except for the inclusion of brief quotations in a review.

International Standard Book Numbers
Paperbound: 978-0-7884-4792-1
Clothbound: 978-0-7884-8064-5

NATIONAL INTELLIGENCER NEWSPAPER WASHINGTON, D C 1859

TABLE OF CONTENTS

Daily National Intelligencer. Washington, D C, 1859: pg 1

Acts passed at last session of Congress: pgs 93-94
Agriculturalists: pg 5
Appointments by the President: pg 31
Army officers: pg 190
Birthplace of Gen Andrew Jackson: pgs 66; 148
Certificates of indebtedness [name and amount]: pg 10
Clipper ship Pomona disaster: pg 168

Commencements:	Columbian College: pgs 95; 213
	Gtwn College: pg 215
	Medical Dept-Gtwn College: pg 101
	National Medical College, Wash: pg 95
	Naval Academy: pgs 192-193
	Princeton College of N J: pg 213
	St John's, Annapolis, Md: pg 243
	St Mary's, Chas Co, Md: pg 256
	West Point: pg 167
	Yale College: pg 236

Death of Hon Henry L Ellsworth: pgs 1; 6
Death of Brvt Brig Gen Archibald Henderson: pg 15
Death of Edward Hudson, U S N: pgs 36; 87
Death of Washington Irving: pg 348
Death of Francis, son of Philip Barton Key: pg 13
Death of Col Francis Lee: pg 34
Death of James Maher, public gardener: pg 138
Death of Don F Melchoir-Hong Kong: pg 40
Death of Horatio Gates Phillips: pg 361
Death of Wm Hickling Prescott: pg 40
Death of Susan B Ringgold: pg 1
Death of Bertram Arthur Talbot: pg 116
Death of Ira J Thurston, Aeronaut: pg 100

Disasters to our Navy, 1798 to 1859: pgs 238-240

Emperor Napoleon reception-Americans present: pg 73

Fire Insurance Co of Alexandria: pg 84
First Things: pg 104
FeeJee Islands-murder and canabalism: pg 161

Geo and Martha Washington, N Y C, Jan 1790: pg 4
George Washington's First Love: pg 282
Harper's Ferry: see index

Jennings Estate: pg 187
John Quincy Adams' chair: pg 81
Jurors, Washington City: pgs 22; 99; 128; 129; 130-131; 202; 352

Marine Corp appointments: pg 82
Methodist Episcopal appointments: pg 103
Midshipmen: pgs 192-193; 218
Military Academy appointments: pg 111
Mount Vernon Estate: pg 232
Mount Vernon Ladies Association: pgs 14; 188; 367
Naval Engineers: pg 262

Officers of the: Frig St Lawrence: pg 161
                   Frig Wabash: pg 362
                   Sloop-of-war Brooklyn: pg 288
                   Sloop-of-war Dale: pg 175
                   Sloop-of-war St Mary's: pg 105
                   Steamer Fulton: pgs 152; 283

Officers of the Washington Corp: pgs 55-60
Officers/soldiers of the War of 1812: see index
Old Sailors: pgs 288; 289
Old Soldiers: pgs 283; 294
Oldest Church: pg 265
Orphans Court-James Dixon: pg 123

Paraquay steamers converted into Men of War: pg 261
Promotions in the U S Army: pgs 112; 222-223

Revolutionary pensioners-Conn: pg 257

Revolutionary Soldiers: pgs 26; 244; 257

St Aloysius Catholic Church: pgs 169; 301; 301; 307; 325
St Vincent Female Orphan Asylum picnic managers: pgs 229-230
Statement of appropriations: pgs 154-156
Steamboat St Nicholas' disaster: pgs 147; 164; 171; 177
Steamer Indian disaster: pg 347
Steamer Princess disaster: pgs 97; 106; 107

Tax sale of Gtwn, D C property: pgs 304-306
Tornado, Morgan Co, Ill: pgs 186-187
Train disaster-Alexandria: pg 250
Train disaster-Chicago: pgs 210-211
Train disaster-Georgia: pgs 2-3
Train disaster-South Bend: pg 209
Trial of Capt Cook, Charleston: pg 321
Trial of Danl E Sickles for the murder of Philip Barton Key: see index

Washington City property sold for taxes: pgs 43-55
Wichita Expedition casualties: pg 180
Will of the late Wm W Cox: pg 178
William and Mary College, Va: pgs 70; 76; 85
Women of the Revolution-pensioned: pg 341

Index: pg 373

Dedicated to my cousin Robert Paul Neff,
b 1927, Wash, D C; mrd 1956, Wash, D C
Mary Catherine Daw, b 1933, Gtwn, D C

PREFACE
Daily National Intelligencer Newspaper Abstracts
1859
Joan M Dixon

The National Intelligencer & Washington Advertiser is hereafter the Daily National Intelligencer. It was the first newspaper printed in Washington, D C; Samuel H Smith, the originator. The same was transferred to Jos Gales, jr on Aug 31, 1810; on Nov 1, 1812, the paper was under the firm of Jos Gales, sr, & Wm W Seaton. The Library of Congress has microfilm of the paper from the first issue of Oct 31, 1800 thru Jan 8, 1870, the final paper. The Evening Star Newspaper of Jan 10, 1870 reports: The Intelligencer is discontinued: the proprietor, Mr Alex Delmar, says that having lost several thousand dollars, & being in poor health, he has resolved to discontinue its publication.

Included in the abstracts are advertisements; appointments by the President; Hse o/Rep petitions; passed Acts; legal notices; marriages; deaths; mscl notices; social events; military promotions; court cases; deaths by accident; & maritime information-officers-crews. Items or events which might be a clue as to the location, age or relationship of an individual are copied.

No attempt has been made to correct the spelling. Due to the length of some articles, it was necessary to present only the highlights of same. Chancery and Equity records are copied as written.

The index contains all surnames and *tracts of lands/places*. **Maritime vessels** are found under barge, boat, brig, frig, schn'r, ship, sloop, steamboat, tugboat, yacht or vessel.

ABBREVIATIONS:

AA CO	ANNE ARUNDEL COUNTY
CMDER	COMMANDER
CMDOR	COMMODOR
ELIZ	ELIZABETH
ELIZA	ELIZA
MONTG CO	MONTGOMERY COUNTY
PG CO	PRINCE GEORGE'S CO
WASH, D C	WASHINGTON, DISTRICT OF COLUMBIA

BOOKS IN THE NATIONAL INTELLIGENCER NEWSPAPER SERIES: 1800-1805/1806-1810/1811-1813/1814-1817/1818-1820/1821-1823/1824-1826/1827-1829/1830-1831/1832-1833/1834-1835/1836-1837/1838-1839/1840/1841/1842/1843/1844/1845/1846/1847/ 1848/1849/ 1850/1851/1852/1853/1854/1855/1856/1857/1858/59. SPECIAL: CIVIL WAR 2 VOLS, 1861-1865

DAILY NATIONAL INTELLIGENCER NEWSPAPER
1859

SAT JAN 1, 1859
Obit-died: on Dec 27, Hon Henry L Ellsworth, at his residence, in his 68th year. He was twin brother to Hon Wm W Ellsworth, formerly Govn'r & now Judge of the Supreme Court of Errors of Conn; & the two were the youngest children of Hon Oliver Ellsworth, 2nd Chief Justice of the U S. He graduated at Yale College in 1810; studied law; was appointed by Gen Jackson as Resident Com'r among the Indian tribes to the south & west of Arkansas; two years later he was called to Wash, & placed at the head of the U S Patent Ofc; about 10 years later, he resigned & established himself at Lafayette, Indiana, in the purchase & settlement of U S lands, & resided there until about 2 years ago, when, in consequence of declining health, he removed to his native State.

The anniversary of the Landing of the Pilgrims was celebrated in a spirited manner at Charleston, S C, on Dec 22. Dr F M Robertson was the orator of the day, & Wm Gregg toasted the projector & successful founder of manufactures in S C.

Obit-died: on Nov 10, Susan B Ringgold, relict of the late Thos Lee Ringgold, U S Army, & only child of Hon A P Upshur, who, at the time of his sudden death, on board the ship **Princeton** in 1844, was filling the high ofc of Sec of State. After this sad event the subject of this memoir, with her mother, retired to her native home in Va, where she remained in strict seclusion till her return to our midst a bonnie bride. Let us think of her, not as lying in cold, quiet *Oak Hill*, but as she is, in Paradise, singing, with husband, father, children, the song of the lab forever.
–Christmas, 1858 -S

John S McKenney, was on Thu last elected Cashier of the Patriotic Bank of Wash, in place of Chauncey Bestor, who has faithfully filled the ofc for nearly 20 years, & who lately resigned it to retire to private life.

Died: on Dec 31, M Rufino Zappone, 2nd son of Americus & Margaret Ann Zappone, aged 2 years & 2 months. His funeral is Sun afternoon at 2½ o'clock, from the residence of his parents, 53 Pa ave, Wash.

Boston, Dec 31. Geo French, formerly first ofcr, & Wm Meeks, 2nd mate of the ship **Waverley**, who were condemned to 10 years' imprisonment for endeavoring to suppress a mutiny in which many coolies were killed, at Manilla, have been liberated through the intercession of Minister Dodge, at Madrid.

Atlanta, Ga, Dec 31. Mr Webb, a bailiff, was shot & killed today by W A Choice. The excitement is at a high pitch.

Augusta, Ga, Dec 31. The morning train from Columbus for Macon ran off the track at Odum's Mills, where the culvert washed away, & J H Miller, engineer, fireman, wood-passer, & W H Snell were killed. 2nd dispatch: the following bodies have been recovered: 2 Misses Guiees, of Salem, Ala; W H Snell, a train hand; a lady & 3 children of Texas; two ladies of Columbus. Those saved: Dr Walker, of Columbus; Dr Phillips, of Ala; S W Blake, of N Y; Conductor Snell, a gentleman from Texas, another from Ala, & 4 others, whose names & residences have not been ascertained. Among the killed are believed to be Thos O'Bryan, of Charleston; W P Dupece, of Houston Co, Laura West, Georgia Van Ness, & Celeste Sharp. [Jan 3rd newspaper: Killed: Mrs Leveritt & 3 children, of Rapides parish, La; Mrs Smith, of Texas; two Misses Guys, of Ala; Mr Miller, engineer; Mr Bucke, fireman; Mr W H Snell, train hand of Columbus. All these bodies have been recovered except the infant & Mrs Leveritt. The racehorse Moidore was on the train & was lost. The cars fell about 30 feet, breaking them into fragments & throwing the passengers into the stream. The first reports were much exaggerated.]

Circuit Court of Wash Co, D C-in Equity, No 1,415. Eliz Braiden, vs Richd Smith et al. This suit is to perfect the title & procure the sale of a part of lot 13 in square 319 in Wash City. On Nov 9, 1841, John P Van Ness leased to Sarah A Payne all that part of lot 13 of square 319, Wash City, for & during the space & term of 7 years, commencing for the same on Oct 1, 1841, at the yearly rent of $50, payable semi-annually; & that there was incorporated in the said lease, an agreement that said Sarah A Payne & her assigns might at any time during said term purchase the fee simple in said premises for $800. That afterwards, about Jun 6, 1843, said Sarah A Payne agreed to purchase said premises for $800 & having made part payment thereof, subsequently sold & assigned said lease & agreement to cmplnt, who as such assignee, made payment on account of said purchase money to said Van Ness. That said Van Ness died in May, 1846, intestate, leaving Cornelius P Van Ness, Gertrude Hoffman, [intermarried with Martin H Hoffman,] Peter Van Ness Van Allen, Matilda E Van Ness, Chas W Van Ness, Edw Van Ness, & Eugene Van Ness his heirs at law. That at the death of said John P Van Ness there was yet due of said purchase money the sum of $200, with interest from Oct 1, 1844. That after the death of said John P Van Ness, Cornelius P Van Ness took out letters of administration on his estate, & the cmplnt paid to him the amount due of said purchase money, with interest. That at the death of said Cornelius P Van Ness, letters of administration, de bonis non, on the estate of said Cornelius P Van Ness were granted by the proper authority to Eugene Van Ness. That said Cornelius P Van Ness, by his will, duly made & executed, devised all his real estate in Wash City to his daughter Christina, giving his wife, Madelina Van Ness, also an interest therein. That by sundry conveyances from the heirs-at-law of said John P Van Ness, their devisees & assigns, all the real estate of which he died seized was vested in Richd Smith, upon certain trusts, among others in trust to fulfill such contracts or assignments if any made & entered into by said John P Van Ness, for the sale & conveyance of any part or parcel of said property. That said Martin H Hoffman

& Gertrude his wife are now deceased, & that all their interest in said estate is now vested in Wm H Philip. That said Peter Van Ness Van Allen has since died intestate. The bill further states that said Eliz Braiden died intestate in Oct, 1856, leaving said cmplnt & Eliz McCollum, Catharine B Scott, Margaret L Scott, Edwin Saunders, Laura Saunders, Albert B Saunders, & John M Saunders, her heirs at law. That said parcel of land is not susceptible of partition, & that it will be for the interest of all parties concerned that the said should be sold. And it appearing that Matilda E Van Ness, Chas W Van Ness, Edgar Van Ness, Eugene Van Ness, Madelina Van Ness, Christina Van Ness, Catharine D Philip, Eliz McCollum, Catharine B Scott, Mgt L Scott, Edwin Saunders, Laura Saunders, Albert B Saunders, & John M Saunders are non-residents. Absent dfndnts are to appear at the ofc of the Clerk of the Circuit Court of Wash Co, D C on the first Monday of May, 1859. –Wm M Merrick, Assist Judge -Jno A Smith, clerk [Jan 5th newspaper: this same Equity-No 1,415, can be found under: Margaret Lyons vs Richd Smith et al.]

MON JAN 3, 1859

Circuit Court of D C-in Chancery. Morris Adler, cmplnt, vs Alex'r Ray, John Davidson, Robt E Clary, & others, dfndnts. The cmplnt, as trustee under a decree of the said court, did, on Sep 4, 1855, offer for sale, at auction, those parts of lots 32 thru 35, in the original plan of Gtwn, D C, & lots 43 & 44, & part of lot 45, on south side of Water st, in Gtwn, of which Allan Scott, died seized; that at said sale Alex'r Ray was the purchaser of the said parcels of land, for $6,000; that he complied with the terms of sale prescribed, & paid to the cmplnt, in hand, one-fourth of said purchase money, & gave him his 3 notes for the residue thereof, date Sep 4, 1855, each for $1,500, bearing interest from the date thereof, & payable severally in 8, 16, & 24 months from said date, that said Ray paid the first of the said notes, but has failed & neglected to pay the said two notes falling due at the end of 16 & 24 months as aforesaid, & judgments have been obtained against him for the amounts thereof respectively, on the common law side of the said court, with interest thereon & cost to suit; that he believes the said Ray has no property, real or personal, out of which the said debt can be made; that he has retained the title to said premises, & is advised that said debt is an equitable lean thereon, & he has a right to have the same sold for the payment of the said debt. The bill states that the said Ray, by his deed, dated Oct 17, 1858, after reciting that he was indebted to Robt E Clary & others, severally, who are made dnfdnts in said case, in divers sums of money, as stated in said deed, did grant & convey to John Davidson, his heirs & assignees, all his, the said Ray's, right & property in the said parcels of land, in trust to secure to the said named creditors the sums of money stated to be owing to them severally. The object of the bill of cmplnt is to obtain a decree for the sale of the said parcels of land, for the payment of said debt & interest thereon & cost of suit, as shown by the said recited judgments; & for as much as it appears that the said Robt E Clary is not a resident of D C, & cannot be found therein, he is warned to appear in this court on the first Monday of May next. –Jas S Morsell, Assist Judge -Jno A Smith, clerk

N Y C, Dec 31, 1858. Michl Cancemi, the Sicilian, who, after a 4th trial for the murder of a policemen, was lately convicted of manslaughter in the first degree, yesterday was sentenced to imprisonment & hard labor at Sing Sing for the term of his natural life.

The Alexandria Gazette commences today its 60th year. It was established in 1800 by the father of the present senior editor. [No name given.]

Died: on Dec 31, in Gtwn, D C, after a long & painful illness, Vincent J Taylor, in his 47th year. He was esteemed & beloved by all who knew him. May he rest in peace!

TUE JAN 4, 1859
N Y C, Jan 1, 1859. Jan 1, 1790. Gen Washington, in the first year of his Presidency under the new Constitutioon, in 1789, resided at the Franklin House, at the head of Cherry st. On New Year's Day, 1790, the snow of yesterday gave way to rain that morning, and the skies cleared away & gave them a fresh & delightful afternoon. He was waited upon by the principal gentlemen of that city. In the evening Mrs Washington took her levee. Introduced by the aids & gentlemen in waiting, after taking their seats, tea, coffee, plain & plum cake were served round. When the hall clock struck nine, Mrs Washington, an undersized & rather portly personage, plain in her attire, rose with great dignity, & looking complacently around the circle, observed, "The General always retires at nine, & I usually precede him." At this signal the ladies instantly rose, adjusted their dress, & after paying their respects, retired.

Hon Jeremiah Clemens, formerly U S Senator from Alabama, has assumed the editorship of the Memphis [Tenn] Eagle & Enquirer. –Times

Saml Cargill & Chas F Bunker were instantly killed on Friday at the Print Works in Manchester, N H, when they were literally torn to pieces between the large wheels of the mill & a post. Bunker was showing Cargill how to make the nightly examination of the wheels, & it is supposed that Bunker was caught in the wheel first, & Cargill, in trying to save him, was caught. Bunker was 22 & Cargill 42. They both leave families.

Criminal Court-Wash, Monday: 1-Gus Gasenheimer found guilty on a charge of larceny of 3 pairs of boots. 2-Terence Corrigan again arraigned for larceny of a quantity of iron from the new gashouse in west Washington: case not tried-inability to procure a jury.

Mrd: on Jan 2, by Rev Andrew G Carothers, Mr John M Maxwell to Miss Eliz Crouse, both of Wash City.

Convocation of Agriculturists from various parts of the Union assembled at the Patent Ofc yesterday upon the invitation of the Com'r of Patents.
Hon Marshall P Wilder, of Mass, chosen Pres.
Ben Perley Poore, of Mass, chosen Sec.
Maine: Dr Ezekiel Holmes
Mass: Hon Marshall P Wilder, Dr Chas T Jackson, Ben Perley Poore.
N H: Levi Bartlett
Vt: Fred'k Holbrook.
N Y: Wm Lawton, Col C C Morrell, Rev A Brown.
Pa: Jas Gowen, Hon J C G Kennedy, Hon John H Ewing, W P Shattuck.
Dela: Ex-Govn'r Geo H Ross
Md: Clement Hill, Joel Blew, Chas B Calvert.
Dist of Columbia: W W Corcoran, Jonathan Seaver, J C Lewis, Dr Chas G Page, Joshua Pierce, E Harte, E Kingman.
Va: Col Wm Garrett, Lewis Bayley.
S C: Jas G Holmes, Hon J H Hammond.
Indian Territory: Col P P Pitchlyn
Texas: W T Mecklin.
Indiana: Hon D P Halloway, Hon E Case.
Ill: Dr John H Kennicutt, Dr L S Pennington.
Mich: Hon H L Stevens
Minn: Dr T T Mann, Hon W W Phelps, J J Noah.
Ohio: F G Carey.
Wisc: Gustavus De Neven.
Calif: A W McRee.
Nevada: Col Jas M Crane.
Oregon: Hon Delazon Smith.
New Mexico: Hon Manuel A Otero

Isabella Burns, the youngest sister of the poet, more generally known as Mrs Begg, died recently at her cottage near Ayr, in her 88th year. Her husband, dying in 1813, left her with a family of 9 children. She had an income of about $100 a year, & maintained herself & family by teaching & sewing. After a number of years an annual pension of 10 pounds was granted to her, & in 1842, a subscription was raised amounting to 400 pounds, part of which, being invested in an annuity, died with her, the remainder going to her children.

For sale: **Nonsuch**, a valuable improved farm, near Wash City, about 2 miles from the Navy Yard Bridge, on the road leading to Upper Marlboro, containing 664 acres, more or less; the dwlg is a comfortable 2 story frame bldg in good repair, & the out-bldgs & Mill, with permanent horsepower, are in tolerable order. The manager, Mr Rowland, will show the same. Apply to the subscriber, 435 6th st, & to John C Brent, atty-at-law, west wing of the City Hall. –Geo W Young

Died: on Jan 1, of congestion of the brain, Mary, youngest child of Jas B & Henrietta Dodson, aged 23 months & 12 days.

In Chancery, Va: Circuit Court of Highland Co, Oct term, 1858. Jacob P Keister & wife, plnts, vs Robt Lockridge's heirs, etc, dfndnts. Notice to John Lockridge, son of Robt Lockridge, deceased, formerly of Bath Co, Va, or, in case of his death, to the widow & children of said John Lockridge, if any, that he or they appear here at the next term of this Court to assert his or their claim, as distributee or distributees, or heir or heirs at law of said Robt Lockridge, deceased. --A Stephenson, clerk

Hartford, Conn, Jan 3. The late H L Ellswoth bequeathed all of his property, excepting $100,000, to Yale College. It is supposed that the College will thus obtain $700,000.
[Jan 6th newspaper: the provisions of the will: $25,000 in trust to his son, Henry W Ellsworth; $25,000 to his daughter, wife of Roswell Smith; $25,000 to the heirs of his son, Edw; $1,500 annually to his wife. The remainder, about $700,000, to Yale College. This sum amounts to more probably than the present entire worth of that corporation.]
[Jan 14th newspaper: New Haven News states that the will of Hon Henry L Ellsworth is to be contested, & adds that for several years his mind has not been sufficiently strong to enable him to transact business without aid.]

Berkeley Springs, Va, 129 miles west of Balt. The undersigned wishes to sell his boarding establishment at this place. --John Strother, Martinsburg, Va.

WED JAN 5, 1859
Senate: 1-Bill introduced for the relief of Isaac S K Ogier, judge of the U S district court for the southern district of Calif. 2-Joint resolution authorizing the settlement of the accounts of Roderick McKee. 3-Ptn from Lt J B Moeller, in relation to his transfer from the furlough to the leave pay list: referred. 4-Ptn from Wm Maxwell Wood, surgeon in the navy, asking to be allowed traveling expenses incurred under order of his commanding ofcr: referred. 5-Ptn from Wm Hazzard Wigg, asking the withdrawal of his grandfather's papers from the Court of Claims, & that they be sent to the Cmte on Revolutionary Claims. 6-Ptn from the widow of C B White, asking to be allowed a pension: referred.

The latest intelligence from ex-Pres Pierce is dated at Naples, Dec 2, 1858, where he had remained a week, but was then making preparation, in obedience to medical advice, go to the Island of Capri, for the benefit of Mrs Pierce, the state of whose health, her friends will be pained to learn, is far from encouraging. She has suffered much from the damp cold air of Florence & its surroundings.

Henry Lane, of Acton, Canada West, came to his death on Sat at Toronto, when his lamp set fire to the bed, he being too intoxicated to help himself.

House of Reps: 1-Cmte of Claims: bill for the relief of Capt John B Montgomery: committed. Same cmte: bill for the relief of Geo W Wood: committed. Same cmte: bill for the relief of Saml H Taylor: committed. Same cmte: bill for the relief of Wm Money: committed. Same cmte: bill for the relief of Jeremiah Moors: committed. Same cmte: bill for the relief of Tench Tilghman: committed. 2-Cmte on Public Lands: bill for the relief of David Moors, father & heir at law of Timothy Moors, deceased: committed. Same cmte: bill to authorize the Sec of the Interior to issue a land warrant to Benj Ward: committed. Same cmte: bill for the relief of Wm Packwood: committed. 3-Cmte on Revolutionary Claims: bill for the relief of Maryett Van Buskirk: committed. 4-Cmte on Indian Affairs: bill for the relief of Willis A Gorman: committed. Same cmte: bill for the relief of Geo Stealy: committed. 5-Cmte on Military Affairs: bill for the relief of the heirs or legal reps of Jean Hudry: committed. Same cmte: bill further explaining the act for the relief of Adam D Stewart & Alex'r Randall, exc of Danl Randall: committed. Same cmte: bill for the relief of the firm of Alden & Williams: committed. 6-Cmte of Claims: bill for the relief of Aaron H Palmer: committed. Same cmte: bill for the relief of Jane J Wingerd: committed. Same cmte: bill for the relief of Miles Devine: committed. Same cmte: bill for the relief of the heirs-at-law of the late Abigail Nason, sister & devisee of John Lord, deceased: committed. 7-Cmte on Invalid Pensions: bill granting an invalid pension to Jos McReynolds: committed. Same cmte: bill granting a invalid pension to Andulotia Pier; to Henry F Bowers; to John O'Leary; to Michl Hanson; to Anselmn Clarkson, of Mo; & Wm T Broaddus, of Va: committed. Same cmte: bill granting a pension to Mary J Maddox; to Sarah Blackwell; to Gregory Patti: committed. Same cmte: bill for the relief of Ebenezer Ricker: committed. 8-Memorial of Mrs Phebe Ann Shockley, widow of Nehemiah Shockley, praying Congress to grant her a pension for services of her husband in the Florida war: referred. 9-Ptn of Gilbert Cooper, of Madison Co, Ill, praying an increase of his pension: referred.

Mr Hugh Frazer Grant, a large rice planter of Glynn Co, was awakened on Dec 25 by an alarm of fire, which accidentally broke out on his premises. His estimated loss is $15,000. –Savannah Rep

Yesterday, at the boarding-house of Mrs Holmead, on 4½ st, Mr Lewis E Grant, of Louisiana, committed suicide by taking prussic acid. He was about 30 years of age, & a clerk in the Navy Dept. He once held the post of colonel in the Mexican service, under Comonfort's administration.

Criminal Court-Wash-Mon. 1-Thos Parker, Saml Spalding, Jos Parrish, & Dennis Magee, charged with riot in Gtwn & resistance to the police: sentenced to 6 months imprisonment in the county jail & a fine of $5.

Mrd: on Dec 29, in Fluvanna Co, Va, by Rev Mr Blackwell, Edw C Edmonds, of Fauquier Co, to Maggie S Tutwiler, daughter of Col M Tutwiler.

Election on Monday in the ofc of the Wash Gas Light Co of the following directors to serve the present year: G W Riggs, Wm G Freeman, & John W Thompson, representing the stockholders of Wash City, & Wm L Gaw & Chas W Rogers, of Phil.

Circuit Court of Wash Co, D C-in Equity 1,388. John F Boone vs Wm C Boone & others. The trustee reported he sold the south half of lot 12 in square 406, in Wash City, to Richd Ela for $5,950, & that the purchaser hath complied with the terms of said sale. -Jno A Smith, clerk

THU JAN 6, 1859
Excellent household & kitchen furniture at auction on Jan 12, at the residence of Dr Tyson, 398 10th st, at I north. -A Green auct

The undersigned trustees of the Circuit Court of D C , passed on Dec 7, 1858, in a cause between John Hooper & others as cmplnts & Wm Bird's heirs & other dfndnts, No 1,202 in equity, will, on Feb 1, 1859, at public auction sell the following property, [or so much & such parts thereof as may be necessary for the payment of the debts of said Wm Bird] in Wash, D C, in lot 14, in square 388, fronting on south F, between 9th & 10th sts west, with improvements thereon; lots 7 & 8 in square 356; lots A, B, E, G, K, & L, in Bird's subdivision of square 463, fronting on 6th st west, south C st, & Md ave, & part of the original lot No ?, in said square 463, with improvement, lots nos 13 & 14 in square 636, on south Capitol, near south B st.
–Wm H Ward, Wm R Woodward, trustees -A Green auct

Senate: 1-Cmte of Finance: from the Court of Claims, the papers of Fred'k Vincent, exc of the estate of Lecaze & Mallet, as called for by resolution of the Senate. 2-Ptn from A G Miller, urging the importance of a law to authorize the district courts of the U S to appoint com'rs: referred. 3-Ptn from Wm Henry Brisbane, formerly of the State of S C, urging the enactment of a law by which all negroes born in the U S, & not convicted of crime, may become citizens of the U S: referred. 4-Ptn from Wm Richmond, a soldier in the war of Mexico, asking a pension: referred. 5-Cmte on the Military Affairs: memorial of Fannie White, widow of a military storekeeper, asked to be discharged from its further consideration, & that it be referred to the Cmte on Pensions: which was agreed to.

The venerable Jas Brown, jr, long the Second Auditor of the State of Va, died at Richmond on Monday, from the effects of an injury he sustained a few days since at the depot of the Richmond & Fredericksburg railroad, in which his ankle & foot were severely wounded by the wheels of the locomotive as it left the depot.

Last Fri, at Atlanta, Ga, Calvin Webb, a city bailiff, was murdered by Wm A Choice. The previous day the deceased arrested Choice on a bail for $10, & on Fri they met on the street when Choice drew a pistol, fired twice, & killed Webb on the spot.

The Hong Kong correspondent of the London News, writing on Oct 29th says: The news of the death of the Emperor of Japan is confirmed. He died of cholera, which disease was carrying off great numbers. The Emperor of Japan being childless, before his death adopted Foer-tsigo, Prince of Ku-sin, aged 16 years, as his child & successor. [Jan 11th newspaper: The Dutch physician, residing in Japan, said the Emperor died of dropsy in the chest. The name of the Emperor was Casaduco. He died on Sep 16. He was 36 years old & had 12 wives. Some say he had no sons. My interpreter said he had one who is between 15 & 16 years old, & who has ascended to the throne. Widows nor daughters are allowed to succeed a deceased Emperor. On the failure to have a son, he is permitted to adopt any one of his pleasure. This young Emperor just concluded a fair, liberal & honorable treaty with the U S, & opened his empire to the return of Christianity, after it had been expelled above two centuries.]

House of Reps: 1-Message received announcing the death of Gen John A Quitman, late a member of the House from the State of Mississippi, since the adjournment of the last session. He died on Jul 17, 1858, at his residence in Mississippi. He was of that opinion himself that his disease was contracted at the Nat'l Hotel in Wash City, from an infection which prevailed there 2 years ago from an unknown cause, where he resided for a time, & was afterwards accustomed to accept the hospitality of his friends. Gen Quitman was a native of N Y, born at Rhinebeck, Dutchess Co, on Sep 1, 1799, & was 59 years of age at the time of his death. He was of German descent, his father, Dr Fred'k Henry Quitman, being a native of Prussia, of German origin, &, after his removal to this country, an officiating minister of the Evangelical Lutheran Church at Rhinebeck. Gen Quitman was himself educated in the ministry; but, pursued the profession of the law; at age 21 he left his paternal homestead to seek his fortune for himself, &, emigrating to the West, remained 2 years in the State of Ohio & became a licensed practitioner of the law. He removed to the State of Mississippi to pursue his profession; & in 1822 settled at Natchez, where in 1824 he was married to the accomplished Miss Turner, the present Mrs Quitman, who, with an interesting family, still survives him. In 1827 he was elected a member of the Judiciary Cmte.

The Petersburg [Va] Intelligencer has been sold to Mr Albion K Moore, once one of the editors & proprietors of the Savannah Republican.

Fire in Gtwn yesterday: first house burnt was owned by Mr B Forrest, the other by Mr F Lutz, of Wash. Fire originated in the grocery store of Mr Geo Bohrer, Gay & High sts. Everything was completely destroyed. The adjoining frame occupied by Mr Boyd as a tin-worker's establishment & Mr Shaffer as a boot & shoe factory was also consumed, with much loss to the occupants.

Mrd: on Dec 23, in Wash City, by Rev C C Meador, Mr Wm Winkler to Miss Fanny Jones, all of Wash City.

Mrd: on Jan 4, in Wash City, at the McKendree Parsonage by Rev Mr Ball, Mr Lewis W Trumbo to Miss Mary S Wroe, all of Wash.

Wash Corp: Mayor's Ofc, Jan 3, 1859. In compliance with resolutions of the Board of Alderman, of Dec 27, 1858, herewith enclosed is a statement containing the certificates of indebtedness issued under act of Sep 8, 1858, all of which are still outstanding & remain unpaid. –Jas G Berret, Mayor Statement showing the date, amount, & to whom issued, of Certificates of Indebtedness: [Oct, 1858]

John Fletcher: $700	Wash Gas Light Co: $3,100.
Wm Tucker: $300.	Wm H Jones: $600.
John Chapman: $1,500.	Robt Payne: $5,700.
John McCollum: $600.	S J Degges: $800.
Thos W Burch: $1,200.	J B Greenwell: $1,000.
Wm Fletcher: $1,500.	P O'Callaghan: $1,200.
John W Tucker: $700.	Saml Curson: $200.
F A A Schneider: $200.	Geo W Eslin: $4,100.
Chas Stewart: $1,500.	Thos Lewis: $100.
J J McCollum: $3,100.	Robt Costello: $700.
Dennis Looney: $3,500.	Patrick Maguire: $1,050.
P Scanlon & Co: $300.	John Agnew: $1,200.
Walter Linkins: $6,400.	Patrick Buckley: $800.
Geo Neitzey: $1,450.	Thos McNaney: $900.
Thos J Barrett: $2,700.	Michl Cullinan: $500.
E E Barnes: $500.	

Died: on Dec 27, at his residence, **Lebanon**, on West river, Md, John Thomas, a gentleman highly respected in the community in which he resided.

Died: on Jan 5, in Wash City, Mrs Mary B, wife of Silas H Hill, aged 47. Her funeral is on Fri at 2 o'clock, from her late residence, E & 6th sts.

FRI JAN 7, 1859
Mr Cass, late American Minister at Rome, took leave of the Pope, & presented Mr Stockton as his successor, on Nov 28th. The Pope sent him next day a marble bust of himself as a testimonial of his regard.

Chancery sale: by decree of the Circuit Court of Wash Co, D C, made in the cause of Wheatley & Walker et al, vs Wm Collins' heirs & administrator: public auction on Jan 28, on the premises, lot 16 in square 28, with an old frame dwlg.
–Walter S Cox, trustee -Jas C McGuire & Co, aucts

John Hancock, a nephew of the Revolutionary patriot of that name, died at Boston on Jan 2, aged 85 years.

Excellent household & kitchen furniture at auction Jan 25, at the residence of Robt Cochran, jr, B st, between 13th & 13½ sts west. –Andrew Wylie, trustee -A Green auct

Senate: 1-Ptn from Peter Tyler, asking the aid of Gov't in enforcing his claims against Peru: referred. 2-Ptn from the widow of Col Josiah Snelling, asking to be allowed a pension: referred. 3-Additional papers presented in support of the claim of the widow of Cmdor Perry to a pension: referred. 4-Ptn from Wm Young, asking the establishment of an additional daily mail between N Y & Boston: referred. 5-Ptn from Thos G Rathbone, asking indemnity for spoliations by France prior to 1800: referred. 6-Ptn from Jas Albertsen, a soldier in the war with Mexico, for a pension: referred. 7-Cmte on Commerce: asked to be discharged from the consideration of the memorial of Abel Hildreth, asking an appropriation to test an invention for keeping up a continual alarm on the coast by the rise & fall of the tides: which was agreed to.

House of Reps: 1-Bill to provide for the settlement of the accounts of the late Lt Col Lewis S Craige for his services in command of the military escort to the Mexican boundary commission: referred to the Cmte on Military Affairs. 2-Cmte of Claims: reported adversely on Senate bill for the relief of Ann L Rodgers: laid on the table. 3-Joint resolution authorizing Townsend Harris, U S Consul Genr'l at Japan, & H C J Henskin, his interpreter, to accept presents from the Queen of England, & authorizing the payment of the salaries of Ministers Resident to the Argentine Confederation, Costa Rica, & Honduras: referred to the Cmte on Foreign Affairs.

Among the prisoners who escaped from the Columbus [O] jail were two imprisoned for the murder of Henry Korrel in Jun last, named Conrad Seibold & John Frononberger. On Jan 2, with the officers pursuing Seibold, he stepped to the end of a bridge, about 20 feet high, placed the muzzle of his single-barrel pistol between his teeth, fired, & fell headlong down the precipice dead.

Obit-died: last evening, in Wash City, Brvt Brig Gen Archibald Henderson, of the U S Marine Corps. He was a native of Va, & has been in the service of his country since 1806. For a long series of years he has been stationed at the Navy Yard in Wash City as Commandant of the Marine Corps.

Died: on Jan 5, in Wash City, Mrs Mary B, wife of Silas H Hill, & daughter of the late Jas M Varnum, aged 47. Her funeral is on Friday at 2 o'clock.

Hon Green B Samuels, one of the 5 Judges composing the Supreme Court of Appeals of Va, died on Wed last at Richmond, to which place he had repaired to be present at the opening of the court on Jan 5. His age was about 65 years, during 11 of which he had been on the Bench of the Supreme Court of Appeals.

Mrd: on Jan 6, at the *Hermitage*, Montg Co, Md, by Rev J G Henning, Henry Polkinhorn, of Wash City, to Rachel Ann, daughter of the late Erasmus Perry.

Criminal Court-Wash-Thu: 1-Wm Austin convicted of petty larceny: sentenced to 1 year in jail & fined $5. 2-John W Groves convicted of petty larceny: sentenced to 9 months in prison & fined $5. 3-Edw Butler found not guilty for assault & battery with intent to kill John Curran. 4-Danl Miller: acquitted of stealing a ham & pencil. 5-Thos Robins: acquitted for the larceny of linen goods, the property of Mr Richd W Carter. 6-Wm Jones, colored, was convicted of simple assault on Officer Suit. 7-Richd Brooks was acquitted for an assault on Geo Thompson. 8-Richd Hill was acquitted of assault & battery with intent to kill Jas O'Day.

SAT JAN 8, 1859
Superior household furniture at auction on: Jan 13, at the furniture warerooms of Geo T Smallwood, on 7th st, near Odd Fellows' Hall. -Jas C McGuire & Co, aucts

Capt Saml C Reid, now in his 77th year, is still hale & vigorous. He is a visiter in Wash City. Capt Reid, is famous as the cmder of the private-armed brig **General Armstrong** during the war of 1812.

Mr Meril Utley, on Dec 25, bore a hole in a log & charged it with powder, & put fire to it. It exploded mortally wounding Mr Utley, who died 3 to 4 hours later. A large family has been left in a most distressing condition. –Hillsborough [N C] Recorder

Senate: 1-Ptn from Geo W Grayson, asking that the heirs of Col Wm Grayson, of the Revolutionary army, may be allowed commutation pay with interest: referred. 2-Ptn from T N Strong in favor of including the Seneca Indians of N Y, engaged in the war of 1812, in the pension bill now before the Senate: referred. 3-Ptn from Lucien Peyronnet, asking to be allowed to locate certain bounty land warrants issued under the act of Feb, 1847: referred. 4-Ptn from Taylor & Maury & other citizens of Wash, asking of Congress authority to construct a railroad from Gtwn along Pa ave to the Navy Yard: referred. 5-Ptn from Lawrence Myers, contractor to furnish iron pipe for the Wash aqueduct, stating that he was unable to comply with his contract on account of delinquencies on the part of the agent of the Gov't, & asking relief at the hands of Congress: referred. 6-Ptn from Wm Rees, asking permission to locate 1,500 acres of public land in one body for the establishment of a normal settlement: referred. 7-Ptn from Adolphus Glavecke, asking compensation for mules & horses illegally seized at Brownsville in Oct, 1857, by the Marshal of the U S: referred.

A monument to the memory of the late Dr Kane is to be erected in the Central Park, N Y. Mr Thos Hicks has furnished the design. Liberal donations have been received.

Valuable tract of land in PG Co, Md, containing 16¼ acres of land, at auction, on Jan 10. This tract is known as *Stony Ridge*, being part of the tract which belonged to Wm Brown, deceased. -A Green auct

Fatal casualties from fire-arms. 1-Francis Key, a youth, aged 15 years, son of the late Philip Barton Key, of Louisiana, was killed while on a visit to a gentleman of the factory district last week. Young Key was ramming the charge of his gun, when the gun went off, lodging nearly the whole contents in his side. He lived about 5 minutes after the accident. 2-Robt Posey, age about 21 years, was killed last week while on a visit to his brother, who resides in Chas Co. Mr Posey was gunning for ducks, & the accident occurred while taking his gun from a boat. He received the contents of both barrels in his side, & never spoke afterwards. He was a young man of amiable manners, unblemished character, & considerable mental endowments. –Leonardtown [Md] Beacon

House of Reps: 1-Cmte on Public Lands: bill for relief of Martin Layman, & asked that it be put upon its passage. 2-Cmte on Indian Affairs: bill for relief of Madison Sweetser: committed. Same cmte: bill for relief of Anson Dart: committed. 3-Cmte on Military Affairs: bills for relief of John S Sanford, adm de bonis non of the estate of Robt Sanford; for relief of Benj & Thos Laurent, & for relief of Chas Stillman: committed. Same cmte: bills for relief of Julius Martin, M E Bronaugh, & Antone Robidoux: committed. 4-Cmte on Naval Affairs: bill for relief of John Allen, of Harrington, Maine: committed. 5-Cmte on Foreign Affairs: bill for relief of the owners, officers, & crew of the brig **General Armstrong**: committed. 6-Cmte on Revolutionary Pensions: bills for relief of Catharine Jacobs, widow of Francis Jacobs, a waiter in the household of Gen Washington; & for relief of Hannah Stroop, widow of John Stroop, deceased: committed. 7-Bills reported with a favorable recommendation: pension to Mary Blattenberger, widow of John Blattenberger. Bills for relief of Abel M Butler; Hannah Little & for other purposes; of the assignees of Hugh Glenn; of Wm Waer; of Jos Hardy & Alton Long; of Enoch B Talcott; of Saml A Fairchilds; of Hall Neilson; of Elias Hall, of Rutland, Vt; & of Shade Calloway. 8-Ptn of Julius Martin, of Calif, for compensation for supplies furnished the military forces operating under Col Fremont in Calif in 1846 & 1847: referred. 9-Memorial of Wm F Bayly, Taylor & Maury, Fitzhugh Coyle, Geo & Thos Parker, Judson Mitchell, Saml Bacon, & H A Willard, residents of Wash City, praying Congress to grant them corporate privileges for the purpose of constructing a passenger railway from Gtwn, through Pa ave, to the Navy Yard: referred.

Died: on Jan 7, in Wash City, Mary Anna, second daughter of the late Capt Jos B & Mary A S Tate, after a few days' illness, in her 5th year. Her funeral is on Sunday at 2 o'clock, from the residence of her grandfather, John Mills, 406 D st, between 6th & 7th sts.

The steamer **Vanderbilt**, Capt Frazee, left N Y on Monday & after passing Huntington, snow commenced falling; on Tue she struck a rock on the Race Point, Fisher's Island, about 12 miles from New London. On board were 72 passengers, of whom 15 were females, with 2 or 3 children, making with the ofcrs & crew, over 100 persons. On Tue the passengers were landed by the small boat, into which they were lowered, & from which they scrambled supplied plentifully with food from the boat & with light by lanterns hung around over the rocks to a wrecking-house but a short distance from the shore. This house contained a large room, with a pine floor made to preserve the bldg should the water flow upon the island. They were made as comfortable as possible, being Arrangements were made with Mr Noyes, the owners of a schnr, on the western shore of the island, to take the passengers to New London, & early on Wed a number of ox wagons conveyed them to the place of debarkation. They saved all their baggage & personal property, & reached Boston at a late hour on Wed. The steamer **Vanderbilt**, valued at $150,000, it is feared will prove a total loss, though it is possible her machinery may be got out.

MON JAN 10, 1859

Mrs M A Comeygs, who was lately appointed vice regent for Delaware of the *Mount Vernon Association*, has been so successful in obtaining contributions that it is predicted that Delaware will make a larger donation than any other State, taking into consideration her population. In the short space of 5 weeks she paid nearly $1,200 into the *Mount Vernon* treasury. She has organized the State with wonderful rapidity.

Geo M Newton, M D, Professor of Anatomy in the Medical College of Georgia, died yesterday, of lockjaw, caused by injuries received in a fall from a buggy some 2 weeks ago. He was reared in this city, where he endeared himself to a large circle of devoted friends. –Augusta Chronicle, 7th.

Meeting of the Columbia Fire Co, held on Jan 7, the following were elected ofcrs for the ensuing year: Pres, Jas A Tait; Vice Pres, Jas A Brown; Sec, Jas McDermott; Corr Sec, Danl A Connolly; Treas, Jos M Adams; Librarian, P S Ennis; Marshal, Thos Robinson; Capt of the Engine, Thos March; Capt of the Hose, Philip S Ennis; 1st Assist Engine Division, C C Edelin; 2nd Assist, S J Lacy; 3rd Assist, D Barnes; 1st Assist Hose Division, Danl Connolly; 2nd Assist, John S Bootes; 3rd Assist, Jas S Brest.

Criminal Court-Wash-Thu. 1-Wm O'Brien convicted of an assault on Davis & Morris Rady: fined $25 & costs. 2-Lemuel Harris, colored, convicted of stealing hose: sentenced to 10 months in jail. 3-Fred'k Betz convicted of stealing sundry gold coins the property of Jas C Reynolds: sentenced to 2 years in the penitentiary. 4-Geo Bryant, a youth, was convicted of stealing jewelry & money from John Kaiser: sentenced to 1 year in the penitentiary. 5-John Simms acquitted of a charge of assault on Jas W Dean. 6-Jas Ragan convicted of assault on John Lacy: fined $12 & costs. 7-Alfred Green, colored, convicted on 4 distinct indictments, charged with stealing coats & caps from sundry persons: sentenced to 2 days in jail & 5 years in the penitentiary. 8-Sarah Weens, colored, convicted of stealing female apparel: sentenced to 6 months in the county jail. 9-John Brittain, an old soldier living at Soldiers' Home, was charged with assaulting Wm Kieth, another soldier of the same place, during a political debate, & acquitted. 10-Danl Barry, an old soldier, charged as a participant in the same assault, was likewise acquitted.

Edw Clark, the efficient architect for the Interior Dept, has prepared a plan & estimates for State houses & prisons for the Territories, which will be submitted to Congress in compliance with the provisions of a resolution passed at the last session. -Union

Orphans Court of Wash Co, D C. Letters of administration on the personal estate of Matthew Trimble, late of Wash Co, deceased. –Jos Trimble, Jas Adams, adms

Navy Dept, Jan 8, 1859. The Sec of the Navy announces to the Navy & Marine Corps the sudden death, in his 76th year, of Brvt Brig Gen Archibald Henderson, the Colonel Commandant of the Marine Corps, which occurred in Wash City on Jan 6, 1859. The deceased joined the Marine Corps on Jun 4, 1806, & was appointed to the command of it on Jul 1, 1834, which he has retained continuously since. He distinguished himself in command of the Marine Guard of the ship **Constitution** under Cmdor Stewart, in her celebrated action with the ship **Cyane** & the ship **Levant** in 1815. He was the brevet rank of Brig Gen for eminent services while in command of the marines in the Indian wars in Florida & elsewhere in 1836-'37. In respect to his memory the flags at the several naval stations & of all vessels in commission for sea service will be hoisted at half-mast & 13 minute guns fired at meridian of the day after the receipt of this order. Ofcrs of the Navy & Marine Corps will wear crape on their left arm for 30 days. –Isaac Toucey, Sec of the Navy. His funeral will be on Jan 10th. At 12 o'clock the funeral procession will assemble in front of the quarters of the late Brvt Brig Gen, from which the procession will move at 1 o'clock; Lt Col Harris to command the escort. Maj W W Russell is charged with the arrangements of the day. –H B Tyler, Adj & Inspector U S Marine Corps. Pall Bearers: Cmdor Smith; Cmdor McCauley; Capt Rudd; Capt Ingraham; W W Seaton; J Bayard H Smith; Surgeon Gen Lawson; Col Craig; Col Cooper; Col Larned; P R Fendall; Thos Blagden. –H P Tyler, Adj & Inspector U S Marine Corps.
+
The funeral of Brvt Brig Gen Henderson will take place from his quarters at the Marine Barracks, in Wash City, at one P M Monday, 10th instant. Officers of the Army, Navy, & Marine Corps, & the friends of the deceased are invited to attend.
+
[Jan 11th newspaper: the funeral of Gen Henderson took place yesterday. Religious services were performed by Rev Mr Morsell, of Christ Church, of which the deceased had been a considerable portion of his long life a consistent member. Rev Dr Pinckney & Rev Mr Hall assisted. It was the coldest day of this winter & the wind was very sharp. The temperature yesterday morning, between 7 & 8 o'clock, was 7 degrees above zero. Gen Henderson leaves a family of 6 children, 3 daughters, all married, & 3 sons, the eldest of whom, Lt Chas Henderson, is one of the officers attached to the marine guard of the expedition to Paraguay. The command of the Marine Corps devolves on Lt Col Harris, heretofore of the N Y station, who will become full colonel, & it is presumed, will hencefort reside in Wash.]

Orphans Court of Wash Co, D C. Letters of administration on the personal estate of Peter Stevin, late of Wash Co, deceased. –Tim J O'Toole, adm

Mrd: on Jan 6, in Wash City, at McKendree Chapel, by Rev Dabney Ball, Mr John B Hill to Miss Mary E Ball, of Wash.

Providence, Jan 9. The schnr **Worcester**, Rhodes master, from Phil for Mobile, with a general cargo, was lost on Dec 10 on the Bahama banks. Capt Elisha H Rhodes & mate, John S Adamson, were also lost.

Supreme Court of the U S, No 104, Dec Term, 1858. Appeal from the Circuit Court of the U S for the Southern District of Alabama. Sidney E Collins, appellant, vs Drury Thompson, Wm F Cleveland, & Jas Campbell. Mr Seward, of counsel for the appellant, having suggested to the Court that Jas Campbell, one of the appellees, had died pending this appeal now here, moved the Court for an order that, unless the proper representatives of the said Jas Campbell, deceased, shall become parties within the first 10 days of the next term of this Court, the appellant shall be entitled to open the record, to have the decree of the Court below reversed if it be erroneous. It is ordered by the Court that, unless the proper reps of the said Jas Campbell, deceased, shall become parties within the first 10 days of the next term of this Court, that then the appellant shall be entitled to open the record, &, on a hearing, to have the decree of the Court below reversed if it be erroneous. –Wm Thos Carroll, Clerk Supreme Court U S

TUE JAN 11, 1859
Senate: 1-Ptn from Roland Gelston, asking indemnity for French spoliations prior to 1800: referred. 2-Ptn from Ann Scott, widow of Wm B Scott, pension agent, asking to be allowed a commission upon the disbursements made by her late husband: referred. 3-Ptn from Carlos Butterfield, asking the aid of Congress in establishing a line of steamers between the principal Mexican & American ports in the Gulf of Mexico: referred. 4-Ptn from Russel Comstock, on the subject of letter transportation: referred. 5-Ptn from Micajah Owen, a soldier of the war of 1812, for a pension: referred. 6-Ptn from Ey Swift, of the Black Hawk war, asking an amemdment of the bounty land laws: referred. 7-Ptn from Saml Crapin, asking that his pension may commence from the date of disability: referred. 8-Ptn from Ezra Clark to the same effect: referred. 9-Ptn from Geo Robbins, a soldier in the war with Mexico, asking a pension in consequence of disease contracted while in the service: referred. 10-Cmte on Pensions: bill for the relief of John Harris, of Warren Co, Ky: recommended that it do not pass. Same cmte: adverse reports on the petitions of Nancy Read & that of Hester Stott. 11-Cmte of Claims: memorial of Radford Cabot, asking indemnity for losses sustained in consequence of orders issued by the cmder of the troops sent to Utah, submitted an adverse report on the same. 12-Bill for the relief of Jas Alburtson: referred.

Court of Claims: Jan 10: Geo C B Mitchell, of Wash City, was sworn an atty of the Court.

A statue of St Peter, modeled after one at Rome, was raised last week to one of the niches in front of the Roman Catholic Church of St Peter, at Phil, in presence of a large number of persons. The figure is 7 feet high, & made of Acadia freestone. A statue of St Paul, of similar size, will soon be raised to a contiguous niche.

Hon Theodore Atkinson, formerly one of the most wealthy men in N H, & who died at Portsmouth in 1799, left a legacy of about $1,000 to the Episcopal Church at Portsmouth, to be expended in bread to be distributed on Sunday to the poor of the parish. The distribution of more than a dollar's value in bread every Sabbath has now been regularly made for about 60 years.

Household & kitchen furniture at auction on Jan 12, at the house of Mrs Luber, on Market st, Gtwn, between Prospect & 1st sts. –Barnard & Buckey, aucts

Mrd: on Dec 23, in Marengo Co, Ala, at the residence of the bride's father, near Uniontown, Mr Wm O Key to Miss Virginia, daughter of J G A Coleman.

Mrd: on Dec 14, in Trinity Church, New Orleans, Miss Catherine Polk, of that city, to Mr Wm D Gale, of Tenn. The bride is the 2nd daughter of the Rt Rev L Polk, D D, Bishop of Louisiana, who officiated at the performance of the ceremony.

Circuit Court of Wash Co, D C-in Equity. Jas S Taggert, against Anna V Farquhar, excx, & Geo W, Sophia C, Matilda L, & Edw Y Farquhar, heirs of the late Edw Y Farquhar. The bill states that lots No 7 & 8 in square 57, in Wash City, with dwlg house thereon, were conveyed to the late Edw Y Farquhar & his heirs, in trust for the cmplnt, her heirs & assigns, who afterwards made a mortgage of said premises to said late Edw Y Farquhar to secure the sum of $3,248.47; that the mortgage debt was fully paid & satisfied to said Edw Y Farquhar in his lifetime, but he departed this life before any release thereof was executed; that the dfndnts above named are his excx & heirs at law, & the object of the bill is to obtain a conveyance of the legal estate, & release of said mortgage from the said dfndnts to the said cmplnt, & her heirs; but, because all the said dfndnts are non-residents of said District of Columbia, the cmplnt is unable to obtain such conveyance & release. Said absent dfndnts are to appear in this Court on or before the third Monday of May next. -Wm H Merrick, Assist Judge -Jno A Smith, clerk

WED JAN 12, 1859
Mrs Warren Fisher, daughter of Dr Winslow Lewis, died at Boston on Sunday from injuries received on the previous Wed, when, whilst she was shopping in Daniels & Co's store, at a part of the bldg lighted by heavy glass plates, an avalanche of snow & ice fell from the roof of the store, &, striking upon the glass, broke a number of panes, one piece of which penetrated the lady's right side between her hip & lower rib, inflicting a frightful wound. The hemorrhage was fearful, but no time was lost in sending her to the doctor's residence where she remained till death put an end to her sufferings.

Norfolk, Jan 11. Dr Thos Williamson, nearly at the head of the list of naval surgeons, has been attacked with apoplexy. He is not yet dead, but no hopes are entertained for his recovery.

Valuable farm in Alexandria Co, Va, for sale. By decree of the Circuit Court of Alexandria Co, Va, rendered at the Nov term, 1858, of said Court, in the suit of Chas W Payne & wife vs John T Donaldson & others, the undersigned will offer at public auction, on Feb 15, 1859, all that tract of land of which John Donaldson died seized, containing about 82 acres, with a small stone dwlg; located in Alexandria Co, about 1 mile from the Gtwn Ferry, & adjoins the lands of the late Andrew Hoover, ___ Ross, & others. -Albert Stuart, Chas E Stuart, Com'rs of sale

Senate: 1-Ptn from Ed Brinley, of the navy, asking to be allowed the difference between the pay of midshipman & that of lt during the time he acted in the latter capacity: referred. 2-Ptn from Capt Zadock Paugburn, asking an appropriation for testing certain improvements in vessels & life-boats: referred. 3-Ptn from Thos R Hedgpeth, asking indemnity for certain depredations committed by Indians: referred. 4-Ptn from Henry B Livingston, an ofcr of the army of the Revolution, asking for half-pay & arrears for services under the resolves of Congress of 1780 & 1785: referred. 5-Ptn from Joel M Smith, asking to be allowed per centage on his disbursements as pension agent at Nashville, Tenn: referred. 6-Ptn from Hiram J Graham, asking the establishment of certain mail routes in Iowa, Kansas, & Nebraska: referred. 7-Ptn from John Gordon, chief messenger in the Post Ofc Dept, asking compensation for extra services: referred. 8-Cmte on Revolutionary Claims: adverse report on the memorial of Hiram C Flagg, asking to be allowed the half-pay to which his father was entitled for services in the war of the Revolution. 9-Cmte on Revolutionary Claims: bill to allow the legal rep of Saml Jones 5 years' full pay in lieu of half-pay for life, made a written report in favor of the bill. 10-Cmte on Foreign Relations: memorial of H Rives Pollard, asking that an adequate salary may be attached to the ofc of the U S Consul at Bangkok, Siam, to which port he had been recently appointed, submitted an adverse report on the same. Same cmte: adverse report on the communication from C L Fox, U S Consul at Aspinwall, asking an increase of his salary. 11-Cmte on Pensions: bill restoring Joshua Mercer to the roll of invalid pensions

Died: on Jan 10, Edw S Cropley, in his 55th year, a native of England, but for the last 30 years a resident of Wash City. His funeral will take place from the residence of Mr C O Wall, on D st, between 6th & 7th sts, at 2 o'clock today.

Died: on Jan 10, in Wash City, of scarlet fever, aged 2½ years, Maria May, the infant daughter of Edw M & Jane S Clark.

THU JAN 13, 1859
A Monster Concert. Jenny Ling, Cruvelli, Artot, & Frezzolini are all to sing at a charitable concert at the Crystal Palace in Paris. Seven thousand performers will take part in this monster concert.

The trial of Marion Cropps, indicted, with Peter Corrie, for the murder of police officer Rigdon, was closed on Tue by a verdict against the prisoner of murder in the first degree. –Balt Am

Chas Reinhart, who was committed to jail in Lexington, Le Sueur Co, Minn, on a charge of having murdered a man named Bodell, was lynched & executed by a mob on Dec 27. The mob was composed of 60 men. He was buried under the tree which had served as a gallows.

Lt Orren Chapmen, of the 1st Dragoons, U S Army, died at St Louis, Mo, on Jan 6.

Hon Lewis D Campbell, ex-Congressman, was struck by some ruffian, & seriously if not fatally injured while on his way from his office to his residence on Tue night. He is in very critical condition. –Dayton [Ohio] Journal

Wash Corp-Jan 10. 1-Cmte of Claims: unfavorable report on the ptn of Christian Miller, & asked to be discharged from its consideration: ptn was recommitted. Same cmte: bill for the relief of Wm J Miller; & of M Pinkins. 2-Ptn of Jos Gerhardt, praying the remission of a fine; same for Wm M Maddox; Barny Shields; & of C Willie: all referred.

Senate: 1-Ptn from Eulogio De Celis, asking remuneration for money loaned & supplies furnished to Col Fremont as Govn'r of Calif: referred. 2-Ptn from Cmdor H J Hartstene, of the navy, asking that certain expenses incurred on account of the barque **Resolute** may be allowed in the settlement of his accounts: referred. 3-Cmte on Military Affairs: which was instructed in inquire & report to the Senate what action, if any, should be taken by Congress to manifest the appreciation of the country of the gallant & meritorious services of Capt Chas Stewart, of the U S Navy, reported a joint resolution conferring the rank of senior flag officer on the active list of the U S navy on Capt Chas Stewart. 4-Cmte on Naval Affairs: memorial of E B Boutwell, a cmder in the navy, asking compensation for certain extra services while in command of the U S steamer **Col Harney** & the U S ship **John Adams**, submitted an adverse report on the same. 5-Bill for the relief of Elias Hall, of Rutland, Vt: passed. 6-Bill for the relief of John Nourse & others: passed. 7-Bill for the relief of Arnold Harris & Saml L Butterworth: postponed.

Dr Hopfar, Dentist, removed his office from 262 Pa ave to the rooms over Kidwell & Lawrence's drug store, 3 doors east of 14th st.

J D Hoover, late U S Marshal for D C, has associated himself with Walter D Davidge, counselor at law, Wash.

The funeral of Mr Edw S Cropley, for a number of years a compositor in this office, was attended yesterday by a large number of his fellow-members of the craft, by whom he was held in much estimation. The funeral services were conducted by Rev W D Haley.

House of Reps: 1-Ptn of Saml C Young, John Rutherford, & others, members of Capt Crozier's company of Tenn volunteers, praying for bounty land: referred. 2-Ptn of Jos Davis, of Calif, for supplies furnished volunteers during the Rogue River Indian war of 1853: referred.

A Sale to Close out Business is this morning at Mr Geo T Smallwood's, on 7th st, nearly opposite this office.

FRI JAN 14, 1859
Trustee's sale of fancy dry goods, at the trimming store of Geo M Cassidy & Co, on Pa ave, between 10th & 11th sts, on Jan 18. –Richd H Laskey, trustee -A Green auct

Dr Williamson, a Surgeon in the Navy, died at Norfolk, Va, on Jun 11.

Trustee's sale: deed of trust from Jas Crutchett, dated Oct 14, 1857: public auction on Jan 27, on the premises, lots M & N in Balt & Ohio Railroad Company's subdivision of lot 4 in square 574, on Indiana ave. –Walter S Cox, trustee -Jas C McGuire & Co, aucts

Senate: 1-Ptn from Rev John Snellwood, of the Protestant Episcopal Church, asking remuneration for losses, injuries, & expenses incurred by the attack on American citizens at Panama on Apr 15, 1856: referred. 2-Ptn from Eliza G Townsend, widow of Maj David S Townsend, late of the army, asking to be allowed a pension: referred. 3-Ptn from Benj Willard, asking remuneration for losses occasioned by the declaration of the war of 1812, & compensation for his services as a commissary during that war: referred. 4-Ptn from B B Meeker, asking the establishment of an overland mail route from Lake Superior to Puget's Sound, with a branch to the Pacific, in Oregon: referred. 5-Ptn from John Needham, asking to be allowed bounty land & pay for services in the war of 1812: referred. 6-Cmte on Public Lands: bills for the relief of Abel M Butler, & for the relief of Hannah Little: recommended that they do not pass. 7-Cmte on Revolutionary Claims: memorial of the heirs of Gen Stephen Moylan, with a bill for their relief. Same cmte: bill for the relief of the *____ grandchildren of Col Wm Thompson, of the Revolutionary army, of S C. [*Could be surviving grandchildren-paper was creased.] 8-Cmte on Commerce: referred the memorial of the assignees of H B Russ, reported a bill for the relief of Richd Cheney. Same cmte: bill for the relief of Capt Douglass Ottinger, recommending its passage.

Jas A Abbott, a well known lawyer of Boston, on Tue, fell over the banisters from the 3rd story of the Coolidge House, & was instantly killed.

House of Reps: 1-Cmte of Claims: bills for relief of Jas Collier & T H Johnson: committed. Bill for relief of Geo K Knight; & bill for relief of Saml Perry: committed. Bill for the relief of Jos C G Kennedy: committed. 2-Cmte on Commerce: bill authorizing the registering of the schnr **Enterprise** to F Wilson, of N Y: passed.

Died: on Jan 12, after a long illness of consumption, Mattie, youngest daughter of Richd R Burr, in her 20th year. Her funeral will be from her father's residence, F & 3rd sts, today at 2:30 P M.

Died: on Dec 29 last, at Rectortown, Va, Mrs Josephine Denham, consort of Mr David B Denham, & daughter of the late Jos Forrest.

Wash City Ordnance: 1-Act for the relief of Mrs Mary Childs: to compensate her for 11 months' service as matron of the Wash Asylum in 1849 & 1850; provided the Corp has never paid any one for said services. Approved, Jan 13, 1859.

SAT JAN 15, 1859
Senate: 1-Ptn from T B Templeton, asking compensation for his services in reporting at the trial of Dr Gardiner, indicted for frauds upon the Treasury: referred. 2-Ptn from J G Lintz, asking to be recompensed for his services as keeper of the public property connected with the improvement of the harbor of Erie: referred. 3-Ptn from Jas & Theodore Walters, asking that certain lots in Wash City may be conveyed to them: referred. 4-Ptn from Geo Squiers, asking to be allowed the balance of salary & outfits due him as Charge d'Affaires to the Republic of Central America: referred. 5-Ptn from Tilman Leake, asking that certain money paid by him for land which had been previously sold & patented by the U S may be refunded, with interest: referred. 6-Ptn from the widow of Thos Reynolds, of the war of 1812, asking to be pensioned in consequence of the losses & suffering of her husband during that war: referred. 7-Cmte on Naval Affairs: memorial of Cmder H J Hartstene, of the navy, asking that expenses incurred by him on account of the barque **Resolute** may be allowed in the settlement of his accounts, reported a joint resolution for his relief: passed. 8-Cmte on Military Affairs: bill for the relief of the exe of Brvt Brig Gen Jas Bankhead, late of the U S Army, submitted an adverse report on the case: ordered to be printed. 9-Cmte of Claims: referred the report of the Court of Claims against the case of Ann W Butler, admx of Gen Richd Butler, reported a recommendation that said report be affirmed. Same cmte: asked to be discharged from the consideration of the ptn of memorial of Jos Brobst, asking payment for certain continental scrip received by John Beeson for indemnity for losses resulting from his expulsion from land on which he had settled in Oregon: agreed to. 10-Cmte on Indian Affairs: authorized the settlement of the accounts of Redick McKee, reported it back with a recommendation that it pass.

Jas McMahon was hung at Newark, N Y, on Wed for the murder of his sister-in-law. He was 37 years old, & served under Gen Scott during the whole of the Mexican war & on the frontier against the Indians.

U S District Court met at Charleston on Jan 11, Judge Magrath presiding, when the following gentlemen were sworn in to act as Grand Jurors:

A S Johnstone, foreman	B S Rhett	L Northrop
R M Green	B O'Neill	J Wood
F Hisch	R H McDowell	J Maguire
W J Robinson	N Tagnalaneri	Wm Ryan
R P Thackam	D Riker	A McBride
J C Simons	T Corcoran	
Jos Zealy	R Thomlinson	

The U S Dist Atty, Jas Conner, after reading the law as set forth in the act of 1800 for the suppression of the slave trade, gave out indictments against the following persons, composing the capt & crew of the ketch **Brothers**, the vessel taken by Lt Stone on the coast of Africa, & taken to Charleston on suspicion of being engaged in the slave trade; Capt Jas Gage, Antonio DeSoto, Antonio Blanco, Jose Silvarra Clara, Jose Antonio Silvarra, Juan A Tenido, J Knick, Chas Wan, John Waser. The jury, after being out about an hour, returned into court with the finding of "no bill in each of the indictments."
-Mercury

The steamer **Niagara** beings intelligence that Mr Erskine, Sec of the British Legation in this city, is to be succeeded by Mr Irvine, late attaché of the British Legation at Vienna. Mr Erskine has been appointed Sec at Stockholm.

Dr Thos Williamson, a surgeon in the U S navy, died at Portsmouth, Va, on Wed, in his 68th year. He was a native of Md, & entered the naval service May 13, 1813, his present commission as a surgeon ranking with cmders, being dated from May in 1824. His sea service under his last commission exceeded 11 years. During a service of 44 years & 7 months he was unemployed only 4 years & 9 months. His name is the fourth in the navy register in his grade.

Tampa [Fla] Peninsular-Jan 1: Mr Kilburn, who arrived at that place on the day previous, states that the celebrated Seminole Indian Chief, Sam Jones, is dead, & that Tiger Tail has been appointed in his stead. Jones was supposed to be at least 110 years old.

Erastus Hogg, a boarder at the Planters' Hotel, Raleigh, N C, had a good natured trial of strength with the barkeeper, named Parish, which ended in a quarrel. Parish drew a sword from a cane & rushed at Hogg. Hogg stabbed Parish, killing him. This was done in the dining room in the presence of a considerable number of boarders.

Died: on Jan 14, after a long & painful illness, John Thompson Polkinhorn, eldest son of R Oliver & Hannah M Polkinhorn, aged 2 years & 6 months. His funeral will be on Jan 15 at 3 o'clock, from the residence of his grandfather, John Thompson.

Died: on Jan 14, of scarlet fever, Ann Catherine, only daughter of Jas & Josephine Stone, aged 6 years & 4 months. Her funeral will take place from the residence of her parents, 333 5th st, on Jan 16 at 10 o'clock.

House of Reps: 1-Cmte of Ways & Means: bill for the relief of Jas P Cook: committed. 2-Cmte of Claims: bill for the relief of Francis A Gibbons & Francis X Kelly: committed. 3-Cmte on Commerce: bill authorizing the Sec of the Treasury to grant a register for the schnr **Wm A Hamil**: passed. 4-Cmte on Public Lands: bill for the relief of Theresa Dardenne, widow of Abraham Dardenne, deceased, & their children: committed. 5-Senate bill to revive & extend an act entitled "An act for the relief of the reps of John Donelson, Stephen Head, & others," approved May 24, 1824, & the several acts continuing the same: committed. 6-Cmte on Revolutionary Claims: bill for the relief of the heirs of Lott Hall, deceased: committed. 7-Cmte on Private Land Claims: bill to issue a land warrant to Danl Davis: committed. Same cmte: bill for the relief of Thos L Disharoon: committed. 8-Cmte on Military Affairs: bill appropriating $700 to Wm B Whiting, to be used in experiments under the direction of the Sec of War: committed. Same cmte: bill for the relief of Joshua Fish: committed. 9-Cmte on Naval Affairs: bill for the relief of G W Palmer & others. 10-Cmte on Foreign Affairs: joint resolution authorizing Townsend Harris, U S Consul-Gen at Japan, & H C J Heuskin, his interpreter, to accept presents from the Queen of England: passed. Same cmte: bill for the relief of Thos W Ward, late U S consul at Panama: committed. 11-Cmte on Invalid Pensions: bill for the relief of Ezekiel Jones; relief of Sarah Hildreth; & bill granting a pension to Moses Grooms: all committed. 12-Cmte on Patents: bill for the relief of Jas G Holmes: provides that the patent he obtained in 1844, for an improvement in chairs for invalids, for 14 years, which has now expired, shall be extended 7 years, provided the application be made within 30 days after the approval of the bill.

Circuit Court of Montgomery Co, [Md] as a Court of Equity. Ptn of Wm B Gaither, adm of Elisha R Gaither. Ann Williams vs Wm Clarke et al. This case is to obtain an order distributing the sum of $417 assigned to Wm Clarke, trustee of Francis Simpson, among the creditors of said Francis, whose claims are still unsatisfied. The ptn states the above sum was assigned to Wm Clarke, as trustee, & that other dividends were assigned to the petitioner & others, leaving considerable balances due them. That Clarke removed from this State, & has since died, leaving heirs whose names are unknown, & no administration has been granted on his estate in this county, & whether any he has been elsewhere is unknown. That the above dividend to him remains uncalled for, & the ptn prays it may be divided between himself & the other creditors of Simpson who are unsatisfied, & that the heirs & adms of said Clarke, if any, may be made dfndnts & answer the ptn; &, for as much as they are non-residents, that an order of publication may be passed. It is ordered that the adm & heirs of said Wm Clarke, if any, appear in this court on or before Jul 4th next. –Jas G Hening, clerk

Mrd: on Jan 11, at New Castle, Dela, by Rev J B Spotswood, D D, Dr Lewis A Edwards, U S Army, to Miss Eliz R, daughter of the late Dr Jas Couper.

Mrd: on Jan 13, near Poolesville, Md, by Rev Mr Cornelius, David T Cissel, of Wash City, to Miss Sarah S, daughter of the late Saml Young, of the former place.

For rent: 3 story brick dwlg house on H st, between 10th & 11th sts, lately occupied by Judge Hillyer. Key may be found at the adjoining house occupied by Gen Geo W Bowman. Apply to J Libbey & Son, 45 Water st, Gtwn.

MON JAN 17, 1859
Trustee's sale of lot 35 in square 100, with a frame dwlg & steam mill: by deed of trust from Nicholas Kuhland & wife, dated Apr 19, 1856, recorded in Liber J A S, No 116, folios 17 et seq, of the land records of Wash Co. Auction on Feb 21 next, on the premises. --Anthony Hyde, trustee -A Green auct

Mr Judson J Hutchinson, one of the members of the Hutchinson family, extensively known as popular singers, committed suicide on Jan 11th by hanging himself at the home of the family in Lynn, Mass. He was about 40 years old.

Willard Saulsbury, has just been elected by the Delaware Legislature to the U S Senate for 6 years from Mar 4 next, & succeeds Hon Martin W Bates, both Democrats. He is about 40 years of age, studied law under Mr Bates, & was Atty Gen of Dela. -Sun

House of Reps: 1-Memorial of Geo D Dods, praying Congress to grant him an appropriation of $200 as a remuneration for expenses incurred in procuring outfit: referred. 2-Ptn of H C Simpson & 45 others, citizens of Wabashaw Co, Minn, against the sale of the public lands in said State: referred.

Criminal Court-Wash-Wed. 1-*David Van Pelt convicted of picking the pocket of Mr J G Buck, in connexion with John & Thos Smith, at the railroad depot in Wash City. Motion made for a new trial. Judge refused a new trial, stating that the case was one of the plainest he ever knew. 2-Emory Baxter convicted of assault on Sarah Mills: fined $20 & costs. 3-Henreitta Savoy convicted of petty larceny: sentenced to 6 months in jail. 4-Thos Stone found guilty of an assault on Peter Magrath: fined $10 & costs. 5-Alex'r Adams was found guilty of an assault on Wm Coxen: sentenced to 1 weeks' imprisonment & fined $1. 6-Henry Williams, colored, found guilty of stealing the keys of the watch-house in the First Ward, in which he had been confined: sentenced to 6 months in jail. 7-Christopher Adams acquitted on a charge of assault. 8-Jas Mahar was found guilty of stealing some silver money: sentenced to 1 year in the county jail. 9-Henry Williams, colored, found guilty of stealing some property of Mr Joshua Pearce: sentenced to 4 months in prison. 10-Eben Ben Fowler, colored, acquitted of the charge of assault. 11-Henry Douglas found guilty for an assault & battery on John P Milton. [*Jan 18th newspaper: John Smith, Thos Smith, & David Van Pelt, each sentenced to 3 years at hard labor in the penitentiary.]

Edw Long, age 19, of Somerset Co, Md, was killed accidentally while out hunting, by the discharge of his gun he was endeavoring to knock down some persimmons with the butt.

Orphans Court of Wash Co, D C. In the case of Francis K Davidson, adm of Ann Talbott, deceased, the administrator & Court have appointed Feb 8 next, for final settlement of the personal estate of said deceased, of the assets in hand.
-Ed N Roach, Reg/o wills

Orphans Court of Wash Co, D C. Letters of administration on the personal estate of Joh H Massey, late of Wash Co, deceased. –Mary C Massey, admx [Joh as copied.]

Died: on Jan 15, in Wash City, after a long illness, of consumption, Mary H, wife of Lt J C Tidball, U S Army. Her funeral will be from the Rugby House, 14th & K sts, on Monday at 12 o'clock.

Died: on Dec 26, after an illness of 12 days of scarlet fever, Perry E, aged 4 years; & on Jan 12, of the same disease, Samuel, aged 2 years, children of Samuel C & Anna E Pennington.

Died: on Jan 16, in Wash City, of scarlet fever, Anthony Delano, aged 4 year & 10 months, youngest daughter of Danl & Matilda B Smith. His funeral is this evening at 2½ o'clock, from the residence of his parents, on K st, between 4th & 5th sts.

Died: on Dec 10, at Vallejo, Calif, of typhoid fever, Mr Robt M Kersey, in his 28th year, formerly a resident of Wash City.

TUE JAN 18, 1859
Excellent marble mantels at auction on Jan 21, at the residence of Mr F Cardoni, 494 Mass ave, between 5th & 6th st, two very elegant Italian Statuary Marble Mantels, carved by one of the finest artists in the country. Also, a lot of fine Italian slabs.
–Wall & Barnard, aucts

Senate: 1-Court of Claims: adverse in the following cases: on that of H McCulloh, exc of Jas H HcCulloh; on the heirs of Dr Jas Thatcher; on Henry W Morris; on Almanzon Huston; & on that of the heirs of Geo Yates: read & referred to the Cmte of Claims. 2-Ptn from Lt J C P De Krafft, of the navy, asking to be allowed mileage for a journey from N Y to San Francisco, performed under an order from the Navy Dept: referred. 3-Ptn from Eliz Osgood, daughter of a lt in the army of the Revolution, asking a pension: referred. 4-Ptn from Eliz Spear, widow of a soldier killed in battle, asking a pension: referred. 5-Ptn from Emily L Slaughter, asking for a pension due her as widow of Cmder A G Slaughter, from Sep 9, 1853: referred. 6-Ptn from Thos E & Edw O Smith, asking compensation for supplies furnished to emigrants on the route to Calif: referred. 7-Cmte on Pensions: bill for the relief of Mary E Lanard.

In the Senate a vote was taken upon the joint resolution introduced by Mr Hale, restoring Cmdor Chas Stewart to the active list of the navy, with the rank of senior flag-officer. The resolution was adopted-yeas 34, nays 14.

Revolutionary Soldiers: During the past year 18 Revolutionary soldiers have died: David Chapin, Gideon Bentley, John Titus, Wm Matteson, Robt Gallup, Zachariah Greene, & David Davis, of N Y; Zacheheus Robinson & Abraham Rising, of Mass; Wm Turkey & Rev John Sawyer, of Maine; Thos Kerowltin & Elisha Mason, of Conn; Geo Wells & Chas Garman, of Tenn; Jas Bushnell, of Vt; Henry Straight & John Frazer, of Ohio. The Sec of the Interior, in his annual report, says there are yet 200 of the patriots of the Revolution living & receiving their pensions.

Senate: 1-Message was received announcing the death of Hon Thos L Harris, late a member of the House of Reps from the State of Ill. Appropriate eulogies on the deceased were delivered by Messrs Douglas, Shields, & Davis. [Jan 20th newspaper: Thos L Harris was born in Norwich, Conn, on Oct 29, 1816, & was 2 years old when his father died, leaving him & a younger brother dependant on a widowed mother for support. He graduated with credit at Trinity College, Hartford, Conn, in 1841; became a student at law in the ofc of Govn'r Toucey, now Sec of the Navy; in 1841 he removed to Amherst Co, Va, teaching school for his support. In 1842 he was admitted to the bar in Va & removed to Petersburg, Menard Co, Ill, & resided there until the period of his death. In 1846 he raised a company of volunteers & was elected their captain. He joined the 4th regt of Ill volunteers under the command of Col Baker; on Jul 4, 1846, he was elected major of the regt. After reaching Mexico the absence & sickness of the col & lt col devolved the command of the regt upon Maj Harris. During his absence in Mexico, Maj Harris was elected by the people to the Senate of Ill. Maj Harris left a wife & 4 small children.]

The War Dept has received the minutes of the Gen Court Martial, convened at *Fort Randall*, Nebraska, for the trial of Lt Lee, 2nd infty, & has confirmed the decision of the Court, honorably acquitting that officer. Lt Lee will therefore resume his duties.

Patapsco Female Institute announces the additional bldgs & improvements commenced a year ago are now complete. Mrs Lincoln Phelps intends to resign her ofc of Principal at the close of the present school year, & Robt H Archer is her successor. –Chas W Dorsay, Pres; Wm Denny, M D, Sec; T Watkins Ligon; E Hammond; John P Kennedy, trustees

Fire in Calvert Co, Md, destroyed the residence of John A Whittington on Jan 11, with about 5,000 lbs of tobacco & a quantity of corn. There was no insurance. The proprietor was on a visit to Va at the time. The fire is supposed to have been accidental.

Petersburg Press, date Wytheville, Va, Jan 11. A large number of persons were assembled on a pond near here today, when Mr Harkreder dropped through the ice. Efforts were made to rescue him, but he sunk to rise no more.

Criminal Court-Wash-Mon: 1-Edw C Eckloff was convicted of assault on Lewis E Burkhead: fined $6 & costs. 2-Michl Barton & Jacob Shaeffer were convicted of assault on John Ragan: fined $8 each & costs. 3-Harry Smith, alias English Harry, was acquitted of an assault on officer Daw on New Year's Day. 4-Terence Corrigan, convicted of stealing iron at the new gas house, was sentenced to 1½ years in the penitentiary. 5-Gus Gasenheimer, convicted of grand larceny, was sentenced to 1½ years in the penitentiary. 6-Henry Douglas, convicted of an assault & battery on John P Milton: sentenced to pay a fine of $25 & costs.

Died: on Jan 17, in Wash City, at the residence of her brother, Col Gardner, on Capitol Hill, Miss Julia Ann Gardner, in her 69th year. Her funeral is this afternoon at 2 o'clock.

Died: on Jan 17, of pneumonia, John C Wade, eldest son of the late John H Wade, of Wash City, aged 38 years. His funeral is tomorrow at 2 o'clock, from the residence of his mother, 6th st, between G & H sts.

Died: on Jan 17, in Wash City, of scarlet fever, Charles A, aged 3 years & 6 months, oldest child of John F & Mary A Ellis. His funeral is this afternoon at 3 o'clock, from the residence of his parents, on 6th st, between E & F sts.

Com'r sale of land by direction of decrees of the Circuit Court of Jefferson, [Va] in the suits of the Hagerstown Bank & others vs Saml Strider, & Saml Strider against the Hagerstown Bank & others, the Com'rs will offer for sale on Feb 21 the following property of Saml Strider: tract of land supposed to contain 424 acres, 3 roods & 20 poles, in Jefferson Co. A portion of this tract, consisting of a grist mill on Elk Branch, containing about 8 acres, 3 roods & 7 poles. Also, a tract, called Saml Strider's **Furnace Farm**, supposed to contain 267 acres, 1 rood, & 23 poles. –Thos C Green, Wm Lucas, Edmund I Lee, Com'rs

Orphans Court of Wash Co, D C. Letters testamentary on the personal estate of Wm Stewart, late of Wash Co, deceased. –Walter Lenox, exc

Valuable farm in PG Co, Md, for sale: contains 100 acres; improvements in good repair. Also, adjoining the farm, 100 to 240 acres will be sold if desired. The above land will be offered at public sale on Jan 27, 1859. –Chas Digges, near Bladensburg

WED JAN 19, 1859
Executor's sale of an extensive & excellent assortment of Household & kitchen furniture at auction on Jan 20, by order of the Orphans Court of Wash Co, D C; at the wareroom of A Green, 396 I st, the personal effects of the late Col Thos H Benton, deceased. -Montgomery Blair, exc -A Green auct

Senate: 1-Bill for the relief of Jas G Holmes: passed. 2-Ptn from J P C Davis, on behalf of the owners of the schnr **Rudderow**, wrecked on the coast of Florida while conveying Gov't stores, asking indemnity for loss of said vessel: referred. 3-Ptn from Asa Sprague & others, of the State of N Y, asking that persons entitled to pensions under the act of Apr, 1816, may be allowed the same from the date of that act: referred.

Criminal Court-Wash-Tue. 1-Jesse B Haw, Wm S Tyler, & L T Lovett were severally tried for assault on Alex'r Bowie & acquitted. The prosecuting witness could not be found.

Letter from St Thomas, dated Dec 27: Jas W Herbert, our Consul here, died last night of yellow fever. He has endeared himself to the whole community by his frank & courteous manners & his zealous attention to the duties of his office.

Trustee's sale: by decree of the Circuit Court for PG Co, Md, sitting as a Court of Equity, wherein Wm B B Cross & others are cmplnts & Trueman Cross dfndnt, the undersigned, as trustee, will expose to public sale, on the premises, on Feb 28, the real estate of which the late Col Trueman Cross died seized & possessed, called **Brookridge**, containing 900 acres; located within 3½ miles of the village of Upper Marlborough & ½ mile of Mount Calvert landing, on the Patuxent; with tobacco houses, corn houses, stable, overseer's house, quarters, all in excellent repair. The manager, Mr Brown, will show the same. -Wm B B Cross trustee

$100 reward: for Box lost from one of the wagons of this company on Dec 25, directed to Adams' Express, Augustine Ga. –W H Trego, Superintendent, Adams' Express Co, Pa ave, Wash, D C.

Died: on Jan 18, Maggie Addison, aged 6 years & 8 months, eldest & last of three daughters of the late Capt Jos B & Mary A S Tate, who have departed this life within the last 5 weeks. Her funeral will take place from the residence of her grandfather, John Mills, D st, between 6th & 7th sts, on Wed, at 2 o'clock.

THU JAN 20, 1859
Trustee's sale of valuable real estate & wharf property: by deed of trust, dated May 1, 1854, recorded in Liber J A S No 73, folio 5, et seq, & a decree of the Circuit Court of Wash Co, D C, wherein John Van Riswick is cmplnt; & Geo Page & others dfndnts: public auction on Feb 23 of lot 3 thru 6 in Page's subdivision of square 390. Also, all the north part of square 472. Also, all that part of said square 472 conveyed to said Geo Page by John Farley & wife. Also, all that other lot, part of said square 472. Also, all that mole or wharf lying due west of said last lot. Also, all that part of said square 472 conveyed to Geo Page by deed from Alpheus Hyatt & others. Also the whole of square 471, fronting 475 feet on each of south K & L sts by 235 feet on each of 6th & 7th sts west. The sale will take place in front of the Powhatan House, near Page's wharf, at the foot of 7th st. –Chas S Wallach, trustee -Jas C McGuire & Co, aucts

Ex-Govn'r Slade, of Vt, Sec of the Nat'l Board of Popular Education, died at Middlebury on Sunday last.

English paper: Francis Baxter, [age 18 years,] son of Mr Thos Baxter, a respectable dealer in glass & china ware, residing in High st, Kettering, was to marry Sarah Morris, age 16, the daughter of a neighbor. On the day of the wedding he committed suicide by shooting himself. His father was opposed to the match, principally on account of their extreme youth, & it is thought this led to the melancholy suicide. [No dates given.]

Senate: 1-Ptn from A Edwards, late register of the land ofc at Kalamazoo, asking to be reimbursed for money paid by him for extra clerk hire: referred. 2-Ptn from Francis Huthmann, asking the return of tonnage & light duties exacted from him & paid on Peruvian, Danish, & German vessels: referred. 3-Ptn from Frances Steeley, a widow, & formerly the widow of David Dolk, killed in the Black Hawk war, asking to be allowed a pension: referred. 4-Ptn from D C Davis, asking compensation for extra services as a watchman in the ofc of Com'r of Indian Affairs: referred. 5-Cmte of Claims: memorial of Capt Wm C Pease, of the revenue cutter service, asking to be reimbursed public money lost while on deposite in the banking-house of Adams & Co, San Francisco, submitted a report, accompanied by a bill for his relief. 6-Cmte on Indian Affairs: memorial of Geo Eitlemann, asking relief on account of injuries received while employed as a laborer at the Sioux Agency, made an adverse report on the same, but at the same time expressed the opinion that the papers constituted an equitable claim upon the Indian dept, & asked that the papers might be referred to the Sec of the Interior: which was agreed to. 7-Resolved: That the Cmte on Pensions inquire into the propriety of reporting in favor of allowing Arabella Riley, widow of the late Gen Bennet Riley, the same pension which has been allowed to the widows of other general officers who died in actual service under similar circumstances.

The fine dwlg house of Alex'r Keech, in Bladensburg district, PG Co, Md, with most of its contents, was consumed by fire on Tue of last week. Mr Keech was not at home at the time. The loss is not far below $5,000; no insurance. Marlboro Gazette

The large steam factory works of Mr Geo Bishop, at Newbern, N C, were destroyed by fire on Monday last. Loss about $14,000.

Orphans Court of Wash Co, D C. Letters of administration on the personal estate of John H T Werner, late of Wash Co, deceased. –Catherine Werner, admx

Orphans Court of Wash Co, D C. Letters of administration on the personal estate of Mary A Campbell, late of Wash Co, deceased. –Reuben Collins, adm

Mrd: on Jan 6, 1859, at the M E Church, Dumbarton st, Gtwn, D C, by Rev Mr Edwards, Worthington Dorsey, of Wash City, to Miss Mary J, daughter of Walter Godey, of Gtwn, D C.

Locust Grove Farm at private sale: 217 acres; commodious dwlg, & out-bldgs. Terms: $6,000 cash; $2,000 on or before Jan 1, 1860; & the balance of the purchase money secured by mortgage of 10 annual equal instalments. –W W Bowie, Govnr's Bridge, Md

FRI JAN 21, 1859
Senate: 1-Ptn from Henry C Rielly, Jno J Speed, jr, & Tal P Shaffner, proposing to complete a telegraphic communication between the Atlantic & Pacific States: referred. 2-Ptn from Chas C Walden, manager & superintendent of a company established for the purpose of connecting the U S with the island of Cuba by means of a submarine telegraph, asking that the Pres of the U S be authorized to contract with him for the transmission of Gov't dispatches: referred. 3-Ptn from Jacob A Whemple & Geo Westinghouse, asking that the Com'r of Patents may be authorized to determine their application for an extension of a patent for an improved grain separator: referred. 4-Ptn from Lewis C Underwood, asking to be allowed to purchase a tract of land as a pre-emption claim: referred.

Geo C Whiting, Com'r of Pensions, has made another important haul of pension-papers forgers; in this case in Wisconsin. In 1856 the Com'r of Pensions broke up a similar gang in Ark, arresting 2 or 3 partners in the nefarious business, Jas R Buchanan, who was convicted, & ___ Ambler, who broke jail. The third, Stammer, escaped before he could be arrested. Clarke, Munroe, & Feutchwanger were recently arrested in Wisconsin. Mr Clarke turns out to be the Mr Ambler who escaped in 1856 by breaking jail in Arkansas. A man named Bennett has also been arrested recently in Brunswick, Ga, for similar offences. -Star

Last Monday at South Franklin, Mass, Miss Susan V Whiting, whilst returning from a party with Ephraim Follett, was shot through the head by Mr Jonathan Wales. She died in about 2 hours. He immediately went into the woods & shot himself. Wales was about 28 & Susan was about 16. Both parties were connected by the intermarriage of near relations.

The Southern papers announce the death of Hon Jas E Belser, some years ago an able & highly esteemed Rep in Congress from the State of Alabama. He died at Montgomery on Sunday evening last.

Mrd: on Jan 11, in Phil, by Rev Fr Walsh, Francis Barry, of Wash City, to Henrietta Virginia, daughter of the late Richd Vermillion, formerly of Roanoke, Va.

Died: on Jan 19, in Gtwn, John E Deakens, in his 53rd year, after a long & severe illness, which he bore with Christian fortitude & resignation. His funeral will be from the residence of his mother, 2nd & Lingan sts, on Friday at 3 o'clock. His relatives & friends, & those of his brother, late Joshua Bateman, are invited to attend.

Died: on Jan 19, at the Marine Barracks, Anne Maria Cazenove, widow of the late Brvt Brig Gen Archibald Henderson. Her funeral will be on Jan 22 at 12 o'clock.

Criminal Court-Wash-Tue. Edgar Patterson was convicted of manslaughter in the death of a colored boy named Bowling. Witnesses for the prosecution: Jos Libbey, Chas Whealey, & Dr C H Cragin. When the verdict of manslaughter was rendered, the prisoner was much affected & wept profusely.

SAT JAN 22, 1859
Appointments by the Pres, by & with the advice & consent of the Senate.
Jas B Bowlin, of Missouri, Com'r to Paraguay.
John P Brown, of Ohio, Sec & Dragoman of the Legation at Constantinople.
Garey W Rokman, of Calif, Sec of the Legation in Chile.
Demosthenes Walker, of Miss, Consul at Genoa.
Robt Dowling, of Iowa, Consul at Cork.
Jos W Livingston, of N Y, Consul at La Union, San Salvador.
Albert Mathieu, of N Y, Consul at Carthagena.
Chas A Leas, of Md, Consul at Revel.
Henry Anthan, jr, of N Y, Consul at Batavia.
G T Ingraham, of Maine, Consul at Laguna.
Edw P Peters, of N Y, Consul at Trebizond.
J W Mandeville, Surveyor Gen of Calif.
Naval Appointments:
Edw Hudson & R T Maccour, to be Surgeons in the navy.
Chas E Lining, John C Bertoletto, T W Leach, M P Christian, Jas J Magee, Benj F Gibbs, Jos C Burnett, & Wm M King, to be Assist Surgeons.
Granville T Pierce & Jas Fulton, to be Pursers.
Henry H Stewart & Alban C Stimers, to be Chief Engineers.
Robt Tansill, to be Capt in the Marine Corps.
Robt L Browning to be 1st Lt.
Henry C Ingraham & J Howard Rathbone, to be 2nd Lts in the Marine Corps.

Col Francis Lee, U S Army, died in St Louis on Jan 19. Col Lee was a native of Pa.

Criminal Court-Wash-Fri: 1-John Maguire was found guilty of malicious mischief in killing a hog, the property of Mr Thos C Magruder: fined $10 & costs. 2-Thos Robbins, alias Dolley Robbins, was found not guilty for larceny of a lot of wheat sacks, the property of Danl S Rench. In another case Robbins was convicted of petty larceny, having stolen sacks, the property of Mr Geo Waters, of Gtwn, & sentenced to be imprisoned in the county jail for 10 months. 3-Edger Patterson, convicted of manslaughter, was sentenced to 4 years in the penitentiary, to commence on Jan 28.

Anthony Elding, a German, while at a grocery store at N Y on Mon, drank 3 pints of gin. He became insensible, was carried to his residence, & died soon afterwards.

Senate: 1-Ptn from F Keilsey, of Conn, asking an appropriation to enable him to build the model of a steamboat on a new principle in order to test the value of his invention: referred. 2-Ptn from Elit Davis, C H Kreamer, & Timothy Malihan, asking compensation for services as doorkeepers or day watchmen: referred. 3-Ptn from Lt T A M Craven, of the navy, asking additional compensation for his services in command of the expedition to make an exploration & verification of the surveys of a ship canal to connect the waters of the Atlantic & Pacific by the Atrato & Truando rivers: referred. 4-Ptn from the adms of John Deaman & Geo Townley, asking a settlement of a certificate to said firm by a commissary in the war of the Revolution for cattle furnished: referred. 5-Cmte on Pensions: bill for the relief of Geo Robbins, with a report. 6-Cmte of Claims: asked to be discharged from the consideration of the memorial of Francis Huttman, & that it be referred to the Cmte on Commerce. 7-Bill for the relief of Thos Laurent, surviving partner of the firm of Benj & Thos Laurent: further consideration postponed. 8-Bills passed-relief of: Geo Ashley, adm de bonis non of Saml Holgate, deceased; of Moses Noble; of the heirs of Lt Nathl Weeks, deceased; of the legal reps of Jas Bell, deceased; of Mrs Henry R Schoolcraft; of the legal reps of Chas G Ridgely, U S Navy; & of W Y Hansell, W H Underwood & the reps of Saml Rockwell. 9-Bill for the relief of Jas Suddards was decided in the negative.

House of Reps: 1-Cmte of Claims: bill for the relief of John Peebles: passed. Same cmte: bill for the relief of Nancy M Johnson, admx of Walter R Johnson, deceased; & for relief of Emilie P Jones, excs of Jas P Jones: both passed. 2-Court of Claims: bill for the relief of Thos Allen: committed. 3-Cmte of Claims: bill for the relief of David Myerle: committed. Same cmte: to settle the accounts of Capt J H Edes: committed. Same cmte: bill for the relief of A C Davenport: committed. 4-Cmte on Public Lands: bill for the relief of Wm Yearwood, sr, of Tenn: passed. 5-Cmte on the Post Ofc & Post Roads: bill for the relief of J G Ferry, for carrying the mail for one quarter from Pittsburgh & Franklin: committed. Same cmte: bill for the relief of Thos Livingston & his securities: passed. 6-Cmte on Indian Affairs: bill for the relief of Henry S Schoolcraft: passed. Same cmte: bills for the relief of Jos E Johnson, adm on the estate of Almond M Rabbitt, deceased; & for the relief of John Johnson, of Ohio: both committed. Same cmte: bill to compensate Israel Johnson for services performed by direction of the Indian agents at the treaty-ground at the forks of the Wabash in 1853: committed. 7-Cmte on Military Affairs: bill to provide for the settlement of the accounts of the late Lt Col Louis S Craige for his services as military escort on the Mexican boundary commission: passed.

Linden Farm in Fauquier Co, Va, for sale: contains about 543 acres; formerly known as **Chapman's farm**, now the property of Alfred B Carter, of Miss; with a fine dwlg house, newly built, & convenient out-houses, also, all new. Apply to Robt Randolph, Atty at Law, Warrenton, Va.

Mrd: on Jan 20, in St John's Church, Wash, by Rev Smith Pyne, Nina Wood, daughter of Dr R C Wood, U S Army, to Edw Boyce, of Gtwn, D C.

Mrd: on Jan 18, at St Matthew's Church, by Rev Fr Walters, Geo Walters, of Howard Co, Md, to Miss Eliza L Clemments, of Wash City.

Mrd: on Jan 20, at St Matthew's Church, by Rev C J White, Peter Cazenave Howle to Mary Louisa, daughter of N T Kieckhoefer, all of Wash City.

Died: on Dec 27, in St Mary's Co, Md, from the accidental discharge of a gun in his hands, Francis Scott Key, in his 14th year, son of the late Col Philip B Key, of the Parish of Lafourche, in Louisiana.

Died: Jan 21, suddenly, in his 20th year, John Woodside Heart, eldest son of John & Eliza Heart. His funeral will be from the Foundry Church, 14th & G sts, today at 3 o'clock.

Died: on Jan 21, Sidney De Camp, aged 1 year, 10 months & 4 days, youngest son of Thos F & Margaret Stewart. His funeral will be tomorrow at 2½ P M, 332 5th st, between I & K sts.

MON JAN 24, 1859
Household & kitchen furniture at auction on Jan 28, at the residence of W H Bawner, E st, between 2nd & 3rd sts. -A Green auct

House of Reps: 1-Adverse reports from the Court of Claims upon the ptns of Cyrus H McCormick & Wm Neill, with the recommendation that the report of the Court be concurred in. 2-Bill for the relief of Chas J Ingersoll, upon which an animated discussion ensued: laid aside with the recommendation that it do pass. 3-Bill to indemnify Henry Leef & John McKee for illegal seizure of a certain barque was taken up; cmte rose & reported to the House. 4-Ptn of Caswell Osborn, of Pulaski Co, Ky, praying Congress to pass a law granting him power to discover the real cause of the milk sickness in the West & Southwest, the amount of public land sufficient to induce the undertaking & to reward the enterprise if successful: referred to the Cmte on Public Lands.

Mr Alfred Vail, one of those originally connected with the Morse telegraph invention, died at Morristown, N J, on Jan 18. He superintended the bldg of the line between Wash & Balt, & was the first to operate & work it.

Chas Hale, Editor of the Boston Daily Advertiser, & son of the respected founder of that able & venerable journal, has been elected Pres of the Senate of Massachusetts.

One of Dupont's powder mills, near Wilmington, Dela, exploded on Thu last, killing Jas Gibbons & John Grant, two of the workmen.

On Dec 28 Thos Hall, of Lynn, N H, who is 79 years of age, walked from his residence to a wood lot, one mile, chopped 3 cords of wood, sled length, & then walked home, & all between the hours of 9½ & 3. This would be a large day's work for a young man.

Sale by order of the Orphans Court of Wash Co, D C, on Jan 26, at the residence of the late Benj M Lewis, on Bridge st, Gtwn, all his personal effects, comprising household furniture & sundry articles. –Josephine M Lewis, admx -Thos Dowling, auct

Criminal Court-Wash-Sat. 1-John Schaub was convicted of stealing firewood from Mr John A Smith: sentenced to 8 months in jail. 2-*John Meader was convicted of a similar offence: motion made for a new trial. 3-Louis Brunett, acquitted for retailing liquors without a license. 4-Wm Dent, colored, convicted of stealing a pair of blankets & counterpane, valued at $13.50: sentenced to 1 year & 9 months in the penitentiary, to commence from & after Jan 23. 5-Michl Corcoran, acquitted of a charge of stealing firewood. [*Jan 25th newspaper: Meader sentenced to 8 months in the county jail.]

Hon L D Campbell, who was so seriously injured by a ruffian blow, struck in the dark, at Dayton, Ohio, is rapidly recovering.

Bray Sanders, convicted of the murder of his wife last Oct, was executed on Jan 14, at Jerusalem, Southampton Co, Va.

$100 reward for runaway, my servant man Dick, [or Richd Nicholls,] as he calls himself, who left my house on Jan 19. He is about 28 or 29 years of age. –P T Berry, Gtwn, D C

Died: on Jan 23, Mr John Warwick, in his 58th year, a native of Phil, but for the last 28 years a resident of Wash City.

TUE JAN 25, 1859
Obit-died: on Jan 19, at St Louis, Col Francis Lee, of the U S Army, of a chronic disorder stated to have been contracted during his service in Mexico. He was a native of the State of Pa, & entered the army in 1822. In 1847 he was promoted to Major of the 4th Infty, which corps he commanded in the valley of Mexico. He was brevetted lt colonel for gallant & meritorious conduct in the terrible battles at Contreras & Cherubusco on Aug 20, 1847. He was brevetted colonel for gallant & meritorious conduct in the battle of El Molino del Rey, on Sep 8, 1847. At the siege of *Fort Brown* in 1846, he was second in command. In 1855 he was promoted to Colonel. He was in his 57th year.

The Pensacola Gaz announces the death of Purser Dudley Walker, U S Navy, who died in that city on Jan 12.

The youngest daughter of John S Williams, in Balt, Miss Maggie Williams, whilst preparing to attend Sabbath school, passed near the hearth grate, the flames of which communicated to her dress. Her cries for help aroused the family, who extinguished the flames. It is hoped she will ultimately recover.

Valuable farm for sale: the farm on which the subscriber resides; adjoining the farms of Messrs Chas Digges & Woolman Gibson: contains 150 acres; with a frame dwlg containing 9 rooms, & out bldgs. Inquire of Thos J Barclay, near Bladensburg.

Senate: 1-Ptn from Mary Chase Barney, sole daughter & survivor of Saml Chase of Md, one of the signers of the Declaration of Independence, asking to be allowed a pension. [She says she stands in need of aid.] Referred. 2-Ptn from J E Reeside, Jay Cooke, & W W Logan, of Phil, asking the privilege of laying down & using a double-track railroad from the Navy Yard gate along 8th st east to its intersection with Pa ave, & to 1st st east, to E st north & Indiana ave to 1st st west, with the privilege of a switch to the depot of the Balt & Ohio Railroad Co: referred. 3-Ptn from Joshua Taggart & other constables of Phil, asking an appropriation of $700 as compensation for service rendered & expense incurred in ferreting out & bringing to justice the perpetrators of the theft of specimen coin from the cabinets of the U S Mint in Aug last: referred. 4-Ptn from Wm Pettibone & other practical bookbinders & residents of Washington, asking the correction of an alleged abuse in relation to the ruling & binding for the Executive Depts: referred. 5-Cmte on the Judiciary: asked to be discharged from the consideration of the memorial of the widow of Brvt Brig Gen Gratiot, & that it be referred to the Court of Claims. Same cmte: adverse report on the bill for the relief of Saml C Phagin & others. 6-Cmte on Pensions: adverse reports on the ptns of Fannie White; of Francis Steeley; & of Mary Willard.

Died: on Jan 23, Chas Thoma, a well know citizen of Wash City. He was born Jun 17, 1814, in Baden, Germany, & emigrated to this country in 1840. A wife & 4 small children are left to lament his death. His funeral will take place at 2 o'clock on Jan 26.

Died: on Jan 18, in Wmsburg, Va, of pneumonia, Mrs Eliz Stoddert Ewell, the widow of the late Dr Thos Ewell, & daughter of the late Benj Stoddert, first Sec of the Navy, in her 74th year. She leaves to her surviving children the recollection of a well spent life.

WED JAN 26, 1859

The celebrated Randall suit, in Kenawha Co, Va, has been decided in favor of Josiah Randall. To M Maupertuis, one of the French claimants, the court decreed 300,000 acres of the land in controversy. Mr R recovers about 2,000,000 acres of land in Western Va.

Mrd: on Jan 23, at Harmony, Monmouth Co, N J, by Rev W B Wilson, Wm Wurdemann, of Wash City, to Miss Lucy M Parsons, of the former place.

Died: on Jan 24, in Wash City, suddenly, Mrs Eliz Beale, wife of Robt Beale. Her funeral will be Jan 27 at 2 o'clock, from her late residence, corner of Pa ave & 2nd st.

Died: on Jan 24, in Wash City, Letitia Atkinson, widow of the late Saml Humphreys, in her 73rd year. Her funeral will take place on Jan 27, at 12½ o'clock, from the residence of her son, Capt Humphreys, 345 19th st.

Circuit Court of Wash Co, D C-in Equity. Jas C McGuire, for himself & other creditors, against C Smith Keech, adm, Anna E Young, widow, & J Terrett Young, Ann L Young, Helen E Young, & Kate McC Young, heirs of Wm L Young. Statement of the account of the personal estate of the late Wm L Young, in the City Hall, Wash, on Feb 7 next. -W Redin, auditor

Senate: 1-Bill to allow to Edw O Cooper & his assigns, being citizens of the U S, the exclusive right of occupying the island or key of Nerassa, in the Caribbean sea, for the purpose of obtaining & selling guano therefrom: referred. 2-Bill for the relief of the widow of Chas Pearson; referred. 3-Bill to grant a register to the schnr **Wm A Hamill**: passed. 4-Ptn from the widow of Chas G Bryant, asking to be allowed a pension: referred. 5-Ptn from W Henry Forbes & others, guardians of the minor children of the mixed blood of the Sioux Indians, asking the enactment of a law to make the scrip issued under the act of Jul, 1854, transferable, & to confine titles to land located under said scrip: referred. 6-Cmte on Foreign Relations: memorial of Jonas P Levy, relative to his claims against Mexico: submitted an adverse report. Recommended that the claim be rejected: which was agreed to. 7-Cmte on Foreign Relations: memorial of J Horsford Smith, asking permission to have built, free of charge, 3 war steamers at foreign ports to be registered as American vessels & employed in the coasting trade, submitted an adverse report on the same; which was agreed to. 8-Cmte on Revolutionary Claims: ptn of the inhabitants of Yates Co, N Y, in favor of pensioning Martha Brown, widow of Silas Brown, of the army of the Revolution' & of the heirs at law of Thos Arnold, an ofcr of the Revolution, submitted an adverse report in each case; which was agreed to. Same cmte: bill for the relief of Henry G Carson, adm of Curtis Grubb, deceased, reported it with an amendment. 9-Cmte on Pensions: bill for the relief of the widow of Isaac Correll for a pension. Same cmte: bill for the relief of Eliz Spear for a pension. Same cmte: adverse report on the following ptns: Thos M Folk, for an increase of pension; Ezra Clark, asking pension to commence from day of his discharge; John Vreeland, asking pension for the service of his father in the Revolution; Harriet Ward, asking that her pension extend back to the death of her husband, which he asked the Senate to concur in, as several of these cases had been previously reported adversely on, & were again before the cmte without an additional testimony, which could be the case without some violation of the rule. The adverse reports were then severally agreed to.

THU JAN 27, 1859
The trial of Peter Corrie for the murder of Police-officer Rigdon, which occupied the attention of Balt Co Court at Towsontown for some 10 days past, was brought to a close this morning. Verdict: guilty of murder in the first degree. The culprit was remanded to prison to await sentence. –Balt Patriot of last night.

Dr Hudson, of the Navy, died on Sunday in Brooklyn. He was 13 years in the service, & a Pennsylvanian by birth.

Senate: 1-Ptn from Israel Johnson, asking compensation for services rendered & supplies furnished to the Miami & Pottawatomie Indians by order of the U S Indian agents: referred. 2-Cmte of Claims: asked to be discharged from the consideration of the memorial of S G Simmons, asking to be relieved from liability for certain public money stolen from his possession in Mexico, & that it be referred to the Cmte on Military Affairs; & the memorial of Richd Roman, asking to be credited with an amount disallowed in the settlement of his accounts: referred to the Cmte on Military Affairs. Same cmte: asked to be discharged from the consideration of the memorial of Sampson P Moses: referred to the Cmte on Commerce. 3-Cmte on the Judiciary: adverse report on the resolution for the relief of Hall Neilson. 4-Cmte on Naval Affairs: bill for the relief of Ann Scott, widow of Wm B Scott. 5-Cmte on Naval Affairs: adverse report on the recommitted memorial of Saml James, Ignatius Lucas, Chas Tillery, & Thos S Bingey. 6-Cmte on Naval Affairs: adverse reports on the recommitted memorial of Jos Humphreys; & to which was referred the memorial of Franklin Kelsey. 6-Cmte on Patents: memorial of Jacob N A Wemple & Geo Westinghouse, asking an extension of a patent for an improved grain separator, reported adversely thereon: which was agreed to.

Trustee's sale of lot 1 in square 257, on Ohio ave & 13½ st, near the Canal; with improvements; in virtue of a deed of trust from Eugene Schwinghamer & wife, dated Jun 7, 1858, recorded in the land records of Wash Co, D C: sale on Mar 4. –A Hyde, trustee -A Green auct

A large barn upon the estate of Dr Wm Gunton, in Spalding's district, PG Co, Md, was consumed by fire on Jan 23, with a large quantity of provender, agricultural implements, & harness. Two of Dr Gunton's servants have been committed to jail, charged with having fired the barn. –Marlboro Advocate

Mrd: on Jan 13, by Rev Dr Hendrick, Rev J Thilman Hendrick, pastor of Zion Church, to Miss Mary F, eldest daughter of Maj G W Mayes, all of Maury Co, Tenn.

Mrd: on Jan 25, by Rev Mr Boyle, Saml A Rainey to Miss Theodosia Jas Donn, youngest daughter of Thos C Donn.

FRI JAN 28, 1859
Adm's sale of the household furniture belonging to the estate of the late Matthew Trimble, deceased. Sale at his late residence on 7th st, between Va ave & L st.
-Jos Trimble, Jas Adams, adms -A Green auct

Household & kitchen furniture at auction on Feb 3, at the residence of Z Dugan; all his personal effects. -Jas C McGuire & Co, aucts
+
Sale of stock of groceries at auction, on Feb 2, at the store of Z Dugan, corner of 9th & L sts. -Jas C McGuire & Co, aucts

Died: on Jan 26, after an illness of 8 days of pneumonia, Margaret Jane, in her 18th year, youngest daughter of John & Mary Espey. Her funeral is on Jan 29 at 2 o'clock, from the residence of her parents, on 20th st, between E & F sts.

Died: at Chicago, Ill, John J Cantine, aged about 53 years, formerly connected with the press in Pa, & more recently an efficient clerk in the ofc of the Third Auditor at Wash. The deceased was a most estimable citizen & leaves many friends to lament his death. [No death date given-current item.]

Mrd: on Jan 5, at the Legation of the U S, in the city of Brussels, Rev W Drury, Episcopal Chaplain, & Mr Verhoutsraeien, the Deacon of St Gudule Cathedral, officiating, Miss Strother, daughter of the late Hon G F Strother, former member of Congress from Va, to Baron Philip Fahnenberg De Burgheim.

Senate: 1-Ptn from Hiram J Graham, asking the organization of a new Territory, to be composed of the western part of Kansas, the southwestern part of Nebraska, & the eastern part of Utah: referred. 2-Ptn from Isaac H Randall, asking compensation for extra service performed by him while a master's mate attached to the Japan expedition: referred. 3-Ptn from Wm Vance & Brothers, asking to be reimbursed for expenses in furnishing outfits to certain volunteers in the Mexican war, but not finally mustered into the service: referred. 4-Ptn from Ambrose S Mead & other citizens of Iowa, asking indemnity for property destroyed by a wandering band of Sioux Indians in the spring of 1857: referred. 5-Ptn from Wm Collicott, asking remuneration for losses sustained through an erroneous entry of land by Gov't agents: referred. 6-Ptn from one of the heirs of Wm Clarke, asking payment for supplies furnished to white families at the request of Gen Henry Dodge in the Black Hawk war: referred. 7-Cmte on Commerce: bill for the relief of Eli M Goff: recommended its passage. 8-Cmte on Revolutionary Claims: bill for the relief of Fred'k Vincent, adm of Jas Lecaze, surviving partner of Lecaze & Mallet. 9-Same cmte: bill for the relief of Haym M Salomon: passed. 10-Bill for the relief of the adm of Benj Wakefield, deceased: referred.

A few mornings since a strolling man, named Tucker, his wife, & 2 children, were found frozen to death in a barn, in Westchester Co, N Y. The previous day they were asking alms, & it is supposed that they did not have enough money for lodging.

Macon, Ga, Jan 27. Little Mary Marsh, of the Marsh troupe, was so seriously burnt last night while performing before an audience that the physician despairs of her recovery. Mrs Marsh & Miss Geogiana Mously were also severely but not dangerously burnt.

For sale: a lot of land containing about 4 or 5 acres, on the Plank Road & Piney Branch Road: with a small frame house, suitable for a gardner. Apply to the subscriber on the premises. –Enoch Moreland

Orphans Court of Wash Co, D C. In the case of Kirk P Mitchell, adm of Eliz Sweeny, deceased, the administrator & Court have appointed Feb 15 next, for the final settlement of the personal estate of the deceased, of the assets in hand. -Ed N Roach, Reg/o wills

SAT JAN 29, 1859
Died: on Jan 28, Martha Elenor, wife of Danl S Harkness, in her 39th year. Her funeral will take place on Sabbath afternoon at 3 o'clock, from McKendree Chapel.

Senate: 1-Cmte of Claims: recommended the passage of the following bills-relief: of John Peebles; of Nancy Johnson, admx of Walter R Johnson, deceased; of Emilie G Jones, excx of Thos P Jones, deceased; & of Asbury Dickens. Same cmte: adverse report on the memorial of Rezin Orme. Same cmte: asked to be discharged from the consideration of the memorial of G Baley & W R Baley, & that it be referred to the Court of Claims: agreed to. 2-Bill for the relief of Jane Smith, of Clermont Co, Ohio: laid on the table. 3-Bill for the relief of Lucinda Robinson, of Orleans Co, Vt: laid on the table. 4-Bill for the relief of Lt Joshua D Todd, of the U S navy: passed. 5-Bills laid on the table: bill for the relief of Wm F Carrington, passed assist surgeon in the U S navy; & relief of Robt Carter, passed assist surgeon in the U S navy. 6-Bill for the relief of A W McPherson: passed. 7-Bills for the relief of Susannah Hayne Pinckney, sole heir of Capt Richd Shubrick, & for the relief of John Hastings, collector of the port of Pittsburg: indefinitely postponed. 8-Bill for the relief of Jos C G Kennedy: passed. 9-Bill for the relief of Arnold Harris & Saml F Butterworth: passed. 10-Bill for the relief of Benj & Thos Laurent: passed.

House of Reps: 1-Cmte on Military Affairs: bill for the relief of Danl Cole: passed. Same cmte: bills for the relief of Brvt Lt Col Martin Burke & Capt Chas S Winder, of the U S army; for the relief of David G Burnett, & to refund to the State of Texas the money advanced by her for the support of certain volunteer troops called into service by Gen Persifor F Smith & the Govn'r of that State for the protection of said State from the incursions of the Indians: committed. Same cmte: bill for the relief of John Patterson: committed. Same cmte: bills for the relief of Rice M Brown & for the relief of Orrin H Rice: committed. Same cmte: bill for the relief of Angelina C Bowman, widow of Francis L Bowman, late capt in the U S army: & put upon its passage. Mr Jones, of Tenn, moved to amend the bill so as to confine the pension to the widowhood, & not during the natural life of Mrs Bowman: passed. 2-Bill for the relief of the legal reps of Francois Guillory. 3-Bill for the relief of J W Hilton.

An official decree in the Moniteur declares that the Cathedral of St Denis is to be hereafter the burial place of the Emperors of France, & thus a long debated question is settled. The Prince Jerome, guardian of the body of his brother, the first Emperor, at the Invalides, held out to the last against the change, but he only obtained this concession that the heart might be retained in the magnificent sarcophagus of the Invalides, while the body will go to St Denis. At the same time the decree creates a chapter of St Denis, of which the almoner of Tuileries is to be head.

Orphans Court of Wash Co, D C. Letters of administration on the personal estate of Benj Wakefield, late of the U S Navy, deceased. –Chas De Selding, adm

Hong Kong Register contains the horrible death which the Mandarins have inflicted on the venerable Don F Melchoir, a French Catholic Bishop in Cochin China. The Bishop, with a heavy chain around his neck, was marched through the streets of the capital by a guard of 500 soldiers; his two young servants were beheaded. The executioners stretched a mat on the ground, placed a small carpet upon it, broke the chain around the neck of the Bishop, & made him lie down on his back upon the matting. The executioner took 2 stakes, which he fixed in the ground on each side of him, & to which his hands were tightly bound with cords, causing great pain. Two others were then placed under his armpits & over the chest of the Bishop, so as to press it tightly. Two other posts were then set up a short distance from his feet. The cord with which the feet were bound was passed around these posts & stretched violently; the feet were pegged down; the loins were similarly secured. An order was then issued first to cut off the feet, then the hands, afterwards the head of the martyr, & lastly to eviscerate him. At this order 5 executioners commenced their frightful duty. They were armed with a kind of billhook or hatchet, purposely blunted in order to inflict greater suffering. They commenced by cutting off the legs above the knee, each limb receiving about 12 blows before it was severed. The same process was repeated with the arms. The power of speech now failed the happy martyr, who, so long as strength remained, had not ceased to call on the name of Jesus.

His head was then struck off after repeated blows; &, lastly, his body was opened & his entrails drawn with a hook. Different parts of the body were wrapped up in a mat & thrown into a pit dug for this purpose. The head was exposed for some days on the southern gate of Nsn-dinh, & then broken to pieces & thrown into the sea.

MON JAN 31, 1859
The case of Geo E Deneale, charged with obtaining money on false pretences from a bank here, was submitted to the County Court this morning, & he was acquitted.
[Feb 2nd newspaper: Geo E Deneale has been honorably acquitted. –Alexandria Gaz]

Wm Hickling Prescott died suddenly on Friday. He was stricken with apoplexy. Mr Prescott belonged to a New England family of high honor. His grandfather, Col Wm Prescott, as is well known, commanded the American forces at the battle of Bunker Hill. His father, Wm Prescott, known in this community, was Judge Prescott, one of the best & wisest men who have ever lived & died among us. His mother was a daughter of Thos Hickling, who for a great many years was U S Consul at the Azores. Mr Prescott was born in Salem, Mass, May 4, 1796, & resided there until his father removed to Boston, when he himself was 12 years old. He entered Harvard College in 1811, & was graduated in 1814. While in college he was deprived by an accident of the use of one eye, & the sight in the other eye was impaired. He constantly was obliged to use the eyes of others for his studies & researches. He married soon after returning from a two year trip to Europe. –Boston Courier

Trustee's sale of valuable coal land, mining equipment, at public auction, on Mar 30, 1859: about 557 acres, being the lands known as the *Allegany Mining Co*, situated in & adjoining Frostburg, Allegany Co, Md. —Chas A Secor, Edw Franks, trustees

Balt, Jan 30. The steamer **North Carolina**, from Balt, bound to Norfolk, was burnt to the water's edge on Friday night. A clergyman, Rev Mr Curtis, [of S C, a minister of the Episcopal Church,] & one of the colored stewards perished. The steamer was a first class boat, & insured for $80,000. [Feb 3rd newspaper: Rev Dr Curtis was hurrying home to attend the funeral of a member of his family. He was a fine writer, & a clergyman of the Baptist Church. At the time of his decease he was principal of a female seminary at Chester, S C. He was in his 78th year. He leaves a son, who is a professor at Lewisburg Univ. —Balt Sun & Nat'l Intell]

Senate: 1-Ptn from R M Hamilton, late Consul of the U S at Montevideo, asking compensation for diplomatic services rendered by him while at that port. [Mr Hamilton refers to his correspondence with the Dept of State from Jul, 1838, to Jul, 1850, as sufficient proof to entitle him to the same remuneration that has been allowed in similar cases.]-referred. 2-Ptn from Pierre Choteau, jr & Co, licensed Indian traders, asking indemnity for goods & merchandise forcibly taken from them by the Sioux Indians at *Fort John*, on the north fork of the Platte river: referred. 3-Cmte on Military Affairs: asked to be discharged from the consideration of the memorial of Eulogis de Celis, asking remuneration for money loaned & supplies furnished to Col Fremont while acting as Govn'r of Calif: referred to the Court of Claims. Same cmte: asked to be discharged from the consideration of the memorial of Chas C Walden, asking that the Pres of the U S be authorized to contract with him for connecting the U S with Cuba by means of a submarine telegraph, & the resolution of the Senate in relation to connecting the fortifications & naval station at Garden Key, Tortugas, & that the memorial & resolution lie on the table. Same cmte: adverse report on the memorial of Capt Koscialouski, asking 3 months' extra pay for his company.

House of Reps: 1-Bill for the relief of Wm Hazlitt Lee was laid aside, with the recommendation that it do pass. 2-Bill for the relief of Eliphalet Brown, jr, was laid aside. 3-Bill for the relief of Katharine K Russell was laid aside, with the recommendation that it do not pass. 4-Bill for the relief of Charlotte Butler was laid aside. 5-Bill for the relief of Jos M Plummer & Mary R Plummer, minor children of Capt Saml M Plummer, laid aside, with the recommendation that it do not pass. 6-Bills for the relief of Henry Taylor & for the relief of John Hopper were laid aside, with a recommendation that they do pass. 7-Bill for the relief of the heirs of John A Hopper was laid aside with the recommendation that it do not pass. 8-Bill granting a pension to Mary A Harris, widow of Thos L Harris, deceased: referred to the Cmte on Pensions. 9-Memorial of Nancy Maygart, praying for an invalid pension: referred.

Died: on Jan 26, at Charlestown, Jefferson Co, Va, Mr Thos P Beall, one of the editors of the Spirit of Jefferson, in his 25th year.

A marriage took place at Prattsville, Greene Co, N Y, at 7 ½ o'clock on the evening of Jan 10th, & at 9 o'clock the same evening, the husband wept beside the bride of death. Here is the sad record: Mrd: in Prattsville, on Jan 10, by P K Salisbury, John Bivens, of Middletown, Delaware Co, to Miss M A Turk, of Prattsville, Greene Co. Died: in Prattsville, on Jan 10th, of asthma & hemorrahage of the lungs, Mrs M A Bivens, wife of John Bivens, in her 29th year.

Boston, Jan 29. A verdict was rendered in the Supreme Judicial Court today against the Boston & Worcester Railroad Co for $20,000 damages, awarded to Mrs Sarah E Shaw, whose husband was killed & herself seriously injured some years ago by a train on this road coming in contact with the plntf's carriage.

Boston, Jan 30. Wm Cranch Bond, an eminent astronomer, & director of the Cambridge Observatory, died last night.

TUE FEB 1, 1859
The patent granted Jan 31, 1845, to Cyrus H McCormick for his reaper expired yesterday. The Com'r of Patents overruled a motion for extending the patent on the ground that the patentee has been sufficiently remunerated.

Judge Price, of Balt, on Sat, overruled the motion for a new trial in the case of Marion Cropps, convicted of the murder of ofcr Rigdon. The prisoner was immediately thereupon sentenced to be hung on such day as the Govn'r may designate.

Died: on Jan 31, after a brief illness, Mary Jessie, daughter of Dr Wm E & Abby Jane Waters, aged 2 years. Her funeral will be on Wed at 2 o'clock, from the residence of her grandmother, 254 C st, between 12th & 13th sts.

Died: on Jan 31, in PG Co, Md, Dr Richd W Bowie, in his 49th year.

In Equity, No 1,459. S B Blanchard against Mary Holmead, widow, & Ada, Cordelia, & Wm Holmead, & Christr C Callan & Susan his wife, heirs of Wm Holmead. On Feb 11th I shall state an account of the personal estate of said Wm Holmead. –W Redin, auditor

Senate: 1-Ptn from Noah Fairbanks, asking that sea-going vessels of a certain tonnage may be required to take with them on every voyage a copy of the directions for making fresh water from sea water: referred. 2-Ptn from Mrs Anne W Angus, widow of a naval chaplain, asking a certain allowance: referred. 3-Cmte on Military Affairs: bill for the relief of F W Lander. 4-Cmte on Patents & the Patent Ofc: to which was referred the memorial of Oscar J E Stuart, reported a bill to authorize the issue of patents in certain cases to negro slaves for the use of their owners. 5-Bill for the relief of Jas P Cook: referred.

WED FEB 2, 1859
Executor's sale of valuable private Library, by order of the Orphans Court of Wash Co, D C. Public auction at my auction room, on Feb 8, the Library of the late Thos H Benton, deceased, amongst which will be found rare & valuable books, such as Congressional Proceedings from 1776 to 1852; Life & Works of John Adams: & Cranch's Reports, Index to Decisions in the Supreme Court.
–Montgomery Blair, exec -A Green auct, corner of 7th & D sts, Wash.

Senate: 1-Ptn from Jas G Clarke, asking compensation for his services as Charge d'Affaires for the U S to Belgium, having acting in that capacity for 2 years in Belgium: referred. 2-Ptn from Jonathan Wiggin, asking a pension on account of injuries sustained in the naval service: referred. 3-Ptn from Danl R Kenney, a soldier in the war with Mexico, asking a pension: referred. 4-Cmte of Claims: bill to settle the accounts of the late Lt Col Lewis G Craig for his services in command of the military escort on the Mexican boundary commission: recommended its passage.

Dr Wm H Ellet, an eminent professor of physics & chemistry, died at N Y on Wed last. He was formerly, for about 14 years, a professor in the college of South Carolina.

The christening of the 26th child of a happy couple named Wonters, at Lierre, in Belgium, is celebrated in the foreign papers. Twenty-two of the children still survive.

Wash City Property to be sold for taxes, May 3 next, unless the said taxes be previously paid to the collector. Years 1857-1858. –Jas F Haliday, Collector

Aldrich, Alex'r
Addison, Anthony & Wm Cockrell
Armitage, Benj
Alexander, Columbus
Ashford, Craven
Adams, Caleb
Arden, Danl D
Appleby, Geo W
Andrus, Horatio N
Arnold, Jos W
Adams, Jas
Allen, Mary E
Adams, Thos N
Avery, Thos
Adams, Washington
Brooke, Ellen M [Due for 1856, in the name of N & B Young, $16.65.]
Barry, Richd [Due in the name of R B Clarke, for 1856]
Brown, Wm, in trust for E Carrico & others
Bush, Wm [Due for 1856 & 1857 in the name of Henry Kinsley.]
Burche, John C, in trust for Catherine Burche
Borland, Alex'r
Bohrer, B S
Bean, Benj
Bayliss, Beckner
Blakeman, Chas W
Bennett, Clement W
Bohn, Cassimer
Brooks, Edw
Beall, Eliza A & Richd J
Burnett, Enoch
Burford, Eliz
Ballenger, Francis
Butler, Geo A
Bryant, Geo [colored]

Butler, Geo W
Bell, Henry
Bateman, Henry E
Butler, Henry, [colored]
Bowen, Harrison P, in trust
Bond, Hugh L
Bealer, H W
Barnes, Hanson
Bontz, Henry &J W Coombs
Brackenridge, John A
Byram, John W
Brereton, John
Barr, Jas R
Boteler, John W, in trust
Bryan, Jos
Bernhard, John
Boyle, John
Boss, Jas H
Brent, John [colored]
Bain, John
Beers, Isaac
Beasley, Jos
Burche, John C, in trust for Catherine
Burche
Beall, John W
Barron, Jas
Barry, Julianna
Brady, John
Birch, Jas H
Baker, John H
Butcher, Jas
Burch, Jacob W
Brunet, Lewis L
Beach, Levi
Borreman, Mary Ann
Baker, Mary & Lucy
Bevan, Mary
Brooks, Mary
Barron, Mgt E & Catherine
Bosse, Martin
Brown, Marshall [colored]
Brady, Nath'l
Burchell, N W & J W McKensie
Bias, Noah
Browning, P W
Bridgett, Richd B
Barry, Richd
Buchley, Rudolph
Beall, Richd J
Briscoe, Richd G
Brent, Robt Y
Brooks, Richd
Brown, Richd
Brown, Robt [colored]
Burche, Susan M
Bowen, Sayles J
Brereton, Saml
Boynton, Sylvanus Co
Brown, Thos [colored]
Benton, Thos H
Barrett, Thos J
Byrne, Thos
Bicksler, Thos J
Barnes, Thos
Barr, Wm
Bagman, Wm
Bird, Wm
Breckenridge, Wm D
Bigley, Wm
Bayly, Wm F & T J Fisher
Brown, Wm H
Bush, Wm
Ball, Wm H
Burdine, Wm
Baldwin, Wm T
Becket, Wm [colored]
Boone, Wm
Bird, Wm Jr
Browning, Wm A, in trust

Callan, Nicholas, in trust for Ellen M Gay.
Cross, Eli & Anthony Holmead, [one-fifth in the name of Holmead, & four-fifths in the name of Cross.]

Carlisle, Jas M, Geo S Gideon, & Walter D Davidge, in trust. [Due for 1855 in the name of Wm H Winder.]
Crutchett, Jas [Taxes due from 1851-1858]
Chafee, Wm E [Due for 1857 in the name of Henry F Wood.]
Costin, Wm [children of,] Bradley & Weightman, trustees
Crutchett, Jas [Taxes due from 1851-1858]
Collins, Reuben, in trust for Mary A Campbell
Cheshire, Archibald
Clements, Aloysius
Crown, Ann R, in trust
Chever, Benj H
Chambers, Benj
Chubb, Chas St J & J M
Chubb, Chas St J
Cushing, Caleb
Collins, Charlotte & Mary E
Coddington, Camilla
Cellar, Chas B
Church, Chas B
Callaghan, Cornelius
Causer, Edw
Chapman, Eliz
Costigan, Eliza
Coombe, Griffith
Crown, Geo W
Cottrell, Geo
Chittenden, Henry A & Henry C Bowen
Clark, John Geo
Carrico, Jas
Colclazer, John J
Cassidy, Isabella
Coombs, Jos J
Coumbe, John T
Cabot, Jos S
Clarke, Jos S & Richd G Briscoe
Carlisle, Jas M
Clarke, Jas T
Coombs, J W
Cahoe, John F
Clarke, Jos S
Coombe, Jas G
Cushley, John
Costigan, John
Cross, Jos
Costen, John T
Coombs, Jos J & John Welch
Coombs, Mary E
Cluskey, Mich W
Callanan, Mary
Caton, Michl
Cavenaugh, Michl
Cullinaine, Mich
Callan, Nicholas, in trust for Jane Lynch
Callan, Nicholas
Carroll, Peter, in trust
Cullenane, Patrick
Crawford, R R
Clarke, Ruth Ann
Callan, Rowena, & Mgt S
Clarke, Richd H, in trust for E Hassler
Coxe, Richd S
Cochran, Robt
Clements, Rachel & Mary E
Chilton, Saml
Coakley, Sarah [colored]
Clarke, Saml
Carusi, S N & Louis
Curson, Saml
Conner, Saml W
Cook, Saml
Corcoran, Thos & W W
Corcoran, Thos
Collins, Thos
Connelly, Thos, of John
Costello, Timothy
Cross, Thos B
Callahan, Thos
Chandler, Walter S
Cock, Wm [colored]
Collins, Wm
Corcoran, Wm W

Campbell, Wm W
Cox, Washington F
Clarke, Wm
Cranch, Wm G
Dulaney, Adam [colored]
Davis, Alex'r McD
Dulin, Armistead
Dulaney, Bladen
Dyer, Benj, in trust
Dyer, Benj F
Davis, Catharine
De Selding, Chas
Dulaney, Caleb [colored]
Dougherty, Cornelius A
Davis, Eliz
Dyer, Ellen C
De Kraft, Edw
Dyer, Edw
Douglas, Earl
Dickins, Francis A
Dainese, Francis
Dyer, Geo F
Davis, Geo A
Davis, Henry S
Dodson, Henry
Douglas, John
Dobson, Jos
Duffey, Jas
Dove, Jos
Dixon, Jas
Daley, John
Drury, John H
Daniel, Jos W
Dorsey, Isaac
Deasey, Jeremiah
Daley, Jas
Dalton, John
Dyer, John F
Downs, John & Wm
Davidson, Mgt
Dodson, Mary E, in trust
Donohoo, Mary
Downey, Michl

Donn, Orlando H
Defalco, Pasquale
Dement, Richd
Duley, Robt W
Davis, Richd [colored]
Daley, Sarah
Douglas, Saml E
Drury, Saml T
Decamp, Sidney
Dawson, Susan & Mgt
Donn, Thos C
Dewey, Timothy
Dutton, Thos
Davis, Thos B
Duane, Wm, in trust
Dove, Wm T
Durr, Wm
Drury, Wm P
Dewees, Wm
Donelan, Wm C
Davidge, Walter D
Donophon, Wm T
Denham, Z W
Evans, Alex'r H
Elder, Basil T
Eckel, Chas, in trust for Ann Dellaway
Eckloff, Edw C
Evans, Estwick
Eakle, Elias H
Evans, Evan
Ennis, Gregory
Evans, Geo
Edelin, Jos
Edwards, Lewis
Elliot, M J & F
English, Patrick, in trust
Emerick, Peter
Ellis, Robt
Everett, Saml & Benj
Easby, Wm, in trust for W E Denham
Eyre, Wilson
Easby, Wm
Evans, Wm A

Foster, Adams, in trust for Susan Burch & children

Favier, Agricol
Fowler, Abraham
Frazier, Benj [colored]
Fisk, Chas B
Finkman, Conrad
Flint, Chas W
Fitzgerald, David
Finch, David
Fowble, David
Falconer, Elisha
Fisher, Elwood
Felsom, Henry
Farrell, Harriet
Fischer, Harriet
Fischer, Harriet, & Thos Gunton
Fearson, Jos N
Faber, John C
Fitzhugh, John W
Fowler, John L
Foy, John
Fitzgerald, John
Fenno, J Brooks
Gwinn, Sarah J, Susannah M, & Francis A
Gladman, B K, & W Dougherty
Green, Ben E
Gardner, Caroline
Garner, Catherine W
Gardiner, Chas Thos
Gallagher, Danl
Greenleaf & Elliot
Gallant, Edw
Gardiner, Edw C
Goddard, Emma A C
Greentrup, Ferdinand
Gordon, Geo
Gillis, Groenveldt, & others
Garrett, Geo W
Grammer, G C
Groot, John R
Gadsby, John
Galligan, Jas & Thos
Garner, Jas W
Galligan, Jas

Fitzgerald, Jas
Fox, John & J W Van Hook
Fowler, Jas J
Fowler, Jos O
Foulkes, J E & wife
Fowler, John L
Ferguson, Jos
Ferris, Mgt
Farrar, Mary
Fredinberger, Michl
Fagan, M Ann
Fowke, Mary
Flannery, Patrick
Frazier, Simon
Flynn, Simon, & G S Donn, in trust
Feran, Thos
French, Thos
Fisk, Theophilus
Fletcher, Wm
Forrest, Wm H
Faherty, Wm P, in trust
Force, Wm Q

Gardner, Jacob B
Garner, J W B
Galligan, Jas & Son
Godfrey, Lewis
Groff, Michl
Gritzner, Max Jos
Green, Owen
Grenan, Patrick
Gibson, Richd
Gouverneur, Saml L, jr
Gross, Susanna
Gregg, Saml
Gregg, Saml, in trust
Greer, Thos J
Gunton, Wm
Gordon, Wm
Goddard, Wm C
Gadsby, Wm & A Newton
Gunnell, Wm H

Hamilton, Chas O [Due for 1857 in the name of Geo Sweeney.]

Henning, Geo C & Georgiana Thompson
Holtzman, Jacob & Robt Cunningham
Herbert, Wm W, in trust for Amelia J Irwin
Havenner, Thos H [Due for 1855, $18.96]
Harris, Angella
Hyde, Anthony
Hager, Ann
Hetzel, A R
Hamilton, Anna M
Haislip & Athy
Heitmiller, Alfred & Anton
Humphries, Anna M
Hays, Bernard
Hart, Bridget
Haslup, Chas G
Havenner, Chas W
Hardy, Dennis, in trust
Hines, Danl, Christopher, & Matthew
Harkness, Danl S
Hall, David A
Hall, David A & J B Kibbey
Holland, Edw
Harrison, Eliz O
Haw, Eliza F
Higbee, Francis & others
Hutchins, Francis
Houzam, Fred'k
Hitz, Florian
Hall, Francis W
Hill, Geo
Hill, Gustavus
Hanson, Grafton D
Hanson, G D, in trust
Henning, Geo C
Hinton, Geo W
Heath, Geo A
Haw, Henry, in trust
Hall, Henry
Heitmiller, Henry, C L
Haskell, Henry W
Hatton, Henry [colored]
Hopkins, John, & Geo W
Herty, Jas, Mary Ann, & others
Jackson, Andrew, in trust for John Jackson

Holtzclaw, John M
Hoover, John T
Hill, Isaac
Hickman, John L
Houston, John H
Hepburn, Jeremiah
Hughes, John
Howard, Jos
Hogan, John
Hoffman, John W
Henlein, Jos H
Henke, Lewis, trustee
Houston, Mary F
Hamilton, Mary A
Hunt, Montgomery
Hill, Mary B
Hutchins, Mary
Hogan, Philip
Harper, Phena
Harrison, Rachel
Hawley, Reuben
Handy, Saml W
Hammond, Sarah
Hyatt, Seth
Hanson, Saml, jr
Howell, Sarah Ann
Hickey, Thornton F
Hunt, Thos J
Holtzclaw, T J & R W Bruff
Hogan, Thos
Hewitt, Wm
Hutchinson, Wm
Harper, Wm M
Ingle, Christopher, in trust
Iseman, John
Indermauer, Jeremiah, jr
Iddins, Saml

Jackson, Andres, in trust for Jno E Fitzgerald
Jenkins, Ann
Jacobs, Cornelius
Jones, David [colored]
Jones, David & B Minor
Jones, Emily G
Jones, Francis Lee, & others
Jewell, Jas G
Johnson, Jas, & Leonard Miller, trustees
Jolly, John
Jones, Joel W
Jones, Mary [colored]
Jeffers, Matthias
Jannings, Paul
Johnson, Richd D
Jones, Saml W [colored]
Jones, Thos S
Jones, Thos W
Jewell, Wm
Johnson, Wm C
Johnson, Wm
Jordan, Wm
Johnson, Wm, of Peter
Jacobi, Wm
Kendall, John E [Pump tax due since Dec 18, 1855, $2.45.]
Kendrick, F P, in trust, [Due for 1857 in name of Bernard Givenny]
King, Martin [Due for 1856 $7.45, tax for paving alley.]
Keese, A E L
Kaiser, Adam
Kleindenst, Antoine
Kidder, Byron A
Knox, Charlotte F
Kroft, Christopher
Kennedy, Christopher
Kiernan, Chas
Kendrick, Francis P
Keating, Geo
Key, Henry S
Klopfer, Henry A
Key, John Tayloe
Keller, Henry
Kuhn, J L
Kidwell, John L
Kurtz, John & others
Kennedy, Jas [colored]
King, John F
Kibbey, John B
Killman, John T
Kleindenst, John P
Kennedy, Jas A
Kelly, Michl
Keehlan, Nicholas
King, Nathan G
Key, Philip
Kurtz, Peter
Kraft, Philip
Kall, Sophia S
Knight, Saml M
King, Saml D
King, Thos
Keen, Wm E G
King, Wm
Kammerhueber, W, Von
Kibbey, Wm B
Lawson, Thos [Pump tax due since 1855.]
Lippard, A F
Leggett, Aaron
Luckett, Alex'r
Lephard A & A F
Lowe, Bennet
Lawrence, Eliz
Lazenby, Elisha
Lacey, Emanuel
Lewis, Esther M
Lamb, Francis
Lacey, Harriet
Loughborough, Hamilton, in trust
Laskey, John
Lee, Jesse
Lovejoy, John N & John Y Donn
Lewis, John [colored]

Lee, Jos [colored]
Little, John E
Lightell, John
Laskey, J M
Lafontaine, J D
Lancaster, John L
Lear, Louisa
Little, Mgt A E & oters
Lafontaine, Mary
Lammond, Peter
Lowry, Rebecca
Lloyd, R B
Lewis, Saunders
Lunt, Saml
Lunt, Sarah & Peter Daggy
Lumpkin, Thos
Law, Thos
Leach, Thos
Linkins, Wm
Lowry, Wm

Marlow, John W [Due for 1857, in name of Estwick Evans.]
Mitchell, A C, in trust for C Goldsborough]
Macomb, Alex'r
McIntire, Alex'r
Macnamara, Anastasia
McKinstry, Ann G V
Middleton, Benj F
Middleton, B F & B Beall
Myers, Benj B
Milburn, Benedict
Mix, Chas E
Mason, Chas
Madison, Catharine
McCorkle, Christiana
McNamee, Chas
McDonald, Danl
Mitchell, Dennis & Rebecca
Mason, E Lorraine
McCarthy, Eugene
Morgan, Edwin C
Milstead, Eliza
McGinniss, Eliz
Morgan, Edwin C, in trust
Maddox, Eliz J
Murphy, Francis J, in trust
Mohler, Fred'k
Meigs, F C [Due for 1855, $8.84.]
McGlue, G T [Due for 1855, $3.86.]
Munroe, Geo [colored]
Myers, Geo
McKnight, Geo B & Martha H
McKnight, Geo B
Morfit, Henry M
Marryman, Horatio R
Marryman, H R, in trust
Mason, Jas M
Mason, Jos
McCarty, John
Mitchell, Isaac W
McBride, John
Mason, John
McKnight, John L
McConkie, John T S
McCutchen, John H G
Maxwell, John S
Merman, Jane
McAvoy, Jas
Montgomery, John B
Morgan, John B
Miller, John
McCollum, John J
McGinnis, John jr
McGuire, Jas C
McCalla, Jon M
McElfresh, Jas P
McKelden, John C
Mulloy, John J
Mitchell, John
McKeon, John B
McCormick, Jas, jr
Mitchell, John [colored]
Mills, John E & Susan
McGee, John S
McGraw, Jas & Eliza A

50

McCleary, Jas
McCollum, John
Martin, Luther J & Mary J
Mackall, Lewis
Morton, Marion, & others
Maher, Michl
McCarthy, Michl
Maxwell, Mary L
McKnight, Martha H
Martin, Mary Julia
Milburn, Mgt, in trust
McGee, Patrick
Mitchell, Perry A [colored]
McKenna, Patrick
Miller, Robt
McPiers, Sarah
McMeehan, Sarah A C
Middleton, Saml
McNancy, Thos
McMinn, Thos
McGill, Thos
McQuillan, Thos

Morton, Wm
McKinstry, Wm
McKinstry, Wm
Mockabee, Wm
Maack, Wm N H
Marshall, Wm
Mohun, Wm P
Mills, Wm McC
McKnew, Z W, in trust
Newton, Augustine, in trust
Nailor, A [Due for 1855, $29.90.]
Nicholson, A A
Nourse, Chas H
Noyes, Crosby S
Neitzey, Geo
Newman, Lewis A
Nelson, Madison
Nugent, Richd H
Norris, Wm B
Noyes, Wm
Nichols, Wm S
Norris, Wm G

Nichols, Wm S, & W W Corcoran, in trust
Nailor, Dickerson, in trust for Wm C Nailor
Naylor, Henry, in trust for Mrs E J Beall
Noble, Mason [Sixth Presbyterian Church]
Osborne, E, & children [Due for 1856, $3.18.]
O'Hare, Christopher
Owen, Edw
O'Leary, Ellen, & Dennis
Oyster, Geo
Orr, Henry [colored]
Owen, Henrietta B
O'Leary, Jeremiah
Owen, Jos
O'Donnell, John & Michl
Owner, Jas
O'Neale, John H

O'Donnohue, Timothy & Peter
O'Donnohue, Timothy
Osgodby, Thos W, in trust
O'Neale, Wm
Parker, Albert
Pacetti, Andrew E
Pendleton, Alex'r G
Powers, Ann
Patterson, Basil [colored]
Pratt, Carey
Pettit, Chas

Polton, Chas A, in trust [Due for 1857 in the name of Chas White.]
Pearson, Peter M & C W Davis Duckett
Pearson, J M Y & A M [Due for 1856, $1.04.]
Peugh, David L [Due for 1856 & 1857 in the name of Saml Register.
Prather, Overton J [Due for 1854 $18.59.]
Posey, Richmond, in trust for Lucy

Phelps, Chas H
Preuss, Chas
Peter, Geo
Parker, Geo
Page, Geo, & Geo Mattingly
Pratt, Henry, & others
Pfeil, John K
Polk, Jas
Pierce, Jos B
Powell, Jas
Porter, John E
Phillips, Jas B
Phillips Jas B
Prout, Jonathan
Pickett, John
Pumphrey, Jackson H
Pierce, John R, in trust
Pfister, Mgt
Pearl, Mary [colored]
Prout, Mary
Peters, Mary [Due for 1856, $11.07.]
Pollard, Richd J
Pleasanton, Stephen
Payne, Saml [colored]
Phillips, Saml
Peugh, Saml A
Platt, S H
Philips, Thos H
Phillips, Thos J
Pitcher, Thos J
Pumphrey, T B, J W, & F A
Parker, Wm H
Philip, Wm H
Philip, W H, & W B Todd
Purcell, Wm F, trustee
Phillips, W D & B F Slocumb
Quirke, Edw
Robinson, John G & Jas Friend [Due for 1856, $6.83.]
Rodgers, Johnson K [Due for 1855, $5.38.]
Rothwell, Andrew
Railey, Benedict J L
Ritchie, Catharine
Rodgers, Edmund Law
Rodbird, Ebenezer
Riggs, Geo W
Rochat, H
Remmely, John C
Roberts, John
Riggs, John M
Ricar, John P C
Ree, Jas, in trust
Ross, Jemima [colored]
Ridgeway, Jos A
Rye, John T
Reeler, Jesse
Rally, Jas
Robey, John H
Ragan, Jas
Rowland, Jas W
Roach, Jas
Rodgers, Lloyd N
Reardon, Michl
Robey, Mary Ann [Due for 1856, $1.60]
Riley, Philander C
Redfern, Saml
Ritchie, Thos
Ryne, Thos
Riley, Wm R
Ruggles, Wm
Rawlings, Washington
Rupp, Wm
Shekell, B O & H N Henning [Due for 1856, $24.21.]
Settle, Barbara, & others [Due for 1856, $5.55.]
Sengstack, C P, jr [Due for 1855, $31.80.]
Sengstack, C P, sr [Due for 1855, $13.46.]
Schley, F A [Due for lightning the street for 1854, $7.23.]
Sweeny, Hugh B [Due for 1856, $1.13.]
Sage, Henry [Due for 1856, $2.98]

Suit, John T B, in trust for Louisa B Suit
Smith, John L, in trust for Mary Williams & others
Smallwood, Wm H [Pump tax due for 1855, $2.59.]
Swartze, Andrew
Small, Andrew
Stewart, Andrew
Stone, Anna Maria
Smith, Archer B
Smith, B F [Due for 1856, $31.36.&
Scrivener, Chas
Schussler, Chas
Simmonds, Cornelia
Smallwood, Danl A
Slater, Eliz
Swann, Edw
Saeger, Eli J & Geo Mathiot
Slater, Eliz
Saeger, Eli J
Shorter, Fanny
Simpson, Gilbert, in trust
Sanford, Geo A
Sweeny, Geo
Sherman, Geo
Small, Geo
Scott, Geo B
Simpson, Gilbert
Saunders, Harriet
Stone, Henry
Sommers, Henry W
Steers, Henry C
Suter, John
Sumby, Jas [colored]
Strange, Jas [Due for 1856, $0.72.]
Smith, John W
Souder Jacob B
Stewart, J E
Simms, Ignatius [colored]
Scrivener, Jas
Stewart, Jas W
Saunders, Jane
Smith, John C
Sears, Jas W
Smith, John A
Smull, Jas T
Spaet, John
Sullivan, J J, & J A Stewart
Smitson, John H
Sheets, John S
Smith, John Geo
Saur, Louis
Speake, Mary Ann
Scholfield, Mary E
Shields, Mary Ann
Sweeney, Mary
Snyder, Nicholas
Sewall, Robt
Saxton, Robt
Schwartz, Robt
Smoot, Saml C
Stettinius, Saml
Shoemaker, Saml M
Sterling, Sherman H
Smitson, Sarah
Sheckell, Theodore
Sylvester, Thos [Due for 1856, $9.89.]
Syphax, Wm F
Stiger, Wm T
Stewart, Wm T
Stonestreet, Wm
Simms, Wm
Tilghman, Amelia
Taverns, Alex'r [Pump tax due since 1853, [assessed to Mary E Allen,] $90.
Thruston, Buckner [Due for 1856, $1.91.]
Thomas, Benj F, in trust for Ann E Bryan
Thomas, Edw M [Pump tax due since Sep, 1855, $1.50.]
Timms, Henry [Due for 1856, $21.16.]
Towers, John T [Due for 1855, $18.18.]
Thompson, Michl, in trust for Mary Peter

Trook, Susanna C [Due for 1855, $2.88.]
Tucker, Wm, in trust for Eliza & Mary A Keefer
Treck, John N [Due for 1856, $1.46.]
Taylor, B Ogle
Thruston, Caroline
Thompson, Christiana
Thomas, Edw A
Tilghman, Frisby
Todsen, Geo P
Taylor, Geo [colored]
Thomas, John H
Toll, Isaac D [Due for 1856, $1.38.]
Taylor, John [3rd]
Thompson, Jas
Totten, Jos G
Tayloe, John, jr
Thompson, Jas
Tobin, John
Towles, Jas, in trust
Thompson, Jos
Talburt, Jane W & Geo W
Taylor, Jos
Twine, Mary
Thaw, Mary Ann
Tyler, Mary M
Thompson, Michl
Twomay, Michl
Travers, Nicholas
Twine, Polly [colored]
Thompson, Saint John
Tabler, Wm J
Talbert, Tobias
Todd, Wm B

Usher, John W, & Joshua Gibson
Van Patten, Chas H [Due for 1856, $2.83.]
Venable, Ellen
Vass, Douglas
Vanderwerken, Gilbert
Vinson, H R F
Vernon, Henry T
Vermillion, H O
Varnell, John T
Van Ness, John P
Varnum, J B
Vessey, Mary J
Van Ness, Mary A W
Veitch, Wm

Winder, Chas H [Due for 1855, $5.34.]
Whelan, Catharine Ann [Due for 1856, $61.42.]
Wiltberger, Chas H [Due for 1855, pump tax, $4.36.]
Watterston, Geo, in trust for Mary Sweeny
Woody, Edw [Due for 1857, in the name of Nathl Frye.]
Williams, Jas [Due for 1855, in the name of Geo W Cochran, $25.87.]
White, W G W, & J L [Due for 1856, $52.53.]
Williams, Thos E [Due for 1856, $19.72.]
Wallingsford, Alfred
White, Ann
Willett, Beniah
Woodward, Chas J
Wilkes, Chas
Ward, Cassandra
Warren, Cyrus M & others
Waters, David S, jr
Worthington, Eliz M
Watson, Edw A
Wheeler, Ephraim
Wood, Ferdinand F
Walsh, Francis S
White, Geo W
Wilson, Geo [Due for 1856, $11.43.]
Wilson, Geo G, in trust
Wright, Geo
Walker, Geo W
Williams, Hannah O
Wild, Havre

Webb, Jos W
Wilson, John
Winder, John H
Walters, Jas, sen, & Thos
Wheatley, John F
Waters, John
Webb, John F
Wirt, John L
Williams, J & J
Wagner, John
Williams, Jos
Wilson, Judith F
Wise, John H
White, John P
Weed, J C & N S
Williams, John
Wilson, Jacob
Washington, Joshua
Wise, John, & Jerome Callahan
Williams, Lemuel
Waring, Marsham
White, Martha R & others
Wright, Matthew [Due for 1856, $1.26.]
Washington, Perrin
Wyman, R H
Waters, R A

Waters, Robt
Williams, Sarah B
Wise, Saml
Wroe, Saml C
Wheeler, Theodore, in trust
Weaver, Thos
Williams, Thos
Ward, Ulysses [Due for 1856, $7.57.
Wilson, Wm
Ward, Wm J [Due for 1855, $111.94.]
Whitlock, Wm D
Webb, Wm B, in trust for Mary Mechlin
Webb, Wm P [Due for 1855, $18.60.]
Wallingsford, Washington
Ward, Wm H
West, Wm H
Webster, Wm A
Wayne, Wm
Walworth, Wm B
Wilson, Wm
Worrell, Wm
Whitmore, Wm
Wilson, Wm T
Young, Alex'r H
Younger, Edw
Young, Notley, heirs of

Young, Nicholas, Notley, Ignatius & Benj, & Sarah E Clagett & C H Wiltberger
Zange, Nicholas

Officers of the Corp of the City of Washington:

Mayor: Jas G Berry
Register: Wm Morgan
Corp Atty: Jas M Carlisle
Tax Clerk: Wm J Donoho
Book-keeper; Edwin J Klopfer
Board of Health:
Dr P C Davis
J B H Smith
Dr R K Stone
Jas E Dunnawin
Dr W G Palmer
Jos Bryan
Dr W P Johnston

Messenger: Wm Q Locke
Collector: Jas F Halliday
Clerks: Reuben Cleary & Wm H Williams
Surveyor: Wm Forsyth

Francis Mohun
Dr G McCoy
J P Ingle
Dr F S Walsh
John D Brandt
Dr J E Morgan
Henry A Clarke

Apothecaries to furnished medicine to the poor:
David G Ridgeley J B Gardiner
Andrew W Hughes Jas D O'Donnell
Valentine Harbaugh D B Clarke
Jas N Callan

Physicians to the Poor:
Philip C Davis, M D J M Grymes, M D
J W H Lovejoy, M D J M Roberts, M D
Geo M Dale, M D J E Willett, M D
J M Toner, M D
Com'r of Health: Chas F Force, M D

Aldermen:
Geo W Riggs Edmund Barry
Wm T Dove-Pres C W C Dunnington
Thos Miller Robt Clarke
Thos J Fisher Aaron W Miller
Thos Donoho John L Smith
Jos F Brown Peter M Pearson
Wm W Moore Erasmus J Middleton-Sec
Francis Mohun Messenger: Jacob Kleiber

Cmte of the Board of Aldermen:
On Finance: Messrs Riggs, Brown, & Smith
Improvements: Messrs T Miller, Moore, & Pearson
Police: Messrs Mohun, Barry, & Smith
Claims: Messrs Barry, Brown, & Pearson
Schools: Messrs Donoho, Dunnington, & Clarke
Fire Dept: Messrs Fisher, Barry, & A W Miller
Elections: Messrs Moore, Fisher, & Clarke
Drainage, Sewerage, & Distribution of Water: Messrs Brown, T Miller, & Pearson
On Unfinished Business: Messrs A W Miller, Dunnington, & Smith

Joint Cmtes:
On the Asylum: Messrs Moore, Donoho, & A W Miller
Health of the City: Messrs T Miller, Mohun, & Clarke
Canal: Messrs Brown & Pearson
Wharves: Messrs Donoho & Smith
Enrolled Bills: Mr Moore
Accounts of Register: Mr Barry
Money Transactions of the Corp: Mr Riggs
Eligibility of Assessors: Messrs A W Miller, Fisher, & Smith
T Count & Destroy Due Bills: Mr Fisher
To attend to the interests of the Corp before Congress: Messrs Dunnington, Riggs, & Clarke

Board of Common Council:
Chas Abert-Pres
John B Turton
Southey S Parker
Wm Orme
Grafton Powell
Chas S Jones
Wm G Palmer
Lambert Tree
Christopher S O'Hare
Stephen D Castleman
Elijah Edmonston
Wm P Mohun
Wm A Mulley
Wm F Wallace
T Van Reswick
Geo A Bohrer
Franklin S Ober
John H Russell
Thos E Lloyd
Chas Wilson
Thos Milstead
Wm A Kennedy-sec
Wm Q Locke-messenger

Cmtes of the Board of Common Council:
On Ways & Means: Messrs Jones, Turton, Tree, Castleman, Van Reswick, Ober, & Lloyd
On Improvements: Messrs Turton, Van Reswick, Orme, O'Hare, Mohun, Russell, & Lloyd
Of Claims: Messrs Powell, Mohun, & Wilson
On Unfinished Business: Messrs Palmer & Milstead
On Elections: Messrs Wallace, Ober, Wilson
On Police: Messrs Mulloy, O'Hare, Parker, Powell, Castleman, Bohrer, & Lloyd
Canal: Messrs Castleman, Orme, Ober, Van Reswick, Parker, & Milstead
Schools: Messrs Tree, Turton, Powell, Mohun, Wallace, Bohrer, & Lloyd
Fire Dept: Messrs Parker, Edmonston, & Milstead
Drainage, etc: Messrs Palmer, Orme, Turton, Mohun, Mulloy, Russell, & Wilson
Corp before Congress: Messrs Jones, Mohun, Lloyd, & Tree
Joint Cmtes:
Wash Canal: Messrs Castleman & Van Reswick
On Money Transactions with Corp: Mr Jones
Asylum: Messrs Turton, Jones, Wallace, & Milstead
Count & Destroy Due Bills: Mr Edmonston
Register of Accounts: Mr Bohrer
Wharves: Messrs Orme, Castleman, & Russell
Health of the City: Messrs Palmer, Parker, Wilson, & Mulloy
Enrolled Bills: Mr Tree
Eligibility of Assessors: Messrs Wallace, Parker, O'Hare, & Edmonston
Com'rs of Improvements:
Jos E Rawlings
R B Owens
Stephen Coster
Saml S Taylor
Board of Trustees of the Public Schools:
Wm B Randolph-Pres
Roger B Ironside
A B Stoughton
Erasmus M Chapin
Jas Laurenson
Mitchell H Miller

John D Brandt
Wm F Price
Francis S Walsh
J E Willett

Fred'k Whyte
Saml Yorke AtLee
Robt Ricketts-Sec
Valentine Harbaugh-Treasurer

Officers of the Asylum:
Intendant: John R Queen
Physician: Dr W H Berry
Com'rs: Geo W Emerson, Geo Mattingly, & Leonard Harbaugh
Sec: John H Noyes
Com'r of the Eastern Section of the Canal: Chas C Edelin
Com'r of the Western Section of the Canal: Wm Wise
Com'rs of the West Burial Ground: Jos Borrows, Thos P Morgan; August Miller-sexton
Com'rs of the East Burial Ground: John D Brandt, Geo W Oyster; John O'Neale-sexton

Inspectors & Measurers:
Flour & Salted Provisions: Jos Lyons
Gauger & Inspector: Florian Hitz
Sealer of Weights & Measures: Hiram Richey
Inspector of Fire Apparatus: John W Martin
Inspectors & Measurers of Lumber: Peter Gallant, Wm Douglass, Saml R Beyer, Thos W Burch, Benj Bean, & S F Gates
Measurers of Grain, Bran, etc: John Wilson & J Z Williams
Wood & Coal Measurers: Jos Z Williams, Saml C Mickum, Richd Wimsatt, John Cumberland, & Wm P Drury

Clerks & Com'rs of Markets:
Clerk of Centre Market: John Waters, Jos Lyons, assist
Clerk of Eastern Market: Sylvester F Gates
Clerk of Western Market: Wm Walker
Clerk of Northern Market: Geo D Spencer
Com'rs of the Centre Market: Wm Orme, Hudson Taylor, & Buckner Bayliss
Com'rs of the Western Market: Wm H Walker & Wm Brown
Com'rs of the Northern Market: Jas T Devine & Theodore Sheckells
Com'rs of the Eastern Market: G W Johnson & Lawrence A Tuel

Assessors:
Wm Riggles
John T Stewart
Zephaniah Jones
Wm Douglass

Wm F Smallwood
Edw Wayson
John H Bird

Superintendent of Sweeps:
Thos J Jones
Thos Robbins
Chas Keller
John T Neale
Jas R Wood
H O Whitemore

Scavengers:
Danl Linkins
Wm Barr
Roger Adamson
Michl Stahl
John Schue

John Mack
Franklin Hutchins
Ernst Loeffler
Police Magistrates:
Saml Drury
Thos J Williams
John D Clark
Wm Thompson
Thos C Donn
Police Dept:
Chief of Police: John H Goddard
Lts of Police: Noble J Thomas, Edw McHenry
Police Ofcrs:
John McDermott
Wm Daw
Wm D Serrin
Jas F Edwards
Wm H Fanning
Jos Williamson
Chas G Eckloff
Jas Ginnaty
Jas H Suit
Patrick Gormly
Wm L Ross
Jacob F King
B T Watson
H W Haskell
Special Police Ofcrs:
Danl Whalen
Robt H Harrison
John M Thornton
Jas Belt
John Kidwell
John W Coombs
Thos J Kelly
Jos S Norwood
Dennis Murphy
Fred'k Schaffer
Michl Fitzgerld
Martin McNamara
Thos Young
John F Carter
Thos J Edmonston
Lawrence Malone

Wm T Bassford
Jas Curtain
Geo N Adams

Patrick McKenna
Jas Cull
Danl Rowland
Thos C Donn

Henry Yeatman
Franklin Zimmerman
H C Harrover
C W Arnold
Jacob Ash
Henry Nash
Reuben Collins
Francis S Edelin
Jas S Smith
John M Loyd
Jas A Gill
S N Chipley
Josiah Beitzell

Jas Rooney
Jas Scarff
Thos Stone
Richd H Gault
Wm O Neale
Saml Handy
Wm Rabbitt
Philip Hutchinson
Jas R Gates
Wm Johnson
Wm McLane
Peter Kraft
Alfred Henning
John Barnes
John Flaherty
Jos Tucker

John T Lewis	Geo H Morgan
Richd Evans	John Browers
Thos Holden	John J Lacey
Peter Goodyear	Alex'r Hume

THU FEB 3, 1859
Stock of groceries, dry & fancy goods, & furniture at auction, on Feb 8, at the residence & store of Mrs Goddard, corner of 12th & G sts. –Wall & Barnard, aucts

Circuit Court for PG Co, Md, in Equity. Clarinda M Edelen vs Susanna S Holt. This bill is to procure a decree for the sale of certain real estate in said county. The cmplnt is seized, as a tenant in common in fee, with the respondent, Susana S Holt, of 275 acres, more or less, of undivided real estate in said county; that the respondent is supposed to reside in Alexandria, Va, beyond the jurisdiction of this Court; that the said respondent, Susanna S Holt, by the inquisition & return to a writ de lunatico inquirendo, issued out of the same Court, some time in 1856, was found to be non compos mentis, wherefore she is incapable of consenting to a sale of said real estate. The bill prays for an order of publication against the said Susana S Holt, warning her to appear in this Court in person, or by her cmte, guardian, or next friend, or his or her solicitor, on or before the 2nd Monday in Jun next. –Chas S Middleton, Clerk of the Circuit Court for PG Co, Md.

Circuit Court of Wash Co, D C –in Equity. Jane E Gray, Chas Sauter & Ann Virginia Sauter his wife, who sues by said Chas as her next friend, Susan Slatford, & Georgianna Slatford, plntf, vs Mary D Dudley, Noble Simms, Randolph Simms, Annie Simms, & Emma Simms, dfndnts. The bill in the above entitled suit is to procure the appointment, by decree of the Court, of a trustee or trustees to make sale of the real estate of Ann Simms, deceased, pursuant to the direction in her will contained, that all her estate, real & personal, be sold, & that the proceeds of sale shall be appropriated & disposed of pursuant to the provisions of said will, to wit: one-third to said Jane E Gray, one-third to said Ann Virginia Sauter, & the remaining third to be held by the executor or administrator of Ann to the use of said Susan Slatford during her life, & at her death what may remain to go to said Georgianna Slatford, her daughter. The real estate consists of two tenenments, with houses thereon, [one a frame house, the other a brick,] in Wash City, D C, fronting 30 feet on 11th st, part of square 353. All the dfndnts named in the preceding caption being proved to the Court to be non-residents of D C. Absent dfndnts are to appear in the Court on or before the first Monday of Jun next. –Jno A Smith, clerk -Chilton & Magruder, solicitors

A horrible affair took place in Alleghany City, Pa, on Monday night. A man named Rodgers, a carpenter, went to bed intoxicated, & by some means not known the house took fire, & himself, his wife, & 3 children were burnt to cinders.

Mrd: on Feb 1, at the F st Presbyterian Church, by Rev P D Gurley, D D, Thos Cromwell to Miss E Serena Lauck, all of Wash City.

Senate: 1-Ptn from S W Megowan, now of Lexington, Ky, asking to be allowed a pension for military services during the war of 1812: referred. 2-Ptn from J H Templeton, asking the payment of expenses incurred by the State of Calif in suppressing Indian hostilities: referred. 3-Cmte on Naval Affairs: adverse report on the memorial of McKean Buchanan, a purser in the navy, praying indemnity for losses occasioned by the illegal orders of his commanding ofcr. Same cmte: asked to be discharged from the consideration of the bills for the relief of Emilie G Jones, excx of Thos P Jones; & relief of Nancy M Johnson, admx of Walter R Johnson: discharged accordingly. 4-Cmte on Patents & the Patent Ofc: bill for the relief of the widow of Chas Pearson, & recommended its passage: passed. 5-Cmte on Foreign Relations: bill for the relief of Jas P Cook, to be referred to the Cmte on Commerce. 6-Cmte on Military Affairs: adverse report on the memorial of David Butler.

Wash Corp-Jan 31. 1-Ptn from Jas McColgan, asking a return of money for an unexpired term of a tavern license: referred to the Cmte of Claims. 2-Cmte of Claims: adverse reports on the ptns of Geo W Hopkins; of Christian Miller; & of Francis Quigley. Same cmte-bills passed: relief of Jos Mansfield; of Agnes Reagan; & of Thos Geary. 3-Papers of Jos Gerhardt to be withdrawn from the files, & referred to the Cmte of Claims. 4-Ptn of Jas Kanalley; of John Van Skiver; & of Herman Mewze; praying the remission of a fine: referred to the Cmte of Claims.

Some months ago two American citizens, visiting the Fejee Islands for the purpose of trade, were murdered & eaten by the cannibals there living. Cmder Sinclair, of the U S sloop-of-war **Vandalia**, fitted out an expedition in Oct last to punish the perpetrators of this outrage. The expedition consisted of 40 seamen & 10 marines, who proceeded from Levuku to Waya in the schnr **Mechanic**, chartered for the occasion, under the command of Lt Caldwell. They went to the town of Lomati, [Waya island] where the attack took place. Lt Caldwell sent a message to the Chiefs of Lomati, demanding the surrender of the murderers; he sent a declaration to the effect that the natives would be glad to eat more Americans. Nothing left to do but to punish the barbarity & insolence of the cannibals; an attack commenced; they found 300 warriors ready for the fight, decked in funeral robes of white, presenting a frightfully grotesque appearance. After an absence of 10½ hours the party returned to the ship, having burnt 116 houses, all the canoes of the cannibals, & having killed a large number of the enemy. Thus the savages were effectually punished for their crimes.

FRI FEB 4, 1859
Trustee's sale: by deed of trust from David Hoester & his wife, dated Jan 7, 1857, recorded in Liber J A S No 126, folios 220 thru 224, of the land records for Wash Co, D C: auction on Mar 9, on the premises, the western half of lot 3 in square 983.
-E C Morgan, A Lloyd, trustees -A Green auct

Mrd: on Jul 27, 1858, by Rev Andrew G Carothers, Mr Jos Darden to Miss Emily E Harkness, both of Wash City.

Senate: 1-Bill proposes to authorize Gilbert Vanderwerken, Bayard Clarke, Asa P Robinson, & their assigns, at their own expense, to contract & lay down a double-track railway in Wash City, through Pa ave & 15th st, from the west gate of the Capitol to High st, Gtwn, with the right to run public carriages thereon, drawn by horse power, for the transportation of passengers, receiving therefore for a rate of fare not exceeding five cents per passenger for any distance; the maintenance & use of the road are to be subject to the municipal regulations of the cities of Wash & Gtwn. 2-Report from the Court of Claims in favor of Thos Fillebrown, with a bill for his relief. Also, adverse reports on the following claims: of Saml J Hensley, Chas E Stuart, Martin B Lewis, Geo McDougall; Herman Hooker & others, heirs & reps of Jas Hooker, deceased Chas St John, exc of Lewis Warrington, deceased; Philip F Voorhies, John Percival, Herman Thorn, & Eliza Hamilton, excs of C B Hamilton, deceased; David G Barnitz, adm of David Grier; Saml F Holbrook & Alex'r Cross: referred to the Cmte of Claims. 3-Ptn from Cmdor Wm Mervine, asking that he may be refunded the amount of a judgment obtained against him for the discharge of an official duty: referred. 4-Ptn from the surviving children of Capt Robt Orr, who was in the expedition with Geo Rodgers Clarke against the Indians in 1781, asking the land promised by the laws of Va: referred. 5-Ptn from Wm Allen, asking to be allowed arrears of pension: referred. 6-Ptn from Harriet B Macomb, widow of the late Maj Gen Macomb, asking to be allowed a pension: referred. 7-Cmte on Naval Affairs: memorial of Edw Brinley, an ofcr in the navy, asking to be allowed the difference between the pay of a midshipman & that of a lt during the time he acted in the latter capacity, submitted an adverse report on the same; which was agreed to. 8-Cmte of Claims: bill for the relief of Thos Crown, praying to be allowed damages occasioned by the abrogation of a contract made by him with Capt Blaney to furnish bricks for the fortifications at Oak Island. 9-Cmte on Pensions: adverse report on the ptn of Marshall Harvey to be placed on the roll of invalid pensions. 10-Cmte of Claims: bill from the Court of Claims for the relief of John Peebles, & recommended its passage. 11-Bill to provide for the settlement of the accounts of the late Lt Col Lewis S Craig, for his services in connexion with the Mexican boundary commission: passed.

Last year the State of Vermont, after waiting 70 years, erected over the ashes of her world-renowned hero, Ethan Allen, a granite column, 40 ft in height, of solid & enduring workmanship; surmounted by a pedestal for a colossal statue of the hero 10 ft high.

The adopted son of Mr Gibbs, foreman in the Niagara Falls Paper Mill, was taken over the cataract on Sat last. The victim was about 11 years of age, & a favorite of all who knew him. The Mill is situated on Bath Island. The boy was playing in the area & lost his balance. —Rochester American of Feb 1

It will be recollected that the statue of John Adams, was lost on its passage from Leghorn to this country, in the ship **Oxford**, over one year ago. Mr Rogers, the sculptor, has executed a duplicate from the original model, & that the invoice has already been received at N Y. When the statue arrives the gallery will be complete; Winthrop, Otis, Adams, & Story forming the finest group of statuary in New England.

Trustee's sale of valuable farm, houses & lots: by deed of trust executed by Jacob Brounstein & Mary J Brounstein his wife, dated Oct 31, 1857, recorded in Liber C S M, No 2, folios 134 etc, of the land records of PG Co, Md: sale on May 1, of all the right, title, interest, estate, claim, & demand at law & in equity of said Jacob & Mary J Brounstein, in & to all that part of a tract of land in said county, described on the plat of said land & premises by Richd Beall, surveyor of the county & State aforesaid, as a part of *Wilson's Endeavor Enlarged*, of *Warring's Lot Enlarged*, beginning at the 4th line of *Maddam's Neglect*, containing 67 acres, 1 rood & 2 perches. Also, part of *Maddam's Neglect*, part of the north end of *Warring's Lot*, & part of *Uncle's Good-Will*, containing 72 acres, 1 rood & 15 perches, more or less. Also, those parts of lots 41 & 42 in Bladensburgh, PG Co, Md, which was conveyed to Lilbourn Mitchell by Wm Beckett & Rosanna S his wife, by deed dated Feb 11, 1837, recorded in the land records of PG Co, Md. Also, another house & lot in Bladensburg, now or formerly occupied by Catharine Suit, widow of the late Edw Suit, & which was conveyed to the said Lilbourn Mitchell by Joshua H Selby & Susan his wife, & others, dated Feb 17, 1851. Also, all that tract or parcel in said county, called *Columbia*, or part of *Columbia*, it being the same property that was conveyed to the said Lilbourn Mitchell & others, by deed dated Feb 17, 1851. Also, all that other parcel of land in said county, called *Columbia*, or part of *Columbia*, which was conveyed to the said L Mitchell by Joshua H Selby & others, by deed dated Feb 17, 1851, recorded in the land records of PG Co, Md, with all & singular improvements, ways, waters, water courses, right, members, privileges, advantages, & appurtenances thereto belonging & all the estate, right, title, & interest, property, claim, & demand whatsoever, at law & in equity, of the said Jacob & Mary J Brounstein, in & to the above. –H Naylor, trustee -A Green auct [Marlboro Gaz]

Died: on Jan 31, in hope of immortality, at his residence in Wash Co, near Wash City, with consumption, Wm Macabee, in his 40th year.

Circuit Court of Wash Co, D C-in Equity: No 1,426. Branch Jordan against Wm G Palmer & Wm Towers, adms, Eliza P Towers, widow, & Jos B Towers, Mary A Towers, Walter L Towers, Laura J Towers, & Wm P Towers, heirs of John T Tower. On Feb 19, at the Court-house, I shall state an account of the personal estate of said John T Towers. -W Redin, auditor

In Chancery, Jan term, 1859. John Foller vs Andreas Fischer. The object of this suit is to procure a decree for a sale of certain real estate in Wash City, D C, which was conveyed on Jul 31, 1854, by the dfndnt to the cmplnt by deed in the nature of a mortgage. On Jul 31, 1854, the said Andreas Fischer, being indebted to the said Foller in the sum of $450, gave his promissory note for that amount, dated the day & year aforesaid, & payabe to said Foller or order three years after date with interest; & conveyed certain real estate, which is described in the bill, unto the said Foller to secure the payment of said indebtedness; that although due & payable no part of said sum had been paid; that the said Fischer is a non-resident. The absent dfndnt is to appear in the court in person or by solicitor on or before Jun 6 next. –Jno A Smith, clerk -Carrington & Lloyd, solicitors

House of Reps: 1-Cmte on Military Affairs: bill to enable the Sec of War to test the utility of a new mode of wrting invented by Jos M Hodge, of Ark: laid on the table. Same cmte: bill for the relief of Edw Ingersoll: committed.

SAT FEB 5, 1859
Trustee's sale of valuable improved real estate, in Fairfax Co, Va: on Mar 9, 1859, on the premises, by deed of trust from Asa Gladmon & Ann Gladmon, his wife, to Lambert Tree, duly executed, & admitted to record in the Clerk's Ofc of Fairfax Co, Va, the tract of land, in said county: containing 271 acres, near *Holmes' Run*, a corner of Adams' sale to Ben H Thornton; corner of Adams' purchase of W B Randolph; Page's sale to Lipscomb; to junction of the Spring Branch. –Lambert Tree, trustee
-Jas C McGuire & Co, aucts

Senate: 1-Ptn from John Brannan, a laborer to the Dept of State, asking compensatin for performing the duties of Librarian of that Dept: referred. 2-Ptn from John Hambleton, asking indemnity for losses occasioned by the Indians on the route between Albuquerque & Calif: referred to the Cmte on Indian Affairs. 3-Papers from the Court of Claims in the case of Saml J Hensley, on which an unfavorable report had been made yesterday, was agreed to be referred to the Cmte on Indian Affairs. 4-Cmte on Finance: asked to be discharged from the consideration of the memorial of B F Rittenhouse, a clerk in the ofc of the Register of the Treasury, asking compensation for extra services: which was agreed to. 5-Cmte of Claims: asked to be discharged from the consideration of the memorial of Thos S Sprague: which was agreed to. 6-Cmte on Public Bldgs & Public Grounds: asked to be discharged from the consideration of the memorial of Wm Gaston Pearson, which was agreed to.

Los Angeles Star of Jan 8. Maj G A H Blake, in command of the 1st dragoons, will be relieved by Col Beall, & will shortly make a visit to his friends in the Atlantic States. Maj Blake has been on service without leave, we believe, for the past 8 years.

House of Reps: 1-Bill for the relief of Capt J C McFerran: referred to the Cmte on Military Affairs. 2-Bill for the relief of J W Hilton, praying compensation for extra mail service: recommended that it do pass. 3-Bills taken up & passed-relief: of Henry Hubbard; of C Edw Habicht, adm of J W P Lewis; of Mrs Ambroise Brou, of the parish of St Chas, Louisiana; of the heirs & legal reps of Olivier Landry, of Louisiana; of Wm H Russell; of Capt A W Reynolds; & of John Kelly. 4-Bill taken up & passed-relief of Sylvester Tiffany: passed. 5-Senate bill to amend an act entitled "An act to authorize the relocation of land warrants numbered 3, 4, & 5, granted by Congress to Gen Lafayette," approved Feb 26, 1845: passed. 6-Bill to provide for the final settlement of the land claim of the heirs of John Underwood, in Florida: passed.

Orphans Court of Wash Co, D C. Letters testamentary on the personal estate of W Macabee, late of Wash Co, deceased. –A Green, exc

On Sunday last were performed the funeral rites of Mrs Tacy Gray, a lady who had passed, by about 4 months, the great age of 100 years. She died at the house of her daughter, in Shippen st, Phil, & up to 3 days previous to her decease was in the enjoyment of most remarkable health. Mrs Gray was with her husband, who was an ofcr in the Navy, on board Com Perry's ship at the battle of Lake Erie. Her recollection of Washington was perfect. She leaves descendants. Her remains were followed to the grave by a very large concourse of people, among whom was a body of the veterans of 1812 & the Revolution. -Phil North Amer

Rev Peter E Green, of the Mississippi Conference of the M E Church, was shot by a man named Fisher, some months ago, near Vicksburg, for receiving Fisher's wife as a member of the church of which Mr Green was the pastor. Fisher had been tried, found guilty, & sentenced to the penitentiary for 7 years.

In Equity, No 1,401. Geo Parker, Thos Parker, & Jos B Bryan, vs Jos Edw Roberts et al. The object of this suit is to procure a sale of the real estate of John Roberts, now deceased, for the payment of his debts, on the ground of the insufficiency of his personal estate. John Roberts died intestate in Apr, 1857, leaving Jos Ed Roberts & Matthew Roberts his heirs at law. At the time of his death said John Roberts was the owner in fee simple of lots 10 & 11 of square 51, in Wash City; that letters of administration were duly granted on the personal estae of said John Roberts by the Orphans Court of Wash Co, D C, to Wm B Magruder; that the said personal estate is most inconsiderable in quantity, of little value, & utterly insufficient for the payment of his debts; that the said John Roberts at the time of his death was indebted to said cmplnts on a due bill, sundry promissory notes & accounts, amounting in the aggregate of $2,968.42, with interest thereon. Said Jos Edw Roberts is not a resident of D C; absent dfndnt to appear in the ofc of the Clerk of this Court, on or before the first Monday of Jun, 1859.
–Jno A Smith, clerk

Mrd: on Monday, in the Sixth St Methodist Protestant Church, Cincinnati, Ohio, at the close of the services by the Pasor, Rev J J White, Mr Robt Brown to Mrs Eliz Warner, both of Wash, D C.

Mrd: on Feb 1, at St Paul's Church, Richmond, Va, by Rev Dr Minnegerode, Alfred, son of Hon Wm C Rives, to *Saide C, only daughter of Jas B Macmurdo, & grand-daughter of the late Bishop Moore. [*Copied as written.]

Died: on Jan 29, at the residence of his father, in Jefferson Co, Va, Dr Cary Selden Alexander, aged 23 years.

Died: yesterday, in Wash City, at the residence of his grandson, Alfred C Shaw, corner of 10th & K sts, Lemuel Shaw, in his 89th year. May he rest in peace!

Died: on Wed last, in Balt, in her 4th year, Annie Sarah, eldest child of Bernard M & Emily J Campbell.

Died: on Jan 9, 1859, at his residence, in Chickasaw Co, Miss, after a brief illness, Capt Geo Bowen, in his 75th year. He was a native of Charleston, S C, & was capt of an artl company engaged in the Creek war of 1814, in which he distinguished himself. By his great industry & energy he became the owner of several thousand acres of land in Mississippi. He was a man of business to the latest period of his life, a good citizen, & true friend.

Private sale of valuable Montgomery land: by power of atty, duly executed by the devise of Gen Widiam Lingan Gaither, deceased, the undersigned will sell about 600 acres of land, being part of the real estate of which the late Gen Gaither died seized & possessed: the land is between his late residence & the village of *Unity*. I am also authorized to sell an eligible lot of 10 acres, fronting directly upon the Wash & Brookeville turnpike, with a comfortable 2 story frame dwlg & good pump of water. I will also sell 2 other farms in Montg Co, within a few hours travel from Wash City. For terms address A B Davis, Brookeville, Montg Co, Md.

MON FEB 7, 1859
Senate: 1-Ptn from citizens of Mass, asking that the bills to extend the patents of E M Chaffee & Nathl Hayward for improvements in the manufacture of India rubber good may not be passed: referred. 2-Bill for the relief of Mrs Eliz M Cook, widow of Maj Thos H Cook, late U S marshal of the district of Texas: referred to the Cmte on Commerce. 3-Bill for the relief of Anna E Bronaugh, widow of the late John W Bronaugh: referred to the Cmte on Naval Affairs. 4-Bill for the relief of Saml A West, Geo McCallough, & Chas Pendergrast: passed.

The birth-place of Andrew Jackson: conclusively established that Gen Jackson was born in Mecklenburg Co, at the house of Geo McCamie, & near to the S C line. It appears that he was born while his mother was on her way to N C. She subsequently resided at Waxaw, & where her son Andrew spent his early youth. It is not difficult to perceive the prima facie reasons on which it have been commonly, if erroneously, supposed that he was a native of S C.

Sale by order of the Orphans Court of Wash Co, D C: handsome match horses, family carriage, 2 milch cows, & farming utensils, at auction, on Feb 10, at the residence of the late Gen Archibald Henderson, deceased, at the U S Garrison, at the Navy Yard.
-Richd H Henderson, adm -A Green auct

Wm Cranch Bond, director of the astronomical observatory at Harvard College, who died recently, was born in Portland, Maine, Sep 9, 1790, & learned the watchmaking business under his father.

Trustee's sale: by deed of trust made & executed by John Higgins, dated Sep 23, 1847, recorded among the land records of Wash Co, D C, in Liber 97, folios 350, [the former purchaser having failed to comply with the terms of sale] I will sell, on Feb 21, at public auction, lot 16 in square 695, with improvements, consisting of 2 small tenements. -Jas Adams, trustee -J C McGuire & Co, aucts

House of Reps: 1-Cmte on Naval Affairs: bills for the relief of Saml A Cole, jr, late a purser in the U S ship **Levant**; explanatory of an act for the relief of Dr Chas D Maxwell, a surgeon in the U S Navy, & for the relief of Cmder H J Hartstene, for the restoration of the barque **Resolute**: they were severally committed. Same cmte: bills for the relief of Sarah Brashears; & for the relief of Mrs Susan C Rhae, widow of Dr J Burrows: severally committed. Same cmte: bill for the relief of Jas H Causten, sole heir & leal reps of John H Causten, deceased, late a purser in the U S navy; & a bill for the relief of Ann Scott: severally committed. Same cmte: bill for the relief of Lucy A Wakefield, widow of Benj A Wakefield: passed. Same cmte: bill for the relief of Otway H Berryman: committed. 2-Cmte on Territories: bill for the relif of John B Motley: committed. 3-Cmte on Foreign Affairs: reported Senate resolution giving the consent of Congress to the acceptance by Capt M F Maury & Prof A D Bache of gold medals from the Sardinian Gov't: passed. 4-Cmte on Revolutionary Pensions: bills for the relief of Nancy Weeks, of Ga; for the relief of the children & heirs of Eluathan Sears, deceased, late of N Y; & for the relief of Saml Winn, only surviving child of Richd Winn, a Revolutionary ofcr: severally committed. Same cmte: bill granting a pension to Robt Purchase, a soldier in the Revolutionary war: passed.

Mississippi Free Trader: Maj Earl Van Dorn: this gallant young ofcr, in consequence of his late brilliant action on the frontiers of Texas, in which he achieved a complete victory over a superior & well trained force of Camanches, is attracting the public attention. He graduated with distinction at West Point. His father, the late Judge Peter Van Dorn, was an old-time citizen of Natchez; a merchant here in 1807, a native [we believe] of N J, & a near connexion of Col Anthony Hutchins, a man of great ability & influence, who came here in 1771, & whose descendants are among the most distinguished citizens of Mississippi & Louisiana. Peter Van Dorn moved to Claiborne Co, & for a number of years presided over the Court of Probate; his mansion was adorned by a most excellent circle of household divinities; he married a Miss Caffrey, of an old N C family, a near relative of Mrs Gen Jackson, & the aunt of the late John Jenkins, of the Vicksburg Sentinel. In her personal appearance she resembled Mrs Jackson. Under these influences young Van Dorn was nurtured. Maj Van Dorn is one of the most active & brilliant ofcrs in the service, a man of high character & fine attainments, destined, if he lives, to great distinction, & the State of Mississippi owes him a sword. We make this motion, & the People & the Legislature will second it.

Boston, Feb 6. Russell's Mechanical Baker, in Commercial st, burnt this morning. The falling walls crushed the adjoining bldgs. Danl Henderson, a fireman, was killed, & Capt Wilson, of the steam fire engine Eclipse, was seriously injured.

Seth Thomas, so long identified with the manufacturing interests of the Naugatuck Valley, died at his residence in Plymouth Hollow, on Jan 28, at the age of 73 years. He was widely known as a clock-maker, his name being scattered over the world on their dial plates. He also was for many years the chief manager of a cotton mill, & a brass foundry. It is said that Mr Thomas was the first man who made clocks in Connecticut.

Fire broke out on Sat in the frame shed attached to the lime kilns of Mr Lawson Hoover, on 27th st, near the canal basin. Considerable damage was done, but the office was saved.

Mr G A Groux, extensively known in Europe & in America for the extraordinary conformation of his chest, which permits a view of the pulsations of the heart, is now in this city, & the medical faculty have already availed themselves of this unique opportunity to make observations so interesting.

N Y, Feb 6. A dwlg-house was burnt in Brooklyn this morning, & Mrs Gill, 2 children, & a servant girl were smothered. Mr Gill was absent in Phil on business. [Feb 9th newspaper: The family of Mr Gill consisted of his wife, Mrs Eliz Gill, Mary & Ellen, aged 2 & 6 years, 2 servants, Ann Keegan & Honora Keegan, sisters, Thos Gill, brother of Mr E Gill, & Mr Otto Graves, a boarder. Mrs Gill, her 2 children, & Ann Keegan suffocated. Thos Gill was dangerously injured; Otto Graves slightly injured; & Honora Keegan was perhaps fatally burnt. Not known how the fire originated. –N Y Courier]

Engraving of all descriptions: D O Hare, engraver, 264 Penn ave, near 12th st. [Ad]

Orphans Court of Wash Co, D C. Letters of administration, with the will annexed, on the personal estate of Alex'r Adams, late of Wash Co, deceased.
–Priscilla L Adams, admx w a

TUE FEB 8, 1859
Court of Claims-Feb 7: 1-Willis Benefield vs the U S: claimant was a soldier in the 2nd regt of Indiana volunteers in the war with Mexico, & received a warrant for 160 acres of land, which was duly located, & a patent was issued from the U S for the same. He took possession of the land, & held it until it was ascertained that it had been previously conveyed to the State of Indiana, under the act of Congress appropriating lands for the benefit of the Wabash & Erie Canal. This claim is for remuneration for the loss of the land so located. The case was submitted. 2-Mary Reeside, admx, vs the U S. This is a claim for a balance of $34,150, retained by the Sec of the Treasury out of the sum ordered to be paid to the claimant by the act of Congress passed on Feb 7, 1857, on the ground that certain drafts said to have been drawn by the claimant's testator were applicable to the payment of a portion of the amount granted by the act of Feb 7, 1857. The object of this suit is to test the validity of said drafts. Hon Jas Cooper, of Pa, for the claimant. Court adjourned.

First class Confectionary at private sale, the establishment of Messrs Atz & Bro, Bridge st, Gtwn, on the most accomodating terms. –Barnard & Buckey, aucts

San Jose Tribune of the 7th says: yesterday an affray took place near Mayneld, between Messrs Thos Seals, Alex'r Robb, & perhaps Saml Crosby, one one side, & two brothers, Jas & Paul Shore, on the other. Paul Shore was shot dead, Jas severely cut with a knife & lacerated by a bloodhound; Seals was shot through the left left; while Robb received a slight contusion by a blow over the head with a pistol. The Shore brothers went to the ranch of Thos Seal, & commenced putting up a house upon the premises which caused the affray. Crosby was the former owner of the ranch. Last evening affairs were quiet.

I will apply to the Com'r of the Gen Land Ofc of the U S for a duplicate of a land warrant for 160 acres of land, issued to me as captain of co K, 11th regt of U S Infty, dated Apr 9, 1852, No 16,070. The above warrant was lost by John McCulloch, of Jefferson Co, Iowa, at Jefferson City, Mo. –Arthur C Cummings, Abingdon, Va

Mrd: on Feb 3, by Rev Chas H Hall, at the church of the Epiphany, Fred'k Schley, of Md, to Florence, daughter of R C Washington, of Wash City.

Died: on Feb 5, at Alexandria, Mrs Margaret McKenzie, widow of the late Capt Jas McKenzie, in her 80th year. Her funeral will take place from the residence of her son, Lewis McKenzie, on Prince st, on this day, the 8th, at 2½ o'clock.

Died: on Feb 6, in Wash City, Willie, only son of Anna M T & Wm Hemphill Jones, in his 6th year.

WED FEB 9, 1859
Senate: 1-Ptn from Danl McAvery, a soldier in the Florida war, asking a pension: referred. 2-Cmte on Private Land Claims: bill to confirm the title in a certain tract of land in the State of Missouri to the heirs & legal reps of Thos Madden, deceased, reported it without amendment. 3-Cmte on Pensions: adverse reports on the ptns of Dorcas Hall; Micajah Owen; citizens of N Y, asking that a pension may be granted to Polly Egbertson; Mary Featherstone & Effie Van Ness. Same cmte: adverse report on the bill granting a pension to Mary Blattenberger. 4-Cmte on Patents & the Patent Ofc: adverse report on the memorial of Richd Imlay, asking an extension of his patent for an improvement in the mode of supporting the bodies of railroad cars: report was concurred in.

Mrs Mary Hartung, who was on trial in Albany, N Y, the past week, for the murder of her husband, Emil Hartung, has been found guilty of murder.

Henry Jumpertz, who has been on trial the past 10 days in Chicago for the murder of Sophia Werner, whose remains were found in a barrel at the Hudson River Railroad depot, N Y, about a year since, has been found guilty of committing the deed.

Yesterday morning, Mr M F Kleiber, residing at H & 5th sts, arose from bed, & some half hour afterwards his wife came down stairs, & found her husband dead on the floor. He had died of heart disease. Mr Kleiber was about 35 years of age, & leaves 4 small children to the care of their widowed mother.

Probably homicide. Yesterday John Ennis, a resident of the Northern Liberties, in Wash City, was shot in Gtwn by Hilleary Hutchings, the keeper of a restaurant on the west side of the street. It was said that Ennis had offended Hutchings' wife, & was pursued by the husband with a revolver in hand. He was overtaken at High & Water sts & there shot at 3 times. His wound is deemed a mortal one. [Feb 10th newspaper: John Ennis died yesterday at the hands of Hilleary Hutchings in Gtwn.]

Petersburg, Va, Feb 8. **Wm & Mary College**, the oldest institution of the kind in the country except Harvard Univ, together with the extensive library & laboratory, was destroyed by fire this morning. All the students escaped. There was insurance on it for $22,000. [Feb 10th newspaper: The burning of Wm & Mary College is a calamity to every Va heart. It was founded in 1693, in the reign of Wm & Mary, who granted it a donation of 20,000 acres of land. In 1693 the Assembly ordered that it should be built in Wmsburg. Its charter was dated Feb 8, 1692. Rev Jas Blair, D D, was the first Pres. He died in 1742 & was succeeded by Rev Wm Stith, author of a History of Va, who died in 1750. Bishop Jas Madison was Pres from 1777 to 1812. His successors were Rev W H Wilmer, Dr J Augustine Smith, Rev Adam Empie, D D, Thos R Dew, A M, Bishop Jones, & B F Ewell, A M, the present President. In the square fronting the college is a statue of Lord Botetourt, one of the colonial governors. A large proportion of the graduates of this college, including Jefferson, Patrick Henry, Winfield Scott, & others, have filled the highest place in the councils & the camp of the nation. –Rich Dis]

Died: on Feb 7, Garret Flannigan, in his 48th year. His funeral is today, at 2½ o'clock, from his late residence, Mass ave, between 1st & 2nd sts.

THU FEB 10, 1859
Extensive sale of very superior carved marble mantles, monuments, headstones, lintels & sills: on Feb 23, at the marble yard of Mr H Parry, who is removing his business to N Y, on Pa ave, between 18th & 19th sts. -A Green auct

Two sheep strayed on the premises of the subscriber. Owner to come forward, prove property, pay charges, & take them away. –Alex'r Feortney, P st.

Died: suddenly, at Susquehanna, St Mary's Co, Md, Francis Scott Key, son of the late P Barton Key, of Louisiana, in his 13th year. [Death date: Dec 27, 1858.]

Died: on Jan 21, at her residence, PG Co, Md, Mrs Margaret P Duckett, in her 42nd year, consort of Dr Thos S Duckett. She leaves her dear husband & beloved children. -H

Senate: 1-Ptn from Henry Roy de La Reintrie, asking compensation for his services in exposing the fraudulent claims of Jose Y Limantour to lands in San Francisco Co & adjacent islands in Calif: referred. 2-Cmte on Naval Affairs: bill for the relief of Lucy A Wakefield, with a recommendation that it do pass. 3-Cmte on Pensions: Jas Monroe, asking arrears of pension, to have leave to withdraw his papers: which was agreed to. 4-Cmte on Naval Affairs: ptn of Anne E Bronaugh, widow of the late John W Bronaugh, to be referred to the Cmte on the Judiciary. 5-Cmte on the Judiciary: bill for the relief of Wm F Wagner, & recommended its passage.

Executor's sale of valuable real estate: the subscriber, as atty for the executors of the late Mrs Mary Herbert, will offer at public sale at Beltsville, on Mar 8 next, all the real estate of said testatrix. This property lies in PG Co, Md, about 1 mile from Beltsville, & contains about 700 acres; with a large & newly built brick dwlg, & newly built necessary out-bldgs. The premises will be shown by Edw Herbert, one of the executors, who lives on an adjoining farm. Further information can be obtained by addressing Alfred Herbert, Wash City, or Edw Herbert, Beltsville, Md, or the undersigned, Upper Marlborough, Md. –C S Keech, atty for Alfred Herbert & Edw Herbert, excs of Mary Herbert, deceased.

Public sale of valuable real estate: by decree of the Circuit Court for Fred'k Co, Md, in equity, the subscriber, as trustee of Christian Smith, late of said county, deceased, will sell at public sale, on Mar 12, that splendid country seat, late the residence of said deceased, known as **Prospect Hill**, adjoining the residence of Col Wm P Maulsby, containing 282½ acres of land; with a large & elegant brickhouse, & numerous out bldgs. Mr Hargate, living on the farm, will show the same. Possession given on Apr 1 next. –Geo Smith, trustee

FRI FEB 11, 1859
Mrd: on Feb 11, by Rev Mr Morgan, Mr John I King to Miss Mary E Oliver, all of Wash.

Senate: 1-Ptn from John Sample, of Mississippi, setting forth that he is the inventor of an invaluable apparatus for the security of human life, known as the tiller-rope protector, & asking the passage of a law authorizing the Sec of the Navy to investigate the claim to the usefulness to the said invention, & to purchase the same for the use of Gov't if found worthy: referred. 2-Ptn from Wm F Fleckner, urging that, in the organization of Arizona Territory, proper provision may be made for the advancement of the Indians; & stating that upon the policy of the present period relating to the organizaition of that Territory depends the future of the aboriginal race of the country; that the present generation must one day account for a race extinct, or a people civilized & elevated: referred. 3-Cmte on Territories: to which were referred the memorials of the Legislature of the Territory of New Mexico, asking an appropriation for the completion of their capitol & penitentiary bldgs, & of Messrs O'Rieley, Speed, & T P Shaffner, proposing to complete telegraphic connexion between the Atlantic & Pacific States, submitted adverse reports in each case. 4-Cmte on Indian Affairs: asked to be discharged from the consideration of the following memorials of: Thos O & Ed O Smith, asking compensation for supplies furnished emigrants on the route to Calif; Gillum Baley & W R Baley for indemnity for losses resulting from Indian depredations; John Hambleton for losses occasioned by the Indians on the route between Albuquerque & Calif; Board of American Indian Aid Association of N Y against any more States being organized out of the public domain without consulting the tribes inhabiting the same: & of D C Davis for extra services as a watchman in the ofc of the Com'r of Indian Affairs: which was agreed to. 5-Cmte on Pensions: bill for the relief of Mary B Dusenberry, recommended its passage. Same cmte: adverse reports on the ptn of Vincent Kokouski; & on the ptn of Jas McCutcheon, an inmate of a military asylum, for continuance of his pension: which was agreed to. 6-Cmte on Commerce: asked to be discharged from the consideration of the bill for the relief of Jas P Cook, & that it be referred to the Cmte on the Judiciary: which was agreed to. Same cmte: adverse report on the memorial of Simpson P Moses in relation to fixing definitively the compensation of the collector at Astoria: agreed to. Same cmte: asked to be discharged from the consideration of the ptn of J C P Davis, in behalf of the owners of the schnr **E S Rudderow**, lost on the coast of Florida while freighted with Gov't stores; of John Barbee, in relation to an invention for the protection of tiller ropes from fires; of Noah Fairbank, in relation to requiring vessels of a certain tonnage to take a copy of directions for making fresh water from salt water; & of Wm H Ward, asking board for the purpose of examining into the various systems of marine signals: which was agreed to.

Died: on Feb 10, Charles Louis, son of G C G & Margaret Saur, aged 3 years, 4 months & 17 days. His funeral is on Sat at 3 o'clock, from the residence of the parents on 4th st, between F & G sts.

We have just been shown a finished plat of the new ***Prospect Hill Cemetery*** on the northeast of the city, & it is certainly very neatly & commodiously arranged. It will be ready to receive its perpetual tenantry in about 2 weeks.

SAT FEB 12, 1859
Senate: 1-Ptn from Chas Minturn, Pres of the Central Steam Navigation Co in the State of Calif, asking compensation for transporting the mails from San Francisco to Oakland & Petaluma: referred. 2-Ptn from Leslie Combs, one of the survivors of the battle on the river Raisin during the war of 1812, asking the passage of a law for the benefit of his few surviving brother soldiers of that war: referred. 3-Cmte of Claims: bill for the relief of Benj Sayre: recommended its passage. 4-Cmte on Commerce: bill for the relief of Mrs Eliz M Cock, widow of Maj Thos M Cock: passed. 4-Cmte of Claims: bills for the relief of Enoch B Talcott, late collector of customs at Oswego, N Y; & for the relief of Capt A W Reynolds: passed. Same cmte: asked to be discharged from the consideration of the reports of the Court of Claims adverse to the claims of Chas V Stewart & Martin B Lewis: which was agreed to.

Orphans Court of Wash Co, D C. Letters of administration on the personal estate of Nancy Dykes, late of Wash Co, deceased. –Chas I White, D D, adm

Memphis Bulletin: On Thu last, at Jackson, Tenn, Mr Geo E Miller, clerk of the bank, was horribly mutilated by a hammer. The keys to the vault were under his pillow, the bank was robbed, & as to whom committed this double crime is a mystery. Mr Miller was a worthy & estimable young man.

The Emperor Napoleon received quite a number of Americans at his last reception & invited them to a court ball. Among them were Hon Hamilton Fish, of N Y, & the ladies of his family; Gen Totten, U S Army & lady; Hon Mr Schroeder, former American Minister to Sweden; Mr Dillon, of N Y, Sec of Legation to Brazil; Mr & Mrs Jerome, of N Y; Mrs & Miss W H Russell, of N Y; Mrs & Miss Fellows, N Y; Mr & Mrs Mildeberger, N Y; Mr & Mrs Robt Potter, N Y; Mr & Mrs Haskell, N Y; Mr W H Kane, N Y; Mrs Elisha Riggs, Wash; Mrs Coleman & daughters, Ky; Mr Roger & family, Charleston, S C; Mr & Mrs McCord, Charleston, S C; Mr Alex'r Brown & family, Balt; Col C W Brush, Balt; Mr Chas March, Portsmouth, N H; Mr F W Smith, Va; & Mr S Egleston, Va.

Dr Solomon Allen, of Westbrook, Maine, returned rather late to his home in that town on Monday, drove his horse into the stable, & was later found lying on the horse-rack dead. It is presumed he fell into the rack & broke his neck. He was an elderly man, much respected & beloved.

To the heirs of David Luckett & Eliz Offutt. The parties named are notified that legacies due to them from the estate of Leven Luckett, deceased, are ready for payment, & will be paid to them upon proper proof of their identity. –Horace Luckett, Adm de bonis non, with will annexed, of Leven Luckett, deceased, at Leesburg, Loudoun Co, Va.

Mrd: on Feb 10, at the McKendree Chapel, by Rev Mr Ball, Mr Geo H Turton to Miss Catharine E L Ourand.

Died: on Feb 11, at the residence of Capt Harwood, U S Navy, Bladensburg, Md, Sarah Maria Bleecker, of Albany, N Y.

From Calif & South America. 1-Chas E Howard, of Balt, died at Panama on Jan 30th.

MON FEB 14, 1859
Senate: 1-Ptn from S L Broome, of the U S marine corps, asking to be allowed the difference between his pay & that of a purser in the navy during the time he acted in that capacity: referred. 2-Bills passed: relief of Guadalupe Estudilio de Arguello, widow of Santiago E Arguello; relief of Monroe D Downs; relief of Rebecca M Bowden, of PG Co, Va; relief of Wright Fore; relief of Dinah Minis; relief of Robt A Davidge; relief of Evelina Porter, widow of the late Cmdor David Porter, U S Navy; & relief of Mary Boyle. 3-Bills indefinitely postponed: continue pension to Katharine M Hamer; & relief of Mrs Jane Turnbull.

Calif Intelligence: 1-Danl Barry, jr, formerly of New Orleans, was killed in a mining tunnel at Spring Hill, Amador Co, on Dec 30, when a rock weighing 300 pounds detached itself & fell upon his head, crushing him to death instantly. 2-Wm Graham was buried alive in a mining claim on Jan 8, near Sand Hill, Yuba Co, when working 15 feet deep. He came to this State 3 months ago from Pittsburgh.

A male Bengal tiger belonging to Van Amburgh's menagerie, now exhibiting in Phil, very dangerously wounded a young girl, Sarah B Noble, aged 15 years on Friday. She was with her brother & had gained admission behind the scenes. She thrust her arm through the cage & attempted to pet the tiger when the tiger seized her by the arm, & lacerated her face at the same time. Her arm was amputated at the Pennsylvania Hospital. She asked to be taken to her father's residence as soon as possible.

Hon Campbell P White, for many years a prominent merchant of N Y C, & formerly one of the Reps in Congress, died at that place on Sat morning, after a brief illness.

Orphans Court of Wash Co, D C. In the case of Jas L Edwards, with the will annexed of Thos R Gedney, deceased, the administrator & Court have appointed, Mar 1st next, for the final settlement of the personal estate of the deceased, of the assets in hand.
-Ed N Roach, Reg/o wills

Mrd: on Nov 28, 1858, by Rev Mr Nadal, Mr W H Henning to Miss Lottie Colclazer, all of Wash.

Died: on Feb 13, Mrs Rebecca Scrivener, aged 83 years. Her funeral will take place from her late residence on E st south, near the Navy Yard, at 2 o'clock P M, on Feb 15, & from Christ Church at 2½ P M

Died: on Feb 11, in Wash City, John H Buthmann, long known here as a wine merchant of strict probity of character & benevolence of dispostion.

Died: on Feb 12, after a very brief illness, Francis Dunbar, eldest son of John D & Rosannah Brandt, aged 8 years & 10 months. His funeral is this afternoon at 3 o'clock, from the residence of his parents on 8th st east.

TUE FEB 15, 1859
Valuable Albemarle land, near Charlottesville & the Univ, for sale: by deed of trust from Monroe Kelly & wife, recorded in the Clerk's ofc of Albemarle Co. Sale on Mar 16, 1859, of: the desirable estate on which Mr Kelly resides, containing 522 3/4th acres of land; adjoins the lands of Benj Sneed, Geo M Bowen, & others; the dwlg has 12 rooms, with outhouses in good order. At the same time I shall offer the personal property of said Kelly, consisting of 12 horses, 20 cattle, milch cows, oxen, sheep, hogs, & household & kitchen furniture; & a good carriage. –John G Lane, trustee

Senate: 1-Ptn from Geo W Armstrong, son & exc of Maj Saml Armstrong, asking compensation for losses & injuries sustained by his father, & for the military & other services rendered by him in the war of the Revolution: referred. 2-Ptn from the heirs of Capt Nehemiah Stokely, of the Revolution, asking for the half-pay promised by resolutions of Congress, that officer never having received the commutation that other officers did or the half-pay: referred. 3-Ptn from the heirs of the legal reps of Brig Gen Wm Thompson of the army of the Revolution, asking the 7 years' half-pay due to his widow & orphan children by the act of Aug, 1780: referred. 4-Cmte on Public Lands: bill for the relief of Sylvester Tiffany: recommended its passage. 5-Bill for the relief of A Baudouin & A D Robert: passed.

The dye house at the woolen factory of Mr Jas Crawford, on the Northeast Creek, Cecil Co, Md, was destroyed by fire Wed. The loss about $3,000, of which $1,500 is covered.

Mrd: on Jan 15, at St Paul, Minn, by Rev E D Neill, G Thos May, formerly of Gtwn, D C, to Emma H Hale, of St Paul.

Mrd: on Dec 2, 1858, in Balt, by Rev Saml Regester, R T Morsell, of Wash, D C, to Mary A, youngest daughter of the late Henry R Pratt.
+
Died: on Feb 13, Mary A, wife of R T Morsell. Her funeral will be from the residence of her husband, 374 L st, this afternoon, the 15th, at 1½ o'clock.

Died: on Sunday, very suddenly, Wm M McCauley, aged 64 years. His funeral will be today at 4 o'clock, from his late residence, 490 Mass ave, between 4th & 5th sts.

Died: on Feb 12, after a long & painful illness, Margaret, wife of Wm S Nicholls, of Gtwn, D C. Her funeral is this afternoon at 3½ o'clock, from her late residence on Gtwn Heights.

Died: on Feb 14, in Wash City, Mary Lee, daughter of the late Capt Thos Lee & Susan B Ringgold, & grand-daughter of the late A P Upshur, aged 7 years & 10 months. Her funeral is today at 3 o'clock, from the Church of the Epiphany.

WED FEB 16, 1859
Mrd: on Feb 14, by Rev Andrew G Carothers, Mr Jas H Sherwood to Miss Mary Abigail Parker, daughter of Wm H Parker, all of Wash City.

Orphans Court of Wash Co, D C. In the case of Wm A Whittlesey, adm de bonis non of Oliver Whittlesey, deceased, the administrator & Court have appointed Mar 12 next, for the final settlement of the personal estate of said deceased, of the assets in hand.
-Ed N Roach, Reg/o wills

Senate: 1-Among the subjects in the topographical memoir & maps of Col Wright's late campaign against the Indians in Oregon & Wash Territories, is the report of an authentic account of the murder of the Methodist Missionary, Dr Klitman, who crossed the plains in 1838 & settled in the valley of the Walla-Walla, where he soon had around him all the comforts of rural life, & where, with his interesting family, he commenced his efforts to instruct & enlighten the savages of that region. The smallpox broke out among the Indians & the missionary family not being afflicted with it created a suspicion in the minds of the Indians that the pestilence had been brought to destroy the red man & obtain their lands. Two Indians were sent to the mission farm & strangely both died. The next step for the Indians was revenge. A selected savage stole into the chamber of the sleeping family & buried his tomahawk in the brain of the missionary & that of his wife, & then other Indians rushed in, & helpless children, male & female employes, were butchered, the house razed to the ground, fences destroyed, & every vestige of a once happy home disappeared. 2-Cmte on Public Lands: bill for the relief of Wm Yearwood: recommended its passage. Same cmte: memorial of Wm Collicott for indemnity for loss sustained in the entry of lands through the errors of Gov't ofcrs, reported a bill authorizing Wm Collicott or his legal reps to enter a quarter section of the public lands. 3-Cmte on Military Affairs: asked to be discharged from the consideration of the memorials of J & R H Porter, & of Jos C Irwin & Co, & that the memorialists have leave to withdraw their papers: which was agreed to.

The sum of $10,000 has already been raised at Wmsburg, Va, for the erection of **Wm & Mary College**, recently burned. The professors have contributed liberally. They have taken measures to continue lectures & recitations without intermission, & the students have unanimously resolved to remain.

Died: on Jan 21, at the residence of her son, Chas M Taylor, Henderson Co, Ky, Eloise Thruston, relict of Maj Edmund Taylor, U S Army, of Jefferson Co, Ky, & the youngest daughter of Col Chas M Thruston, [of Revolutionary memory,] formerly of Fred'k Co, Va, & late of Louisiana.
+
Died: on Jan 24, at Murfreesboro, Tenn, Mrs Mary E Poyles, 4th daughter of the late Eloise Thruston & Maj Edmund Taylor, U S Army.

Died: on Feb 10, at New Orleans, La, Addison T Pickrell, in his 49th year. He was a native of Gtwn, D C, & for the last 24 years resided in the former city.

Died: on Feb 9, at *Edge Hill*, Lucretia Hart, wife of J K Pitzer, of Roanoke Co, Va, & eldest daughter of the late W S Derrick, of Wash, D C.

Health Report: Ofc of the Com'r of Health, Wash, Feb 15, 1859. Monthly report of deaths in Wash City for Jan, 1859: 78. –Chas F Force, Com'r of Health

Situation as a teacher wanted. A young married gentleman, who has been educated at one of the best colleges in the country, & has taught school several years, desires a situation as a teacher in some good school. –Warren H Kean, Wash, D C

THU FEB 17, 1859
Circuit Court-Wash-Wed. 1-John W Shiles vs Saml Strong: verdict for the plntf, with interest on debt. 2-Matilda Smith [colored] vs Thos Martin: this was a ptn for freedom, & the jury gave a verdict for petitioner. 3-Jas Fitzpatrick, adm of Patrick Fitzpatrick, vs Peter Monahgan: verdict for plntf, damages $119, & interest till paid. 4-Ptn of Benj M Martin, on a habeas corpus for the possession of his 2 children, now in custody of their mother, his wife. On account of the tender years of the younger child, it should be for the present retained by the mother, not to be removed from D C, whilst the elder should be handed over to the father.

Mrd: on Feb 15, in Wash City, by Rev Andrew G Carothers, Lt Henry B Tyler, U S Marines, to Miss Mary M Edwards, both of Wash City.

Mrd: on Feb 16, in Long Meadow, Mass, by Rev John W Harding, Dr Henry B Noble, of Wash City, to Maria R, daughter of Jas Bliss, of Long Meadow, Mass.

Died: on Feb 11, at Flatbush, Long Island, near N Y C, Emily, wife of Chas C Walden.

Died: on Feb 9, Mrs Eliz Hagan, in her 78th year.

Died: on Feb 14, at St Joseph's College, Perry Co, Ohio, Rev P D Noon, O P. A solemn requiem service will be performed in St Dominic's Church, [Island] Feb 18 at 10 o'clock.

The Poughkeepsie journals announce the suicide of Mr John F King, formerly of Kansas, & correspondent of various journals. No cause was assigned by him for the act. He was a gentleman of respectable family connections, & bore the reputation of an honest man.

Mrs Wordsworth, widow of the poet, died at Rydal Mount, England, on Jan 17, having reached the venerable age of 90 years.

Senate: 1-Ptn from John B Bennet, relative to his pre-emption rights under a contract to carry the mail from Highland, Kansas, through Nebraska, to the Nyoway river: referred. 2-Ptn from Archibald Henderson, asking to be allowed a pension for services in the war of 1812: referred. 3-Cmte on the Judiciary: bill for the relief of Anne E Bronaugh, widow of the late John W Bronaugh: reported its passage. 4-Cmte on Pensions: asked to be discharged from the consideration of the bill for the relief of Jas Albertson: which was agreed to.

For rent from Jun 1 next, or earlier if desired, the large dwlg house, 27 Indiana ave, now occupied by Hon Geo Taylor, of N Y, & previously by the Peruvian Minister. Apply at the subscriber's ofc, 499 7th st, or address through the Post Ofc. —Thos Blagden

Yesterday an imprudent robbery was made on Mrs Sarah Moore, an aged lady, living on F st, between 9th & 10th sts. While entering the door of her residence, a valuable gold watch, attached to a button by a gold chain, was torn from her bosom, by a man who had been asking her directions. The watch stolen was a patent lever, made by Wm Robinson, of Liverpool, No 14, 935, with the initials S M on the back.

House of Reps: 1-Cmte on Invalid Pensions: bills granting a pension to Hestor Sargent Barton; & for the relief of Mrs Rachel McMillan: committed. Same cmte: bill for the relief of Myra Clark Gaines. This bill grants a pension not exceeding $50 a month to Mrs Gaines during her natural life: passed. 2-Bill for the relief of Wright Fore: passed. 3-Bill for the relief of Evelina Porter, widow of the late Cmdor David Porter: passed.

Hartford, Conn, Feb 15. Dr L P Brockett, formerly of the firm of Brockett & Hutchinson, booksellers of this city, was arrested today for forgery. The amount of paper now out is from $15,000 to $20,000. Dr Brockett had been looked upon as a man of strict integrity.

Notice. Being in infirm health & desirous of settling all claims against the estate of my late husband, Gov Saml Sprigg, as well as against myself, I request all persons having claims will forward them to the subscriber at Wash City, D C.
—Violetta Sprigg, Northampton, PG Co, Md.

Orphans Court of Wash Co, D C. Letters of administration on the personal estate of John H Buthmann, late of Wash Co, deceased. —A E Buthmann, admx

FRI FEB 18, 1859
Senate: 1-Ptn from Ed A Collins, of N Y, setting forth the justice of his claim against the Gov't, as sustained by the opinion of Atty Gen J S Black, & asking that the Sec of the Navy may be authorized to pay the same, with legal interest upon moneys withheld from time to time: referred. 2-Cmte on Judiciary: bill for the relief of Jas P Cook, with amendments. Same cmte: memorial of Cmdor Wm Mervine, U S Navy, asking to have refunded the amount of a judgment recovered against him for the discharge of an official duty, submitted an adverse report on the same, & asked to be discharged from the consideration of the subject: which was agreed to. 3-Cmte on Commerce: adverse report on the memorial of Jas H Causten, atty in fact for the legal reps of Saml Smith, Jas A Buchanan, & others: which was agreed to. 4-Cmte on Finance: bill for the relief of Smallwood Earle & Co, asking to be allowed the fine illegally imposed upon them, & paid to the collector of the customs at N Y. 5-Cmte on Indian Affairs: memorials of Pierre Choteau, jr, & Co, licensed Indian traders, asking indemnity for goods forcibly taken from them by the Sioux Indians, & of Ambrose S Mead & others, of Iowa, asking remuneration for property destroyed by a wandering band of Sioux Indians, asked to be

discharged from their further consideration: which was agreed to. 6-Cmte on Pensions: adverse reports on the ptns of Eliz Osgood, daughter of an ofcr of the Revolution, asking for a pension; & of Danl McArery, a soldier in the war of Florida, for a pension. 7-Cmte on Private Land Claims: to which was recommitted the memorial of Wm Sawyer & other citizens of Ohio, asking to be confirmed in their titles to certain lands in that State, submitted an adverse report on the same: which was agreed to.

Late on Monday a crowd collected in front of Vandyke & Thurber's store, attracted by the cries of thief, who had been caught in the act of stealing some beef from the store, & was immediately arrested. Being an old offender the crowd made & adjusted a noose to his neck, & being thrown over a high post, he was drawn up by the excited crowd. He was left hanging until daylight, when the authorites cut him down & buried him. -Hastings [Minn] Ledger of Jan 30.

Wash Corp, Monday: 1-Ptn from David Bell for the remission of a fine: referred to the Cmte of Claims. 2-Ptn from John Van Reswick, Geo E Kirk, & 237 other citizens of the 7th Ward, asking that the proposed 7th Ward market-house may be placed in Va ave, at the intersection of D st south: referred to a select cmte on the subject. 3-Cmte of Claims: bill for the relief of Jos Mansfield: passed. Same cmte: bill for the relief of Simeon Collins: determined in the negative. Same cmte: bill for the relief of Agnes Ragan. Same cmte: bill for the relief of Thos Walsh: passed. 4-Bills for the relief of Patrick Dacy & wife; for the relief of Enoch Tucker; for the relief of S J Biggs: severally referred to the Cmte of Claims. 5-Ptn from Wm H Parker; of A Block; of Patrick Daly; of Danl Almon; of Jessie Anderson: each for the remission of a fine: each referred to the Cmte of Claims. 6-Bill for the relief of Geo McCollum: passed.

The co-partnership existing under the firm of McLean & Munroe is this day dissolved by mutual consent. Mr McLean will use the name of the firm in closing up the business. -Wm McLean, Geo A Munro. Wm McLean will continue the Lumber business at the old stand, 13th & Canal.

Circuit Court-Wash-Thu. 1-Lewis & Charity Gassawy vs Adam Rose, in which the petitioners [colored persons] pray for their freedom. Verdict for the dfndnt, the jury believing the title to freedom not made out. 2-U S vs Jos Bryan, surety of Saml Davison King, formerly Surveyor-General of Calif, said King having been a defaulter to the Gov't in a sum exceeding $14,000.

The Readings from Shakspeare, by Mrs Fany Kemble Butler, will commence on Wed next, at Philharmonic Hall.

Mrd: on Feb 17, in Wash City, by Rev G W Samson, Mr Porterfield Graves, of Staunton, to Miss Sarah Crone, of Richmond, Va.

Died: on Feb 16, in Wash City, Miss Mary A W Quincy, well known as a teacher in Wash for more than 20 years. Her father, who was of the eminent Quincy family of Boston, held an ofc in Wash City, received from Gen Jackson, until his death several years since. Miss Mary, having previously been a teacher in Boston, on removing to Wash continued her pursuit, in which she was engaged till her death. Her funeral procession will leave the residence of her family, on 11th st, between L & M, today, at 2½ o'clock.

Miss Harriet Fanning Read will read the Merchant of Venice, at Philharmonic Hall, Feb 21, at 8 o'clock. Tickets 50 cents.

Died: the last of Jan, at his residence, in Tin-Pot, Fauquier Co, John Fox, aged 84 years. He was unmarried, & leaves a large estate, principally in slaves, between two & three hundred. But the most remarkable thing that can be said of him is, that he has been a subscriber, & a punctual payer for, & a render of, the Nat'l Intelligencer ever since its establishment by Saml Harrison Smith.

SAT FEB 19, 1859
Senate: 1-Court of Claims: returned the papers of Wm Gaston Pearson, called for by Mr Kennedy to be returned to the Senate; which papers were referred to the Cmte on Public Bldgs & Grounds. 2-Ptn from Catherine Beatty, only child & heir of Barret de Klyn, asking to be paid certain loan ofc certificates, issued by authority of the Continental Congress, for moneys loaned to carry on the war, & which have never been paid: referred. 3-Ptn from Mary A Moore, widow of a late postmaster at San Francisco, asking compensation for service performed by her husband as collecting & disbursing agent of the Post Ofc Dept: referred. 4-Cmte on Foreign Relations: bill to allow to Ed R Cooper & his assigns, being citizens of the U S, the exclusive right of occupying the island, or Key of Navassa, in the Caribbean Sea, for the purpose of obtaining & selling guano therefrom, recommended that the bill be indefinitely postponed. 5-Cmte of Claims: House bills for the relief of Shade Calloway; relief of Cassius M Clay; & for the relief of the assignees of Hugh Glenn: recommended their passage. Same cmte: asked to be discharged from the consideration of the House bill for the relief of Lydia Fletcher, & that it be referred to the Cmte on Military Affairs: which was agreed to. 6-Cmte on Pensions: bill for the relief of Mrs Ann Smith, widow of the late Brig Gen Persifor F Smith, reported it without amendment, accompanied by a written report. Same cmte: bill for the relief of Abby S Chaplain. 7-Cmte on the Post Ofc & Post Roads: asked to be discharged from the consideration of the memorial of Jos Taylor, postmaster at Gratiot, Ohio, asking to be allowed for postage stamps destroyed by fire while in his possession: which was agreed to. 8-Cmte on Commerce: memorial of Thos Brown, adm of Geo Fisher, deceased, reported a joint resolution relating to the claim of Geo Fisher, late of Florida: resolution passed. 9-Cmte on Indian Affairs: bill for the relief of Tilman Leak. 10-Cmte on Public Lands: bill for the relief of Elias Yulee, late receiver of a land ofc in Wash Territory, substituting a new bill, accompanied by a report. 11-Cmte on Foreign Relations: bill for the relief of E Geo Squier, for balance of salary & outfit due him as

Charge d'affaires to the Republics of Central America: which was agreed to. 12-Bills which were passed: relief of Leonard Loomis; of John F Cannon; of Francis Carver; of Robinson Gammon; of Fred'k Smith; of David Watson; & of the reps of Henry King, deceased. Also, Act granting an invalid pension to John Lee, of the State of Maine. Also, Act to authorize the claimants in right of John Huertas to enter certain lands in Florida. 13-Following bills were laid on the table: relief of Mgt Whitehead; of Wm Bullock; & of John C Rathbun. 14-Act for the relief of Dr Geo H Howell: indefinitely postponed.

N Y C: the chair, so long used by John Quincy Adams, in the old House of Reps, was presented on Tuesday to Mr Wm E Robinson, at his residence in West 32nd st. [Feb 21st newspaper: The N Y letter regarding the chair of John Quincy Adams is an error. Both the chair & desk of Mr Adams while he was a member of the House are in the possession of Mrs John Adams, of Wash City, his estimable daughter-in-law.]

Mrd: on Feb 16, in Fred'k Co, Md, by Rev M A Stewart, Mr J W Kay, of Iowa, to Miss S Janette *McDuell, daughter of the late Geo *McDuel, of Wash City. [*2 spellings.]

The London papers of recent date announce the death of Henry Hallam, the distinguished historian & author. He was born in 1778, & was educated at Eton & Oxford, but since he left the Univ has resided in London. In 1818 he published his first work. Mr Hallan died on Jan 22, at the age of 80 years.

The undersigned informs his friends & the public that he has purchased the Rupp's Hotel & Restaurant, 484 Pa ave, which he will open on Feb 22, under the name of Columbia Hotel. –Geo A Springman

MON FEB 21, 1859
Senate: 1-Cmte on Military Affairs: memorial of James & Mills, for the purchase by Gov't of their invention of the safety fuze train, for the use of the army & navy, the Sec of War having given it as his opinion that the purchase at present is neither necessary nor advisable; & on the memorial of Assist Surgeon P S Simpson, for extra services performed at the hospital of Key West, on the ground that the time of ofcrs belongs to the Gov't. 2-Cmte on Patents & the Patent Ofc: bill for the relief of Fred'k E Sickels, for an improvement in the steam engine. 3-Cmte on Military Affairs: bill for the relief of John T Wright, owner of the steamer **America**. 4-Cmte on the Post Ofc & Post Roads: bill for the relief of Saml A Fairchilds: passed. 5-Bill for the relief of Mrs A E Childs: referred to the Cmte on Pensions.

Mexico: Gen Miramon has, after restoring his father-in-law [Zuloaga] to the Presidency, called another council, & had himself again elected President; so that the lallador Zuloaga against yielded the chair of State & retired to private life.

Marine Corps: The following promotions have been made in consequence of the decease of the late Brvt Brig Gen Henderson, & the commissions issued to the parties: Maj Jas Edelin to be Lt.Col, vice Lt Col Harris promoted to the Col Commandant. Capt Ben Macomber to be a Major, to fill the vacancy occasioned by Maj Edelin's promotion. 1st Lt John C Grayson to be a Capt, to fill the vacancy occasioned by Capt Macomber's promotion. 2nd Lt Edw Jones to fill the vacancy occasioned by Lt Grayson's promotion. Lucien L Dawson has been appointed a 2nd Lt to fill the vacancy occasioned by Lt Grayson's promotion. Fred'k N Wise, of Ky, appointed a Purser in the navy.

Chancery sale of valuable tract of land near Wash, by deed of trust of the Circuit Court of D C duly passed on Feb 14, 1859, in a certain chancery suit pending in said court, wherein S B Blanchard is cmplnt & Mary A Holmead et al dfndnts: sale on Mar 16, 1859, at public auction, of 20 acres, 2 roods, & 39 perches, more or less, in Wash, D C: beginning at the south branch of Piney Branch; part of the tract of land which Wm Holmead died seized, & adjoins the lands of Gen Walbridge & Thos Blagden.
-Wm J Stone, trustee -Jas C McGuire & Co, aucts

Died: on Feb 19, in Gtwn, Dr Wm H Berry, of Wash, in his 32nd year. His funeral will be on Feb 21 at 3½ o'clock, from the residence of his father, P T Berry, 121, corner of Congress & Dunbarton sts, Gtwn.

Died: on Feb 19, in Wash City, John Albert Dahlgren, only son of John D & Rosannah Brandt, aged 3 years & 9 months.

Obit-died: on Feb 8, 1859, at Troy, N Y, Mrs Warren, relict of the late N Warren, in her 71st year. A mother in Israel had fallen. She built at her own expense a beautiful little chapel, [the Church of the Holy Cross,] & provided a faithful clergyman, Rev Dr Tucker. Without the distressing ordeal of protracted sickness or wasting disease, she leaves behind her a memory fair as the lily of the valley, fragrant as the rose of Sharon.

TUE FEB 22, 1859
Superior rosewood piano & excellent household & kitchen furniture at auction on Mar 1, at the residence of W Hope, of the British Legation, on 13th st, between L st & Mass ave. All his furniture & effects. -Jas C McGuire & Co, aucts

Senate: 1-Ptn from Thos Sullivan, asking to be enrolled on the pension list: referred. [This old soldier had served faithfully for 20 years, & was honorably discharged, as no longer able to perform the arduous duties of a soldier, & alike unable, by his long service in the army, for any pursuit of civil life.]

Valuable real estate for sale: by decree of the Circuit Court of PG Co, [Md,] as a Court of Equity: public sale on Mar 11, 1859, of the real estate of the late Mary Berry, containing 824 1/4th acres, in said county, with a good comfortable dwlg house, kitchen, & all necessary out houses. A B Berry will show the land. –C C Magruder, trustee

Dissolution of copartnership under firm of Howell & Morsell, by mutual consent, Feb 21st. The business will be conducted by J W Morsell. –Wm P Howell, jr; J W Morsell.

Circuit Court of Wash Co, D C. Wheatley & Walker et al vs Wm Collins' heirs & administrators. The trustee reports he has sold lot 16 in square 28, to Peter & Jas O'Day for $580, & they have complied with the terms of sale. –Jno A Smith, clerk

Died: on Feb 21, in Wash City, Mrs Mary Greenleaf, wife of Mr C Greenleaf. Her funeral will be on Feb 23 at 3 o'clock, from the residence of her husband, 334 9th st.

Died: on Feb 21, in Wash City, Mrs Mary Jane Shinnors, in her 66th year. Her funeral is this evening at 3 o'clock, from her late residence, 1st & L sts.

WED FEB 23, 1859
Senate: 1-Ptn from Wm Dease, setting forth that he enlisted at Rochester, N Y, in 1855, & was immediately marched to Nebraska Territory, where he had all the fingers on both hands frozen off up to the knuckle joints, & is unable to perform labor of any sort; in Jul, 1858, he was admitted to the Military Asylum, where he remained until Feb 5, 1859, when he was arbitrarily & without just cause dismissed; now without property or friend able to support him, thrown early in life, mutilated & maimed in his country's service, upon the cold charity of the world, he appeals to that country in whose service he was disabled for such support as Congress may deem him entitled: referred. 2-Ptn from Geo W Dorrance, Chaplain at the Penitentiary, asking that the recommendation of the Board of Inspectors in regard to his compensation may be carried into effect, either by increasing his pay, or, if not, to take $300 from the salary of the clerk & give it to the chaplain: referred. 3-Ptn from Jno Reeves, of Brooklyn, N Y, asking that the U S Minister at Constantinople may be instructed to submit to the Sultan his claim to remuneration for services while employed & detained at Constantinople to construct vessels of war for the Turkish Gov't: referred. 4-Ptn from Jos M Taylor, asking to be relieved from a judgment recovered against him as security for a defaulting postmaster: referred. 5-Ptn from Sampson McCown & Danl D Burress, making a like request: referred.

U S ship **Saratoga**, Vera Cruz, Feb 1, 1859. Wedding on board a man-of-war, a few days since. A merchant in Vera Cruz, Mr Dewhurst, & the father of an American lady, Mr Markoe, also an American merchant, & resident of this city, solicited permission from Capt Turner, commanding the **Saratoga**, to solemnize the nuptials of Mr Dewhurst & Miss Markoe, under the American flag, on board the **Saratoga**. The Capt readily gave his consent.

THU FEB 24, 1859
Sprague & others of N Y, asking that pensioners under the act of Apr, 1816, may be allowed from the date of that act.

Circuit Court of Wash Co, D C-in Equity. Selden, Withers & Co, for themselves & other creditors of A A Nicholson, vs Augustus A Nicholson's widow, heirs & adms. I will proceed to audit the account of Augustus A Nicholson, deceased, on Mar 19 next, at my ofc, in Wash, at 11 o'clock. –Walter S Cox, Special Auditor

Fire Ins Co of Alexandria, Va. Incorporated 1814: Capital & surplus $140,000.
Board of Directors:

Wm Gregory	John B Daingerfield	Thos McCormick
Robt Jamieson	Edw S Hough	D B Smith
Thos R Keith	Jas P Smith	C W Wattles, Sec
John H Brent	Robt G Violett	T M Hanson, Agent

520 7th st-opposite the Intelligencer Ofc.

Senate: 1-Ptn from J P Durbin, on behalf of the Methodist Missionary Society, asking payment for certain land in Oregon, taken as a site for a military post. 2-Cmte on Foreign Relations: memorial of R M Hamilton, late Consul of the U S at Montevideo, asking compensation for diplomatic services rendered whole at that port, submitted an adverse report, recommending that the claim be rejected: which was agreed to. 3-Cmte on Military Affairs: asked to be discharged from the consideration of the papers in relation to the claims of Majors & Russel, & that they be referred to the Cmte of claims: which was agreed to. 4-Cmte on Indian Affairs: asked to be discharged from the consideration of the reports of the Court of Claims adverse to the cases of Martin B Lewis, of Chas V Stuart, & of Saml G Wensley: which was agreed to. 5-Cmte on Pensions: asked to be discharged from the consideration of the House bill providing an increase of pension to Peter Van Buskirk, of Wash City. Same cmte: adverse report on the House bill for the relief of Danl Cole. Same cmte: adverse reports on the following ptns: that of Margaret Halsey; of Sarah S Hine; of David Merry; of the widow of Peter Lewis Morris; & of Asa

Mystic Hall Seminary for Young Ladies: Mrs Thos P Smith, Principal; Rev Edw J Stearns, A M, Chaplain. The Institution is situated 15 minutes' ride from Boston by the Lowell Railroad, in the midst of an amphitheatre of hills, with lovely villages sleeping among them, while the Mystic River gives new beauty to the whole. Address: Mystic Hall Seminary Box, Boston, Mass.
Reference: parents & guardians of the pupils, among whom are the following:
Wm L Hanscom, U S Naval Contrator, Portsmouth, N H
S B Phinney, Collector of Customs, Barnstable, Mass
Hon R P Spaulding, Cleveland, Ohio
Philo Chamberlain, Cleveland, Ohio
Elon Comstock, Editor of the N Y Journal of Commerce, N Y
C C Betts, Pres of the Brooklyn City Railroad, Brooklyn, N Y
Rev J I Helm, A M, Principal of Edgehill School, Princeton, N J
Dr Alphonzo Brooks, Princeton, Mass
Dr I S P Lord, Batavia, Ill
Rev E P Marvin, Medford, Mass

Corp of Wash, Feb 21. 1-Cmte of Claims: asked to be discharged from the consideration of the ptns for remission of fines: of Jas Kenally; of W H Parker; of Danl Almon; of Patrick Daley; of Jas Kelly; of Patrick Sullivan; & of Jas Reed. 2-Ptn from Jacob Printz for the remission of a fine: referred to the Cmte of Claims. 3-Cmte on Drainage: asked to be discharged from the consideration of the ptn of Fred'k Stutz & others, asking for a reservoir at the corner of E & 11th sts: cmte discharged accordingly. 4-Bill for the relief of Chas D Maxwell: passed.

Circuit Court-Wash-Wed. 1-Mgt Lyons, admx of Eliz Bradin, vs O E P Hazard, returned a verdict for plntf, with damages for the amount in suit & interest. 2-W & H C Noyes vs Jos Hyle. The jury gave a verdict for dfndnt. The Court then adjourned.

Mrd: on Feb 22, in Wash City, by Rev G W Samson, Mr Saml P Robertson to Miss Lizzie Wilkins, all of Wash City.

Died: on Feb 21, in Balt, Celester Hunter, youngest daughter of Alfred & Susan Hunter, of Wash.

Died: on Feb 11, at the residence of her mother in Columbia, Ky, Corinna A, daughter of Eliz & the late R R Peebles.

Died: on Feb 23, Nicholas P, the beloved son of Mr John N Singleton, aged 3 years. His funeral is this afternoon at 3 o'clock, from his father's residence, 448 E st.

FRI FEB 25, 1859
Senate: 1-Ptn from Erastus Smith & 236 other citizens of Cleveland, Ohio, in favor of the passage of the homestead bill now pending in the U S Senate. 2-Cmte on Public Lands: bill for the relief of the heirs or legal reps of Francois Guillory, & recommended its passage. Same cmte: memorial of Wm McClelland & other citizens of Nebraska, asking the confirmation of their titles to certain lands, reported a general bill to legalize certain informal entries of town lots in the Territory of Nebraska. Same cmte: bill for the relief of John B Bennet. 3-Cmte on Commerce: adverse report on the memorial of Zadock Pangburn, asking an appropriation to test certain improvements in vessels & lifeboats. 4-Bill for the relief of Wm F Wagner: passed.

The 166th Anniversary of **Wm & Mary College**, in Va, was celebrated last Sat. A poem was read by St Geo Tucker, & an address delivered by ex-Pres Tyler. A the evening dinner toasts were responded to by Gov Wise, Hugh Blair Grigsby-of Norfolk, Gen Taliaferro, O J Wise, Dr Garnett, Professor Joynes, & others.

Died: on Wed, Erskine, son of Anne & the late Francis H Kleiber, in his 8th year.

Died: on Feb 24, Julia, only daughter of Chas & Helen De Selding. Her funeral is on Saturday at 1 o'clock, from her father's residence, corner of B st south & 9th st, Island.

On Tue, soon after the opening of the Atlantic Bank, in Brooklyn, the paying teller, Mr Oscar S Field, was absent from his accustomed desk, a very unusual circumstance. On opening the vaults a bag of gold containing $1,000 was missing, & $10,000 in notes of other banks. It became evident Mr Field had absconded with the money. He had been an employee of the bank for some 6 years. It is possible that the amount of defalcation will exceed the sum of $60,000. –N Y Com Adv

On Feb 8 the dwlg of Mr Zimmerman, in Clark's Valley, near Lykenstown, Pa, was destroyed by fire, & 3 children, the eldest about 13 years of age, were burnt to death. Mr Zimmerman was at work near Pinefrove, & Mrs Zimmerman & her eldest boy had gone to a neighbor's when the fearful occurrence took place.

Court of Claims: Feb 23. 1-Nancy D Holker, admx, vs the U S: claim for the avails of 37 War Ofc certificates, issued under the authority of the U S Congress during the Revolutionary war; certificates were destroyed by fire in 1780; in 1816 Congress fixed the specie value of these certificates at $5,805, & ordered them to be paid, with interest from a certain date. The petitioners claimed the specie value to be $12,400, & brought this suit to recover the difference, with interest. Judge Scarburgh delivered the opinion of the Court, adverse to the claim.

A very sudden affliction has visited the family of Mr Robt Stratton, 320 Eutaw st, Balt. Last night Miss Laura Stratton, aged 16 years, attended the ball of the Independent Greys, at the Md Institute, with her brother & Miss Walters, & on the return home Miss Stratton complained of a pain at her heart. Her brother hastened to the drug store of Mr Emory, who came to her relief, along with Dr McSherry, a physician, but on arrival the vital spark had fled. Her death was attributed to congestion of the heart. –Balt Patriot, 23rd

Asher A Skillings, a man of immense weight, died in N Y on Sat of disease of the liver. Two years ago he weighed 460 pounds.

SAT FEB 26, 1859
Senate: 1-Bill for the relief of Kennedy O'Brien, a soldier in the war with Mexico: passed.

Positive sale of valuable farm near Wash City at auction: on Mar 7, on the premises, the farm of Mr Jos Gingle's, containing 49½ acres, with a good dwlg & other necessary out-bldgs; adjoins the farms of Messrs Thos Wilson, Geo W Riggs, & Dr Condict, being the first farm after passing over the Sligo branch. -A Green auct

Mrd: on Feb 24, by Rev Stephen P Hill, D D, Lawrason Riggs to Mary T Bright, daughter of Hon Jesse D Bright, of Indiana.

Mrd: on Feb 24, at Trinity Church, by Rev Geo D Cummins, D D, of Balt, Rev Walter W Williams, of Leesburg, Va, to Alice, youngest daughter of Jos H Bradley, of Wash City.

Mrd: on Feb 23, by Rev Fr Alig, Mr Andreas Englehart to Margaret Braun, both natives of Germany.

Mrd: on Feb 22, at Lancaster, Pa, by Rev H A Boardman, D D, of Phil, Oliver Phelps, jr, of Canandaigua, N Y, to Sarah L, daughter of the late Geo B Porter, Govn'r of Michigan.

Died: on Feb 18, 1859, at the Univ of Va, in her 33rd year, Mrs Lucy Landon Davis, wife of Prof John S Davis, & oldest child of Mr Wm M Blackford, of Lynchburg, Va. United at an early age to the man of her choice, she enjoyed for years as much unshadowed happiness as the world can bestow. For several years she had been in declining health, & for many months prior to her death was confined to her chamber. The duties of friendship, as well as those of filial & sisterly affection, were discharged with a kindly cordiality. She leaves her husband & children to mourn her loss.

Public sale of valuable land: by deed of trust from Chas Digges to the undersigned for the payment of his debts, duly executed, & recorded in one of the land record books of PG Co: public sale of all the real estate of the said Chas Digges, containing 100 acres of land. Auction on Mar 18, of about 40 acres; 2 miles from Bladensburg. Mr Chas Digges on the premises. –D C Digges, trustee

MON FEB 28, 1859
Senate: 1-Cmte on Commerce: bill for the relief of Francis Huttman: passed. 2-Bill for the relief of Wm Rich: passed.

Trustee's sale of Exchange Hotel: by deed of trust from David A Hall, dated Aug 1, 1842, recorded in the land records of Wash Co, D C, in liber W B No 95, folios 160 thru 163; public auction on Mar 14, 1859, of part of lots 4 & 5 in square 490, being the same property which was conveyed by the Bank of Wash to said David A Hall by deed dated aforesaid, with improvements thereon. This property fronts on C st north, between 4½ & 6th sts west, known as the Exchange Hotel. –Jas Adams, trustee
-Jas C McGuire & Co, aucts

The McMicken bequest of $400,000 to the city of Cincinnati has been declared valid against the suit of his relatives, who will carry the case up to the U S Supreme Court.

Mrs Bratt, of Pittsburg, Pa, was sued by Mrs Allison for slander. The jury on Monday rendered a verdict of $1,500 for the plntf. Same plntf vs Miss Mills is now being tried, & as the dfndnt is said to be wealthy, smart damages are looked for in the event of her conviction.

Household & kitchen furniture at auction on Mar 2, at the residence of Hon Johsua Hill, 469 6th st, between D & E sts. –C W Boteler, auct

Circuit Court-Wash-Sat. Mary E Bronaugh vs T J Robinson: on May 31, 1855, dfndnt purchased 6 slaves from the plntf for $1,650. In the fall of 1857 the plntf took out her replevin under which the slaves were taken from the possession of the dfndnt, & sold to a trader in Alexandria for $3,000. Plntf contends that the sale to dfndnt was void, for the reason that a large part of the purchase money for the negroes was made up of usurious loans made to her by the dfndnt prior to the date of the sale, & that the bill of sale given by her to dfndnt, though absolute on its face, was intended only as a security for the usurious loans made to her, & that the purchase money was far less that the value of the negroes. On the part of the dfndnt it is contended that there was no usury in fact in the transactions between the parties prior to the sale; & even if that had been the case the bill of sale was a new transaction which settled all matters between the parties; that the full value was paid for the negroes; & that the bill of sale was absolute & so intended to be by the parties at the time. The case was withdrawn for the present term in order to afford opportunity for plntf to adduce new evidence.

A new & beautiful painting by artist Leutze, the subject is Moore's "Paradise of the Peri," will be exhibited in Mr Franklin Philps's Bookstore. Mr Leutze has become a resident of Wash, & had opened a studio, for the present, over Messrs Blanchard & Mohuns' store, at the corner of 11th st.

On Sat fire broke out in the brick bldg & grocery store on K st & 22nd west, owned & occupied by Mr Jas Kennedy. There was an insurance of $1,500 on the property.

Mrd: on Feb 25, at the Foundry Chapel, by Rev J Lanahan, Rev Humphrey C McDaniel to Mary A Leech, daughter of D D T Leech.

Mrd: on Feb 23, in Martinsburg, Va, by Rev Mr Davis, Capt Jas McIntosh, U S Army, to Miss Judith Phelps.

Died: on Feb 22, of pneumonia, in her 74th year, at the residence of her son-in-law, A P Crenshaw, in Chas City Co, Va, Mrs Eliz H Parker, widow of the late Judge Richd E Parker, of the Court of Appeals. She has left her sorrowing children here to rejoin her husband & children there, in heaven.

Died: on Feb 26, of scarlet fever, Jas Skirving, only son of Maria & W H Beardsley, aged 2 years, 6 months & 28 days. His funeral will be today at 10 o'clock, from the residence of his father, 275 D, between 13th & 14th sts.

Died: on Feb 24, at Upper Marlboro, Margaret Chew, in her 13th month, the only child of Danl C & Bettie C Digges.

Calif: Collector Sutherland, of Sacramento, died on Feb 2. He was formerly from Phil.

St Louis, Feb 26. Hon Edw A Hannegan, formerly U S Senator from Indiana, died at the Planters' House here last night.

Orphans Court of Wash Co, D C. Letters of administration on the personal estate of Dr Wm H Berry, late of Wash Co, deceased. –P T Berry, adm

TUE MAR 1, 1859
Senate: 1-Ptn from Francis M & Henrietta L Green, children of Lt Col John Green, asking to be allowed a pension: referred.

Court of Claims: 1-Mary Williams vs the U S. A claim for damages arising from the U S troops taking possession in Dec, 1835, of Harford plantation, in Florida, during the Indian troubles in that Territory. Mr Polk opened the argument for the claimant. The Court adjourned.

Gtwn election: resulted in the re-election of the present incumbent of the Moyoralty, R R Crawford, by a plurality of 19 votes. Crawford-551; Addison-532; Magruder-50. For Councilman the following were elected: Stake-565; E Pickrell-561; Dunlop-550; King-589; Bangs-553; Hyde-564; Teney-564; D L Shoemaker-576; Offut-588; Lazenby-549; Marbury-571.

Orphans Court of Wash Co, D C. In the case of Zachariah Chandler, adm of Geo R Griswold, deceased, the adm & Court have appointed Mar 22 next, for the final settlement of the personal estate of the deceased, of assets in hand.
-Ed N Roach, Reg/o wills

Orphans Court of Wash Co, D C. In the case of Wm Poulton, adm of Thos Lamb, deceased, the administrator & Court have appointed Mar 22 next, for the final settlement of the personal estate of the deceased, of assets in hand. -Ed N Roach, Reg/o wills

The venerable Rembrandt Peale, now in his 81st year, intends to sell in Phil the entire collection of paintings & studies in his studio, & has thrown his rooms open for inspection.

Mrd: on Feb 23, in Wash City, in the Church of the Epiphany, by Rev Chas H Hall, Cary Carter, of Augusta, Ga, to Emilie, oldest daughter of the late Geo H Jones, of Va.

Died: on Feb 28, in his 79th year, Anthony Smith, who at the time of his decease & for 63 years, with a short intermission, was a resident of Gtwn. His funeral will take place today, Mar 1, at 4 o'clock, from his late residence on Montgomery ave.

Died: on Feb 27, in Wash City, Philip Barton Key, aged 39 years. His funeral will take place this afternoon at 2 o'clock, from his late residence, 388 C st, this afternoon, at 2 o'clock. The remains will be taken to Balt for interment.

Rev Dr Packard, Theological Seminary of Va, wishes to receive into his family two young Ladies to be educated with his daughter. A very competent teacher resides in the family. Terms, $300 per session of 10 months, one-half payable in advance.

Prof Henry Marix, 454 D st north, between 2nd & 3rd sts, formerly Prof of Modern Languages in the Univ of Leipsie, Germany, desires to teach the modern languages in private families or in public institutions of learning.

I have this day associated with me J Richd Burroughs, & will do business in the style of Smoot & Burroughs, 119 Bridge st, Gtwn. –John H Smoot

Mrs A Speir will be open on Mar 2, for the benefit of the ladies who wish to purchase their hats early: 275 Pa ave, Wash.

WED MAR 2, 1859
House of Reps: 1-Bill passed placing Mary A Harris, widow of Thos L Harris, on the pension roll at $30 per month during her widowhood.

A young lady, Susan Tuck, of Lebanon, Ky, was about to be married to Mr Thomas, of that place, when her wedding dress caught fire & she was fatally burnt. Her sister, Mrs Bury Harrison, who came to her assistance was also fatally burnt. The marriage ceremony was performed while she lay upon her couch, suffering intense agony.

A young man, Orlando C Parsons, formerly a clerk in the N Y post ofce, committed suicide at his boarding-house in Balt, yesterday, by shooting himself through the head. He had been disappointed in securing a clerkship in the State Dept, as shown by a letter from Gen Cass found in his pocket. He was out of means, & in a fit of despair.

Private sale of desirable farm in PG Co, Md, 6 miles from Wash, containing 240 acres, with bldgs all nearly new, being built 6 years ago, the dwlg is large & convenient. -Richad Q Bowling, post ofc in Wash, D C.

Died: yesterday, in Wash City, Mary M Wood, wife of Phineas F Wood & daughter of the late Wm H Bayne, aged 19 years. Her funeral is this afternoon at 3 o'clock, from her late residence, 90 South C st.

New Orleans, Feb 28. The steamboat **Princess** from Vicksburg for New Orleans, when near Baton Rouge on Sunday, exploded her boiler & was burnt to the water's edge. About 400 persons were on board. About 200 were killed or drowned, mostly Louisianians & Mississippians. Among the killed are J W Seymour, of Baton Rouge; ___ Calhoun, of Marysville, Ky; H B Murphy, of St Louis; J J Hodges, of Miss; Chas Bannister & L Howard, reps at Baton Rouge; & Saml Watts, of Va. Unrecognized bodies were found along the shore.

THU MAR 3, 1859

Senate: 1-Ptn from Tal P Schaffner, asking that authority may be given to render him such aid as may be practicable in carrying out his plans for laying a telegraph between Europe & America, via Greenland, etc, by permitting the Gov't ships to transport his surveying party: referred. 2-Cmte on Public Lands: bill for the final settlement of the accounts of Abraham Edwards, late receiver of the land ofc at Kalamazoo.

On Tue last Wm D Massey was re-elected Mayor & S J McCormick, Auditor of the city of Alexandria, without opposition. Other municipal ofcs chosen at the time: C S Hallowell, surveypr; John A Field & Wm H Smith, collectors of taxes; S R Shinn, gauger of liquors; & Geo Davis, superintendent of police.

House of Reps: 1-Come of the Whole: bill for the relief of Anthony Caslo, a soldier in the war of 1812: passed. Same cmte: bill for the relief of Jas Collier: passed. Same cmte: bill for the relief of John Pickell, late a lt in the U S army: passed.

Mrd: on Mar 1, in Wash City, by Rev Andrew G Carothers, Mr Wm A Thompson to Miss Maria J Anderson, both of Wash City.

Mrd: on Mar 1, by Rev Mr Chipchase, Mr Geo W Blandford, of PG Co, Md, to Miss Laura Virginia Bowen, of Wash City.

Orphans Court of Wash Co, D C. Letters of administration on the personal estate of Horatio N Andrus, late of Wash Co, deceased. –Eliz A Andrus, admx

Obit-died: Surgeon Edw Hudson, U S Navy, was ordered to the U S frig **Niagara**, he joined her on Sep 12, 1858, & conveyed captured negroes to Monrovia. The miserable state of these unhappy creatures enlisted his warmest sympathy, & his unremitting attentions to them is regarded as sowing the seeds of fatal disease in his hitherto robust & healthy frame. He returned home in Dec, complaining of great lassitude, grew gradually worse, until he expired on Jan 23, peacefully in the bosom of his afflicted family. He had just reached the highest rank in his profession, with a devoted young wife & all to make life bright & enticing, he yielded all without regret to his Master's call. He embraced the Catholic religion about 3 years ago.

The house of Mr Elley, 288 H st, between 17th & 18th sts, is for rent.

Died: on Jan 31, near Clifton, Ohio, Richd Randolph, formerly of Culpeper Co, Va. He was born in Prince Wm Co, in May, 1795, & was long a member of the Va bar. Some years ago, having bought land near Clifton, & finding that it required his personal superintendence, he settled upon it. It increased rapidly in value. The hand of death was laid upon him where no kindred hand, no friend of early life could smooth his pillow & whisper words of sympathy & consolation.

Wash Corp-Mon: 1-Bills for the relief of Thos Walsh; of David Fowble; of Ernst Loefler; & of Jas T Lloyd: each passed. 2-Bill for the relief of John Van Skiver: rejected. 3-Ptn of Jas T Nally; of Louis Velter; of Patrick Sullivan; & of J J Rolles, each praying the remission of a fine: referred to the Cmte of Claims.

Louisville, Mar 2. A collision today at Hawesville, resulting from an old political feud. Cicero Maxwell, prosecuting atty, while addressing the Court, was interrupted by Thos S Lowe, who grossly insulted the former. Some friends fired, wounding Low & killing John Alldredge. Law was committed to jail for protection from the mob. [Mar 8th newspaper: on Mar 3rd Thos S Lowe was assassinated, in the Hawesville jail, by a blood thirsty & cowardly mob. He received some 16 or 18 balls in vital parts & died instantly. Glutted with vengeance the mob then retired. Lowe leaves a family, who reside in Hawesville. His father lives in this city. He was a cool, determined, & most dangerous man. -Louisville Courier of Mar 4.]

FRI MAR 4, 1859
Valuable lot at auction: by order of the Orphans Court of Wash Co, D C, confirmed by the Circuit Court of Wash Co, D C, in Chancery, passed Nov 23, 1858, in the case of Wm A Richardson, Guardian: public sale on Mar 24 next, on the premises, lot 16 in square 245, fronting on 13th st west, between M & N sts, Wash City. –A Lloyd, trustee -A Green auct

Senate: 1-Cmte on the Judiciary: bill for the relief of Francis Dainesse, & recommended its passage.

House of Reps: 1-Cmte of Claims: bill for the relief of Wm M Harris: passed. 2-Bill for the relief of Frances Ann McCauley: passed.

Died: on Mar 3, in Wash City, Elizabeth, infant daughter of Mose & Mary W Kelly, aged 3½ months. Her funeral will take place this afternoon at 4 o'clock, from the residence of her parents, 372 west 4th st.

Circuit Court-Thu: 1-John F Ferguson vs Jos & H A Willard: suit to recover $175 supposed to have been stolen by some person not known when a guest at the hotel of the dfndnts. Verdict for plntf to the full amount. 2-Richd B Lloyd vs Geo T Langley, to recover per centage for effecting, as alleged, the sale of a house, the property of dfndnt.

St Louis, Mar 3. A band of Apaches stole a number of horses & mules from San Elizario. They were pursued by a detachment of the mounted rifles from **Fort Bliss**, under command of 2nd Lt Henry M Lazella. An engagement occurred, resulting in the withdrawal of the troops, with a loss of 3 killed & 6 wounded, including Lt Lazella, who received a mortal wound in the lungs. About a dozen Indians were killed. The troops number 22 & the Indians 200.

SAT MAR 5, 1859

Senate: 1-Private bills considered & passed-relief: of Geo B Bacon; Mrs Ann Smith, wife of the late Gen Persifor F Smith; of John Perry; of Stuart McGowan; of Abby S Chaplin; of Lucy A Wakefield, widow of Benj Wakefield; & of Abram Edwards, late register of the land ofc at Kalamazoo, Mich.

List of Acts of the Session of Congress just closed:

1-Relief of:

- Mary Bainbridge
- Leonard Loomis
- John F Cannon
- Mary Boyle
- John Campbell
- John Duncan
- Monroe D Downs
- Wm F Wagner
- Saml A Fairchilds
- Dinah Minis
- Wright Fore
- Francis Carber
- Robinson Gammon
- Fred'k Smith
- David Watson
- Robt A Davidge
- Jas G Holmes
- Wm Yearwood, sr, of Tenn
- Mrs Henry B Schoolcraft
- Capt Douglass Ottinger
- Henry Hubbard
- Marlin Layman
- Myra Clark Gaines
- Kennedy O'Brien
- Wm Rich
- Capt A W Reynolds
- Eli W Goff
- Frances Ann McCauley
- Mary B Dusenbury
- Jane Turnbull
- Jas Collier
- John Perry
- Wm M Harrison
- Edw Ingersoll
- Assignees of Hugh Glenn
- Ferdinand Coxe
- Jas A Glanding
- A Baudonin & A D Roberts
- Legal reps of Henry King, deceased
- Rebecca M Bowden, of PG Co, Va
- Elias Hall, of Rutland, Vt
- Jos Hardy & Alton Long

2-Relief of:

Anthony Caslo, a soldier of the war of 1812
John Pickell, late a lt in the U S army
Lucy A Wakefield, widow of Benj Wakefield
Roswell Minard, father of Theodore Minard, deceased
Evelina Porter, widow of the late Cmdor David Porter, U S Navy
Heirs & legal reps of Oliver Landy, of the State of Louisiana
C Edw Habicht, adm of J W P Lewis
Enoch B Talcott, late collector of customs at Oswego, N Y
Mrs Ambroise Brou, of the parish of St Chas, La
Thos Laurent, surviving partner of the firm of Benj & Thos Laurent
3-Right of John Juertas to enter certain lands in Florida. 4-Assignment of land warrant No 35,959 issued to John Davis. 5-Invalid pension to John Lee, of the State of Maine.

6-Settle accounts of the late Lt Lewis S Craig for his services in command of the military escort on the Mexican boundary commission. 7-Sec of the Treasury to grant a register for the schnr **William A Hamill**. 8-Confirm to the heirs or assigns of Bernardo Segui title to lands in East Florida. 9-Final settlement of the land claim of the persons claiming as heirs of or under John Underwood, as purchasers or otherwise, to certain land in Florida, & to confirm the title to the proper owner or owners. 10-Resolution for the relief of Michl Paprenitza. 11-Joint resolution authorizing Townsend Harris, U S Consul General at Japan, & H C J Heuskin, his interpreter, respectively, to accept a snuff-box from the Queen of England. 12-Joint resolution to correct a clerical error in an act for the relief of Isaac Body & Saml Fleming. 13-Joint resolution giving the consent of Congress to the acceptance by Capt M F Maury & Prof A D Bache of gold medals from the Sardinian Gov't. 14-Resolution for the relief of Wm Hazzard Wigg. 15-Resolution conferring the rank of Senior Flag-Ofcr in the active service list of the U S navy on Capt Chas Stewart.

Mr John Marron, Third Assist Postmaster Gen, died at his residence in Wash City the night before last, of an affection of the heart. Mr Marron was a native of Ireland, but has been in this country from his childhood, entering the Gen Post Ofc as a clerk when a young man, rose by his merit gradually to the high position of Third Assist Head of the Dept. He was about 60 years of age, & has left a most estimable family.

Mrs Mary Taylor, of Lee, Mass, had a surprise party of her 15 children on her 100th birthday lately.

John C Haines, Republican, was re-elected Mayor of the city of Chicago on Tue last.

Mrd: on Mar 1, at *Hillandale*, the residence of her brother, Miss Nannie F Colston to Mr John B Minor, Prof at Law at the Univ of Va.

Died: on Mar 3, John Marron, Third Assist Postmaster Gen, in his 60th year. His funeral will be from his late residence, N Y ave, between 9th & 10th sts, at 10 o'clock A M today.

Died: on Mar 3, in Wash City, Caroline Laurens, wife of Lt John N Maffit, U S Navy, daughter of the late Hon John Laurens, of Charleston, S C. Her funeral will be from her late residence on K st, near 13th, Franklin Row, Mar 6 at 2:30 o'clock.

Died: on Mar 4, in Gtwn, Sarah E, wife of Levi Davis, in her 38th year. Her funeral will take place from her late residence, 145 Beall st, Gtwn, today at 3:30 P M.

Wash City Ordnance: Act for the relief of Enoch Tucker: to pay him $35, it being in full for damages sustained by his carriage & harness on Nov 8, 1858, by being precipitated down an embankment on N Y ave, near North Capitol st. –Chas Abert, Pres of the Board of Common Council. Wm T Dove, Pres of the Board of Aldermen. Approved, Mar 4, 1859. –Jas G Berret, Mayor

The Annual Commencement of the Nat'l Medical College took place on Thu in the lecture room of the Smithsonian Institution. Prayer was by Rev Dr Samson; faculty present being Profs Holston, Johnston, Ruggles, Waring, Wurtz, Tyler, Stone, Riley, & Crow. The graduates on this occasion were:

J W Fennell, of Ala
D W Russell, of S C
W G Mathis, of Tenn
J M Trevey, of Va
H B Martin, of Md
Wm Walton, of Ohio
Joshua Way, of Ohio
C E R King, of Va
P M Martin, of Va
Wm G Williams, of Md
John E Atwell, of Ohio
Thos E Williams, of Va

F C James, of N C
W R Moye, of S C
W D Murray, of N Y
G P Fenwick, of D C
A N Williamson, of N C
John A Drake, of N C
B V Sweringen, of Ohio
J R Sowers, of Va
A B Campbell, of Ill
Thos M Johnson, of Wisc
C W Hines, of D C
P A Gardiner, of Md

Honoray degrees delivered to: Dr John Ordromax, of N Y; & Dr P J Gardener, of Md

Lands on College Hill for sale: the Trustees of Columbian College have for sale that portion of their land lying south of the College commons fronting on Boundary st & 14th st extended, & containing in all 21 acres. Address through the Wash Post Ofc, Rev Jos Hammitt, Treasurer Columbian College.

Oxford Female Seminary, Oxford, Chester Co, Pa: the 40th half-yearly session will commence on the first Wed in May. –Rev John M Dickey, or Rev Saml Dickey, Principals, Oxford, Pa. References: Rev P D Gurley, D D; Oliver Defore, Gen Land Ofc; Dr O Munson; Maj H L Harvey, Navy Dept

MON MAR 7, 1859
Mr Ten Broeck & Mr Robt Harlan, two well known men of the turf, have left N Y for Liverpool, taking with them another stock of American thoroughbred horses.

Dr Wm Newton Mercer, of New Orleans, has made an additional donation of $2,500 to the Md Agricultural College. The aggregate amount of his contributions is now $7,500.

Obit-died: Jas Carnahan, D D, long time Pres of Princeton College; born Nov 15, 1775, & died at Newark, N J, on Mar 2. –N J papers

Mrd: on Mar 3, by Rev Mr Buck, of Rock Creek Church, Miss Mary A Taylor, of Montg Co, Md, to Chas Batchelor, of N Y.

Mrd: on Feb 24, at Sackett's Harbor, N Y, by Rev Mr Brayton, Capt G N Hollins, U S Navy, to Louisa S Sterrett, of Balt, Md.

Mrd: on Jan 12, by Rev Edw Strong, of New Haven, G W Alston Jenkins, of N Y, to Miss Clara B Williams, only daughter of T W Williams, of Janesville, Wisc.

Died: on Mar 5, in Wash City, Mary Wheat, wife of the late John Wheat, in her 77th year. Her funeral is this day at 3 o'clock, from her residence on 4½ st, corner of N st, [*Greenleaf's Point.*]

Died: on Feb 11, at the residence of her husband at Carthage, Tenn, Mrs Lucy B Pickett, wife of Col Jos G Pickett, & youngest daughter of the late Saml P Howard.

Died: on Dec 20, 1858, at Calcutta, India, Marie Jessie Clemence Eliz, only daughter of Mr & Madame Gauldrie Boilleau, born at Gtwn, D C, Jun 28, 1856, & grand-daughter of the late Hon Mr Benton.

Died: on Mar 5, of pneumonia, James Lownds, infant son of John L & Virginia Lownds Smith, aged 1 year & 7 days. His funeral will take place from the residence of his parents, 565 12th st, [Island,] on Mar 7 at 12 o'clock.

Died: on Mar 6, James Edmund, infant son of Jos F & Mary Isabel Hodgson. His funeral is this afternoon at 3 o'clock, at 405 7th st, between H & L sts.

Died: on Mar 6, Lucy Petronella, infant daughter of Geo K & Virginia P Boyd, aged 5 months & 12 days. The Saviour said: "Suffer little children to come unto me, for of such is the Kingdom of Heaven". Her funeral will be on Mar 8 at 4 o'clock, from 513 10th st, south of C st.

TUE MAR 8, 1859

Mr John La Mountain is busily engaged in Troy, N Y, in making preparations for the construction of the balloon with which he hopes to be able to cross the Atlantic during the coming seson. If he does not succeed in crossing, it is to be feared, he will share the fate of those who go down to the sea in ships. –Troy Times, Feb 19

Hon Henry S Geyer, late a U S Senator from the State of Missouri, died at St Louis on Sat last. He was an eminent lawyer, & as a citizen universally respected.

On Oct 28 last the ship **Flora McDonald**, then on a voyage to Liverpool, encountered at sea the British barque **Jane Black**, bound from Quebec to Limerick, with lumber, in distress & water-logged, & took off the captain & crew, 17 in number, then in a starving condition. In the Liverpool Times of Feb 12 we find a notice of the arrival of the deserted barque at the very port of her destination, she having been carried by the wind & waves to the river Shanon. She is now the property of the underwriters, they having long since paid the insurance on her. –Cork Constitution.

Mr Obadiah A Bowe, for some time past connected with the editorial dept of the N Y Sun, died this afternoon. He was a native of Vt, & a printer by profession, connected with the press in some capacity for over 30 years. –N Y, Mar 6

The fine packet steamer **Princess**, Capt Jackson, commanding, burst her boilers, took fire, & burnt to the water's edge, at Conrad's Point, on Sunday. List of killed & wounded, as far as ascertained:

Son of W B Stuart, Fayette, Miss
Jas Yale, Natchez
W L Glover, Natchez
Col Coffey, Grand Gulf
Dr Richards, Point Coupee
John M Bell, N O
H 'W Sherberne, Baton Rouge
Chas Bannister, Rep from N O
L Huarck, Rep from N O
Capt Jackson
John Clark
One pilot lost
Jas Ized, clerk
S H Lurty
L D Brewer
C B Phillips, Bayou Sara
Hall Wilcox, Rodney
Jos Clark, 2nd clerk
Judge Boyce, a nephew of Mr Murphey
Mr Brandon, clerk of the Court of Natchez
Two brothers named Marks from Fayette, Miss
Mr Cockburn, of the house of Oakey A Hawkins
Claxton Taylor, of Baton Rouge, assist engineer, cut in two

J F Scott, Tensas
Augustus DeLee, Clinton
F Surget, Natchez
J J Hodges, Franklin, Miss
A Harbour
Mr Vigne, Point Coupee
F A Cheatem, Baton Rouge
Geo Evans, Natchez
J M Carr, New Carthage
Philip Stevens, Baton Rouge
Andrew, colored waiter
C M Kinston, New Orleans
Saml Waits, Va
Edw Quig, barkeeper
Mr Baxter, Rapides
J D Comeaus, Baton Rouge
Mr Allen, Baton Rouge

Hurt but not seriously:
Judge Farrar, Point Coupee
Philip Brandon, Wash, Miss
Miss Lizzie Stone, Natchez
Mrs F Surget, Natchez
Mrs Reeves, Tensas

Mr Delaney, Baton Rouge
Judge Burk, Baton Rouge
Mr Brewers & servant, died since
J W Seymour, Baton Rouge
Mr Calhoun, Ky

Died: on Feb 26, in N Y, aged 76 years, Col Thos L McKenney, a native of Md, & for many years a resident of Wash City. He was an active ofcr of volunteers in this District during the war of 1818, & was superintendent of Indian trade & joint com'r with Gen Cass to make treaties with Indian tribes in the Northwest.

Mrd: on Mar 3, by Rev Geo W Samson, Prof Edw S Fristoe, of Columbia College, to Miss Julia Laub, of Wash.

A telegraphic dispatch from Sacramento brings us the unwelcome intelligence of the death of Thos W Sutherland, one of our oldest Calif residents. He was born in Phil, & was a son of Dr Sutherland, who was a member of Congress from Phil for several years, & a warm friend of the Pres of the U S. In 1849 Mr Sutherland came to Calif & commenced the practice of the legal profession in Los Angeles, where he soon rose to the bench, & was appointed Judge of the southern district of Calif in 1850, an ofc he filled until late in 1852, when he settled in this city. He received the appointment of Collector of the port of Sacramento from Pres Buchanan, which ofc he held at the time of his death. Judge Sutherland leaves a wife & a son to mourn his premature death. He was indisposed but 3 or 4 days, & was cut down in the prime of life by congestion of the brain. –San Francisco paper

WED MAR 9, 1859
Hon Aaron V Brown, Postmaster Genr'l, expired at his residence in Wash City yesterday, of pneumonia. He had prepared his friends a day or two to anticipate his termination. Mr Brown was in his 64th year; a native of Va; educated at the Univ of N C; removed to Tenn & rose to eminence. He was called by Pres Buchanan to take the place in his Cabinet as Postmaster Genr'l.

Hon Robt M McLane, of Balt, formerly Minister to China, has been appointed by the Pres & Senate Minister Plenipotentiary to Mexico, vice Mr Forsyth, who has returned home.

Alex'r N Zevely, the efficient Chief Clerk to the Third Assist Postmaster Genr'l, has been promoted, by appointment of the Pres & Senate, to the ofc of Third Assist, made vacant by the death of the lamented Mr Marron.

Chas Phillips, the eminent Irish barrister, died in London on Dec 31, 1858. He was an excellent lawyer, & held at the time of his death the office of Comr'r of the London Bankruptcy Court. He died in his 72nd year.

Laws of the U S: Public No 33. 1-To Eliz C Perry, per act Mar 2, 1821, $312.50.

The undersigned, trustees, under a decree of the Circuit Court of D C, passed on Dec 7, 1858, in a cause between John Hooper & others as cmplnts & Wm Bird's heirs & other dfndnts, [No 1,202 in equity,] will on Apr 1 offer the following property, for the payrment of the debts of said Wm Bird, in Wash City: parts of lots 7 & 8 in square 353, fronting on D st south, between 11th & 12th sts west, in Bird's subdivision of square 463, fronting on 6th st west, south C st, & Md ave, & part of original lot 2 in said square 463, with improvements; lots 13 & 14 in square 636, near south B st. At the same time, at the risk & cost of the former purchaser, lot 14 in square 388. –Wm H Ward, Wm R Woodward, trustees   -A Green auct

Both executed. Fleming, the telegraph operator, & O'Leary, who were both found guilty of murder at the last Assizes, were executed at Toronto, Canada, Mar 4, in the presence of many spectators.

Criminal Court-Wash-Tue. Grand Jury:
Thos Carbery, foreman
Saml Bacon
Thos Blagden
John P Ingle
Benj O Tayloe
John M Brodhead
Stephen D Castleman
Lewis Johnson
Chauncey Bestor
Edw C Dyer
Stephen P Franklin
Darius Clagett
Thos Thornley
Erastus M Chapin
Sayles L Bowen
Edw M Linthicum
David English
Valentine Harbaugh
Robt Beale
Geo Poe, jr
Geo McCeny
Lewis Carbery
Robt White
Robt Clarke

Petit Jury:
David Hepburn
Saml H Howell
Richd E Simms
Jas Fullalove
Thos R Brightwell
Archibald White
Wm Bond
Reuben Worthington
Wm Dawson
Warren Lowe
John E Neale
Abraham Butler
Jos Bryan
Rezin Arnold
John Scrivener
Chas M Skippen
Saml R Sylvester
Lewis Brooks
Jas L Davis
Bennet Sewell
Robt A Griffin
John Smith
Jos L Savage
Wm M S Hopkins
Lewis Wright
Paul Stevens
N Boyd Brooks
Henry M Hurdle
Lawrence Iardella
Geo E Kirk

+

Criminal Court-Wash-Tue: 1-Chas McIlvaine Matthews, admitted an atty & counselor of this Court. 2-Chas Willis, who was put on trial in 2 cases for assault & battery on Lawrence Lippard, & in both acquitted. 3-Lawrence Kane stood charged with assault & battery on Eliz Usher in Sep last: guilty & sentenced to a fine of $6. He was praying in commitment till fine & costs were paid; & was accordingly remanded to jail.

The subscriber will sell at public sale on Mar 10th, the farm on which he resides, containing 148½ acres, adjoining the farms of Messrs Chas Digges & Woolman Gibson, 1 mile from the Bladensburg Depot; improvements consists of a comfortable frame dwlg & all necessary out-bldgs. -Thos J Barclay, near Bladensburg.

Adrien, Mich, Mar 7. The remains of Mr Ira J Thurston, the lost aeronaut, were found near Toledo last Sunday, & fully identified. He fell from the balloon last Sept. [Mar 14th newspaper: On Mar 5, a son of Mr Hoag was searching in a piece of woods for some lost sheep, on the farm of Mr Salmon Miner, on Indiana road, about 6 miles from Toledo, when he discovered articles of clothing & bones, which satisfied him that a dismembered human body had decayed & portions of it eaten there by animals. In the pockets were found a Lepine silver watch, jack-knife, & a buckskin purse containing $1.36 in money. Gloves were found in a coat pocket. Mr Thurston, last seen near Knight's Station, on Sep 16 last, when carried away by the escaping balloon.]

Orphans Court of Wash Co, D C. Letters of administration on the personal estate of Philip B Key, late of Wash Co, deceased. –W A Maury, adm

THU MAR 10, 1859
Excellent household & kitchen furniture at auction on Mar 14, at Forrest Hall, Gtwn, the furniture of the late Col Humphreys. -Bernard & Buckey, aucts, Gtwn

The funeral of Hon Aaron V Brown, Postmaster Genr'l of the U S, is appointed for this day, & will move from the Executive Mansion, the doors of which will be opened at 10 A M. The funeral services will take place at 12 o'clock M, in the East Room. Pallbearers:
Mr Fitch, of Ind   Mr Floyd, Sec of War
Mr Johnson, of Ark   Judge Catron, Sup Court
Mr Thompson, Sec Inte'r   Judge Clifford, Sup Court
[Mar 11th newspaper: the cortege was formed & in procession moved down 15th st to Pa ave, thence to the **Congressional Cemetery**. The remains were placed in a vault until the time appointed for their removal to Tennessee.] [Mar 16th newspaper: The remains of the late Hon Aaron V Brown, accompanied by his son, in charge of Senators Nicholson & Johnson, reached Nashville, Tenn, on Mar 14. Mrs Brown, the widow, will leave this city [Wash,] in a few days for her home in Tenn.]

Mr Aaron Kehew, 83 years old, & Mrs Sarah Batchelder, 90 years old, were both found dead in their beds Sat. Coroner Walter was called in both cases, but held no inquest in either, Dr Stone having certified that death was caused in former from disease of the heart, & in the latter from congestion of the lungs, with complication of ossification of the heart.

Wash Corp-Wash-Mon: 1-Ptn from Mrs Rebecca Van Horn for permission to add to her brick bldg a frame addition: referred to the Cmte on Police. 2-Bills for the relief of Jas T Lloyd, & for the relief of E Loeffler, were referred to the Cmte of Claims. 3-Ptn from Wm Rupp, asking to be refunded a portion of the amount paid for a tavern license: referred to the Cmte of Claims. 4-Ptns of Henry Better; of Patrick Sullivan; of Jas T Nally; of Louis Vetteir; & of Jos Anderson, each praying the remission of a fine: referred to the Cmte of Claims.

Hon Geo W Jones, of Iowa, late a Senator in Congress from that State, has been appointed Minister Resident to New Granada.

Mrd: on Wed, in Wash City, by Rev John C Smith, Mr Thos H Oakshott to Miss Mary P Campbell, all of Wash City.

Died: on Mar 6, at Beaverdam, Botetourt Co, Va, of typhoid fever, Jas Madison Allen, in his 19th year, son of Judge John Jas Allen.

Hemp farm in Saline Co, Mo, at auction, on long credit, in pursuance of the decrees of the Circuit Court of Saline Co, Mo, rendered in the suit of Peyton A Brown vs Susan A Brown & others, at the May & Nov terms, 1858: sale on May 11 next, of the farm of Henry J Brown, deceased. It contains about 250 acres; the dwlg house was burnt about 3 years since; there is an office with 2 rooms, below & one above stairs, making a comfortable dwlg. Apply to T W B Crews, Marshall, Saline Co, Mo, or to E S Brown, Sunny-Side post ofc, Cumberland Co, Va. Mr Isbell, the overseer on the farm, will show the same. –Jacob H Smith, Sheriff of Saline Co, Mo

Orphans Court of Wash Co, D C. Letters of administration on the personal estate of John Marron, late of Wash Co, deceased. –Eliza Ann Marron, admx

Orphans Court of Wash Co, D C. Letters of administration on the personal estate of Richd Randolph, late of Wash Co, deceased. –Wm B Randolph, adm

FRI MAR 11, 1859

Annual Commencement of the Medical Dept of Gtwn College took place last evening at the Smithsonian Institution. Faculty present: Drs Noble Young, Liebermann, Snyder, Eliot, Morgan, Antisell, & Willett, accompanied by Rev Dr Early, Pres of Gtwn College, & Rev Mr Curly, of the same institution, & Dr Eliot, dean of the faculty. Graduates who received the degree of doctor of medicine were Reuben Cleary, of D C; Lucius Smith, of Ohio; Jos T Howard, of D C; Geo W Hill, of Ohio; F C Christie, of N Y; J Wells Herbert, of Md; Dent Burroughs, of Md; E Lyon Corbin, of N Y; & Augustus R Sparks, of Iowa. The Valedictory was pronounced by Dr Thos Antisell.

Hon John M Moore, of Vicksburg, one of the most prominent men on the bench in Mississippi, died suddenly at his plantation, in Isaquena Co, on Feb 16, from injuries received by a fall from a doorway, which at first were deemed trivial, but in a short time terminated fatally.

Mrd: on Mar 8, at Trinity Church, by Rev Dr Butler, Dr J V D Middleton, of Ala, to Helen E, daughter of David H Burr, of Wash City.

Mrd: on Mar 8, in Wash City, by Rev Mr Hall, Jas M Cupit, of Providence, R I, to Viginia J Gaines, of Wash.

Mrd: on Thu, in Wash City, by Rev John C Smith, Mr Wm H B Butler to Miss Sarah E Wright, both of Alexandria, Va.

SAT MAR 12, 1859
We have received a copy of the life & adventures of the famous frontier man, Kit Carson, the Nestor of the Rocky Mountains, written by Dr DeWitt C Peters. –Taylor & Maury's

A letter has been received from Lt Beale by his family residing at Chester, dated at Santa Fe on Feb 3 last. He had just returned to that place from Taos, where he had been upon a visit of a few days to his old friend, Kit Carson, who returned with him.

Public sale of 2 fine farms in PG Co, Md: by decree of the Circuit Court for PG Co, as a Court of Equity, the trustees will expose to public sale, on the premises, on Apr 1st next, all the real estates of the late John Brooke, containing 940 acres, more or less. **Mount Calvert**, the home place, contains 620 acres; a commodious brick dwlg house, with farm bldgs & overseer's house. **Brooke Hill** adjoins the above estate, contains 320 acres, more or less. R B B Chew will show the premises. –R B B Chew, Trustee for the sale of **Mount Calvert**. –C C Magruder, Trustee for the sale of **Brooke Hill**.

Somebody is circulating a petition in this city for signatures to be sent to the Pres of the U S, praying for the pardon of Cyrus W Plummer, the murderer of Capt Archibald Mellen, jr, on board the ship **Junior**, of this port. On what grounds Plummer may be set at liberty we are not advised. Plummer admitted that the verdict of murder was what he expected. –New Bedford Mercury

Mrd: on Mar 8, at St Matthew's Church, by Rev Fr Waldron, Rosina, daughter of R B Lloyd, of Wash City, to Capt Thos J Mackey, Inspector of Surveys for Kansas & Nebraska, assisted by Gov Black, of Nebraska, & Gen Heningsen, late of Nicaragua.

Died: on Mar 11, in Gtwn, D C, William Henry, son of Geo & Anna H Waters, aged 12 years. His funeral is on Mar 12 at 4 o'clock, from his father's residence, 37 Market st.

Died: on Mar 11, of pneumonia, infant son of John F & Amanda L Mullowny, aged 3 months & 7 days.

Died: on Feb 15, at Yazoo City, Miss, Alfred Johnson, aged 46 years. He was a native of N C, & a son of Gen Robt Johnson, of that State; but for 20 years had been a resident of the Southwest. In the neighborhood where he died he was beloved & respected.

Died: Mar 5, near Salem, Roanoke Co, Va, Hugh Derrick Pitzer, aged 1 month & 3 days.

MON MAR 14, 1859
Died: on Mar 13, Eliza T, wife of John H Bradley, jr. Her funeral will take place from the First Presbyterian Church, 4½ st, today, Monday, at 12 o'clock.

The Gettysburg [Pa] Compiler gives an account of the loss of a little boy, 4 years of age, a son of Mrs Oyler, of Cumberland Co, who strayed from home. After two days & nights the dead body of the little fellow was discovered nearly 9 miles from his home. The little dog, the child's playmate, was found nestled in the child's bosom. The faithful dog had tramped quite a path around the lifeless body of the sleeping boy, thus betraying the affection that it had for the youth.

Last Wed St Mary's Church, of the <u>Order of Redemptionists</u>, at Oswego, N Y, was thronged for some interesting religious exercises, when the flooring gave way. One man, Lawrence Murray, was taken out dead; also, Mrs Mary Carlin, Mrs Bridget Langdon, & Mrs Margaret Henessy.

The Balt Conference of the Methodist Episcopal Church, lately in session at Lewisburg, Va, closed its labors on Mar 9th. The following is a list of appointments for this city & vicinity: Wash District: L F Morgan, P E-Wash; Foundry, B H Nadal; Wesley Chapel, D Ball; Waugh Chapel, T M Carson; McKendree, W Hamilton; East Wash, W M D Ryan; Ebenezer, [to be supplied;] Ryland, S Rogers; Gorsuch, J H M Lemon; Union, J N Coombs, W O Lumsden, Sup; Fletcher & Providence, H N Sipes, M A Turner, Sup; Asbury & Mount Zion, J M Grandin; Rockville, S Register, [one to be supplied,] B Barry, Sup; Elkridge, H C Westward; Bladensburg, W H Wilson, John A Williams; Patapsco Circuit, W Prettyman, Geo C Kramer, C A Reid, Sup; Patapsco Station, T McGee; Woodville, H C Daniel; Patuxent, F S Cassidy. Alexandria District: B N Brown, P C-Alexandria, J Lanahan, W S Edwards, A Griffith, Sup; Gtwn, W B Edwards; West Gtwn & Tennalytown, J H Ryland; Fairfax, W G Coe; Stafford, W Champion, H Lever, Sup; Fredericksburg, J A McCauley; St Mary's, B H Smith, R R Murphy; Charles, C G Linthicum, W Bagley; Montg, S Cornelius, W E Magruder; Mount Vernon, S M Dickson; Leesburg, J Landstreet; East Loudoun, D Thomas; West Loudoun, J H March; Warrenton, E D Owen; Rehoboth, J P Etcherson.

A young man, Wm C Carroll, residing at 276 Houston st, N Y, accidentally shot his mother on Friday, wounding her so severely that it is thought she cannot recover. He was preparing a pistol to shoot rats, when it accidentally discharged. She is 61 years old.

Mrd: on Mar 11, by Rev Andrew G Carothers, Mr Dawson Burgess, of Fauquier Co, & Miss Margaret Clowser, of Fred'k Co, Va.

Mrd: on Mar 9, at Balt, by Rev Mr Rich, Dr Edw J Griffith, of Balt Co, Md, to Miss Nellie Griffith, of Balt.

Mrd: on Mar 13, in Wash City, by Rev G W Samson, Mr Jas L Drumright, of Goochland Co, Va, to Miss Lucis M Richardson, of Fluvanna Co, Va.

Died: on Mar 7, at Val Verd, PG Co, Md, in her 83rd year, Mrs Priscilla Maddox, relict of the late Notley Maddox & daughter of Col Truman Skinner, of the army of the Revolution.

TUE MAR 15, 1859
Mrd: on Mar 1, at Christ Church, New Orleans, by Rt Rev Leonidas Polk, Wm F Howell to Mary Minnie, daughter of Rev W T Leacock.

Mrd: on Mar 14, by Rev Andrew G Carothers, Mr Rouzee Rains to Miss Rebecca Paign, both of Stafford Co, Va.

Died: on Mar 14, in Gtwn, Mrs Nancy Martel Miller. Her funeral will take place from her late residence, corner of Beall & Green sts, this evening at 3 o'clock.

First Things: 1-The first carriage said to be built in America was made in Dorchester, Mass, by a man named White, for a private gentleman in Boston. 2-The first stage-coach to Boston from N Y stated Jun 24, 1772, from the "Fresh Water. The fare was 4d, N Y currency, per mile. It reached Hartford, Conn, in 2 days, & Boston in 2 more. 3-The first grand jury in America met in Boston Sep 1, 1635, & presented 100 offences. 4-The first insurance office in New England was established at Boston in 1724. 5-The earliest institution for savings of any kind was established in Berne, Switzerland, in 1787. 6-The first attempt to establish a post ofc system in the American colonies was made in 1693 by Thos Neale, to whom a royal patent for this purpose had been issued; but his arrangements were very limited & imperfect. The utmost contemplated by Neale was a post ofc in each couty, & his actual operations came far short of this. 7-Henry Cruger was the first American who sat in the British House of Commons, elected in 1774 as one of the two reps of Liverpool in Parliament, his colleague being Edmund Burke. He defended America during the Revolutionary war, & upon his return to N Y after the peace was elected to the State Senate, while he was still a member of the British House of Commons, his term of service not having expired. 8-The first Methodist Chapel erected in the world was built in Bristol, England, in May, 1739. 9-The first mint in the U S was put in operation in 1793. 10-The first iron rails for a road bed were laid down at Whitehaven, England, in 1738. 11-The first actual model of a steam carriage was constructed by a Frenchman, Cugnot, who exhibited it before the Marshal de Saxe in 1763. The first English model of a steam carriage was made in 1784 by Wm Murdoch. 12-The first Normal School on this side of the Atlantic was established at Lexington in 1839. 13-The first degree of Doctor of Divinity conferred at Harvard was conferred upon Rev Increase Mather, in 1692, then Pres of the University. 14-The first agricultural association which was formed in this country, The Philadelphia Society for promoting Agriculture, was established in 1785. Mr Matthewson, of Rhode Island, received a gold medal for the best sample & greatest quantity of cheese exhibited. 15-The first cattle show held in this county was held in Pittsfield, Mass, in Oct, 1810. –Boston Transcript

Criminal Court-Wash-Sat. 1-Lewis Bell found guilty of grand larceny in stealing 2 pictures: sentenced to 2 years confinement at hard labor in the penitentiary. 2-John Baptist, colored, convicted of larceny: sentenced to 10 months in jail. 3-Danl Moone alias John Dumb was proved to have stolen a large Bible, valued at $15, but the jury, believing him to have been insane at the time of the act, found him not guilty. He will be sent to the infirmary. 4-Arthur Alexander, colored, guilty of stealing a pair of boots, the property of Wm Valentine: sentenced to 9 months in jail.

Macon, Mar 14. A letter has been received here from Albany, stating that Col Jos Bond, of this city, was murdered at that place on Sat by one Lucius Brown. Col Bond was one of the largest cotton planters of the South, a popular & public spirited citizen. The difficulty is believed to have originated by Brown's having whipped one of Col Bond's negroes.

A movement is on foot to surround the tombstone of Byron, at Harrow, with a neat iron railing, & subscriptions are asked for the purpose. It seems that the vandalism of unscrupulous persons, in chipping off pieces of the tomb, has been carried so far that a very considerable portion of the inscription is now deficient.

St Louis, Mar 13. The loss of the Neasho & Alburquerque mail of last Nov is confirmed by the arrival here of John Hall, the conductor, who makes affidavit to the effect that when about 2 days' march behind Lt Beale's party he was attacked by 40 Comanches, badly wounded, & taken prisoner The mail was destroyed. Hall escaped from the Indians in Feb, & after enduring great hardships reached the settlements in safety.

WED MAR 16, 1859
Sale of fine Paris made rosewood furniture & excellent household effects at auction, Mar 22, at the house recently occupied by Hon J C Breckinridge, Vice Pres of the U S, & Hon Mr Stephenson, & Hon Jas B Clay, 466 6th st, between D & E sts. –C W Boteler, auct

The U S mail steamer **Star of the West**, arrived at N Y from Aspinwall on Mar 5, brings Cmder Davis & the ofcrs & crew of the U S sloop-of-war **St Mary's**, which arrived at Panama on Feb 20 from Acapulco. On the 21st Cmder Davis handed over the command of the St Mary's to Capt Thornburn. List of the returning ofcrs of the **St Mary's**: Cmder, C H Davis; Lts: Maury, McCorkle, & Ward; Surgeon: J W Taylor; Purser: W A Ingersoll; Lt of Marines: E McD Reynolds; Assist Surgeon: Stewart Kennedy; Boatswain, P J Miller; Carpenter: E A Cassidy. <u>Panama Star & Herald</u>: The ofcrs & crew now returning home relieved the ofcrs & crew under the command of Capt T Bailey in Dec, 1856. In the following May Capt Davis, in the **St Mary's**, at San Juan del Sud, saved the life of Walker & his filibusters after the surrender at Rivas. Subsequently the **St Mary's** visited the Guano Island in the North Pacific, & surveyed them, & then proceeded to the Sandwich Islands, San Francisco, & lastly to the Mexican coast, where her presence & the action of Capt Davis tended materially to protect American life & property.

Closing out sale of Buthmann's stock of Wine & Liquors, on Mar 19th, at the store of the late Mr Buthmann, on Pa ave, between 4½ & 6th sts. –A E Buthmann, admx -Jas C McGuire & Co, aucts

Mrs Phebe Washburn, of Lenox, aged 92 years, was visited on Mar 19, her birthday, by 5 children, 14 grand-children, 10 great grand-children, & 1 great-great-grandchild.

Household & kitchen furniture at auction on Mar 18, at the residence of J R McGregor, 492 E st, between 2nd & 3rd sts. -Jas C McGuire & Co, aucts

Trustee's sale of improved real estate in Wash City: by decree of the Circuit Court of Wash, D C, passed on Jan 23, 1859, in a cause in which Christiana McClery & others are cmplnts, & Lawrence W James & others are dfndnts. Public auction on Apr 7, on the premises, the south part of lot 13 in square 253, fronting on 14th st west; with a 2 story brick dwlg house. –Gilbert Rodman, trustee -J C McGuire & Co, aucts

New Orleans Delta of Mar 3-steamer **Princess**. We have made out the following list of dead, including all who are missing. Any other classification would be a mockery. We have included among the killed those who have since died of their wounds. Killed: Capt Jackson, H W Sherburn, J C Taylor, J W Seymour, of Baton Rouge; H B Murphy, Rapides Parish; John J Hodes, Miss; John Clark, ofcr; Mr Brandon, Jas Gale, W L Glover, Natchez; Col Coffee, Miss; L Huard, Chas Bannister, members of the Louisiana Leg; Dr Richards, Pointe Coupee; John M Bell, New Orleans; John Hagan, Iberville; Mr Marks, Miss; Jas Izod, clerk of the boat; Mr Calhoun, Maysville, Ky, Master Stewart, Miss; Jos Clark, 2nd clerk; Peter Hearsey, 2nd engineer; Edw Quig, barkeeper; Wm Kingston, New Orleans; Mr Carrey, barkeeper. Wounded: S H Lurty, sheriff of West Feliciana; Mr Brewer, lawyer of Bayou Sara; W B Phillips, merchant of Bayou Sara; Wm Vernon, sheriff of Concordia; H Wilcox, Rodney, Miss; John F Scott, Texas; Auguse Delee, Clinton, La; F Lurget, Natchez; Mr Cockburne, New Orleans; W Harbour, J Vignee, Point Coupee; F Cheathath, Baton Rouge; Mr Baxter, Rapides; Mr Corneau, Mr Aliery, Baton Rouge; L D Reeves, member of Legistlature from Tenn; F C Laville, member of Legislature, New Orleans; T Davenport, Miss; Judge F Farra, Point Coupee; Philip Brandon, Miss; Miss Lucy Stone, Mrs F Surget, Natchez; Mrs W H Winter, Washington City; M Bourgeois, Point Coupee; Mr Hudson, Bayou Sara; Geo Evans, Natchez; Philip Stevens, Baton Rouge; J M Carr, New Carthage; E Flood, Bardstown, Ky; Miss T Smith, Natchez; Edw Williams, Texas; Jos Delaney, Judge Boyce, Avoyelles; L Canonge, New Orleans; E Lacouel, Point Coupee. The list does not include the hands or crew of the boat, among whom the mortality must have been great.

I certify that Saml Burress, farmer of Wash Co, D C, brought before me as a stray, trespassing near his enclosures, a Bay Mare. Owner is to prove property, pay charges, & take her away. –F S Myer, J P

Orphans Court of Wash Co, D C. Letters testamentary on the personal estate of Mary A Miller, late of Wash Co, deceased. –F W Jones, exc

Criminal Court-Wash-Tue. 1-Chas R L Crown found guilty for assault & battery on Mr Robt W Barnard: sentenced to pay a fine of $30 & costs. 2-Erasmus Salyard, charged with larceny, was tried & acquitted.

Died: on Mar 14, in Wash City, at his residence, 11th & I sts, Hon Vespasian Ellis, aged 59 years & 4 months. His funeral is this afternoon at 3 o'clock.

Died: on Feb 28, at Evergreen Cottage, Fairfax Co, Va, Marian Louisa, daughter of August A Von Schmidt & Sallie V Lee, aged 9 years & 7 months.

Died: on Mar 15, Mary Ann McGlue, in her 15th year, daughter of G T & Hester McGlue. Her funeral is on Thu at 3 o'clock, from Union Chapel, on 20th st.

Died: on Mar 5, at Water Proof, Tensas Parish, La, Mr J F Scott, from injuries received on board the ill-fated steamer **Princess**. He was an affectionate husband, a loving father, & an exemplary Christian. –J W W

Circuit Court of Wash Co, D C-in Chancery, No 1,364. Edw H Fitzgerald et al vs Thos C Fitzgerald. Thos Carbery, trustee, reported that having failed to sell the property at public sale, for want of bidders at sufficient prices, did offer the same at private sale, on Oct 18, 1858, & sold to Jos C Ives that part of said property being part of square 106, on the following terms, viz $2,500 in cash, & the residue in 2 equal payments of $2,170 each, at one & two years respectively from date, with interest. –John A Smith, clerk

THU MAR 17, 1859
Affray between two little brothers. The Spencer [Owen Co, Ind] Journal says that on Sat week the 2 & 4 year old sons of Mr A Goodwin, of Green Co, got quarreling as to which one should have possession of an axe. The elder one succeeded in getting the axe, & immediately struck his brother in the head, killing him almost instantly.

Criminal Court-Wash-Wed. 1-Philip Kegan was found not guilty of stealing a coat.

The body of Thos Jasper, of Culpeper Co, Va, was found yesterday in the canal. In his pocket was a purse containing $386. Conjecture is that he fell into the canal when intoxicated.

In Equity, No 1,388. John F Boone, jr, against Wm C Boone & John J Dyer, his guardian ad litem, A A Smith, R H Clarke, T J Massie, & Thos J Fisher. Parties named are notified that on Apr 8, at my ofc in the City Hall, Wash, I shall state the account of the trustee. -W R Redin, auditor

Mrd: on Mar 13, at the Fourth Presbyterian Church, Balt, by Rev J L Lefevre, Geo H Stewart to Miss Laura E Sayre, eldest daughter of Jas T Sayre, all of that city.

Died: on Mar 14, Elizabeth, wife of Alex'r McCoy, & eldest daughter of the late John Knoblock, sr, formerly of Wash City.

Orphans Court of Wash Co, D C. Letters testamentary on the personal estate of Chas R Queen, late of Wash Co, deceased. –Mary Ann Queen, excx

Orphans Court of Wash Co, D C. Letters testamentary on the personal estate of Anthony Smith, late of Wash Co, deceased. –A Hyde, exc

FRI MAY 18, 1859
Chickering Piano Forte, & excellent household & kitchen furniture at auction on Mar 24, at the residence of Capt T J Page, U S N, in the center house of the De Menou Bldgs, on H st, between 13th & 14th sts, we shall sell all his furniture & effects.
-Jas C McGuire & Co, aucts

Mrd: on Thu, by Rev John C Smith, Carey Gwinne to Miss Maria O, daughter of the late Anthony Preston, all of Wash City.

Died: on Mar 3, in Wash City, Caroline Laurens, wife of John Laurens, of Charleston, S C, & daughter of John N Maffitt, U S Navy. [Paper creased-this is what it APPEARS to be.]

Died: on Mar 17, of typhoid fever, Ida Caroline, daughter of Jas & Caroline H Skirving, aged 4 years, 7 months & 17 days. Her funeral will be from her father's residence, 423 11th st, this morning, at 10 o'clock.

Died: on Mar 14, at the residence of her parents, in Prince Wm Co, Va, Eva Percy, daughter of Edmund & Mary L Berkeley, in her 9th year.

Store for rent: the 4 story brown stone bldg on Pa ave, near the Nat'l Hotel, occupied by Mr B J Semmes, for many years in the wholesale Grocery & Liquor trade, will be rent on Apr 1. Mr Semmes being about to remove to the South. -M G Emery

Criminal Court-Wash-Thu. The Grand Jury yesterday found an indictment against Danl E Sickles for the murder of Philip B Key. Mr S F Butterworth has not been called as a witness by the Grand Jury. [Mar 19th newspaper: Sickles was merely presented, but has not yet been indicted.] [Apr 5th newspaper: Criminal Court-Wash-Apr 4. Trial of Danl E Sickles: present was Mr Sickles, sen, & Mr Bagioli, father of Mrs Sickles. Witnesses for the Gov't: Dr R H Coolidge, Dr R K Stone, Rich N Downer, Francis Doyle, Thos E Martin, Jas N Reed, Eugene Pendleton, Philip V R Van Wyck, Jos Dudrow, Edw Delafield, Abel Upshur, & Edw M Tidball.]

Obit-died: John Connell, on Mar 9, aged 76 years, at Tusculum, near Wilmington, Delaware. He was a native of Marcus Hook, in Pa; a Phil merchant. His knowledge of public & international law was most extensive; long employed as agent of the claimants on Congress for redress for French spoliations prior to 1800. He was happy in his domestic relations with the estimable wife who survives him. He was deprived in rapid succession of 2 lovely children at an early age. He was suddenly stricken in his declining years by having snatched from him, his only son, by an awful casualty, who had arrived at his majority, a rising minister of theGospel. From this blow Mr Connell never fully recovered.

N Y, Mar 17. The body of Hon Mike Walsh was found this morning near a bldg on 8th ave. It is probable he met his death by accidentally falling into the area & breaking his neck. All the democratic headquarters in the city have their flags at half-mast. [Mar 19th newspaper: Mr Walsh's old watch, chain, & diamond ring were missing, & the presumption at first was that he had been murdered. In the absence of any external injuries, beyond a scalp wounded, it is believed he came to his death when he fell down the steps while intoxicated. –N Y Express] [Mar 21st newspaper: Mike Walsh came to his death by apoplexy, on Mar 17, produced from being precipitated down the stone steps of the area of 136 8th ave.] [Mar 22nd newspaper: The impression is becoming general that the death of Hon Mike Walsh was produced by violence. His remains were conveyed to **Greenwood Cemetery.**]

A respite has been granted to the four condemned men at Balt, Gambrill, Crops, Corrie, & Cyphus, from this day until Apr 8 next. The sheriff desires to make known to them that this extension of time is allowed them for the purpose of enabling them to prepare to meet their solemn fate, & that all hope & expectation of further Executive clemency must be entirely banished from their minds.

SAT MAR 19, 1859
Capt Zachariah F Johnson, a Capt of the U S Navy, residing on Lexington st, Balt, died of apoplexy quite suddenly on Wed. He was a native of PG Co, & had been in the service nearly 41 years, of which 16 years were spent in active service at sea, 4 years & 6 months on shore, or other duty, & 20 years unemployed. He was at the time of his death awaiting orders. His funeral was attended by the various U S Army & Navy ofcrs of the city & port of Balt.

Miss Theodosia Smith, daughter of Geo P Smith, a young lady of 19 years, was in a singing rehearsal under Mr Hall, in the basement of St Paul's Church, on Mar 14. Suddenly she had some affection of one foot, saying her foot was asleep. She could not rise & when assisted, she fell back unconscious & never revived. She died about 12 o'clock. The physicians called say that there was enlargement of the lungs, & that she died from paralysis of the lungs. –Cleveland Herald

Criminal Court-Wash-Fri: 1-Hilleary Hutchins & John Jones were indicted for the murder of John Ennis in Gtwn. 2-Pink Coakley, colored, was found guilty of assault, & sentenced to 1 week in jail. 3-John Collins was found guilty of assault, & sentenced to one month in jail & pay a fine of $10 & costs. He was also prayed in commitment till fine & costs are paid. 4-Geo Brown alias Brooks, colored, was found guilty on 2 charges of larceny of 3 umbrellas, from Messrs S T Shugert & C N Parmelee, & found guilty in both. Sentenced to 6 months on each case.

Reward for runaway slave Henry, the property of Edw Harding & his grandchildren, who ran off from the residence of Jas A Clagett, near New Balt, in Fauquier Co, on Mar 12. Henry is 20 years old. –B E Harrison, trustee, Lagrange, near Thoroughfare, Prince Wm Co, Va.

Died: on Mar 18, Samuel L, infant son of Ellen C & the late Saml L Brown, aged 4 months. His funeral will be on Sunday at 3 o'clock, from the residence of J Harbaugh.

MON MAR 21, 1859
Foreign Obit: 1-Countess of Sandwich, sister to Lord Cowley, the special British Envoy to Vienna, died in London, Feb 21, after a short illness. The deceased Countess was the 2nd daughter of the late Field Marshal the Marquis of Anglesey, by his 2nd marriage. She was born on Jun 16, 1812, & married, on Sep 6, 1838, the Earl of Sandwich. 2-Lady Delamere died at her residence in London, Feb 24. She was 2nd daughter of the Earl & Countess of Kinnoul. She married in 1848 Hon Hugh Cholmondeley, who has since succeeded to the title of Baron Delamere. She had not long entered her 31st year. 3-Gen Sir Alex'r Leith, well known for his gallantry & achievements during the Peninsular war, died at his seat of Freefield, Aberdeenshire, Scotland, Feb 19, in his 85th year. 4-The Countess de Chateaubriand, nee d'Orglande, has just died of a decline at Pau, in her 20th year. The deceased was married about 15 months ago to the grand nephew of the celebrated writer. 5-The death of Mr Abel Smith, the head of the large London banking firm of Smith, Payne & Smith, has occurred at the age of 71. [No death date given.] 6-M Houry, the learned Orientalist, & professor to the Hereditary Prince of Persia, has just died at Teheran. 7-Field Marshal General Count Dohna, of the Prussian army, has just died from disease of the nerves. 8-M Dubessey, a member of the French Council of State, & an active supporter of the Imperial Gov't, has recently died at Paris. 9-The Venerable Archdeacon Froude died at Darlington, England, Feb 16, at the age of 89. 10-The Countess Clauzel, widow of the Marshal Clauzel, has just expired at Nousseau, near Chartres. 11-At Leipsic, the Prince Otho de Sconberg-Waldenberg has recently died.

Fatal duel at New Orleans on Mar 11, between Edw Locquet, a cotton broker, of New Orleans, by Emile Hiriart, operatic critic of the Delta. The weapons were shot guns loaded with balls & the distance was 40 paces. Mr Locquet was struck by a ball near the heart, passing through on the opposite side, causing his death almost instantly.

The Pres has appointed the following Cadets at large for 1859 to enter the Military Academy: 1-Jas M Wright, son of Col Geo Wright, 9th Infty, brevetted for meritorious conduct in Florida, & at Contreras, Churubusco, & Molino del Rey.
2-Henry H Lee, son of the late Col Francis Lee, brevetted for gallantry at Contreras, Churubusco, & Molino del Rey.
3-Josiah H V Field, son of the late Capt Geo P Field, killed while leading his company at the storming of Monterey.
4-Thos Ward, son of a soldier who died in the army, after a service of 30 years.
5-Saml C Clark, son of Maj M Lewis Clark, Missouri btln, distinguished at Sacramento, grandson of Govn'r Wm Clark, of Missouri, & grand nephew of Gen Geo Rogers Clark.
6-Thos Rowland: father died of disease contracted in the Mexican war, ancestors distinguished in the Revolution.
7-Geo D Ramsay, jr, son of Maj Geo D Ramsay, Ordnance Corps, brevet for gallantry at Monterey.
8-Jas B Washington, lineal representative of Geo Washington.
-Jas R Tyler; Edw Y Buchanan

Adm's sale of the household & kitchen furniture at auction on Mar 25, at the residence of the late P Barton Key, on C st, between 3rd & 4½ sts. –W A Maury, adm
-Jas C McGuire & Co, aucts

Trustee's sale: by deed of trust from W von Kammeshueber & his wife, dated Mar 18, 1858, recorded in Liber J A S No 150, folios 342 thru 346, of the land records for Wash Co, D C: sale on Apr 22 next, on the premises, all of lots 7 & 9 in square 874, with improvement thereon, which is a 2 story frame house. –Chas Walter, trustee
-A Green auct

Obit: 1-Hon Wm T Haskell, an ofcr of the Mexican war, & formerly a member of Congress from the State of Tenn, died in the lunatic asylum at Hopkinsville, Ky, last Sunday. He was attacked with insanity a year or so ago. 2-Rev Jas Kendall, D D, died at his residence in Plymouth, Mass, on Thu, at the advanced age of 89 years. He was ordained pastor of the First Church in Plymouth Jan 1, 1800, & labored faithfully for about 40 years, until the infirmities of age compelled him to relinquish a portion of his pastoral duties. 3-Mr Timothy Sweeny, aged 122 years, died at Fairview township, Butler Co, Pa, on Feb 27. He was born in 1737, in Carahan, parish of Ardfert, county Kerry, Ireland, & emigrated to this country in 1837, being then 100 years old. He was never known to have had an hour's sickness, even up to the day of his death, but was always remarkably stout & healthy, having the full use of his faculties to the last.
4-Judge Strawbridge, for several years Judge of the 4th District Court of New Orleans, died in that city on Mar 11, in his 74th year. He was a native of Md, but emigrated to New Orleans some 40 years ago.

Promotions of the Army; since Dec last.
Engineer Corps: Capt J G Barnard, to be major; 1st Lt W H C Whiting, to be Capt; 2nd Lt J B McPherson, to be 1st Lt; Brevet 2nd Lt E P Alexander, to be 2nd Lt; Brevet 2nd Lt H M Roberts, to be 2nd Lt.
Ordnance: Brevet 2nd Lt C C Lee, to be 2nd Lt.
First Dragoons: 2nd Lt A B Chapman, to be 1st Lt; Brevet 2nd Lt Leroy Napier, jr, to be 2nd Lt.
1st Artl: Capt E D Keyes, to be major.
3rd Artl: 1st Lt G P Andrews, to be Capt; 1st Lt J H Lendrum, to be Capt; 2nd Lt T M Saunders, to be 1st Lt; 2nd Lt H V DeHart, to be 1st Lt; Brevet 2nd Lt Augustus G Robinson, to be 2nd Lt; Brevet 2nd Lt Edw R Warner, to be 2nd Lt.
2nd Regt of Infty: Lt Col Dixon S Miles, to be Colonel.
3rd Regt of Infty: Maj Electus Backus, to be Lt Col: Capt Caleb C Sibley, to be Major; 1st Lt Henry B Clitz, to be Capt; 2nd Lt Alex'r McD McCook, to be 1st Lt; Brevet 2nd Lt Wm H Bell, to be 2nd Lt.
5th Regt of Infty: 1st Lt Augustus H Seward, to be Capt; 2nd Lt Alex'r Chambers, to be 1st Lt; 2nd Lt Lucius L Rich, to be 1st Lt; Brevet 2nd Lt Bryan M Thomas, to be 2nd Lt; Brevet 2nd Lt Wm J L Nicodemus, to be 2nd Lt.
7th Regt of Infty: Brevet 2nd Lt Asa B Carey, to be 2nd Lt.
8th Regt of Infty: 1st Lt Thos G Pitcher, to be Capt; 2nd Lt Wm Craig, to be 1st Lt; Brevet 2nd Lt Royal T Frank, to be 2nd Lt.

Excellent household & kitchen furniture at auction on Mar 29, at the house of Mrs Nesbet, 386 C st, between 3rd & 4½ sts. -A Green auct

Household & kitchen furniture at auction on Mar 22, at the residence of the late Vespasian Ellis, on N Y ave, between 11th & 12th sts. -Jas C McGuire & Co, aucts

Some 6 weeks ago Jos Wright was bitten by his own dog, & nothing occurred to cause alarm until last Wed when he experienced a great deal of pain in the arm which the dog had fastened his teeth. Wright suffered until Sunday morning, when he became raving mad, & his disease was declared to be hydrophobia. He expired on Mar 13, leaving a wife & infant child. –Cincinnati Enquirer, Mar 15.

The sad tidings have flown with lightning speed from the distant South & have told us that Dr Thos Dent Mutter is no more. A long & painful illness had warned us that ere long such tidings might come. Dr Mutter was born in Richmond, Va, in Apr, 1811, & was descended from a family of Scotch extraction, though originally coming from Germany, having settled in Scotland, near Glasgow, soon after the revocation of the edict of Nantes. He commenced his medical education in Alexandria, Va, & graduated at the Univ of Pa. In 1840 or 1941, at age 29, was appointed Prof of Surgery in the Jefferson Medical College. Phil, Mar 18. -T M B, jr [No death date given-current item.]

Horses, cows, milk, carts & harness, farming implements, at auction, on Mar 23, at the residence of Chas De Bevoise, on B st, between 12th & 13th sts. -A Green auct

Orphans Court of Wash Co, D C. The case of Elias Travers & Jos Travers, excs of Nicholas Travers, deceased, the execs & Court appointed Apr 12 next, for final settlement of the personal estate of said deceased, of assets in hand.
-Ed N Roach, Reg/o wills

TUE MAR 22, 1859
A gentleman, Ellis Waldrup, residing near Brown's bridge, on the Chattahoochee river, Geo, & his wife, on Mar 11, left their 4 children, 2 girls & 2 boys, the eldest 12 years old, & walked to a neighbor's house a quarter of a mile off, to see a sick person. They left their children asleep. On returing home they found their house in flames & the children had all perished.

Criminal Court-Wash-Mon. 1-John McNancy, a mere boy, was put to trial for petty larceny, having stolen, in company with another minor, Chas Schenig, some harness, the property of Dr W H G Newman. Both were convicted & sentenced to 6 months in jail.

Mrd: on Mar 20, in Wash City, by Rev John C Smith, Dr Benj Hodges to Miss Ann Eliza Queen, all of Wash City.

Died: on Mar 21, in Wash City, Alice Mary, infant daughter of Hon Geo E & Therese Pugh, after a lingering illness, with pneumonia. Her funeral will take place at Brown's Hotel, at 2 o'clock today, after which the remains will be removed to the railroad depot, to be conveyed to Cincinnati.

Lewis Hickman, White-washer, informs his friends & the public that he is now on hand & ready to serve them. Orders left at my house, 668 L st, between 3rd & 4th sts, or at Wm D Shepperd's bookstore, 7th & D sts, will be thankfully received.

Surgeon Saml Jackson, U S Navy, died at his residence in Brooklyn on Mar 16. He was appointed surgeon from the State of N Y on Jul 10, 1812, & was 72 years of age at the time of his death. Latterly the infirmities of age rendered him unfit for active service, & he was furloughed in consequence.

Indianapolis, Mar 21. Hon O H Smith, ex-U S Senator died on Sat.

WED MAR 23, 1859
Ex-Govn'r David Campbell, of Va, died in Abingdon, Va, on Mar 19, aged 80 years. He was a major in the 12th Regt U S Infty during the war with Great Britain, & served with great credit on the Northern frontier.

Railroad accident in Canada, on Friday night, when between Flambro & Dundas, many lives were lost. The storm had washed away the bank & the engine ran into a chasm nearly 20 feet deep with the baggage car & 2 passenger cars. Killed as far as ascertained: Jones Boyer, of Chicago, Ill; Alexander Braid, of Hamilton, C W; G Morgan, engineman; W Milnes, brakeman; 2 names not reported. Wounded, some seriously: Henry Post, of Buffalo, N Y; W W Smith, of Kalamazoo, Mich; F D Adams, wife & children; E D Bryant, of Pontiac, Mich; Thos Sackett, of Livingston Co, N Y; Adam Wilson, of Mamilton Co, C W; Hiram Cook, of Cleveland, Ohio; Columbus Desser, of Detroit, Mich; J B Smith, of Livingston Co, N Y.

The subscriber has determined to decline farming, & offers his highly improved farm, near Rockville, in Montgomery Co, Md, which contains 296 acres of land, on the Barnesvill road, at private sale or exchange for Wash City property. Improvements consist of a large 2 story brick dwlg, & out bldgs. If the farm is not sold by Apr 7 next, it will be for rent. --Jos Thompson

Died: on Mar 21, in Gtwn, after a lingering & painful illness, in her 34th year, Anna M Smith, daughter of Saml S Fearson. Her funeral will take place from her father's residence this day, at 3 o'clock.

Died: on Mar 22, in Wash City, after a protracted illness, Mrs Fred'k Lakemeyer, aged 35 years & 10 months. Her funeral will take place on Mar 24, at 2 P M, from the residence of her father, John C Roemmelle, 18th & K sts.

THU MAR 24, 1859
Correspondence of the Journal of Commerce, Key West, Mar 12, 1859. The U S Marshal has arrested Capt Mathias Lind, master of the slave brig **Tyrant**, of Rochland, Maine, reported in our despatach of Mar 10th as having been ashore on the Marquesas. The crew, 9 in number, were arrested by Marshal Moreno within an hour after the issue of the warrant. Capt Lind was taken a few days later. He is the only one detained. The crew were examined & discharged. The brig **Tyrant**, Capt Lind, waa cleared at the port of NY on Nov 15 last by the master for Loando.

Mrd, in Iredell Co, by Jacob Fraley, on Jan 20th last, after a close courtship of 23 years, Mr Reuben Barbaour to Miss Sarah Thompson, both aged about 60 years.
-Iredell [N C] Express

Hotel Villa Nardi, Sorrento, Feb 11, 1859. It was pleasant to find here letters & papers from home awaiting our arrival. It would be difficult to convey to you the extent to which I have enjoyed the repose which, for the first time in 25 years, it has been my privilege to command. For Mrs Peirce, exception from care & exciting causes of solicitude is indispensable. Your friend, Franklin Pierce [To Hon B M Farley, Hollis, N H.]

Wash Corp-Mon: 1-Ptns from Timothy Gleesen; from Danl McLaughlin; from John Kelly; from Peter McDonough; from Jas Sumby; & from Moses Smith; each for the remission of a fine: referred to the Cmte of Claims.

The New Orleans Picayune of Mar 11th says warrants for 3 executions had been received by the sheriff of that city, to take place on the Fri succeeding. Peter Smith, Henry Hass, & Jos Lindsay are the names of the doomed men.

Mrd: on Mar 22, at McKendree Chapel, by Rev Dabney Ball, Mr Geo W Baylis, of Va, to Miss Mary E Bushby, of Wash City.

Mrd: on Mar 23, in Gtwn, D C, at the residence of John W Bronaugh, by Rev Mr Tillinghast, Ralph King, of N Y, to Mildred M, youngest daughter of the late Dr John Bronaugh, of Prince Wm Co, Va.

Mrd: on Mar 23, at the church of the Epiphany, by Rev C H Hall, Mr W S Crawford to Miss Fannie Thompson, only daughter of Mr S Cole, of Wash City.

Died: on Mar 4, at the residence of his brother-in-law, Col W F Wilson, of acute bronchitis, Dr Thos Geo Clinton. His remains will be brought to Wash for interment, & notice of their arrival given to his friends. A lovelier, happier death never occurred on earth. [The place of the residence is impossible to read.]

Died: on Mar 11, at his residence in Chas Co, Md, after an illness of 3 weeks, of pneumonia, Dr P H Hamilton, in his 43rd year.

Foreign: The young Prince of Prussia has been named Wm Victor Albert.

The Life & Adventures of Kit Carson, the Nestor of the Rocky Mountains, from facts narrated by Himself, by De Witt C Peters, M D. Price in cloth, gilt back & side, $2.50; library sheep $3; half calf, antique, $3.50; full Turkey $6. Autograph letters from Christopher Carson, asserting that this is the only life of himself which he has ever written or dictated. A paper signed by two of the most prominent citizens of New Mexico, Lt Col Ceran St Vrain & Chas Beaubian, late circuit judge, stating that of their own knowlege this is the only authentic biography of Christopher Carson which has ever appeared. –Taylor & Maury's Bookstore, 334 Pa ave.

FRI MAR 25, 1859
Excellent household & kitchen furniture at auction on Mar 30, at the late residence of V Luce, recently occupied by Gov Wright, of N J, 14 & H sts. -Jas C McGuire & Co, aucts

Mrd: on Mar 23, at the church of the Epiphany, by Rev C H Hall, W S Crawford to Miss Fannie Thompson, only daughter of S Cole, of Wash City.

The 17th Earl of Shrewsbury, Bertram Arthur Talbot, died in 1856, in possession of large estates regarded as annexed to the earldom. This title of nobility was supposed to have become extinct on his death, & he accordingly devised his whole estate in trust for Lord Edw Howard, who married Miss Augusta Talbot, a convert to Romanism, about whom there was much talk a few years since, on account of the efforts of the Catholic clergy to induce her to enter a convent, bestowing her great wealth upon the church. On the Earl's demise, however, Henry John Chetwynd, Earl Talbot, claimed the title of Earl of Shrewsbury, as did also the Duke of Norfolk, for his son, Lord Edw Howard, above named, then a minor. The title was decided, by the House of Lords, to belong to Earl Talbot who thereupon set up a claim for the estates also. This Earl had been bred a Catholic, but conformed to the Established Church. He settled his estates upon 3 Protestant trustees, in favor of Geo Talbot, his cousin, for life, with remainders to persons designated. The heir to his title was Gilbert Talbot, a Jesuit priest, who accordingly became the 13th Earl, while his younger brother George took estates as tenent for life. All the parties who could claim under the will, died before him; as did all the trustees, except the Bishop of Salisbury, himself a Talbot, unrecognised in the Earl's will, except as a trustee. Geo Talbot aspired to the handoff a sister of Vicount Fitzwilliam, & a Protestant. She consented to the marriage, & the terms of marriage settlement were agreed upon, direct reference being had to the penal statutes against Roman Catholics, & in such manner as to preserve the landed estate to Geo Talbot & his heirs, according to the will of the Earl in his favor. The Bishop of Salisbury was not so holy a man as his titles would imply that he ought to be. He formed an ambitious scheme for keeping this vast property in his own family. The marriage was solemnized & a son was born to the Talbots. After a long controversy the House of Lords set all the parties aside, attaching the estates to the Earldom, now held by Gilbert, [a Jesuit priest under a vow of celibacy,] & decreeing that the estate should ever after follow the title, in whosoever vested. The old statue of Geo I, empowering the next of kin to seize the lands of any one educated a Roman Catholic who had not conformed before the age of 18, was not repealed until 1843, during the lifetime of the late Earl & the minority of the present claimants. This case excites a deep interest in Great Britain, & the feeling between the 2 religious parties is similar to that created by the famous "Convent" affair, in which one of the same persons was immediately concerned, in 1850. –Cincinnati Gazette

Obit-died: on Mar 19, Hon Oliver Hampton Smith, at Indianapolis, in his 65th year, after a protracted illness. He was born near Trenton, N J, in Oct, 1794, & emigrated to Indiana in 1817. In 1824 he was appointed Prosecuting Atty for the 3rd district, & filled the ofc with credit for 2 years; was then elected to Congress & served one term; & in 1836 he was elected to the U S Senate. On retiring from official life, he had in the meantime, changed his residence to Indianapolis, & resumed the practice of law.

Criminal Court-Wash-Thu. 1-John Faley was convicted on a charge of assault. 2-The rioters, Chas Berret, Alex'r W Mosely, Frank Stier, & Alfred P McCrabb, found guilty, & each fined $5 & costs. 3-John H N Pumphrey was convicted of petty larceny in stealing a pair of boots.

SAT MAR 26, 1859

Mr Saml Yeager, who left Easton, Pa, on Mar 14 for N Y, intending to return the next day, has not since been seen or heard from. He was a prominent merchant of Easton, & his disappearance has caused much excitement amongst his fellow-citizens of that place. Mrs Yeager has offered a large reward for any information leading to the recovery of the body of her husband, whether dead or alive. [Apr 9th newspaper: the Easton [Pa] Express of Apr 4 says that Mr Yeager has been discovered at Charleston, S C. Two of his fellow townsmen started for Charleston to bring him home to his friends & family.] [May 2nd newspaper: the body of Saml Yeager, the missing Easton merchant, has been found in the Ohio river, at East Liverpool, 45 miles below Pittsburg. His papers & money were found upon the corpse. The coroner's verdict: accidentally drowned.]

On Monday last the wife of Mr Saml Hyde, a workman in the mill of the Hamilton Co, at Lowell, Mass, with a young child in her arms, went into see her husband. While there her clothes became entangled with a revolving shaft, by which she was carried round with fearful velocity, & so horribly mangled that she died before reaching home. The child escaped injury.

Duxbury Hall, the fine bldg at Chorley, Lancashire, England, was the residence of Wm Standish, & recently was almost totally destroyed by fire. This ancient & stately residence for centuries of the Standish family has a connexion with the history of the famous Puritan, Capt Miles Standish. Capt Miles Standish was born in Chorley, near which ***Duxbury Hall*** is situated, & according to his own account he was the rightful heir to the Standish lands & living surreptitiously detained from him. Duxbury, Mass, where Capt Standish settled, after fighting the battles of the Puritans, was named after the seat of his ancestors, & a representative of his descendants some years since visited England to make good the American Standish claim to the estate, but without effect.

Daring robbery in Balt on Thu. The Pastor's residence attached to the Church of the Immaculate Conception was broken into by some daring robber. The burglar entered the chamber of Rev Mr Giustiniani, who, upon arising from his bed, was knocked down with a billy, or slung-shot, & left insensible on the floor, while the villain rifled his pockets. Rev Mr Quigley, the associate pastor, being in an adjourning room, was awakened by the noise, & alarmed the neighborhood, but the burglar, after firing a shot at him, escaped the police. The injuries of Rev Mr Giustiniani are so serious as to cause apprehension of a fatal termination.

Valuable farm & pleasant residence in Fairfax Co, Va, at private sale: by decree of the Circuit Court for said county; sale of ***Collingwood***, in said county, on the Potomac river, the residence of the late H Allen Taylor: contains about 240¼ acres; with a new & commodious frame dwlg, kitchen, & other out-houses, of the best materials. If not sold, it will be offered at public auction on Apr 16. –W Arthur Taylor, John A Washington

In Ralls Co, Mo, on Thu of last week, Mrs Rebecca Hayden, a widow lady, & her 4 children, while attempting to cross Salt river, were all drowned. They were in a buggy, which they endeavored to drive across the ford, when it upset.

Criminal Court-Wash-Fri. 1-John H N Pumphrey was found not guilty of stealing a pair of boots from Wm Mela. 2-Charlotte Medley, colored, was found guilty of assault & battery & sentenced to 4 weeks in jail. 3-John Wagoner was found not guilty for stealing a goose. 4-Saml Wolf was found guilty on Wed for assault & battery on John Johnson, & sentenced to pay a fine of $10.

Died: in Wash City, Robt Washington Fenwick, eldest son of K M A Fenwick, aged 5 years & 9 months. [No death date given-current item.]

Died: on Mar 25, Fielder B Plummer, aged 43 years. His funeral will be on Mar 27 at 2 o'clock, from his late residence, 319 G st, between 12th & 13th sts.

Died: on Mar 24, in Gtwn, D C, Timothy O'Donnoghue, in his 64th year. His funeral will take place from his late residence, on 1st st, at 10 o'clock, on Mar 28.

Died: on Jan 22, in Owensboro, Ky, Mrs Ada P Waters, in her 26th year.

Savannah, Mar 24. Passengers by the Florida steamer state that Major Gregg, chief engineer of the Florida railway, was shot dead at Jacksonville on Sat by Alfred T Sears, in consequence of a previous difficulty. Both were natives of Mass. The body of Maj Gregg is enroute to his former residence in Mass. The murderer, who is imprisoned, has a family in Mass. [Apr 28th newspaper: Augusta, Apr 27. The jury in the case of Alfred Sears, for the murder of Maj Gregg, the engineer on the Florida railroad, have returned a verdict of voluntary manslaughter. The court sentenced the accused to pay $1,000 & to be imprisoned for 12 months.]

New Orleans, Mar 22. Three criminals, Henrich Hass, Peter Smith, & Jos Lindsey, were hung today, all on one scaffold. They all confessed their crimes just previous to their execution.

MON MAR 28, 1859
Her Britannic Majesty's Legation, Wash, Mar 13, 1859. In Oct last the crew of the British vessel **Jane Black**, of Limerick, were rescued from the sinking wreck of their ship by a boat from the American vessel **Flora McDonald**, of Balt, & dispatched to their relief by Capt Caldwell, & commanded by his chief mate, Mr R Barclay. In recognition of this humane action, her Majesty's Gov't desire to present with their warmest thanks to Capt Caldwell & Mr Barclay the telescopes which I have the honor to transmit to you in a separate packet. –Napier, to Hon Lewis Cass, Sec of State.

Capt Newton C Givens, of the 2nd U S Dragoons, died at San Antonio, Texas, on Mar 9, 1859.

Mr & Mrs Bramwell, an old gentleman & lady long residents of North Madison, were accidentally killed on Monday by the running away of a horse attached to the buggy in which they were riding. The accident was unknown until yesterday, when the bodies were discovered. It appears that Mr Bramwell died instantly, & Mrs Bramwell lived a short time after the occurrence. The horse was found near by the place, & the buggy was broken to pieces. –Indianapolis Sentinel of Mar 23.

At a recent sale of pictures in N Y good prices were obtained. List will show the estimation in which the different artist are held: Winterhalter's famed painting "Florinda," the gem of the collection, was sold to Wm H Webb for $3,150; Verbeekhooven's "Mother" was sold to a German gentleman for $2,200; the "Moses" of Baume brought $570; Schlessinger's "Speaking Likeness": brought $515; Casilear's "View of Lake George" brought $510; Church's "Tribute to Cole," $510; a repetition of Gignoux's "Dismal Swamp," $600; Hillmacher's "Whist Party," $410; Muller's "Primavera," $400; Grosse's "Creation," & "Nativity," each $396; Cole's "Promethoeus," $370; Mignot's "Winter Scene," $345; Landscape by Casilear, $305; Autumn Scene, by Mignot, $300; Hart's "Lake on the Hills," $295; Gignoux's "Moonlight on the Saguenay," $290; De Metz's "First Tooth," $260; Lambert's "Love Merchant," $245; Hillmacher's "Concert," $215; Holfield's "Bread of Life, "Landscape & Cattle," by Hinckley, of Boston, "Rabbits at Play," by Hays, each $100.

Superior Rosewood piano forte, French plate mirrors, chandeliers, china, & household & kitchen furniture at auction on Apr 5, at the residence of Lord Napier, H st, between 17th & 18th sts. -Jas C McGuire & Co, aucts

Mount Vernon Ladies' Association of the Union: since the signing of the contract for the purchase of *Mount Vernon* between Mr Washington & the Association, on Apr 6 last, the Association has paid $158,333 of the sum of $200,000 required to secure the title to *Mount Vernon*, $150,000 of which has been paid in a little more than 3 months. Who can longer doubt that the Association will attain all the sacred objects in view? $41,666, with interest thereon, is yet to be provided for, being the 4th installment, due Feb 22, 1862. Since last report, Jan 7, five more Vice Regents have been appointed: Mrs Mary Pepperell Jarvis Cutts, for Vt; Mrs Magdalen Gordon Blanding, for Calif; Miss Lily Lytle Macalester, of Pa; Mrs Sarah F Johnson, for Ark; & Mrs Harriet V Fitch, for Indiana; making 30 States now legally composing the Association. Mrs Alice H Dickinson, has, for reasons of a domestic character, felt herself obliged to resign the Vice Regency for N C. –Susan L Pellet, Mar 28, 1859

On Sunday night, Mar 13, John Potter, jr, & Jas Nance, residing in Menard Co, Ill, 6 miles from Petersburg, were killed by a stroke of lightning, during a storm.

A fearful case of poisoning occurred at N Y on Wed at the boarding house of Mrs Emily Beetham, 14th st & 4th ave. Mrs Beetham died on Thursday, & Mr Robinson on Friday night. Mgt Burke, the cook, was arrested & committed to prison. Mrs Beetham was a widow, with 2 or 3 children, & kept several boarders, some of them medical students.

Jas Stephens, of N Y, has been convicted of having murdered his wife by administering poison to her with her medicines. It was proved that Mrs Stephens, who died on Sep 27, 1857, died under suspicious circumstances. Just before her death Mr Stephens purchased arsenic, for which he had no particular need. He had cherished the hopes of a second marriage. After the body was disinterred, it was found to contain traces of arsenic. [Mar 30th newspaper: Bella, his little daughter, aged about 6 years, attended the trial.] [Oct 7th newspaper: The Court of Appeals having affirmed the decision of the Court of Oyer & Terminer in the case of Stephens, for poisoning his wife, the prisoner will be hung, unless the Govn'r should interpose.]

The father of young Busch, who was acquitted of murder in Chicago, a day or two since, gave the jury who cleared him a champagne supper on the evening after the verdict was rendered. Eleven of the jurors attended.

John W Farmer, a resident of Detroit, Mich, for nearly 40 years, extensively known as the compiler of valuable maps of Mich & Wisc, fell or threw himself from the 4th story of the Windsor st Hospital in that city on Thu, & was killed.

Circuit Court of Wash Co, D C-in Chancery, No 1,038. B W Kennon against M C Kennon, M C Williams, Mary Peter, & others. Wm Redin, trustee, reported the sale to Jas Estlin, of 9 acres or thereabout, part of the small farm called **Mount Pleasant**, in this District, at the price of $1,800. –John A Smith, clerk

Orphans Court of Wash Co, D C. In the case of Nathan Darling, adm of Christopher K Darling, deceased, the administrator & Court have appointed Apr 19 next, for the final settlement of the personal estate of the deceased, with the assets in hand.
-Ed N Roach, Reg/o wills

Criminal Court-Wash-Sat. 1-Edw Dubant found guilty of assault on Chas Everett, & fined $8 & costs, & prayed in commitment till fine & costs are paid. 2-Francis Schaffer charged with an assault on Francis Libbey, sentenced to pay a fine of $15 & costs.

Died: on Mar 21, at **Yarrow**, near Bladensburg, Md, Dr Hanson Penn, in his 61st year. For more than 20 years an earnest communicant of the Protestant Episcopal Church. His illness was painful & protracted, lasting nearly 10 months' duration. He has been gathered unto his fathers, in the communion of the Catholic Church, in the confidence of a certain faith. -C

Mrd: on Mar 23, at *Shirley*, the residence of Mr Hill Carter, by Rev Dr Wade, Lt W H F Lee, U S Army, to Miss Charlotte G Wickham, daughter of the late Mr Geo Wickham, of Richmond.

Harris [Marquerite Co,] Mar 26. Two residents of this place, Jonathan Post, a Baptist preacher, & his wife, were both killed yesterday by their son, while the latter was in a state of phrenzy. The murderer is about 30 years of age, & has been insane for several years, although he was considered harmless until this sad occurrence. He made no effort to escape. He will be confined in a place of safety.

TUE MAR 29, 1859

Tribute to the late Hon Oliver H Smith, from the Indiana State Journal. He died on Sat after a tedious illness of nearly a year, which for several months confined him entirely to his house. He died, as he lived, a firm & sincere Christian. Oliver Hampton Smith was born on Oct 23, 1794, at Smith's Island, on the Delaware river, some miles above Trenton, N J; he attended school at a little place nicknamed Lugar; in 1813, on the death of his father, he left home & went to N Y on an excursion; worked in cotton or woolen mill for sometime in Pa before he came west; in 1817 he came to this State & settled first at Rising Sun; in the winter of 1818 he removed to Lawrence, studied law, & in Mar, 1820, was admitted to the bar by Judge Miles C Eggleston. He obtained his license & went to Versailles, Ripley Co, but left there very soon, & in May of 1820 went to Connersville, where he made his first plunge into the heady current of pioneer life. He served in the Legislature 1822-1823; was appointed by Gov Hendricks prosecuting atty; served 2 years; was elected to Congress in 1826; served during 1827 & 1828, with such men as Tristram Burgess, John Randolph, Saml L Sothard, McDuffie, & others. His chief claim to distinction lies in his great efforts in the cause of railroads.

Mr Chas C Fulton, one of the proprietors of the Balt American, sailed from N Y on Sat in the steamship **City of Washington** for Liverpool. The principal object of the trip is to repair his health. He is making a tour of England, Ireland, & Scotland, & portions of France, Germany, & Italy, & will furnish the readers of the American with his impressions of the Old World.

Criminal Court-Wash-Mon: 1-Emmanuel Mason, colored, charged of unlawfully harboring a slave, his son, aged 11 years, the same being the property of Mrs Forrest. He was found guilty, & motion entered for arrest of judgment, to be argued probably today. 2-Alfred Hunter, indicted fort the sale of improper books & prints, has been waiting for trial. The principal witness for the prosecution, a salesman in traverser's employ, was not to be found.

Died: on Mar 28, Mrs Margaret Hogan, in her 58th year, late of the county of Limerick, Ireland, & sister of John Sinon. Her funeral will be from her late residence, corner of 4½ st & Md ave, on Mar 30 at 10 o'clock.

Died: on Mar 27, in Wash City, Virginia Frances, wife of Frank A McGee, & daughter of Dr E C & Adaline Robinson, of Norfolk, Va, aged 26 years. Her funeral will take place from the residence of Mr S Massie, on 9th st, between E & F sts, on Tue at 11 o'clock.

WED MAR 30, 1859
Gen Geo W Bowman, at present Superintendent of the Public Printing, has become sole proprietor of the Washington Union newspaper, & will take full possession of it on Apr 11 next. –Union

Last week at Westchester, Pa, in the case of Catharine G Ogier vs the Pa Railroad Co, the suit was brought to recover damages sustained by the loss of her husband, Dr Ogier, who was accidentally killed by the cars in East Whiteland township, Chester Co, about a year ago. She claimed damages to the amount of $20,000. The arbitrators were Messrs Jos Dowdall, Saml J Dickey, & John M Kelton, who came to an agreement for $15,000. It is a great consolation to know that railroad companies have money if they have no souls.

Murderers to be executed. 1-Peter Corrie, Marion Cropps, Henry Gambrill, & John H Cyphus, convicted of murder, in Balt, on Apr 7. 2-Isaac Freeland, in Fayette Co, Ga, on Apr 15, for the murder of Claiborne Vaughan. 3-Mrs Hartung, for the murder of her husband, & John Wilson for killing Patrick McCarty, in Albany, on Apr 27. 4-Henry Jumpertz, who murdered a woman, Michl McNamee, for killing his wife, & Michl Fann, in Chicago, on May 6. 5-Burns, for the murder of a man named Burks, in Cincinnati, on May 27.

Orphans Court of Wash Co, D C. Letters of administration, with the will annexed, on the personal estate of Chas Thoma, late of Wash Co, deceased. -J Eliz Thoma, admx, w a

Died: on Mar 28, Geo Noble Wallingsford, of PG Co, but for the last 5 years a resident of Wash City. His funeral will be on Wed at 3 o'clock, from the residence of J W Shields, 408 14th st, near I st.

Died: on Mar 29, suddenly, Azariah Charles, youngest son of Edw H & Emily Fuller, aged 6 years & 4 months. His funeral will be from his father's residence, on Mar 31 at 2 o'clock.

THU MAR 31, 1859
Obit-died: on Mar 21, Dr Hanson Penn, in his 61st year. He was an affectionate husband & protector to his family. –H

Died: on Mar 20, at **Mount Prospect**, Bedford Co, Va, Virginia Steele Allen, in her 36th year, eldest daughter of Hon Robt Allen.

Died: on Mar 30, in Wash City, Harry Carothers, infant son of Jas G & Susan Ellis, aged 2 years & 8 months. His funeral is this afternoon at 3 o'clock, from the residence of his parents, 389 6th st, between G & H sts.

Died: on Mar 29, in Wash City, Amanda B, beloved wife of Walter D Wyvill, & only child of Wm B Lewis, aged 21 years. Her funeral is this evening at 4 o'clock, from her late residence, 453 Pa ave.

U S Patent Ofc, Wash, Mar 29, 1859. Ptn of Chas J Woolson, of Cleveland, Ohio, praying for the extension of a patent granted to him on Sep 9, 1845, for an improvement in cooking stoves, for 7 years from the expiration date of said patent, which takes place on Sep 9, 1859. –S T Shugert, Acting Com'r of Patents

Orphans Court of Wash Co, D C. Jas Dixon & others [heirs of Jas Dixon, deceased,] vs Jas Walker, adm of Jas Dixon. Jas Dixon, a native of Scotland, emigrated to the U S & located in Wash City about 30 years ago, became a citizen by naturalizaton, after which he acquired property, both real & personal, in D C. He has recently departed this life intestate, & the administration of his estate has been committed by this Court to Jas Walker. The deceased left no issue, but as next of kin he left 3 sisters, viz: Jeanett, Eliz, & Margaret, & the children of a deceased brother, Wm, all being liens. The sister Margaret has 2 sons in this District who have been naturalized. The question is who are the parties entitled to the estate? The personal estate will be distributed according to the law of the last domicil of the deceased, that being in this case D C. When the heirship in the case shall be legally established, the Orphans Court of Wash Co, D C will pronounce a decree of distribution of the said personal estate. A foreigner is able to take & hold lands in this District & to convey & transmit them to his foreign relation, but it only extends to such lands as may be acquired before naturalization. As soon as the foeigner becomes a citizen of the U S by naturalization he relinquishes all allegiance to a foreign Power, & landed property acquired in this District subsequent to such naturalization cannot be transmitted to foreign heirs or relation. But can the two nephews of the deceased who have been naturalized inherit? They must claim through their mother, who is a foreigner, & it is well settled that at common law no person can claim lands by descent through an alien, since he has no inheritable blood. The claim of the two naturalized sons of the sister of the deceased is invalid.

A little boy, the son of Mr Edw Fuller, living near the Nat'l Observatory, was drowned on Tuesday, having accidentally fallen into the canal whilst fishing from its banks.

Teacher wanted. The trustees of Belair Academy, Harford Co, Md, will receive applications for a principal until Apr 16 next. –Harry D Gough, sec

Orphans Court of Wash Co, D C. Letters testamentary on the personal estate of Timothy O'Donnoghue, late of Wash Co, deceased. –Sarah O'Donnoghue, Jas O'Donnoghue, & Peter O'Donnoghue, excs

FRI APR 1, 1859
Pre-emptory sale of china, glass, crockery ware, at auction, on Apr 6, at the warehouse of T Purcell & Son, 269 B st, between 6th & 7th sts. –Wall & Barnard, aucts

Public sale of a valuable improved farm & farming implements, stock & corn, on Apr 19, the farm on which he resides, containing 148½ acres, adjoining the farms of Messrs Chas Digges & Woolman Gibson. Apply to Mr J M Jackson, at Hanover's, or to the subscriber. –Thos J Barclay, near Bladensburg

John H King, Landscape Gardener, 35 High st, Gtwn, D C. [Ad]

Locomotive blown to pieces on Wed, on the Reading railroad, at the Falls bridge. The engineer, Josiah Missimer, was blown into the river & no trace has yet been found of him. John Foley, the brakesman, was blown 50 yards, & his body was found upon the tow path. Mr Missimer was a married man. Mr Foley was unmarried.

Fire in Gtwn yesterday, in the dwlg-house & store of Mrs Hurley, at the corner of High st & Cherry alley. The force of the water from a new hydrant, fed from the aqueduct reservoir at Little Falls Branch, soon diminished the fire.

Criminal Court-Wash-Wed. 1-Jas McFall found guilty & sentenced to pay a fine of $5 & costs. 2-Chas T Griffin, a city watchman, found guilty for assault on Jos B Wolling, the latter being one of a party of persons pulling a fire-engine on Pa ave: sentenced to pay $5 & costs. 3-Thos Groom alias Thos Bredd, colored, guilty of petty larceny, sentenced to 1 year in jail. 4-Chas Coombs, found guilty of assault, shooting several times at the house of Mr Ferry, sentenced to 3 months in jail & fined $10 & costs.

Mrd: on Mar 28, by Rev Andrew G Carothers, Mr Thos T Hurdle to Miss Harriet A Collins, both of Wash City.

Mrd: on Mar 29, by Rev B F Bittinger, Mr Thos Taylor to Miss Hester Barnetson, both of Wash City.

Mrd: on Mar 16, at Brooklyn, Ohio, by Rev Lewis Burton, John Chas Williams, of Milwaukee, Wisc, [formerly of Md,] to Sophia M, daughter of J Lockwood, of the former place.

SAT APR 2, 1859
N Y, Mar 31, 1859. 1-The recent death of Capt Wylie, of the steamship **City of Manchester**, on board that vessel when near Liverpool, on her outward bound trip, has created much regret. He was quite a favorite. 2-Judge Roosevelt sentenced Jas Stephens, convicted of murdering his wife by poison a year ago, to be hanged on May 20.

A letter from an ofcr of the U S steam-frig **Powhatan**, dated Hong Kong, Jan 29th, states that Lt Chas W Place, of the sloop-of war **Germantown**, died at Manilla on Jan 29. The poor fellow got his foot mashed between 2 guns while trying to have them moved aft in a gale of wind. His leg was amputated, & he died soon after. His wife resides in Portsmouth, Va.

The old mansion of Gov Wylly on the Charter-Oak Pl, Hartford, is being demolished, to make way for a modern house. The old mansion was built 222 years ago for the royal Govn'r of the Colony, & the frame, of solid English oak, was sent out from England.

Sea side summer resort: Fairfield House, under the management of Wm R Butts, Fairfield, Conn, will be opened about May 1, 1859. There will be no public bar on the premises. [Ad]

Circuit Court of D C, -Equity Docket, Jan Term, 1859. Wm S Nichols against Chas H Van Patten. John Marbury, trustee, sold lot 5 in square 14, to Stephen D Castleman, for the sum of $950, & Castleman has complied with the terms of sale. –John A Smith, clerk

Mrd: on Mar 31, at Rockville, Md, by Rev Mr Russell, Warfield T Browning, of Wash City, to Miss Carolyn M Cinnamond, of Balt, Md.

Died: on Mar 31, in Wash City, at the boarding house of Mrs Clark, on E st, in his 78th year, Jas Hervey Bingham, formerly of Claremont, N H. His funeral will take place on Sunday afternoon, at 3 o'clock.

Died: on Mar 31, of pleurisy, Mr Harden S Wait, in his 30th year. He was a native of the State of Vt, & for the last 2 years was engaged on the U S Wash Aqueduct. His funeral will take place from the residence of Mr C G Morrison, 380 E st, today at 2 o'clock P M.

Died: yesterday, Chas W Hazeltine, aged 19 years. His funeral is this afternoon at 3:30 o'clock, from the residence of his mother, on 8th, between D & Pa ave.

MON APR 4, 1859
Examination has been going on at N Y, before U S Com'r Betts, in which the dfndnt, Mr I Churchill Woods, is charged with making a number of false vouchers, which were presented to the Sec of the Interior for payment. Mr Woods has been arrested & held to bail in the sum of $10,000. N Y Evening Post

The propellar **Lady of the Lake**, from Cleveland to Dunkirk, blew up near Fairport on Sat week. A deck hand named Miller had his head blown off, & Timothy Murphy, the cook, is supposed to have been killed, as he cannot be found. Chester M Stoddard, the engineer, was scalded; John Herron, 2nd engineer, had his leg broken & was scalded; Saml Hogan, the fireman, had his arm & shoulder broken, & was seriously scalded.

Henry Duvall, convicted of murder in Balt was on Friday sentenced to be hung. He killed Christian Fisher a few months since.

Piano forte, & household & kitchen furniture at auction on Apr 7, at the house recently occupied by Gov Stevens, on 12th st, between E & F sts. –Jas C McGuire & Co, aucts

Trustee's sale by decree of the Circuit Court of D C, passed in a cause wherein Saml S Hetzel is cmplnt, & Margaret J Hetzel & others are dfndnts. Public auction on May 9, of parts of lots 10 thru 13 in square 104, in Wash City, which front upon F st, on the south thereof, 70 feet & 7 inches, extended back of the same width, 92 feet or thereabouts, with a 3 story dwlg house & other improvements thereon, the whole having been the residence of the late Capt A R Hetzel.

Criminal Court-Wash-Fri. 1-Eugene Lanahan & Geo Long were put on trial for assault & battery & committing an affray at Miller's tavern, on Pa ave, on Feb 13. Lanahan was acquitted & Long found guilty.

Yesterday the appearance of a hat, shawl, & coat on the wharf foot of 3rd st east, led to a search of the water, which resulted in finding the body of Chas A Appleton, who had evidently committed suicide a few hours previously. He was a native of Maine, resided more recently in N Y, & was aged about 30 years. He was temperate in his habits. His kinsman, Hon John Appleton, took charge of the remains.

Monongahela city, Wash Co, Pa, Thu. The wife of Capt Bentley, of that place, subject to periodical attacks of insanity, got possession of her husband's pistols, the same which he uses when in command of his troop, the Ringgold Cavalry, & discharged them at Mr Bentley. The gentleman's injuries are very severe, & little hope of his recovery. It was the intention today to have placed her in the Western Pa Hospital. –Pittsburgh Chronicle

Died: on Apr 3, of scarlet fever, Eliz Jane Lanthall Stone, eldest daughter of Mary F & Wm J Stone, jr, aged 4 years & 9 months. Her funeral will take place from her father's residence, on 5th st, above Louisiana ave, on Apr 4, at 4 o'clock.

TUE APR 5, 1859
Trustee's sale, by decree of the Circuit Court of D C: public auction on Apr 27, of lot 13, in Reservation D, in Wash City, D C, all the real estate, legal & equitable, of John M Springman therein to pay the sum of $259.65, principal, interest, & cost on a judgment of said court at law against said Springman, at the suit of Archibald McDaniel. The lot is at the corner of Md ave & 6th st west, improved by a good dwlg house; it will be sold subject to a lien thereon for $1,000 due the estate of Jos Morrison, deceased, with interest, under a deed of trust from said Springman to Fred'k Whyte, dated Aug 16, 1855, & payable in 5 years. –Jno Marbury, trustee -Jas C McGuire & Co, aucts

Crime in N Y during the first quarter of the present fiscal year which ended on Thursday.
Bridget Kennedy, killed by Dead Rabbits.
Henry Fry, fatally stabbed by Arthur May.
Mrs Beetham & Mr Robinson, fatally poisoned.
Mich Raley, stabbed at by Concklin, alias Smith.
Philip Wold, slung-shotted by John Martin.
John Smith, shot at twice by A D Richards.
Wm McElroy, a boy, stabbed to death by Thos Miller, a boy.
Bryan Perrigan, beaten to death by rowdies.
Chas J Sturges, shot by J D Pfromer.
Harry Jennings, shot by John Jennings.
Barney Fitzpatrick, a boy, stabbed by D Wardell, a boy.
John Van Wart, stabbed to death by W E Moore.
John Aiken, stabbed by Sam Taggart.
Wm Butler, stabbed by Wm Boland.
This does not include the bodies of unknown men found in the river-N Y C.

Obit-died: on Wed last, Hon Chas C Stratton, formerly Govn'r of N J, at his residence in Swedesboro, N J, aged 63 years. He served in Congress from 1837 to 1839, & from 1841 to 1843.

Obit-died: The venerable Thos H Willie is no more. On Sat last, in his 79th year, after an illness of 2 weeks, he quietly breathed his last. Thus our town is bereft of its oldest citizen, both in years & length of residence. –Oxford [N C] paper

This is to give notice that Wm Henry Lee, who, when last heard from by his mother, Eliz Hagan, late of Wash, D C, was in Pittsburg, Pa, [or his daughter Ann or Nancy,] can hear of something that will result to their benefit if they, or either of them, can be heard from within one year from Feb 9, 1859, by addressing Jas Rhodes, exc

Died: on Mar 24, at New Phil, Ohio, Mary E, wife of Mercer Matlock, of that place, & daughter of Jacob Janney, of Wash, D C, in her 48th year.

Wanted, a Coachman [white] of experience, & who understands well the care & management of horses. Apply at **Tudor Place**, Gtwn Heights.

WED APR 6, 1859
In Orange, N J, a few days ago, a man named John Koch, while engaged in painting on the 3rd story of a house, fell to the ground & was taken up for dead. He was conveyed to his residence, laid out, & funeral arrangements were made for Sunday. A few hours before the funeral, he exhibited signs of returning animation, & the young man began to converse with his friends. The physicians pronounce his present condition as critical.

Trial of Danl E Sickles for the murder of John Barton Key: examined for the jury & refused: Mr Geo J Johnson; set aside: Mr W B Jackson, Mr John Garrett, Thos L Potter, Geo B Barnard-a minor, Robt C Brook, A P Hoover, Jas J Barrett, Z Gilman, & Geo Rhodes, jr. Also set aside: Mr Philip Hauptman, Wm H Harrover, Jas W Sears, Francis Miller, Jos Gawler, Henry A Clarke, Richd W Carter, Wm R Riley, Wm H Tenney, Jos B Moore, & Jos W Nairn. Mr Jas Kelly was the first juror accepted & sworn. Talesman refused: W M Galt, Jas E Smith, Jno W Ott, Ephraim Wheeler, Jas W Colley, Geo E Jillard, E E White, Jas A Riley, Theo F Boucher, Thos J Galt, Wm Baldwin, Thos Orme, Saml Duvall, Robt M Sutton, C S Whittlesey, Wm Dowling, Richd H Darnell, John G Dorry, John H Wilson, Esau Pickrell-had sympathy with the prisoner, Benj F Guy, Geo M Wight, Jas Goddard, Chas B Church, John F Bridget, Wm H Craig, Geo M Sothoron, T J S Perry, Thos Milburn, Jas B Dodson, N C McKnew, Hilleary L Offutt, John W Dyer, Mr Michl R Coombs, Edw Lennie, A F Offutt, & Robt A Hooe. Mr Wm H Morrison, B B Mayfield, E B Tucker, Josh B Jenkins, & John T Given.were refused, being sympathizers decidedly with the prisoner. Additions to the jury: Jonas B Ellis, John Moore, A Lewis Newton, Alex Minifie, Mr Wm C Harper, Mr Henry Knight, John H Smoot was called, but failed to appear, understood he was sick & might be excused-excused accordingly. Mr Anthony Hyde asked to be excused as being a member of the bar of the Circuit Court. He was excused.

At St Louis, last Friday, three boys, Anthony Leite, Nicholas Trautwein, & Theodore Debold, were convicted of the murder of Hugh Downie, & sentenced to the penitentiary for life. The two first were sentenced to be hanged, but the Govn'r consented to spare their lives by allowing the court to imprison them.

Obit-died: Capt John M Otey, late Cashier of the Bank of Va, of Lynchburg. He was born in 1792, at Liberty, Bedford Co, Va, & was the 2nd son of Maj Isaac Otey, a man of great worth, & distinguished by his fellow-citizens as their representative in the House of Burgesses of Va for a quarter of a century, from 1797 to 1822. In 1808 Capt Otey was placed by his father in the Land Ofc at Richmond, where he remained a short time, & transferred to the Chancery Ofc. At the commencement of the war with Great Britain, in 1812, he determined to go to Canada, & enlist in the U S Cavalry commanded by Capt Selden. Gov Barbour repaired to the quarters of Capt Selden & demanded his discharge, as he was only 17 years of age. The Capt refused at first, but at length yielded to the remonstrances of the Govn'r; & when he spoke of returning the bounty, the Capt replied: He has refused both bounty & pay, & I would sooner discharge any 6 of the other recruits then part with him. When Richmond was threatened by the British he enrolled himself under Capt Radford's mounted riflemen, & went as a private to the defence of that city. On Aug 8, 1812, he was appointed discount clerk of the Farmers' Bank of Va, which was recently chartered. We cherish the ones who survive in weeping for the husband, the father, & friend. –H [No death date given-current item.]

Mrd: on May 5, by Rev Dr Sunderland, Thos T Houston, U S Navy, to Susie, youngest daughter of Peter D Posey, of Montg Co, Md.

Died: on May 4, after a lingering illness, Mr Henry B Robertson, the crier of the Circuit & Criminal Courts of this District, in his 79th year. His funeral is this afternoon, at 3 o'clock, from his late residence, 227 Pa ave.

Trustee's sale of valuable farm in Montg Co, Md. At the request of Mrs Rebecca Winn, & by deed of trust executed by Jas Donnelly & wife, dated Aug 13, 1855, recorded in Liber J G H, No 5, folios 282 thru 284, of the land records of said county, [made to cure a certain debt therein named, due & payable to Mrs Rebecca Winn,] I shall offer at Public sale, on May 10 next, on the premises, a parcel of land called *Williamsborough*, in Montg Co, Md, containing 398½ acres of land, more or less, [it being the same land which was conveyed by the said Rebecca Winn to the said Jas Donnelly,] together with all & singular the improvements, privileges, hereditaments to the same belonging or in any manner appertaining. –B F Middleton, trustee

THU APR 7, 1859
Died: on Apr 5, Susan A Harrison, wife of Robt M Harrison, & eldest daughter of the late Saml Harkness, in her 60th year. Her funeral will be on Apr 8 at 2 o'clock, from her late residence, 274 Vt ave.

Trial of Danl E Sickles for the murder of Philip Barton Key, yesterday. First talesman called, Robt M Coombs, said his mind was so fixed about the case that no evidence could change his opinion. Set aside. Geo W Hinton, set aside. Wm H Arnold was refused, having a strong sympathy in the case. Geo M Goodall had a decided opinion. Also set aside: Mr Adam Grinder, Mr Thos Parker, Thos E Young, & Jas W Coombs. Mr Hiram H King was challenged. Mr Wm G Deale would try to render an impartial verdict, but was not quite certain about it. Mr Jesse D Wilson was accepted by defence & sworn, making the 9th juror. Mr John A Ruff & Mr Jno E Leach had formed an opinion, & were refused. Mr Jas Noakes had sympathy for both sides. Would do any man justice. John McDermott was sworn in as the 10th juror. Leonidas Coyle, Andrew J Duvall, Fras A Tucker, & Francis Mattingly were all refused. Wm H Stanford, Alex'r Bully, Thos G Ford, Thos E Baden, John P Dennis, Zadock Williams, Jas T Macintosh, & Wm Utermuhle: all refused. Michl Green had opinions; he was refused. Job W Angus was refused. Elijah Edmonston was refused. John B Wiltberger, challenged. A Lommond, Thos Mosher, Geo F Varnell, Wm H Marlow, Jas Skirving, John H Semmes, Benj S Kinsey, Alex Forrest, John Pettibone, all refused. John G Robinson, Jos Davis, Wm Hughes, all challenged. Mr Wm M Moore was sworn, making the 11th juryman. High Leidy, Thos J Magruder, Joshua L Venable; Saml Pumphrey, & Jas B Greenwell: all refused. Robt Cohen was challenged. Jas L Barbour, Jas S Tophan, & Thos C Wheeler: all refused. Mr Wm H Baum, Wm H Upperman, Hiram Richy, Stephen Coster, John R Mitchell, Harmon Burns, John Miller, Reuben B Clark, Franklin Tenney, Jas P Bartholow, Danl B Clarke, Jeremiah Hepburn, & J F B Purcell: all refused. Mr Wm Cooper was challenged. Mr A S Wight was sworn as the 12th & last juror.

Fauquier White Sulphur Springs, well known celebrated Water Place for sale. At a Circuit Court of Fauquier Co, held on Sep 23, 1858, Thos Green, plntf, against Isham Keith & others, dfndnts in Chancery. And the Fauquier White Sulphur Springs, plntf against Thos Green & others, dfndnts in Chancery. These causes, consolidated by a former decree of the Court, came on this day to be further heard on the papers formerly read, & the report of Com'r Jas V Brooke, of Aug 7, 1858, to which there is no exception, & was argued by counsel. On consideration whereof the Court doth adjudge, order, & decree that said report be confirmed, & that unless Thos Green, the plntf in the first & one of the dfndnts in the 2nd named suit, shall pay to the Fauquier White Sulphur Springs, or to their authorized agent & atty, the sum of $4_,742.68, with interest on $35,314.22, part thereof from Dec 15, 1857, until paid, together with the cost of these suits; & to Wm B Phillips, or to his duly authorized agent or atty, the sum of $4,400, with interest from Dec 15, 1855, until paid, within 6 months from the date of this decree, then & in the event of the non-payment of said sums of money, the Court doth direct that B H Shackelford, Robt E Scott, Saml Chilton, E M Spilman, & by consent of parties by counsel, Isham Keith, any one or more of whom may act if the others decline, be & they are hereby directed, as Com'rs of this Court, to sell the real & personal estate in the bill & proceedings mentioned; said real estate consisting of about 1,013 acres of land, in Fauquier Co, including the Hotel Bldgs & Springs, to the highest bidder, after 30 days' notice by publication in the Warrenton newspapers, & in the Nat'l Intelligencer, & by handbills of the time & place of sale. The Court reserves all questions relating to the debts of Jas Lyons, Henry A Wise, & Julia A Peyton, on their application by counsel, reported by Com'r Brooke, or such future order as may be deemed right.
–John S Byrne, clerk
+
The sums of money referred to in the foregoing decree not having been paid, the undersigned com'rs, will offer for sale, on the premises, on May 12, 1859, the entire real & personal property therein mentioned on the terms of said decree. –B H Shackelford, Robt C Scott, Saml Chilton, E M Spilman, Isham Keith, Com'rs

FRI APR 8, 1859
Jury in the Canl E Sickles trial for the willful murder of Philip Barton Key:

Rezin Arnold	Wm Bond	Jesse B Wilson
Jas L Davis	Jas Kelly	John McDermott
John E Neale	Wm C Harper	Wm M Moore
W M S Hopkins	Henry Knight	Alpheus S Wight

Witnesses for the prosecution-present & sworn:

Dr R H Coolidge	Jos Dudrow	Robt J Dillon, of N Y
Dr R K Stone	Abel Upshur	Thos Woodward
Richd N Downer	Edw M Tidball	Reuben Worthington
Francis Doyle	Cyrus McCormick	Jas N Reed
Thos E Martin	John M Seely, jr	Henry Hepburn
P V R Van Wick	Jonah D Hoover	

Those absent:
Eugene B Pendleton
Hon Richd Brodhead, of Pa
Hon Geo Eustis
Danl Dougherty, of Pa
Barry Hayes, of Pa
Edw C West, of N Y
Hon Hiram Walbridge, of N Y

E W Cone, of N Y
Welcome Beebe, of N Y
C K Alburtis, of N Y
Hon J B Haskin, of N Y
Ambrose C Kingsland, of N Y
Jas Pumphrey, of Wash City

First witness called, Mr Jas N Reed, followed by P V R Van Wyck, Edw Delafield, jr, Thos E Martin, Richd M Downer, Francis Doyle; Abel Upshur, Cyrus McCormick, & Edwin M Tidball;

The steamboat **Augusta**, Capt Frazer, which left Augusta for Savannah on Friday last, caught fire & burnt to the water's edge. The engineer, Mr H G Day, & two negroes were drowned, & one negro was burnt to death.

Letter from Middleburg, Loudoun Co, Va, to the Alexandria Gaz, says that "Our village was thrown into gloom this morning by the sudden death of Col Humphrey B Powell." He was in the enjoyment of his usual health on Tue night. He died on Wed morning.

Disappeared, from his residence, corner of Va ave & 7th st, on Apr 6, John A Cassell, bricklayer. Any information concerning him will be thankfully received by his afflicted family.

Mrd: on Apr 5, by Rev Mr Pyne, Hon Geo Eustis, of Lousiana, to Miss Louisa Morris Corcoran, only daughter of Wm W Corcoran, of Wash, D C.

Mrd: on Apr 6, by Rev Andrew G Carothers, Mr Thos J Frazier to Miss Ann Rebecca Childress, both of Wash City.

Mrd: on Apr 6, by Rev Andrew G Carothers, Mr Edw S Logan to Miss Margaret C Spotts, both of Wash City.

Died: yesterday, Wm H Winter, in his 47th year. His funeral is on Sunday next, at 2 o'clock, from his late residence, N J ave.

SAT APR 9, 1859
Excs' sale at public auction of valuable bldg lots belonging to the estate of the late Timothy O'Donnoghue, deceased, viz: lots 16, 18 thru 20, subdivisions of square 183, on 19th st west, between L & M sts; lot 4 in square 136, fronting on 18th & N H ave; lot 5 in square 454, fronting on G, between 6th & 7th sts. –Sarah O'Donnoghue, Jas O'Donnoghue, & Peter O'Donnoghue, excs -Wall & Barnard, aucts

Trial of Danl E Sickles, Apr 8. Mr Thos Woodward was first called & examined by the District Atty. Also examined: Eugene B Pendleton, Chas Winder, Dr R R Stone, Mr Jas N Reed, & Mr P V R Van Wick-recalled.

Execution of 4 murderers yesterday in the jail yard, at Balt, Md: Henry Gambrill, Marion Crops, Peter Corrie, & Cyphus, alias Stephens, a colored man. [Apr 12th newspaper: The bodies of the four men were delivered to their relatives for interment, those of Cropp, Corrie, & Cyphus were committed to the tomb without any public demonstration. Henry Gambrill was buried in **Baltimore Cemetery** on Sunday, when the funeral attracted a large concourse of spectators & sympathizing friends.]

The U S Marshal Tyler, at Detroit, convicted of manslaughter in the killing of Capt Jones, of the brig **Concord**, on Nov 29, while serving process upon him, was sentenced in the U S Circuit Court on Monday. He was fined $1, & to be imprisoned in the jail of Wayne Co, Mich, for 30 days. Tyler had been kept in prison for over 4 months.

Sale on Apr 11, in front of the premises, all that lot of ground on the north side of Gay st, between the residences of Mr Redin & Robt Dicks, in Gtwn, being 57 feet front & 120 feet, enclosed by a stone wall mounted with an iron railing. –Barnard & Buckey, aucts

Jas B Foley, proprietor of the Screven House, at Savannah, was thrown from his buggy a few days ago, & has since died.

Rev Jas B Donelan, who was for many years the pastor of St Matthew's Church in Wash City, has been appointed pastor of the Cathedral at Chicago.

Mrd: on Apr 7, in Phil, by Rev Dr Ducachet, of St Stephen's Church, P M Dubant, of Wash, to Sue L, daughter of the late John A Bender, of Phil.

MON APR 11, 1859
The Columbus [Geo] Enquirer announced the death, on Mar 31, of Hon Hopkins Holsey, in his 60th year.

Four persons burnt with their house: Mrs Potter, an old lady, her 2 sons, aged 40 & 35, & a grand-child, aged 10 years, were burnt, with their house, in Lee, Me, on Apr 6. Another son saved himself by jumping from the attic window. They were the only occupants. [Apr 16th newspaper: It has since been disclosed that the son who escaped, Marshall Potter, murdered the entire family & then fired the dwlg. He said: "I am guilty."]

On Monday Detroit was the scene of a foul murder. Edw H Benedict, an American mechanic, stabbed his wife in a fit of drunken passion. She died shortly after of her wounds. The husband was pursued & captured.

Household & kitchen furniture at auction on Apr 13, at the residence of Mrs General Hamilton, in thewestern house of the De Menou Bldg. –Jas C McGuire & Co, aucts

We learn from a friend of the sudden death of Mr Van Rensselaer Perry & his wife, for many years residents of the n e part of Lewiston. Mrs Perry died on Mar 26, & Mr Perry on Mar 27. Old age was probably the cause in both cases, he being 79 & she 72 years old. They had lived together 55 years. –Niagara Falls Gaz of Apr 6.

Having disposed of the Union newspaper to Mr Geo W Bowman, my connexion with it has ceased. The books & papers belonging to the Union establishment have been placed in the hands of Mr Jas M Towers, 408 D st, near 7th. –C Wendell, Wash, Apr 9, 1859.

TUE APR 12, 1859
The trial of Jas Green, in Warrenton, Va, for the killing of Mr Carver, at the Fauquier Springs last Sept, has just terminated in acquittal.

Died: on Apr 10, Mrs Lilias Arnot Dickins, wife of Asbury Dickins.

Trial of Danl E Sickles for the murder of Philip Barton Key. We will show that between Jan 25 & Feb 25 Mrs Sickles & himself [Philip Barton Key,] were seen to enter a house on 15th st from 6 to 8 times. Key had hired the house for an express purpose, & had an intimacy with Mrs Sickles as close as her husband had. Key became a subject of kitchen comment; he was called by the servants "disgrace;" that was the name given to him by the kitchen dept of Mr Sickles' house. The servants felt the pressure of his infamous attention to Mr Sickles' wife.

WED APR 13, 1859
Mr Edw H Delano, Naval Constructor at the Charleston Navy Yard, died on Sat last at the age of 48 years.

At Cahoes, N Y, on Monday, the dress of Miss Alice Russell accidentally took fire whilst engaged in household duties, & though her father went speedily to her relief, she died in a few hours.

On Friday at the Oriskany Valley Woolen Mills, Margaret Brien, about 16 years of age, was in the carding room when suddenly her dress caught in the machine, revolving her violently around. She died in a few minutes. –Utica [N Y] Observer

A verdict for $7,000 has been obtained at Burlington, Vt, against the Vt & Canada Railroad Co in suit brought by the adms of Mr Ebden N French, who was killed by the explosion of a locomotive on the road, in July, 1855. The company was found guilty of culpable negligence in permitting the locomotive to run when in an unsafe condition.

Trial of Danl E Sickles-Apr 12. John J McElhone sworn & examined-he resides in Phil. Rev Smith Pyne sworn & examined-a clergyman of the Episcopal Church-resides in Wash. Jonah D Hoover, & Robt J Walker, sworn & examined. Both reside in Wash City. John H Goddard, Chief of Police of Wash City, sworn & examined. Francis Mohun sworn & examined: resides in this District & has lived here about 40 years, since 1819 or 1820. Bridget Duffey sworn & examined: I live in Mr Sickles' house as nurse & lady's maid, & partly chamber maid. I have lived in Mr Sickles' family since Nov last.

By deed of trust from Geo W Butler & wife, dated Nov 6, 1855, I will offer at public auction, on Apr 21, on the premises, lot 9 in square 583, with frame dwlg & out-houses thereon, in Wash City. –Jno C C Hamilton, trustee -A Green auct

Circuit Court of D C, sitting in Chancery. Miller & wife vs John & Catharine Mason et al, heirs at law of Alex'r Macomb. Public auction on May 5, all the right, title, interest, & estate of the parties to the above cause in the following lots, in Wash, D C: lots 12 & 13 in square 25; lot 3 & 14 in square 32; lot 15 in square 33; lots 1 & 13 in square 37; lot 3 in square 40; lot 6 in square 41; lot 4 in square 42; & lots 28 thru 30 in square 126. -J B H Smith, trustee -A Green auct

Died: on Apr 11, after a painful illness, Robt J H Handy, in his 33rd year. His funeral is today at 3 o'clock, from the residence of his brother, corner of Md ave & 4½ st.

Died: on Apr 10, Mrs Lilias Arnot Dickins, wife of Asbury Dickins. Her funeral is on Apr 13 at 11 o'clock.

Died: on Apr 9, at Alexandria, Va, Andrew, son of Andrew & Mary Caroline Wylie, aged 11 years & 8 months.

THU APR 14, 1859
Trial of Danl E Sickles for the murder of Philip Barton Key: 1-Miss Octavia Ridgley called & examined: resides at 15th & N Y ave, Wash City. Resides with her mother & step-father at Mrs Hyatt's. Thinks she has resided there about 6 years. 2-Bridget Duffy recalled & examined. 3-Wm W Mann sworn & examined-resides at Buffalo, N Y; a lawyer. He arrived on the day of Mr Key's decease; had known him by sight perhaps 4 years.

Court of Claims, Apr 13, 1859. Geo N Butt, survivor of John D Black, vs The U S. The plntf claims under a contract with Capt Montgomery, U S Army, for transporting military stores from Preston to **Fort Belknap**, Texas, in 1851 & 1852; & he claims that the Gov't refused fully to execute the same, whereby he has sustained large damages. The case was submitted.

On Friday a small bldg at New London, Conn, occupied by Michl Pheney, was completely destroyed by fire, & Mrs Pheney & her 2 children burnt to death. The father of the family was absent at the time. The family was probably asleep at the time.

Wash Corp: 1-Ptn from Fred'k Koons for permission to erect a frame stable in the rear of his lot, No 7, in square 530: referred to the Cmte onImprovements. 2-Ptn from S A H Marks & others for paving certain squares: referred to the Cmte on Improvements. 3-Ptns of Wm Dellaway; of Christian Zang; of Jas Casparis; & of Jas Muntz; for the remission of fines: referred to the Cmte of Claims.

Circuit Court of D C, in Equity, No 1,419. John Van Reswick vs Geo Page et al. Chas S Wallach, trustee, reported he sold at public auction 5 certain parts of square 472, in Wash City, which were conveyed by a deed of trust, dated May 1, 1854, from Geo Page to J T Fenwick & Richd Wallach, filed in said cause, to Jos Bryan for the sum of $11,600; & all the estate, right, interest of Geo Page in & to square 471, in said city, to John Van Reswick for $775; & that Bryan & Van Reswick have complied with the terms of sale. –Chas S Wallach, Solicitor for Cmplnt -Jno A Smith, clerk

Died: on Apr 12, suddenly, John M Willson, formerly of Balt, but for the last 30 years a resident of Wash City. His funeral will be on Apr 14 at 2 o'clock P M, from his late residence, on 4½ st, between N & O sts, **Greenleaf's Point.**

FRI APR 15, 1859
Trial of Danl E Sickles: 1-Geo D Woolridge sworn & examined; resides in Mongaup valley, Sullivan Co, N Y. On Feb 27th he resided at 534 12th st, Wash City. 2-Chas G Bacon sworn: resides in this District; had been acquainted with Mr Key about 18 months before his decease. 3-John Keiler sworn: resides in Wash; knew the late Mr Key some 3 or 4 years. 4-S S Parker sworn: resides in this District; knew Mr Key as long as he could remember. 5-Wm Ratley sworn: resides in this District; had known Mr Key for 2 or 3 years, by sight. 6-Jeremiah Boyd sworn: resides in this District; knew Mr Key about 4 or 5 years. 7-Fred'k Wilson sworn: I saw Mr Key & Mrs Sickles & a little girl coming up the avenue near 17th st. Mrs Sickles & the little girl went into Green's furniture store. Mr Key stood outside reading a letter. 8-Thos J Brown sworn: resides in N Y C. 9-Jacob Wagner sworn: I reside in Wash City; I am a locksmith.

Obit-Ex-Govn'r Tilghman M Tucker died in Alabama on Apr 3. At the time of his death he resided in North Louisiana, where he had lived for several years. He was best known in Mississippi where he had filled several offices of trust. -Mississippi

Lord Murray, a distinguished lawyer, died Mar 8, at his house in Edinburgh, in his 81st year. He was the last, except Brougham, of those distinguished men who reflected such luster on the Scottish capital throughout the first 30 or 40 years of this century-Jeffrey, Playfair, Sidney Smith, Thos Brown, Horner, & Cockburn.

Superior cabinet furniture, French plate mirrors, superb French mantel sets, silver-plated ware, crystal, horses & carriages & harness, etc, at public sale, on Apr 27, at the residence of le Compte de Sartiges, [French Minister,] on the Heights of Gtwn, nearly opposite the gateway of **Oak Hill Cemetery**. -Jas C McGuire & Co, aucts

Hon Geo M Bibb died yesterday at his residence in Gtwn, believed to have been between 80 & 90 years of age. He was a long time U S Senator from the State of Ky & Chancellor of that State, & subsequently filled the ofc of Sec of Treasury in the administration of Pres Tyler. He died of pneumonia.

Sad accident at the U S arsenal, *Greenleaf's Point*, on Tue last, by which Mr John M Wilson, an old resident of Wash City, & a most estimable man, came to his death. In returning from inspecting some lumber, he fell accidentally through a hatchway in the 2nd story of the bldg, & fell against a railway some 16 feet below. Although promptly removed to the hospital, he died during the night. He had been engaged in the arsenal for over a quarter of a century, & at the time of his death was a foreman. He leaves a widow & 5 children. -Constitution

Circuit Court of Montg Co, as Court of Equity, Mar Term, 1859. Wm B Canfield, Ira C Canfield, & Jos Meredith, trading together as copartners under the name of Canfield, Brother & Co, vs Henry A Klopfer, Christian G Klopfer, & Ann A Klopfer. This suit is to procure a decree for a sale of certain mortgaged premises in said county, which were, on Sep 23, 1858, mortgaged by the dfndnts, Henry A Klopfer, Christian G Klopfer & Ann A Klopfer, his wife, to Wm B Canfield, Ira C Canfield, & Jos Meredith, trading as above stated. On Sep 23, 1858, the Klopfers conveyed certain real estate, which is described in the bill & its accompanying exhibit, unto the said Wm B Canfield, Ira C Canfield, & Jos Meredith, by way of mortgage to secure the payment of $759, which was then due & owing from the said Klopfers to the same Canfield Co; & that Henry A Klopfer, Christian G Klopfer & Ann A Klopfer reside out of the State of Md. Absent dfndnts to appear in person or by solicitor, on or before the 2nd Monday of Nov next. -Jas G Henning, clerk

Mrd: on Apr 12, by Rev P D Gurley, D D, Mr Geo J Musser to Miss S Lizzie Hutchinson, all of Wash City.

Mrd: on Apr 12, at Calvary Church, N Y, by Rev F L Hawkes, D D, Henry S Fitch, of Chicago, [only son of Hon Graham N Fitch, U S Senator from Indiana,] to Ellen R Hetzel, daughter of the late I Newton Hetzel, M D, of Harrisburg, Pa.

Died: on Apr 13, of consumption, Miss Susan B, daughter of the late Edmund & Eliz W Bradford, in her 19th year. Her funeral will take place this evening at 3 o'clock, from the residence of her mother, 436 K st, between 6th & 7th sts.

Circuit Court of D C, in Chancery, No 1,456. Mary M Williams against Theophilus Connell & others. A Lloyd, trustee, sold part of lot 17 in square 451, with improvements, to R S Wharton, for $915, & he has complied with the terms of sale. –Jno A Smith, clerk

SAT APR 16, 1859
Trial of Danl E Sickles: 1-Rev C H A Buckley sworn: resides in West Winsted, Conn; has known Mr Sickles since 1838; they were associated together as classmates in the N Y Univ. In 1840, in N Y C, Prof Da Ponte died. He was kind of a patron or guardian of Mr Sickles. Mr Sickles broke out into a spasm of passionate grief, & with frantic energy rushed up & down the grave-yard shrieking, so much so that it was impossible for us, who were his friends, to pacify him with words. We were obliged to take hold of him & by friendly force restrain him, & take him out of the cemetery. 2-John M Seely sworn: resides in this District; painter by trade, resided on 12th st near 15th. 3-Lewis Poole sworn: lived, in Feb last, on L st, between 15th & 16th sts. I know the brick house on 15th st, midway between K & L sts, & was there when the lock was taken off & changed. 4-Jesse B Haw sworn: knew the late Philip Barton Key; saw him last on the morning he was shot, up by Lafayette square, going up the avenue in the direction of Gtwn. I had known him about 5 or 6 years, I guess. 5-Maj Hopkins sworn: I am the coachman of Col Freeman of Wash City, & have been for between 5 or 6 years; his house is on H st, between 15th & 16th sts. 6-Mrs Nancy Brown sworn: I live on 15th st, my husband is the President's gardner; I knew Mr Philip Barton Key; I last saw him the day on which he was shot; I saw him go into the house on 15th st, next door to where I live. Mr Brady said that he should insist that Mr Key was killed in an act of adultery within the meaning of the law, & that just before Sickles left his house & home on Feb 27, & shortly before he met Key, the latter had used his handkerchief in front of said house as a signal to procure Mrs Sickles to leave the house, join him, & proceed to said house in 15th st, & that Sickles saw the said Key so use his handkerchief, & knew what was its meaning. Mr Key had hired a house on 15th st, in Wash City, for the exclusive purpose of meeting therein with Mrs Sickles, & the key of such house was found on the person of the deceased after his death, & was one of those which have been produced in this trial. The said house was rented for the unlawful & wicked purpose aforesaid; that such key, in the possession of the deceased, was one of those found in his pocket after his decease & produced on this trial, & that Sickles knew of the aforesaid design, intent, & preparation of said Key. At that time, Sickles met Key on Feb 27, at Madison ave, & just before he shot, Key was on his way to the home & house of Mr Sickles, with the unlawful & wicked design to cause & procure Mrs Sickles to leave said house, & proceed with him to the aforesaid house on 15th st, said Key having the key of the front door lock in his possession to be used in procuring admittance. Key was in the habit of exhibiting & using his handkerchief before Mr Sickles' house & home as a signal, on perceiving which Mrs Sickles was to leave said house & proceed to the house on 15th st, & she had done so in pursuance of such signals, which said facts had, shortly before the meeting between Key & Sickles on Feb 27, come to the knowledge of said Sickles, who immediately before the killing had himself seen the said Key using his handkerchief before the residence of said Sickles for the purpose above stated.

The ship **City of Baltimore** brought intelligence of the death of the celebrated Marquis of Waterford, while hunting upon his estate, near Curraghmore, Ireland, on Mar 29; lacking only one month of being 48 years of age. In his 16th year he succeeded to the title of his father, & an income of L10,000 per annum. –Boston Courier

The following missionaries are about to sail from Boston for Calcutta: Rev C W Judd & wife, Rev J W Waugh & wife, Rev E W Parker & wife, Rev J R Downey & wife, & Rev J M Thoburn.

Mr Jas Maher, the public gardener, died yesterday, aged nearly 67 years. He was a native of Ireland, & came to this city from Phil early in the administration of Gen Jackson, who gave him the office he held at the time of his death, & which he kept uninterruptedly through all intervening changes of Administration for a space of nearly 30 years. Mrs Maher, his wife, proceeded him to the grave in Oct last.
+
Died: on Apr 15, Jas Maher, Public Gardener, in his 67th year. His funeral will take place from his residence on E st, between 13th & 14th sts, on Monday next, at 10 o'clock.

Obit-died: This intelligence copied from the Norwich [Conn] Courier of Apr 12, will fall with a heavy weight upon a large circle of friends in this city by whom Mrs Foster was no less loved than admired for those qualities of head & heart. Mrs Joanna Boylston Foster, wife of Hon Lafayette S Foster, of this city, died on the Sabbath, of a fatal & mysterious malady, malignant sore throat. She was descended from one of the oldest & highly respected of our Norwich families, connected on her mother's side, with another scarcely less prominent. Her whole life passed in this her native place. As one of a band of brothers & sisters around whom clustered sweet memories of childhood, she ever retained for each her fullness of appreciation & constant love. Her sickness was short.

Died: on Apr 14, after a brief illness, Hon Geo M Bibb, formerly of Ky, in his 82nd year. His funeral will be on Apr 17 at 3½ o'clock, from the late residence of the deceased, corner of 2nd & Fayette sts, Gtwn, D C.

Died: on Apr 13, of pneumonia, after a short illness, Bartold, third son of H Mela, aged 12 years.

Augusta, Apr 15. Mrs Senator Toombe fractured her leg yesterday morning by jumping from a buggy when the horse was beyond control. She received no other injury, although her life was in imminent danger. The accident occurred near this city.

MON APR 18, 1859
Trial of Danl E Sickles: 1-Peter Cagger sworn: member of the bar; resides in Albany, N Y; has known Sickles for upwards of 12 years; saw Mr Key once, in Jun, 1858; I was introduced to him by Mr Sickles.

Hon Edw V Whiton, Chief Justice of the Supreme Court of Wisc, died at his residence in Janesville, a few days since, in his 55th year. He was a native of Mass, & emigrated to Wisc in 1835, among the early pioneers of that Territory.

Excellent household & kitchen furniture at auction on Apr 26, at the house recently occupied by Judge Loring, on I st, between 15th & 16th sts. -Jas C McGuire & Co, aucts

Mrd: on Apr 14, in Wash City, Rev Mr Marvell, Mr Eugene Carrington to Miss Cora, daughter of Capt Chas Dimmock, all of Richmond, Va.

Died: on Apr 17, in Wash City, of typhoid fever, Mrs Jacqueline S Pendleton, 2nd daughter of Eliza B & the late Robt Mills, of S C. Her funeral will take place from her mother's residence, Capitol Hill, 553 N J ave, on Apr 19 at 2 o'clock.

TUE APR 19, 1859
Trial of Danl E Sickles: 1-Mrs Nancy Brown recalled & examined: the last time I saw Mr Key was on the Wed before he was shot; at the brick house on 15th st. He unlocked the door & put the key in his pocket. He came out of the house in about an hour. Mrs Sickles went in the back way & came out the back way. When Mr Key came out he first came out the back way & let her out at the gate, & then came back & went out the front door. In Oct Mr Key rode up on his horse, at the time I was going out at the gate on my way to church. He asked me if I knew whether that house was occupied, & I told him it was not. He asked me if I knew who owned it & I told him John Gray. He came another time & tied his horse to my tree. I asked him if he did not know that was against the law. He said no. I told him it was, & that I did not wish him to tie his horse there again. He said he would not. 2-Danl Ratcliffe sworn: Mr Key has resided since Nov last in C st, near 4½ st, about a mile from 15th st. Mr Key was a widower. He had 4 children, as I understood. Mrs Key has been dead for 4 or 5 years. 3-John M Seeley, recalled & examined: I reside at 361 L st; I noticed them two or three times perhaps up to Feb 12. 4-Chas Mann sworn: I am acting as a policeman now. There were 2 rooms & a kitchen on the lower floor of John Gray's house, furnished in plain style. The rooms were carpeted. In the second story there were 2 chambers, communicating with each other, I think, with folding doors; the furniture was a bedstead, a bed, a washstand & pitcher, & there may have been a bureau there. There were soiled towels lying about the floor; the bed looked like it had not been made for some time; & there were some cigarettes there. 5-Mrs Sarah Seeley sworn: I am the wife of John M Seeley; I knew Philip Barton Key when he was a boy & when his father lived in Gtwn; I knew him well. I live on L st, & can seen into that portion of the yard & saw him go in 3 times. I saw them pass in through the back alley. These visits were all in Feb, as far as I can recollect. My daughter brought my attention to Mrs Sickles. 6-Jas Ginnity sworn: I am a policeman in this District: I've known Mr Key for the past 5 to 7 years; on Feb 16th last, I saw Mr Key & the lady with him; I left them & they went down 15th st. 7-Miss Matilda Seeley sworn: I am the daughter of Jno M Seeley; I saw Mrs Sheckles go to John Gray's house in Feb, about 2 weeks before Mr Key's death. 8-John B Haskin recalled: Mr Sheckles

had to go to NY & asked me to call at his house to see if Mrs Sheckles wanted anything. My wife & children were with me & we had been to Gtwn to get some shoes. We opened the front door & the door in the library being opened, I entered without knocking. Mrs Sickles & Mr Key were seated at a round table; Mrs Sickles became flustered. Entering my carriage my wife said Mrs Sickles was a bad woman.

Orphans Court of Wash Co, D C. Letters of administration on the personal estate of Harding S Wait, late of Wash Co, deceased. —Asa W Wait, adm

Excellent household & kitchen furniture at auction on Apr 28, at the residence of John Farley, U S C S, 175 G st, between 19th & 20th sts. -A Green auct

Valuable lot at auction, by order of the Orphans Court of D C, confirmed by the Circuit Court of D C, in Chancery, passed Nov 23, 1858, in the case of Wm A Richardson, Guardian: public sale on May 5, on the premises, lot 16 in square 245, fronting on 13th st, between M & N sts, of Wash City. —A Lloyd, trustee -A Green auct

Trustee's sale of valuable improved property on 6th st, between G & H sts, at public auction, on May 12, by deed from Geo McNaughton & wife, dated Aug 5, 1858, duly recorded in Liber J A S No 159, folios 178; sale of lot 12 in square 486, with a 2 story brick dwlg house, with back bldg & bakery attached. —Chas S Wallach, trustee
-Jas C McGuire & Co, aucts

Mrd: on Apr 14, by Rev Mr Scrivener, Mr Stephen W Randall, of PG Co, Md, to Miss Catharine Vanfleet, of Wash.

Died: on Apr 17, in Gtwn, Virginia Moncure, infant daughter of J E & F E Stewart, formerly of Martinsburg, Va. Her funeral is tomorrow at 4½ o'clock, from 55 Bridge st.

Died: on Apr 17, in Wash City, of scarlet fever, Wm Hungerford, son of Wm H & Henrietta V Minnix, in his 2nd year. His funeral is today at 10 o'clock A M.

WED APR 20, 1859
At Glenwood, Mills Co, Iowa, on Apr 4, while Rev Wm Watson, pastor of the Methodist Church, was preaching a funeral sermon, he was arrested for passing counterfeit money. The people in attendance were incensed at the officer & thrust the officer from the house. In the cellar of Rev Watson's house was found inks, presses, paper, rolling machines, & the apparatus for the manufacture of counterfeit bills. He is about 40 years old, a man of family. He was taken, & in default of bail was committed to the county jail to wait trial.

Obit-died: on Apr 17, 1859, in Wash City, at the residence of her mother, Mrs Jacquelin S Pendleton. The close of her life was calm.

Trial of Danl E Sickles: 1-E B Hart sworn: I reside in N Y C; am surveyor of the port of N Y; have known Mr Sickles about 12 years. 2-John Thompson sworn: I reside in N Y; was coachman of Mr Sickles from Nov 16, 1857 until Feb 4, 1859. Mrs Sickles went alone from the house in the coach when I drove her. She would go out from 12 to 1, & generally remain out from 4 til 5; the usual dinner hour was 5 o'clock. When Mrs Sickles went out in the coach Mr Key would always join her somewhere on the streets. There were very few days when out in the carriage she did not meet Mr Key. 3-Geo W Emerson sworn: I reside in this District; occupation is that of butcher; I have known Mr Key some 4 or 5 years; I known Mrs Sickles; I have had a stall in the market for 13 years; Mrs Sickles was in the habit of obtaining her meat from me. 4-John Cooney sworn: I am the private coachman of Mr Sickles; have been since Feb 8, about 4 weeks before the death of Mr Key, & I took the place of John Thompson. I had lived in Wash City about 3 months before I became Mr Sickles' coachman.

The death of the Marquis of Waterford took place while his lordship was hunting with his own hounds, at Castle Morris, county of Kilkenny. The Marquis' horse missed his hind legs on the bank, & dropped his fore legs into a small cut on the other side, which threw the animal on its knees & nose, so that his lordship was thrown off on his face. He was entirely unconscious & never afterwards spoke, living about 10 minutes. The marquis left no issue, & the title & estates descend to Hon & Rev John Beresford.
–Kilkenny Moderator [No death date given-appears to be a recent item.]

Mrd: on Apr 7, in Wash City, at St John's Church, by Rev Smith Pyne, J S Henry, of Ky, to Kate, only daughter of the late John A Kearney, Surgeon in the U S Navy.

Died: on Apr 16, Clara Stewart, infant daughter of Saml W & Catherine E Owen.

THU APR 21, 1859
Trial of Danl E Sickles: 1-Geo B Woolridge was recalled: I could not say what hour it was when Mr Sickles returned to his house after killing Mr Key. 2-John J McElhone was called, but did not answer. He had returned to Phil since he was last examined. 3-Alfred A McGaffey sworn: resides in Wash City, at the present; I am a contractor; I have known Mr Key since Jan or Feb, 1858. 4-Chas G Bacon recalled: I went to the eastward side of Cmdor McCauley's house & walked rapidly to the 2nd tree from the corner, the tree where Mr Key was killed, & it took me 30 seconds. 5-John McDonald sworn: I hired with Mr Sickles as groom & footman on Feb 10, 1859. When John Cooney went out with the coach I always accompanied him. 6-Felix McClosky sworn: I reside in the city of Brooklyn; I was in Wash City on Feb 27 last. 7-Chas Lee Jones sworn: I visited the house in 15th st owned by John Gray in company with Mr Pendleton; on Monday, 8 days after the murder. I went into the house, by previous appointment. I met John Gray, who I had not known by name, but when I saw him I recognized him as a colored man I had known as a waiter or in some capacity in Wash City for many years.

Orphans Court of Wash Co, D C. Case of Jos F Hodgson & Wm Flaherty, adms of Jas Handly, deceased, the administrators & Court appointed May 14 next, for the final settlement of the personal estate of said deceased, of assets in hand.
-Ed N Roach, Reg/o wills

Mrd: on Apr 20, at Kalorama, by Rev Smith Pyne, Dr Geo Maulsby, U S Navy, to Anna M, daughter of the late Thos Lovete, of N Y.

Died: on Apr 19, in Wash City, in his 54th year, Fred'k Dankworth, a native of Phil, [lately attached to the U S Coast Survey ofc,] & for the last 20 years a resident of Wash City. His funeral is on Friday next, at 3 o'clock, from his late residence, 612 Md ave, near 12th st, Island.

Died: on Apr 10, 1859, at his residence, in Uniontown, Fayette Co, Pa, Alex'r Hamilton Campbell, M D, in his 43rd year.

FRI APR 22, 1859
Trial of Danl E Sickles: 1-Albert Greenleaf sworn: I was present at the club-house when Dr Miller was there on the evening of the death of Mr Key. 2-Jacob F King sworn: present at the club-house on the evening of the death of Mr Key. I got there while the examination was going on at the coroner's inquest. I stayed thereuntil the body was removed to Mr Tayloe's house. 3-Abel Upshur recalled: I observed the manner & appearance of Mr Sickles on the occasion of the death of Mr Key; he appeared to be cool. 4-Edw M Tidball recalled: Mr Sickles was rather cool & deliberate on the occasion of the death of Mr Key. 5-Chas Howard sworn: Mr Key was my brother-in-law. I returned to Balt, I think, on the Thursday of the week after the death of Mr Key. 6-Wm Daw sworn: I was present at the house of Mr Sickles immediately after the death of Mr Key. I accompanied Mr Sickles there from Judge Black's house. Mr Mann, Mr Suit, Mr Butterworth, & Mr Sickles were in the carriage. I rode on the outside with the driver. 7-Jas G Berret sworn: I am Mayor of Washington. I was present at the house of Mr Sickles on the afternoon of the day when Mr Key was killed. I went with the Chief of Police. 8-Jas H Suit sworn: I accompanied officer Daw from Judge Black's house to Mr Sickles' house. I was in the hack. Mr Mann was with me. 9-Miss Octavia Ridgely called & examined: I was in Mr Sickles' house at the time he returned from Judge Black's on the afternoon of Sunday, Feb 27. I was in the basement, or rather on the same floor with the street. I remained down stairs. I saw Mr Sickles getting out of the carriage. 10-J H McBlair sworn: I was present at Mr Sickles' house the evening of the death of Mr Key, Feb 27th. I went there about 15 minutes after the occurrence. Mr Woolridge, Miss Ridgely, & Mr Slidell were present when I was there.

The Balt Patriot announces the death in that city yesterday of Rev Dr Henry V D Johns, Rector of Emanuel Church, an eminent divine of the Protestant Episcopal Church.

Hon Wm C Bouck, of Schoharie, died at his residence in that county, on Apr 19, at the age of 73 years. Albany Argus: He held the first offices of the town of his residence in Schoharie, & in 1812 was appointed by Gov Tompkins Sheriff of the county. He lived on the same farm occupied by his father & grandfather, & which was a part of the tract on the Schoharie creek patented by the later & others from George II in 1755. –Con Adv

Died: on Apr 21, in Wash City, Hugh Lockerey, in his 46th year. His funeral is today at 2½ o'clock, from the residence of Jas Lynch, East Captiol st, Capitol Hill, between 1st & 2nd sts.

Supreme Court of the U S, No 237, Dec, 1858. Chas M Micken, appellant, vs Franklin Perin. Appeal from the Circuit Court of the U S for the Easter District of Louisiana. Mr Taylor, of counsel for the appellee, having suggested to the Court that Chas McMicken, the appellant, had died since the order of appeal was granted in this cause, leaving as his proper reps Eliz Randall, Chas Cair; Naomi Wood, wife of Wm Wood; Mary Ann Powers, wife of Wm Wood; Mary Ann Powers, wife of Wesley Powers; Eliz Jennett; Louis Carrigan, wife of ___ Carrigan; Henrietta Twish, wife of Wm Twish; Andrew Lear; Chas Lear & Geo Lear; Emiline Johnson, wife of ___ Johnson; Andrew McMicken; Lizzie McMicken, wife of D P Stille; & the minors, Chas M, Clyde, & Mary Ellen Perin, represented by their guardian, F Perin; now here moved the Court for an order that, unless the proper reps of the said Chas McMicken, deceased, shall become parties within the first 10 days of the next term of this Court, the appellee shall be entititled to have this appeal dismissed. –Wm Thos Carroll, Clerk Supreme Court U S

SAT APR 23, 1859
Trial of Danl E Sickles: 1-John J McElhone, Richd Brodhead, & Jas Haldemar were called as witnesses for the prosecution, but neither of them answered. 2-Jos Dudrow recalled: When the last shot was fired I was 35 or 40 feet from where they were. 2-Edw Delafield recalled: I saw Mr Sickles on Feb 27th last, coming down Madison square. When the thing was over Mr Sickles walked off quietly. He put the pistol in his pocket afterwards. 3-Chas H G Lewis sworn: I am connected with the ofc of the Congressional Globe. The reporters employed on those days for the Globe were Mr Hincks, Mr Smith, Mr McElhone, Mr Andrews, & Mr Hayes. 4-Francis H Smith sworn: I am one of the official corps of reporters of the House of Reps.

In the 86th year of his age, in the 64th year of his practice, while yet engaged in the adjudication of weighty causes, the film of blindness had suddenly settled upon the sight of the great lawyer, Danl Cady. When Mr Cady came to the bar Geo Clinton, of Revolutionary immortality, was Govn'r of the State of N Y. Mr Cady made his first motion in the Supreme Court in 1798. Alex'r Hamilton heard it. His perfect moral organization was a large part of his professional character. –N Y Tribune

Beautiful country residence on the Heights of Gtwn at auction on May 2, on the premises; lately occupied by B T Hodges; on the New Road & the Ridge Road, & contains 15 acres, with a nearly new & commodious brick dwlg, barn, stables, & servants' houses. The view is unsurpassed in this region of the country. –Barnard & Buckey, aucts

Died: yesterday, in Wash City, Miss Eliz T Price, late of Phil, in her 65th year. Her funeral is this afternoon, at the residence of her brother-in-law, Hon Chas Naylor, 4 4½ st, preparatory to the removal of her remains to Phil. [No time given.]

Died: on Apr 21, at the residence of his grandfather, Jas McClery, John Charles, infant son of J Charles & Indiana Gardiner, aged 9 months.

MON APR 25, 1859

Trial of Danl E Sickles: 1-Richd Brodhead sworn: I am acquainted wit Mr Sickles, but not intimately. I saw him the the day of the death of Mr Key. I was walking in Washington with a friend, Mr Haldemar, [a son of Jacob Haldemar,] of Harrisburg.

Interior Decorations: John Markriter, 486 7th st, Wash. [Ad]

Last Oct Jas A McCorkle, Cashier of the People's Bank, Richmond, Indiana, suddenly disappeared, carrying with him some $15,000 belonging to the bank. Mr W J H Robertson, deputy sheriff of the county, was employed to ascertain the whereabouts of the absconding cashier, & has been absent the whole winter in this undertaking. News has just been received that McCorkle was found at San Antonio, Texas, & that he has left New Orleans with his prisoner on his way to Richmond.

Died: on Apr 23, Mrs C Malvina, wife of Rev B F Bittinger, aged 31 years. Her funeral is today at 4 o'clock, from the residence of her father, Jos Libbey, 46 First st, Gtwn.

Drowned: found drowned, on Apr 24, in the Potomac river, near Geisboro, Mr John Alfred Cassell, in his 52nd year. His funeral will be from his late residence, 7th & Va ave, this day, at 3 o'clock, to proceed from there to St Patrick's vault, where his remains are deposited, & thence to **Mount Olivet Cemetery**.

Died: on Mar 27, in Paris, Wm Stettinius, son of John F Clark, in his 27th year.

Died: on Thursday last, at his residence, near **Prospect Hill**, Fairfax Co, Va, Col S M Ball. He was a most estimable gentleman; for many years an active & useful citizen of his county; elected several times to the Legislature. As a husband, father, & friend, he was truly beloved, & his memory will be cherished by all who knew him.

TUE APR 26, 1859

Rev W W Arnett, pastor of Emmanuel parish, [Protestant Episcopal,] church at Cumberland, Md, died on Apr 21. He had but recently returned from a visit to Cuba.

Trial of Danl E Sickles: 1-Among the Jews, by the law of God, the adulterer & adulteress were both stoned to death. In Greece, Lycurgus decreed that adultery should by punished the same as murder. The Saxons, by their law, burnt the **_adulteress_** to death, & over her ashes reared a gibbet, on which the adulterer, her accomplice, was hanged. In France, under the law of Louis the Debonair, both parties suffered capital punishment. 2-Mr Brady: Look, your Honor, at Danl E Sickles. Look at Teresa, that was his wife. Look at the woman whom I knew in her girlhood, in her innocence, & for whom in the past, as now, I pray the good & merciful interposition of Heaven to make her future life a source of happiness. She is the mother of a child, she is a girl, accessible to the influence of a master intellect. Look at that young child, standing between its father & mother.

The funeral of the late Rev H V D Johns took place on Sunday last from Emmanuel Church, Balt, attended by a large concourse of friends. The impressive burial service of the church was read by Rev Chas Howard & Rev A C Coxe. Dr Johns was in the prime of his usefulness, say between 40 & 50. He was a brother to Bishop Johns, of Va.

Suit for estranging the affections of a wife is now in progress at Columbus, Ohio. In the Superior Court of this county, Judge Matthews presiding, a suit for damages laid at $15,000 was taken up on Mondy last. The plntf is a young man, Lucius A Bowers. In the spring of 1858 Miss Mary E Kent, a young lady resident in Licking, was admired by 2 young gentlemen, one of whom is plntf in this action, the other being Mr Aaron D Griffin, both residents of this county. The lady chose the former & married him in April. Soon after they removed to Illinois, & in a short time Griffin induced the wife to forsake her husband & return to Ohio. Letters from Ira A Preston to Margartet Preston, his wife, to the wife of Bowers, & other influences brought to bear upon her are alleged to have assisted in her alienation, & Preston & wife are, with Griffin, made parties dfndnt to the suit which is brought by the husband, Bowers, to recover damages caused by the separation, thus taking from his possession the control of which the wife was the expectant. Messrs Galloway, Warden, & Wright appear for the plntf, & Messrs Swayne, Barber, & Andrews for the defence.

The residence of our deceased townsman, Chas Willson, is a house of mourning, & his family is suffering the deepest of affliction. Mr Willson died of apoplexy; & the mail contained his mother's obituary to his son Charles, who resides at Princton, Wisc. His mother died on the previous day age 90 years. Mr Willson had just written the address of his son upon the wrapper of the paper when he fell to the floor, dead. His daughter, about 18, received a shock, her nervous system being anything but favorable. Few of the friends of the family repaired to the house of her son to attend the funeral of his mother. Much to their surprise they found the corpse of the mother in one apartment, the corpse of her son in another, & the fair daughter prostrated & senseless in another.
–Rochester Union, Apr 22.

A shooting affray occurred at New Orleans on Apr 19th, between J M Vernon & Jos C Bossier, co-proprietors of the Louisiana Courier, which it is feared will terminate fatally for Mr Bossier. Mr Vernon was arrested. –Picayune

Distressing suicide. Mr John R Gilmer committed suicide yesterday, by throwing himself on the Washington railroad, near the depot, in front of the wheels of a locomotive when in motion. Mr Gilmer was a lawyer by profession, & a son of Gov Thos W Gilmer, of Va, & more recently Sec of the Navy, who was killed by the explosion of the peacemaker gun on board the U S steamer **Princeton** in 1843. Mr Gilmer has been recently the conductor of the Exponent, a newspaper published at Charlottesville, Va. Mr Gilmer, it appears, was about 30 years of age. Roger A Pryor took charge of the remains of the deceased, which are to be sent to Va for interment.

Superior household & kitchen furniture at auction on May 2, at the residence of Sir Wm Gore Ouseley. –C W Boteler, auct

Stray horse taken up at the Farm of Capt Carberry, in Wash Co, D C. Owner will please call, pay charges, & take him away. –Jas Halpin, manager

Cyrus W Plummer, the leading mutineer of the whale ship **Junior**, has been convicted in Boston of the murder of Capt Mellen, of that vessel, & was on Thutsday sentenced to be hung on Jun 24. He read to the Court a long statement, avowing his innocence, & declaring that he saved many lives instead of committing murder. The other 3 prisoners tried with him were convicted of manslaughter.

WED APR 27, 1859
Trial of Danl E Sickles: The clerk directed the prisoner to stand up. He then put the question to the jury, to which the foreman responded not guilty. The verdict was received by the audience with an overwhelming burst of applause, which all the efforts of the court could not restrain or check for some minutes. Mr Stanton moved that the prisoner be discharged from custody, which motion was granted by the Court. Mr Stanton desired, in behalf of Mr Sickles, to thank the Jury, & also that he [Mr Stanton] wished to shake hands with the jurors before they retired. Mr Sickles was borne along by the crowd, seeming quite overcome by his feelings, towards the jury-box, & received the congratulations of the jurors & of his many friends who crowded around him. He was then escorted to a carriage in waiting & drove to the residence of Mr McBlair, near Lafayette Square, where in a more private manner he continued to receive the congratulations of his friends.

Nearly new household & kitchen furniture at auction on May 3, at the residence of Mr O Dietz, on E st, at 2nd st. -A Green auct

Norfolk, Apr 26. Hon John Letcher has returned home, being too ill to continue the Gubernatorial canvass.

Orphans Court of Wash Co, D C. Letters of administration on the personal estate of Ferdinand Greentrup, late of Wash Co, deceased. –Adam Raab, adm

THU APR 28, 1859
Adm's sale of a handsome gray horse belonging to the estate of the late Philip Barton Key, at the Auction Store of A Green, 526 7th st, on Apr 30. –W A Maury, adm -A Green auct

Wm Lyons was a rebellious convict on Tuesday in the District Penitentiary. He is employed at shoemaking, & was ordered by the Warden to take a certain position with his work- bench, which he refused to do, accompanying the refusal with oaths & severe blows upon Deputy Warden, McC P Sengstack, jr, who had come to assist his father, the Warden. Deputy Warden drew his revolver & fired at his assailant, but the ball took effect in Jos Cunningham, who had run up to assist. Happily the shot was not fatal.

Mrd: on Apr 26, at the Church of the Epiphany, by Rev Dr Hall, Mr Edw A Pollard, of N Y, to Miss Adelaide M Barry, of Wash City.

Louisville, Apr 25. The steamboat **St Nicholas** was on her way from St Louis to New Orleans, when an explosion took place near Island Sixty, on Sunday. The boat & cargo are a total loss. The following are dead or missing: Capt McMullen, of that boat; Mrs Gline, the clerk's wife; Mrs Dunnican, clerk's cousin; Miss McKnight; Mrs Christopher; unknown lady with a babe; Wm Faulkner, of McGregor's Landing, Iowa; another unknown lady; John Jenkins, 2nd engineer; Wm Tew, 1st engineer; John Bond, cabin boy; Jas Wood, 1st cook, of Hillsborough city, Pa; the barber; Miss Jackson, a chambermaid, of St Louis; Edw Stephens, pilot, of St Louis; John Limbeck, fireman. Badly scalded: Benj V Gline, 1st clerk, of St Louis; J S Acutt, of Warrenton, Miss; Jacob Langhorn, of Pittsburg; R J Stuart, of Staunton, Va; Thos Carter, of Tamaqua, Pa; Ella Kennedy, of Brunswick, Mo; Rose St John, of New Orleans, chambermaid; Wm Pennibacker, of St Louis, watchman; Fred'k Miller, Geo McIngle; Andy Slick fireman; D Kapps, of Farmington, Ill; O W Reynolds, of Sioux City. [May 2nd newspaper: Mr B B Stuart, of Staunton, Va, badly scalded; Capt McMullen, dead; Gideon J Pillow, jr, son of Gen Pillow, of Tenn, dead. At the time of the accident Capt McMullen, Capt Glime, the clerk, & Mr Reid, the pilot, were on watch. Capt McMullen fell below, & his leg was caught in some timbers; &, although efforts were made to extricate him, he was burnt to death, while his cries for help were distinctly heard by those around him. Mr Gillman, 2nd clerk, was in his birth, & when he awoke to consciousness was on his mattress, floating in the river, a 100 yards from the boat. He reached the shore without assistance, though badly scalded.]

Alexis Clerel De Tocqueville, one of the most illustrious writers of France, died recently at his residence, near Lannes. He was a great grandson of the famous philosopher, Malesherbes, & was born on Jul 29, 1805. –N Y Evening Post

Birthplace of Gen Jackson. Monroe, N C, Mar 22, 1859. Old Andrew Jackson, the father of Gen Andrew Jackson, with several of his brothers in law, to wit, Geo McCamie, John Leslie, Saml Leslie, Jas Crawford, & Jas Crow, who married the Misses Hutchinson, sisters of Mrs Jackson, all came to this country from Ireland & settled in the Waxsaw settlements, lying partly in North & partly in South Carolina. That Andrew Jackson, senior, came in 1765 & settled on Twelve Mile Creek, N C, at a place where Mrs Martha Laney now lives, near Pleasant Grove camp ground, which place was then comprised in what was then called The Waxsaw settlement, taking its name from a tribe of the Catawba Indians called the Waxsaw tribe, & from which also the Waxsaw Creek took its name. That in the latter part of the winter of 1766 & 1767, & before the birth of his son Andrew, old Andrew Jackson died at the above named place on Twelve Mile Creek, N C. That soon afterwards his mother removed from Twelve Mile Creek, N C, to live with her sisters on Waxsaw Creek, & more expecially with her brother-in-law, Jas Crawford, of S C, who was the wealthiest among them. She stopped on her way at the house of Mrs Margaret McCamie, in N C, & whilst there gave birth to her son Andrew. As soon as she had recovered she proceeded to Mr Jas Crawford's, in S C, & remained there with her children until 1780 or 1781, upon the invasion of S C & N C by Lord Cornwallis, when she retreated with her son Andrew in the vinicty of Charlotte, N C, & shortly afterwards died near Charleston, D C. Andrew, now 14 years old, his mother & brothers all being dead, removed into N C, where he finished his education under Mr McCullock, & began the study of the law with Spruce McCay, & John Stokes, in Salisbury, N C; was licensed to practice law, & remained in Salisbury until the spring of 1788, at which time he went with Judge McNairy to Tenn. These facts are taken from his biographers from the time he was 13 or 14, & were all within the entire recollection of Gen Jackson himself. Mrs Mary Cowsat was then living in S C, where she was living when Jackson was born, within half a mile of Geo McCamie's house in N C, & stated that she was sent for to attend to Mrs Jackson on the night of Andrew's birth; & it was she who received Jackson in her arms at the house of Geo McCamie's, in N C. So her grandsons Jas Faulkner, Thos Faulkner, & John Lathan has often heard his mother, Mrs Sarah Lathan, the daughter of Sarah Leslie, assert that she too was present with her mother on the night of Andrew Jackson's birth; & concurs in the fact that it was at Geo McCamie's, in N C; so Benj Massey, Jas, Thos, & Saml Faulkner & others have often heard her say the same. Mrs Eliz McWhorter, who lived in N C within a mile of Geo McCamie's, was also sent for as an assistant on the night of Andrew Jackson's birth, & was present & said that he was born at Geo McCamie's, in N C. She also took her son Geo McWhorter, a lad a little over 5 years of age, with her the next day to visit Mrs Jackson at McCamie's. This is the recollections & statement of Saml McWhorter, the grandson of Mrs McWhorter, of what he has often heard his father & his grandmother relate. There are certificates of Mrs Jane Wilson & others who corroborate Saml McWhorter's statement, & another certificate corroborating the statement of the others.
–S H Walkup

Died: on Apr 27, in Wash City, William Thomas, aged 3 months, infant son of John H & Mary Wallace. His funeral will take place this evening at 3:30 o'clock, from the resident of his parents, on 8th st, between G & H, No 419.

Died: at Jaffa, Syria, Jan 5, 1859, Yacoub Serapion Murad, for nearly 20 years consular agent of the U S for Jaffa & Jerusalem. Travellers will remember the kind attention received from Mr Murad & his brothers, Simeon & Lazarus. –N Y Post

FRI APR 29, 1859
Baltimore & Ohio Railroad: Washington Branch: will run between Wash & Annapolis Junction, commencing on Apr 27, leaving Washington daily, except Sunday, at 3:45 P M, & the Junction, on its return, at 5 P M. –T H Parsons

Explosion on Apr 3 when the steam ferry-boat **Contra Costa** blew up while crossing the bar, near Oakland. Persons killed were David Cadey, M G Smith, Geo McDowell, Henry A Ostrander, & Matthew McQuinn.

San Jose, Mar 28-trial of Thos Scale for the murder of Paul C Shore, in which Crosby was said to be implicated, came up this morning in court before Judge McKee. Shots were fired in front of the court house between Crosby & young Shore, a brother to Paul. Crosby & young Shore on one side; Shore, Jas Bareley, & others on the other. A bullet struck a stranger, from Grass Valley, formerly from Missouri, named L P Ferguson. Bivan was shot through the leg. Shore wounded in both legs.

Rt Rev Geo Washington Doane, D D, Protestant Episcopal Bishop of N J, died on Apr 27, at his residence in Burlington, N J. He was born in Trenton, N J, May 27, 1799; ordained a deacon in 1821; was Prof of Belles Lettres & Rhetoric in the New Wash College [now Trinity,] Hartford, Conn; became Assist Minister of Trinity Church, Boston, in 1828, & Rector in 1830. In 1832 he was consecrated Bishop of N J; the year after he became the Rector of St Mary's Church at Burlington.

Trial of Danl B Vondersmith, of Lancaster, Pa, for frauds commited upon the U S Pension Bureau, terminated yesterday at Phil. He was arraigned on 6 indictments, & found guilty on two of them, the remaining four being thrown out under the act of limitation.

Hon Nathan Dayton, formerly a Judge of the Supreme Court of N Y, died suddenly of apoplexy, while dressing, on Tuesday morning, at his residence in Lockport. He was in his 64th year, & has for nearly 30 years taken rank with the most eminent lawyers of Western N Y.

Died: on Apr 28, in Wash City, Paul Stevens, aged 68 years. His funeral is tomorrow at 10 o'clock, from the residence of Mr Jos Whitney, on 14th st, between D & E sts.

The Army Medical Board convened in Phil & recommended the following gentlemen for appointment in the Medical Staff of the Army: 1-Geo Suckley, M D, N Y; 2-Dewitt C Peters, M D, N Y; 3-Chas H Alden, M D, Pa. Assist Surgeons: Alex'r B Hasson & Jonathan Letherman. -Surgeon General's Ofc, Apr 27, 1859

Judge Wright, of the 3rd judicial district, on Mon, granted a stay of proceedings in the case of Mrs Hartung, who was to have been executed in Albany on Wed. Application for a new trial will commence next week. It appears that this case will not be disposed of before the trial of Rhineman, indicted as an accomplice of Mrs Hartung.

Chancery sale of valuable improved property on 7th st, by decree of the Circuit Court of Wash Co, D C, in equity, in the cause of Williams & Kennedy vs Jas Williams et al, No 698: public auction on May 20, of the northern part of lot 9 in square 457, in Wash City, fronting on 7th st, with a 3 story brick house. —Walter S Cox, trustee
-Jas C McGuire & Co, aucts

I will sell that beautiful property, near Staunton, Va, known as the site of **Eastwood School**, adjoining the grounds of the Va Institution for the Deaf, Dumb, & Blind. The house is handsome & commodious. I also offer for sale a farm of 251 acres, 2½ miles from Staunton. —Pike Powers, Staunton, Va

For sale: a beautiful Country seat & Farm of 365 acres within a mile of Staunton, Va, with a large brick mansion, & all the conveniences of a gentleman's residence. Apply to John L Peyton, Staunton, Va.

Last week died one of the oldest bookworms of Paris, M Veinant, author of Bibliotheca Scatologica, & editor of the Farces of Fabarin. A sum of 85,000 francs [L3,400] has already been offered for the collection.

On Wed a poor man, Uriah Ager, residing in Fred'k st, Gtwn, committed suicide by cutting his throat with a razor. He is said to have been a drinking man, & had become despondent from fear of future want.

Mrd: on Apr 26, in the 4½ Presbyterian Church, by Rev Byron Sunderland, Mr John W Stevens, of Ky, to Miss Rosa M Cawthon, of Va.

Mrd: on Apr 26, by Rev Mr Waldron, Dr N S Lincoln to Mrs Margaret E Ridgate.

Mrd: on Apr 26, in St Matthew's Church, by Very Rev N D Young, John B Brooke, of Marlboro, PG Co, Md, to Miss Helen Hill, of the same county.

Mrd: on Apr 26, by Very Rev N D Young, John T Talbert to Sarah E King, of PG Co.

Mrd: on Apr 28, at Trinity Church, by Rev Dr Butler, Wm A Saxton, of Huntingdon, Pa, to Sallie S, youngest daughter of the late Jas Abercrombie, of Balt, Md.

SAT APR 30, 1859
Geo O Atherton, teller of the Southern Bank of St Louis, was arrested there on Apr 26, for having abstracted from the bank the sum of $53,000. This had been taken from time to time from the deposits of the Bank, & the fraud concealed by an ingenious device. He says he has loaned the greatest part of this money $47,000, to a firm of which his brother-in-law is a member. He was committed to jail to await his trial by the Criminal Court.

John M Crane, editor & publisher of the Bonham Independent, was shot & killed in Bonham on Monday last, by M C Saddler. A difficulty had previously taken place, & Crane was the aggressor. Col Crane was 36 years of age, & leaves a wife & 2 small children. –Dallas Herald, Apr 6

From Liberia. 1-Dr John Z Forney, American Commercial Agent for Liberia, died at Monrovia on Feb 9. 2-Chief Justice Day died at Monrovia on Feb 15, in his 62nd year.

On Wed, at N Y, Miss Matilda Sawyer, a beautiful & intelligent young lady, almost 22 years of age, lost her life when the camphene lamp near her bed upset, exploded, & set fire to the bed clothes. She boarded with Mrs Holmes, & was engaged to be married in a few days.

The ***Fort Smith*** [Ark] Herald announces the death, at Belle Grove Institute, on Friday, by accidental burning, of the daughter of Rev Mr McManus, Chaplain in the U S army at ***Fort Arbuckle***. Miss Maria McManus' clothes caught fire & she died the next day. She was boarding there, & her father & mother are at ***Fort Arbuckle***.

Jas Porter, the famous Ky giant, died at his residence in Portland, Ky, on Sunday night, in his 50th year. He died of disease of the heart. He was 7 feet 9 inches in height. He was a gentleman of intelligence, modest & retiring, the very soul of honor & honesty.

Excellent household & kitchen furniture at auction on May 5, at the residence of Dr Maxwell, U S N, 267 I st, between 17th & 18th sts. -Jas C McGuire & Co, aucts

Mrd: on Apr 28, at Christ Church, Gtwn, by Rev Dr Norwood, G French Bowie to Cornelia, daughter of the late Dennis Magruder, of Missouri.

Mrd: on Apr 28, by Rev S A H Marks, Mr Thos Cuddy, of Newport, R I, to Miss Annie M Gardner, formerly of Balt, Md.

Mrd: on Apr 28, by Rev Smith Pyne, D D, John F Cabot, of Phil, to Sophie, daughter of the late Rev Wm Hawley, of Wash City.

Mrd: on Dec 28, 1858, by Rev A G Carothers, M John R Leake to Miss Kate E Warren, all of Wash.

Mrd: on Apr 28, at **Meadow Farm**, Prince Wm Co, Va, by Rev Mr Towles, Dr Wm A Bradley, jr, of Gtwn, D C, to Bettie, daughter of Dr J W F Macrae.

Mrd: on Apr 28, at **Rosedale**, by Rev Fr Lynch, Fielding Lewis, of Va, to Mary Imogen, daughter of the late John Green.

Died: at Marietta, PG Co, Md, of scarlet fever, Philip Landsdale, in his 5th year, son of E B & Caroline L Duval. [No death date given-current item.]

Norfolk, Apr 29. St Paul's [Catholic] Church in Portsmouth, presided over by Rev Jos Plunkett, was entirely destroyed by fire last night. Only the pictures & vestments were saved. It was the work of an incendiary. The church was erected in 1853 at a cost of $23,000, & was insured for only $10,000.

MON MAY 2, 1859
Officers attached to the steamer **Fulton**, Lt commanding John J Almy, arrived yesterday at the Wash Navy Yard, from Paraguay & the River La Plata, having left Montevideo on Mar 17, stopping on her way at St Catherines, Pernambuco, & Barbados for coal. She sailed from the Wash Navy Yard on Sep 23 last; the first steamer to reach the River La Plata. John Van McCollom, John B Stewart, Robt Selden, & Marshall C Campbell, Lts; Robt H Clark, Purser; Henry O Mayor, Passed Assist Surgeon; Thos K Porter, Midshipman; Harman Newell, 1st Assist Engineer; John A Grier, 2nd do; Walter P Burrows, 3rd do; Jas B Houston, 3rd do; Jas De Kraft, 3rd do; Albert P Hulse, Capt's Clerk; Geo B Glenn, Purser's Clerk.

Appointments by the Pres: Geo Gideon; Harman Newell; Andrew Lawton; & John Faron: chief engineer in the navy, Apr 26, 1859. Obadiah B Curran, postmaster at Ithaca, N Y, Apr 26, 1859. Simeon M Johnson, of N Y, consul at Havre, Apr 27, 1859.

John Lehman was recently sentenced, at Urbana, Mo, to imprisonment for life for a heinous crime, & a day or two after, having been convicted of horse stealing, was sentenced by a stern Judge for an additional term of 8 years.

Sale of real estate in Wash City, by deed of trust executed on May 11, 1855, recorded in Liber J A S, No 100, folios 375 thru 380, by Thos Green of the first part, Wm J Ward, of the 2nd part, & B H Shackelford & Isham Keith of the 3rd part, the undersigned of the 4th part, I shall, as trustee under the said deed, by direction of the excx Beverley Tucker, deceased, sell on Jun 23 next, at public auction, all of square 173 with the bldgs thereon, having a front of 70 feet on 17th st, & entending back to B st. –P M Thompson, trustee -Jas C McGuire & Co, aucts

Mr Thos S Sutter, of N J, has been appointed Public Gardener, vice Jas Maher, deceased.

Mrd: on Apr 28, by Rev A G Carothers, Mr Hugh McAllister to Miss Caroline Reeves, both of Fairfax Co, Va.

Mrd: on Apr 28, at *Rose Hill*, by Rev Bishop McGill, of Richmond, Va, Geo E Mattingly, of Wash, to Louisa M, eldest daughter of Peter D G Hedgman, of Stafford Co, Va.

Died: on Apr 29, Henry, son of Chas H & Catharine Kreamer, in his 9th year.

Died: on Mar 29, at his residence in PG Co, Md, Jas M Duvall, in his 23rd year.

Died: on Feb 25, of consumption, in San Francisco, Calif, Emily Austin, wife of Alex'r G Abell.

Landscape & Plain Gardening: John F Weber, Bladensburg, Md. [Ad]

Isaac Hill has removed his Wood & Coal Yard to 4th & I st. [Ad]

TUE MAY 3, 1859
Trustee's sale, by deed of trust from W von Kammerhueber & his wife, dated Mar 18, 1855, recorded in Liber J A S, No 150, folios 342 thru 346, of the land records for Wash Co, D C, I, Chas Walter, will sell, on May 4, on the premises, all of lots 7 & 9 in square 3̲74 or 8̲74, with improvements, with a 2 story frame house. –Chas Walter -A Green auct

Accident on Thu at Cincinnati: Mr Geo Matschack, painter, engaged in painting a 3 story bldg, fell from the top of the bldg and died of his injuries within an hour or two of being taken home. John Sturm, apprentice, fractured his ancle.

Orphans Court of Wash Co, D C. In the case of Wm R Simmons, adm of Richd Shaw, deceased, the administrator & Court have appointed May 24 next, for the final settlement of the personal estate of the deceased, with the assets in hand. -Ed N Roach, Reg/o wills

John Mills, Justice of the Peace, Conveyancer, & Gen Agent: ofc 442 7th st, between F & G sts, opposite the Patent Ofc. [Ad]

Board in the Country: extensive additions to our former residence. Address, through the Post Ofc at Wash City, Lewis Bailey, Fairfax Co, Va.

New Silk Dyeing Establishment, John T Berkley, Pa ave, between 9th & 10th sts. -Wm Bell, J T Berkley

WED MAY 4, 1859
Orphans Court of Wash Co, D C. Letters of administration on the personal estate of John M Millson, late of Wash Co, deceased. –Rebecca H Millson, admx

Criminal Court-Wash-Tue. 1-Jas Miller was tried for an attempt at burglary on the dwlg house of John Freiz & with assault & battery on Anna E Freiz. The trial was not concluded. 2-Danl Long convicted of assault & battery, sentenced to a fine of $13. [May 5th newspaper: Jas Miller was acquitted.]

Mrd: on Apr 25, Easter Monday, by Rev L J Gilliss, John Thos Clements to Miss Fannie E Warner, all of Wash City.

Mrd: on May 3, at Trinity Church, by Rev Dr Butler, Oliver J Ruger, of Syracuse, N Y, to Miss Fannie C, eldest daughter of Col C Mortimer, of Va.

Mrd: on Apr 27, at St John's Church, Tallahassee, by Rt Rev Bishop Rutledge, Maj Robt Gamble to Laura Wirt, youngest daughter of Judge Randall, of Fla.

For sale at public auction, *Nonsuch*, the subscriber, having divided this tract of land into lots ranging from 40 to 128 acres, will dispose of each lot at public auction on May 24, on the premises. Land lies on the public road leading from Washington to Marlborough. Apply for information to John C Brent, ofc, City Hall, of 435 6th st. –Geo W Young

THU MAY 5, 1859
Jacob Shafer, residing on H st, near 7th, last evening made an attempt upon his life by shooting himself in the right ear with a pistol, but whether the pistol was loaded with ball or not does not yet appear to be quite certain. The cranium in the vicinity of the ear is much torn, but at the time of writing this Shafer had so far recovered as to reply when spoken to.

Catalogue sale of the Library of the late P Barton Key, on May 3, at the auction rooms. -W A Maury, adm -Jas C McGuire & Co, aucts

Died: on Apr 12, in PG Co, Maud, only daughter of John Hunter, correspondent of the Associated Press.

Statement of Appropriations:
1-Act for the relief of Jos Hardy & Alton Long, for the amount of rent exacted by the U S agents of lead mines from Jos Hardy, for lead mined & smelted upon the land of the Ottowa, Pottawatomie, Chippewa, Winnebago, or other tribes of Indians prior to the purchse thereof by the U S: indefinite.
2-Act for the relief of Elias Hall, of Rutland, Vt, for balance due him for his services as superintendent of repairs of small arms & for subsistence, expenses, & losses while engaged in the service of the U S during the last war with Great Britain: $516.52.

3-Act for the relief of Thos Laurant, surviving partner of the firm of Benj & Thos Laurant: for the amout paid by the firm to Maj Gen Winfield Scott, in Mexico city, for the purchase of a house in said city, out of the possession of which they were since ousted by the Mexican authorities: indefinite.

4-Act for the relief of C Edw Habicht, adm of J W P Lewis: for the balance of his accounts as U S agent for the construction of a lighthouse on Sand Key, in Fla, as stated by the accounting ofcrs of the Treasury: $2,238.47.

5-Act for the relief of Henry Hubbard: for his services as U S agent charged with the safe keeping of the public property at the harbor of Ashtabala, Ohio, as certified by the Bur of Topographical Engineers, with interest, at the rate of 6% per annum, from Jun 11, 1846, from which time payment is shown to have been delayed for want of appropriation: indefinite.

6-Act for the relief of Capt Douglas Ottinger: in full compensation for the use of his invention of the life or surf car by the U S, & also to enable him further to test the practicability of adapting such cars to the rescuing of passengers & crews during violent gales at sea: $10,000.

7-Act for the relief of A Boudouin & A D Robert: for the damage sustained by them arising from the sinking of a flat-boat of ice, at New Orleans, by a steamboat in the service of the U S: $2,000.

8-Act for the relief of Dinah Minis: to pay to her or her legal reps, the sums due on loan ofc certificates, #93, for $37.27 2/3; & #104, for $81.66; all dated Aug 19, 1791, & signed by Richd Wylly, com'r of loans-on the surrender of the said original certificates at the Treasury Dept: indefinite.

9-Act for the relief of Robt A Davidge: for his services as a temporary clerk in the ofc of the 1st Comptroller of the Treasury from Mar 26 to Apr 30, 1857: $118.90.

10-Act for the relief of Saml A Fairchilds: for expenses & services in arresting & bringing to trial certain persons charged with robbing the U S mails, & to pay to him whatever sum he may show, by proper evidence, his expended: $802.50

11-Act for the relief of the rep of Henry King, deceased: for the services of said Henry King in the 3rd Md regt, & in the commissary dept, during the Revolutionary war: $1,817.86.

12-Act for the relief of Wm H Russell: for his salary, as collector of the port of Monterey, Calif, from Mar 13 to Jun 23, 1851: $839.66.

13-Act for the relief of Capt A W Reynolds: to pay the amount of the award of the arbitrators, R T Matthews, Chas I Biddle, & Rush Van Dyke, in the case of the U S against A W Reynolds, with legal interest from Sep 4, 1857, till paid; & to pay to the parties legally entitled the costs, as stated in said award, upon the presentation of the proper evidence & certificates from the U S district court: indefinite.

14-Act for the relief of Wm Rich: for the difference between the compensation allowed to a sec of legation & that to a charge d'affaires, for the period during which he acted in the latter capacity: $830.

15-Act for the relief of Francis Ann McCauley: to pay to Francis Ann McCauley, widow of Danl S McCauley, deceased, late consul general of the U S at Alexandria, Egypt, the

sum of $4,200, for compensation for judicial services performed by her said husband while holding said ofc from Aug 14, 1848, to Oct 26, 1852: $4,200.
16-Act for the relief of Eli W Goff: for damages & losses sustained by his efforts faithfully to execute the revenue laws of the U S: $5,000.
17-Act for the relief of Edw Ingersoll: for the amount of a judgment with cost against him for the hire of carriages use by the board of com'rs, while in the discharge of their duties at Springfield armory: $335.32.
18-Act for the relief of Jas Collier: For the amount, with its interest at the rate of 6%, due from the U S to said Collier in certain action tried & determined in the circuit court of the U S for the southern district of N Y, held on Nov 30, 1855: indefinite.
19-Act for the relief of the assignees of Hugh Glenn: for the balance of a judgment certified by the U S district court for the district of Ky, at the Dec term, 1822, in favor of Hugh Glenn, in a suit wherein the U S was plntf & the said Hugh Glenn dfndnt: $6,971.26
20-Act for the relief of Enoch B Talcott, late collector of customs at Oswego, NY: for the amount lost by him by the robbery of the custom house there, on Dec 9, 1857, whilst he was collector of customs for that district: $452.97
21-Act for the relief of Ferdinand Coxe: for his salary as charge d'affaires at the court of Brazil, from May 12, 1853, to Aug 16, 1853, inclusive; the said sum being the difference between said Coxe's salary as sec of legation & the full salary of charge d'affaires: $662.69.
22-By the resolution for the relief of Wm Hazzard Wigg: to examine & readjust the accounts of Wm Hazzard Wigg, stated under authority of the act of Congress for his relief, approved on Mar 3, 1853, & ascertain the alleged clerical error whereby the sum of $1,560 is supposed to have been withheld: $1,560.

Circuit Court of Wash Co, D C-in Equity. Margaret Chandler, Danl S Chandler, Mary Chandler, Joshua Humphreys, & Margaret Ann his wife, vs Wm Chandler, Walter Hay, Benj E Gantt, Walter C, Mary S W, Ann H, Edw C, Lucy, Richd, Catharine S, & Jane C Gantt, Margaret R Chandler, & Mary J, & Wm L Chandler, & ___ Browne, & ___ Taylor & Mary his wife. Special auditor to report if the lots mentioned in the bill are susceptible of partition between the complnts & dfndnts; & if not, whether it will be for the benefit of the minor dfndnts in said cause & of the widow, Margaret Chandler, & of the other parties, that the same be sold. The parties are notified to attend before me on May 16, at my ofc in Wash, to be heard & offer evidence touching the premises.
—Walter S Cox, Special Auditor

Elias Neville, who has been on trial for several days in the Superior Court at Halifax, N C, for the murder of a man named Phillips, has been found guilty & sentenced to be hung. The Court ruled out the evidence offered by the prisoner to show an attempt, the day before the homicide, on the part of the deceased, to commit an offence upon the prisoner's wife, & the communication of the facts to him immediately preceding the homicide. An appeal to the Supreme Court has been taken.

FRI MAY 6, 1859
We announce the death of Hon J Phillips Phoenix, who died this morning, at his home in N Y C. N Y Express

Orphans Court of Wash Co, D C. Letters of administration on the personal estate of John M Willson, late of Wash Co, deceased. –Rebecca H Willson, admx

Ex-Judge Vondersmith has been sentenced to 21 years imprisonment, to pay a fine of $5,000, & to refund to the Govn't $30,000, the proceeds of his forgeries of pension certificates. Vondersmith is 56 years old.

New Book: The Life of James Watt, by Jas Patrick Muirhead, M A, with illustrations, 1 vol 12 mo; cloth, $1.25. For sale at Taylor & Maury's Bookstore, 334 Pa ave.

The most valuable far in the Southwest Mountains for sale: on May 24, my *Rockwood Farm*, at public auction: contains 324 acres of land. –John Willis, Post Ofc, Orange Court-house, Va.

In Equity, No 1,488. John C Roemmele against Margaret Foley & John & Martin Foley, jr, admx & heirs of Martin Foley. The above named are to appear at the Court house on May 17th, for a statement of the account of the personal & real estates of said M Foley. -W Redin, auditor

In Equity, No 1,366. Geo & Thos Parker & Jos B Bryan against Jas Kennedy, Mary Kennedy, John Magee, & Horatio Browning, adms, heir, & endorser of Patrick Magee. The above named are to appear at the Court house on May 12th, for a statement of the account of the personal & real estates of said P Magee. -W Redin, auditor

Mrd: on Wed, by Rev John C Smith, Geo W Conn to Miss Margaret Ann, daughter of Archibald O Douglass, all of Wash City.

Mrd: on May 5, at the residence of the bride's father, by Rev Saml Rodgers, Mr Harrison P Carter, formerly of Va, to Miss Mary E, daughter of Rev Jas S Petty, of Wash City.

Died: on Apr 12, in Prince Edward's Island, Maud, only daughter of John Hunter, correspondent of the Associated Press.

SAT MAY 7, 1859
The Balt American says: "Col Johnson, brother-in-law of Mr Minister McLane, who was sent by the War Dept to Mexico in the hope that he might secure the right to construct a military road from Arizona to the Gulf of Calif, through Sonora & Chihuahua, which should serve as an entering wedge towards the acquisition of those provinces, has returned without accomplishing anything.

Household & kitchen furniture at auction on May 10, at the residence of the late Jas Maher, corner of 13½ & E sts, by order of the Orphans Court of Wash Co, D C. –Edw C Dyer, Thos J Fisher, excs -Jas C McGuire & Co, aucts

Cmder John S Paine, of the U S Navy, died at his residence in Portland, Maine, on May 2. He entered the service in 1813, &, with the exception of a few intervals, occasioned by illness, continued in actual service for the next succeeding 40 years. In 1853 his health had become so impaired by the fevers contracted while in the service that he was prevented being called upon for actual service, & he was placed upon the retired list. He was about 60 years of age.

Danl Davis, engineer of the steamer **Ocean Spray**, was convicted on an indictment for manslaughter, growing out of the destruction of that vessel by fire, whereby some 10 lives were lost. This is the first conviction ever had under the law of Congress providing for the protection of lives & property on board of steamboats. The case of the engineer on board the ship **Col Crosman**, under a similar indictment for manslaughter, is now on trial in the same court, the U S Circuit Court. –St Louis Republican, Apr 20

New Store! Groceries! -E E O'Brien, s w corner 9th & L sts. [Ad]

Catastrophe on the Pa Railroad, near Greensburg, this morning, when the locomotive exploded, killing John Dodds, the engineer, & Mr Woods, the conductor, instantly, & Jos Speelman, engaged as a fireman on the train, so injured, that he died soon after. -Pittsburg Chronicle of Monday

To Nancy & Phebe Clark, daughters of Jas Clark, of Amelia Co, Va, who left said county about 1796, & went to Albemarle Co, Va, since which time nothing has been heard of them. This is to inform them that their father, Jas Clark, has since died & left an estate, & they are entitled to their portion of said estate. My address is Mulberry Inn, Dinwiddie Co, Va. –Phineas Fowlkes, Com

Notice. I take this method of returning my sincere & heartfelt thanks to all those kind friends & neighbors, as also the press, who manifested such zeal & untiring efforts in searching out the whereabouts of my late husband, John A Cassell, whose mysterious disappearance caused so much solicitude on their part as well as mine. –Eliz E Cassell

Mrd: on May 5, in Wash City, by Rev E A Knight, Mr Elexius Marceron to Miss Martha E Thompson, all of this place.

Mrd: on May 4, at Charleston, S C, in the Huguenot Church, by Rev T R G Peck, Lt J R Hamilton, U S Navy, to Mary Louisa Hamilton, daughter of Wm S Whaley, of S C.

Died: on May 6, in Wash City, Mrs Jane L, beloved wife of Theodore Sheckels, aged 34 years, 8 months & 11 days. Her funeral will be from her late residence, 371 north 7th st, on May 7, at 4 o'clock.

MON MAY 9, 1859

Household & kitchen furniture at auction on May 11, at the residence of Mrs Burk, 456 9th st, between E & F sts. -A Green auct

Public sale of undivided interest in square 133, on Jun 11, on the premises, by an order of the Orphans Court of Wash Co, D C, confirmed by the Circuit Court of Wash Co, D C, I shall sell the undivided 1//3rd interest of the minor children & heirs of Margaret Randolph, deceased, to said square, in Wash City. --Margaret Eaton, Guardian -Jas C McGuire & Co, aucts

Suicide: The Albany Argus says Henry W Preston, once a favorite actor, & for some years manager of the theatres in Albany, drowned on May 3. Of late years he had indulged in drink to excess, & was very poor. An acquaintance heard a fall & a splash.

For rent, furnished or unfurnished, the pleasant residence at N J & I st, formerly occupied by Hon S A Douglas, & last by Hon Bayard Clarke. --J Madison Cutts

Teacher wanted: a Southern lady, as assistant in a young ladies' seminary, located in the village of Lowndesboro, Ala. Address Thos C Bragg, Lowndesboro, Ala.

Mrd: on Apr 18, by Rev B H Nadal, T Hamilton Quinn, of Detroit, Mich, to M Virginia Clarke, of Va.

Valley View will be open for the reception of a few select families from Wash & Lower Va about the middle or last of June. *Valley View* is an old country residence, on the Manassas Gap railroad. Address E S Fisher, Markham Station, Fauquier Co, Va.

TUE MAY 10, 1859

The death of Prof W C Larrabie is announced in the Indianapolis Journal. He was a native of Maine, & nearly 60 years of age. He had been superintendent of public instruction of Indiana, & was one of the proprietors of the Indianapolis Sentinel. [No death date given-current item.]

Alex'r Bell, only surviving son of Mr Bell, residing on 12th st, between G & H sts, was drowned yesterday in the Potomac river, near the Little Falls bridge. He had been fishing with a friend, & the two entered the river to bathe, & as he was an expert swimmer it is supposed that he was attacked by cramp or alarmed by the force of the current. He was in his 21st year, & a student of medicine with Dr Garnett.

The friends of Washington Irving will be glad to hear that his health is now becoming quite settled. He made his first appearance in N Y the other day for the first time in months. He is now past 76 years of age.

The claim of Mrs Cunningham to the estate of the murdered Dr Burdell was set at rest forever yesterday in N Y. Chas Edwards, the counsel for the heirs, took an order dismissing the appeal, for want of appearance on the part of the lady. This put a quietus on all the proceedings, & the lady is once more plain Mrs Cunningham, & not a doctor's widow.

Equity, No 1,456. Mary M Williams against Theophilus Connell, Jane E Connell, Robt A, Sarah W, John F, Jas S, Mary V, & Wilkerson G Williams, & John L Smith. The parties above named, the Guardian ad litem, & the trustee in the cause, are to appear at my ofc in the City Hall, Wash, on May 19, when I shall state the trustee's account, & the distribution of the trust fund & the shares of the parties in the same. –W Redin, auditor

Mrd: on May 5, at Fred'k City, Md, by Rev Mr Seymour, Geo E Curtis, of Gtwn, D C, to Sophie A, daughter of the late Cmdor Stephen Cassin, U S Navy.

WED MAY 11, 1859

Household & kitchen furniture at auction on May 13, at the residence of the late J A M Duncanson, H st, between 9th & 10th sts. Also, by order of the Orphans Court of Wash Co, D C., we shall sell a smart servant, about 22 years old, an excellent cook, washer, ironer, & a fine seamstress, & first rate general house servant. –Martha D Duncanson, admx -J C McGuire & Co, aucts

Criminal Court-Wash-Tue. Hilleary Hutchins & John Jones indicted for the murder of John Ennis of Gtwn on Feb 8 last, were arraigned on May 2. Hutchins is charged with having held the pistol which took Ennis' life; Jones is charged with being a principal in the 2nd degree, having aided, abetted, & countenanced the commission of the deed. Witnesses: Mr Saml Boots, Surveyor of Gtwn, deposed to having made the map handed to the jury, & testified to its accuracy. Crampton Harper saw Hutchins on Potomac st. Mr Cornelius Stribling, a merchant, was a witness. Dr Johnson Eliot examined the wound before death. There was no post mortem examination. Murray Donaldson, age 13, was examined. Mr Wm H Edes testified that Ennis was carried into Murphy's house, & that Ennis said Hutchins had shot him. Chris C Fearson testified to complying with a suggestion of Mr Edes to take Ennis home in the hack after he had been shot. Chris Crouse went with him & David Stacon sat on the box. Wm Mattingly testified to seeing Ennis on Water st.

John Heart, of S C, appointed Superintendent of Public Printing, vice Geo W Bowman, resigned.

The U S frig **St Lawrence**, from Montevideo on Mar 11th, has arrived in Boston. List of her present ofcrs: Flag Ofcr, French Forrest; Capt, John B Hull; 1st Lt, P U Murphy; 2nd Lt, John H Parker; 3rd Lt, H C Blake; 4th Lt, J G Walker; 5th Lt, Wm P Buckner; 6th Lt, W H Dana. Major of Marines, J G Reynolds; Surgeon, Saml Barrington; Passed Assist Surgeon, Geo Peck; Assist Surgeon, Francis L Galt; Chaplain, M R Talbot; Purser, C W Abott; Lt Marines, A W Stark; Midshipmen, R L Phythian, R R Wallace, W E Evans, Geo S Shryock; Boatswain, Wm Smith; Acting Gunner, Robt Owens; Carpenter, W F Leighton; Sailmaker, Geo Thomas; Flag Ofcr's Sec, Geo L Brent; Capt's Clerk, Geo A Sanger; Purser's Clerk, M R Moore. The **St Lawrence** has been absent from the U S since Oct 13, 1856, at which date she sailed from Norfolk.

The sentence of death was yesterday a second time passed upon Stephen H Houser for the murder of John Farrish. The crime was perpetrated at a wayside house in Gasconade Co, 6 years ago. Farrish, as an ofcr, had arrested Houser. Mary Hennessy was the sole person in the house. Houser cut Farrish's throat & stabbed him 4 times. He fled to Calif where he remained in security for 3 years. When he ventured out, he was recognized & arrested. He was found guilty. –St Louis Dem, May 5

Fire & loss of life-from the Watertown [N Y] Reformer of May 6. This afternoon, before assistance could arrive, the east end of the village, the well-known woolen factory, was a mass of ruins. Miss Angeline Sloan, aged about 21, jumped from the 4th story, & died in about half an hour. Mrs Vincent White jumped from the 3rd story, & cannot survive; her spine is broken. Miss Maria Greenwood, aged about 18, jumped from the 4th story, & was badly injured, but may recover. Miss Silvia Blodget jumped from the 4th story, & her life is despaired of. John Shepherd was an object of excruciating suffering, from deep burns. He may survive, but it will be a wonder. Jas M Griffin escaped from the weavers' room with his 7 year old child between his legs. He was badly burnt on his left arm. His child was slightly burnt. Mr & Mrs Marshall were both badly burnt; both may recover. Thos Farrar, badly burnt on the left arm. Thos Osborn was badly burnt. Mrs Eliz Frasch, aged about 26, jumped from the 4th story; cannot survive. Mary Harris, broken ankle, jumped from the 3rd story; is doing well. Mary A Huntley, aged about 24, burnt very badly, but may recover.

On Sat last a train on the Va Central Railroad ran into the carriage of Rev Horace Stringfellow, of Hanover Co, containing Mr, Mrs, & Miss Stringfellow, & Mrs Dr Nelson, of Powhatan Co. The carriage was crossing the track & was not discovered in time to prevent the collision. One of the horses was killed. Mr Stringfellow was terribly wounded; Mrs Stringfellow was badly but not dangerously cut about the head; Miss Louisa Stringfellow was slightly injured, & Mrs Nelson escaped injury. Mr Stringfellow was some years ago pastor of Trinity Church in this city.

Wm Morton Watkins, class of 1792, of Farmville, Va, is said to be the oldest living graduate of Princeton college, & is now 87 years old. He & Bishop Hobart were roommates.

From the Detroit papers: the sentence of 30 days' imprisonment imposed by the U S District Court upon Tyler, for the killing of Capt Jones, expired on May 3. The Grand Jury of St Clair Co, where Jones died, have found an indictment against Tyler for murder, & he has been re-arrested & taken to St Clair Co for a second trial.

In the U S District Court at Pittsburgh, on Thu, indictments were found against John McCleary, Lavinia McCleary, his wife, Jas McCleary, & Eliza McCleary, for counterfeiting the gold & silver coin of the U S.

The Chicago Times gives an accout of the execution there, on Friday, of Michl McNamee for the murder of his wife. The trap fell instantly & the wretched man fell, but, the jerk was so severe that the leather collar broke & the poor man fell 10 feet flat down on the stone floor of the prison below. He was raised by the vigilant ofcrs & carried up the stairs. A length of rope was placed around his neck, & again the wretched man was placed in the proper position on the drop, & launched into the space below. This time the work was better done. The poor man struggled violently, & swung to & fro for some minutes, but his struggles ceased after 10 or 12 minutes.

Spring & Summer Millinery, at Miss E E McDonald, 71 Bridge st, Gtwn, D C. [Ad]

Desirable country residence for rent. A family wishing to spend the summer in the country could not find a more delightful location. Address R D Hall, Beltsville, Md.

Died: on May 9, of consumption, Mrs Ann Hepburn, wife of Jeremiah Hepburn, aged 48 years. Her funeral is this morning at 10 o'clock, from her late residence, 23 East Capt st.

THU MAY 12, 1859
Circuit Court of Wash Co, D C. Re-application for the sale of real estate of J A M Duncanson, deceased: small family carriage & harness, & family horse, at auction, on May 14, in front of the auction rooms. -J C McGuire & Co, aucts
+
By decree of the Circuit Court of Wash Co, D C, passed in said case on May 6, 1859, sale, on the premises, on Jun 6 next, sale of lot 2 in square 374, with improvements-a large brick dwlg house & out-bldgs, it being the residence of the late J A M Duncanson; also, east part of lot 2 in said square; & lot 5 in said square, on the north side of H st, between 9th & 10th sts. We shall also sell part of lot 7 in square 558, at 3rd & L sts north. On Jun 7th, we shall sell lots 34 & 7 in subdivision of square 448; also ½ of lot 5 in square 440. On Jun 8: we shall sell lots 13 thru 15 in square 327; located on 12th st, between Md ave & south G st, on the Island. –W B Todd, F Mohun, J Clark, J Towles, Com'rs -A Green auct

Horace Vernet is going to be married, at the age of 67. The illustrious painter has gained the heart of a widow, Madame Marie Amelie Fuller, whose first husband was M de Bois Richeux.

Chancery sale of valuable improved property: by decree of the Circuit Court of Wash Co, D C, in Chancery, made on Nov 5, 1858, in a certain cause, No 1,409 pending in said court, wherein Abigail C Wood is cmplnt & John M McCalla is dfndnt, on Jun 4 next, public auction of all the right, title, & interest of said dfndnt in & to the western part of lot 18 in square 533 in Wash City, fronting 26 feet on Indiana ave, with a 3 story brick dwlg house & back bldg, the said property being subject to a life annuity of $400.
-W Y Fendall, trustee -Jas C McGuire & Co, aucts

Hon A B Greenwood, of Ark, appointed Com'r of Indian Affairs.

Wash Corp-May 3. 1-Cmte of Claims: bills for the relief of: Peter Lynch, Jas Spaulding, John Allen, & Jas Casparis: passed. Same cmte: asked to be discharged from the consideration of the ptns of of Jas Welsh; Patrick Howlin; Danl W Lane; A Block; & Geo Brown, for the remission of a fine. Same cmte: asked to be discharged from the consideration of the ptn of Patrick Ryan, praying damages for injuries done to his hack & horses: discharged accordingly. Same cmte: adverse to the ptn of Patrick Sullivan, praying the remission of a fine.

The death of the Rt Rev Dr Christopher Bethell, Lord Bishop of Bangor, the oldest prelate on the Episcopal bench, occurred Apr 9. The deceased was born in 1773, & therefore attained the good old age of 86, being 5 years older than the Bishop of Exeter, & 7 years older than the Archbishop of Canterbury.

Mrd: on May 10, in Wash City, by Rev Fr White, Michl Joyce, of Wash, to Miss Catharine O'Connor, of Montg Co, Md.

Mrd: on May 11, J S Wilson to Julia A, daughter of Col Gasynski, of Poland.

Runa Rockwell was married to Rachel Darling 68 years ago, on Nov 11, 1790, he having been born in Feb & she in May of 1773, so that neither was 18 years old when they married. They celebrated their golden wedding more than 18 years ago. They have lived till quite recently on a farm in Ridgefield, Ct, which belonged to Mr Rockwell's father & grand-father, & which he has recently given to a grandson. A tavern was kept here long before the Revolution, as well as long afterwards, & when the British burnt Danbury the father of the present senior Rockwell conveyed his wife & this child, then 4 years old, out of the British line of march, & then shouldered his musket & joined the defenders of Ridgefield. Both he & his wife are still hale in body, clear in mind, & fluent in speech.
-Tribune

FRI MAY 13, 1859
Capt Jos St Aug Bossiere, who was recently shot in a fray at New Orleans by John M Vernon, died on May 1, from his wounds. Mr Vernon was re-arrested & committed to prison to await an examination.

A telegraphic dispatch received yesterday from Memphis announces the death of Mr B Baldwin Stuart, of this place, who had been lingering 2 weeks from injuries received by the explosion of the steamer **St Nicholas**. He was on his way to marry a daughter of the far South. —Staunton Spectator

In N Y, 2 or 3 days ago, John Schmidt, German, killed himself for loss of his wife. She had abandoned him on the plea that he did not supply her with fashionable clothing, & on Thursday swallowed laudanum.

Trial of Hilleary Hutchins & John Jones: 1-Thos Cogan testified to being in Gtwn at the time of the shooting. 2-Jas B Adams, clerk to Mr Stribling, saw Ennis come down the alley. 3-Mr Thos J Williams, police magistrate, had taken the declaration of the deceased shortly before his death. 4-Geo Golding testified to being with Brown at Hutchins' on Feb 8. 5-Mr Baker Thorn testified to being in Gtwn on the occasion of the killing. 6-Mr J Carter Marbury, a member of the Washington bar, saw Hutchins on Feb 8. 7-Mr Ebenezer Irwin testified to the fact of the shooting. 8-Mr Wm G Newman has his establishment next door to Justice Reaver's ofc. 8-Mr Hannibal Clagett Addison was at the door of his warehouse on Water st when he saw Hutchins shoot a man. 9-Ofcr Jefferson Robinson arrested Ennis on Hutchins'-charge against him for throwing stones the previous night. 10-John Donaldson, Capt of the Gtwn Police, made an examination of the premises. 11-Mr Chas Grimes testified to riding with Mr Addison in his buggy from the city. 12-Jas Brown saw Ennis at Mrs Brown's, near the fish dock. 13-Jas W Redrick saw Ennis, Brown, & Golding go into Cox's. 14-Mr Henry Thecker did not know Ennis at all. 15-Grafton Harper was recalled; saw no pistol in Ennis' hand or possession when he went up from the fish dock. 16-Saml Godfrey testified to being with Mr Redrick at Cox's. 17-Jas L Warwick was in Hutchins' when Brown & Golding were there. 18-Mr D J Cox called for the defence; keeps the restaurant close to the Canal bridge, in Market space; had seen John Ennis once; the day he was shot. 19-John Potter lives in Gtwn, & knew John Ennis well. 20-Alex Giles testified he was the other man with Jones & Hutchins at the time Potter called. 21-Mr O'Rourke testified that he knew John Ennis well.

Mrd: on May 9, in Balt, by Rev Dr Heiner, Mr Wm Finley, of Wash City, [formerly of Balt,] to Eleanora, youngest daughter of Saml Jennings, of Balt.

Mrd: on May 11, in Wash City, at the English Lutheran Church, by Rev J G Butler, Mr Wm B Noerr to Miss Mary Virginia, eldest daughter of Amon Duvall, all of Wash City.

Died: on May 12, Lewis R Hammersley, in his 35th year. His funeral is tomorrow at 4:30 o'clock, from his late residence, 13th & F sts north.

Cleveland, May 11. Bushnell, one of the Oberlin rescuers, was today sentenced to 60 days imprisonment in the county jail, & fined $600 & costs. The Ky ofcrs have been arrested on the charge of kidnapping.

SAT MAY 14, 1859
Public auction on May 12 next, by deed of trust from Wm Stonestreet, dated Feb 16, 1858, duly recorded: sale, on the premises, part of lot 3 in square 724. -A Green auct

Valuable improved property on Pa ave, between 21st & 22nd sts, at auction, on May 23, part of lot 14, in square 75, it being the residence of the late Mrs F D Lear, with a brick house; & on lot 15 in square 75, with a good 2 story brick house. -A Green auct

Trial of Hilleary Hutchins & John Jones: 1-J McKinley called for the defence; was living at Hutchins' at the time of the shooting. 2-Benj McGraw knew Ennis. 3-Capt John H Goddard was placed on the stand for the defence. 4-Michl Ruple lives next door but one from Hutchins. 5-Mr J W Boucher heard of the stoning on Monday. 6-Dr Cissel had known John Potter for about 4 years. 7-John Hammond was at a ball with John Ennis on the evening before Ennis was killed. 8-Mr Isaac Sickles saw John Ennis at the ball; as did Robt Johnson. 9-Thos Morgan was at Burch's, on 9th st.

Troy Female Seminary, in operation for nearly 50 years. Circulars may be obtained by application to the principals, Mr or Mrs John H Willard, Troy, N Y.

For sale: one of the most desirable plantations in Louisiana, 15 miles above Alexandria, on Bayou Rapide, in the parish of Rapides, La, containing 1,900 acres of land; with a very good frame dwlg, partly built last year. Apply to the proprietor, on the plantation, or to Mr J Fenwick Young, Wash, D C. –Madison McAfee, Jackson, Miss. -Messrs Block, McAfee & Co, New Orleans, La.

Mrd: on May 12, in Wesley Chapel, by Rev John Lanahan, Wm J Sibley & Dorothea Lowndes, daughter of Wm P Jackson, all of Wash City.

Died: yesterday, Eliz Oliver, wife of Henry Baldwin, jr, in her 24th year. Her funeral will take place at the Church of the Ascension this morning at 11 o'clock. The interment will take place at the family vault at **Kalorama**.

Died: on May 13, after a lingering illness, Alice Stuart, daughter of John C & Ann E Bowyer, in her 14th year.

MON MAY 16, 1859
New Orleans True Delta of May 5: the wife of Hon Pierre Soule died last night, at his residence on Rampart st. We sympathize with Mr Soule in this unexpected bereavement.

Among the Americans in Rome on Apr 16, were ex-Pres & Mrs Pierce; Gen Dodge, late U S Minister to Spain; Senator Sumner, of Mass; Senator Clingman, of N C; Gen Totten, U S Army; Mrs Gen Scott, & a large number of others.

Executor's sale of saddle horse, saddle & bridle, belonging to the estate of the late Jas Maher. –E C Dyer, Thos J Fisher, excs -Jas C McGuire & Co, aucts

Chancery sale of valuable lot of ground: by decree of the Circuit Court of Wash Co, D C, in equity in cause No 1,442, wherein Mary Lyndall is cmplnt & Richd Barry, Wm B Lyndall, & others are dfndnts: public auction on Jun 8 next, of lot 1 in square 879, on East Capitol st & 8th st east. –Richd Barry, trustee -Jas C McGuire & Co, aucts

Prof Dennison Olmsted, LL D, expired at his residence at New Haven, Conn, on May 13, aged 68 years. He graduated at Yale College in 1813. He was beloved as a teacher & a man universally.

Chancery sale of valuable improved property: by a decree of the Circuit Court of Wash Co, D C, in Equity, in a cause, No 1,463, wherein Jas C McGuire & others are cmplnts & Anna E Young & others are dfndnts: auction on Jun 9 next, of part of lot 12, in subdivision of square 74_. Also, a right of way across part of said lot from the outer cellar door of the brick dwlg houses on the premises. –Richd H Clarke, A Austin Smith, trustees -Jas C McGuire & Co, aucts

Dr Wm Sawyer died at his residence, in Boston, last week. He was born in Boston, & was in his day a physician of considerable eminence, but for the past few years has been confined to his house & bed by his infirmities. He had reached his 89th year, & was the oldest living graduate of Harvard Univ, having graduated in 1788. By his death Hon Josiah Quincy, Senior, of the Class of 1790, becomes the oldest living graduate. Of the Class of 1796 four only are now living, -Traveller

The Port Clinton [Ohio] Democrat says that Mrs Peter Perry, whose husband was drowned last week, has since died from the effect of the loss of her husband. Four small children are left orphans, having been rendered fatherless & motherless in just 10 days.

Orphans Court of Wash Co, D C. Case of Sarah H Nourse, guardian. Sarah H Nourse, guardian, reported that she sold to Jos W Nairn, lot 8 & part of lot 9, in square 377, in Wash City, for the sum of $5,000, & he has complied with the terms of sale. -Wm F Purcell, Judge of the Orphans Court -Ed N Roach, Reg/o wills

$100 reward for runaway, negro man Wm Mason, about 25 years of age. He has a sister in Wash, D C, owned by Mrs J M Cutts. –John Hamilton, living near Port Tobacco, Chas Co, Md.

Yesterday some evil disposed hand set fire to the stables & outbldgs attached to the dwlg house on 7th st, between D & E, occupied by Mr David A Winsor. Mr Winsor's loss as tenant will reach $1,000; that of the proprietor of the stables, Mr Geo E Kirk, about $500. The dwlg house also suffered some damage.

Died: on May 14, in Wash City, John Maguire, jr, in his 19th year.

Died: on May 14, in Wash City, Constantine, son of Johanna & Isaac Hill, aged 3 years & 4 months. His funeral is this evening at 4½ o'clock, from the residence of his parents, 9th st, between G & H sts.

TUE MAY 17, 1859
After the sermon, John Hilton arose & addressed the congregation, recently, in the Baptist Church, Yarmouth, Nova Scotia. He sat down & he fell from his seat a corpse.

The undersigned will offer at public auction, in Leesburg, on Jun 13 next, the highly improved far in Loudoun Co, Va, called Somerville, containing 800 acres, binding on Goose Creek, late the property of Mrs Martha S *Blincoe; with a 2 story dwlg, overseer's house, & barn. –The Heirs [Difficult to read-possibly Blincoe.]

Criminal Court-Wash-Mon. 1-John Ogleton, colored, alias John Peeps, guilty of petty larceny in stealing a saw: sentenced to 5 months in jail. 2-Francis Shannon was found guilty of assault & battery on one Slater: sent to the county jail for 2 months.

Mrd: on May 6, in Hamilton, Canada, at the residence of Thos Morton, by Rev Dr Rice, Isaac N Cary, formerly of Wash City, now of the city of Toronto, to Mary E Bibb, of the town of Windsor, Canada.

Died: on May 14, in Alexandria Co, Va, of congestion of the bowels, William J Dawson, son of Thos B & Eliz Dawson, in his 16th year.

Died: on May 16, of scarlet fever, Albert Hunter, son of Thos J & Mary A Galt, aged 5 years & 5 months. His funeral is this afternoon at 4 o'clock, from the residence of his parents, 10 Louisiana ave.

WED MAY 18, 1859
Visitors to *West Point* to attend the annual examination of the military academy, Jun 1, 1859: Hon Augustine Haines, of Maine; Col John T Heard, of Mass; Col Rufus L Baker, of Conn; Gen Geo E Danforth, of N Y; Geo W Cass, of Pa, Capt Thos J Lee, of Md; Hon John Kerr, of N C; Ebenezer Starnes, of Ga; Maj Wm Beard, of La; L R Page, of Miss; Dr John P Barnes, of Ala; Col John Johnston, of Ohio; V P Van Antwerp, of Iowa; Chas Eldridge, of Wisc; Gen J Carraway Smith, of Fla; Gen S B Loury, of Minn; & Ethelbert Hibben, of Oregon.

The Columbia Hotel at Bristol, Va, was burnt on Wed last, with nearly all its contents. The proprietor, Col J C Grant, & his wife, barely escaped with their lives.

A private letter from *Camp Floyd*, dated Apr 21, announces the death of Capt Geo H Paige, Assist Quartermaster of the Army.

Three Years' Lease of the Union Hotel, corner of 1½ & E sts, & valuable vacant lot at 14th & E sts, at public auction, on May 20, on the premises. The Union Hotel was recently occupied by the late Jas Maher, & for many years known as the ***Indian Headquarters***. The vacant lots at 14th & E sts, was formerly occupied as a wood & coal yard. –E C Dyer, Thos J Fisher, excs -Jas C McGuire & Co, aucts
+
Executor's sale of valuable Nursery of Shade Trees belonging to the estate of the late Jas Maher: sale on May 25, on 16th st west, between O & P sts north. –E C Dyer, Thos J Fisher, excs -Jas C McGuire & Co, auct

Dr Abbott, the collector of the valuable gallery of the Egyptian Antiquities, died on Mar 30, at a village near Cairo, Egypt. He was born in London about 47 years ago, & at age 23 received the appointment as surgeon on board a British man-of-war. The Historical Society is now considering the propriety of his collection. –N Y Times, May 10.

Information a day or two by telegraph of the shipwreck of the N Y clipper ship **Pomona**, Capt Chas Merrihew, off Wexford, on the coast of Ireland; owned by Messrs Howland & Frothingham, of N Y C. She left Liverpool on Wed with a crew of 36 sailors in addition to the capt, Chas Merrihew, & with 380 passengers for N Y. The capt, when nearing Tuscar, seems to have lost his reckoning & mistaken his position, for a little after midnight the ship was driven on to a sand bank some 7 miles off Ballyconigar, near Blackwater, the sea making a clear branch over her & sweeping her decks. The capt & 1st mate remained on the sinking ship, the only ofcr in the boat being the 3rd mate, Stephen Kelley, who reached shore with 18 others of the crew, & 3 passengers. List of survivors: Mathew Lees, Bartholomew Reilly, John Raber. Crew: Stephen Kelly, 3rd mate; Richd Long, boatswain; Michl Moriarty, John Smith, Richd Emmett, Thos Barnes, Thos Jordan; John Sullivan, Harry Millar, Rodolph Thom; Jeremiah Williams, Geo McIlvillis, Geo Nott, John Rodgers, Chas Jackson, Chas Thompson, Jas West, Wm Murphy, & John McCormack, seamen; John Meehan, passenger's cook. <u>Cabin passengers lost:</u> Mrs Paxton, a retired officer's widow, & her 3 children. <u>List of the English:</u> Chas Parkinson, John Webster, John Chapman, Wm Randall, Geo Radford, Geo Pale Thorpe, Thos Charnley, Jas Fewkes & wife, John Milles, [or Miller,] Mary Miller, John Primley, Geo Armitage & wife, Fred'k Sugden, Wm Ackroyd, John Edmundson; David, Eliz, Wm, Jos, Mary Ann, & Chas Doubleday; John Seddon; Mary, Wm Ann, Mary Jane, Eliz, & Sarah Ann Whitley; Henry Smith, Betty Giles, & Emma & Harvey Shaw. Scotch passengers: John McCollum & wife, Robt Lyle, Thos Wilson, Wm Taylor, Margarett Scott, John Graham, Jas Keene, & Adam McCoffrey. None of the foregoing were saved. Irish who had engaged passage did not sail in the **Pomona**: Alfred Palmer, Patrick Clary, Teresa O'Neill, Michl Scott, Catharine Looney, Catharine Neilson, Geo Heyn, Catharine Fitzgerald, Thos Taswell, Margaret Casey, Catharine Norman, Bridget Divine, & Robt Mullins.

On May 14, a sailboat containing 4 persons was upset & immediately sunk off the harbor of Wilmington, N C, & all on board drowned: Chas Jennings, of Portsmouth, Va, aged 26; Isaac Taylor, of Pawtucket, R I, aged 21 years; Chas Simpson, of N Y, aged 21 years, [all three seamen;] & Chas Farrow, of Wilmington, aged 15 years.

Excellent household & kitchen furniture at auction on May 23, at the residence of A H Mechlin, 345 19th st, between I & K sts. –C W Boteler, auct

Elegant & superior household & kitchen furniture at auction on May 24, at the residence of Hon Geo Taylor, 27 Indiana ave-***Blagden's Row***, between 3rd & 4½ sts. –C W Boteler, auct

Rich & beautiful farm for sale. I offer my farm *Airley*, in Fauquier Co, Va, adjacent to **Catlett's Station**; containing 1,466 acres: with a commodious dwlg & the usual out-bldgs. Refer to my atty, Rice W Payne, Warrenton, Va. –C J Stovin, P O **Catlett's Station**, Fauquier Co, Va.

Criminal Court-Wash-Tue: 1-Wm Knooks was found guilty of assault & battery. 2-Jas Stanford, colored, was found guilty of petty larceny & sent to the county jail for 1 year.

Mrd: on May 17, at the Church of the Epiphany, by Rev C M Butler, D D, Mr E H Miller to Miss Mary Farnham, all of Wash City.

Mrd: on May 12, at Eudora, by Rev Thos A Ware, Henry E Peyton, of Fauquier Co, Va, to Mary Eliz, daughter of Noble S Braden, of Loudoun Co, Va.

Died: on May 16, Mrs Harriet Fischer, relict of the late Wm Fischer. Her funeral is this afternoon at 4 o'clock, from her late residence. Her friends & those of her brother, Wm Gunton, are requested to attend without further notice.

Died: on May 12, in Balt, Paul Moreau, infant son of Hon D M Barringer, of N C.

THU MAY 19, 1859
The new ***Church of St Aloysius Gonzaga*** is advancing rapidly towards completion, & it is the hope of its learned & esteemed Pastors to have it consecrated to Divine worship early in June. Mrs Young, the accomplished soprano, & other musical talent are now vigorously rehearsing beautiful sacred music.

Jas H Johnson was hung on May 13, at Washington, Rappahannock Co, Va, for the murder of his wife.

Orphans Court of Wash Co, D C. Letters of administration on the personal estate of Jacquelin S Pendleton, late of Wash Co, deceased. –J W Webb, adm

Mrd: on May 17, by Rev Andrew G Carothers, Mr John Leach, jr, to Miss Sarah Wilson, both of Wash City.

Mrd: on May 18, in Balt, by Rev Archbishop Kenrick, Alex'r Johnson to Julia C, daughter of Jos N Hart, of Wash.

Died: on May 17, in Wash City, Geo W Ballenger, in his 44th year. His funeral will be this afternoon at 2 o'clock, from his late residence, Va ave, between 3rd & 4½ st.

Died: on May 18, in Wash City, Alexander C Reno, aged 15 months, infant son of Mary C & Capt J L Reno, U S Army. His funeral is today at 5 o'clock P M from the residence of Wm B B Cross.

Paris, May 7. The death of the venerable Baron Humboldt, of Berlin, is announced.]May 21st newspaper: Alex'r Von Humboldt expired on May 6th last at Berlin; born in 1769.] [May 27th newspaper: Berlin, May 10, 9 A M-the solemn funeral procession of Alex'r Von Humboldt is now on its way to the Cathedral. A line of carriages of immense length closes the procession. The Prince Regent & all the Princes & Princesses are assembled in the Cathedral, awaiting the arrival of the great philospher's mortal remains.]

Austin, Texas, May 11. Capt Brayer entered the Upper Reservation on May 3 with 50 men, killed 15 Indians, & fled. A party of dragoons & Indians were pursuing him. Great excitement existed. The Indians on the Lower Reserve had left their farms for Capt Rio's encampment.

FRI MAY 20, 1859
Henry C Ware, of Youngstown, Ohio, entered a gas receiver to make some repairs without taking the requisite precautions for a supply of fresh air, & was dead when taken out, after being in the receiver 20 minutes.

A day or two ago a young lady, Mathilde Sawyer, residing in Port Jervis, was making her wedding dress, when the fluid in the lamp was nearly consumed. She attempted to fill it with one of the wicks burning. The can burst setting her dress on fire, & she was so burnt that she expired in a short time.

In Equity-No 1,450. Michl Griffith & others, against Michl Cooney, adm, & Danl A Cooney, heir at law of John Cooney. The parties above named, the guardian ad litem of the minor, & creditors of John Cooney are to appear on May 31, at the court house, for an account of the personal & real estate of said John Cooney. –W Redin, auditor

Died: on May 18, at Balt, Mrs Mary Taylor Key, in her 75th year, relict of the late Francis S Key, for many years a resident of Wash City, & author of the patriotic & highly popular song known as "The Star Spangled Banner."

Thos Jefferson Sulter, the new public gardener, has entered upon his duties & has confided the special charge of several divisions to: Mr John Warr, of the Pres' grounds, conservatory, Lafayette Square, & the grounds south of the Pres' House; Mr Jas Stone, of the Capitol grounds, the Circle, the enclosed triangular spaces on Pa ave, & of the trees planted by authority of Gov't on various avenues; Michl Griffith, of the Smithsonian grounds & a portion of the Mall between 12th & 14th sts. Mr Sulter will divide his time in visiting the various sections every day. -Sun

Foreign-May 19. 1-Dr Dionysius Lardner is dead. 2-The Duke of Leeds is dead. [May 23rd newspaper: Dr Lardner was 69; born in Dublin in 1790; his father was a lawyer; young Lardner graduated in 1817 from Trinity College, Dublin.]

Syracuse, May 18. As the morning express train from Buffalo to N Y was passing the crossing a mile west of Jordan, a cow sprang on the track throwing off the baggage & 3 passenger cars. Thos S Gifford, conductor, was instantly killed, & some 15 injured.

SAT MAY 21, 1859
Nonsuch, advertised at auction on May 24, by Geo W Young; & at the same time, his household & kitchen furniture & farming utensils. The property lies on the road leading from Washington to Marlboro. -A Green auct

Obit-died: on May 11, Dr Tomlinson Fort, in his 73rd year; commenced the practice of medicine in 1810; member of the Ga Legislature, & in 1825-6, was elected to Congress, where he served one term, & then resumed his practice. He was made Pres of the Central Bank of Ga & presided over it until its charter expired. -Milledgeville [Geo] papers.

Hon R J Dawson, of **Fort Wayne**, Ind, the Democratic candidate for Congress for the last election, died on May 16.

Rt Rev Michl Portier, Catholic Bishop of the diocese of Ala & Fla, died at Mobile on May 14. He was a native of France, born at Lyons on Sep 7, 1794; came to the U S in 1819, landing at New Orleans; removed in 1825 to Mobile, having been nominated in that year Bishop of the diocese of Ala & Fla.

A Memphis paper of May 9th tells of the death of the oldest son of Hon Alex H H Stuart. B B Stuart is dead; a few days since we announced the said fate of young Gideon J Pillow, of Tenn. It now becomes our paiful duty to announce the death of B Baldwin Stuart, [age 23 years,] of Staunton, Va, who died at Gayoso House last night from injuries received in the late disaster to the steamer **St Nicholas**. It was just 2 weeks last night since the sad accident occurred. Great credit is due to Dr J H Erskine, his physician. His father & mother have been here in the city for several days, & also Dr Lochett & son, friends of his from Louisiana.

Criminal Court-Wash-Fri. 1-Danl Rowland, a magistrate, was found guilty for charging fees beyond the legal allowance & fined $30 & costs.

Hon Mr Keitt, of S C, reached Wash last evening, accompanied by his bride. He was married at Mandeville, S C, on Wed last, to Miss Sue Sparks. They are on their way to Europe, designing to go out in the ship **Persia** on her next trip. -Star

Mrd: on Apr 28, in New Orleans, at the Church of the Jesuits, by Rev Fr Duffoo, Lt L J Smith, of New Iberia, La, to Ann Virginia, daughter of the late Maj Parke G Howle, of Wash.
[See notice in May 23rd newspaper.]

Mrd: on May 16, at Havre de Grace, by Rev Mr Geyer, Mr Geo S Conn, of Wash, to Miss Maria A Donohoo, daughter of the late Capt John G Donohoo, of the former place.

Died: on May 14, at the residence of her brother-in-law, John Bowie, Miss Sarah S Gantt, daughter of the late Mr Levi Gantt, of PG Co, Md, aged 74 years.

Pittsburg, May 20. Christian Jacobi & David S Evans were executed here this afternoon. They were both convicted of having murdered their wives. Evans declared his innocence; Jacobi delined speaking.

MON MAY 23, 1859
Executor's of Edw H Pendleton, deceased, will offer at public auction, on Jun 2, lot 12 in square 580-improved; lot 1 in square 535; & parts of lots 3 & 4 in square 630.
–P P Pendleton, Henry B Tyler, excs -Jas C McGuire & Co, aucts

Excellent furniture in the Navy Yard at auction, on May 25, at the late residence of Cmdor Rudd. -A Green auct

Three young men, two brothers Knight & one named Ed Green, were swamped in a skiff near Long Bridge yesterday, & Green was drowned. He was about 22 years of age, & resided on 13½ st, Island; body was recovered. The Knights were rescued by a boat.

Mrd: on Apr 28, in New Orleans, at the Church of the Jesuits, by Rev Fr Duffoo, Doct L J Smith, of New Iberia, La, to Ann Virginia, daughter of the late Maj Parke G Howle, of Wash. [See notice in May 21st newspaper.]

Circuit Court of D C, in Equity, No 1,401. Thos & Geo Parker & Jos B Bryan, against Jos Edw Roberts, Matthew Roberts, Sarah Roberts, & Wm B Magruder, adm, widow, & heirs at law of John Roberts. The parties named, the guardian ad litem of the minors, & the creditors of the said John Roberts, to appear on May 28 at the Court-house for an account of the personal & real estate of said John Roberts. –W Redin, auditor

In Chancery, No 1,202. John & Jas Hooper vs Ebum Bird, Abel Bird, John H Bird, Susan C Bird, Margaret H Bird, Ann E West, & Robt Henry & Chas Bird & others. Trustees, Wm H Ward & Wm R Woodward reported they sold, in Feb & Apr last, the real estate of Wm Bird, deceased,:Wm T Glaze became the purchaser of part of original lot 2 in square 463, for $1,475; John P West, of lots in subdivision of part of square 463- lot G for $1,600; lot K for $860; & lot C for $99.16; John H Bird, of lots A & B, in square 463, for $378; Wm R Riley, of lot 14, in square 388, for $520-sold at the risk & cost of a former purchaser; & Chas A Alexander, for parts of lots 7 & 8 in square 353, for $625;
& that said Chas A Alexander hath assigned his said puchase to Jane E Gray; & the purchasers have complied with the terms of sale. –Jno A Smith, clerk

Circuit Court of D C-in Equity, No 1,419. John Van Reswick against Geo Page & others. By order of the Court I am directed to state the trustee's account in the said cause, & the amount of any incumbrances on the premises sold to Jos Bryan prior to the claims of said Van Reswick, & whether said Bryan's purchase money is sufficient to satisfy all indebtedness of said Page to said Van Reswick, or for which he is liable & which is secured by the deed of May 1, 1854, or any other deed or agreement of said Page binding the property mentioned in such deed. Parties to attend at my ofc, in City Hall, Wash, on Jun 2 next. –W Redin, auditor

TUE MAY 24, 1859
Chancery sale of very valuable property in Wash City, by decree of the Circuit Court of D C, passed on Mar 24, 1859, in cause between John R Woods & others, cmplnts, & Anna Josephine Brisco, Richd C Brisco, Walter C Brisco, Maria Jane Brisco, & Theodore H Brisco, heirs at law of Richd G Brisco, & others, dfndnts, No 1,227 in equity: public auction on Jun 17 of part of lot 14 in square 255; west half of lot 2 in square 350; & part of lot 9 in square 382. On Jun 22: lot 11 in square 408; & east half of lot 2 in square 633. –Wm R Woodward, trustee -A Green auct

Public sale of valuable bldg lots on the Island, on 6th st west, by the last will & testament of Hanson Barnes, deceased, & an order of the Orphans Court of Wash Co, D C: sale on Jun 16, of lots 18 & 19 in Wm B Todd & Wm H Gunnells' subdivision of square 465. -Alex'r Lee, adm C T A -A Green auct

Valuable lot at auction, by order & decree of the Orphans Court of D C, in Chancery, passed on Nov 23, 1858, in the case of Wm A Richardson, guardian: public sale on Jun 9 next, of lot 16 in square 245, fronting on 13th st, between M & N sts, in Wash City. -A Lloyd, trustee -A Green auct.

Valuable lot at auction: by order & decree of the Orphans Court of D C., confirmed by the Circuit Court of D C, in chancery, in the case of Isabella Johnston, guardian: public sale on Jun 10 next, lot 4 in square 531, subject, however, to the right of dower of the widow. –Isabella Johnston, guardian -Jas C McGuire & Co, aucts

Died: on May 23, Thos W Jones, in his 42nd year. His funeral will be tomorrow at 4 o'clock P M, from his late residence, 303 south B st, Capitol Hill.

Died: on May 23, in Wash City, of dropsy, Edmund Le Roy, eldest son of Dr R B & Mary W Ironside, aged 5 years & 2 days. His funeral is tomorrow at 4 o'clock, from the residence of his parents, 426 N st, corner of Vt ave.

Leslie, the artist, whose death is announced by the Vanderbilt, was born in England, but was the son of American parents, educated in Phil until 16, when he returned to England. He has been a royal academician for 33 years. Two pictures of his were exhibited in London the present year: Hotspur & Lady Percy, & a scene from the Heart of Mid Lothian-Jeannie Deans & Queen Caroline.

The Portsmouth Journal records the death of Mr Jacob Brown, at age 92. His entire property, accumulated during 70 years of active life, amounts to about $50,000. [No death date given-current item.]

Fatal duel at Mobile dated yesterday: Henry G Vick was killed in a duel with Mr Stith, at Mobile. Mr Vick was a native of our city, the only son of Col Henry W Vick. -Vicksburg Southron

Circuit Court of D C, in Chancery. Andreas Fischer vs Geo W Bergershausen, Geo Stoessel, & Chas Walter. This suit is to procure an injunction to enjoin & restrain the dfndnts, their agents, etc, from selling or disposing of certain real estate in Wash City, being part of lot 4 in square 449, & to annul certain deeds made by cmplnt to said Bergershausen, & by said Bergershausen to said Stoessel [dfndnts] of said property. The bill states that said cmplnt, being the owner of said real estate, the said Bergershausen represented that he would purchase the same for a certain sum therein named cash; that say cmplnt, relying on such representations, caused a deed in fee simple to be prepared in favor of the said Bergershausen, &, not suspecting any fraud or deception, delivered said deed to said Bergershausen; that the said Bergershausen had no intention of buying his said property, & that the said deed was fraudulently obtained by said Bergershausen. The bill further states that when the cmplnt discovered the fraud practiced he demanded a return of said deed, but said Bergershausen, instead of returning the deed, had the same recorded among the land records of D C. And, said cmplnt is informed that the said Geo W Bergershausen has made a deed for said property in favor of said Geo Stoessel, of Germany; that the same passed to said Chas Walter, & is now in his possession; that the said deed is null & void, & was made by said Bergershausen the better to carry out his original fraudulent design towards said cmplnt; & that said Bergershausen, after obtaining said deed from cmplnt, suddenly left Wash City; that said cmplnt went after him, & that said Bergershausen has promised to surrender said deed; & said Bergershausen & said Stoessel are non-residents. Absent dfndnts are to appear in this Court on or before the 1st Monday in Oct next. –Jno A Smith, clerk

Many persons in Wash are now laying down water pipes to be fed by the Potomac water supplied by the Gov't, & of sizes less than those which it is most likely will prevail through the city. The minimum pipe to be laid along the streets for general supply shall be 6 inches in diameter; this should be regarded by private citizens, or they may find themselves in unpleasant conflict with the city authorities.

The Pres of the U S has pardoned Alex'r Eggleston, who, for a year past, has been undergoing the sentence of the Criminal Court to 3 years in the county jail for riot & assault on a funeral procession. [May 25th newspaper: The offences for which Eggleston was sentenced were for an assault & for resisting a police officer.]

The 11 year old son of Mr J H Philips, draughtsman in the Patent Ofc, yesterday, fell from a large tulip poplar tree on E st, near 6th, into which he had climbed to gather flowers. He was very much injured & his life is in danger. [May 25th newspaper: the little boy is doing well & gives hopes of final recovery.]

WED MAY 25, 1859
Hon Wm D Bishop, recently appointed Com'r of Patents by the Pres, has entered upon the discharge of the duties of that ofc.

Naval: 1-List of the ofcrs of the U S sloop-of-war **Dale**, just arrived at Portsmouth, from the coast of Africa: Cmder, Wm McBlair; Lts, E L Winder, Francis G Dallas, Hunter Davidson, A Boyd Cummings, & Wm P A Campbell; passed assist surgeon, S Allen Engles; assist surgeon, Richd C Dean; purser, John S Cunningham; boatswain, Chas Hasker; gunner, John Gaskins; carpenter, John A Dixon; sailmaker, S G King.
2-U S brig **Dolphin**, Com Steadman, & brig **Bainbridge**, Lt Com M Woodhull, were at Buenos Ayres Mar 29.

Circuit Court of D C: yesterday the suit of Lucy M Darrell against Walter T Brooke, & the issue involved was the validity of a will of the brother of the dfndnt, Capt B E Brooke, of the Marine Corps, deceased, in which plntf is legatee. The Court granted 5 instructions, under which the jury gave a verdict for plntf without leaving the box, thus establishing the will. The property willed is about $4,000, & is wholly personal. [May 26th newspaper: Regarding the last will & testament of the late Capt Benj E Brooke, of the Marine Corps. This document gave all his effects to his niece, Miss Lucy M Darrell, the propounder of the will, except his gold watch, which it gave to his brother, Walter T Brooke, the contestant, or, in technical language, the caveator of the will. The words of the will are: "To Wm S Darrell, clerk in the Gen Post Ofc, Wash, D C, for Lucy Martha Darrell, his daughter, to whom I wish all my effects to be given except my gold watch, which is to go to my brother, Walter T Brooke, clerk in the Gen Land Ofc, Wash, D C." It is not written by the testator, nor signed or sealed by him, nor was it witnessed. The pecuniary amount is nearly $6,000.]

Excellent household & kitchen furniture at auction on May 31, at the residence of Capt John Patrick, 8th & La ave. -Jas C McGuire & Co, aucts

Mrd: on May 18, at Society Hill, S C, the residence of the bride's father, by Rev Mr Lafar, Hon Lawrence M Keitt, a Rep in Congress from S C, to Miss Susan Sparks.

Valuable homestead farm for sale or exchange for good improved Wash City property: contains 190 acres, in Montg Co, Md, near the 7th st turnpike road; dwlg is 3 stories; with a Switzer Barn, & other out-bldgs. –J M Johnson, Real Estate Agent, 480 7th st.

Valuable estate in Fauquier for sale: I offer my present residence, with six, nine, or eleven hundren & fifty acres attached thereto. The house is large & well built of brick, with necessary out-houses. Apply at the post ofc, the Plains station, Fauquier Co, Va. -Robt E Peyton

Circuit Court of Wash Co, D C-in Equity. John Hooper & Jas Hooper vs Abel Bird, Margaret Bird, Chas Bird, Eburn Bird, John H Bird, Susan C Bird, Margaret H Bird, John P West & Ann E West his wife, & Wm H Ward, heirs & adm of Wm Bird, deceased. The above named & the creditors of Wm Bird, deceased, are to appear before me at my ofc in Wash on Jun 17 next. –Walter S Cox, special auditor

THU MAY 26, 1859
Excellent household & kitchen furniture at auction on May 25, at the late residence of Capt Rudd, in the Navy Yard. -A Green auct

Wash Corp-Mon. 1-Wm H Keilholtz nominated by the Mayor as Com'r of the Eastern Market vice John Castell, declined: referred to the Cmte on Police. 2-Mayor nominated E L Childs as a member of the Board of School Trustees of the 2nd district, vice Erastus M Chapin, resigned: referred to the Cmte on Schools. 3-Ptn of E O Sanderson; & of Alex'r Davis, for the remission of fines: referred to the Cmte of Claims. 4-Bill for the relief of Robt A Waters: passed. 5-Cmte of Claims: bills passed-for the relief: of B J Semmes, Jefferson Baldwin; of Wm Aler; of John Kaehler; of John T Nally; of Jas E Horseman; of Patrick Sullivan; & of Gilbert Vanderwerken.

The inventor of <u>Lucifer matches</u> Mr Jno Walker, of Stockton, England, died recently at the age of 78. For a considerable time he realized a handsome income from the sale of his matches in boxes at 1s 6 d each.

A Little Rock [Ark] man, Cosgrove, has been convicted of the murder of a youth named Lester, & sentenced to be hung on Jun 10. Threats were made to hang the culprit immediately upon the rendition of a verdict provided that verdict was a favorabl one!

On Monday Mr Gifford was conversing with a friend in Syracuse in regard to the death of Mr Bowen, when he remarked it is a mere matter of time with all of us. He was killed by a railroad accident on the following Wed.

Valuable farm at trustee's sale: by a decree of the Circuit Court for St Mary's Co, in Equity, passed Mar 24, 1859, the undersigned will offer at public sale, in Leonardtown, on Jun 21, that valuable estate of which the late John H Bean died seized, called **Part Piney Point**, containing 280 acres, together with 20 acres of detached wood land; improved by a commodious dwlg, & necessary out-bldgs. Mr Jos A Hammett, who resides on the premises, will show the same. –R Ford, trustee

Died: on Mar 9, at Rio de Janeiro, of yellow fever, Nathan H Topping, in his 36th year.

FRI MAY 27, 1859
Adm's sale of wines etc, at the Auction Rooms, on May 30, imported by the late B Schad. –Chas Mades, exc -Jas C McGuire & Co, aucts

In searching for the body of his son, who was drowned through the explosion of the steamer **St Nicholas**, Gen G W Pillow discovered 23 bodies, but his son has not yet been found.

Adm's sale, by order of the Orphans Court of Wash, D C, of the personal effects of the late J A Cassell, deceased. Household & kitchen furniture at auction on May 31, at the late residence of John A Cassell, deceased, Va ave & 7th st. -A Green auct

Mrd: on May 26, in Wash City, at Wesley Chapel, by Rev Dabney Ball, Geo Z Colison to Miss Caroline Furguson, all of Wash City.

Died: Apr 23, at **Camp Floyd**, Utah, Lt E Kane Botts, 7th Regt of Infty, in his 21st year. [May 28th newspaper: died, Apr 23, at **Camp Floyd**, Utah, Lt E Kane Potts, 7th Regt of Infty, in his 21st year.]

SAT MAY 28, 1859
At Denver City, Kansas, Apr 18, two old friends, Capt R F Bassett & John Scudder, fell into a quarrel about opening some post ofc letters. Scudder drew a pistol, a struggle ensued, & when Basset started to go away Scudder fired hitting the Capt. He walked a short distance, fainted away, & in a few hours died. Scudder was bound over to the sheriff, but escaped a day or two after.

Circuit Court of Wash Co, D C, in Chancery, No 1,221. John Van Riswick vs Mary A Ayton, widow & admx, & others, children & heirs at law of Richd Ayton, deceased. The trustee, Chas S Wallach, reported that on Jun 21, 1857, he sold lot 17 in square 435, to John Van Riswick at & for the sum of $286, & he has since complied with the terms of said sale. –John A Smith, clerk

Orphans Court of Wash Co, D C. Letters of administration on the personal estate of John D Schnier, late of Wash Co, deceased. –Margrethe Schnier, admx

Died: on May 24, in his 5th year, after a few hours' illness, Richard Beckett, youngest son of Jas M & Mary E Peyton Torbert.

MON MAY 30, 1859
The will of the late Wm W Cox, of Chas Co, Md, contained the following clause: "I also devise & bequeath that my negro woman Kitty, & her children, John, Catharine, Sarah, & Charles, shall work for themselves by paying the executor annually one cent per year hire." This bequest [the Port Tobacco Times says] fails, in the opinion of Judge Crane, & he has declared it null & void, as against the policy of the laws of the State, as exhibited by repeated acts of the Legislature of Md.

Circuit Court of D C –in Equity, No 1,420. Geo & Thos Parker & Jos B Bryan against Catharine McGee & Chas McGee, reps of Owen McGee, deceased. Parties named & creditors of said Owen McGee, are to meet at my ofc in City Hall, Wash, on Jun 8 next, for an account of the personal & real estate of said Owen McGee. –W Redin, auditor

Mrd: on May 25, 1859, at **Oaken-Brow**, in King Geo Co, Va, by Rev Thos E Locke, Thos M Lewis, M D, of Westmoreland, to Alice, youngest daughter of the late Chas Taylor, of King Geo Co.

Died: on Apr 23, in Shasta City, Calif, from rupture of a blood vessel of the heart, S N Briceland, formerly Lt of the U S Navy, & a native of Steubenville, Ohio.

TUE MAY 31, 1859
Rev Wm H Odenheimer, D D, of Phil, has been elected Bishop of the Protestant Episcopal Church in N J, by the Convention of that diocese. [Current item.]

A teaspoon was recently ploughed up on Stockbridge on the farm formerly owned by Timothy Woodbridge, a Judge of the Common Please Court in 1761, bearing the initials of himself & wife. The field had not been ploughed for 100 years, but the spoon was as good as new.

Trust sale of real estate, by deed of trust executed to the undersigned, as trustee, by David Fisher, dated Jul 21, 1857, recorded in the land records of Wash Co, D C, in Liber J A S, No 152, folios 266 thru 268: public auction on Jun 20, of the south half of lot 14 in square 250, between H & I sts, Wash City, with all the bldgs thereto.
–Sam Chilton, trustee -A Green auct

The landing of the Pilgrims of Md was celebrated at Mt St Mary's College on May 11. Addresses were delivered by Masters John McLaughlin, of Balt, & St Clair Jones, of Louisiana.

Died: on Apr 23, in Shasta City, Calif, suddenly, from rupture of a blood vessel of the heart, Isaac Newton Briceland, formerly Lt of the U S Navy, & a native of Steubenville, Ohio, but for the last 5 years a resident of Shasta, where he was universally respected & beloved.

Died: on May 30, after a protracted illness, Napoleon Koscio_ski, Capt in the U S Infty during the Mexican war-a Polish exile of 1830. Friends & brother Masons are requested to attend his funeral this day, May 31, at 4 o'clock, at the Wash Infirmary.

Died: on May 29, at the residence of her mother, Mrs Hannah Ward, in PG Co, Md, Miss Ellen Ward, in her 20th year. An invalid & sufferer for 8 or 10 years, but in possession of a strong confidence of a happy immortality. Her funeral will take place from the residence of the late Wm J McCormick, Capitol Hill, today at 11 o'clock.

Circuit Court of D C in Chancery, No 1,445. Augusta McBlair, Julia Ten Eyck, & others against John G McBlair, Augusta Ten Eyck, Wm Gadsby, Ann S Newton, Margaret S Chapman, & others, devicees & heirs of the late John Gadsby. I am directed to show whether it is expedient or not to decree a sale of the real estate of the late John Gadsby, in square 167, in Wash, with bldgs thereon. Meet at my ofc in City Hall, Wash, on Jun 8 next, where I shall commence the execution of said order. –W Redin, auditor

WED JUN 1, 1859
Suspension Bridge, May 30. Orliff Olson, clerk of the Grand Trunk railway, at Toronto, was found dead yesterday on the river bank, having fallen from a precipice, a distance over 200 feet. He came to Toronto to celebrate the Queen's birthday, since which he had not been heard of.

Dr John G T Nolston, Prof of Surgery Nat'l Medical College, residence & medical ofc: 536 7th st, near Pa ave, Wash. Over Reily's Confectionary. Ofc hours: 7 till 9 A M, 3 to 5 P M. [Ad]

On Sunday, Jun 15, 1856, 4 prisoners, Moore, Croggon, Bailey, & John H Ray, escaped from the jail of this county. The latter three were part of the then well remembered Naylor gang, which had kept our citizens so long in nightly terror of robbery & violence. In the course of some days all were re-captured except Ray. He went to Va & committed a felony there, was tried, convicted, & sentenced to the Richmon State Penitentiary. The term of his punishment will expire on Jun 6, but the Govn'r of Va has pardoned him out. Yesterday he was brought here & lodged in the edifice from which he escaped.

Obit-died: on Apr 12, in Wash City, after a brief illness, Mr Lewis Robt Hamersley, in his 38th year; a native of Lancaster, Pa, & was bred to the bar. He came to Wash City was known as a prompt & efficient officer. As husband, father, & brother, the deep felt grief of those who mourn his loss in silent anguish attests their affection & his value. –W

Dentistry: Dr D B Closman, 536 7th st, & Pa ave, over Reily's Confectionery store. [Ad]

Died: on May 19, 1859, at his residence, Fleming Co, Ky, Gen Danl Morgan, aged 68. He was son of Capt Simon Morgan, who served with distinction as an ofcr of the Revolutionary war, & brother of the late Cmdor Chas Morgan; was a native of Fauquier Co, Va, but had resided more than 40 years at his late residence.

Circuit Court of D C, in Equity, No 1,465. Richd W Bryan & wife, Ruel K Compton & wife, Geo W Tubman & wife, Chas H Lane & wife, & Mary E Briscoe, cmplnts, against Jane H Dement, widow, John P Dement, Wm B Dement, & Thos Dement, dfndnts. The Court having directed an account to be taken of the real & personal estates of Richd Dement, deceased, & of the debts owing by him, & an inquiry whether it is necessary to sell any part of such real estate, in aid of the person, for payment of said debts; & whether or not it will be to the interest & advantage, not only of the creditors of said Richd Dement, but of the cmplnts & dfndnts above named, his widow & heirs at law, that lots 20 & 21 in reservation no 11, in Wash City, with dwlg houses thereon, should be sold, for the purpose of paying any such debts, & of division among the said widow, in lieu of her dower right, & said heirs at law; notice is given to attend to my ofc in City Hall, Wash, on Jun 23 next. –W Redin, auditor

THU JUN 2, 1859
Died: on Jun 1, after a long & painful illness, Mary, beloved wife of C Stewart, aged about 34 years. Her funeral will take place today at 3 o'clock, from her late residence, 304 8th st north.

Orphans Court of Wash Co, D C. Letters of administration on the personal estate of Benj E Brooke, late of the U S Marine Corps, deceased. –Lucy M Darrell, admx

News by the ship **Asia** announces the death of Jos Sturge, known in England as identified for a lifetime with popular & reform movements, & as an uncompromising opponent of abuses in Church & State. Mr Surge was one of the Society of Friends, & was more distinguished perhaps for his opposition to Church rates than for any other political course of action.

Napoleon Delaplace, a respectable Frenchman, who has been for many years intimate with the family of Rev Dr Verren, pastor of the French Protestant Church in Church st, N Y, on Sunday shot the son of his friend, in the street, & without the least provocation. Delaplace is about 50 years old, & was taken before Justice Brennan, at the Tombs, &, very much to the chagrin of Rev Mr Verren, who did not want him prosecuted, committed for examination. It is believed he is a lunatic, as there was no cause for his conduct.

Orphans Court of Wash Co, D C. Letters testamentary on the personal estate of Patrick Corbet, late of Wash Co, deceased. –Michl Griffith, John Connors, excs

Fort Belknap, Texas, May 22. Express arrived from *Camp Radziminski* with report that on May 16 Maj Van Dorn had a fight with the northern Camanches on a prong of the Arkansas river, killed 40 & took 36 prisoners. Lt Lee & Capt Smith wounded. Several soldiers wounded & 2 killed. The express leaves for Camp Cupee.
–Wm Burkett, Postmaster

Mr John Hadleston Read died at Charleston, S C, on the 23rd ult. He was born in 1788, & was the son of Dr Wm Read, of the Continental army, under Gen Washington. He was graduated at Princeton College, & in early life was an aid to Brig Gen Read. For many years he has been the Pres of the S C Society of Cincinnati, a position which he held at the time of his death.

On the 17th ult the dwlg of A W Parker, of Giles Co, Tenn, was destroyed by fire, & 3 of his daughters, one between 15 & 16 years, another between 12 & 13, & the youngest aged about 7 years, perished in the flames. Two were entirely consumed; the other was rescued by her father, but she was badly burnt & died in about 28 hours.

The residence of Mr Levi Pennyfield, in Montg Co, some 10 miles from Wash City, was destroyed by fire on Friday night last. Two promising lads, sons of Mr Pennyfield, who were asleep at the time could not be reached, & were burnt to death. One was 13 & the other 9 years old.

Orphans Court of Wash Co, D C, May 31, 1859. In the case of Margaret R Wirt, admx of John L Wirt, deceased, the admx & Court appointed Jun 25 next, for the final settlement of the personal estate of the said deceased, of the assets in hand.
-Ed N Roach, Reg/o wills

From the Georgia Gaz: died: on May 18, 1859, at his residence in Greenesboro, Ga, Hon Francis H Cone, one of the most eminent lawyers of the South. He was born in East Haddam, Conn, on Sep 5, 1797, at the family mansion, where his ancestors had lived for more than 150 years. He died the proprietor of his paternal acres, bequeathing them to one of his sons. His father was a soldier in the war of Independence, & participated in several of the sanguinary conflicts of that great struggle. He received his education in Yale College, & graduated with honor in the class of 1818.

Obit-died: on the 16th ult, at her residence on C st, Mrs Harriot Fischer, relict of the late Wm Fischer, & sister of Dr Wm Gunton, of Wash City. Mrs Fischer was a native of England, but had for the greater portion of her time resided in Wash. She had intense devotion towards her daughter & grandchildren.

FRI JUN 3, 1859
Died: on May 31, at Leavenworth, Kansas Territory, after a short illness, Alexander O, son of W O Slade, of Fairfax Co, Va, in his 20th year.

Circuit Court of Wash Co, D C-in Equity, No 1,229. Geo Fitzhugh & Martha L Smith, against Wm Bell, exc, & Leonidas Smith, Jas M Smith, Amelia W Smith, Philip Smith, Catherine A Smith, John Boutwell Smith, Ida Smith, Appollos Smith, & Camilla Smith, heirs at law of Jas M Smith, late of Wash City, deceased. The bill in this case is that the said Martha L Smith, formerly Martha L Boutwell, in 1845, married the said Jas M Smith, & before the said marriage, by agreement between the said parties, the property of the said Martha L was conveyed [the said Jas M Smith uniting in said deed] to the said Geo Fitzhugh, in trust for her sole & separate use; that after the said marriage the said Jas M Smith borrowed from the said trustee, in 1853, the sum of $3,000, to be employed & that the same was employed in bldg upon & improving a lot in Wash City, & afterwards by his deed, dated May 1, 1853, conveyed the said lot to the said Geo Fitzhugh to secure the said debt, in which deed [recorded Sep 21, 1853] the said trust deed from said Jas M & Martha L is in part recited, & the lot thereby conveyed to secure the said debt is described as situated on 12th st, between G & H sts; that the said loan was for a period of 5 years, &, if it was not paid, the trustee was empowered to sell the said property. The bill further sets up that the said Jas M Smith, in his life time, converted to his own use some of the personal property which had been settled by the said deed of May, 1845, to the use of said Martha L, to the amount of about $1,130, which also was to have been secured by a deed on the same property; that no part of either of said debts has been repaid to the said cmplnts or either of them; that the said Jas M Smith died in 1853, having made his will, & appointed said Wm Bell his executor, & leaving the other dfndnts his heirs at law & all said dfndnts reside out of D C. That the said deed from Jas M Smith to Geo Fitzhugh, to secure the said $3,000, is imperfect & insufficient to carry the fee at law, being made to him & his successors instead of heirs, whereas it was intended to vest in him a fee; & thereby he is unable to sell the property. The bill asks for an account of the debts due to the said trustee by said Jas M Smith, & a sale of the said property to satisfy them. Absent dfndnts to appear in this court on or before the 3rd Monday of Oct next. –John A Smith, clerk

Mrd: on Thu, by Rev John C Smith, Wm Thompson [*Paper creased.] daughter of John R Nourse, all of Wash City.

Mrd: on Jun 2, in Wash City, at the E st Baptist Church, by Rev Dr Samson, Robt W Fenwick, of the Scientific American, to Miss Annie E Munson, of Falls Church, Fairfax Co, Va.

Mrd: on May 31, in Wash City, by Rev Dr Cole, Wm T Marshall, of Balt, to Sallie A King, of Wash City.

SAT JUN 4, 1859
In Pontotoc Co, Miss, a man named Holladay waylaid & shot L E D Roberts, a planter, while he was going to church, a few days ago. The neighborhood captured him & hung him. This is the 3rd case of lynching that has occurred in the county within 2 years.

Tornado in Central Ill; letter to the St Louis Republican, dated Jacksonville, Ill, May 27: a house belonging to Jos Fry, about 8 miles s e of here was destroyed; the tenant's wife, Mrs Richd Rout, a child of Mr Geo Vanzant, & a Portuguese boy were all killed. A house belonging to Mr Beford Brown was blown down & his son Saml was killed. A house belonging to & occupied by Mr Barnabas Barrows was destroyed, & 2 of his children are missing. A house 9 miles south of here, owned & occupied by Mr Jesse Henry, was blown down. A house s e of here belonging to Jacob Samples was destroyed, & his son-in-law, a man named Thomas, killed. A man, Jonathan Carlyle, was killed, & his house torn down. On the Great Western railroad 2 cars standing on a switch were run off & turned over on the track. The rain fell in torrents with thunder & lightning.

Friday a small boat upset in the Delaware, & Saml Reiff, 18, & another lad, the son of Alderman Reinl, were drowned. Their bodies were not recovered. –Phil Press, Sat

Fourth District Court-San Francisco: Apr 30, 4 men convicted of murder were sentenced. Wm Morris, guilty of murder in the 1st degree for killing B H Doak, to be hung Jun 10; Henry Wappner, for murder in the 1st degree, killing Louisa Vollmer, to be hung Jun 17; John Reynolds, guilty of murder in the 2nd degree, for killing Chas Mulloy, sentenced to the State prison for life; Geo Gilman, for murder in the 2nd degree to be imprisoned in the State prison 10 years, for killing Shubal S Russel by accident having fired at Whitemore, the keeper of a hotel.

Trustee's sale of a small track of land in Alexandria Co, Va, on Jul 8, on the premises, by deed in trust dated Jun 19, 1856, recorded in Liber R, No 8, page 487, of the land records for said county, containing 33 acres, 3 roods & 30½ perches, with a small dwlg house, half a mile from the farm of the late Andrew Hoover. –Andrew P Hoover, trustee -Jas C McGuire & Co, aucts

Sad accident on Thu, whereby 2 worthy mechanics, Geo Streeks & Wm Offutt, sustained injuries so severe that Streeks has since died & Offutt is scarcely expected to live hour by hour. Partners by trade, they were painting one of the lofty walls in the interior court of Willards' hotel, & were about to stop for the day. Streeks let drop the paint pot he was using, about 35 feet, but pushing the ladder with too much force, it swung too far outward, & he fell over the ladder. Offut moved to save his companion & was thrown over the edge. Mr Streeks died yesterday. Mr Offutt was taken to the Infirmary, where he is lying at this time with fracture of the leg & bones of the chest & several contusions. Mr Streeks lived on 20th st, & leaves a widow & 2 small children. [Jun 6th newspaper: Mr Offutt is doing well & will probably completely recover. He continues at the Infirmary.] [Jun 17th newspaper: Mr W R M Offutt had his left leg amputated on Tue. He died yesterday. His funeral is today at 2 P M.]

J Carbery Lay has opened an ofc, 447 9th st, Wash, as an agent for the transaction of all kinds of business; procuring patents, pensions, back pay, real estate, deed, etc.

Burglary & arson. Michl Doyle, Thos Dillon, John O'Brien, & Mich Macnamara were found with the articles stolen from the stores of Mr Clark & Mr Leddy, grocers on the Island. Information was derived from Mr Jas Larcombe, from a statement made by Robt Binnicks, who were employed in a stonecutter shop together. Binnicks also told him of 4 houses, the property of Mr Geo E Kirk's stable, occupied by Mr David A Winsor as tenent, & the burning of the stable of Mr Ward. The result: discharge of John O'Brien on bail, furnished by his father, for $2,000; discharged Jas Keenan in $500 bail, furnished by his father, & committed for trial, in default of bail, Lizzie Bowen, Wm Richards, Michl Doyle, & Robt Binnicks. [Jun 6th newspaper: Thos Dillon has made a full confession of the many dark crimes charged to have been committed by the united party.]

Mr Geo Henry Moore, Librarian of the N Y Historical Society, lately repeated before the Pa Historical Society his Lecture on the Life & Character of Maj Gen Chas Lee, of the Revolutionary army. Gen Lee was born in England, & entered the British army at age 11; embarked to America in 1773; always been known that Gen Lee was rash, arrogant, conceited, & too much disposed to sacrifice great interests to his own vanity; official documents depicts him in still darker colors. Lee's ambition was to be the cmder-in-chief of the American army; he was created the 2nd Maj Gen in the service, being ranked only by Washington & Gen Ward. He constantly depreciated Washington, & by letters to the New England Govn'r & to parties Congress, to place himself in the position of Washington. After the surrender of ***Fort Washington*** his whole career was marked by disobedience of orders until he was taken prisoner by a detachment of British dragoons under Col Harcourt. He was taken to N Y & lodged in the City Hall, in mortal fear of being put to death as a deserter from the British army or a rebel against the British Gov't. He penned a document, addressed to Lord & Gen Howe, containing a plan betraying the American cause to the British Gov't. Lee again disgraced himself at the battle of Monmouth. He died, without his treason being discovered. He was followed to his grave at Christ Church by all that was most distinguished, both civil & military then in Phil. He was buried with the honors of war; but the traitor, like the murderer, connot rest in peace.

Mrd: on May 22, in Wash City, by Rev Mr Bates, Mr Hiram Leslie to Miss Mary Hinton, of Wash City.

Circuit Court, in Chancery, at Halifax Co, May 14. Eliz Jas Murphy, alias Eliz Jas Sadler, plntf, against Wm W Breedlove, late sheriff of Halifax, & as such adm of Jas Murphy, deceased, dfndnt. The plntf seeking by this suit to recover of the dfndnt the residue [after the payment of debts] of the estate of Jas Murphy, who was born in that part of the dominion of Great Britain called Ireland, & who died in Halifax Co, Va, in 1848, intestate; the court, on the motion of the plntf by counsel, doth order & require that all & every person or person who claim an interest in the said residue as distributee of the said Jas Murphy, deceased, do appear before this Court on or before the next succeeding term of this court. –Jas Medley, jr, clerk -E Barksdale, jr, P Q

Died: on Jun 1, in Balt, Virginia Frances, aged 10 weeks & 2 days, only child of Frank A & the late Virginia F McGee, of Wash.

Valuable farm for sale: by last will & testament of Dr Hanson Penn, late of PG Co, Md, deceased: public sale on Jun 20, at his late residence near Bladensburg, Md, a tract of land on which he died seized & possessed, called **Yarrow**, containing from 100 to 166 acres; adjoins the lands of John C Rives; main dwlg has been erected but a few years. Title is indisputable. –N C Stephen, exc of Hanson Penn

Assassination: St Louis, Jun 3. Jos *Charles, one of the oldest & most respected citizens of St Louis, was shot & mortally wounded on the street this morning by J W Thornton, formerly a tell of the Boatman's Saving Institution. Thornton was tried & acquitted about a year ago of a charge of having stolen $20,000 from the bank, & Mr Charles was one of the principal witnesses against him. [Jun 6th newspaper: Jos *Charless died this morning, Jun 4.] *Two spellings of Charles/Charless. [Jun 8th newspaper: Mr Thornton was charged with the embezzlement of $19,000; Mr Charless was one of the witnesses against him; the trial resulted in Thornton's acquittal. Mr Charless' wife & family request that no violence be used against the prisoner.]

St Louis, Jun 2. The case of Miss Effie Carstang, [age 30 years, daughter of a deceased Methodist clergyman, of humble circumstances,] vs Mr Henry Snow, [age 65 & immensely wealthy,] for a breach of promise of marriage, was decided by the jury today, rendering a verdict for the full amount of the petition of the plntf, $100,000. The counsel for the dfndnt will file a demand to have the verdict set aside, & also petition for a new trial. [Jun 6th newspaper: Snow pursued Miss Effie for 2 years, bestowing gifts upon her. He gave her an elegant piano. The wedding dress was procured & suddenly Mr Snow discontinued his visits. He had the piano removed to his own residence, on the pretence that it was wanted for a musical party. The wealth of the dfndnt was proved to be over a million dollars.]

MON JUN 6, 1859

Chancery sale of valuable house & lot on 4½ st, near Pa ave: by decree of the Circuit Court of Wash Co, D C, No 1,310: public sale on Jun 30 next, all the right, title, & interest of Jas Williams, dfndnt in said cause, in & to lot 27, in Reservation No 10, with a 2 story brick dwlg house. –Chas S Wallach, trustee -Jas C McGuire & Co, aucts

Battle with the Comanches. Our troops in Texas under Maj Van Dorn made another successful scout, & gained a complete & decisive victory over the Comanche Indians. Lt Lee was badly wounded, but it is hoped that he will soon recover. Capt Smith was severely but not dangerously wounded. 49 Indians were killed, 38 captured, & 3 escaped unhurt. –Letter dated in camp, on Big Turtle Creek, May 14.

Mrs Abigail Centre, of Manchester, N H, committed suicide on Tue last by swallowing strychnine. She had just quarreled with her husband.

Hon Cyrus Spinck, member of Congress elect as the successor of Philemon Bliss, in the 14th Congressional district of Ohio, died on Monday last, stricken with apoplexy. He had not yet taken his seat in Congress. —Cleveland Plaindealer

Wm H Robertson, late acting Consul at Havana, died there on May 28 of pulmonary disease. The body had been embalmed, & is to be sent to Phil for burial.

Michl O'Brien, convicted of murder, was hung at Albany, N Y, on Fri last. John H Byers, also convited of murder, was hung at Welland, Canada, on May 31. He was a negro, who escaped some 9 years ago from a Southern State.

Died: on Jun 5, in Wash City, Wm Edwin, eldest son of John & Martha Castel, in his 15th year. His funeral will be on Tue at 4 o'clock, from the residence of his father, 8th st east, between G & I sts.

Died: on Jun 1, in Jefferson Co, Va, of consumption, Richd Henderson, in his 58th year, leaving a widow & 12 children as well as an aged mother & other friends to mourn their irreparable loss.

Orphans Court of Wash Co, D C. Letters testamentary on the personal estate of Harriot Fischer, late of Wash Co, deceased. —W Gunton, exc

TUE JUN 7, 1859
Tornado near Jacksonville, Morgan Co, Ill, on May 26. Houses destroyed: Wm McBride's, near Manshcester, Scott Co, Ill; house of Masters; residence of Wm Wyatt; house of Wm McDonald, himself & wife seriously injured; house of Jesse Henry, family members wounded; Mr Cowell's house, his wife & daughter were dangerously injured; houses of David Taylor & Mr Cowan completely smashed to pieces, but no one of the families much hurt; Mr Sweezy's house blown to atoms, his wife & 7 children escaped with bruises; house of Geo Brown destroyed; house of Mrs Wood, widow, destroyed, some 5 or 6 children in the house were not seriously injured; Mr Robinson's house destroyed, his father & mother seriously injured. The house of Mr Jos Fry, occupied by Richd Rout & Geo Vanzant, renters, torn to atoms. Mr Rout took up a child aged 12 months, & losing his grasp upon the babe it was blown into a cistern & drowned. Mr Scott was killed, & a son of Mr Barrows received a compound fracture of the skull- considered dangerous. The house of Mr Swigart was torn to pieces; he, his wife, & 3 children were saved from death by being blown under the bodies of 3 or 4 large oaks. The house of Wm Craig was torn to pieces. The house of Mr Kirby destroyed, he, his wife, & 2 children much injured. House of Jonathan Carlisle blown away; Mr Carlisle himself blown a considerable distance, found with a piece of timber entirely through his head, & life extinct. His mother & a young lady living in the family are both seriously injured, with little hope of recovery. Peter Davenport's house was unroofed. Jacob Samples, seriously injured, his mother killed, 2 of his daughters badly hurt. Leander

Thomas' house demolished, himself killed, his wife & child slightly injured. Mrs Thomas, with her young child, were found buried beneath the ruins. She received little or no injuries. The houses of Mr Hynes, Mr Long, & Mr Scott were all blown to pieces. Mr Scott & his wife were seriously injured.

The Jennings' Estate. The undersigned, having been requested to go to England to look after said estate, thinks it best to call a convention of the descendants of Cornelius Dabney & Sarah, Saily, or Sallie, his 2nd wife, whose maiden name was Jennings, & died in Albemarle Co, Va, about 1787, & spoke of Wm Jennings & his estate, saying his descendants would get it. She had 6 children-John [my grandfather;] Mary married Christopher Harris; Eliz married Danl Maupin—Harris & Maupin went to Ky about 1788; Cornelius died a young man, & it is thought left no heir; Frances married John Maupin. Great grandmother Dabney left 35 grandchildren, nearly all the names are in my possession. A convention of the above named persons will attend in Charlottesville, Albemarle Co, Va, on Oct 5, 1859. –Chas Brown

Two valuable Va farms for sale: my farm, adjoining Warrenton, Fauquier Co, on the one side & the lands of R C Scott on the other, containing 232 acres; with a large frame dwlg. I will also sell another farm, adjoining the lands of Hon W W Payne & R E Scott, containing about 100 acres. Refer to my atty, Rice W Payne, Warrenton, Va.
–John Smith

Valuable real estate in Gtwn at auction. The subscribers, excs of the late Gen Jas Thompson, deceased, will expose for sale at public auction on Jun 15, all the right, title, & interest of said deceased in the following property in Gtwn, D C, to wit: parts of lots 60 & 61, Old Gtwn, with 2 dwlg house thereon, on the east side of Jefferson st. Also, part of lots 60 & 61, fronting 33 feet, more or less, on Jefferson st, running back with the line of the Canal 107¼ feet. Also, s e part of lot 151, fronting 30 feet on Gay st, 80 feet on west side of Montgomery st. Also an undivided third of lot 223, fronting on 6th st, north side, 150 feet deep. –W H S Taylor, jr; J B H Smith, excx

The case of Andrew Rothwell & others vs the heirs of Wm Dewees & others, in which the title to valuable real estate on the Island was involved, was decided at the late term of the Circuit Court, confirming the title of the dfndnts. The principle involved was, that one co-tenant, without the consent of his companions, cannot buy up an outstanding incumbrance or an adverse title to disseise & expel his co-tenant. Thus plntf in this case in the purchase made by him of the property in controversy is a trustee for himself & wife & the other heirs of the deceased Wm Dewees. For the plntf Jos H Bradley, sr; for dfndnts Edw Swann.

Local Item. We observe that John Cunningham, formerly of the Navy Dept, but some 2 years since appointed Purser in the Navy & sent on duty in one of the vessels of the African squadron, has returned to his home in this city in good health.

Mrd: on Jun 4, at the Wood Park, Orange Co, Va, by Rev Jos Ernest, A F Hayward, of Tallahassee, Fla, to Belle, 2nd daughter of Col Geo Willis.

Mrd: on Jun 2, by Rev Dr Cole, Henry Brown to Miss Annie E Oliver, all of Wash City.

Mrd: on May 18 last, at New Orleans, La, at the residence of Mr Chas Pride, by Rt Rev Bishop Leonidas Polk, Mr Thos S Powell, of Wash City, to Miss Hannah F Rowland, of the former place.

Yarbrough House [in Raleigh, N C,] for sale: at public auction on the first Monday in July next. –Dabney Cosby

WED JUN 8, 1859
White children recovered from Indians: Superintendent's Ofc, Utah, Great Salt Lake City, May 4, 1859. I succeeded recovering 16 children & have them now in my possession. It is said these are all that remains of probably 140 men & women, & children of the Mountain Meadow massacred in Sep, 1857. These children are about 3 to 9½ years old, intellectual & good-looking, not one mean looking child amongst them. 1-Calvin, 7 or 8, does not remember his name, says his family lived in Horse Head, Johnston Co, Ark, & he had a father, mother, & 5 older borthers; killed brothers Henry, Jas, Wm, & Larkin; & 4 sisters, Nancy, Mary, & Martha, his father Jos & his mother Matilda. 2 & 3: Ambrose Miram Taggit, about 7, & Wm Taggit, about 4½ ; the elder says they had a father, mother, & 2 older brothers killed. He says they lived in Johnston Co, & when they left the States had a grandfather & grandmother living. 4-Prudence Angeline, 6; & Annie; had father, mother, & 2 brothers, named Jas & John, all killed. 6-A girl about 4½, says her name is Frances Hawn or Kern. 7-A boy about 3. I have no account of this boy. Those with whom he lived called him Wm. 8-Eliza W Huff, 4. 9-Sophronia or Mary Huff, about 6. 10-Chas Francher, 7 or 8. 1-Annie, about 3½, had a sister. 12-Betsey about 6. 13-Jane, about 4. Have no account of these: 14, 15, & 16: Rebecca, Louisa, & Sarah Dunlap. I learned the children resided in the same neighborhood. –J Forney, Superintendent of Indian Affairs

Ladies' **Mount Vernon Association**: report of the Sec: the additional sum of $10,000 has been paid over to Mr Washington by the treasurer during this month [March] leaving but a little over $30,000 of indebtedness. –Susan L Pellet

Distressing accident. Henry T Barnes, 16, son of the senior editor of the Tribune, was found hanging by a strap from one of the ladders at Detroit, where he had been practicing in a gymnasium. Life was entinct. He connected himself with the Baptist Church about a year since, with an elder brother & sister, & had derived great happiness from his new experience & his church relations.

Mrd: on May 24, in Portsmouth, Ohio, in All Saints Church, by Rev Dr Burr, Mr Thos F S Hall to Miss Sallie Rigdon.

Died: on Jun 6, Clara Brumidi, a native of Rome, Italy, aged 36 years.

Thos O'Donnell was arrested & secured in the county prison for trial for the assault & beating of Justice Curry in his own ofc at the Navy Yard last evening.

Mayor's Ofc, Wash, Jun 7, 1859. Gentlemen elected members of the Board of Aldermen & the Board of Common Council, viz:

Alderman:
Wm B Magruder	Wm F Price
Wm F Bayly	Francis McNerhany
Thos Donoho	Edw M Clark
Wm H Ward	

Board of Common Council:
Chas Abert	W J C Duhamel
John B Turton	E F French
Thos P Morgan	John W Meade
Wm Orme	Thompson Van Reswick
Grafton Powell	F S Ober
Chas S Jones	J H Russell
Lambert Tree	Jas Boisseau
P M Martin	Danl B Clark
Theodore Sheckels	John T Cassell
Elijah Edmonston	John T Given
Wm P Mohun	
-Jas G Berret, Mayot	

The police on Monday & yesterday made exertions to arrest Alex'r Eggleston on a charge of violently assaulting & beating an elderly man at 7th & H sts. Eggleston is believed to have left the city. He is the same who a few days since was pardoned out of jail by the Pres of the U S on the condition of leaving the city, which he has complied with.

THU JUN 9, 1859
The West Point Cadets have written a letter to Miss Cunningham, commonly known as the Southern Matron, enclosing $448, their subscription to the ***Mount Vernon*** fund-$2 from each Cadet.

Mrd: on May 31, in Wash City, by Rev Mr Knight, Mr Chas Stewart, of Callas, Maine, to Henry Ann, 5th daughter of the late Notley S Adams, of Wash City.

Hamilton, Canada, Jun 7. John Mitchell was hung this morning for the murder of his wife. Mitchell confessed the murder.

Headquarters, Wichita Expedition, Camp on Small Creek about 15 miles south of old *Fort Atkinson*, May 13, 1859. I have just come up with an engagement with a party of about 90 to 100 Comanches; 49 are dead on the field, 50 killed a few days previously; 5 wounded; 36 are prisoners of my guard; 100 animals captured; the whole camp is destroyed. Lt Fitzhugh Lee, acting Adj was dangerously wounded; Capt E K Smith– quite severely wounded. Private Willis Borrows, of Co G, killed. Wounded:
Sgt Thos Elliott, Co A, slightly
Pvt Eugene Camees, Co A, dangerously
Pvt Patrick Kenevane, Co A, severely
Pvt Wm Moore, Co A, slightly
Sgt W P Leverett, Co A, dangerously, since dead.
Sgt Peter Alba, Co B, severely
Pvt Isaac Chrisman, Co B, slightly
Pvt Wm Hartly, Co B, slightly
Sgt J W Spangler, Co H, severely
Pvt Rouson, Co H, severely
Cpl Geo Nichols, Co H, slightly
-Earl Van Dorn, Brvt Maj Capt 2nd Cavalry
to Capt John Withers, Assist Adj Gen, San Antonio, Texas
P S: This band of Comanches is a part of the same with whom we had the affair in Oct- Buffalo Humps.

The following is a list of army ofcrs who have permission to go beyond the U S, with the understanding that they are to put themselves in communication with the antagonizing armies in Italy, as as to note military operations, vis: Col W W Loring, mounted riflemen; Lt Col G B Crittenden, mounted rifles; Maj G A Blake, 1st Dragoons; Maj H Brewerton, of engineers; Lt Col E J Steptoe, 9th infty; Maj T B Toner, engineers; Capt H B Citz, 3rd Infty; Capt J A Palmer, 2nd Cavalry; Capt T Seymour, 1st Artl; Lt Geo W Carr, 9th Infty; Lt J C Kelton, 6th Infty; & Lt John Pegram, 2nd Dragoons.

FRI JUN 10, 1859
A party of *Pike's Peak* emigrants, consisting of Aaron Davis, Danl Skinner, Jonah Robinson, & Jacob Wilt, from Gallipolis, Ohio, returned to this city yesterday, having been as far as *Fort Kearny*, on their way to *Pike's Peak*. They started in March last, with a number of others from Meigs Co, with the intention of trying their fortunes in the new El Dorado. At the Fort Mr Davis' party found about 1,000 persons who had come back without gold, but with an abudance of rags, & with an appetite that bordered on starvation. The largest amount of gold in possession of any one, was $2. They saw the tail of the elephant only, & had no desire to see the entire animal. –Cincinnati Gaz

San Antonio, Texas, May 27. The health of Maj Gen Twiggs has changed for the better, but not so decided as to warrant the expression of a confident opinion of his recovery. His only daughter, the wife of Col Myers, U S Army, left New Orleans to attend him, & has reached San Antonio.

Family relations of the Czar & the Emperor. A son of Eugene Beauharmais, who was married to the daughter of the King of Bavaria, married a sister of the present Emperor Alex'r of Russia. Eugene was the son of the Empress Josephine, the first wife of Napoleon. One of her grandsons is the present Emperor of France. Another is the husband of the sister of the Emperor of Russia. One of her grand-daughters by Eugene is the present Queen of Sweden. Another grandson, who is now dead, married the Queen of Portugal. Still another grand-daughter by Eugene is the Empress of Brazil. –Cincinnati Enquirer

Mrd: on Jun 8, in Wash City, by Rev G W Samson, Peter Gooding to Amanda M, daughter of Mordecai C Fitzhugh, both of Fairfax Co, Va.

Mrd: on Jun 7, in Gtwn, D C, by Rev Dr Norwood, Mr Ryland R Weisiger, of Va, to Miss Mary M, daughter of Geo D Abbot, of the former place.

Died: on Jun 9, in Wash City, Caspar, infant son of John & Emily F Wiley, aged 1 year & 5 months. His funeral is this evening at 5 o'clock, from the residence of his parents, 419 5th st, between E & F sts.

Thirty-three Stars must be on the national flag from & after Jul 4th next. This is in compliance with the act of Congress passed Apr, 1848. Oregon was admitted at the last session of Congress as a State of the Confederacy.

Circuit Court of Wash Co, D C: Jas E Morgan & Jas F Slater vs Chas Slater & Saml A Peugh. The object of this bill is for a decree for a sale of the real estate of which the late Eliz Slater died seized. Eliz Slater died in 1855, seized of the real estate mentioned in the bill & largely indebted to cmplnt, Morgan; that letters of administration were granted to dfndnt, Peugh; that her personal property is insufficient to pay said debt; that said real estate is not susceptible of division among her heirs at law; & that the said Chas Slater is an absent dfndnt & prays a decree for a sale of same to pay said debt to said Morgan & that the residue be divided among said heirs. Absent dfndnt to appear at the clerk's ofc of said court on the 3rd Monday of Oct next. –Jno A Smith, clerk

Board in the Country: 8 miles from Alexandria, 10 from Washington. –Mrs Emma Bartlett, Falls Church, Fairfax Co, Va.

SAT JUN 11, 1859
Excellent household & kitchen furniture at auction on Jun 16, at the residence of J H Bradley, jr, 4½ & D sts. -A Green auct

Furniture & effects of the Mexican Minister at auction on Jun 16, at the residence of Gen Robles, Minister, on I st, between Vt ave & 16th st. -Jas C McGuire & Co, aucts

Thos Whipple, for 40 years one of the most active & influential politicians of Rhode Island, died at his residence in Coventry, on Wed, aged 71 years. He was the first elected as representative from the town of Coventry in 1817. In 1820 he was made a judge of the Court of Common Pleas in his native county, in 1827 was elected to the Senate; from this period to 1849 he was elected Lt Govn't, & was frequently returned to the House of Reps. He was last a member of that body in 1856.

Washington Taylor, notorious counterfeiter, with 3 other prisoners, Wm Askins, Wm H Bean, & Jas Fulce, made their escape from the Camden, N J jail on Wed.

Dr King, the wife poisoner, was hung at Coburg, Canada, on Thu. He made a speech on the gallows, declaring his guilt & willingness to die.

Univ of Va, Jun 3, 1859. Shooting affair at this place this morning between Mr J M Bentley, of Ky, & Chas Gachet, of Alabama. The former was seriously, if not fatally wounded. Mr Gachet was admitted to bail. The difficulty originated about the medal which was awarded by the Columbia Society to Mr S L Arrington, of Ala. Mr Baker, of Ky, was contending for it. The night of the election, 3 gentlemen joined the society for the purpose of voting for Mr Arrington. –Richmond Enquirer

Ann Smith College, Lexington, Va, will commence on Sep 1. –Wm N Page, Principal; Miss Sally Lacy Assist in English & Scientific Depts; Maj R E Colston, of Va Military Institute, Prof of French; Prof J L Campbell, of Wash College, Lecturer in Natural Sciences; Dr E A Ludwig, Prof of Music & Drawing; Rev Wm S White, D D, Weekly Lecutres on Scriptures. –Wm N Page, Principal, Lexington, Va

Died: on Jun 7, at Hedgesville, Berkeley Co, Va, Mrs Jane Catharine Wever, consort of Col Caspar W Wever, of Weverton, Md, aged 68 years. She was a meek & lowly follower of the Lamb for some 50 years, & was a bright example of the true Christian.

Died: on Jun 8, at Balt, after much suffering, Mr Robt W Reed, formerly of Winchester, Va, in his 44th year.

MON JUN 13, 1859
The Naval Academy graduates: acting midshipmen who recently graduated at the Naval Academy, arranged in the order of merit, viz:

Wilburn B Hall, Lou
Alfred T Mahan, NY
Saml W Averett, Va
Geo C Remey, Iowa
A Slidell MacKenzie, N J
Norman A Farquhar, Pa
Saml D Greene, R I
Henry R Claiborne, Lou
Chas H Swasey, Mass
Geo A Borchert, Ga
Theodore F Kane, N Y
Beatty P Smith, N Y
C M Schoonmaker, N Y
Hilary Cenas, Lou
Roderick Prentiss, Ind
Roderick L McCook, Ohio

Saml H Hackett, Pa
Gilbert C Wiltse, N Y

Thos S Spencer, Conn
Walter R Butt, Wash Ter

Mr Henry K Brown, the sculptor, with his friend Dr Gibbes, was descending a hill near Columbia, S C, when a span of frightened horses in a heavy farm wagon came suddenly upon them & dashed the wagon to pieces. Dr Gibbes escaped with a few bruises, & after a few days, Mr Brown is now so far recovered that he thinks he will be able to come to Washington for his appointment with his colleagues of the Art Commission.

Sale of pair of horses, calash, & harness, etc, at auction, by order of the Orphans Court of Wash Co, D C, in front of my store, the property belonging to the estate of Mrs Jacqueline S Pendleton. –J W Webb, adm -C W Boteler, auct

Appointment by the Pres: Lafayette M Stiff, of Ala, receiver of the land ofc at Centre, Ala.

Gtwn: my home for a brief period in years long gone; my favorite haunt was the shaded height that skirts the town on the north, **Parrott's Woods**; on the west was a rope-walk, & adjacent to it the elegant mansion of Mr Parrott. Years passed on; another home & other cares were mine. Lately I visited that grove. It is now the resting place of the dead. No spot could have been chosen for a rural cemetery more fitting than this one. It is understood that it is the grant mainly, if not entirely, of our public spirited fellow-citizen, Wm W Corcoran, to the town, or to some religious society of Gtwn. -H

Duel near New Orleans on May 30th between two men named Garcia & Percival, over some trifling matter. Garcia was stabbed in 5 places with a knife & died the next day.

Circuit Court for Montg Co, in Equity. Jas Kilgour & John M Kilgour et al vs Lawrence A Jamieson et al. The object of the bill in this case is to obtain a decree for conveyance from the dfndnts, heirs at law of Mary Ann O'Neale, late of said county, deceased, for all those parts of **Conjurer Detected**, part of **The Token of Love**, & part of **What's Left**, containing by supposition 339 acres, more or less, & which were sold by the late Mary Ann O'Neale to Eleanor Busey, as appears by a bond of conveyance from the former to the latter dated Aug 31,1839, a copy of which is fixed, marked exhibit A. The bill alleges that the purchase money was fully paid by Busey to O'Neale, who by her last wll constituted the late Wm Chiswell her executor, & expressly authorized him to convey the same. Chiswell dying before executing the conveyance, Henry A Jamieson was appointed by the Orphans' Court of said county administrator with the will annexed of said O'Neale, & subsequently by the County Court of Allegheny Co, was appointed trustee to complete the trusts contained in said bill. The cmplnts are advised that the legal estate in said premises have descended to the dfndnts heirs at law of said Mary Ann O'Neale, deceased, viz: Lawrence A Jamieson, of Pa, Henry A Jamieson, Thos D Jamieson, Eliz Bynn, widow, [since dead,] Henrietta Jamieson, Cecilia Jamieson, Catharine, wife of John R Brooke, Rosetta, wife of Richd B Jamieson, all of Alleghany

Co, Md; also, Susan, the wife of John A B Leonard, of Montg Co, Ellen, the wife of J Madison Cutts, & Rose Greenough, widow, of the District of Columbia, & Mary, the wife of John Rowan, of Pa. After the death of Miss O'Neale, Eleanor Busey sold the above lands to Stephen M Lyddane & Thos Lyddane, & afterward, the Eleanor Busey having intermarried with Wm N Austin, the said Austin & Eleanor, his wife, conveyed the said lands to the said Stephen M Lyddane, & the said Lyddanes have sold the same to the cmplnts, Jas & John M Kilgour. The bill prays that all the right, title, & estate, at law of in equity, of the said Mary Ann O'Neale, & the dfndnts, her heirs at law, may, by a trustee to be appointed for that purpose, be conveyed to the cmplnts, Jas & John M Kilgour, & for other & further relief. Non-residents of the State of Md are to appear in this Court on Jun 4 next. –Jas G Hening, Clerk Circuit Court for Montgo Co, Md.

White Hall, Cape Island, [Cape May,] N J, is now open for the reception of visiters. -Saml S Marcy, Proprietor

Mrd: on Jun 7, by Rev Mr Rogers, Signor Antonio Buckignani to Mrs Margaret L Eaton, all of Wash City.

Mrd: on Jun 1, at St Paul's Church, Balt, by Rt Rev W R Whittingham, Mr Wm G Woolford to Miss William Anna Dashiell, both of Somerset Co, Md.

Died: on Jun 11, in Wash City, after a brief illness, Mary L, consort of the late Fielder B Plumer, in her 38th year. Her funeral is this afternoon at 5 o'clock, from her late residence, 319 G st, between 12th & 13th sts.

Died: on Jun 5, at Yadkinsville, N C, in his 44th year, Robt Williams, merchant.

Died: on Jun 11, of scarlet fever, Aaron Lawrence, eldest son of Catherine Glover & Robt H Marcellus, & grandson of Rev Aaron A Marcellus, of N Y, aged 2 years, 8 months & 12 days.

Died: at 11 o'clock, Edward S McPherson, of Wilmington, Dela, son of H H & Eliz H McPherson. [No death date given.]

TUE JUN 14, 1859
The Missouri Senate is holding an extra session for the purpose of trying Judge Albert Jackson, of the 15th judicial circuit, impeached by the House of Reps for alleged official misconduct. In general he has been deficient in courtesy to the bar, & that he has played cards. [Jun 27th newspaper: Judge Jackson is acquitted.]

The Austrian General [Benedeck,] who was wounded in the thigh near Casale, & was obliged to have his leg amputated, has died of the operation. It was whilst superintending one of the unsuccessful attempts to cross the Po, at Frassinetto, that he was wounded.

A destructive fire in Culpeper court-house, Va, on Thursday, destroyed the bakery occupied by Mr Hogg, & the residence of Mrs Jamieson, Robt Williams, & A Pinkard, besides several out-houses. All insured except Hogg.

Jerry Dangerfield, an old lighterman, was found drowned at City Point, Va, on Sunday.

Circuit Court of Wash Co, D C-in Equity. Edw Wheeler, Ann M Wheeler, John A Baldwin & Martha R Baldwin, Philip Whitwright & Eleanor Whitwright, Wm Carter & Caroline Carter, Jas E Morgan, vs Eliz M Garner, Thos M Garner, & the heirs of Richd McConchie. The bill states that lots 19 thru 22 in square 117, were conveyed to Richd McConchie in trust for Barbara McConchie & her heirs; that said Barbara McConchie has died intestate of said property, whereby & by sundry conveyances the equitable title has become vested in the parties aforesaid except said Richd McConchie; that said Richd McConchie has also died, whereby the legal title has passed to his heirs at law, but said heirs are unknown. It further shows that the property is not susceptible of specfic partition among the parties interested, & that it will be for the advantage of all parties to sell the same for the purpose of division, & it asks a decree accordingly. It further shows that the dfndnts are all non-residents. Absent dfndnts are to appear in this Court, on or before the first Mon of Nov next. –Jas Dunlop, Chief Judge -Jno A Smith, clerk

Piney Point Pavilion, St Mary's Co, Md, will be ready for the reception of visiters on Jun 20th. Charges moderate. –W W Dix, proprietor

WED JUN 15, 1859
Public sale of most desirable property in Wash, on Jun 28, on the premises, on Pa ave & C st north, now occupied by C Stott, druggist, & others, being part of lot 5 in square 460. -A Green auct

Public sale of real estae, under deed of trust executed by Saml Strong & wife, dated Nov 24, 1858, recorded in Liber J A S No 165: public auction on Jul 11 next, of all the right, title, interest, & estate, at law & inequity, of the said Saml Strong & wife, in & to all that tract of land lying partly in Wash Co, D C, & partly in PG Co, Md, being part of a tract called **Chillum Castle Manor**, containing 106 acres, together with improvements. -H L Stevens, trustee -A Green auct

Sale of horses, colts, cattle, wagons, carts & wood, at public auction, on Jun 21, at **Linden**, the residence of Theodore Mosher, on 7th st road. -A Green auct

The Emperor of Russia has presented a diamond broach, valued at $5,000, to the wife of Capt Hudson, in acknowledgment of courtesies extended to some Russian officers by him while engaged in laying the Atlantic cable.

The steamboat **John G Lawton** exploded on Thu last, 40 miles from Savannah, Ga, & Master Jas Strobhart was killed, 5 white & 5 colored persons were missing, & several of the crew & passengers severely injured.

At Phil on Wed Richd Vickers, age 36 years, came to his death from taking an overdose of laudanum. A physician had his wife give him small doses. He said it was not enough, & when she was absent he took another dose, the effects of which he died. He was 13 years in the U S Army, & crossed the Rio Grande with Gen Taylor, & was wounded during an engagement for which he received a pension from the Gov't. He leaves no children. -Ledger

A daughter of Mr David Keller, of Stroudsburg, spilt some fluid, which ignited her clothes instantly. She died in a few hours. –Harrisburgh [Pa] Telegraph

Ramsay Crooks, a well known & highly esteemed merchant of N Y C, died on Monday in his 73rd year. In early life he was engaged in the Fur Co under John Jacob Astor, & resided for many years in the n w portion of this continent, now known as the State of Oregon & Territory of Washington.

Orphans Court of Wash Co, D C. In the case of Martha D Duncanson, admx of John A M Duncanson, deceased, the admx & Court appointed Jul 5 next, for the final settlement of the personal estate of said deceased, of the assets in hand. -Ed N Roach, Reg/o wills

Mrd: on Jun 14, by Rev Fr Boyle, Mr Howard H Young, of Fairfax Co, Va, to Miss Florence E Darrell, daughter of Wm S Darrell, of Wash City.

Mrd: on May 10, at Sacramento, Calif, Hon Edw Stanly, formerly of N C, to Miss Cornelia Baldwin, sister of Judge Baldwin, of the Supreme Court of Calif.

Mrd: on Jun 8, at the plantation of the bride, in Madison Point, La, Hon Sherrard Clemens, of Wheeling, Va, to Mrs C E Groves, widow of Horace H Groves, deceased.

Died: on Jun 14, in Gtwn, Andrew Wilson, the youngest child of Alex'r & Anna M Smith. His funeral is this afternoon at 4 o'clock, from the residence of his grandfather, Saml S Fearson.

Died: on Jun 12, at West River, Lucy Ashby, only daughter of Thos H & Helen Gibbs, aged 20 months.

THU JUN 16, 1859
Mrd: on Jun 14, in Trinity Church, by Rev Joshua Morsell, Lt Jos S Skerrett, U S Navy, to Miss Maggie Love, daughter of Capt Algernon Sidney Taylor, of the U S Marine Corps.

Died: on Jun 15, William Leon, infant son of Theodore & of the late Jane L Sheckels, aged 4 months & 17 days. His funeral is this afternoon at 2½ o'clock, from the residence of his father, 371 7th st west.

Died: on Jun 15, Mrs Catherine, wife of Geo Ailier, & mother of P Thyson, in her 77th year. Her funeral is on Friday at 10 o'clock A M, from her residence, 407 7th st, between H & I sts.

Trustee's sale of brick dwlg house on 14th st, between F & G sts, by decree of the Circuit Court of D C, passed on Jan 23, 1859, in a cause in which Christiana McClery & others are cmplnts, & Lawrence W James & others are dfndnts; public auction on Jul 8 next, of the south part of lot 13 in square 253, in Wash City, fronting 22 feet 10½ inches on 14th st, between F & G sts north, running back with that width 100 feet to a wide public alley. –Gilbert Rodman, trustee -Jas C McGuire & Co, aucts

A valuable Negro man belonging to Jas S Garrison, of Princess Anne, while hauling the seine on Lynnhaven beach, about 10 days ago, was pierced in the leg by the sting of the fish called a stingray. He died on Monday last. The immortal Capt John Smith, while exploring the shores of the Chesapeake, lost one of his companions by the same mishap, at the mouth of the Rappahannock, that goes by the name of Stingray Point to this day. -Norfolk Herald [Capt Smith himself was wounded near Rappahannock river by one of those dangerous fish, & suffered greatly, but he finally recovered.]

The conviction & sentence of Felix Sanchez on Sat makes 4 culprits now under the sentence of death in N Y C, who, unless the higher courts interfere, will be hanged at the same time, on the same gallows, on Jul 22, viz:
Jas Stephens, for poisoning his wife
Jas Shepherd, for arson, burning his wife to death
Quimbo Appo, for murdering his landlady
Feliz Sanchez, for murdering his father-in-law

Oswego, N Y, Jun 14. Two murders in the eastern part of this county. One of the victims was the notorious Marvin Green, the parish bully, & the other was Soloman Rima, who was killed by his father, Geo Rima, the mail carrier between Richmond & Redfield.

FRI JUN 17, 1859
Missionaries embarked Jun 13 on the barque **Race Horse** to enter upon their work in the East, under the auspices of the American Board of Comr's for Foreign Missions. They were Rev J F Clarke & wife, who will connect with the missions in North Armenia; Miss Maria A West, who returns to resume her duties as teacher at the Female Seminary at Bebek; Miss Myra A Proctor, who will join the Seminary at Aintab as teacher; & Mrs J W Parsons, who, with her 2 children, returns to join her husand in missionary labors. -Boston Journal, Jun 13

Hon Geo W Dargan, Chancellor of the State of S C, died at Columbia, in that State on Jun 12. He was born in 1802, hence in the 58th year of his age.

Annual exhibition on Tue at the West Point Academy. The following are graduates, arranged in the order of general merit; all admitted to the West Point Academy during the months of Jul & Aug, 1854, their ages respectively at the time being from 16 to nearly 18 years:

1-Wm E Merrill, at large
2-Saml H Lockett, Ala
3-Chas R Collins, Pa
4-Chauncey B Reese, N Y
5-Orlando G Wagner, Pa
6-Robt F Beckham, Va
7-Moses H Wright, Tenn
8-Edw G Bush, Ill
9-Francis L Guenther, N Y
10-Elias B Carling, Md
11-Martin D Hardin, at large
12-Eugene M Baker, N Y
13-Jonathan N Hall, Mich
14-Roderick Stone, Minn
15-Francis J Crilley, Pa
16-Allen L Anderson, Ohio
17-Edwin H Stoughton, Vt
18-Caleb H Carlton, Ohio
19-Jos Wheeler, jr, N Y
20-John J Upham, Wis
21-Abraham K Arnold, Pa
22-Henry A F Worth, at large

Messrs Merrill, Lockett, Collins, & Reese are recommended for appointment in the Engineers, Topographical Engineers, Ordnance, Artl, Infty, Dragoons, Mounted Rifles or Cavalry, being all the corps in the service. Messrs Wagner, Beckham, & Wright are recommended for all the above corps except the Engineers. The orator of the day was Hon John Kern, of N C, introduced by Col Delafield.

Mrs Mary Dunlap, wife of Saml Dunlap, residing in Albany, Ga, was killed by lightning on Jun 4th. –Albany Patriot

Norwich [Ct] Courier: an accident on the Hartford & Providence railroad on Sat, killed Mr & Mrs Meech, when the train came around a curve & struck their carriage. Mrs Meech died instantly. Mr Meech died within the hour.

Three Italians, all natives of Genoa & residents of Richmond, Va, were drowned on Wed last in James river. Their names are Francisco Gevasco, Pietro Mozante, & Jacoma Conio. They were from 23 to 25 years of age. Conio had been a soldier in the Scadinian army, & went through the whole active service of the siege of Sebastopol with the Allies.

Fire last evening in the frame ofc & lime & cement store of Mr W H Campbell, adjoining the canal bridge on 7th st. The fire party accidentally struck down Mr Washington Offutt, a painter by trade, who has been employed at the Navy Yard for a considerable time. He is about 30 years of age, & a cousin to Mr W R M Offut who died yesterday from injuries sustained from a fall while painting at the Willard Hotel. Washington Offutt was taken to the drug store of Z D Gilman, examined by Dr Boyle, & recovered sufficiently to be taken to his home in Gtwn.

Geo Walston, an employe in Garrison's soda & mineral water manufactory in Louisville, was killed on Sat by the explosion of a sold fountain. He was killed almost instantly.

Mrd: on Jun 14, in the Presbyterian Church, on 4½ st, in Wash City, by Rev Dr Sunderland, Myron C Riggs, of the Treasury Dept, to Miss Rebecca, eldest daughter of John Thaw, of the same Dept.

Died: on Jun 16, Mary E, youngest daughter of the late Alex'r Shepherd. Her funeral is this morning at 9 o'clock, from the residence of the family.

Died: yesterday, from an abcess of the stomach, John P, 2nd son of Jas & Mary McGrann, aged 5 years, 3 months & 19 days. His funeral will take place this afternoon at 5 o'clock, from his parent's residence, 291 B st.

Obit-died: on Monday, at his residence in this city, after a lingering & excessively painful illness of several months, Rev Hippolytus De Neckere, S J, beloved pastor of St Johns' [Roman Catholic] Church. He came to Fred'k a confirmed invalid, suffering with the terrible disease which terminated his useful life. He was called to his reward in the very prime of life. [Taken from the Fred'k citizen-published in Fred'k, Md-of Friday last.] -K

SAT JUN 18, 1859
The dwlg house belonging to Wm P Pumphrey, & temporarily occupied by Richd O Mullikin, a few miles from Marlboro, Md, was destroyed by fire on Sunday night last, together with all the furniture, jewelry, plate, & clothing, of its inmates. So rapid were the flames that Mr Mullikin & family barely escaped from the devouring element. This is the second time Mr Mullikin has been burnt out within a few months.

We learnt yesterday that Mr Washington Offutt, who was run over on Thursday, was then in a hazardous condition. His residence is on G st, at the Navy Yard, having removed thither from his former residence in Gtwn.

Died: on Jun 15, at Lothian, West River, Md, Philip J Thomas, in his 77th year.

Died: yesterday, in Wash City, Richard Grafton Hyatt, infant son of Margaret Ann & the late Richard G Hyatt.

N Y, Jun 16. Judge Roosevelt has ordered the arrest of Edw Belknap on the complaint of the Union Bank for fraudulently certifying checks while teller of that institution. The amount of the alleged embezzlement is $16,000. His bail was fixed at $30,000.

MON JUN 20, 1859
Mrd: on Jun 16, in Wash City, by Rev Stephen P Hill, Henry L Reynolds, of Mobile, to Mary Wilson Hill, of Wash City.

Mrd: on Jun 15, at St Luke's Church, Phil, by Rev Dr M A De Wolf Howe, Edw B Jacobs to Emily Caroline, youngest daughter of David Reeves.

Executor's sale of improved & unimproved real estate. The undersigned, excs of the last will & testament of Wm Easby, deceased, in conformity with the directions contained in his will, & by the decree of the Circuit Court of D C, sitting in Chancery, No 1,066, whereas Agnes M Easby is cmplnt, seeking an admeasurement of dower & other relief in equity, & Horatio N Easby & John W Easby, Henry King & Marian his wife, Cecilia J Hyde, Wm R Smit_ & Wilhelmina his wife, are dfndnts, will sell at auction, on Jul 12, numerous parts or parcels of real estate in Wash City. –Horatio N Easby, John W Easby, Agnes M Easby, excs -Jas C McGuire & Co, aucts

By decree of the Circuit Court of D C, in Equity, in a cause pending in said court wherein Geo & Thos Parker & Co are cmplnts & Mary Kennedy & other dfndnts, [No 1, 366,] I will proceed to sell, at public auction, on Jul 12, the east part of lot 9 in square 72, in Wash City, having a front of 20 feet on K st north, extending back that width 75 feet to the rear line of said lot. –W J Stone, jr, trustee -Jas C McGuire & Co, aucts

Correspondence of the London Times. Portsmouth, Jun 3. The ship **Eastern Monarch** left Kurrachee on Feb 22 last, with the following ofcrs & troops on board, for Gravesend: Col Allan, 81st regt, in command; Capt Molesworth, 27th regt, lady & 3 children; Capt Manning, 24th regt; & Capt Stopford, 52nd regt; Lt Clive, 52nd; Lt Gresam, 27th regt; Quartermaster Neville, 70th foot; Assist Surgeon Kidd, 27th regt, in medical charge; 352 men, invalids from various regts in the northwestern province of India; 30 women, & 53 children. Fifteen deaths occurred on the passage home. Lt Col Muter, of the 60th rifles, & lady, & Lt Whish, of the Bombay artl, also came home passengers by the ship. Capt Morris was cmder of the ship; Mr Narracott the chief mate. Touched at St Helena; called at Spithead for supplies, when an explosion took place blowing the cuddy skylights on the poop & carrying away the poop ladders. The after part of the troop deck felt the greatest effects of the explosion. The women & children were berthed in this part of the ship, & one woman & 5 children were killed or suffocated by the explosion.

On Sat at Richards' brickyard, on the Island, a young man, Mr Lemuel Howell, employed in the establishment, &, while passing too near the machinery for the manufacture of pressed brick, his clothing became intangled in the fly wheel. The rapid motion of the wheel took the young man from his feet, & he was precipitated among the press-brick machinery & crushed to death. He was an unmarried man, & resided with his parents on N J ave, near L st. -Constitution

The twin daughters of Abraham Guise, of Gettysburg, Pa, died there recently at age 44 years. They were born & raised together; never separated for a single night; took the same disease, [measles;] died within a few hours of each other, & were buried side by side in the same grave.

Two lads were killed by jumping from a dray, day before yesterday. Two sons of Mr Van, Robt Albert, 14, & Theodore Lewis, 16 were killed. What makes this case more singular is, that Mr Van has lost all his sons by accident-the two above being the last of 11 boys. -Cincinnati Times

Circuit Court of Wash Co, D C-in Equity. Hugh Heaney vs the heirs-at-law of Milton M Bussard, deceased. This bill filed in this cause states that on Dec 7, 1835, Periander L Bussard & Milton M Bussard, heirs-at-law of John R Bussard, of Loudoun Co, Va, deceased, being seized & possessed of a large estate, real & personal, as tenants in common, entered into & made a certain agreement to divide said estate, real & personal, between them, by which agreement said Milton M Bussard, in consideration of certain agreements & covenants on the part of said Periander L Bussard to be done & performed, agreed & bound himself, his heirs, excs, & adms, to relinquish all his right, title, & interest in & to all that piece or parcel of ground lying in Wash City, D C, known as being part of lot 21 in square 168, with improvements, to said Periander L Bussard, his heirs & assigns; & that said Periander L Bussard, having done & performed the agreements & covenants on his part to be done & performed, by deed dated Jun 30, 1838, recorded in Liber W M No 69, folio 477,of the land records for the county & District aforesaid, conveyed said parcel of ground & premises, with the appurtenances, to the said cmplnt, Hugh Heaney; that the said Milton M Bussard has since died without having made & executed any deed or conveyance of said right, title, & interest in & to said parcel of ground & premises, with the appurtenances, to the said Periander L Bussard, or to the said cmplnt, & that who are the heirs-at-law of said Milton M Bussard, deceased, capable of inheriting said right, title, & interest, is entirely unknown to & cannot be ascertained by said cmplnt. The object of the bill is to procure a decree for the conveyance of the said right, title, & interest in & to said parcel of ground & premises, with appurtenances, by the said dfndnts, heirs-at-law of said Milton M Bussard, deceased, to the said cmplnt, his heirs & assigns, at the vesting of the title to the same in said cmplnt, his heirs & assigns. Dfndnts to appear in this Court on or before the first Monday in Nov next. –Wm M Merrick, A J -Jno A Smith, clerk
-C S Wallace, Solicitor for cmplnt

Mrd: on May 10, 1859, at Grace Church, in the city of Sacramento, Calif, by Rt Rev Bishop Kipp, D D, Hon Edw Stanly [formerly member of Congress from N C] to Miss Cornelia M D Baldwin, sister of Judge Baldwin, of the Supreme Court of Calif, daughter of Capt Jo C Baldwin, formerly of Staunton, Va.

Died: on Jun 18, Alice Ramsay Potts, daughter of the late Saml I & M A Potts, in her 17th year.

Died: on Jun 19, Emma Frances, infant daughter of Geo A & Louisa Shekell, in her 2nd year. Her funeral will take place today at 3 o'clock.

St Louis, Jun 17. Geo H Lamb, who was convicted of the murder of his wife by drowning her in the Mississippi river in Dec, 1857, expiated his crime this afternoon. The gallows were erected in the jail yard, & the execution took place at twenty minutes after one o'clock.

TUE JUN 21, 1859
The 12 year old daughter of Harrison Bateman, of Rockingham Co, Va, went with her younger brother to water the cow, when some difficulty arose between them. The brother struck her in the temple with a stone. She later went to her room to rest and when she awoke she was speechless. She soon expired. –Valley Democrat

Died: on Jun 19, in Wash City, after a long & painful illness, Rumina Adelia, wife of Rev J E Parker, of Michigan, aged 36 years. Her funeral is this day at 4 o'clock P M, at the family residence.

Died: on Jun 20, in Wash City, of pneumonia, after an illness of 5 weeks, James Butler Purcell, infant son of Hon Wm F & Mary F E Purcell, aged 2 years & 4 months. His funeral is this afternoon at 5 o'clock, from his father's residence, on Capitol Hill, 316 Delaware ave.

June Term of the Criminal Court-Wash:	Grand Jury:
Wm Gunton, foreman	Geo Mattingly
Geo A Bohrer	Jos Bryan
Stanislaus Murray	Pierce Shoemaker
Eleazer Lindsley	Benj Beall
John F Coyle	Whitman C Bestor
Jas L Edwards	John P Pepper
Francis Mohun	Jos F Brown
Bladen Forrest	Saml McKenney
Philip T Berry	Selby Scaggs
Jos N Fearson	Wm Orme
Wm A Bradley	John Purdy
John Pettibone	Jehiel Brooks

The New Albany [Ia] Ledger says: on Wed Miss Eunice Cooper, a young lady, living in Clark Co, Ind, was struck by lightning & instantly killed. She was in a field near her mother's house.

WED JUN 22, 1859
Lt Duer, cmder of the surveying steamer **Vixen**, died at Apalachicola on Jun 14.

Application was made to the Pres of the U S last week for a pardon to Cyrus W Plummer, now under sentence of death at Boston, Mass, for the murder of Capt Mellen during a mutiny on board the ship **Junior**. The Pres declined to arrest the due course of law.

The U S barque **Release**, Lt Commanding Wm A Parker, one of the Paraquay expedition, has arrived in N Y in 50 days from Montevideo. She brings home as passengers the crew of the late American barque **Austria**, which was destroyed by fire at Buenos Ayres on Apr 7 last. The American squadron sailed from Montevideo for Buenos Ayres Apr 29. Officers & crews all well.

At Campbell Court-house, Va, on Wed last, a difficulty occurred between John D Alexander, clerk of Campbell Co court, & Dr David Bass, in which Mr Alexander shot Dr Bass with a shot gun, & Dr Bass snapped a pistol at him twice. The wound of Dr Bass is not certainly fatal, though exceedingly dangerous.

Hygeia Hotel, Old Point Comfort, Va, located at **Fort Monroe**, will be ready for the reception of visiters on Jun 10. –Jos Segar, Proprietor

Mrd: on Jun 21, at Wesley Chapel, by Rev D Ball, Mr Henry R Champayne, of Balt, to Miss Airey E Wirt, of Wash City.

Died: on May 14, at Florence, Italy, in her 18th year, Martha M, daughter of Cmder S B Bissell,
U S Navy. She had gone to Italy for the benefit of her waning health, & died in the full communion of the Catholic Church, of which she had been a devout member for several years.

Died: on May 3, suddenly, near Fountain City, Kansas, in his 27th year, Edmund Bradley French, only son of Col Edmund French, of Wash City, formerly of Troy, N Y. He lately occupied the post in the U S Patent Ofc, & discharged his duties with marked ability; but, having embibed the spirit of adventure from an excursion to the Falls of St Anthony, he found civil employment irksome, & abandoned it to prosecute a more active career in the stirring scenes of the far West. With comrades & a large party of emigrants, he overcame the dangers of an expedition to **Pike's Peak**, having arrived on May 1 at Fountain city. By the accidental discharge of his fellow-sportsman's rifle, he was shot through the body, & only lived long enough to write a few words of farewell to his family. He lies buried at the foot of Rocky Mountain, on the banks of the Containe que Bouille, near the old Spanish **Fort Puebla**. A grave-stone marks his resting place.

Died: on Jun 21, in Wash City, after a brief illness, John Cartlitch Wiley, son of John & Emily F Wiley, aged 4 years & 21 days. His funeral is this afternoon at 4 o'clock, from the residence of his parents, 419 5th st.

THU JUN 23, 1859
Public sale of valuable bldg lots on the Island, on 6th st west, by the last will & testament of Hanson Barnes, deceased, & on order of the Orphans Court of Wash Co, D C: auction on Jun 28, of lots 18 & 19, in Wm B Todd & Wm H Gunnell's subdivision of square 465, fronting 23 feet 9 inches on 6th st west, between south D & E sts, 120 feet deep.
-Alex'r Lee, Adm, C T A -A Green auct

Criminal Court-Wash-Tue: 1-John H Roy guilty of robbing the dry goods store of Mr John W Lathan, on 19th st, in Mar, 1856; also of robbing the watchmaker's establishment of Mich Hoffa, on Pa ave, between 11th & 12th sts. The Judge understood him to be a married man, & should have supposed that his affection for his wife would have prevented him from the commission of these serious crimes. He was sentenced to 2 years imprisonment & hard labor in the penitentiary, 6 years in all.

Mrd: on Jun 22, in Wash City, by Rev Dr Morgan, Rev T Banks McFalls, of Balt Methodist Episcopal Conference, to Lou E Gobright, only child of L A Gobright, of Wash City.

Died: Jun 15, in Wash City, Jilson J Dove, formerly of Loudoun Co, Va, in his 39th year.

FRI JUN 24, 1859
London Star of Jun 11. The mail steamer **Ethiope**, Capt French, arrived on Thu at Liverpool, with the West African mails. By its arrival we have details of the loss of her Majesty's sloop **Heron**, on May 9, 200 miles from the cost of Africa. She was caught in a tornado & instantly capsized. 107 of the crew were lost. Capt Truscott, his gunner, boatswain, 16 seamen, 4 Portuguese & 2 Kroomen saved themselves in a boat, which was picked up by the ship **Iriam** & conveyed to Sierra Leone. Cmder Truscott, Geo Heydon, boatswain, & Kettle, a private of marines, died on board the **Ethiope**, on the passage to Liverpool, of yellow fever. Previously to her loss the **Heron** captured a slaver, after a chase of 12 hours. The slaver had arrived at Sierra Leone in charge of Lt Chapman & a prize crew.

By decree of the Circuit Court of Wash Co, D C, in Chancery, passed on May 27, 1859, in a cause wherein John C Roemmele et al are cmplnts & Foley's heirs are dfndnts, I shall sell, on Jul 18 next, the north 22 feet of lot 28 in square 105, fronting on 18th st west, between I & H sts, with a neat nearly new 2 story brick house.
–John F Ennis, trustee -A Green auct

Valuable improved property near the Capitol at public auction on Jun 28: sale of parts of lots 11 & 12 in square 659, adjoining the residence of the late Mrs Pendleton, fronting on N J ave, with a well built brick dwlg house, brick carriage house & stable attached.
-Jas C McGuire & Co, aucts

Amongst the items of the Persia's news, the American people will regret the announcement of the death of Mr Gamadiel Bailey, the proprietor & editor of the Nat'l Era, of this city. He was a native of Mount Holly, N J. Seeking relief from a wasting disease in a foreign clime, he died before reaching land, on board the ship **Arago**, on Jun 5. He was accompanied on his intended tour by his eldest son, Mr Marcellus Bailey, who took the remains of his father to Havre, in order to bring them home in the steamer **Vanderbilt** for the U S. He is expected in N Y about Jul 3.

John Morris, stonecutter, about 26, died on Jun 20, in Columbia, S C, by falling from the 3rd story window of his boarding-house. He had seated himself on the window to smoke.

Tragedy at Brooklyn on Wed, when 2 brothers, Thos & Chas Mackey, 10 & 6 years old, quarreled. Chas stabbed Thomas, fatally wounding him. He carried him to his mother, & he died in about 15 minutes.

For sale: the best farm in the neighborhood of Wash, on the Rockville Turnpike, 4 miles from Gtwn, improved a few years ago by John C McKelden: contains 116 acres; dwlg house is plain but comfortable, with back bldgs. Inquire of Mr Keith, the owner, or overseer, Mr Scott, on the premises, or Barnard & Buckey, Gtwn, D C.

Valuable property at private sale, ***Spa Spring Woods***, adjoining the town of Bladensburg, embracing over 200 acres. Also, a number of lots in the village of ***Ellaville*** containing from 3 to 10 acres. –Chas B Calvert, near Hyattsville, PG Co, Md.

Case before Judge Merrick on Tue. John Witmer, of Wash Co, Md, bought certain slaves from the late Gen Lingan, of Md. One of the women thus purchased gave birth to a child who was named Agnes Robinson. The mother of Agnes was set free at some time after the birth of Agnes. Agnes herself was also manumitted by her master, John Witmer, in 1847. Shortly afterwards Agnes came to Wash City to live, with the full knowledge of Danl Witmer, the son of John Witmer, about 1849 herself became a mother. Danl Witner now claims Agnes & her child as fugitives, asserting his property in them under a bill of sale dated 1844. The father, John Witmer, died last summer, & the son made no claim on Agnes until after the death of his father. Further, the bill of sale under which he claims was never recorded in Wash Co, Md, until the present month, though the girl had visited for a considerable time Danl Witmer's place of abode in that county. The Judge held the matter under advisement until Wed, when he refused to allow the introduction of any evidence save such as would go to show that she was not the child born since the residence of Agnes here. Agnes & her daughter were then delivered into the custody of the claimant.

Mrd: on Thu, in Wash City, by Rev John C Smith, Wm L Milburn to Miss Catharine M Eldred, both of Alexandria, Va.

Mrd: on Jun 17, by Rev Dr Tustin, Caspar Smith to Miss Eliz Mayers, both of Harford Co, Md.

Mrd: on Jun 21, in Balt, Md, by Rev N J B Morgan, Columbus V Emich, of Balt, to Ann E Snyder, of Alexandria, Va

Circuit Court of D C-in Chancery, 1,520. Saml J Diggs vs Geo Atkinson & Wm Atkinson. The object of this suit is to procure a conveyance of the legal title to part of lot 8 in square 450, in Wash City. The bill of cmplnt in substance states that said dfndnts, Geo & Wm Atkinson, claiming to be owners in fee simple, as tenants in common, of lot 8 in square 450, by an instrument of writing, under seal duly made & executed on Feb 8, 1836, authorized & empowered one David A Hall to sell certain property in Wash City, including lot 8, at public or private sale, for cash or on credit, & to give full receipts & discharges for the purchase money, & to convey the same to the purchaser thereof, by a good & sufficient deed, with covenants of warranty & title. That said Hall, acting as atty for & in the name of said Geo & Wm Atkinson, on Oct 30, 1838, sold said lot 8 to one J A M Duncanson, for a full consideration in money, & its market value at the time, & on the same day executed & delivered a deed to said Duncanson for the same, containing a covenant of general warranty, & said purchase money was duly paid to said Hall, at atty as aforesaid; that said Duncanson afterwards, namely, on Mar 21, 1839, conveyed to said cmplnt in fee simple all the north part of said lot 8, which has a front on 7 st west of 25 feet, & extending back with width the depth of the lot. It appearing to the satisfaction of the Court that said Geo & Wm Atkinson do not reside in D C: they are ordered to appear in the ofc of the Clerk, on the first Mon of Nov next. –Wm M Merrick, A J -John A Smith, clerk

Criminal Court-Wash-Thursday. 1-Thos C Kirkley was found guilty of assault & battery on a free negro boy, Chas H Dent, by him hired & employed. It appears by evidence that Dent, an indentured apprentice to traverser, had his hands tied behind him, & was severely beaten; he was then tied up by the neck with a rope & left for several hours, his feet barely touching the floor, in a great state of suffering. His cries reached the ears of neighbors, who came to his assistance. Kirkley was sentenced to 6 months in the county jail & fined $20.

SAT JUN 25 1859
Trustee's sale of valuable pieces of land in Montg Co, Md, by deed of trust dated May 24, 1855, recorded in Liber J G H, No 4, one of the land records for said county, in said State, we will sell at public sale, on Jul 16, the tract of land called ***Discovery***, or ***Beall's & Edmonsion's Discovery***, near the land of John Caffey; containing 100 acres of land, more or less. Also, part of a tract called ***Beall's & Edmonsion's Discovery***, as conveyed to Henry Baggerly & Chas Phillips, containing 15 acres, more or less. The improvements consist of a small house & a young orchard in good condition. –Wm H Ward, Jas Y Davis, trustees -Wall & Barnard, aucts

A fine obelisk to Lt Herndon, who was lost in the steamship **Central America**, which is to be placed on the grounds of the Naval academy at Annapolis, has just been completed at Quincy, Mass. The shaft is 18 feet long, 4 feet square at the base, tapers to 1 foot 6 inches at the top, & will rest upon a pedestal 4 feet high, 6 feet square. Upon one side is "Herndon;" upon the other "September 12th, 1857."

Three farms, two of 400 acres each, & one of 337 acres, in Prince Wm Co, Va, for sale: the subscriber, desiring to leave the State, now offers his land for sale: lying north of & immediately upon the turnpike leading from Thoroughfare to Gainesville, 2 stations upon the Manassas Gap Railroad. –Cassius Carter

Court of Equity: State of N C, Alamance Co-Spring Term, 1859. Saml Thompson against Jane & Martha Thompson. It appearing to the satisfaction of the Court that the next of kin of Jas Thompson, to wit, Jane & Martha Thompson, are non-residents of the State of N C, & are supposed to reside in Arkansas, & are the children of the said Jas Thompson, who left an estate in Alamance Co, N C; the said Jane & Martha Thompson are to appear before the Clerk & Master of said county & State, within 6 months, to satisfy that they are the next of kin, or be forever foreclosed from any interest in said estate. Witness, Isaac Holt, Clerk & Master of our said Court. –Isaac Holt, C & M

Notice: Thos H Nelson, late of Craven Co, N C, in & by his last will & testament, hath devised & bequeathed all of his real & personal estate "unto his nephews & nieces, the children of his brother, Wm C Nelson, & the children of his sister, Eliz Wise, [except her son, Jas B_ggs."] The estate of the said Thos H Nelson, deceased, hath been settled, & the subscribers, his executors, are desirous to account with his nephews & nieces as aforesaid, &, as they do not reside in the State of N C, & are unknown to the executors, are to prove their identity, & to come forward & receive their estate.
–John H Nelson, Jas H Mason, trustees, Newbern, N C

Mrd: on Jun 11, at Trinity Church, Galveston, by Rev Benj Eaton, John Thornhill, of New Orleans, to Miss Bettie A, daughter of Alex'r S Withers, of Va.

Mrd: on Jun 24, at Brown's Hotel, by Rev D Ball, Mr G V McGlue to Miss Victoria Smith, both of Va.

Died: on Jun 2, at Coventry, Conn, Mrs Mary S Porter, wife of Dr John B Porter, Surgeon U S Army, aged 29 years.

Chambersburg, Pa, Jun 24. Hon D F Robison, ex-member of Congress from this district, died today from disease contracted at the Nat'l Hotel in Wash in the spring of 1857.

MON JUN 27, 1859
The Republican State Convention of Iowa, on Jun 22, nominated the following: for Govn'r-S J Kirkwood; for Lt Govn'r-N S Rush; for Supreme Bench: L P Love, L D Stockton, & Caleb Baldwin.

Orphans Court of Wash Co, D C. Letters testamentary on the personal estate of Thos W Jones, late of Wash Co, deceased. —Margaret A Hutchinson, excx

Died: on Jun 26, in Wash City, Miss Eliz H Evans, daughter of Benj Evans, in her 28th year. Her funeral is this afternoon at 4 o'clock, from the E st Baptist Church.

Criminal Court-Wash-Sat. 1-Chas Stewart, free colored, found guilty for an assault with intent to kill Greenberry Hurley, agent for J Gibson, restaurant keeper, G & 7th sts. 2-Wm Lawrence, colored, guilty of an assault on a small white boy: sentenced to 8 months in jail. 3-Cornelia Jane Hall, colored, & Antonio Lauri were found guilty of stealing each a pair of shoes: each sentenced to 6 months in jail. 4-Wm Boston, colored, guilty of grand larceny in having stolen a shawl valued at $6: sentenced to 1 year in the penitentiary. 5-Michl Queen convicted of stealing a goblet, the property of Miss Laura Donoho: sentenced to 1 year in the penitentiary.

Died: on Apr 16 last, at Hong Kong, China, Lt Chas Deas, U S Navy.

The steamship **Washington** arrived at Panama on Jun 12 & sailed the next day for San Francisco. The frig **Roanoke** & sloop-of-war **St Louis** were at Aspinwall. The sloop of war **Vandalia** & the sloop of war **St Mary's** were at Panama. Lt Lambert, U S N, died on board the ship **Cyane**, on May 27, at Point Yeason [?] [The [?] is as written.]

TUE JUN 28, 1859
Valuable farm for sale near Port Royal, Caroline Co: on Aug 2, on the premises, 600 acres, being a portion of the estate called *Gay Mont*, the residence of the late John H Bernard; no bldgs except a good overseer's house & a double cabin for negroes. Address Powhatan Robertson, Racoon Ford, Culpeper Co, or M P Scott, Warrenton Springs, Fauquier Co, Va. —Powhatan Robertson, M P Scott, excs of J H Barnard

Orphans Court of Wash Co, D C. Letters of administration on the personal estate of Andrew D Birch, late of Wash Co, deceased. —Susannah C Birch, admx

Died: on Jun 23, after a short illness, at the *Vale of Benjamin*, his residence in PG Co, Md, Zachariah B Beall, in his 35th year. He had many estimable qualities, which endeared him to a large circle of friends & acquaintances.

WED JUN 29, 1859
Mrd: on Jun 22, at Morley's Hotel, Trafalgar Square, London, by Rev Frederic C Finch, Geo May, of Balt, to Eliz Arabella, youngest daughter of the late John J Palmer, of N Y.

In the death of Prince Metternich, which took place on Jun 11, Europe has lost one of her most celebrated statesmen, whose council's at one time dominated every European Cabinet. He was born at Coblentz on May 15, 1773, & therefore completed his 86th year before he died.

Died: on Jun 28, after a severe & painful illness, Washington Lewis, in his 62nd year. His funeral is on Thu morning, from his late residence, 581 I st, between 4th & 5th sts.

Died: on Jun 28, after a long & painful illness, Janet B, relict of the late Enock W Smallwood, in her 48th year. Her funeral is on Jun 30, at 4 o'clock, from her late residence, corner of south A & 6th sts east.

Chicago, Jun 28. Accident last night on the Michigan Southern railroad near South Bend. It was caused by the washing away of a culvert. Among those killed are the express messenger, the engineer, fireman, the baggage-master, Mrs E P Gillett & child, of Stone Mills, of N Y, & Thos Wisham, of Mich City. Wounded was W J Hawk, of Charleston, Va. The passengers were, for the greater part, residents of the West.

THU JUN 30, 1859
Circuit Court of D C-in Chancery, #1,522. Wm W Corcoran & Geo W Riggs vs Henry C Mathews, Wm M Corcoran, Christopher N Thom, Sarah C Thom, W Alex'r Kirk, Martha E Kirk, John C Fremont, Richd Taylor Jacobs, & others. The object of this suit is to procure the appointment of a trustee in the stead of Thos Corcoran, deceased, to carry out the trusts of the deed herein after mentioned. The bill alleges, on or about May 14, 1845, the late Thos Hart Benton & wife conveyed to the said Thos Corcoran, his heirs & assigns, all that part of lot 28 in Reservation 10, in Wash City, in trust to secure the payment of a certain indebtment of $4,000 from the said Thos Hart Benton to the said cmplnts, Wm W Corcoran & Geo W Riggs; that the said debt is past due & unpaid; that since the execution of the said deed the said Thos Corcoran hath departed this life, having first duly made his will, thereby devising all his real estate to Henry C Matthews, his heirs & assigns, in trust to sell & dispose of the same, & to divide the proceeds thereof among the heirs at law of the said Thos Corcoran are as follows, ot wit: Wm M Corcoran, Sarah N Thom, Emily Corcoran, Martha E Corcoran, who hath intermarried with one W Alex'r Kirk, & Jas W Corcoran; that since the delivery of the said deed the said Thos Hart Benton hath also departed this life, having first duly made his will, thereby giving & devising the said parcel of ground to Wm Carey Jones, John C Fremont, Richd Taylor Jacobs, Montgomery Blair, Saml Phillips Lee, & the survivor of them, his heirs & assigns in trust, for the sole & separate use of Eliza P C Jones, the wife of the said Wm Carey Jones; but it is necessary that the said Court should appoint a new trustee in the place of the said Thos Corcoran, deceased, to execute & carry out the trust in the said deed limited & set forth, & that the said Wm M Corcoran, Christopher N Thom, Sarah C Thom, W Alex'r Kirk, Martha E Kirk, John C Fremont & Richd Taylor Jacobs, are non-residents, living beyond the limits of the District. Said absent dfndnts are to appear in the ofc of the Clerk on the first Monday in Nov next. –Wm M Merrick, A J -Jno A Smith, clerk

Trustee's sale of valuable real estate: by deed of trust from Chas H Winder & wife, dated Mar 14, 1855, recorded in Liber J A S No 103, folios 59, of the land records of Wash Co, D C: sale on Jul 11th next, of lot 1 in square 170, in Wash City; also, all that part of lot 2 in said subdivision, adjoining said lot 1, on 18th st west. –W D Davidge, trustee
-A Green auct

Obit-private advices from China announce the death at Shanghai, on Apr 9, of Rev Wm Allen Macy, one of the missionaries of the American Board. He was a nephew of the late Benj F Butler, & left this country for his missionary field in Nov, 1854. He was attacked by the disease [a malignant form of small-pox] which cut short his career. -N Y Post

Died: on Jun 29, in Wash City, after a lingering illness, Jane H, wife of John Lane, aged 49 years. Her funeral will be this afternoon, at 2½ o'clock, from her late residence, Temperance Alley.

Died: on Jun 29, in Wash City, Washington Deane, infant son of John S & Mary Hollingshead, aged 18 months.

Annual Commencement of Columbian College took place yesterday in the E St Baptist Church; officiating chairman was Dr Ruggles; prayer by Rev John C Smith; first orator was Mr Chas W Hassler, of Wash; next was one by Mr Saml R White, of Bedford Co, Va; next was Mr Jos F Deans, of Norfolk Co, Va; then a poem in blank verse, by Mr W A Harris, jr, of Pike Co, Mo; 6th oration by Mr John H Wright, of Nansemond Co, Va. Mr John T Griffin, of Nansemond Co, Va, traced the history of the principal of human self-gov't from the commencement of the Christian era. The next oration was by Mr Wm S Wright, of Nansemond Co, Va.; the last one by Mr Wm Y Titcomb, A B, of Alabama. Medals were awarded to Mr Wm S Wright, of the senior class; the second to Mr John Pollard, jr, of the jr class; honorable mention to Mr John M Clampitt, of Wash. Degrees conferred on: candidates for the Degree of Bachelor of Philosophy: Wm Alex'r Harris, jr, of Mo. Candidates for the Degree of Bachelor of Arts: Jos F Deans, John Thos Griffin, Trezevant Harrison, of Va; Chas Wm Hassler, of Wash; Saml Richerson Waite, John Henry Wright, Wm Stephen Wright, of Va. Degree of Master of Arts: Edw J Cuil/Cull, D C. In Course: Jas G Board, Mahlon A Hensley, of Va; Bradford A Lincoln, of N Y; Marshall W Read, of Va; Wm Y Titcomb, of Ala; Chas H Uttermuhle, of Wash. The degree of Dr in Divinity was conferred on Rev Jas P Boyce, of S C, & that of A M on John R Thompson, of Richmond, Va.

Chicago, Jun 28. Accident last night on the Michigan Southern railroad near South Bend. It was caused by the washing away of a culvert. Among those killed are: Hartwell, express messenger; engineer & fireman, both named Chulp; Babbington, baggage-master; C W Smith, road master; Mrs E G Gillet & child, & Stone Mills, of N Y; & Thos Mishaw, of Mich City. Also killed: Henry Fleckinger, of Reading, & E P McCullough, of Lawrenceburg, Pa. Wounded: Fred Miller & Augustus White, of Holmesville, Ind; E M Knapp, of Hudson, Wisc; Miss Hattie Knapp, Auburn; J K Gardner, Jonesville, Mich;

Chas Sherman, Boston; Wm Flannery, P Myers, P Quinn, C Anderson, & W R Anderson, all of Ainsworth, Ill; A D Piser, Chicago; D P Rhodes, Cleveland; Miss Moore, Freeport; Mr & Mrs A G Gurry, Brooklyn; C Jackson & Miss C Nielder, Waukesha, Wis; Messrs Walworth, father & son, & C Bennett, Adrian, Mich; Oscar Warpeton, M H Regan, lady, & daughter, Rockford, Ill; S C Rose, Coldwater; W G Hawks, Charlestown, Va; C Yaw & lady, Otsego Co, N Y; A Vansyck, wife & 4 children, of Warren, Ohio-himself & one child seriously; Stephen H Arnold, Decatur, Iowa; Mary Coates, Youngstown, Ohio; & Miss D D Porter, Hudson, Mich. E C Smith, banker, N Y, was fatally injured. [Jul 1st newspaper: also died & bodies found: Mary Ann Curran, of Dunkirk; & Mrs Tiswold & 4 children. Mrs Regan, of Rockford, has died since the accident at Rankin.]

FRI JUL 1, 1859
The Navy Dept has received the intelligence of the death of Lt S S Bassett, who died on board the ship **Bainbridge** on May 6 last, at Buenos Ayres.

Household & kitchen furniture at auction on:Jul 5, at the residence of the late Mrs Laird. -Barnard & Buckey, aucts

Mrs Mary B Francisco, widow of the celebrated Peter Francisco, of Revolutionary memory, died in Fincastle, Va, on Jun 8, at the residence of her son-in-law, Jos V Carper. Mrs Francisco was born in England, in Brompton, the western suburb of the metropolis, on May 12, 1782. By the death of her parents she was early left an orphan. At the age of 5 years she became a member of the family of her grandmother, Mrs Randolph, who resided in London. At about age 15 years she sailed to America, landed upon Va soil, & became an inmate of the household of her uncle, Gov Randolph. Having remained 2 or 3 years in the family of the Govn'r, she was received into the family of her uncle, Philip L Grimes, of Brandon, Middlesex Co, with whom she resided until her marriage with Maj West, a wealthy planter of Va. Of this marriage she left 3 daughters, whose families are respected citizens of the State which she adopted as her home on her arrival in the U S. Being left a widow, she married Peter Francisco, the soldier of Revolutionary memory. -Richmond Enquirer

Pioneer Mills for sale: situated on the river front within a few yards of the Orange & Alexandria & Manassas Gap Railroads, with wharves, grain elevator, engines & boilers, & a cooper's shop. Apply to Fowle & Co.

The recent English papers announce the death of Rev Dr Burns, who was known as the Father of the Free Church of Scotland. He died in May in his 81st year; ordained in 1800; removed to Kilsyth in 1820, where his pastoral labors of 39 years lasted. He left 2 sons in the ministry, one in China, & the other the minister of the Free Church in Dundee..

Mrd: on Jun 28, in Wash City, at the Church of the Ascension, by Rev Dr Pinckney, Dr John Hunter to Miss Mary E Brooke, daughter of the late Walter Brooke, of PG Co, Md.

Mrd: on Jun 30, in Wash City, at Trinity Church, Mr John Hyatt, of PG Co, Md, to Marion, eldest daughter of B F Middleton, of Wash City.

SAT JUL 2, 1859
Breach of promise case in the cause of Effie C Carztang vs Henry Shaw, in which a verdict of $100,000 damages was given to the plntf, a short time ago, at St Louis, was argued on Tue last in the Court of Common Pleas of that city. A new trial was granted.

Fauquier **White Sulphur Springs**. This well known Watering Place for sale. Circuit Court of Fauquier Co, held on Sep 23, 1858. Thos Green, plntf, against Isham Keith & others, dfndnts in Chancery. And the **Fauquier White Sulphur Springs**, plntf, against Thos Green & other, dfndnts in Chancery. These causes, consolidated by a former decree of the Court, came on this day to be heard on the papers formerly read, & the report of Com'r Jas V Brooke, of Aug 7, 1858, to which there is no exception, & was argued by counsel. On consideration whereof the court doth adjudge, order, & decree that said report be confirmed, & that unless Thos Green, the plntf in the first & one of the dfndnts in the second named suit, shall pay to the **Fauquier White Sulphur Springs**, or to their authorized agent & atty, the sum of $41,742. 63, with interest on $35,314,22 part thereof from Dec 15, 1857, until paid, together with the costs of these suits; & to Wm B Phillips, or to his duly authorized agent or atty, the sum of $4,400, with interest from Dec 15, 1855, until paid, within 6 months from the date of this decree, then & in the event of the non-payment of said sums of money, the court doth direct the B H Shackelford, Robt E Scott, Saml Chilton, E M Spilman, &, by consent of parties by counsel, Isham Keith, any one or more of whom may act if the others decline, be & they are directed, as Com'rs of this court, to sell the real & personal estate in the bill & proceedings mentioned; said real estate consisting of about 1,013 acres of land, in said county, including the Hotel Bldgs & Springs, to the highest bidder, after 30 days' notice by publication in the Warrenton newspaper & in the Nat'l Intelligencer & by handbills of the time & place of the sale. The said com'rs shall have the power to sell said real estate in whole or in separate parcels, as they may deem most judicious. Said Com'rs shall sell the personality at the same time & place with the real estate, & upon such terms as they may think most judicious. The court hereby reserves all questions relating to the debts of Jas Lyons, Henry A Wise, & Julia A Peyton, on their application by counsel, reported by Com'r Brooke, for such future order as may be deemed right. Said com'rs are not to act under this decree until they shall have respectively executed bonds, with approved security, before the Clerk of this court, in the penalty of $60,000, conditioned for the faithful discharge of their duties under this & any future decree that may be entered in this cause; & they are to report their proceedings to the court. –John S Byrne, clerk
The sums of money referred to in the foregoing decree not having been paid, the undersigned, com'rs, will offer for sale, on the premises, on Aug 17, 1859, the entire real & personal peoperty therein mentioned, on the terms of said decree.
-B H Shackelford, Robt C Scott, Saml Chilton, E M Spilman, & Isham Keith, Com'rs

The 112th annual commencement of **Princeton College** of N J was celebrated on Tue & Wed last. Honorary degrees were conferred: degree of LL D on Hon Jas A Pearce, Md; Hon Richd S Field, N J; & Fred'k A Packard, Pa. Degree of DD on Rev John Dorrance, Pa; Rev R H Thornton, Canada West; Rev Jas Smith, Prof in the Presbyterian Theological Seminary, Nova Scotia; Rev E R Craven, Newark, N J; & Rev D M Holliday, Peekskill, N Y. Degree of A M on Rev M Street, Phil; W J Cheney, Phil; Silvester M Chadbourne, Me; Geo B Sears, Newark, N J, & Geo W Alexander, D C.

The 105th annual commencement of **Columbian College**, N Y, took place on Tue last: address by Pres King; degree of A B conferred on 27 persons, who composed the graduating class. The honorary degree of D D bestowed on : Rev A S Leonard, Rev Geo H Haughton, & Rev Lot Jones, of N Y C; Rev A G Mercer, Newport, R I; Rev W A Dod, Princeton, N J; & LL D upon Prof Wm M Gillespie, of Union College, Schenectady, & Saml Tyler, of Fred'k Md.

Circuit Court of D C-in Equity, No 1,037. Francis Wheatley, use Judson Mitchell, against Chas H Winder & Wm H Winder. The subscriber, trustee in above cause, reported that he sold,on Jun 20, 1859, 4 lots of ground in square 170, Wash City, being subdivisions of lots 6, 5, 4, & 3, the last named lots being part of the original subdivisions of original lots nos 9 & 10, which lots were made to front on F st north; that at such sale Hamilton G Fant became the purchaser of lot 1 at the price of $897.25; & Columbus Alexander became the purchaser of lot 2, 3, & 4 for $2,472.03. –W Redin, trustee -John A Smith, clerk

MON JUL 4, 1849
The Pres left Wash City this morning for his summer residence at the *Old Soldier's Home*. On Jul 18 he proposes setting out for Bedford Springs, where he will stay for 2 weeks. He will be accompanied by his niece, Miss Lane, Sec & Mrs Floyd, & probably Mrs Sec Thompson. –Constitution

Household & kitchen furniture at auction on Jul 11, at the residence of R C Walker, 439 11th st, between G & H sts. -A Green auct

On Jun 20th the citizens of LeClaire were startled by the death of Mr A J Jansen, from the effects of the sting of a bee. He was stung by a bee on the neck near the jugular vein. He had gone to the premises of Mr Maloy, near Princeton, to purchase a hive of bees.

Improvements going on now in Wash City: 4 story dwlgs on 3rd st, between 4th & E sts, by Chas Walker; two 4 story dwlgs on E st, between 9th & 10th sts, by Thos Walker; two 4 story, brown front, E st, between 3rd & 4th sts, just completed, & owned by J W Shiles; three 4 story dwlgs, 3rd & Mo ave, owned by P W Browning; three 3 story dwlgs, 6th st, between M & N, by Thos Lewis, bricklayer; two 2 story, M st, near 1st st, owned by Campbell & Berker.

Dissolution of co-partnership, between the undersigned, in the Coach & Cabinet Hardware, by mutual consent. –John R Elvans, G R Thompson. John R Elvans will continue the business at the old stand, 309 Pa ave, between 9th & 10th sts, under the name of John R Elvans & Co.

The remains of the late Dr Gamaliel Bailey, who recently died on his way to Europe, will arrive in Wash City this morning, & the funeral services will take place at Trinity Church tomorrow, Jul 5, at 10 o'clock. [Jul 6th newspaper: The body was taken to the Congress Burial Ground, where the solemn service of the Episcopal Church was read. He was a most faithful & devoted husband & father.]

Montgomery, Jul 1. Five bills of indictment having been found by the grand jury against N Mannery, a former express agent, for the embezzlement of $50,000 in money, committed to the care of Adams' Express Co, & Mannery failing to appear, his bail has been forfeited.

Mrd: on Jul 2, by Rev Dr Nadal, Addison M Smith, of Wash City, to Sallie D, daughter of Col Israel M Jackson, of PG Co, Md.

WED JUL 6, 1859
Hon Wm O Goode, of Va, a member of the House of Reps from the Petersburg district for several years, & a member elect of the next Congress, died of consumption on Jul 3, at his residence near Boydton, Mecklenburg Co. His health had been feeble for some time past.

Mrs Everett, the estimable wife of Hon Edw Everett, of Mass, died at Boston on Jul 2.

Trustee's sale: in compliance with the terms of a deed of trust from Thos Norfleet to me, dated Aug 11, 1858, recorded in Liber J A S No 112, pages 485 etc, one of the land records of Wash Co, D C: sale on Jul 18, all the right, title, & interest of said Thos Norfleet in & to part of square 399, in Wash City. Said interest being a leasehold for 99 years from Ulysses Ward, dated Mar 1, 1856, recorded in Liber J A S, No 114, pages 505, etc. –Thos C Donn, trustee -A Green auct

Mrd: on Jun 15, at San Antonio, Texas, by Rev Fr Dubuis, Capt John Withers, Assist Adj Gen U S Army, to Miss Anita Dwyer, of San Antonio, Texas.

Mrd: on Jun 28, by Rev Mr Tillinghast, at St John's Church, Gtwn, Thos C Wheeler, formerly of Montg Co, Md, to Nannie, daughter of W B Chew, of the former place.

Died: on Jul 4, Christina, wife of Jas Casparis, aged 36 years. She was a native of Switzerland, but has resided in this country for 28 years. Her funeral will be on Jul 6 at 3 o'clock P M, from her late residence on Capitol Hill.

Died: on Jul 3, Adelaide, aged 5 months & 2 days, only daughter of Dr W V H & Adelaide J Brown.

Died: on Jul 5, Jane Stone, youngest daughter of B W & M L Ree, aged 18 months. Her funeral is this morning at 10 o'clock, from the residence of her parents, F & 14th sts.

THU JUL 7, 1859
Sale of real estate in Wash City, by deed of trust, executed on May 11, 1855, recorded in Liber J A S No 100, folios 375 thru 380, of the land records of Wash Co, D C, by Thos Green of the first part, Wm J Ward, of the 2nd part, B H *Shackeford & Isham Keith of the 3rd part, & the undersigned of the 4th part, I shall, as trustee under the said deed, by the direction of the excx of Beverly Tucker, deceased, sell on Aug 19 next, at public auction, the square south of square 173, except that part of the same situated at the s e corner thereof, having a front of 70 feet on 17th st, extending back 100 feet. –P M Thompson, trustee -Jas C McGuire & Co, aucts -*Shackeford as written

Trustee's sale of south part of lot 17 in square 196, at auction, on Jul 12, by deed of trust from Wm A Ducket to the subscriber, dated Jun 19, 1858, recorded in Liber J A S No 156, folios 410 thru 413, of the land records for Wash Co, D C; with a frame dwlg-house. -Edw C Carrington, trustee -A Green auct

John Rosamond, late Postmaster at White Hill, Choctaw Co, Miss, was convicted at the late term of the Federal court at Pontotoc, of having stolen money & stamps from the mail, & sentenced to 12 years' imprisonment in the penitentiary.

Explosion of a fireworks factory in Phil, occupied by Saml Jackson, pyrotechnist, took fire yesterday. Chas Beck, 22, at the work at the time, was killed.
–North American of Jul 4.

Annual Commencement of **Gtwn College** took place yesterday in the large hall of the College; music by the Marine Band; Orations by Jas O Martin; Chas G Andry; Robt Y Brown; Henry S Foote; Jas H Dooley; Francis X Ward; John B Gardiner; Jos P Orme; Clement S Lancaster; John E Dooley; Jas F McLaughlin; Robt F Lovelace; John F Marion; & Jas P Neale. Degree of LL D was conferred on Alex'r Dimitry & Geo W Watterston, both of Louisiana; & Augustin Jos Morales, N Y. Degree of M D was conferred on: Reuben Cleary, of D C; Lucius Smith, Ohio; Jos T Howard, D C; G W Hill, Ohio; F C Christie, N Y; J Wells Herbert, Md; Dent Burroughs, Md; E Lyon Corbin, N Y; & Augustus R Sparks, Iowa. Degree of A M was conferred on Wm X Wills, of Md; Robt Ray, Louisiana; Robt C Combs, Md; John Rieckleman, Ohio; & Danl G Major, Calif. Degree of A B was conferred on John P Marshall, of Md; Robt Lovelace, Louisiana; Benj Sheckell, D C; Jas P Neale, Md; Jas O Martin, Louisiana; John B Gardiner, Md; Francis X Ward, Md; Clement S Lancaster, Pa; & Peter S Brank, Louisiana. Degree of A B was conferred on the following students of the College of the Holy Cross, near Worcester, Mass: Chas Stone & Jas Tracy, of Mass.

Criminal Court-Wash-Tue. 1-Catharine McCarick was found guilty of assault, & recommended to the mercy of the Court: sentenced to 4 weeks in jail. 2-Emanuel Miller found guilty of stealing a calf: sentenced to 1 year in the penitentiary. 3-Thos Price, colored, found guilty of assault: sentenced to 1 year in jail. 4-Margaret Russell found guilty of an assault: sentenced to 3 months in jail. 5-Hilleary Hutchins, convicted of manslaughter on Sat last: sentenced to 8 years in the penitentiary. 6-Lewis Arthur, indicted for stealing a gold watch chain & seals from Felix Dennis: sentenced to 18 months in the penitentiary.

Disappeared from the house of Geo Mathiot, Delaware ave & C st, Mary Eliz Kirby, aged 12 years. Any one giving information of her will receive the grateful thanks of her distressed mother. Residence at Mrs Boggs', East Capitol st.

Orphans Court of Wash Co, D C. Letters testamentary on the personal estate of Enoch Moreland, late of Wash Co, deceased. –Caroline Moreland, excx

Rosedale Cottage to be rented or leased for one or five years; located on the Rockville turnpike. Apply to E Harte, on the premises, or at 373 Pa ave.

Died: on Jul 5, in Wash City, Mrs Sarah J Richardson, in her 34th year. Her funeral will take place this afternoon at 4 o'clock, from her late residence on 6th st, between M & N.

Died: on Jul 3, Margaret R, relict of the late John L Wirt, in her 38th year.

FRI JUL 8, 1859
P St George Cocke has presented to the Va Military Institute $20,000 for the establishment of an Agricultural Dept at that institution.

Criminal Court-Wash-Thu. 1-Mr O E P Hazard was tried on an indictment for assault & battery on Mr Groux & wife, but the jury found him not guilty. 2-Laura Smith & Anna Green, were convicted of keeping disorderly houses.

$200 reward for runaway negro man Tom, aged about 32 or 33. Ran away from the subscriber living in the Forest of PG Co, Md. –Benj Lee, Post Ofc Upper Marlborough

Died: on Jul 7, after an illness of 7 months, Mr Wm Feeney, aged 54 years, a native of the county of Longford, Ireland, & a resident of Wash City for the last 30 years. His funeral will take place this afternoon at 4 o'clock, from his late residence on D st, between 14th & 15th sts.

Died: on Jul 6, in Gtwn, D C, Brvt Maj Saml Chase Ridgely, U S Army. His funeral will take place this afternoon at 3½ o'clock, from the residence of his brother, W G Ridgely, on First st.

Died: on Jul 7, infant child of Robt & Louisa Waters, aged 4 months & 17 days. The funeral will take place this morning at 10 o'clock, from their residence, 422 D st.

SAT JUL 9, 1859
A gentleman named G W Childs fell from the steamer **George Page** as she was passing early yesterday from Wash City to Alexandria. He was on his way home, which was in Louisa Co, Va, from Bethany College, near Wheeling. He had sunk to rise no more before assistance could be rendered. Nothing appears to be known as to the cause of the mishap. [Jul 12th newspaper: the body of the young student G M Childs, who drowned on Fri last, has been found & sent to his friends in Louisa Co, Va.]

Accidents from fireworks on Jul 4 at Pittsfield, N H: fatal injuries to Benj F Leavitt, of Chichester, & Mr Calvin Garland, of Barnstead. Mr Leavitt is about 46 years of age, an overseer in a factory in Pittsfield, but went to Calif some 8 or 9 years since; returned & redeemed his father's homestead from all incumbrances, & settled upon it. Mr Garland is about 28, an only son of Saml Garland, of Barnstead, & a worthy man.

Orphans Court of Wash Co, D C. Letters of administration on the personal estate of Vespasian Ellis, late of Wash Co, deceased. –Wm H C Ellis, adm, Norfolk, Va.

Circuit Court of Wash Co, D C-in Equity. Martha Wales & others vs the heirs at law of Isaac H Wales. Trustee's sale of improved property, by a decree passed on Jun 14, 1858, in the above cause: public sale on Aug 8, in front of the premises, eastern part of lot 17 in square 687, on North B st, between 1st st east & Capitol Square, with a good 2 story brick house. –Edw G Handy, trustee -A Green auct

Died: on Jul 7, Mary Dement, wife of the late Walter Dement, of St Mary's Co, Md, aged 83 years. Her funeral will be from Trinity Church on Sat at 10 o'clock.

Died: on Jul 8, in Wash City, after a short illness, Virgil Maxcy, aged 4 years & 10 months, son of Jos & Hannah M Mattingly. His funeral is this afternoon at 2 o'clock, from 522 Mass ave.

Died: on Jul 8, Matilda Brooke, infant daughter of Stanislaus & Mary H Murray, aged 8 months & 15 days. Her funeral is this evening at 4 o'clock, from the residence of her parents on 5th st, opposite the City Hall.

MON JUL 11, 1859
Chicago Journal, Jul 5: R H Bacon, connected editorially with the Daily Times, fell overboard from the steam tug **Salvor** yesterday, while on an excursion to Waukegan. He was a native of the vicinity of Boston, about 37 years of age; a graduate of Hamilton College, N Y, & studied at Cambridge Univ for the Ministry, to which profession he was admitted in 1848, when he settled as a Unitarian Minister at Rochester, N Y.

N Y Post: Rev Kingman A Nott, pastor of Broome st Baptist Church, drowned on Thu, in company with several friends, while bathing in the Raritan river. He may have been seized with a cramp.

Administrators sale of household & kitchen furniture at auction on on Jul 14, at the residence of the late John L Wirt, 391 North Capitol st, Capitol Hill, by order of the Orphans Court of Wash Co, D C. –Florian Hitz, adm de bonis non -A Green auct

Mr Jas Wright, an old citizen of Cincinnati, but who moved to Vanceburg, Ky, last Aug for the purpose of devoting his attention to getting out timber for the manufacturing of spokes & hubs, was engaged in the woods when in turning over a log, a rattlesnake suddenly sprung at him & struck its fangs into the back of his hand. He ran to town, & when he reached there he was entirely blind, his body & head covered with spots of the same color of those of a rattlesnake. He expired the next morning. –Cincinnati Gaz

Orphans Court of D C. Case of Wm A Richardson, guardian of Margaret Richardson, et al. Asbury Lloyd, trustee, reported he sold lot 16 in square 245, [being a resale] to Geo W Hauptman, for the sum of $1,264.80, & Hauptman has complied with the terms of sale. –Wm F Purcell, Judge of the Orphans Court of D C. -Ed N Roach, clerk

The Mayor has appointed Mr Wm Cooper as police magistrate for the 7th Ward, vice Mr D E Rowland.

Criminal Court-Wash-Sat. 1-Henry Rennigee, charged with assault & battery on a while child only 3 years of age, his wife's sister's child, submitted his case, & was sent 3 months to jail. 2-Bernard McNerhany was convicted of beating Deborah Wife: fined $3, in consideration of his having already been nearly 2 weeks in jail. 3-Manual Glasco was convicted of a felony in killing & making way with a cow, the property of Mrs Foley.

TUE JUL 12, 1859
Naval: the following ofcrs have recently passed their final examination, & are now passed-midshipmen in the navy, arranged in the order of relative merit:

Geo A Bigelow	Le Roy Fitch	Jas C Moseley
R F Crawford	Jos W Harris	Geo H Perkins
R L Pythian	Thos H Eastman	Geo Blodget
Aug P Cooke	Chester Hatfield	W W Allen
W E Evans	Chas J McDougall	Nathl Greene
Geo S Shryock	Thos R Porter	

Died: on Jul 9, in Wash City, Jas Sutton, in his 34th year. His funeral is this evening at 4 o'clock, from his late residence on 5th st east, between F & G sts north.

Died: on Jul 8, in Wash City, of scarlet fever, Kate Eliz, aged 3 years, only child of Jos & Margaret A Plowman & grandchild of W B Wilson.

The Court of Princess Anne, Va, decided that their own jail was an unsafe depository for the prisoner Walter S Land, [charged with a most atrocious murder,] & order his removal to the jail of this city for safe keeping. Yesterday the Deputy Sheriff, Mr Henry Lewis, having secured the prisoner in irons, procured a rockaway to which he consigned him in the custody of Mr Willougby Williams, an elderly man of 55 or 60 years of age, while he, Lewis, followed behind in a gig. They had not proceeded but 4 miles when Land suddenly threw himself from the carriage, sprang to his feet & dashed into the woods. The fugitive made his escape. A reward of $100 for his apprehension has been offered. -Norfolk Herald

Excellent furniture & household effects at public sale on Jul 28, at the residence of Lt I Green, on I st, between 13th & 14th sts. -Jas C McGuire & Co, aucts

Obit-died: Hon Thos G Carey died on the 30th at his summer residence in Nahant, at age 67 years. He was born in Chelsea, Mass, Sep 7, 1791; graduated at Harvard College in 1811, in the same class with Hon Edw Everett, Rev Dr Frothingham, Chas P Curtis, Hon John C Gray, & Hon Peter O Thatcher, & began the practice of his profession in Boston. He married Mary, a daughter of the late Hon Thos H Perkins, of this city. One of his daughters is the wife of Prof Agassiz, & another the wife of Prof C C Felton, of Harvard College. -N Y Express

Trustee's sale of handsome bldg lot on the Island at auction, on Jul 25, by deed of trust from Chas Coleman, dated May 11, 1859: sale of lot 1 in square 499, unimproved: fronts on 4½ st, at south K st, running back 75 feet. –Chas Walter, trustee -A Green auct

Harrisburg, Jul 4. Hon Jas Burnside, of Bellefonte, died suddenly on Fri last. He had been sitting at the door, when his nephew, Harvey Mann, drove up in a buggy with his mother, a sister of Judge Burnside, who had come to pay them a visit. The horse was a new one, & after Mrs Mann had got out the Judge said to his nephew that he believed that he would get in & take a short ride with him. He got in, & young Mann was about following him, when he slipped, &, touching the horse, started him. The horse dashed down a steep stoney st & threw the Judge out. Blood gushed from every feature, & when he was picked up he was dying. The event created the greatest grief in the town.

On Sunday Mr Jas Sutton, a watchman at the marble yard of the Post Ofc extension in Judiciary Square, died suddenly. He had eaten a hearty dinner & was not apparently out of health. The disease was hemorrhage of the lungs, giving him not more than 10 minutes' respite between the attack & death. He was buried yesterday.

On Sat the son of Col Wm P Young, [about 12 years of age,] who had been fishing at Rock Creek, with several of his companions, had his left hand shattered from the explosion of a pistol which he at the time held in his hand. It was necessary to amputate it, as far up as the wrist.

Criminal Court-Wash-Mon. 1-Geo Fisher, colored, was convicted of an assault & battery with intent to kill with an axe Eliza Jane Byas, colored: sentenced to 4 years in the penitentiary. 2-Theodore Hurdle, Geo Sullivan, & Eugene Sardo were indicted for assaults, in June, on John Brown & Geo A Jones: all of them acquitted. 3-Allen Fleetwood alias Brooks was indicted for stealing 3 heifers from W H Rowland, but the place where the stealing occurred proving to be in PG Co, Md, the traverser was acquitted, but held by the Marshal for a requisition from the Govn'r of Md. [Jul 14th newspaper: 1-John Sherwood, charged with an assault on a slave, the property of a gentleman in Gtwn, was acquitted. 2-Moses & Martha Bridwell, tried for keeping a disorderly house: discharged.]

Died: on Jun 25, at the residence of her father-in-law, Geo M Potts, in the city of Fred'k, Rebecca B, wife of Lt Richd Potts, U S A, now on duty at **Fort Ripley**, Minn, in her 29th year.

Died: on Jul 10, in Wash City, Clarence Westwood, aged 4 years, son of Chas K & E C King. His funeral is today at 5 o'clock P M, from the residence of his father, 167 H st.

WED JUL 13, 1859
Criminal Court-Wash-Tue. 1-John Ellis submitted his case in a charge of assault & battery against a colored woman, & was fined $5 & costs. 2-Two cases of assault & battery against Peter Hyde were tried & he was acquitted on both.

The citizens of Chelmsford, Mass, proposed to erect a monument in honor of the Revolutionary heroes of that place, on Jul 4, but had to postpone it until Sep 22, & invited Ex-Pres Pierce to be present. Letter of reply from Ex-Pres Franklin Pierce dated Langen Swalbach, Duchy of Nassau, Jun 2, 1859. Your kind letter of Apr 13, which reached Rome after my departure, was returned to Paris, & only came to me yesterday. This reply will probably not be received before the day designated, but my heart will be there. I enclose herewith a check for $50, which you will please to place in the hands of the cmte as a contribution to the monument. Your friend & servant, Franklin Pierce
[To Chas H Dalton, Boston, Mass.]

The daughter of John Rafferty, of Cincinnati, has been killed when she was pitched over the banisters from a 2nd story of the house, & received fatal injuries by the fall.

In May last Jasper Rouzy shot Jas Oldham in Milledgeville, Lincoln Co, & fled. Last Monday he was captured in Bradfordsville; taken to Stamford, the county seat of Lincoln, & placed in jail. A mob of some 80 persons attacked the prison, carried off the prisoner, & hung him from a tree. Rouzy asked that his body be given to his wife.
–Louisville [Ky] Democrat

Mrd: on Jul 6, at Sag Harbor, Long Island, by Rev E Hooper, Lt Oscar F Stanton, U S N, to Miss Carrie E, daughter of the late Chas F Gardiner.

Commencement at **Alnwick Female Seminary**, PG Co, on Jun 30. Essay by the Valedictorian of the class, Miss E Harris, of Wash; diplomas awarded to Miss Harris, of this city, Miss Heath, of PG Co, Md, & Miss Dent of St Mary's Co, Md. Miss Mary Tyson, Principal.

THU JUL 14, 1859
At Markheidenfelt, in Bavaria, there lives a man 68 years of age, named Johannes Schlottembeck. He is a master chimney-sweep, a vocation more honorable in Germany than in this country. He is now living with his 3rd wife; & on Jun 16 last his 36th child was christened at the parish church. By his first consort he had 7; by his 2nd consort, 11; & by his 3rd, 18 children, of whom half are girls & half are boys.

The daughter of Jos Charless, recently assassinated at St Louis, carrying out the intentions of her father, has given $20,000 to endow the Professorship of Physical science inWestminster College, a Presbyterian institution located at Fulton, Missouri.

Mr J Glass, Postmaster in New Brighton, was arrested there yesterday on a charge of counterfeiting. –Pittsburg Chronicle, Jul 9.

Capt Jas Ray, a boatman employed on the Delaware & Hudson canal, was attempting to fill a lighted lamp from a can containing nearly a gallon of burning fluid, when the fluid caught fire & the can exploded. Mrs Ray & her sister were dreadfully burnt, so much so that Mrs Ray has died. Her sister's recovery is doubtful. Capt Ray & their child escaped with slight burns.

At Balt, on Tue, Wm W Taylor was brutally murderded on the pavement at the corner of Henrietta & Light sts by two men named Geo Burke & Thos Eaton, who were drunk. Eaton was arrested & a search is on for Burke. Taylor was from Accomac Co, Va, where his parents reside. He was 26 years of age, & a shoemaker by trade. After he was shot he was carried to his boarding house, where he died in a few minutes. -Exchange

Jas Hayes died at Salem on Jun 29 from the effects of drinking a solution of corrosive sublimate at the great fire on Jul 8th, the solution having been given him in mistake for gin, by Danl Crowley, who stole it from the Essex House.

Mrd: on Jun 29, in St Paul's Church, Newport, Ky, by Rev P J Jeffries, Lt Wm G Robinson, U S A, to Gwinthlean Macrae, daughter of Maj Macrae, U S A.

Fine farm for sale in Knox Co, Tenn: contains 250 to 260 acres of land; with a cottage or dwlg house quite comfortable for a small family; four years ago the whole place was valued at $30,000, of which this is the handsomest half. Address Dr Saml Martin, of Campbell Station. –Mary P Williams

Army promotions & appointments since the publication of Gen Orders, of Mar 15, 1859:

Promotions:

Corps of Engineers: 1st Lt Edw B Hunt, to captain, Jul 1, 1859, having served 14 years continuous service as lt.

2nd Lt Wm P Craighill, to 1st Lt, Jul 1, 1859, vice Hunt, promoted.

Corps of Topographical Engineers: 1st Lt Wm F Smith, to captain, Jul 1, 1859, having served 14 years continuous service as lt.

2nd Lt Chas N Turnbull, to 1st Lt, Jul 1, 1859, vice Smith, promoted.

1st Regt of Dragoons: Brvt 2nd Lt Richd H Brewer, to 2nd lt, Mar 29, 1859, vice Evans, deceased.

2nd Regt of Dragoons: 1st Lt John Buford, jr, to capt, Mar 9, 1859, vice Givens, deceased.

2nd Lt Francis C Armstrong, to 1st lt, Mar 9, 1859, vice Buford, promoted.

Brvt 2nd Lt Solomon Williams, to 2nd lt Mar 9, 1859, vice Armstrong, promoted.

1st Regt of Cavalry: 2nd Lt Eugene W Crittenden, to 1st Lt, May 4, 1859, vice Perkins, cashiered.

Brvt 2nd Lt Andrew Jackson, jr, to 2nd lt, May 4, 1859, vice Roane, deceased.

4th Regt of Artl: Brvt 2nd Lt Geo H Weeks, of the 1st artl, to 2nd lt, Feb 10, 1859, vice Roane, deceased.

Brvt 2nd Lt Jas Hallonquist, of the 3rd artl, to 2nd lt, Feb 24, 1859, vice Bennett, deceased.

2nd Regt of Infty: 2nd Lt Alfred E Latimer, to 1st lt, Apr 18, 1859, vice Paige, deceased.

Brvt 2nd Lt Wm G Robinson, of the 7th infty, to 2nd lt, Apr 18, 1859, vice Latimer, promoted.

6th Regt of Infty: Brvt 2nd Lt Chas E Jesup, of the 10th infty, to 2nd lt, May 31, 1859, vice Lee, resigned.

7th Regt of Infty: Brvt 2nd Lt Geo N Bascom, of the 9th infty, to 2nd lt, Apr 23, 1859, vice Potts, deceased.

10th Regt of Infty: Brvt 2nd Lt Oliver P Gooding, of the 4th infty, to 2nd lt, Feb 5, 1859, vice Reed, deceased.

Appointments:

Quartermaster's Dept: 1st Lt Tredwell Moore, of the 2nd infty, to be assist quartermaster, with the rank of capt, May 21, 1859, vice Paige, deceased.

Medical Dept: Kirtley Ryland, of Mo, to be assist surgeon, Apr 28, 1859, vice Henry, resigned.

Richd G Lay, of the Dist of Columbia, to be 2nd lt, Jun 20, 1859, vice Lee, resigned.

Cadets: Graduates of the Military Academy, attached to the army with the Brevet of 2nd Lt, in conformity with the 4th section of the act approved Apr 29, 1812, to rank from Jul 1, 1859. The number prefixed to the name of each indicate his rank among those of the same date:

Corps of Engineers: 1-Cadet Wm W Merrill; 2-Cadet Saml H Lockett; 4-Cadet Chauncery B Reese.

Corps of Topographical Engineers: 3-Cadet Chas R Collins; 5-Cadet Orlando B Wagoner; 6-Cadet Robt F Beckham.

Ordinance Dept: 7-Cadet Moses H Wright.

Dragoon Arm: 12-Cadet Eugene M Baker, 2nd regt; 19-Cadet Jos Wheeler, jr, 1st regt.

Cavalry Arm: 21-Cadet Abraham K Arnold, 2nd regt.
Artl Arm: 9-Cadet Francis L Guenther, 1st regt; 10-Cadet Elias B Carling, 2nd regt; 11-Cadet Martin D Harden, 3rd regt; 13-Cadet Jonathan N Hall, 4th regt.
Infty Arm: 8-Cadet Edw G Bush, 6th regt; 14-Cadet Roderic Stone, 1st regt; 15-Cadet Francis J Crilly, 5th regt; 16-Cadet Allen L Anderson, 2nd regt; 17-Cadet Edwin H Stoughton, 4th regt; 18-Cadet Caleb H Carlton, 7th regt; 20-Cadet John J Upham, 9th regt; 22-Cadet Henry A F Worth, 8th regt.

For sale: a farm of 500 acres in Albemarle Co, Va: adjoins the one on which I reside, & the lands of E S Pegram, J H Lewis, & others; with a frame dwlg house, & necessary outbldgs. Apply to Wm C Rives, jr, Cobham, Albemarle Co, or to Mr T W Brown, at Cobham depot. –Wm C Rives, jr

FRI JUL 15, 1859
Trustee's sale of improved property on 6th st, between G & H sts, at public auction, on Aug 9, by deed from Geo McNaughton & wife, dated Aug 5, 1858, recorded in Liber J A S, No 159, folios 175: sale of lot 12 in square 486, fronting 25 feet on 6th st, with a 2 story brick dwlg-house. –Chas S Wallach, trustee -J C McGuire & Co, aucts

Trustee's sale of household & kitchen furniture at auction on Jul 20, at the residence of E Hart, on 7th st road, near the first toll gate. –J B Holmead, trustee -A Green auct

Brick house & lot at auction on Jul 21, belonging to the heirs of the late Leven D Travers, & sold by consent of all the heirs, viz: lot 26 in square 743, with a good 2 story brick house, with back bldg; located on N J ave, between L & M sts. After the above sale I shall sell lot 4 in square 701; property fronts on N st. Title indisputable. -A Green auct

There is a man by the name of Hyde in Cincinnati who is 110 years of age, & has been married 7 times.

Lt Simoen S Bassett, of the U S brig **Bainbridge**, was buried at Buenos Ayres May 7 with military honors. The deceased had been in delicate health for some time, & on May 6 was seized with convulsions, under which he sank. His remains were deposited in the Foreign Protestant Cemetery. He was a resident of this city & entered the navy in 1841.

Shocking accident yesterday at the Navy Yard, in this city-the bursting of a heavy ships gun, which was undergoing trial on the battery platform for the purpose of fixing her range, under the general direcion of Capt John A Dahlgren. The gun was made at the West Point Foundry, N Y, in 1850. Wm Nokes, of Wash, & Jas Wilson, of Brooklyn, N Y, were killed. Mr Beauchamp is dangerously bruised; Jas Roach-seriously injured; Chas Stewart is much cut; McMellon is badly cut; Periwig Ludwig, a stalwart Frenchman-a concussion; Andrew Wilson considerably injured; Dennis Leary, Conner, Holmead, & Gormley were wounded, but not dangerously.

Ex-Pres Pierce & his wife have arrived in Paris, & were to leave for London on Jun 30.

Orphans Court of Wash Co, D C. Letters of administration, with the will annexed, on the personal estate of John Crome, late of Wash Co, deceased. –Chas Walter, adm

An arrest was made yesterday, by Deputy Marshall Phillips, of John Carlos Gardner, whose connexion with the famous trial for false swearing on a document presented to the Mexican Commission by his brother, about 7 years ago, will be generally remembered. He was arrested on an indictment for perjury during his brother's first trial.

Valuable farm for sale: the subscriber offers his farm, on Hanson Branch, PG Co, Md: contains about 216 acres, & adjoins the lands of Dr Gunton & Dr Roberts, both of Washington. Improvements consist of a large barn, with a house for servants. Apply through the Old Fields Post Ofc, PG Co, Md. –F Tolson

Mrd: on Jul 6, in Immanuel Church, by Rev O A Kinsolving, Thos U Dudley, jr, of Richmond, to Fanny B, daughter of Dr Wm B Cochran, of Middleburg, Va.

Mrd: on Jun 28, at the residence of Judge Mason, Minister of the U S at Paris, Miss Kate Spencer, daughter of Dr Henry W Spencer, Consul at Paris, & J Murray Giles, of N Y.

Died: on Jul 14, in Wash City, Mr John B Boone, of a protracted illness, in his 57th year. His funeral is this afternoon at 4½ o'clock, from his residence, 10th, between E & F sts.

Died: on Jul 14, in his 11th year, John A Linton, son of Wm & Julia Linton. This little boy had unfortunately ventured into the canal to bathe, & was drowned. His funeral will be on Jul 15, at 5½ o'clock, from the residence of his father, C st, between 3rd & 4½ sts.
+
Yesterday John A Linton, in his 11th year, son of Mr Linton, of the Treasury Dept, was drowned. He had gone in bathing & got out of his depth.

Boarding, by day, week, or month, with or without rooms. Mrs M A Mills, 504 Pa ave, near 3rd st, Wash. [Ad]

Halifax, Jul 14. Hon Rufus Choate died on Wed morning. His remains go to Boston for interment. The Bench & Bar are preparing an address of condolence to his family.
[Jul 18th newspaper: Mr Choate was born in the town of Essex, in Mass, Oct 1, 1799; 1819 gradatue of Dartmouth College-with the highest honors of his class; entered law school at Cambridge, & after a few months went to Washington, in the ofc of Mr Wirt. He returned North & was admitted to the bar in 1824; commenced practice in Danvers, but in 2 or 3 years removed to Salem.]

SAT JUL 16, 1859
Mrd: on Jul 14, by Rev Mr Bates, Wm M Warren, of Wash City, to Miss Annie Appleby, formerly of Fred'k, Md.

Died: on Jul 6, at Greenwood, PG Co, Md, Alfred H Wells, in his 52nd year.

Died: on Jul 12, at Florence, Mass, Maggie, eldest daughter of Geo W Bo_ling, of Petersburg, Va.

Drowned, on Jul 8, at Naples, Ill, Chas L Walters, son of the late Wm Walters, formerly of Wash City, but more recently a resident of Springfield, Ill.

The trial of Ofcr Norwood for an assault on Col Jas E Stewart, was tried on Thu, resulting in Norwood's acquittal. The ofcr is to arrest him if disorderly.

Criminal Court-Wash-Fri. 1-Bridwell & wife on 2 charges of keeping a disorderly house, were found guilty, with a recommendation to the mercy of the Court. 2-Robt Binnix, about 19, stone-cutter by trade, was arraigned on 7 indictments for arson & one or two for burglary, committed during Apr & May last. Wm Looney, Jas Keenan, & Michl Doyle, young men, were also arraigned connected with the case of Binnix. Binnix & Doyle indicted for the burglary of the store of Mr Hugh Leddy, on 6th st, of flour, bread, tobacco, cigars, & stockings, which they conveyed to the house of Eliz Bowen, living on the Island. Thos Dillon was a witness for the prosecution, & presents himself as having participated in the burglary. Jas Larcombe coupled himself with the transaction.

Dr Wm S Woodside, whose failing health has for some time past prepared his friends for a fatal result, died on Wed at his residence in Balt. He was for many years connected with the Balt & Ohio railroad; at one time as master of transportation, &, both before & after his retirement from that position, as paymaster.

Loch Willow School, Augusta Co, Va: a boarding school for boys, preparatory to the Univ or Colleges of Va. –Jed Hotchkiss, Principal, Churchville, Augusta Co, Va.

MON JUL 18, 1859
Gen Tom Thumb [Chas E Stratton,] is expected home from Europe, where he has been for 3 years. He is now over 21 years of age, having attained his majority in Jan last. He has secured a comfortable independence, & intends to settle down at Bridgeport, Ct, his native place.

Trustee's sale of lot 1 in square 257, by virtue of authority contained in a deed of trust from Eugene Schwinghamer, dated Jun 17, 1858, recorded in Liber J A S No 166, folio 32, of the land records of Wash Co: sale on Aug 17 next; with the improvements, privileges, hereditaments, & appurtenances to the same belonging. -A Hyde, trustee -A Green auct

Orphans Court of Wash Co, D C. Letters of administration on the personal estate of Mary A Balzer, late of Wash Co, deceased. –Chas S Wallach, adm

Died: on Jul 16, Edward Kingsford, son of Dr W V H & Adelaide J Brown, aged 5 months & 15 days.

TUE JUL 19, 1859
2nd Annual Centennial Celebration of the town of **Woodbury, Conn** formed on the ground where the old church in Woodbury once stood. Most of those who dressed as Puritans were lineal descendants of the first settlers of Woodbury, the Atwoods, Minors, Judsons, & the Curtises. Capt Hurd, 85 years old, & Mrs Atwood, aged 72, dressed in ancient costume, & riding a horse *85 years of age. [*Copied as written.]

On Jul 10th, a fire occurred in Greensboro, Caroline Co, Md, by which the dwlg of Mrs Julia McGonigal, the storehouse of G H Moore, & the residence of Mr Joshua McGonigal, were entirely consumed. Total loss about $8,000.

A man kills the murderer of his father: from the St Louis Republican, a correspondent writing from Vernon Co, Mo, dated Jun 7. On May 26, Mr John Denton, a resident of this county, came across a man in Nevada city by the name of Jas Hardwick, whom he arrested for the murder of his [Denton's] father in Kansas about a year since. Denton had Hardwick handcuffed & placed him securely under guard in the court house. Denton stated that he was going to take his prisoner to Little Osage, in this county, for security. Denton returned to Nevada & stated that Hardwick had got away from him. Four days after this Hardwick's body was found in the prairie, & Denton was arrested for his murder. Hardwicke had told Denton that he was one of the men who shot down the old man Denton, while he was standing in his door.

Brookland School, at Greenwood Depot, Albemarle Co, Va. Wm Dinwiddie, M A, Principal; John C Dinwiddie, John Murray, M A, Jas M Garnett, M A, Instructors. [Ad]

On Sat last a lad named Baldwin, whose father is a blacksmith residing on C st, between 9th & 10th sts, was drowned, as supposed, accidentally. When his body was found he had a full suit of clothing on just as when he left his parents' house.

Died: on Jul 16, in Wash, Richd W Varden, in his 46th year.

WED JUL 20, 1859
Criminal Court-Wash-Tue. 1-Robt Binnix & Michl Doyle both guilty of setting fire to some houses, the property of Mr Ward, on the Island. Thos Dillon was convicted of setting Mr Potentini's ice-house on fire. Prisoners were remanded to jail.

Mrd: on Jun 30, in Decatur, Ill, by Rev S Stampee, J F Miller, of the same place, to Miss Laura E Peddecord, of Wash City.

Orphans Court of Wash Co, D C. Letters of administration on the personal estate of Nathan Blodget, late of Phil, Pa, deceased. –Julia A Briton, admx

Francis A Dickens continues to undertake the agency of claims before Congress & other branches of the Gov't, including com'rs under treaties, & various public ofcs. His ofc is on 15th st, opposite the Treasury Dept, next door to the Bank of the Metropolis. [Ad]

THU JUL 21, 1859
Adm's sale of land warrant: by order of the Orphans Court of D C., at public auction, on Jul 25, for cash, at the auction rooms, 9th & Pa ave, one land warrant for 160 acres of land, belonging to the estate of Michl Schott, deceased. –A Shucking, adm
-Wall & Barnard, aucts

N Y, Jul 19. The Forest divorce suit has taken another step. The Judge of the Supreme Court adjudges Mr Forrest to pay temporary alimony, at $200 at month, & to pay $1,500 fees for the lady's counsel & costs of reference. They had been married 40 years. She charges her liege lord with cruelty & with having an income of $10,000 a year. Though tired of matrimony, the lady is quite eager for alimony.

Lt Bayard E Hand, of the U S Navy, died at Wilmington, N C, on Jul 16, after a short illness. He was one his way to join the steamer **Fulton** at Norfolk, having just returned from the Paraquay expedition, being one of the ofcrs in command of the ship **Southern Star**. He was a native of Rome, Ga, about 28 years of age.

Obit record in the N Y paper: Died in this city, suddenly, Jul 14, Leidai D Lockwood, formerly of Chesapeake, Md, leaving all her property [$150,000,] to her niece, Miss Sarah E Lockwood.

Steam firewood saw-mill. The undersigned will deliver sawed & split hickory, oak, & pine wood, of any length & size, to any part of Wash City, at the shortest notice, at very handsome prices. –G L Sheriff, Yard, 4½ st, Canal Bridge [Ad]

Adm's sale of Fla property. The adm on the estate of the late W H Howard, will sell, at public auction, Dec 19 next, a valuable plantation in Florida, the property of said estate. The plantation is in Marion Co: contains 1,632 acres in one body. –Geo W Howard, Ocala, Marion Co, Fla. –R L Myers, Wash, N C -Adams & Frost, Charleston, S C

Criminal Court-Wash-Wed. 1-Geo H Smith was convicted of assault & battery on Michl Cragin: sentenced to 1½ years in jail. 2-Mary Sheahan was acquitted on a charge of assault & battery on a child. 3-Jas Keenan, convicted of arson, sentenced to 3 years in the penitentiary. 4-Michl Doyle sentenced to 7 years, being 4 years for a case of burglary & 3 for arson. 5-Wm Looney sentenced to 3 years in the penitentiary for burglary.

Window Awnings of colored striped goods, made & put up. Geo Willner, Upholsterer, 464 9th st, between D & E sts. [Ad]

Died: on Jul 19, Anna Eliz, infant daughter of Saml & Eliz Virginia Pyne, aged 9 months & 13 days. Her funeral is today at 3 o'clock, from Mrs A Sweeny's, No 5 A st, Capitol Hill.

Died: on Jul 15, at his residence near Shippensburg, Pa, Mr Jos P Nevin, aged 48 years. He was faithful to his trust as the head of a family, & liberal in his contributions to the church to which he was attached.

FRI JUL 22, 1859
Hon Jacob Bond I'on, a distinguished citizen of Charleston, died last Sunday. He was formerly Pres of the S C State Senate, & during the war of 1812 was a captain in the U S artl.

Col S C Stambaugh, recently appointed the Surveyor General for the Territory of Utah, reached this city to receive final instructions from the Com'r of the Gen Land Ofc. -Star

Household & kitchen furniture at auction on Jul 27, at the residence of Mrs M Ringgold, corner of 9th & F sts. -Jas C McGuire & Co, aucts

Peoria Transcript, Jul 16. A short time ago Mr Thos Beard residing near Wash, Tazewell Co, who was one of the victims of the Michigan Southern Rairroad disaster at South Ben, died. He was on his way to Sandusky, Ohio, to meet his father, Mr Thos Beard, sen, residing in Tioga Co, N Y, who was coming out to visit his son. Thurday the father arrived in this city & stopped at Buckeye House. During the night he fell through a window, thinking he was on the first floor, & dreadfully injured himself. He is 80 years of age. He was hurrying forward in order to reach Washington in time to attend his son's funeral, which is to be held tomorrow. He was alive last night, but without any prospect of recovery.

Hon John W Nash, Judge of the Petersburg [Va] Circuit, died at his residence in Powhatan, on Sunday last. For some years his health had been infirm, & of late very feeble. –Richmond Whig

Orphans Court of Wash Co, D C. Letters of administration de bonis non on the personal estate of John Crome, late of Wash Co, deceased. –C H J Crome, adm d b n

Orphans Court of Wash Co, D C. In the case of David Walker, adm of Jos T Walker, deceased, the adm & Court appointed Aug 13 next, for the final settlement of the personal estate of the said deceased's estate, of the assets in hand. -Ed N Roach, Reg/o wills

SAT JUL 23, 1859
Trustee's sale: by deed of trust from Andrew Swartz, dated Aug 30, 1856, public auction, on Jul 30th next, part of lot 17 in square 169, in Wash Co, D C, together with all & singular improvements. –Geo W Beall, trustee -Wall & Barnard, aucts

Annual Commencement of **Harvard Univ** on Wed last. Honorary degrees announced:
Dr of Laws: Geo Burrell Emerson, of Boston; Geo Perkins Marsh, of Burlington, Vt; Henry Wadsworth Longfellow, of Cambridge; Chas Sumner, of Boston.
Dr of Divinity: Rev Cyrus Bartol, of Boston; Rev Richd Salter Storrs, of Brooklyn, N Y; Rev John Calvin Stockbridge, of Boston; Rev Howard Crosby, of N Y.
Master of Arts: Albert Pike, of Little Rock, Ark; Richd Salstonstall Greenough, of Boston; Wm Jas Rolfe, of Lawrence; Wm Edw Dorsheimer, of Buffalo, N Y.

Our foreign journals brought by the ship **Africa** announce the death of Oscar, King of Sweden. He was born Jul 4, 1799, & was the son of Bernadotte, whom he succeeded as King of Sweden & Norway on Mar 8, 1844. His health & mental powers failed some years ago & since Sept, 1857, he has not administered the Gov't, having left it in the hands of his son, Prince Charles, who succeeds him under the title of King Charles XV. The new King was born May 3, 1826, & was married Jun 19, 1850, to a Dutch Princess, by whom he has several children.

The British mail steamer **Alma**, which left Aden Jun 11, with some 320 people on board, was wrecked the following morning upon a dangerous reef in the Red Sea. All the passengers escaped to land, with great difficulty. The British war steamer **Cyclops** was at anchor & hastened to the relief of the wrecked passengers. The crew, chiefly Lascars, deserted the vessel on the first appearance of danger, & the escape of the passengers was very remarkable.

St Vincent Female Orphan Asylum Grand Pic-Nic on Aug 8. Managers on the ground during the day:

Capt Goddard	H C McLaughlin	Jas Lackey
Dr J C Duhamel	Thos J Fisher	Robt Mahorney
John C Brent	Capt Carbery	Jas Lincoln
J C Fitzpatrick	John McDermot	Wm Harvey
C S Jones	John F Coyle	Patrick Jordan
Richd Clarke	Gregory Ennis	Richd Simms
R H Laskey	Col Hickey	Andrew Joyce
Wm H Ward	Jas Harvey	Thos Botentint
F Mohun	John D Clarke	H J McLaughlin
Peter Gallant	John F Ellis	Dr Walsh
Hiram Richey	Jas Fullerton	Wm T Dove
Edw Simms	Eugene Daley	Jacob Dyson
C Gautier	T V Shiel	Jas Coleman
Geo Savage	Dennis Callahan	Wm Flaherty

John F King	R Echorn	John Tonis
Jos Flashell	A C Shaw	Wm E Dant
Jas E Johnston	Sylvester Gates	Richd B Owens
D Connolly	Edw Allan	Martin King
Andrew Carroll	John Wise	
Hugh Donoho	Thos Magher	

Cmte from the Young Catholic Friends' Society:

Of Wash:

F McNerhany	J J Kane	Wm E Kennedy
Wm Ryan	Philip J McHenry	Jos Keenan
L Neumeyer	V E King	

Of Gtwn:

Lewis Carbery	Francis Harper	W Albert King
John Stakes	John J Bogue	Jas O'Donnoghue
Richd Pettite	Dr Kidwell	

Died: Jul 16, at Rockaway, L I, Mrs Mary Louisa Adam, wife of Wm C Johnson, of Utica, N Y, & grand-daughter of John Quincy Adams, the 6th Pres of the U S. Mrs Johnson was for many years a resident of Wash City, & whilst here, as well as the place of her late residence, was respected & loved by a wide circle of friends.

Died: Jul 18, at Annapolis, Md, Anna, daughter of Lt J Taylor Wood, U S Navy, aged 22 months.

Handsome residence & valuable real property for sale: the undersigned offers the estate on which he now resides, in Chas Co, Md, containing 500 acres of land of superior quality; located in a peninsula of country formed by the junction of the Potomac & Wicomica rivers, called Piccawaxen. Improvements consist of a commodious 2 story brick dwlg with numerous out bldgs. Mr H Luckett, now living with me, or my son, will show the premises. Address me at Allen's Fresh post ofc, Chas Co, Md. –John H Digges

Valuable farm for sale: by decree of Chas Co Circuit Court, the com'rs will sell at public sale, on Sep 1 next, the farm of the late Gen Wm Matthews, in Chas Co, Md; located on Gilbert Swamp; contains 768 acres, including the widow's dower. –Thos Carrico, Peter Wood, Thos O Bean, Wm S Keech, Geo W Carrico, Com'rs

MON JUL 25, 1859

Dr Jas P Screven, formerly Mayor of the city of Savannah, Geo, died at the Hot Springs, in Va, on Jul 16. He was in his 60th year, & had been for some time in ill health.

Hon Danl M Barringer, of N C, to hom was tendered the mission to Central America, has formally declined it.

Miss Mary Caroline Beiser, a native of N Y C, about 18 years of age, drowned on Fri while bathing at Coney Island. Miss Cornelia Gilley & the deceased were carried out by the current. Miss Gilley was floating on her back about 1/4th of a mile from shore when rescued. The body of Miss Beiser was recovered & conveyed to the residence of her father. -Courier

Orphans Court of Wash Co, D C. Letters testamentary on the personal estate of John B Boone, late of Wash Co, deceased. –Jane E Boone, Richd H Clarke, excs

Mrd: on Jul 19, by Rev Dr Gurley, Francis Lamb to Annie E Ridgely, both of Wash.

Died: on Jul 20, Enos E Berkley, in his 40th year.

Died: on Jul 7, at Mount Airy, Richmond Co, Va, Mrs Anne Neilson, relict of Mr Robt Neilson, of Balt, & daughter of the late Benj Ogle, of Belair, PG Co, Md.

Died: on Jul 23, at Calorama, Fauquier Co, Va, Wm Edward, aged 9 months & 5 days, only child of Ed T & Jane E Matthews.

Died: on Jul 21, in N Y C, Frank Brooke, youngest son of Robt & Caroline Brooke, aged 21 years & 11 months.

TUE JUL 26, 1859
Mr Lucius M Joslin, of Worcester, Mass, on Sat, feeling a little unwell, took what was supposed to be epson salts. He found he had mistakenly taken oxalic acid which was purchased 3 years ago. His wife gave him ground mustard & saved his life.

Obit-died: on May 31 last, Gen Cyrus Spink, at Wooster [Ohio.] He was born in Berkshire Co, Mass, Mar 24, 1793; & was 67 years of age. Both on his father's & his mother's side he came of Revolutionary stock. His father, Shibnah Spink, served through a large part of the Revolutionary war, & was at the battle of Long Island, & suffered the winter encampment at Valley Forge in 1777-78. His mother, Delight Spink, had a brother in the American army at Valley Forge, & he died during the terrible winter. The parents of Gen Spink were of the Quaker denomination, & his father was one of the few of that belief who took up arms in defence of the rights of his country. One of Gen Spinks' sisters ultimately became a preacher among the Quakers. Shibnah Spink & family removed from Berkshire Co, Mass, to Chautauque Co, N Y, somewhere about 1800. From then Gen Spink set out to seek his fortune in Ohio in the spring of 1815; appointed deputy county surveyor-took the oath of office on Oct 18, 1815; & he was married to his surviving companion, then Nancy Campbell Beall, daughter of Gen Reason Beall, Feb 19, 1819, 40 years ago last Feb.

Rev Geo McQueen departed this life, after a short illness, on the Island of Corcico, near the western coast of Africa, on Mar 25 last. He entered on his missionary work in Africa in 1853.

On Jul 22, Henry Lehne, who kept a pistol gallery at the Montg [Va] White Sulphur Springs, was killed by the accidental explosion of a pistol which he was loading. He was recently the proprietor of a saloon at Richmond, Va.

Died: on Jul 24, Penelope Earls, wife of J S Blackford, of Gtwn, aged 49 years.

Died: on Jul 17, after a short illness, of typhoid fever, Louisa E, eldest daughter of E A Eliason, of Gtwn, aged 24 years. Sudden & overwhelming has this event come upon us. Only a few days before health & life seemed bright & joyous to her.

WED JUL 27, 1859
Mount Vernon Estate, as occupied by Gen Washington at the time of his death, is divided into 2 unequal parts: the portion in the elbow of the Potomac & between that & Hunting Creek, called *River Farm*, consisting of about 2,000 acres. The other portion, between *Little Hunting Creek* & *Dogue Creek* consisted of about 6,000 acres, in the form of an irregular square, divided into 4 unequal farms: *Mansion House Farm*; *Union Farm*; *Dogue Run Farm*, & the *Muddy Hole Farm*. Washington's will devises the property east of *Little Hunting Creek* to Geo Fayette Washington & Lawrence Augustine Washington; about 2/3rds of the land between *Little Hunting Creek* & *Dogue Creek*, including the *Mansion House Farm*, to Bushrod Washington; & the residue, being the southwesterly part of this tract, to Lawrence Lewis, & his wife Eleanor Parke Lewis. Since the death of Washington the greater part of the *Muddy Hole Farm* & the *Union Farm*, some 1,600 acres in all, was purchased by Mr Aaron Legett, & a part of the *Union Farm* by Mr David Walton. The Ladies of the U S have purchased the *Mansion House Farm* & upwards of 200 acres, leaving still in the hands of Mr John A Washington about 1,000 acres of that part of the estate, extending from the Potomac to Little Hunting Creek, between the *Mansion House Farm* & the property of Mr Leggett. Mr Chalkley Gillingham has made for himself an exceeding pretty place in the pine woods by the long mill race constructed by Washington. The residence of the Lewis family remains, belonging to Mr John Mason, of Maine. –C Cushing

The Mobile papers announce the death of Hon John Gayle, Judge of the U S District Court of Ala, who died at his residence near Mobile on Jul 21. He was in his 67th year of his age, & his health had been declining for sometime previous to his death.

By order of the Orphans Court of Wash Co, D C, we shall sell the wood yard of the late J B Boone, on 10th st, the unexpired term of lease, stock of wood, office, & stable; also a good horse & cart. –Jane E Boone, Richd H Clarke, excs -Jas C McGuire & Co, aucts

Henry P Baldwin, the forger, on his way to Utica, escaped from the custody of Sheriff Bloom, of Cincinnati. He made a sudden spring from the car at 40 miles per hour, & was lost by the Sheriff. The cars were stopped & no trace of him could be found. [Aug 1st newspaper: Baldwin has been rearrested. He was examined before a police justice at Rome & committed on 2 charges in default of bail in $1,000 in each.]

Terrible gunpowder explosion on Jul 20, at Camargo, Ky, when fire was accidentally communicated to a keg of powder in the store of Dr Daniel. Injured: Alfred Yocum & his daughter, John Willoughby, Jas Ballard, Nicholas Willoughby, Wm Covey, a daughter of Dr Daniel, & a negro boy. Alfred Yocum is dangerously injured.

Died: on Jul 25, in his 58th year, Jeremiah Orme, one of the oldest & most respected merchants of Gtwn, D C. His funeral is this afternoon at 4 o'clock, from his late residence, at the corner of First & Market sts, Gtwn, D C.

THU JUL 28, 1859
On Sat Mr Chas Chapman, of New Haven, was suddenly taken with a sudden fit while sitting on the steps of his father's house, fell to the sidewalk & soon died.

Andrew Howitt drowned in New Bedford on Sunday morning. He was in the Mexican war with Taylor's army, & had 5 bullets shot into his breast & arm, two of which were never extracted. The wounds he received caused an aberration of mind. He received a pension from the Gov't of $96 a year.

Died: on Jul 27, in Wash City, Patrick F Hartnett, in his 65th year. His funeral is this afternoon at 5 o'clock, from his late residence, 568 M st, between 7th & 8th sts.

Died: on Jul 27, in Wash City, Elizabeth, infant daughter of Horatio N & Elizabeth B Easby, aged 11 months. Her funeral will be today at 4½ o'clock, from the residence of her parents.

Died: on Jul 23, in St Louis, Archibald E Orme, aged 74 years, a native of PG Co, Md. He emigrated to St Louis with his family when that city was in its infancy, & was one of its most enterprising citizens. He was beloved & esteemed by all who knew him.

Died: on Jul 16, at his residence, in Clarke Co, Va, Wm Fitzhugh Randolph, aged 63 years, youngest son of the late Wm Randolph, of Cumberland Co, Va. He entered upon the practice of law in early life & soon became highly distinguished as an advocate, but being stricken down by paralysis in its worst form, which deprived him of speech & of his physical powers, he had for many years led a life of inacton & of great bodily suffering. In the shades of the old <u>Chapel Grave yard</u> now sleep the remains of him who was loved by those who knew him best.

Died: on Jul 27, Rev Edw Kingsford, D D, in his 71st year. His funeral will be this afternoon at 4:30 o'clock, from the First Baptist Church, 10th st.

FRI JUL 29, 1859
Leeds [Eng] Intelligencer. Died: on Jul 20, aged 45, Mr Peter Matterson, of Low Dunsford, near Boroughbridge. He & his ancestry have been the owners & occupiers of the farm on which he died for more than 800 years. The farm was not entailed, & the owner has always been a Matterson, without adoption.

The celebrated Pottawatamie chieftain, Shau-bee-nay, died at his residence on his farm near Morris, Grundy Co, Ill, on Jul 19, aged about 75 years. In recognition of his services & position he received from the Federal Gov't, since 1829, the annuity of $200, & some years since purchased 20 acres of land, about 5 miles south-east of Morris, where he resided until his death. He was by birth an Ojibway, but marrying among the Pottawatamies, according to Indian custom, he identified himself with his wife's people.

The London papers record the death of Lt Gen Proctor, who played an important part in the last war between the U S & Great Britain, having commanded the 82nd regt at the battle of **Fort Erie**, & subsequently shared in the campaign along the Niagara frontier. He was colonel of the 97th regt. He died a few days since at his seat in Wales suddenly from disease of the heart. He had been 60 years in the army.

Mr H C Bailey, a young man formerly employed as book-keeper in the Bank of Troy, was killed at Plattsburgh on Thus last. Mr Torry shot Mr Bailey dead for some motive not mentioned.

Valuable real estate at public sale, under authority of a deed of trust from Saml A Masters & wife, dated Apr 1, 1857: sale on Aug 20, of a lot of ground in Alexandria city, beginning on Henry st. A tract of land in Loudoun Co, Va, containing 119 acres, 2 roods & 38 perches more or less. Also a tract of land adjoining the above, containing 401 acres, 1 rood & 20 perches, more or less. These lands bind on the Middlet Turnpike road. The bldgs are excellent & nearly new, consisting of a frame dwlg house, a large barn, & other necessary out-bldgs. –Francis L Smith, L Louis Kinzer, trustee

Mrd: on Jun 8, 1859, at Oregon city, Oregon, by Rev D Rutledge, Lt Henry C Hodges, U S A, to Miss Annie, daughter of Ex-Gov Geo Abernethy.

Mrd: on Jul 18, in Balt, by Rev Mr Dashiels, of Charles st M E Church, Edgar S Price, of Alexandria, Va, to Miss Marian V Bankhead, of Balt.

Mrd: on Jul 26, in Gtwn, by Rev Mr Edwards, Mr Emmanuel B Caton to Miss Susie Rose, both of Wash.

Mrd: on Jul 27, by Rev B F Bittinger, Mr Asa L Carrier to Miss Nevilley B Beall, all of Wash.

Died: on Jul 11, in Washington, Ky, David Bronaugh, 2nd son of David Bronaugh & Ann Sandidge, late of Spottsylvania Co, Va, in his 65th year, having patiently borne his great suffering since Sep 26 last, on which day he was seized with a violent paralytic stroke.

SAT JUL 30, 1859
Orphans Court of Wash Co, D C. Letters of administration on the personal estate of Peter Adams, late of the State of Va, deceased. –C Ingle, adm

The funeral of Dr Kingsford was held on Thu last at the 10th st Baptist Church, attended by a large number of people of Wash City: scriptures by Rev Dr Samson; discourse by Rev Dr Hill.

Rev J L Bartlett, Pastor elect of the Western Presbyterian Church, will be installed on Sabbath evening, by the Presbytery of D C. Rev Mason Noble, Moderator of the Presbytery, will preside; Rev Byron Sunderland, D D, will preach the sermon; Rev J C Smith, D D, will deliver the charge to the Pastor; & Rev Wm McLain will deliver the charge to the people.

Criminal Court-Wash-Fri. John Jones, Neil Morgan, & John Walker, on trial for riot on the occasion of the shooting of John Ennis by Hilleary Hutchins in Feb last. The jury convicted John Jones & Neil Morgan, but acquitted Walker.

Mrd: on Jul 28, by Rev P D Gurley, D D, Mr Henry C Lauck to Miss Siddie I McClery, both of Wash.

Died: on Jul 26, 1859, at his residence, **Prospect Hill**, PG Co, Md, Mr John M Brown, aged 57 years.

Died: on Jul 8, at Edward's Depot, Mississippi, of consumption, Mrs Eliz M Byrne, wife of John S Byrne, of Vicksburg, formerly of Wash City.

MON AUG 1, 1859
Col Titus, late of Kansas, & formerly of Alabama, has gone into the siler-mining business in Arizona.

Portugal: the Queen of Portugal died on Jul 16, from a severe attack of sore throat. It will be remembered that she married only a few months since.

Clinton Academy, Gtwn, D C, has removed to 107 West st, near Wash st, to the bldg heretofore occupied by Mr P A Powers. Next annual session will commence on Sep 5. -Geo Arnold, M A, Principal

Commencement at Yale College on Thu last. The graduating class numbered 105. The honorary degrees conferred are as follows: Honorary Master of Arts: Orlando W Wight, of Brooklyn, N Y; Wm R Donaghe, M D, N Y; Prof Wm H Brewer, of Wash College, Pa; Saml J Burr, Brooklyn, N Y; Oscar M Smith. Dr of Medicine: John B Trask, Calif, recommended by the Medical Society of Conn; Asabel Thompson, Farmington, Conn. Dr of Laws: Saml B Ruggles, N Y; Fred'k A P Barnard, Pres of the Univ of Mississippi. L L B: Ezra A Brainard, Henry M Dutton, Richd Z Johnson, Saml C Keeler, Milton Kinkhead, John Latta, Cyrus Northup. Bachelors of Philosophy: Henry A Dubois, Wm D Dwight, Alexis U Harriott, Geo D Seeley, Geo H Smith, Sutherland D Twining, Franklin Booth.

New Boot & Shoe Manufactory-504 Pa ave. –John Mills, Agent [Ad]

TUE AUG 2, 1859
Hon Richd Rush died on Jul 30 at his late residence in Phil. He was removed from an active participation in public affairs in his late years. He was descended from an honorable Revolutionary ancestry. Mr Rush was born on Aug 29, 1780; in 1811 he rose to the station of Atty Gen of the Commonwealth of Pa. He was appointed by the Pres the Comptroller of the Treasury at Wash, where he cemented with Madison a personal friendship such as his father maintained with Jefferson.

N Y, Jul 31, 1859. Among the passengers by the ship **Northern Light**, just arrived from Aspinwall, are Gen Lamar, U S Minister to Nicaragua; Mr Wells, Sec to the Gen; Manuel M Malierino, ex-Pres of New Granada; John S Stephenson & Chas S E Jones, bearers of dispatches from Wash from the U S Legations in Chile & New Granada.

In virtue of 2 writs of fieri facias, issued by F J Murphy, Justice of the Peace, for Wash Co, D C, I will expose to public sale, for cash, on Aug 25, all David Westerfield, jr's right, title, claim, & interest in & to part of square at a point on the line of 3rd st west, together with all & singular improvements thereon; seized & levied upon as the property of David Westerfield, jr, & will be sold to satisfy fieri facias No 1,709 & 4,135, in favor of Hamilton & Leach, & Thompson, Hamilton & Co. –J H Wise, constable

Criminal Court-Wash-Mon. 1-Jas McGee found guilty of assault: sentenced to pay $5 & costs. 2-Lewis Higdon found guilty of an assault: sentenced to pay a fine of $5 & costs. 3-Segent Groves was found guilty of an assault on Christian Umbaw.

Mrd: on Jul 18, in Lexington, Ky, by Rev Mr Morrison, A P Hill, U S Army, to Mrs Kitty G McClung, of the same place.

Died: on Jul 30, after an illness of 3 weeks, at the residence of Mr Absalom A Hall, Anne Arundel Co, Md, Edw Everett Hall, infant son of Baruch & Virginia B Hall, aged 4 months.

Circuit Court of Wash Co, D C. The Mayor, Recorder, Aldermen & Common Council of Gtwn vs Eliz Jewell, Ann Jewell, Thos Jewell, Henry C Jewell, Wm Jewell, Geo Jewell, Jas G Jewell & Frances his wife, Thos B Dawson & Eliz his wife, & their children, Mary J, Dawson, Annie J Dawson, Kate A Dawson, Richd J Alnutt, Wm Alnutt, Jas N Alnutt, Robt D Alnutt, & Mary C Alnutt, children of Catherine Alnutt, deceased, the widow, execs, & heirs at law of Wm Jewell, deceased. The bill which is a creditor's bill states that Wm Jewell, deceased, was indebted to the cmplnts in the sum of $1,200; that his personal estate is insufficient to pay his debts; that he died seized of certain real estate in D C & elsewhere, which is particularly set forth in the bill; that in 1855 he made his will, which, since his death, has been duly admitted to probate, devising certain interest in said real estate to the dfndnts above name, & all his personal estate to his widow, Eliz Jewell & making the said Eliz Jewell, & Thos Jewell, & Ann Jewell, executors of his said will. It further states that the children of Eliz Dawson & Catherine Alnutt aforesaid are all minors, & that all the dfndnts, except Thos Jewell & Ann Jewell, reside out of D C. The object & prayer of the bill is to have the personal estate applied to the debts & any deficiency made up by a sale of part of the real estate. Absent dfndnts to appear in this Court, in person or by solicitor, on or before the first Monday in Jan next. –Jas Dunlop, Chief Judge, Circuit Court of Wash Co, D C -Jno A Smith, clerk

Died: on Monday, after a painful illness of scarlet fever, Rose E, daughter of Edmond & Eugenia Brooke, in her 4th year. Her funeral will be from the residence of her parents at **Queensborough**, on Tue at 4 o'clock.

Died: on Aug 1, in Gtwn, R M Boyer, aged 82 years. His funeral is this afternoon at 5 o'clock, from Mrs Lang's tavern.

Died: on Aug 1, in Wash City, Francis Albert, son of John F & Mary E Bridget, aged 10 months. His funeral is this afternoon at 4½ o'clock, from the residence on D st, between 1st & 2nd sts.

WED AUG 3, 1859
News of the death of Mr Hopkins, the newly appointed Consul of the U S at Kingston, Jamaica, has been received at N Y. He died on Jul 14.

A son of S D Evans, of Haverhill, Mass, while playing with a pistol, Monday last, was accidentally shot by the hammer of the pistol slipping while he was attempting to cock it. The wound will probably prove fatal.

Public auction, by deed of trust from John N Trook & wife to Jas J Fowler, dated Jun 27, 1851, recorded in Liber J A S, No 30, folios 227 thru 230, of the land records of Wash Co, D C: sale on Sep 1: lots 6, 7, & 8 in square 464; lots 9, 10, & 11 in said square; adjoins the dividing line between the houses of Mrs Margaret Milburn & John N Trook; together with the bldgs & improvements thereon. –Jas J Fowler, trustee
-Jas C McGuire & Co, aucts

Rosewood piano forte, household & kitchen furniture at auction on Aug 9, at the residence of Mrs H M Pyfer, 9th & E sts. -A Green auct

The trial of Wesley B Fisher, at Ottawa, Ill, closed last week, & he has been sentenced to be hanged on Aug 17. He murdered his wife by shooting her in a moment of mad jealousy, & then ineffectually attempted to commit suicide by drowning himself. He is represented to be a reckless, hardened man. –Chicago Journal

Edw Falconer, a temperance lecturer, was arrested at N Y on Sunday last for preaching in the street, in violation of a city ordinance. He was held to bail to answer at the Court of General Sessions.

Died: yesterday, in Wash City, suddenly, Mr Matthew Wilson, printer, aged about 50 years. His funeral will take place this afternoon at 3 o'clock, from Mr Hancock's.

Died: on Jul 30, at Fairfax Court House, Va, Aaron W Daggett, in his 61st year.

Died: on Aug 2, John Andrew, only son of John & Mary Treadway, aged 1 year, 2 months & 10 days. His funeral will be from the residence of his parents on E st, between 11th & 12th sts, today at 4 o'clock.

Died: on Jul 26, 1859, in Buffalo, N Y, Martha Eliz Sherman, daughter of Robt D Sherman, aged 16 years.

Died: on Aug 2, after a long & painful illness, Elanora, aged 1 year, infant daughter of John H & Georgianna Bird.

Died: on Jul 29, at Springfield, Alexandria Co, Col Wm Minor, in his 83rd year. In the war of 1812 he was actively & usefully employed in the military operation in this neighborhood, having a command in the militia, & was subsequently a magistrate of the county. He was much esteemed by a large circle of relatives & friends.

Cincinnati, Aug 2. Hon Horace Mann, LL D, President of Antioch College, in this State, died there this afternoon. He was formerly from Mass, & a staunch friend of a general education.

THU AUG 4, 1859
Disasters to our Navy, collected from authentic data exhibits all the disasters that have happened to our naval marine from 1798 to 1859.
Vessels lost:
The sloop **Albany**, 20 guns, Cmder J T Gerry, Gulf of Mexico, 1814.
The schnr **Alligator**, 12 guns, Lt T M Dale, Carysfort Reef, 1852.
The ship **Boston**, 18 guns, Cmder G F Pearson, West Indies, 1846.
The brig **Boxer**, 14 guns, Lt J Porter, off Balize, 1817.

The brig **Chippewa**, 14 guns, West Indies, 1816.
The ship **Concord**, 18 guns, Cmder W Boerum, east coast of Africa, 1843.
The steamer **Edith**, 2 guns, Lt J McCormick, Calif, 1849.
The schnr **Enterprize**, 12 guns, Lt J Gallagher, Little Curacoa Sea, 1823.
The ship **Epervier**, Lt J T Shubrick, at sea, 1815.
The bomb brig **Etna**, 11 guns, [cmder's name not given,] New Orleans, 1812.
The schnr **Ferret**, 3 guns, Midshipman M S Booth, West Indies, 1825.
The schnr **Ferret**, 8 guns, Lt L Kearney, Stony Inlet, 1814.
The schnr **Grampus**, 12 guns, Lt E A Downs, off Charleston, 1843.
The Gun **Boat No 158**, Lt U P Levy, Bay of Honduras, 1823.
The schnr **Helen**, 4 guns, [cmder's name not given,] Delaware Bay, 1815.
The brig **Hornet**, 18 guns, Master Cmder O Norris, off Tampico, 1829.
The ship **Insurgent**, 36 guns, Capt P Fletcher, at sea, 1800.
The schnr **Lynx**, 6 guns, Lt J R Madison, at sea, 1820.
The schnr **Onkahye**, 2 guns, Lt O H Berryman, West Indies, 1840.
The ship **Peacock**, 18 guns, Lt Wm L Hudson, Columbia river, 1841.
The brig **Pickering**, 14 guns, Lt B Hillar, at sea, 180.
The schnr **Porpoise**, 4 guns, Lt B Hillar, at sea, 1800.
The schnr **Revenge**, 12 guns, Lt O H Perry, off Newport, 1811.
The pilot boat **Sea Gull**, 2 guns, Passed Midshipman J W E Reed, off Cape Horn, 1839.
The schnr **Shark**, 12 guns, Lt N M Howison, Columbia river, 1846.
The schnr **Sylph**, 1 gun, Lt H E V Robinson, West Indies, 1831.
The brig **Truxton**, 10 guns, Cmder E W Carpenter, Tuspan bar, 1846.
The ship **Wasp**, 18 guns, Master Cmder Blakely, at sea, 1814.
The schnr **Wildcat**, 3 guns, Lt B Kennon, West Indies, 1824.
The sloop **Yorktown**, 16 guns, Cmder John Marston, Island of Mayo, 1850.
Vessels captured:
The sloop **Alligator**, 1 gun, Sailing-master R Shephard, New Orleans, 1819.
The sloop-of-war **Argus**, 16 guns, Master Cmder Wm H Allen, English channel, 1813.
The frig **Chesapeake**, 36 guns, Capt J Lawrence, off Boston, 1813.
The ship **Eagle**, 3 guns, Lt Sydney Smith, Lake Champlain, 1813.
The frig **Essex**, 32 guns, Capt David Porter, Valparaiso, 1814.
The ship **Frolic**, 18 guns, Master Cmder J Bainbridge, off Havana, 1814.
The sloop **Growler**, 3 guns, Lt Sydney Smith, Lake Champlain 1813.
The schnr **Growler**, 2 guns, Lt D Deacon, Lake Ontario, 1813.
The schnr **Julia**, 2 guns, Sailing-master Traub, Lake Ontario, 1813.
The brig **Nautilus**, 12 guns, Lt Wm M Crane, off N Y, 1812.
The schnr **Ohio**, 1 gun, Sailing-master M Cally, Lake Erie, 1814.
The frig **President**, 44 guns, Capt Stephen Decatur, off N Y, 1815.
The brig **Rattlesnake**, 14 guns, Lt J Renshaw, at sea, 1814.
The schnr **Retaliation**, 14 guns, Lt W Bainbridge, West Indies, 1798.
The schnr **Scorpion**, 2 guns, Lt D Turner, Lake Huron, 1814.
The brig **Siren**, 16 guns, Lt J N Nicholson, at sea, 1814.
The schnr **Somers**, 2 guns, Lt Conklin, Lake Erie, 1814.

The schnr **Tigress**, 1 gun, Sailing-master Chaplin, Lake Huron, 1814.
The brig **Viper**, 10 guns, Lt I D Henley, at sea, 1813.
The brig **Vixen**, 12 guns, Lt G W Reed, at sea, 1812.
The brig **Vixen**, 14 guns, Capt Thos Hall, at sea, 1813.
The schnr **Wasp**, 18 guns, Master Cmder J Jones, at sea, 1812.
Vessels burnt:
The ship *****Argue**, 18 guns, Washington City, 1814.
The ship *****Boston**, 28 guns, do, 1814.
The ship *****Columbia**, 44 guns, on the stocks, 1814.
The ship *****General Green**, 28 guns, Capt C R Perry, Wash, 1814.
The ship **Greenwich**, 16 guns, Lt J M Gamble, Marquesas Islands, 1814.
The ship **John Adams**, 28 guns, Capt C Morris, Hampden, Maine, 1814.
The steamship **Missouri**, 10 guns, Capt J G Newton, Gibraltar, 1814.
The schnr **Sea Horse**, 1 gun, Sailing-master Johnson, New Orleans, 1814.
*These vessels were burnt by order, to prevent them falling into the hands of the enemy during the invasion of Washington in 1814.
Vessels broken up:
The ship **Alert**, 20 guns, at Norfolk, 1829.
The ship **Congress**, 36 guns, at Norfolk, 1836.
The ship **Cyane**, 34 guns, at Phil, 1836.
The ship **Erie**, 18 guns, at Boston, 1841.
The ship **Guerrier**, 44 guns, at Norfolk, 1841.
The schnr **Hornet**, 5 guns, at Norfolk, 1820.
The ship **Iowa**, 44 guns, at Norfolk, 1842.
The ship **Louisiana**, 16 guns, at New Orleans, 1821.
The ship **Macedonian**, 38 guns, at N Y, 1835.
The ship **Natchez**, 18 guns, at N Y, 1840.
The steamship **Princeton**, 9 guns, at Boston, 1849.
The ketch **Spitfire**, 3 guns, at Norfolk, 1820.
The bomb brig **Vengeance**, 3 guns, at N Y, 1818.
The bomb brig *****Vesavius**, 11 guns, at N Y, 1829.
The ship **Washington**, 74 guns, at N Y, 1843.
Vessels blown up:
The schnr **Caroline**, 14 guns, Cmder I D Henley, New Orleans, 1814.
The steamship **Fulton**, 30 guns, Cmdder J T Newton, Brooklyn, 1829.
The ketch **Intrepid**, 4 guns, Master Cmder R Somers, off Tripoli, 1804. [*Possibly Vesavius-very light print.]

Rev Dr Kenrick, Archbishop of Balt, arrived in St Louis on Thu last, & is staying with his brother, the Archbishop of St Louis. These gentlemen, own brothers, & both archbishops, have not, it is stated, seen each other but twice in 18 years, owing to the heavy labors imposed upon them by their archbishoprics.

The death of Rev Dr Jas W Alexander, of N Y, took place on Jul 31 at a watering place in Va, to which the deceased had repaired in search of health. Dr Alexander was the eldest son of Rev Dr Archibald Alexander, long time a professor of theology in the Princeton Seminary. Born in Louisa Co, Va, in 1804, he graduated at Princeton College in 1820.

Mrd: on Aug 2, at Christ Church, by Rev Alfred Holmead, Mr Wm H Thompson, son of Wm Thompson, to Miss Emma Jones, daughter of Mr Cornelius Jacobs, all of Wash City.

Albany, Aug 3. Fatal accident on the Northern Railroad last night near Schagticoke. Known killed: Mrs Schuyler, of Albany; Mrs Cooley, wife of the conductor, Albany; Chas Berthelon, brakesman, Albany; Chas Plimpton, mail agent, Vt; David Russell, express messenger, Albany; Patrick Connolly, brakesman, Greenbush. Wounded: C S Cooley, conductor, Albany, badly; Thos McCarrick, new boy, right leg broken, & otherwise injured; Mich Flannerty, Troy, passenger, badly injured, supposed internally.

FRI AUG 5, 1859
Bloody affair at Waterbury, Conn, on Sat, at a German house, Meyer's Hotel, in which Jas Shannon was stabbed & probably fatally injured by John Riggs. Riggs was arrested.

Madame Jenny Lind Goldschmidt is to visit Ireland in the autumn for the purpose of singing in cratorios. She intends giving the Messiah for the benefit of the Mercers' Hospital, in Dublin.

Translation from a recent Paris Journal des Debate by M Jomard, of the French Institute: Obiutary of the late Robt Walsh. He died at Paris, where he had filled the post of Consul General. This literateur, by his attainments, his impartiality, & the elevation of his character, was a happy inter-medium, a point of union between 3 great nations, his own, England & France. Robt Walsh was born in Balt, in 1785, of an honorable family, originally Irish, his father, Count Walsh, Baron Shannon, having come to this country while young, being of the elder branch, the younger following Jas II to France. Robt Walsh was educated in 2 Catholic Colleges of America. He died Feb 8, after a short illness, 74 years of age, leaving a large inconsolable family.

Gen Earl Cathcart died on the 17th ult at his residence at St Leonarn's on Sea. He was brother of Gen Cathcart who was killed at Inkermann, & was brought up to the military profession. He entered the army in May, 1799, & for the first 16 years saw much active service, having served in the Heider expedition in 1790; in Naples & Sicily during 1805-06; at the Walcheran expedition in 1809, in 1812, taking part in the battles of Barossa, Salamanca, & Vittoria, during the campaigns of 1815 in the Netherlands & France. He was present at Waterloo as one of the Royal Staff Corps. In 1837 he was appointed Cmder of the Forces in Scotland, & Govn'r of Edinburgh Castle; in 1845 he was made Govn't & Cmder in 'chief of Canada, Nova Scotia, & New Brunswick.

Foreign intelligence: a dispatch from Brescia announces the death of the Duke of Abrantes, [son of the famous Junot,] who was wounded at the battle of Solferino. The thigh had to be amputated, & the patient did not long survive the operation. The Duke was Chief of the Staff of one of the divisions of the army of Italy.

Albany was startled Aug 2 by the intelligence that the Trestle Bridge of the northern railroad had fallen, carrying with it the through train from Eagle Bridge. The bridge spanned a chasm of about 40 feet in breadth & 30 feet in depth. Killed: C Plympton, mail agent; David S Russell, express agent; Chas Berthelong, brakeman; *Pataick Connelly, machinist; Howard A Wright, of this city; & Dennis Cahill, laborer. Mrs Geo M Griffen, of this city, & 3 children were in the passenger car-she seized them & went to the rear of the car, which remained on the bank, & escaped. Mr Cooley, conductor, wife & child, & Mrs John Cooley, mother of Mrs Cooley: Mr Cooley snatched the child, but its mother & grandmother were both instantly killed. His wife & mother-in-law went up in the train with him for a ride. [*Copied as written.]

Trustee's sale: by decree of the Circuit Court for PG Co, in equity, in the case of Ann Eliza Brent & Henry Waring Brent vs Mary Victoria Brent & others: public sale on Sep 8 next, at the late residence of Jas R Brent, deceased, on the premises, that tract of land of which he died seized & possessed, **Friendship**, lately known as **Brentville**, containing about 350 acres. It is located a quarter of a mile of *Scaggs' Crossing*, on the Balt & Wash railroad, within 2 miles of Beltsville. Improvements consist of a commodious frame dwlg, & every desirable bldg, all of which have been erected but a few years. -N C Stephen, C C Magruder, trustees

Miss Bates, the sister of Hon Edw Bates, of St Louis, recently emancipated the last of 32 slaves, who formed part of her inheritance, & whom she had gradually set free as they became prepared to take care of themselves in freedom. Judge Bates emancipated the last of his slaves several years ago.

Mrd: on Aug 4, at St Matthew's Church, by Rev E Q S Waldron, Patrick O'Hagan, of Balt, to Lizzie A, 2nd daughter of Mr Jas Stuart.

SAT AUG 6, 1859
Lisbon [17th] Correspondence of the London News. The death of the young & beautiful Stephanie, Queen of Portugal, took place this evening. She passed along the streets but 12 months ago a blooming bride. The Queen's illness commenced on Monday last, when her Majesty accompanied the King to Vendas Norvas to inspect the proving of a new rifled cannon. The day was burning hot, & at first it was thought she had a slight sunstroke, but at last was recognized as the fatal disease diptheria.

On Monday last a steam grist & saw mill, belonging to Jas H Gibbons, in the lower part of PG Co, Md, was entirely destroyed by fire. The loss is estimated at $10,000. No insurance.

St John's College, Annapolis, Md: Annual Commencement on Aug 3. Bachelor of Arts conferred upon the graduating class: Wm Hersey Hopkins, Jas Edgar Richardson, Thos St Geo Pratt, John Riggs Brown, Adolphus Thos Pindle, John Wm Brewer, & Richd Rawlings Goodwin. English diplomas were awarded to Dennis Claude Handy & Jefferson Dent Loker. Degree of Master of Arts was conferred upon the graduating class of 1856 as follows: Marshal Chapman, B A; Hammond Claude, B A; Philip G Clayton, B A; John A Conner, B A; Louis G Gassaway, B A; Thos B Kent, B A; Wm G Ridout, B A; Alvan C Wilson, B A. The honorary degree of Dr of Laws was conferred upon Rt Rev Wm Rollison Whittingham, D D, & Hon Roger B Taney, Chief Justice of the U S. The Alumni Prizes of fifty & twenty-five dollars, were awarded to Wm Hersey Hopkins of the senior class, & Dorsey Thompson of the jr class, respectively, for having made the highest attainments in scholarship in their several classes.

Trustee's sale on Sep 9, by deed of trust from Gottlieb Schlegel & wife, dated Apr 16, 1857, recorded in Liber J A S No 133, folios 212 thru 215, one of the records for Wash Co, D C: part of lot 6 in square 488, with a 2 story frame house.
–John Angermann, trustee -Jas C McGuire & Co, aucts

Memphis Criminal Court: Matthew McDowell, on trial for the murder of W H Johnson, was found guilty of murder in the 2nd degree & sentenced to 10 years' imprisonment in the penitentiary. The murder of Johnson was committed 12 years ago, & nothing was known of the crime until McDowell confessed the crime.

Henry Grattan, the younger, is dead. He was once member of Parliament for Meath, & only surviving son of the great Henry Grattan. He died suddenly on the 16th ult, at his residence in the county of Wicklow. He leaves no male issues; he leaves 2 daughers, both recently married, who will inherit the large estates in Ireland. Disease of the heart is said to have been the cause of his death.

Dr Jas J Irby, being in Hamilton, Geo, on Aug 26, was, while taking out the cushions of his buggy previous to a rain, struck by lightning & instantly killed. He leaves a wife & children, & a large circle of friends, to mourn.

Jas Mullen, convicted of the murder of Jas McGlone, on Jul 28, 1858, was hung at New Orleans on Jul 30.

Mrd: on Aug 4, by Rev Dr Gurley, Jacob Bigelow to Mrs Rebecca M Ogden, daughter of the late Jas Moore, of the Treasury Dept.

Died: yesterday, in Wash City, Mr Alex'r Murphy, aged 67 years. His funeral is tomorrow at 2:30 o'clock, from his late residence, 460 Mass ave, between 5th & 6th sts.

Died: on Aug 4, at Balt, after a short illness, Wm H Topping, of Wash City, in his 40th year. His funeral will be from his late residence, 408 13th st, this morning at 10 o'clock.

Died: yesterday, of whooping cough, Eugene J, youngest son of Geo E & Mary Helen Jensenney, of Winchester, Va, in his 19th month. His funeral will take place from the residence of his grandfather, John S Gallaher, 369 F st, at 4 o'clock this afternoon.

Died: on Aug 2, near Gtwn, D C, Mary, infant daughter of Hugh & Eliza Caperton.

MON AUG 8, 1859
The pension agents in N C report the death of one Revolutionary soldier & pensioner for the half year ending Jun 30, 1859, viz. John Hammond, of Robeson Co.

List of Revolutionary soldiers on the rolls of the States of Georgia & Alabama who are regularly receiving their pensions, & their age in 1859: Georgia:
Micajah Brooks, Polk Co, age 98 years.
Wm Coggin, Gordon Co, age 104 years.
John Hames, sen, Murray Co, age 107 years.
John McMillion, Habersham Co, age 99 years.
John Nicholson, Union Co, age 96 years.
Alabama: Reuben Stevens, Chambers Co, age 97 years.

Trustee's sale of small frame house & lot on north M st, between 12th & 13th sts west, by deed of trust from Jas McDonald & wife, dated Nov 17, 1858, recorded in Liber J A S, No 164, folios 432, of the land records for Wash Co, lot 31 in subdivision of square 282. -John C Harkness, H Naylor, trustee -J C McGuire & Co, aucts

Died: on Aug 5, of whooping cough, at the residence of his grandfather, John S Gallaher, in Wash City, Eugene J, youngest son of Geo E & Mary Helen Senseney, of Winchester, Va.

Accident of the S C Railroad on Thu. The engine F H Elmore, with tender, left Charleston, & the boilers exploded, killing: Thos Kingdon, about 40, leaving a wife & children; H Von Delkin, about 30, leaving a wife & children; Adam Dougan, about 35, leaving a wife & children; L M Chitty, 24, leaving a wife; & A Mitchell, 35, leaving a wife & children.

The Memphis Appeal says Mr Wm Fairchild, his wife & child, while riding in a buggy near Utica, Hinds Co, Miss, a few days ago, were all killed by the falling of a tree, which was thrown on the buggy, crushing them to the earth.

TUE AUG 9, 1859
Died: on Aug 7, in Gtwn, Eliz Dick, in her 85th year. Her funeral will take place from the residence of Judge Dunlop, in Gtwn, on Aug 9, at 10 o'clock.

Died: on Aug 7, Georgella Hilt, only child of D C W & Julia F Ourand, aged 10 months & 26 days.

The late Richd Rush, who died on Jul 30th, would have been 79 years old if he had lived a month longer. He was appointed by Govn't Snyder Atty Gen of the State of Pa; then he was promoted by Pres Madison to succeed the late Judge Duvall as Comptroller of the U S Treasury-that was in 1811. His distressing illness lasted for several months; his arrangements for death were made with composure. Surrounded by the children with whom cultivated as companions, Richd Rush lived long in delightful intimacy, he calmly left this world for a better. Their excellent mother, for 40 years his constant counselor, preceed her husband a few years ago.

Circuit Court of D C in Chancery, No 1,368. Emily Cassin vs Steph J Cassin et al. Jos R Cassin, trustee, on Apr 25, 1859, sold lot 16 & part of lot 15, in square 5, in Wash City, with dwlg house thereon, to J Williams, for $2,600, & on Apr 26, he sold lot 28, in Beall's addition to Gtwn, & part of lot 3, with a dwlg house thereon, to John L Kidwell, for the sum of $1,860, & also lot 161, in Beall's addition to Gtwn, with 2 story brick dwlg house, to John E Cox, for $1,980; also lot 95, in Beall's addition to Gtwn, with 4 story brick bldg thereon, to J Thos Davis, for $6,509; & also lot 96 & 97, adjoining the above, to Jos Libbey, for $6,500; & also lots 97 & 97, adjoining the above, to Jos Libbey, for the sum of $1,200; the purchasers have complied with the terms of sale.
–Jno A Smith, clerk

Died: on Aug 8, William Alfred, aged 10 months & 16 days, only son of Alfred H & Margaret E Marlow. His funeral will be from his father's residence, on East Capitol st, between 4th & 5th sts, this evening at 5 o'clock.

Desirable farm in Albemarle, Va, called *Forest Hill*, for sale; formerly the residence of John Watson, deceased, & more recently that of his widow, will be sold by the undersigned, as exc of the decedent, on Sep 8, 1859. Farm contains about 1,025 acres, opposite the farm of Benj H Magruder, & adjoins the lands of Jas T Marshall, Geo F Stachlin, Mrs Macon, & others. It is located 6 miles below Charlottesville. Improvements are a frame house & numerous out bldgs. Full possession given on Jan 1 next. –Jas R Watson, exc

Trustee's sale of valuable real estate, by decree of the Circuit Court for PG Co, in Equity, passed in a cause wherein Isaac Gibson & others are cmplnts, & Abraham Wingerd & others are respondents, the subscriber, as trustee, will sell at public sale, at the dwlg house on Sep 7 next, all that tract of real estate of which the late John P Wingerd died seized & possessed, containing 150 acres, more or less. It is located in Bladensburg district, PG Co; adjoins the lands of the late Thos W Cumming, Dr Fairfax, & others. The house is a large new frame dwlg, & other necessary out-houses. Information will be given by Mr McDaniel, who lives in the log house on the farm, or by Mr Chas Digges, who lives near by, or the subscriber at Upper Marlboro, Md. –Shelby Clark, trustee

Died: on Aug 8, John George, only son of R & A E Eichhorn, aged 11 months & 22 days. His funeral is at 4 o'clock P M, from the residence of his parents, corner of 3rd & F sts.

WED AUG 10, 1859

Taking passage today at Warrenton for Alexandria was a venerable gentleman, who with his wife, married daughter & her husband, & 2 grandchildren entered the cars bound to their homes in Balt. Before they had been in motion 5 minutes the old gentleman's head fell back & he died, of heart disease. He was Rev Thos McGee, a Methodist Minister, connected, we think, with the Balt Conference. He had been on a visit to a son living in Warrenton. Mr Thomas, his son-in-law, said his family had been warned of his condition. –Alexandria Sentinel of Monday
+
Died: suddenly, at Warrenton, Va, Rev Thos McGee, of the Balt M E Conference, in his 65th year.

Obit-died: on Aug 2, at Yellow Springs, Ky, Hon Horace Mann, formerly of Mass, & late Pres of Antioch College, in Ohio. He was born in Franklin, Mass, on May 4, 1796. -N Y Times

Orphans Court of Wash Co, D C. In the case of Rebecca Sears & Jas W Sears, jr, excs of Jas W Sears, deceased, the excs & Court have appointed Aug 30th for the final settlement of the personal estate of the deceased, of the assets in hand. -Ed N Roach, Reg/o wills

Two convicts of the Ohio Penitentiary, W B Shade, alias Richd Dort, & John Sweeny, on Aug 3, attempted to escape. Shade was shot by the guard & mortally wounded. Sweeny was shot in the legs & neck, & will probably recover.

Mrs U H Lawrence will open on the first Monday in Sept a School for Children between the ages of 4 & 9 years. References: Randolph Coyle, Prof Wm MacLeod, C Bestor, Dr J B Gibbs, & Fitzhugh Coyle.

Died: on Tue, Col Wm Doughty, in his 87th year. His funeral is on Wed at 4 o'clock, from his late residence on 3rd st, Gtwn, D C.

Died: on Aug 9, in Wash City, Isabella, wife of Joel C Green, in her 26th year. Her funeral is this afternoon at 4 o'clock, at the Wesley Chapel, corner of 5th & F sts.

Died: on Aug 7, at his residence, in PG Co, Md, Thos P Ryon, in his 71st year.

Died: on Aug 9, in Gtwn, after a long & painful illness, Mr Philip Gormley, in his 52nd year, a native of the county of Longford, Ireland, but for the last 30 years a resident of the District of Columbia. His funeral will take place on Thursday evening at 4 o'clock, from his late residence, on Jefferson st.

THU AUG 11, 1859

G P R James, the novelist, has determined to leave Venice & return to Va, for the purpose of making that State his permanent abiding place.

The Paris papers of Jul 26th publish the text of the preliminaries of peace agreed upon & signed at Villafranca, by the Emperors Napoleon III & Francis Joseph; between his Majesty the Emperor of Austria & his Majesty the Emperor of the French. The two Sovereigns will favor the creation of an Italian Conference. The Confederation shall be under the honorary presidency of the Holy Father, etc. Done at Villafranca, Jul 11, 1859.

Thos Ewbank, the late Com'r of Patents, was born May 11, 1792, in Barnard Castle, Durham, England; at age 13 was apprenticed to a tin & copper smith, plumber, & shot maker. He recently published "Thoughts on Matter & Force."

Revolutionary pensions in Conn: with their age in 1859:
David Bostwick, Litchfield Co, 98 years
John Brooks, Fairfield Co, 96 years
Benj Cobb, Middlesex Co, 98 years
Jacob Hurd, Middlesex Co, 97 years
Nehemiah W Lyon, Fairfield Co, 100 years
Wm Williams, Litchfield Co, 97 years

On Sat Harrison T Wheeler & Geo W Marshall, were arrested in Boston for having circulated forged checks, purporting to be drawn by Allen, Neale & Co, Brokers, 18 State st; Gideon Beck, auctioneer, 92 Federal st; Babson & Co, Fisher Dealers, & others, to the amount of nearly $2,000. The parties arrested are accused of having been engaged in buying goods & paying for them with forged checks since Jun 8.

Mrd: on Aug 9, in Wash City, at the Church of the Ascension, Rev Dr Pinckney, Mr Townsend D Seaton, of Loudoun Co, Va, to Mrs Mary Peyton Johnson, of Wash, D C.

Died: on Aug 10, in Wash City, Philip C Johnson, aged 64 years. His funeral is this afternoon, at 5 o'clock, from his late residence, 266 F st, between 13th & 14th sts.

Died: on Aug 3, in Gtwn, D C, Gen Geo W Biscoe, in his 71st year.

FRI AUG 12, 1859
Cleveland Herald: on Sunday Elisha T Sterling, one of Cleveland's old residents, was found upon Bank st, covered with blood, under circumstances indicating foul play. Mr Sherman who was with Mr Sterling, said he saw him fall down the stairs. The medical gentlemen who examined Mr Sterling's wounds insinuate that his death was probably caused by a severe blow from a club in the hands of some person to them unknown. [Aug 16th newspaper: The City Councils of Cleveland, Ohio, have offered a reward of $2,000 for the arrest & conviction of the murderer of the late E T Sterling. The county has also offered a reward of $1,000. The sum offered by Mr W J Warner will make the reward amount to $3,500.]

Household & kitchen furniture at auction on Aug 17, at the residence of David Callaghan, 4½ st, between I & K sts, Island. -A Green auct

Mr Wm A Perrin, of Stanton, was bitten by a rattlesnake at Stribling Springs on Sat last, & died from the effects of the poison on Sunday. He had caught the snake & was playing with it at the time the wound was inflicted.

Died: on Aug 11, in Wash City, Gen John Mason, in his 64th year. His funeral will be from his late residence, 122 Pa ave, tomorrow at 10 A M.

Died: on Aug 10, in Wash City, after a painful illness, Henry Clay Bacon, aged 7 years, youngest son of Washington & Sarah R Bacon. His funeral is this afternoon at 3 o'clock, from 317 6th st west.

Orphans Court of Wash Co, D C. Letters of administration on the personal estate of Timothy Downs, late of Wash Co, deceased. –Ellen Downs, admx

SAT AUG 13, 1859
The Firemen's parade at Shippensburg had a melancholy termination in the loss of Capt Jas B McCartney, who in attempting to reach the platform, when the train stopped, missed his hold, & slipped under the car. He was still living, but horribly mangled, when he was brought to town to his father's residence. He died about 3 hours later.
+
On Fri was found the dead body of Sylvester Retinger, a member of the Hope Company of Chambersburg, & a former resident of Bedford Co. He was returning from the parade at Shippensburg, when he lost his hat & went back for it. That was the last time he was seen, until his body was found. –Carlisle [Pa] Herald, Aug 10

In Equity, State of N C, Cleaveland Co. Spring Term, 1859. In the case of Robt Smith et al vs John Miller et al. The plntf, Wm R, Jas M & Newton Smith, died, at spring term, 1857, file a petition against the dfndnts, John, Jonathan, Mathew, & Jas Miller, heirs at law of Jane Miller, deceased; the heirs at law of Eliz Vinzant, deceased; of Margaret Smith, deceased; of Hugh Smith, deceased; of John Smith, deceased; & of Wm Smith, deceased; for the sale of the real estate of Jas Smith, deceased, who died at his residence in Cleaveland [formerly Rutherford] county in 1842. The land of said Jas Smith, deceased, have been sold, & whereas the dfndnts are non-residents of the State of N C, & many of them have not been heard of for more than 20 years, notice is given that they are to appear at the court-house in Shelby on the 11th Monday after the 4th Monday in Sep, 1859, or the proceeds of the estate of Jas Smith, deceased, of Cleaveland Co, N C, will be paid over to the plntfs in this case. -Witness, Thos Williams, clerk & master.

The St Louis Democrat of Monday says: some 4 weeks ago a Frenchman, Louis Laclere, a laborer, was bitten on the arm & wrist by a dog. He died on Sunday night.

Lafayette Institute, 309 F st, between 11th & 12th sts, will commence on the first Monday in Sept. –L C Loomis, A M, Principal Professor

Gen Ed Watts, & well known citizen of Va, died on Aug 9, at his late residence in Roanoke. –Richmond Whig

Falls Plantation on James River for sale: for the purpose of settling the estate of the late Jos Marx, deceased: contains 1,000 acres; comfortable dwlg & excellent barns & out-bldgs. The slaves & stock will be sold with the land, or separately, if the purchaser may prefer. Apply to Saml Marx, exc, of Jos Marx, deceased.

Mrd: on Jul 11, 1859, by Rev Dr Carothers, Mr Anthony M Trunnell to Miss Harriet A Hazel, all of Wash City.

Died: on Aug 8, at Chester, N H, Elizabeth Chester, child of Edmund F & Margaret A French, of Wash City, aged 9 months.

Died: on Aug 12, in Wash City, Wm A, son of Joshua & Susanna Devan, aged 6 weeks & 2 days.

MON AUG 15, 1859
Orphans Court of Wash Co, D C. Letters testamentary on the personal estate of Jeremiah Orme, late of Wash Co, deceased. –G W Orme, exc

N Y, Aug 13, 1859. 1-The latest news from Havana, by the Quaker City, states that the mortality at that place was increasing, & that 2 Americans, Mr Turner, of New Haven, & Mr J B Phillips, of Phil, lately of St Louis, had died. 2-Lt Stamford, of N C, attached to the revenue-cutter **Harriet Lane**, died today.

Mary & Gertrude Lemist, daughters of Mr Geo H Lemist, formerly of Boston, now a resident of N Y, & Miss Bradford, a daughter of Jas Bradford, a lawyer in Sheffield, Mass, were drowned at the latter place on Wed last when bathing in the Housatonic river.

The Annapolis Gaz states that Mr Benj Hutchinson, a young man of that city, died on Monday from injuries received on Sat on the Wash Branch railroad. He imprudently put his head out of a window whilst the cars were in motion & struck it against a bridge post, causing a wound which resulted in death.

A bold robbery was perpetrated on Sat at the residence of Mr Chas F Wood, on 9th st, between E & F sts, when Mrs Wood had gone to market. Money & a gold watch were taken.

Mrd: on Jul 11, 1859, by Rev Dr Carothers, Mr Anthony N Trunnell to Miss Harriet A Hazel, all of Wash City.

Railroad accident yesterday on the line of the Alexandria, Loudoun, & Hampshire railroad. The disaster was caused by the material train being thrown, in coming in contact with a cow, against the supporters & braces of the bridge, knocking them away, causing the fall of the structure. Killed were Thos Hanretty & Chas Daily. Hanretty left a wife & 4 children. Severely injured were Jas Gallaher & Patrick McCarty, who are both at the Almshouse; also Bartholomew Murphy, Jerry McCarty, & Thos Welsh, also of the Almshouse. Patrick Sullivan, John Dogan, John Donnelly, Timothy Sullivan, Anthony Dunn, Jas McFarlan, Peter Cariene, Thos Creed, P L Davis, Jas Grady, & John Penn were bruised & injured. –Alex Gaz

On Tue last an assault was committed in Gtwn by a young man, Henry Funk, on another young man working in the same shop with him, Thos Hawkins. Funk struck his victim from behind, as the latter was washing his hands. Funk is in jail.

Mrd: on Aug 9, in Emmanuel Church, Middleburg, Va, by Rev Wm Sparrow, D D, Rev O A Kinsolving, [Rector of that Church,] to Lucy Lee, eldest daughter of Gen Asa Rogers, of Loudoun.

Mrd: on Aug 9, at Annapolis, Md, Jas Buchanan Henry, of N Y, to Mary H Nicholson, daughter of Col Jos H Nicholson, of the former place.

Foreign: 1-Ex-President Pierce passed through Liverpool, en route for the lake district. He was expected to sail for N Y in about a fortnight. 2-The Earl of Minto, father-in-law of Lord John Russell, is dead.

TUE AUG 16, 1859
Mrd: on Aug 2, in Wash City, by Rev Geo F Doggett, Alfred Ray, of Wash Co, D C, to Ella M Gatch, daughter of Capt Nicholas Gatch, of Balt, Md.

Mrd: on Aug 11, in Darnestown, Montg, Md, by Rev Danl Motze_, Lawrence Reinhart to Miss Ernestina Rebecca Richter, all of Montg Co, Md.

On Sat last, 2 little boys, children of Mr Thos K Taylor, were drowned at Naudian's Landing, Delaware. They slipped into a hole. Their ages were 9 & 12 years old.

On Aug 2, in the court-house at Tuskegee, Ala, Mr David Nuckolls, a young gentleman of that town, was mortally wounded by a pistol shot, & died on Friday. Nuckolls was shot by some unknown person after some words passed between him & Mr Thos B Jones, in reference to the election.

Book-bindery, fixtures, & presses at auction, on Aug 19, at the establishment of J W Arnold, 228 C st, between 10th & 11th sts. –Wall & Barnard, aucts

Hon John Minor Butts was born in Dumfries, Prince Wm Co, Va, on Sep 16, 1802, son of Benj Botts, who was one of the leading counsel of the celebrated Aaron Burr in his trial for treason. On Dec 26, 1811, Mr Botts lost both his parents in the memorable conflagration of the Richmond theatre. From that period, though but 9 years old, he was left to his own care. At age 18 he was licensed to practice law.

In Balt, on Sat, lightning struck Mr Geo H Hall & his son William, killing them both instantly. The younger son, who was with them, was severely shocked, & when he recovered hastened to the city to impart the sad news to his mother. The bodies were brought to the city. -Balt Exchange

Death in the pulpit. At the Methodist Church at Morehouse, La, a week ago last Sunday, Rev John B Spencer sank speechless. He died in a few hours.

Orphans Court of Wash Co, D C. In the case of Wm J Wheatley, exc of John Johnston, deceased, the executor & Court have appointed Sep 6 next, for the final settlement of the personal estate of said deceased, of the assets in hand. -Ed N Roach, Reg/o wills

Notice is given that application has been made to the Mayor of Wash City for a deed to be given to the subscribers for lot 1 in square A, by virtue of a bond of conveyance executed by the Com'rs of Low Grounds, dated Apr 22, 1825, to David Munroe, who, at public sale made by said com'rs on said day, was the purchaser.
–Wm H Ward, Thos B Entwistle, trustees

Was committed to Carroll Co Jail, on Aug 1, a negro woman, as a runaway, Jane Brown, who says she is free & came from Wash. The owner is to come forward, otherwise she will be discharged according to law. –Wm Wilson, Sheriff of Carroll Co, Md

WED AUG 17, 1859
Orphans Court of Wash Co, D C. Letters testamentary on the personal estate of Enos E Berkley, late of Wash Co, deceased. –Wm Dixon, exc

Obit-died: on Aug 12, at Tomkinsville, Staten Island, N Y, in his 31st year, Arthur Delancey Stanford, 1st Lt of the U S revenue cutter **Harriet Lane**. Arthur D Stanford lies dead at my house. Such was the appalling dispatch received by the afflicted family of the subject of this brief notice. He was born in Gtwn, D C; the dream of his youth was to enter the service of his country; & for the last 8 years this dream has been fulfilled. He was a devoted son, a loving brother, a firm friend, & a sincere Christian.

Child lost: a free colored girl, about 12, disappeared from her parent's home in Wash City on Aug 12, & cannot be found or heard of. Her name is Josephine, & her parents name is Holmes: 14th st, between L & M sts. A suitable reward will be given for returning her to her afflicted parents, or information that may lead to her recovery.

Orphans Court of Wash Co, D C. Letters of administration on the personal estate of Philip C Johnson, late of Wash Co, deceased. –R C Johnson, adm

Orphans Court of Wash Co, D C. Letters testamentary on the personal estate of Gamaliel Bailey, late of Wash Co, deceased. –Margaret L Bailey, excx

For rent, with or without furniture, 266 F st, between 13th & 14th sts, residence of the late P C Johnson. Apply on the premises.

Mrd: on Aug 13, at the St Chas Hotel, in Wash City, by Rev W McLain, C W Allen to Miss Sarah M Stover, of Va.

Died: on Jun 18, 1859, at Somerville, West Tenn, at the residence of Hon Thos Rivers, his son-in-law, Col Thos Dillard, in his 69th year, of a carbuncular affection. The deceased was for more than 40 years a resident of Lynchburg, Va, a Christian, intelligence as a citizen, & fidelity as a public ofcr.

Died: on Aug 16, Margaret, relict of the late Thos H Greene, of Norfolk, Va, in her 24th year. Her funeral will take place on Thu at 11 o'clock, from the residence of Dr Cornelius Boyle, 27 4½ st.

Died: on Aug 16, in Wash City, Mrs Susan C Carroll, in her 24th year. Her funeral will take place from the residence of her father, Thos Clarke, 405 G st, today at 3 o'clock.

THU AUG 18, 1859

Excitement in Minnesota: a mob in Wright Co, Minn, having hung Oscar F Jackson after he had been tried for a heinous offence & acquitted, & then rescued a man who had been arrested for participating in the lynching, Govn'r Sibley issued a proclamation, calling out the military to restore order in the county, which was declared to be in a state of insurrection. Several parties were arrested.

Trustee's sale of a farm near Bladensburg, Md, on Sep 23, 1859, by deed of trust from Robt Strong, dated Jul 25, 1856, recorded in Liber J A S, No 117, folios 6, of the land records for Wash Co, D C, & in Liber C S M, No [blank,] folios 321, of the land records for PG Co, Md, I shall sell on Sep 23, in the auction room of Jas C McGuire, a parcel of land lying in D C & partly in PG Co, called **Chillon Castle Manor**. Also, as appurtenant to the land hereinbefore granted, a perpetual right of way through, over, & along the adjoining land of Wm Scott from the land hereby granted to the public road, as the said right of way was granted by said Scott to said Strong & his heirs & assigns, & his own & their household, family, servants, carriages, horses, wagons, carts, cattle, flocks, & herds, & to & for all persons going to & returning from said land. –Thos J Fisher, trustee –Jas C McGuire & Co, aucts

$100 reward for the thieves who stole 20 sheep within the last 6 weeks from my slaughter-house, between N Y & N J ave, Wash City. —John Hoover

Cincinnati ofcrs boarded the flat-boat **Blue Bird** on the Ohio river, on Thu of last week, & arrested John Johnson, about 50 years of age & upwards, an engraver by trade, with his 2 sons, Elijah, only 19 or 20, & Ira, about 22 or 23, for counterfeiting. He is one of the most extensive, if not the most extensive counterfeiter in the West, shrewd & slippery.

More counterfeiters arrested, in Troy, N Y, on Sunday last, by Deputy U S Marshals Shartuck, of Syracuse, & Olmstead, of Rochester, with Deputy Sheriff Stafford, of Canajoharie, arrested Amos I Haight, Caroline his wife, & Dallas his son, 182 3rd st, on a charge of manufacturing & uttering counterfeit coin, & Fred'k M Gantz & Polly his wife, at their house on Ida Hill, on double charges of counterfeiting & forgery. They left this morning for Auburn, where the U S Court is now in session.

Jos K Roberts, **Rose Mount**, near Bladensburg, PG Co, Md, wishes to engage a governess to teach a little boy & girl, 11 & 9 years old, to commence about Sep 1. A member of the Episcopal Church preferred.

Mr W Henry Palmer has determined to remain another season in Wash, to receive pupils for instruction in the Piano Forte. Apply by letter to Mr W H Palmer, Post Ofc, Wash.

FRI AUG 19, 1859
Washington Jas Taylor, a painter, aged 19 years, was killed at New Orleans on Aug 11 by falling from the top of the portico of the St Chas Hotel, where he was at work. He & his brother-in-law had a rude sort of trestle work erected on the balcony, & when Taylor returned from dinner, & stepped on one of the boards, it snapped in two, & he fell 57 feet, striking his head, crushing to pieces the skull, & of course killing him instantly.

Murder in Alexandria. Two sailors, John Riley & Wm King, both of them belonging to the ship **Charles Wood**, lying at Alexandria, got into a fight there on Tue, in which Riley was worsted. Riley rushed upon King with a sheath knife & inflicted a mortal wound, from which he died in 45 minutes. Riley was arrested & committed to jail.

Died: on Aug 18, in Wash City, Margaret A, daughter of Simeon & Sarah Matlock, aged 23 years. Her funeral will take place from the residence of her father, on 8th, between G & H sts, this evening at half-past 3 o'clock.

Died: on Aug 18, in Wash City, after a painful illness of 12 months, Mrs Eliz Tibbett, formerly of St Mary's Co, Md, but for the last 30 years a resident of Wash City, aged about 80 years. Her funeral will take place Sat at 10:30, from St Peter's Church, Capitol Hill.

Died: on Aug 10, in Millwood, Va, Jane, the beloved wife of Jas H Clarke, a devoted wife, tender mother, & sincere friend. Her death is a glorious illustration of the triumph of Christian faith.

Teacher wanted, a gentleman of liberal education, to board in my family, & take charge of a vacant dept in my school. –Caleb S Hallowell, High School, Alexandria, Va.

Orphans Court of Wash Co, D C. Letters testamentary on the personal estate of Wm Doughty, late of Wash Co, deceased. –John T Bangs, Mary A Doughty, excs

Supreme Court of the U S, No 91, Dec Term, 1858. Appeal from the Circuit Court of the U S for the State of Michigan. Eber B Ward, survivor of himself & Saml Ward, deceased, owner of the steamer **Detroit**, appellant, vs Chas Thompson. Mr Alfred Russell, of counsel for the appellant, having filed a suggestion of the death of Chas Thompson, the appellee, pending this appeal in this court, now here moved the court for an order on the proper reps of the said appellee to be made parties pursuant to the 28th rule of this court; on consideration whereof, it is now here ordered by the court, that unless the proper reps of the said Chas Thompson, deceased, shall become parties within the first 10 days of the ensuing term of this court, that then the appellant in this cause shall be entitled to open the record, &, on hearing, to have the decree reversed if it be erroneous. –Wm Thos Carroll, Clerk Supreme Court U S

SAT AUG 20, 1859
Cincinnati Times of Aug 17. Last evening at 8th & Plum sts, Eugene De Marbais, druggist, shot his wife, & then himself, neither wound being fatal. His wife urged him to shoot her first, & then to shoot himself. They had a daughter, Adele, who was placed with the Marshal troop of juvenile comedians. The Phil American speaks disparagingly of both the parties. It says they were well known in Phil, & were both bad characters, he was a swindler of the deepest dye, both in Richmond, Va, & in Phil. He was a chemist by trade, & quite skilfull in it.

Died: on Friday, in Gtwn, Wm Waters, in his 92nd year. His funeral is on Sunday at 10 o'clock, from his late residence, 119 West st.

Died: on Aug 4, at **Box Hill**, Fauquier Co, Va, Rebecca, daughter of Geo & Laura Armistead, aged 1 year, 1 month & 4 days.

Closing out sale for cash only in order to remove to the store now occupied by Wm R Riley, 8th & Pa ave. Closing out in order to save trouble & expense of removal: Geo F Allen, Pa ave, south of 10th sts.

MON AUG 22, 1859
Orphans Court of Wash Co, D C. Letters of administration on the personal estate of John Mason, late of Wash Co, deceased. –Morris S Miller, adm

Letters of Col Hiram Fuller, late editor of the N Y Mirror, published in the N Y Express, & written from London & Paris, he pays the following happy compliment to ex-Pres Pierce: "but of all, the strangers of distinction in Rome none is more courted or respected than our much abused ex-Pres, Franklin Pierce. I see some of the American papers are urging General Pierce's name as a candidate for the next Presidential term, but it is utterly useless. Nothing can induce him to accept a second nomination, nor a public office of any grade. He was a brave general; a patriotic President; an honest man. His enemies found it easy to abuse but impossible to impeach him.

Excellent household & kitchen furniture, & piano forte, at auction, on Aug 24, at the Mount Vernon Hotel, kept by John Miller, south N & 6th sts, near the Southern Mail-boat wharf. -A Green auct

Farm stock, implements, hay, & family horse, at auction, on Aug 31, at the farm of Dr Cockerill, on the road past the Soldiers' Home, the entire personal effects.
–Wall & Barnard, aucts

Excellent household & kitchen furniture at auction on Aug 25, by order of the Orphans Court of Wash Co, D C, at the residence of the late P C Johnson, on F st, between 13th & 14th sts. –R C Johnson, adm -Jas C McGuire & Co, aucts

Two murders have been committed in Ulster Co, N Y. 1-A daughter of Jas Vandervoort, of Lloyd, was engaged at the house of Mr Albertson in making a shroud for the body of his wife, when her father came in & commanded her to go home, threatening her with personal injury if she refused. Young Albertson interfered & he was stabbed in the breast & expired shortly afterwards. Vandervoort has been arrested. 2-On Sunday a man name Cunningham was murdered by 3 brothers, Thomas, Augustus, & Peter Brehany. Thomas has been arrested, & is now in the Monticello jail. The other two are still at large.

Little Miss Fanny Temple, of Boston, who recently castigated a man in the street with the raw & ravenous hide because she thought he had slandered her, has been arrested, fined $25 & costs, & sent to the House of Correction until that amount is paid. Ladies, beware!

Local Matter: Mr Edmund French, engineer & paymaster under Capt Bowman, was investigated for fraudulent inaccuracies in his account. The aggregate amounts for which false entries have been made in vouchers does not yet exceed $4,500; but it is feared the amount will increase. Mr French was arrested by the Chief of Police, & gave as bail B O Tayloe, in the sum of $10,000.

TUE AUG 23, 1859
The N C Christian Advocate states that 3 missionaries from the Southern Methodist Church will sail for Japan in Nov, including Rev M L Wood, of N C Conference; Rev Mr Allen, of the Ga Conference; & Rev Mr Stewart, of the Tenn Conference.

Entire stock of groceries, wines & liquors, at auction, on Aug 30, at the Store-room of Shekell & Miller, their entire stock of goods. -Jas C McGuire & Co, aucts

On Sat an accident took place on the road near the residence of Chauncey Brooks, which resulted in the death of a Sister of Charity, known as Sister Cyprian. The deceased, with another lady & the driver of the Mount Hope Hospital carriage, named Wm, started from that institution to visit the new bldg now in course of erection on Fred'k road. The animal attached to the vehicle became frightened & ran off at top speed. The sister concluded to jump out. Unfortunately, her feet struck an intervening object, causing her to fall upon her head, which struck a rock with such violence as to fracture her skull; the spirit fled, & the good woman was a corpse. She was in her 45th year, regarded as one of the best of nurses, & had been serving as such at the above institution for the last 6 or 7 years. -Balt American

A young married woman, wife of John Nichols, of Bridgeport, Conn, was burnt to death on Wed when a can of burning fluid burst.

A son of Mr David Nelson, of Spencer, N Y, aged 9 years, on Aug 8, took hold of a cow's tail, & the animal dragged him over fences, through brush, & into the creek, when the agonized father succeeded in extricating his boy. The lad died on Aug 14.

Distribution of premiums, **St Mary's Female Institute**, near Bryantown, Chas Co, Md, Jul 28, 1859:

Anna Surratt, PG Co, Md
Alice Berry, PG Co, Md
Mary M Dyer, Wash, D C
Louisa McLean, Wash, D C
R Gardiner, Chas Co, Md
Celestia Waring, Chas Co, Md
L Wilson, PG Co, Md
Synphronia Bryan, PG Co, Md
J Radcliff, Chas Co
Mollie Queen, Chas Co
Mary Dobbyn, Wash, D C
N R Digges, Chas Co
Hanna Sasscer, PG Co
Mary Smith, Gtwn, D C
Fannie Lancaster, Chas Co
M Campbell, Chas Co
Mary Collins, Wash, D C
Mary Holmes, Chas Co
Mollie Digges, Chas Co
Nannie Jameson, Chas Co
Louisa Burroughs, Chas Co
E Gardiner, Chas Co
Zarah Mattingly, Chas Co
Mittie Carrico, Chas Co
Charlotte Reynolds, Wash, D C
S Kelcher, Wash, D C
Alice Burch, Chas Co
C Mattingly, Chas Co
Josephine Lloyd
Leonora Coolidge
Regina Gardiner

Young Ladies Institute, a Boarding & Day School, 30 4½ st, Wash, D C. The 12th year of this institution will commence on the 2nd Mon of Sep, 1859. –Chas H Norton, A M, Principal

Indiana divorces worth nothing in N Y. The case of Julia E Clark against Alvin B Clark, which was tried before Judge Bacon at the last term of the Supreme Court, in June last, in Lewis Co, N Y, has been decided in favor of the plntf upon all the issues of the case. The court held that a divorce obtained in Indiana, when the party goes there for the purpose of procuring such divorce, & then returns to the State of N Y, is wholly inoperative & void.

Wash Select School, 10th & G sts, will be resumed on Sep 1. –Saml Kelly, Principal

Mrs Kingford's Seminary, 415 E st, Wash, will be resumed Oct 1st, 1859.

Circuit Court of D C, in Chancery, No 1,366. Geo Parker, Thos Parker, & Jos B Bryan, vs Mary Kennedy, et al. Wm J Stone, jr, trustee, sold the east part of lot 9 in square 73, in Wash City, fronting 20 feet on K st, to Jas Kennedy, for $517.50. –Jno A Smith, clerk

Orphans Court of Wash Co, D C. Letters of administration on the personal estate of Matthew Wilson, late of Wash Co, deceased. –Thos C Wilson, adm

Orphans Court of Wash Co, D C. Letters of administration on the personal estate of Geo H Fulmer, late of Wash Co, deceased. –Mary N Fulmer, excx

Died: on Aug 22, in Wash City, in her 23rd year, Mrs Cecelia C, the beloved wife of Calvin G Lownds. Her funeral is this afternoon at 4 o'clock, from the residence of her father, John L Smith, 565 12th st, Island.

Died: on Aug 22, after a lingering illness, Eliza Ann, eldest & only daughter of John & Mary Espy, in her 20th year. Her funeral is on Aug 24 at 3:30 o'clock P M, from the residence of her parents, 20th st, between E & F sts.

Died: on Aug 11, in Centreville, Appanoose Co, Iowa, Rev Matthew Smith, who was well known in Wash City, where he frequently preached the gospel of our Lord Jesus Christ. His disease was typhoid fever of the high type. The sympathy of relatives & friends in this city cluster around his young widow in her distant home.

WED AUG 24, 1859
The Roll of Honor: list of Revolutionary soldiers, supposed to be alive, pensioners on the roll of the State of Mass, with their age in 1859: Reuben Burt-95 years; Micah Balcom-100 years; John Bourne-100 years; Rufus Farnham-93 years; John Goodnow-97 years; Reuben Gulliver-97 years; Erastus Morgan-95 years; Abraham Rising-100 years; Benj Smith-94 years; Jas Sawen-98 years; Joel Shepard-94 years; Moses Thompson-97 years; Saml Thompson-99 years; & Saml Yendall-90 years.

Gtwn College, D C: studies will resume on Sep 5. –John Early, S J, President

On Sunday a young man, B F Felt, residing at 222 Gold st, N Y, shot himself in the head with a pistol, causing a wound which is thought must prove fatal. He has been married about a year, & was out riding Sunday. On his return his wife reproved him for having been drinking & he went to his room & shot himself. No hope for his recovery.

The College of St James, Md: the 18th session begins on Sep 28. –John B Kerfoot, Rector, P O College of St James, Md.

Died: on Aug 21, at his residence in Winchester, Va, Col Jas P Riely, in his 51st year. He was Clerk of the County Court of Fred'k Co, & Teller of the Bank of the Valley of Va. He was a gentleman of great popularity & influence, & universally esteemed.

Died: Aug 23, in Wash City, Charles Keller, aged 18 months & 18 days, youngest son of Saml Brett & Marie C Waite. His funeral will take place on Aug 25 at 11 o'clock A M.

THU AUG 25, 1859
Hon John W Davis, of Indiana, died at his late residence in Carlisle, Ind, on Aug 22, aged 60 years.

Letter from Raleigh, N C, dated Aug 19, says that on that day a son of Hon Kenneth Rayner, about 13 years old, was hunting with a shot-gun, in company with his younger brother, when the gun went off accidentally, passing through the head of the elder, & producing instant death.

Mrs Matthia Schrote was shot at Balt on Tue by the falling on the floor of a pistol which her grandson had accidentally knocked off the mantel. Her foot received a very serious wound.

A young man, John Henry Kimball, was recently arrested in San Francisco on a charge of vagrancy. In 1850, says the Atlas of Jul 24, this same man possessed property valued at $200,000.

Another murder in Balt on Tue. Humphrey O'Sullivan was shot dead whilst on Holliday st. He was with friends, when, without provocation, he was shot in the head. Verdict of the Coroner's Jury: Thos Hoffman & Robt Miller did feloniously, willfully, & of their malice aforethought, kill & murder the said Hugh O'Sullivan, by a pistol fired by either Hoffman or Miller. Hoffman is a young man who has been arrested on various charges of assault, & burglary. Robt Miller has always been identified as Hoffman's friend.

Died: on Aug 24, in Wash City, Rev L Durbin Walter, in his 27th year. His funeral will be from the McKendree Chapel this afternoon at 4 o'clock.

Mrd: on Aug 23, at St Patrick's Church, by Rev R J O'Toole, Mr Henry J McLaughlin & Miss Mary C, daughter of Geo W Keating.

FRI AUG 26, 1859
The Pres has appointed the following gentlemen justices of the peace for Wash Co: Jos Peck, O E P Hazard, & F S Myer.

Lost child found: On Aug 15 search was begun for a little daughter of Benj Morse, residing near the lower end of Greenwood Lake, who strayed from home. She was found on Thu by Anthony Rhinesmith who was in an exploring party. The little girl was only 3 years & 7 months old, & subsisted without food & slept on the ground. Her parents had given up hope of every seeing her again. –Paterson [N J] Guardian, Aug 22.

Trustee's sale of valuable real estate; in the Circuit Court for PG Co, in Equity: Jas S Morsell, guardian of Jas N Morsell, & others, vs Jas N Morsell & others. By decree of said Court passed on Jul 6, 1859, the trustee will offer to public sale, on the premises, on Sep 15 next, all that tract of land called **Harper's Grove**, of which the late Jos N Baden died seized & possessed, containing 250 acres, more or less, in said county, within 2 miles of the village of Nottingham, on the Patuxent river. The dwlg house is not in very good repair. Mr Galt, who lives on the place, will show it. –Jas S Morsell, trustee

Died: on Aug 24, in Wash City, Dr Grafton D Hanson, in his 76th year. His funeral will be from his late residence, Pa ave & 3rd st east, this afternoon at 4½ o'clock.

Died: on Aug 25, Thomas Foster, infant son of Robt & Malinda Downing, & grandson of Thomas Foster, late of Winchester, Va. "Suffer little children to come unto me, & forbid them not, for of such is the Kingdon of Heaven."

Home School, 52 Sharp st, near Lombard, Balt. The 4th session will resume on Sep 5. -Mrs R W Cliffe, Principal, aided by the most efficient instructors.

Orphans Court of Wash Co, D C. Letters testamentary on the personal estate of Susan Evans, late of Wash Co, deceased. –F S Walsh, exc

SAT AUG 27, 1859
Jesse Williams, an old & wealty citizen of Caldwell Co, who has been under guard at Princeton, charged with murder, stealing, & cruelty to his slaves, was taken from jail on Thursday night, & after being carried off a distance of 7 miles, was hung by a party of citizens. His two sons, John & James, who are also guilty of numerous crimes, escaped death by absconding. About the same time, Dr Singleton & Messrs Mansfield, Morse, & Straumal, supposed to be connected with Williams in his villanies, were severely punished, & ordered to leave the country.

Valuable & highly improved farm, 2½ miles from the Long Bridge, in Fairfax Co, Va, at auction, on Sep 5. On the premises, that handsome farm on which Mr F D Stuart resides, in Alexandria Co, Va; contains 30 acres; new house with numerous out bldgs. Also, for sale, 2 horses, 3 cows, carriage, buggy, wagon, & farming utensils. -A Green auct

Household & kitchen furniture at auction on Aug 30, at the residence of J Underwood, 586 N J ave, Capitol Hill. -A Green auct

On Aug 18 a large number of the citizens of Nashville, Tenn, were assembled to witness the presentation of the gold box which had belonged to Gen Andrew Jackson. In the absence of Col Andrew Jackson the box was presented by his son-in-law, Dr John M Lawrence, & received by Gen Gideon J Pillow for Gen Ward B Burnett, of N Y, at this time officially employed in the Territory of Kansas. Dr Lawrence read the remarks of Col Jackson: My venerated father, Gen Andrew Jackson, in his last will & testament, bequeaths this gold box, presented to him by the Mayor, Aldermen, & Commonality of N Y C, to that patriot residing in N Y C who shall be adjudged by his countrymen to have been the most valiant in defence of his country & his country's rights.

Richmond [Va] Dispatch, writing from Norfolk, states that on Tue of last week Capt John Doughty was washed from the deck of his sloop about 5 in the morning, off *Smith's Island*; he was picked up by Capt Conkling, after having been swimming 8 hours & carried into Alexandria, from which place he came to Norfolk, & proceeded to his residence in Northampton Co, where it was generally supposed that he was drowned. He must have swam nearly 15 miles, & that with his clothes on except his boots, which he pulled off in the water. When rescued he was nearly exhausted.

MON AUG 29, 1859
The name of the man carried over the Niagara on Mons Blondin's back is Harry Colcord. He is Blondin's agent. There was a rope tied to the waist of each, & it was arranged that if either fell the other was to throw himself on the opposite side of the rope.

At N Y, on Friday night, Mr David J Peters was seriously injured by the accidental discharge of a pistol. At the bar of a hotel he recognized a friend, Mr Thos Kerr, & shook hands with him, after which, in paying a bill, a pistol dropped from his vest & discharged its contents into Mr Peters. The next morning the ball was extracted, & Mr Peters was considered out of danger.

Book just issued: Forty four Years of the Life of a Hunter, being the reminiscences of Meshach Browning, who still lives, at a very advanced age, in the Alleghany Mountains of Md, the scene of his hardy & intrepid exploits. The book was written by himself, & revised & illustrated by Mr E Stabler. Browning was born in 1781, & while a boy moved into the Alleghany region & settled there for life.

Jumpertz, the murderer of Sophia Werner in Chicago, has been granted a new trial by the Supreme Court of Illinois. There seems to be a great deal of sympathy for him there. Probably it is on account of the slight character of his offence. He only killed the young woman, cut her up into convenient pieces, & packed her in a pork barrel. That was really all. –Louisville Journal

Nicholas Watkins was recently killed at St Louis by John Davis while in the act of perpetrating a burglary. He was stabbed, causing his death in a few minutes.

Resolutions authorizing the Govn'r of the State to receive a flag tendered to the State of N C by Lt Guthrie, of the U S Navy. Whereas John Julius Guthrie, a lt in the U S Navy & a native of the State of N C, now on official duty at the Nat'l Observatory, Wash, D C, did, on Nov 20, 1856, capture & carry off as a trophy of war a Chinese flag from the first of 4 barrier forts captured in a combined engagement by the vessels **San Jacinto, Portsmouth,** & **Levant,** on the part of the American naval force, & other vessels under the command of Rear Admiral Seymore, on the part of the English, in the Canton river. [Ratified Feb 15, 1859. –Graham Davis, Private Sec, Raleigh, Aug 22, 1859.]

Paraguay chartered steamers converted into men of war:
1-The vessel **Mystic** was formerly the vessel **Memphis**, of the Cromwell stock; built in Phil, of oak, in 1853, overhauled in 1857. She went in commission on Tuesday for service on the coast of Africa, & will carry 4 or 6 guns, & about 90 men: her ofcrs are: Lt Wm E LeRoy, commanding; Lts D McN Fairfax, Milton Haxton, H M Garland, jr; Acting Master, N Green; Passed Assist Surgeon, W C Harrison; 1st Assist Engineer, Wm Roberts; 3rd Assistants, Jas Plunket, J S Finney, & H McMurtrie.
2-The vessel **Sumpter** was another of Cromwell's craft, & was known as the vessel **Atlanta**; built at Phil in 1853. This vessel is also in commission, destined for the coast of Africa. Her ofcrs are: Lt J F Armstrong, commanding; Lts W B Fitzgerald, J B Stewart, J A Greer; Acting Master G H Perkins; Passed Assist Surgeon, J H Otis; 1st Assist Engineer, T J Jones; 3rd Assistant, E B Litch, W H Glading, J L Plumley.
3-The vessel **Mohawk**, which was known as the vessel **Caledonia**, was built in Phil in 1853. It is ready for commission at Brooklyn, & will carry 4 guns, 90 men, & is to join that portion of the home squadroon whose attention will be devoted to the overhauling of slavers. Her ofcrs are: Lt T A Craven, Commanding; Lts A Barbot, E T Speddon, C C Carpenter; Acting Master, G Hatfield; 1st Assist Engineer, J S Albert; 3rd Assist Engineers, E S Dick, Jas Wallace, & E C Patten.
4-The vessel **Anacosita** was built in Phil in 1856; her old name was the vessel **M W Chapin**. She is now plying between Norfolk & Washington, carrying stores, shot, ammunition, etc.
5-The vessel **Pulaski** is the ill-fated vessel **Metacomet**, that left N Y for Rio & broke down when a few days out, rendering it necessary for her to put into Pensacola for repairs. The **Pulaski** is at Pernambuco, where she recently arrived to meet the storeship, her ofcrs being desirous of getting her as near home as her machinery would allow. She was built in N Y in 1854.
6-The vessel **Crusader**, alias the vessel **Southern Star**, is now at Phil fitting out for the home squadron. She was built this year in Murphrysboro, of oak. She sailed from Norfolk the first week of Nov, carrying two 11 inch guns & 1 howitzer, for Montevideo, & returned in comparative safety; of course she had a break down, but it resulted in no serious consequence: her ofcrs are: Lt Commanding, John N Maffit; Lts, Thos L Phelds, Thos Rooney, & A E K Benham.

Muncy [Pa] Luminary of Aug 23: near Red Bluff, on the Sacramento river, Calif, on May 12th last, the residence of Col E A Stevenson, late Indian agent, was set on fire by an Indian boy in his employ, early in the morning, & the entire family of Col Stevenson, consisting of his wife & 3 children, together with the wife of Mr Kronk & 2 children, perished in the flames. Col Stevenson was absent at the time. Mrs Stevenson was the daughter of the late Jonathan Marcy, of Wilkesbarre, & the niece of Rev Geo C Drake, of this borough.

Naval Engineers: candidates communicated to the Navy Dept as having passed the examination of the Board of Naval Engineers at N Y. They are ranged in the order of merit, & will be warranted as 3rd assist engineers:

Wm Carey Selden, Wash
S W Cragg, Balt
H S Davids, Norfolk
A B Campbell, Brooklyn
R Driver, Wilmington
R H Fitch, Fair Haven, Mass
Jas Atkins, Augusta, Maine
Edw Scattergood, Phil

W W Miller, Wheeling, Va
C F Mayer, jr, Balt
E S Boynton, East Hartford, Conn
H A Delins, Brooklyn, N Y
J H Bordley, Balt
David Smith, Andover
F A Wilson, Brooklyn
John E Neill, N Y

Balt papers-obits: 1-Mr Geo Brown died at age 73 years; born in Ireland, came to this country in early manhood; was Pres of the Merchants' & Mechanics' Banks, & for many years has been the head of the house of Alex'r Brown & Sons. He was an influential member of the Presbyterian Church. His death will be lamented by all, & by none more than those who will miss the bounty which his large fortune enabled & his own kindness prompted him yearly to bestow. 2-Mr Jas Swan, age 67, for a long time Pres of the Mechanics' Bank, died. He was held in high esteem by the community in which he had passed an upright life, & a large circle of relatives will sincerely deplore his loss.
[No death date given for either-current item.]

Died: on Aug 23, in Christian peace, at the Epiphany Church House, Mrs Alice *Cartin, a native of England, in her 21st year; & on Aug 27, her infant daughter, aged 13 days. [*The last letter in Carti_ is possibly an "n"; print is not real clear.]

Died: on Aug 28, in Gtwn, D C, Henry, infant son of Geo & Martha Hill. His funeral will be this afternoon at 4½ o'clock, from the residence of his father, Bridge st, Gtwn.

In virtue of 2 writs of fieri facias, I will expose to public sale, for cash, in Wash City, on Sep 21 next, all David Westerfield, jr's right, title, claim, interest, & estate in part of square north of square 583, in said city, with improvements thereon; seized & levied upon as the property of David Westerfield, jr, & will be sold in favor of Hamilton & Leach, & Thompson, Hamilton & Co. –J H Wise, constable

Boston, Aug 27. 1-Ex-Pres Pierce & wife arrived in America. 2-Rev Dana, an eminent Presbyterian clergyman, of Newburyport, died this morning. He was 89 years of age.

Orphans Court of Wash Co, D C. Letters of administration on the personal estate of Hon Geo M Bibb, late of Wash Co, deceased. –Robt G Thrift, adm

$1,500 reward for runaways, 3 negro men, Gabriel, 24; Minor, 22; & Jim, 20. Gabriel & Jim are brothers. All chew tobacco. –Enoch Foley, Haymarket, Prince Wm Co, Va

TUE AUG 30, 1859
Gen Wm Clarke died in Jackson, Miss, on Monday of last week. He represented Bolivar Co in the State Legislature, & was colonel of the 2nd regt Mississippi Rifles in the Mexican war.

The jewelry store of Mr Benj Barton, of Alexandria, was entered by robbers Friday night & robbed of jewelry & watches of the value of $5,000. It is supposed they entered an unoccupied store adjoining.

The Cincinnati papers state that M De Marbais & his wife are both likely to recover from the wounds self-inflicted during their temporary madness.

The mother of the late Hon Mike Walsh, Mrs Catharine Sammis, of 206 West 21st st, was dreadfully burnt last Thu by the explosion of a fluid lamp. She died on Sat, age 60 years.

Rev Dr John A McClung, pastor of the Presbyterian Church at Maysville, Ky, was found drowned at Niagara falls, where he had been spending the summer. His father was a celebrated jurist in the early annals of Ky, & his mother was a sister of the celebrated Chief Justice Marshall. Mr McClung was educated at Princeton for the ministry. He had removed to Indianapolis, & then to Maysville, near the place he was born. [No death date given-current item.]

Died: on Aug 29, in Wash City, Mary Malvina, consort of P J Torney, & youngest daughter of the late Geo Peacock, of Cecil Co, Md. Her funeral will be from her late residence, 552 Pa ave, between 1st & 2nd sts, this evening at 3 o'clock.

Died: on Aug 26, suddenly, of hemipligue, at Berkeley Springs, Va, Capt Chas McGill, in his 67th year. For 26 years he was engaged as a seaman in the merchant service, & sustained a high reputation for nautical skill & efficiency. He was born in PG Co, Md, & sailed from the port of Balt. He died, as he had for a long time lived, in the fullest hope of Christian's faith. -T

Died: on Aug 2, in San Francisco, Calif, Margaret M, wife of W E Granwell, U S Coast Survey, & daughter of Mrs E Manning, of Wash City.

Died: on Aug 27, in Wash City, Edw Mead, of Balt, aged 54 years.

Died: on Aug 29, at Wildwood, Montg Co, Md, Elouise Campbell, infant daughter of F L & Virginia Moore.

Boston, Aug 27. Ex-Pres Pierce was serenaded this evening at the Tremont House by his friends, & made a very eloquent speech. After alluding to the death of Mr Choate, he stated that the object of his visit to Europe, the restoration of the health of Mrs Pierce, was partially accomplished. He then alluded to his gratification at being on New England soil once more.

WED AUG 31, 1859
Executor's sale of household furniture & effects at auction, on Sep 1, at the residence of the late Col Wm Doghty, near 3rd & High st, Gtwn, D C. –Barnard & Buckey, aucts

It is our duty this week to record the death of Mr Tattersall, for many years at the head of the well known establishment at Hyde park corner. He died at Dover on Aug 22, in his 67th year. He was for many years a large breeder of blood stock, & has owned & exported some of the best stud horses in the world. –London Field

Wash Ordnance: 1-Act for an appropriation for draining James' creek, between I & O sts south: $150. –Approved, Aug 26, 1859

Saddle horse for sale, a thorough bred 5 year old bay mare. Can be seen at the stable of the owner on Gtwn Heights. –Edw Boyce

Orphans Court of Wash Co, D C. Letters of administration, with will annexed, on personal estate of Saml C Ridgely, late of U S army, deceased. –Wm G Ridgely, Adm W A

During my absence from Wash City I appointed Nicholas Callan, Notary Public, No 213 F st, my atty in fact for the transaction of my business. –Junius Boyle, U S Navy

THU SEP 1, 1859
Mr John Lever, of the Galway line, has offered to charter the steamship **Great Eastern** for her first voyage to the U S, paying the owners $100,000. Sometime in Sept we may expect the **Great Eastern** in American waters.

Trustee's sale of lot, on Sep 23, by deed in trust from Pasquale Defalco, dated Jun 2, 1855, recorded in Liber J A S, No 121, folios 296, of the land records for Wash Co, D C: sale of lot 6 in square 1,113, fronting 160 feet on Mass ave, at the corner of 18th st east, 154 feet 6 inches on 18th st east. -Jas C McGuire & Co, aucts

Mrs Cecilia Young will continue her instruction in Vocal Music Sep 1, at her residence, 404½ 12th st, between I & K sts. Gtwn pupils apply to Miss Harrover's Seminary.

The copartnerhsip existing under the name of Bradley & Taylor is this day dissolved by mutual consent, Mr Geo L Taylor withdrawing from the firm. Wm A Bradley, jr, is authorized to use the name of the firm in liquidation. –W A Bradley, jr, Geo L Taylor [Wm A Bradley, jr, will continue to carry on the Commission & Forwarding business at 166 Water st, Gtwn.]

On Sunday last a poor & aged woman, Alice Brady, residing on Capitol Hill, was found by the side of her bed dead. She had been addicted to intemperance, & to that cause was her death assigned by the coroner's jury which sat next day on the case.

Mrd: on Aug 9, at the Legation of the U S, at Paris, by Rev Mr Swaile, Mary Ann Mason, 3rd daughter of Hon John Y Mason, U S Minister to France, to Archer Anderson, of Richmond, Va. Immediately after the ceremony the bride & groom left Paris for a tour in Switzerland & Germany, prior to their return to the U S.

Mrd: on the 30th ult, by Rev Mr Meadows, Mr Orlando R Delphy to Mrs Jane E Flowers, both of Wash City.

Died: on Aug 31, in Wash City, after a lingering illness, Jas R May, in his 26th year. His funeral will take place from his late residence, 13th st, between N Y ave & I st, on Friday at 2 o'clock.

Died: on Aug 26, in Alexandria, Mrs A Emerson, in her 72nd year, after a short but painful illness. She was one of the oldest & most respected of the inhabitants of Alexandria. None knew her but to love her; none named her but to praise.

FRI SEP 2, 1859
Scaffolding fell at the gas works at Buffalo on Monday & Jacob Langenbech is supposed to be fatally injured. Caspar Stein is terribly hurt. David Kling, & Mr Linderman, & 2 Germans were less dangerously injured. Rotten timber in the scaffold gave way.

The U S District Court, Pensacola, adjourned on Aug 19 after a long session. Thomas, of the barque **Rawlins**, convicted of manslaughter, was sentenced to 3 years in the penitentiary in the District of Columbia.

The 6 year old daughter of Mr & Mrs King, living about 4 miles from Kalida, Putnam Co, became lost in the woods and was found 9 days later. She had died but a few hours before being found. –Columbus [O] Statesman, Aug 28th.

Maj A J Donelson, who died recently at Lafourche, La, was not Andrew Jackson Donelson, the adopted son of Gen Jackson.

While a young man, W H Jennison, was witnessing Mons De Lave crossing the Genesee river, on Wed, on a rope, he fell over the Falls, & was instantly killed.

A new shot gun has been perfected at *Colt's Armory*, which will probably be in the market next winter. It is made for 5 charges, on the revolver principle, & is loaded & fired with great facility.

Hotel & Restaurant, long known as the Casparis House, Wash, D C, is for rent or lease. Address Jas Casparis, Capitol Hill, Wash, D C.

Obit-died: suddenly, on Aug 24, at her residence near Romney, Hampshire Co, Va, in her 54th year, Mrs Ann M Gibson, wife of David Gibson. Just 9 months ago her step-daughter, Mrs Susan A Sherrard, lovely in person, lovelier in spirit, was called away. -H

Died: yesterday, David Westerfield, sr, in his 77th year, a native of the State of N J, but for the last 50 years a resident of Wash City. His funeral will take place from the residence of his son James, on N st, between 9th & 10th sts, this afternoon at 2 o'clock.

N Y, Sep 1. The long pending trial of Dr Smithurst, for the murder of Miss Banks, at Richmond, terminated in a verdict of guilty & sentence of death. [Smithurst got up a fictitious marriage with Miss Banks, having at the time a wife living, & slowly poisoned her to get possession of her money.

Orphans Court of Wash Co, D C. In the case of Florian Hitz, adm de bonis non of John L Wirt, the administrator & Court have appointed Sep 24 for the final settlement of the personal estate of the deceased, of the assets in hand. -Ed N Roach, Reg/o wills

SAT SEP 3, 1859
Household & kitchen furniture at auction on Sep 9, at the residence of Mrs Beck, 11th & Pa ave, over the Music Store No 327. -A Green auct

Hon Nathl H Claiborne died at his residence, in Franklin Co, Va, on Aug 15, in his 83rd year. He served that State many years in Congress, & was loved & respected by all who knew him. The only formal speech, we believe, he ever made in Congress was in support of the famous claim of Amy Darden, & the speech was successful.

Public sale: the undersigned offer for sale their farm, lying partly in Montg Co, & partly in D C; contains 104+ acres; house is little but sufficient for workmen & horses; also will be sold horses, cows, hogs, & poultry. Sale on Oct 3. –Patrick Cummins

Died: on Sep 1, in Wash City, John Connelly, in his 40th year. His funeral will be on Sep 4 at 3 o'clock, from his late residence on 7th st, between G & H sts.

Yesterday a train of 14 wagons arrived at *Fort Leavenworth* from Utah. It left Salt Lake City on Jun 26. Maj Eastman & Lt Elwood, 5th infty; Maj Whiting, 7th infty; Lt Carroll, 10th infty, & Lt Tyler, 2nd dragoons, came in with the train. Accompanying the train are also 15 of the children who escaped the terrible massacre at Mountain Meadows, in Utah, some 2 years since. That unparalleled outrage, perpetrated by Mormons under the guise of Indians, startled our whole country. A company of 145 persons had started from Arkansas in the spring of 1857 for Calif, supplied with an excellent outfit, & when they reached Mountain Meadows, whilst encamped, they were butchered by Mormons disguised as Indians, & some Indians. 17 of the children were taken by the Indians. The object of the assailants was evidently plunder. Also came in with the train, under the especial care of Sgt Black, were the 3 Foster children. The father & mother lived in Conn. The father espoused the Mormon faith several years ago, & left for Salt Lake City, carrying with him his 3 little girls. The mother remained behind, & all efforts to retain her children were abortive. About a year ago the father died, & now, through the efforts of the Sec of War, her children have been reclaimed, & will soon be with their mother.

MON SEP 5, 1859
Telegraphic dispatch from Lexington announces the death of the venerable Robt Wickliffe, Sep 1; his age must have been 85. He has been a resident of Fayette Co since youth; the largest land & slaveholder in Ky; one of the wealthiest men in the State. He leaves 3 children, Mrs Preston, wife of Hon Wm Preston, of Wash City, Minister to Spain, who is now with her husband in Europe, Mrs John Preston, wife of John Preston, of Wash City, & Mrs Judge Wolley, of Lexington. -Louisville Journal

Dr Julian Xavier Chabert, well known as the Fire King, died a day or to ago in N Y. He was 67 years of age. He became a kind of chemist & quack doctor, & made almost all kinds of prepartions for diseases, as well as poisons for flies & insects, & Lucifer matches.

Philip Reed, postmaster at Poolesville, Md, has been arrested on a charge of embezzling letters from the mail. He was examined on Friday, & held in $1,000 bail to answer.

Ex-Pres Pierce reached his home in Concord on Fri & was received at the Nashua depot by a deputation of citizens from Manchester, accompanied by the Amoskeag Veterans, & much enthusiasm was manifested. A special train conveyed him & his escort to Manchester, when a procession was formed & marched through the principal streets. He was then escorted to Concord, where similar demonstrations of respect awaited him.

The School taught by Mrs E Goodrich Smith will be continued, from Sep 12, at 382 C st, under the principal supervision of Miss Jennie Ross.

Died: on Aug 31, at Rockville, Md, Lt Richd Forrest, U S Navy.

Died: on Aug 30, at the Rectory, in Cople parish, Westmoreland Co, Va, Thos Bennett Dashiell, aged 72 years.

Died: on Aug 31, at the Sweet Springs, Monroe Co, Va, Howard, infant son of Theodoric & Fannie A Lee, aged 7 months & 20 days.

Orphans Court of Wash Co, D C. In the case of John R Minor, exc of Jas M Minor, deceased, the executor & Court have appointed Sep 27 next, for the final settlement of the personal estate of said deceased. -Ed N Roach, Reg/o wills

TUE SEP 6, 1859
The Republicans of the 14th Congressional district of Ohio have nominated Hon Harrison G Blake, of Medina, to fill the vacancy caused by the death of Hon Cyrus Spink, of Wayne.

Accident on Friday of last week at Amherst Court-house, Va, when a very deserving young man, John Mays, in the employment of Dr Landon Davis, was accidentally shot & killed when his gun became entangled in the bushes & exploded.

Orphans Court of Wash Co, D C. In the case of John Hitz, adm of Gephart Bergmann, deceased, the administrator & Court have appointed Sep 27 next, for the final settlement of the personal estate of said deceased. -Ed N Roach, Reg/o wills

WED SEP 7, 1859
Trustee's sale of property near the corner of 2nd st east & Md ave; on Sep 20, by deed of trust from J A F Todtschinder & wife, dated May 30, 1853, recorded in Liber J A S, No 60, folios 4 thru 7, of the land records for Wash Co: parts of lots 9 & 10 in square 758, having a front of 20 feet on Md ave, with a small frame dwlg house. -Jas C McGuire & John H Semmes, trustees   -Jas C McGuire & Co, aucts

Thos S Gholson, of Petersburg, Va, has been elected a Judge of the 5th judicial circuit of Va, to succeed the late Judge John W Nash

Bennett M DeWitt has become the sole proprietor & publisher of the Va Index, a well conducted Democratic paper published at Richmond.

Army Intelligence: 1-Brvt Maj Gen Jno E Wool, commanding the Dept of the East, is to proceed to make an inspection of **Fort Adams**, R I, & of **Fort Independence**, Mass. 2-Capt Andrew J Smith, 1st dragoons, is to accompany the recruits to be sent, on Oct 20 next, to the dept of Oregon. 3-Col Fauntleroy, of the U S dragoons, has been ordered to duty in New Mexico, where his rank makes him the cmder of the military dept of New Mexico in the absence of Gen Garland, now here, & an invalid.

Hon Thos A Hendricks, who is now a candidate for the nomination of Govn'r of Indian, has resigned his position as Com'r of the Genr'l Land Ofc, & his resignation has been accepted by the Pres.

Executor's sale of horses, mules, buggy, cart, wagons, & harness, at auction; on Sep 9, at the late residence of Enos E Berkley, deceased, on south G, between 12th & 13th sts. Also, on Sep 14, sale of corn, potatoes & cabbage, at the farm of the late Enos E Berkley, in PG Co, Md, about 6 miles from Wash, on the Marlborough road, near the *Long Old Fields*. -Wm Dixon, exc -A Green auct

The U S storeship **Supply**, Cmder Henry Walker, left the navy yard, N Y, on Sat, & proceeded to quarantine, where she anchored. She is bound to Loaudo, cost of Africa, for the purpose of establishing a new store depot for the use of the squadron. Her ofcrs: Cmder, Henry Walker; Lts, J Downes, O F Stanton, Geo Brown; Master, N W Allen; Assist Surgeon, A M Vedder; Capt's Clerk, T M Brower; Purser, H A Walker.

N Y, Sep 5: the corner-stone of St Peter's [Catholic] Church was laid yesterday in the presence of 20,000 spectators. The site will occupy 14 lots at the corner of Hicks & Warren sts, Brooklyn. Bishop Loughlin, assisted by 6 clergymen, officiated.

Ex-Govn'r Wallace, of Indianapolis, one of the oldest residents & lately Judge of the Court of Common Pleas, died of apoplexy on Sep 4.

Saml C Bennett, of Cairo, Green Co, N Y, a member of the legal profession met with a singular accident a few days since, which resulted in his death. He was standing upon the piazza of the hotel in Cairo, with Mr J Pearson, when, during a conversation, Mr Pearson playfully slapped him upon the back, causing him to lose his balance, & he fell forward from the stoop, striking his head with great force. He lingered badly hurt until Thursday, when death came to his relief.

Orphans Court of Wash Co, D C. Letters testamentary on the personal estate of Chas McGill, late of Wash Co, deceased. –Robt T McGill, exc

Orphans Court of Wash Co, D C. Letters of administration on the personal estate of John S Haw, late of Wash Co, deceased. –Jesse B Haw, adm

Mrd: on Sep 1, at the residence of John T Walter, jr, **Chester's Gap**, Warren Co, Va, by Rev W G Lumpkin, Moses Nelson, of Fred'k Co, Va, to Miss Eliz Haines, formerly of Rappahannock Co, Va.

Died: on Sep 6, in Wash City, of consumption, Miss Emma Wannall, aged 18 years, daughter of Wm Wannall. Her funeral will take place this afternoon at 4 o'clock, from the residence of her uncle, Chas P Wannall, corner of N Y ave & 9th st.

John McGee offers for private sale his farm, a little n e of Tenally Town, containing about 41 acres, & where he now resides.

THU SEP 8, 1859
Excellent & nearly new furniture & household effects at auction, on Sep 14, at the residence of John H Knott, on G st, between 14th & 15th sts-all his household effects. -J C McGuire & Co, aucts

Architect & Engineer, Wm R Hutton, ofc 322 Pa ave, over Wall's & Stephen's. [Ad]

The Geneva [N Y] Gaz announces the death, at that place, on Aug 29 last, of Cmder Luther Stoddard, of the U S Navy, in his 46th year. He entered the navy a youth of only 12 years, & his slight form made him seen, as he was indeed, a child. His health had long been delicate, but failed rapidly the last winter, & he was compelled to retire from active duty to the home of his childhood, where he died with the faith & hope of a Christian.

A new & spirited Whig paper, The Sandy Valley Advocate, has been commenced at Catlettsburg, Ky, by Jas J Miller, formerly of this city.

Fire broke out on Tue in the stables of Mr Joshua Batemen, living on 1st st, near the old Trinity Church. It communicated to the back shed of his house, which, with the stables, was destroyed. The fire is said to have been incendiary.

The Pioneer & Democrat, of Olympia, Wash Territory, of Jul 29, come dressed in mourning lines, as a token of respect & sorrow for the late Chas H Mason, Sec of Wash Territory, who died at Olympia on Jul 22. He was 29 years old.

Stephen D Dillaye, said to have been implicated in the late extensive forgeries at Pittsburg, Pa, arrived in N Y C from Syracuse last Monday, in custody of detective Devoe. The arrest was made on a requisition from the Govn'r of Pa, & the accused was to be forwarded to Pittsburg in custody of the Chief of Police of that city.

Trustees of Public Schools met on Tue: 1-Boys selected for competition to compete for the scholarship in the Columbian College donated by Mr Riggs: Jas McKendree Davis, Geo Graham, Jas E Douglass, Jas L Boss, J Abbott Moore, Robt H Mitchell, John L Cameron, & A V Grey. The parents of the selected pupil are to guaranty his remaining the full period at the College. 2-The decease of Miss Emma Wannall, sub-assist in the 2nd School District School, on Tue, was announced by Mr Miller in feeling terms, & a resolution of condolence with the family of the deceased was passed.

Mrd: on Sep 6, by Rev Richd Norris, Capt John E Smith, of Balt City, Md, to Miss Amanda M Robbins, of Balt Co.

Mrd: on Aug 25, at the residence of Col Williamson Simmons, in PG Co, Va, by Rev J E Joiner, Rev Geo F Doggett, of Va Conference, to Mrs Virginia F Hughes.

Died: on Sep 7, John Henry, son of R C & Sophia May Washington, in his 17th year. His funeral is this afternoon at 4 o'clock, from the residence of his parents, 306 F st north.

Died: on Aug 30, at the residence of his son-in-law, Mr John Neville, in New Orleans, aged 93 years, Patrick Fenelon, a native of Tullow Co, Carlow, Ireland.

FRI SEP 9, 1859
Deputy U S Marshal, J J Courtney, of the district of Texas, was recently killed in the town of Birdville, Texas, by Col A G Walker, editor of the Birdville Union. The immediate cause was a political discussion, an old quarrel. Col Walker was held to bail in the sum of $2,500.

Executor's sale of valuable nursery shade trees, belonging to the estate of the late Jas Maher, on Sep 20, on the premises, together with the unexpired lease on the ground in the nursery of the late Jas Maher, on 16th st west, between O & P sts north.
–E C Dyer, Thos J Fisher, excs -J C McGuire & Co, aucts

Inquests were held on Sep 6 at the N Y Hospital upon the remains of Ann Ryan & Eliz Selby, 2 servant girls, who died on Monday from carelessly handling burning fluids, while lighting fires. One was burnt on Staten Island, the other at 134 Orchard st.

Mary A Donohue, age 5 years, whose parents reside at 103 East 15th st, in playing with friction matches, set fire to her clothing, & was so badly burnt, that she died in a few hours. Inquest was held yesterday. –N Y Commercial

Murder trial in England. The long pending trial of Dr Thos Smethurst for the murder of Miss Isabella Bankes, at Richmond, near London, has terminated with a verdict of guilty. The Lord Chief Baron said: Dr Smethurst, you kept her sister Louisa Bankes from seeing Isabella when she was dying, when you yourself were introducing a strange atty to make a will in your behalf. The prisoner was removed to Horsemonger Lane jail, where he will be executed next Monday fortnight.

Col Saml Green, a gentleman of the old school, a printer & editor, well known throughout the eastern section of Conn, died at the residence of his son, Dr G S Green, 425 Main st, Sep 5. He was 91 years old, we presume the oldest printer & editor in this State.
-Hartford Times [Sep 12th newspaper: Col Saml Green died on Sep 6 at age 92 years. He continued to publish the New London Gaz until 1838, since which time he has lived with his son, where he died.]

The steamer **Mount Vernon** for N Y, left this port yesterday, with the freight of this city & Washington, & the following passengers: From Wash, C W Angell & lady, Mrs Gorden, Mr Olcott, R H Clarke, Jos H Bradley, jr, John R Brown, Miss C Brown, Miss R B Smoot, Mr Miles, Mrs Miles, Miss E Emmert, Miss Emmert, & Miss Downs. From Alexandria, Geo D Fowle, M D Corse, & W A Taylor. –Alexandria Gaz

Orphans Court of Wash Co, D C. Letters testamentary on the personal estate of Geo W Biscoe, late of Wash Co, deceased. –A M Biscoe, excx

Mrd: on Sep 7, at Rock Creek Church, by Rev J A Buck, Lt Robt Selden, U S Navy, to Augusta N, daughter of the late Maj Geo W Walker, U S Marine Corps.

Died: on Aug 30, at her residence, *Flower Hill*, Montg Co, Md, in her 42nd year, Mrs Rachel Muncaster, wife of Edwin M Muncaster.

Balt, Sep 8. Rev Geo W Burnap died here this morning of disease of the heart, after a few hours' illness. [Sep 12th newspaper: Rev Burnap was Pastor of the First Independent Church of Balt City; [about 30 years,] he had spent last evening with his wife at a friend's house, & returned home in his usual good health. –Balt Patriot, Sep 8]

SAT SEP 10, 1859
Mrd: on Sep 8, at St Patrick's Church, by Rev Fr Boyle, Mr Thos Sinon to Miss Susan White, all of Wash City.

Mrd: on Sep 9, in Wash City, at Wesley Chapel, by Rev D Ball, Mr Caleb E McElfresh to Miss Agnes J Wiber, all of Wash City.

Trustee's sale of valuable improved property at auction, by deed of trust by Thos McNaney & wife, dated Feb 11, 1859, recorded in Liber J A S No 169, folios 347 thru 351, of the land records of Wash Co, D C: sale of lot 13 in square 68, with improvements thereon. –E C Carrington, trustee -A Green auct

Very superior farm of 143 acres, 5 miles from Centre Market, Wash, at auction: on Sep 20, on the premises, the beautiful farm on which Mr T J Barclay resides, lying on the Northwest Branch, in PG Co, Md, near the District line, adjoining the farms of Messrs J F Clark, Diggs, & Gibson. The house is a good 2 story frame dwlg, with barn & other necessary out-bldgs. -A Green auct

N Y, Sep 9. The Harmonia Hotel at Hoboken was destroyed by fire today. Mr Baese, the proprietor, & 3 of his daughters perished in the flames. Mrs Baese was severely injured by leaping from a window. The eldest daughter also leaped from a window, but was caught by a Mr Herring in his arms. This person was on a ladder endeavoring to assist the inmates of the bldg to escape

Died: on Sep 8, in Wash City, after long years of painful sickness, Mrs Amelia Gardner, consort of David A Gardner. Her funeral is today at 3 o'clock, from the Foundry Church.

The following midshipmen in the U S Navy have been warranted by the Dept as masters:

Geo A Bigelow	Leroy Fitch	T R Porter
Robt T Bradford	J W Harris	J C Moseley
Robt L Pythian	F H Eastman	G H Perkins
A P Cook	R R Wallace	G M Blodgett
W P Evans	Chester Hatfield	W N Allen
Geo S Shryrock	C McDougal	Nathl Green

MON SEP 12, 1859
Willie Widdie, age 5, was burnt on Monday by the camphene accident at Mr G W Clifford's, before noticed, & died yesterday. He was taken from the almshouse some years since by a member of Mr Clifford's family for adoption. He was a great favorite with all who knew him. –Alex Gaz

Prof Ross, well known Hellenist & archaeologist, in a fit of mental depression, engendered by prolonged illness, committed suicide at Halle on Aug 8.
–Vienna Cor of London Telegraph

The late Geo Brown, a merchant of Balt, recently deceased, has left bequests of $50,000 to the House of Refuge in that city; $25,000 to the First Presbyterian Church, Balt; & $20,00 to Princeton College, N J.

Geo Bentley was killed on Thu, at New London, Conn, in attempting to get upon a train of cars while in motion. He fell between the cars & both his legs & one arm were severed from his body by the car wheels.

Farm at Sandy Spring, Montg Co, Md for sale: contains 92 acres, farm of Esther S Moore: with a large frame dwlg & numerous out bldgs. Jas Moore, on the premises, will show the farm. Reference may be made to G H Reese, Pratt st, Balt; Edw Stabler & Wm H Stabler, near the premises, & for terms to the subscriber, on the premises. An indisputable title will be made to the purchaser. –Esther S Moore

TUE SEP 13, 1859
Two Revolutionary worthies have lately passed away in Indiana, Jas Garrison, aged 98, & Geo Holman, aged 98. Jas Garrison was born in Rowan Co, N C, & entered the service in 1781 in the company under Capt John Lopp. He finally settled in Indiana in 1827. Geo Holman was born in Md, & moved to Monongahela, Pa, about 1774, & in 1776 located at the mouth of the Ky river. From 1777 to 1784 he was in various skirmishes with the Indians, 3 years of which time he was a prisoner among them. In 1787 he was in the expedition up the Wabash river under Gen G R Clark. He moved to Indiana in 1805.

Wm Owney, of Southampton Co, Va, died a few days since, aged 100 years & 5 months. He was engaged in the battle of Brandywine, & also at Petersburg, Va, when Arnold paid that town a visit. The old soldier had never taken medicine in his life, & in his last illness positively refused to have it administered.

Henry Stowall, jr, an American merchant doing business in Manchester, England, committed suicide on Aug 21. He received a letter from his partner in America which contained a very discouraging account of the state of trade here. He hung himself.

Addie Williams, a seamstress, committed suicide in Phil, on Monday, by swallowing an ounce of laudanum, purchased with the last penny she possessed. A local paper describes her as only 25 years of age, & possessed of as fine a person as the finest lady you will meet in Chestnut st. She could not obtain work to support herself.

In Buffalo, a day or two ago, Hugh Hurley, foreman in a soap factory, fell into one of the large vats in which Hurley was boiling, & was literally boiled to death. It is supposed he was attacked by a fit while passing the vat, & fell in.

A man named Edrington, who was in custody of a sheriff on a charge of murder, jumped overboard from a steamer on the Ohio on Sep 1, intending to swim ashore & escape, but was drowned in the attempt.

I have this day associated with me my brother, Philander C Riley, in the general Dry Goods business: No 36, Central Stores, west bldg, between 7th & 8th sts.
–Wm R Riley & Brother [Sep 13, 1859.]

Died: on Sep 3, in Anne Arundel Co, Mrs Sarah Ann, relict of the late John M Duval, in her 43rd year, leaving a large circle of relatives & friends to mourn her loss. She was an affectionate mother, a kind neighbor, & was loved by all who had the pleasure of her acquaintance.

The Indianapolis, Ind, papers announce the death, from apoplexy, of Ex-Govnr' Wallace, Judge of the Marion Court of Common Pleas. He graduated at West Point with credit in 1821, & served a portion of the time as Assist Prof of Mathematics. He studied in Franklin Co, where he studied law, in the practice of which he soon acquired a high professional reputation. He was elected to the Legislature several times; in 1834 elected Lt Govn'r; & then elected Govn'r. In 1840 he was elected to Congress, where he served one term. In 1850 he served as a member of the Constitutional Convention, & was called to the ofc of Judge of the Common Pleas Court of Marion Co, which he held at the time of his death. He was 61 years of age.

Died: on Sep 12, in Wash City, Chas St John Chubb, in his 31st year. His funeral is on Wed at 5 o'clock, from his late residence 307 I st.

European Intelligence: Leigh Hunt, the author, died in London on Aug 28 at the advanced age of 74 years.

French & English Select School for Young Ladies, No 6 Louisiana Ave, Miss Violetta Jones, Principal.

Hon Amasa Parker met with a serious accident, as well as his wife & daughter. They had been on a visit to a friend at **Fort Washington**, when upon leaving in their carriage the horse took fright & plunged down a precipice, overturning the vehicle, & injuring all within. Mr Parker was severely cut upon the head & injured considerably in the side. The ladies were less hurt, but are still confined to their beds.

WED SEP 14, 1859
Portland papers contain reports of the condemnation of Capt John A Holmes, master of the ship **Therse**, convicted of the murder of Geo W Chadwick, one of the crew. The defence, says the Boston Courier, was insanity, which does not appear to have had any foundation than was derivable from the brutal fierocity of the beating which was continued until Chadwick was dead.

A correspondent of the Charleston Mercury, writing from Denver's Spring, N C, tells of a Revolutionary soldier named Mr Henry residing there who was in the battles of King's Mountain. He is nearly 95 years years old, & still reads without spectacles. He was a mere boy at the time of the battle, but stood his ground when Ferguson's troops charged with the bayonet, & in consequence had a thrust through the hand & into his thigh. He became a distinguished criminal lawyer. He has a manuscript an account of the battle prepared by himself, with the aid of Vance, another of the participators in that battle. He says that Sumter's original name was not the Game Cock, but Tuck; but he was so called by one Gilmore, who owned a blue hen famous for her game chickens; that a celebrated fighter named Tuck was one of his blue hen's chickens, & in compliment to Sumter's pluck Gilmore gave him the cognomen Tuck, which was afterward changed into the Game Cock.

Georgia paper: The late M A Bowder left by his will the sum of $100,000 to the Glenville College & Military Institute. The interest on this large sum is to be applied to the payment of professors' salaries & the education of poor boys.

Mr G N Fisler, a native of Phil, aged about 30, & for a long time head book-keeper in a large establishment in San Francisco, was engaged to be married to Miss Pico, of San Jose, sister to the wife of Mr A C Campbell, a well known lawyer, & of the first native California family in the State. The parties were sincerely attached to each other. The wedding had been fixed for Aug 16. On the morning of the wedding day the bridgegroom died suddenly from an attack of pneumonia-the house of feasting & merriment was converted into the house of prayer & lamentation.

From Salt Lake of Aug 19, 1859. Lt Gray, with a party of 42 U S dragoons, surprised a force of Indians, 150 in number, who were concerned in the late massacre of emigrants on the Calif road. Sgt Pike, of Co I, 10th Infty, was murdered by Howard Spencer, a Mormon. The murderer made his escape.

The case in which Henry Shaw, of St Louis, appeals from the verdict of $100,000 as damages to Miss Emma Carstang, for breach of promise, is soon to come off again in that city. At present a commission is engaged in taking testimony in N Y.

Mrs Eliz Pascall & her daughter Eliz, who were terribly burnt on Thursday, at their residence, 345 8th st, died the following morning. Mrs Pascall was 59, & her daughter was 25. –Albany Statesman

At Balt on Monday a young woman, Mary Virginia Myers, was fatally burnt when filling an ethereal lamp while it was burning. She was 19 years of age. She ran from her mother's house to a street pump. There was no possible hope that she could survive

On Sat last Wm Edwards, of Raymond, Me, was arrested for the alleged murder of a female named Sarah J Verrill, about 11 years ago. The accused at the time resided in Poland. The girl, who is said to have been a low character, also resided in that town. Last week Joshua Edwards, a brother of the accused, made a confession, stating that he & Wm murdered the girl by chaining her on a pile of brush, then setting fire to it, & burning her alive. –Albany Knickerbocker

Orphans Court of Wash Co, D C. Letters of administration on the personal estate of Philip Gormley, late of Wash Co, deceased. –Margaret Gormley, admx

Orphans Court of Wash Co, D C. Letters of administration on the personal estate of Almira S Reab, late of the State of Georgia, deceased. -W E Kennaugh, adm

Mrd: on Sep 12, in Wash City, by Rev Mr Hamilton, Mr Wm Drane to Mrs Eliza Brereton, all of Wash City.

THU SEP 15, 1859
P H Hutchinson, whose grandfather was a son of Govn'r Hutchinson, of Mass, states, in a communication to a British journal, that the family have MSS of his ancestor that have not been printed. Among them is a diary kept from 1774 until his death in 1780, & a verbatim account of his interview with George III, on his first arrival in England. The same ship which carried over Govn'r Hutchinson's son, in 1776, also carried over the family of Copley, the artist, among whom was the present Lord Lyndhurst, who then was 4 years old. Mr Hutchinson states that the Govn'r's salary of L2,000 a year was continued until his death, that he lived on terms of friendship with all the first persons, & visited, with his family, the King. There are at the State House MSS of the Govn'r, consisting of his private letter-book, portions of which only have been printed. –Boston Post

The oldest Church in America was built in 1681, in the town of Hingham, Mass, & is still occupied as a place of worship. The bell rope hangs down in the middle of the house, where it was placed in order that the bell might be rung instantly to give alarm of any sudden Indian incursion. There are many of the old fashioned square pews in the house, enclosed by what resembles more a high & substantial unpainted fence than any thing to be seen in a modern church. The old house is good for 200 more years. This old church has an old pastor, Rev Joshiah Richardson, having preached in it for 53 years.

The steamer **Anglo-Saxon** brings intelligence of the death of Jas Henry Leigh Hunt, who died at London on Aug 20; born in Middlesex, in Oct, 1784, & was partly American in descent, Stephen Shewell, of Phil, being his maternal grandfather. His mother's aunt was the wife of Benj West, the celebrated American painter; his father was a West Indian, & the son passed his early youth in the West Indies, & at one time, we believe, resided in Phil. Young Hunt commenced his literary career at a very early age, being only 18 when, in connexion with his brother John, he issued the first number of the Examiner, which soon acquired great popularity. Hunt was an intimate friend of Byron, Shelley, & Hazlitt. For many years he has enjoyed a pension from the Gov't, & his son is now the editor of one of the leading literary periodicals in London. –Journal of Commerce

Chas Fred'k Anderson is the architect whose plans for the 4½ st Church were awarded the advertised premium by a unanimous vote. He can be consulted on all subjects connected with his professional pursuits. He is an American citizen, but was educated in Europe. His studio is at 456 11th st, between G & H sts, Wash.

The Trustees of Antioch College, Ohio, have elected Rev Thos Hill, of Waltham, Mass, to the Presidency of the institution, made vacant by the death of Horace Mann.

Mrd: on Sep 5, in Wash City, by Rev John N Coombs, Mr Chas H Clark, of Gtwn, to Miss Mary A Wheeler, of Balt.

Mrd: on Sep 11, by Rev John N Combs, Mr John Purcely to Mrs Sarah Rollins, both of Wash City.

Mrd: on Sep 12, by Rev John N Combs, Mr Wm L Golden to Miss Harriet Jane Spelman, both of Wash City.

Mrd: on Sep 13, by Rev John N Combs, Mr Geo Cochran to Miss Ann Maria Spelman, both of Wash City.

Washington Female Seminary, under direction of Mrs Eliza W Smith, [late Principal of Mystic-Hall Seminary.] Address personally at G st, or by letter, addressed box 702, Wash.

FRI SEP 16, 1859
To the editors of the Nat'l Intell: Gentlemen: Permit me through the medium of your paper to correct an error which has recently had an extensive circulation in our newspapers North & South. It is this: that Cmdor Chas Stewart is "the last of the gallant band of heroic men who have made their country's glory immortal." The allusion of the writer of the paragraph from which I have made this quotation was no doubt to those officers of the navy who were engaged in successful conflicts with British ships of war during out last contest with Great Britain, & who were honored by Congress with swords or medals "for their gallantry & good conduct." Cmdor Stewart is not the last of that band. The following are the names of those who still survive: Capts Wm B Shubrick, John T Newton, Isaac Mayo, Geo C Read, Jos Smith, & John D Sloat. The above named ofcrs were lts during the war of 1812, & have since been promoted. Since their promotion they have at different periods commanded squadrons. Lt of Marines, Jas L Edwards, is now a private citizen. –An **Old Soldier**

Shields, the Jumper, who advertised he was going to jump off the bank at Niaraga Falls on Friday, was drowned this morning. He was drawn under water by the suction of a whirlpool. His body has not been recovered. –Buffalo Advertiser, Tue

Nine years since Mr T F Walton, residing in Hamilton, Butler Co, infected with the gold fever, went to Calif, leaving his wife at home. Not hearing from him for 2 years, Mrs Walton supposing him dead, was granted a divorce, probably on the ground of lack of support. She remarried, & 2 years later that husband died. Several years more passed when Mr T F Walton turned up. He courted her again, & they married at the Walnut st house on Sep 9. –Cincinnati Commercial, Sep 10

The Rockdale mill, near Balt, the property of Mr Geo P Kane, was destroyed by fire on Wed. It was fully insured.

Wm H Campbell, having associated with him his son, Leo C Campbell, will continue the Hardware business at the old stand of Campbell & Coyle, under firm of Campbell & Son.

Mrd: on Sep 13, at Northumberland, Pa, by Rev Dr Hosmer, of the Unitarian Church, Buffalo, N Y, Harry Toulmin, of Mobile, Ala, to Fanny Biddle, daughter of Jos R Priestley, of Northumberland, & grand-daughter of the late Dr Priestley, of England.

Died: on Sep 15, in Wash City, Arabella Wade, daughter of W B & A A Donaldson, aged 2 years & 5 months. Her funeral is this afternoon, at 3½ o'clock, from the residence of Mrs Wade, 390 6th st.

St Louis, Sep 13–from Salt Lake. Lloyd Pike was assassinated by a Mormon, named Spencer, while attending court at Salt Lake. The assassination of Frank McNeill & Sgt Pike is believed to have been done by order of Brigham Young.

SAT SEP 17, 1859
The Ex-Pres of Costa Rica, Don Juan Rafael Mora, who was so summarily turned out of his country has arrived in N Y, accompanied by the following friends, Mr Arguillo, his sec, C Mendina, C Mendina, jr, A Bonilla, & Francisco Avaya. The four latter gentlemen are merchants.

On Thu Mr Wore, bricklayer, who was employed on the bldg of an extension to the residence of Capt Scott, on Gtwn heights, adjoining the Lee's hill reservoir, fell from a scaffolding about 30 feet. He was injured on the spine & head, & his right foot at the ancle injured so as almost to force it from the rest of the limb.

Mrd: on Sep 15, at Wesley Chapel Parsonage, Rev Dabney Ball, Mr Jas T Walker to Miss Virginia G Watkins, all of Wash.

Mrd: on Sep 15, by Rev John Robb, Mr Jas B Smallwood to Miss Annette Morrow, youngest daughter of the late Wm Morrow, all of Wash City.

Mrd: on Sep 11, by Rev A G Carothers, F J O'Brien, of Gtwn, to Miss M A Hoover, all of Wash City.

Died: on Sep 15, in Wash City, of a lingering & distressing sickness, Miss Sarah Cochrane Polk, a native of Somerset Co, Md, but for many years a resident of Wash City. Her funeral will take place today at 4 o'clock, from 447 Pa ave, near 3rd st.

MON SEP 19, 1859
In the Palmer [Mass] Journal of Aug 3: Died-26, May 20th, wife of De Witt Clinton Packard, of Providence, R I." We also find the following: many months ago in Belchertown, a young man sought & received the promise of the hand of a young lady, whose home was in the lap of luxury, whose personal & mental attractions made all pleasant around her, & she trusted his promise. He removed himself to a distant State. Because he had exposed himself to the penalty of the law, he came back & married her in a hasty ceremony. He left her in the street promising to return. That promise was not fulfilled. She and their baby, partaking of its mother's grief, soon died. The mother's obituary is above. The young woman died of a broken heart. [Her first name was not given.]

Died: on Sep 18, Mrs Eliz Kelly, in her 62nd year. Her funeral will take place on Sep 20 at 10 o'clock A M, at her late residence, 376 13th st.

Edw Phillips, about 16, left his father's house on Sep 12th for a shooting excursion near Bergen, N J. He did not return home as expected, but his dog came home alone. The body of the youth was found beside a rail fence, with a gunshot wound in the abdomen, & his fowling piece, which was discharged, lying beside him. There is little doubt that he was shot while climbing the fence by the accidental discharge of his own gun.

Naval Ofcrs of the war of 1812: In addition to the half dozen mentioned by the Old Soldier, the following names of ofcrs equally recipients of the honorable mention he refers to; many of whom, also, have commanded, & some are now in actual command of squadrons. I name them in order in which they stand on the Register, to wit:

Wm D Salter, now capt
Philip Voorhees, now capt
Jno Paul Zantzinger, now capt
Thos Harris, surgeon
Wm J McCluney, now commanding Home Squadron
Stephen Champlin, capt
John H Aulick, capt
J B Montgomery, capt
French Forrest, capt
E A F Vallete, [now Lavellette,] capt

Chas T Platt, cmder
Thos A Conover, capt
Hiram Paulding, capt
Frank Ellory, lt
Saml L Breeze, capt
John H Graham, capt
David Geisinger, capt
Horace B Sawyer, capt
-An Old Sailor

Patrick S O'Conner, age 27 years, a native of Petersboro, Canada West, respectably connected, made arrangements for a leap of 90 feet into Niagara river on Tue. He swam out into the river & dove down once or twice. He then went down in a small whirlpool & rose, but could not escape from the current which drew him down, & so he sank to rise no more. His body may sometime be found near the mouth of the river or on Lake Ontario. -Rochester Union of Wed.

Mrd: on Sep 15, at Trinity Church, by Rev Dr Butler, Mr J M Binckley to Mary Louisa, daughter of Harvey & Jane Michel, all of Wash City.

Mrd: Sep 15, at Trinity Church, Shepherdstown, Va, by Rev C W Andrews, D D, Lt Wm F Lee, U S Army, to Lillie M Parran, daughter of the late Dr Richd Parran, of Jefferson Co, Va.

TUE SEP 20, 1859
Boston Journal of Fri: boy incendiaries, Michl Riley, Wm Cofran, Thos Gordon, Geo C Martin, & Dennis Dwyer, charged with setting the House of Reformation, at Deer Island, on fire on Aug 21, were sentenced: Riley-10 years hard labor; Cofran-9 years; Gordon-3 years. Martin & Dwyer entered a nol pros, & Martin was discharged. Dwyer is held in custody to answer to an indictment for being an accessory before the fact.

The Wheeling papers of Friday state that the body Jas Stewart, of the firm of W & J Stewart, foundrymen, was found on Thu. An elder brother of the deceased, & senior partner in the firm, has been arrested & lodged in jail.

Mrd: on Sabbath evening, by Rev John C Smith, Henry Roberts to Miss Marion F Edwards, all of Wash City.

Fraud on the Pension Ofc. Examination on Sep 12, at Binghamton, N Y, before the U S Com'r, Chas S Hall, of certain parties charged with perpetrating frauds to a considerable amount on the Pension Ofc. The circumstances of the case are these: In 1855 John Manhart, of Van Etten, Chemung Co, a Revolutionary pensioner, died, leaving a widow, Rebecca Manhart. Within 3 or 4 years the widow again married, one Henry R French, with whom she now lives. During the spring of 1858 Jas Van Etten applied to Thos Maxwell, of Elmira, to obtain a pension for Mrs French, stating she was at that time the widow of John Manhart, & still unmarried. The papers were accordingly made out, stating, among other things, that Rebecca Manhart was & still continued to be the widow of John Manhart, & were sworn to by Van Etten & his wife, together with Mrs French, she signing her name & representing herself as Rebecca Manhart; Van Etten having made an arrangement with Mrs French whereby he was to receive all the money obtained except $200, which was to be paid to her, together with the proceeds of a bounty land warrant for 160 acres, which was applied for at the same time. The Pension Ofc required the additional proof that the Mrs Manhart in question was the widow of the indentical John Manhart who had received a revolutionary pension. Van Etten, who was the instigator & getter up of the fraud, accordingly procured the signatures of several of his neighbors to an affidavit containing the additional evidence, stating to them that it was merely a certificate that John & Rebecca Manhart had lived together as man & wife; & took the papers to Justice Patchin, of that town, & induced him to add the jurat to the affidavits, without the persons whose signatures were attached having ever appeared before him, & made oath to the affidavit. On this proof the Dept at Wash granted a pension to Mrs French, alias Manhart, of $96 per annum, commencing in Feb, 1858, together with a bounty land warrant for 160 acres. One year's pay was drawn subsequently & before the fraud was discovered, the sum obtained from the Gov't in all amounting between seven & eight hundred dollars. On Fri last, on the complaint of S C Boynton, of the Pension Ofc, who had been detached from the Dept for the investigation of the fraud, warrants were issued by Com'r Hall against Jas Van Etten & Catharine, his wife, & Justice Patchin, charging them with perjury & making fraudulent writings in order to obtain money from the U S. On Sat last the parties were arrested & brought to Binghampton on the following day. The parties declining to make any statement, & introducing no exculpatory testimony, Van Etten was held to bail in the sum of $4,000, & in default thereof was committed to jail in Albany Co. Mrs Van Etten was bound over on her own recognizance to appear at the next term of the U S Circuit Court to be held in Albany. Patchin, having waived, on the advice of counsel, an examination, was held to bail in the sum of $1,000 to appear at the same court. Mrs French, though as liable to punishment as any of those arrested, having made a clean breast of the matter, & refunded nearly all the money she had received, besides being over 70 years of age, was used as a witness instead of being put under arrest. In case of conviction, the punishment in these cases is imprisonment from 1 to 10 years, or an imprisonment not exceeing 5 years & a fine not exceeding $1,000. –Binghampton Republican

Died: on Sep 16, Robert, youngest child of Jas & Margaret Selden, aged 6 weeks.

Died: on Sep 19, William H, youngest son of Jeremiah G & Sarah E Matlock, aged 1 year & 2 months.

We learn from the Fred'k [Md] Citizen that Mrs Ritchie, daughter of Col W F Maulsby, & wife of John Ritchie, was dangerously injured by the explosion of a camphene lamp. Her clothing & articles in the room were all afire. Her arms are frightfully burnt, as well as other parts of her person. We are gratified to learn that she is out of danger.
Affray between 2 prominent business men occurred at the ofc of the Middlesex Mills, in Boston, on Sat, between Dr J C Ayer, of Lowell, & Richd S Fay, jr. Ayer stabbed Fay in a dangerous locality, over the right groin. Dr Ayer surrendered to the police.

Died: on Sep 19, in Wash City, Col Edw Brooks, a soldier & ofcr in the war of 1812. He distinguished himself in battles, & was a high-minded honorable man in all the relations of life, above all, he was a devout Christian.

Died: on Sep 15, in Wash City, Maj Francis Holden, aged 54 years, formerly of Boston, Mass, but for many years a resident of Wash. He, in 1847, commanded Co D, of the Georgia volunteers, in the Mexican war, under Gen Scott's division; in 1835 served in the Florida war, & was afterwards, for his gallantry, appointed brigade inspector of the Florida militia. He was followed to his last resting place by the order of Masons & Odd Fellows, of which he was a worthy member.

I have for sale, on easy terms, 1,750 acres of land lying on the west side of Raquett Lake, Hamilton Co, N Y. –Arthur W Fletcher, 430 F st, Wash.

Public sale of valuable land, in PG Co, Md, by deed of trust from Jas Crandall & wife, to secure payment of a certain debt to Elisha C Hubbard, which deed is recorded in the proper ofce of PG Co, Md: public auction, on the premises, Oct 21, 1859, of *Magruder's Plains Enlarged*, consisting of 45½ acres, being part of what was known as the old *Wallingford Place*; with a good dwlg house, barn & stabling. –Edwin Martin, trustee

WED SEP 21, 1859
Excellent household & kitchen furniture at auction on Sep 27, at the residence of Wm C Johnson, on F st, between 13th & 14th sts, all his effects, together with a portion of the furniture of the late John Quincy Adams. -Jas C McGuire & Co, aucts

Naval Intelligence: a letter from Woosung, China, dated Jun 16, states that in firing a salute on the U S steam-frig **Powhatan**, Wm Wilson, 1st quarter gunner, whilst ramming home a cartridge, was blown overboard. He was picked up by a boat & taken on board the steamer, & it was found that his right arm was so shattered as to render amputation necessary near the shoulder. He also lost one of his eyes, & the other was much injured. But little hope was entertained of his recovery. Another quarter gunner was injured at the same time by having his thumb split open whilst upon the vent of the gun.

A telegraphic dispatch published yesterday announced the loss of the U S war steamer **Fulton** which went ashore on Santa Rosa Island, near Pensacola, during the gale of the 16th. She was built at the Brooklyn navy yard in 1837. Her ofcrs were: Lt-Commanding John J Amy; Lts: M K Warrington, J B Stewart, Robt Selden, & R P Chapman; Purser Robt H Clark; Assist Surgeon Edwin R Denby; Acting Master M C Campbell; Engineers: 1st Assist Harmon Newell, 3rd Assists R W McClery, Wm Roberts, W P Burrow, & J B Houston.

Hon Albert H Tracy, an old & wealthy resident of Buffalo, N Y, died in that city on Sep 19, aged 66 years. He was a member of Congress from 1819 to 1825.

The plain old mansion at Baton Rouge, La, long the residence of Gen Taylor, was recently torn down. When the Fort of Baton Rouge was taken by the Spaniards under Don Bunardo de Galvez, in 1779, it was the residence of Col Dixon, the English cmder. It was subsequently occupied by the Spanish cmder, & more recently by the family of the hero of Buena Vista.

Naval Ofcrs of 1812. The name of Philip F Voorhees, now a captain in the U S navy, was omitted. That name should be added to the list of ofcrs of the navy who were honored by Congress for their gallantry & good conduct in the war of 1812. Thos Harris, surgeon, should have been inserted in that list. In the article signed Old Sailor, I suppose, he intended to say that the gentlemen on that list were in successful naval engagements during the war of 1812. On examining Force's Register for 1830, I find that only two on the Old Sailor's list were commissioned ofcrs when the battles were fought. Their names are above. In my former communication I did not say that my list contained the names of warrant ofcrs. When the term ofcr is used either in the naval or military service, it is invariably understood to signfy a commissioned ofcr. If the Old Sailor will take the trouble to read the resolutions of Congress of Jan 6, 1814, he will find that the distinction in the 2nd resolutionis there clearly made. –An Old Soldier

The firm of Jas Wilson & Co is this day dissolved by mutual consent. –R S T Cissel, J Humphreys: Sep 21, 1859. A new co-partnership has been formed under the style of A E Beall & Co, for the purpose of manufacturing & selling Soap & Candles. –A E Beall, R S T Cissel, J Humphreys, Green st, Gtwn.

Phil, Sep 20. Hiram P Leslie, the swindler of several school & music teachers, was tried for larceny of the wearing apparel of one of his victims. He was sentenced to 3 years' hard labor in the penitentiary, the extreme penalty provided.

New Orleans, Sep 20. A fatal affray occurred here last night between Dr Robt W Graham & Ernest Toledano, in which Graham was shot dead. The cause of the encounter was a political difficulty.

THU SEP 22, 1859
Executor's sale of furniture, buggy, ploughs, & harrow, Sep 24, at the Auction Rms of Jas C McGuire, aucts, a part of the effects of the late Jas M Minor. –John R Minor, excs

The Republican Court in the days of the first Pres: The Presidential Mansion in Phil was the property of Robt Morris, & had been the headquarters of Sir Wm Howe during the occupation of Phil by the British army in 1777-78.

Trustee's sale of groceries, wines, & liquors, on Sep 27, at the store of J P Levy, 464 7th st, corner of F st. –M A Mitchell, trustee -A Green auct

Montg Co Agricultural Fair, held lately at Rockville, Md, the premium for the best saddle & harness was awarded to John Appleman & Son, of Middletown, Md. Best yoke of oxen R P Dunlop received $8; best stallion, quick draft, H W Blint, $20; Wm P Howser a discretionary premium of $20; for best gelding, H Martin, $10; for best 3 year old colt, J C Cook, $10; for best pacer, Allen Dorsey, $10; for best blooded mare, E Boice, $5; for best Devon cow, T W Stonestreet, $5; for best sheep, N C Dickerson, $5; for best hogs, J G England, $5; for best tobacco, A B Davis, $2.50.

Madame Poitezin, widow of the well known aeronaut, recently made a balloon ascension at Rouen, France, accompanied in the car by her assistant in the costume of Sancho Panza, while below was suspended a donkey, mounted by a new Dulcinea del Toboso, whose white toi_et was visible when the balloon itself could hardly be perceived. The descent was effected in safety at Franqueville.

Wash Corp, Sep 19. 1-Ptn of Mary Keating; of M Jordan; of Thos McLaine; of Thos Fitzpatrick; of Patrick Scanlon; & of J R Worster: praying for the remission of a fine: referred to the Cmte of Claims. 2-Ptn of C W Pettit & others for grading & paving an alley in square 564: referred to the Cmte on Improvements. 3-Ptn of W Q Locke, asking an increase of salary as messenger to the Mayor: referred to the Cmte of Ways & Means.

Orphans Court of Wash Co, D C. Letters of administration on the personal estate of John Connelly, late of Wash Co, deceased. –Rebecca Connelly, admx

FRI SEP 23, 1859
The inauguration of Hiram Powers' statue of Danl Webster, took place in Music Hall on Sat, in Boston.

An incorrect list of the ofcrs of the steamer **Fulton** is going the rounds of the press. The books of the Navy Dept show her present ofcrs to be as follows: Cmder, G G Williamson; Lts, E Thompson, J H Rochelle, & E E Potter; Master, W E Evans; Assist Surgeon, F M Gunnell; Purser, C C Jackson; 1st Assist Engineer, G W Alexander; 2nd Assist, G H Riley; 3rd Assists, Jas DeKraft, R L Harris, & H X Wright; Capt's Clerk, A P Halse; Purser's Clerk, W J Bennett.

By deed of trust from Wm S Martin & Mary E Martin, his wife, to Thos G Clayton, dated Mar 16, 1857, recorded in Liber J A S, No 134, of the land records of Wash Co, D C, the subscriber will sell on the premises on Oct 5, a piece of improved property in square 465, on the Island, being parts of lots 43 thru 46; located between D & E sts south & 6th & 7th sts south. –T G Clayton, trustee -A Green auct

Household & kitchen furniture at auction on Oct 4, at the residence of Chas Eliot, jr, on H st, between 17th & 18th st-all the furniture effects. -Jas C McGuire & Co, aucts

SAT SEP 24, 1859
A large tobacco house on the plantation of Mrs Grace H Clagett, near Upper Marlborough, PG Co, Md, was entirely demolished during the storm on Sat night.

Dr E H Barton, of Louisiana, died recently at Charleston, S C. Dr Barton acted as an army surgeon in our war with Mexico.

Rev Geo Bush, a distinguished theologian & scholar, died at Rochester, N Y, on Monday, at age 63 years. He was a graduate at Dartmouth College, & afterwards studied theology at the Princeton Theological Seminary.

Rev Henry E D Hennis, pastor of the Catholic Church in New Bedford, died on Wed last. He was highly & deservedly respected by all who knew him.

Died: on Sep 18, at the residence of her husband, Chicago, Ill, Sallie F, the wife of B I Semmes, aged 21 years & 7 months.

For sale: the best farm in the neighborhood of Wash, on the Rockville Turnpike, 4 miles from Gtwn, improved a few years ago by John C McKelden. The tract contains 116 acres of land; dwlg house is plain but comfortable, with back bldgs. Inquire of Mr Keith, the owner, or of the overseer, Mr Scott, on the premises, or Barnard & Buckey, Gtwn, D C.

Orphans Court of Wash Co, D C. Letters of administration on the personal estate of Richd M Bowyer, late of Wash Co, deceased. –Thos M Bowyer, H L Offutt, adms

MON SEP 26, 1859
It was announced a short time since that the body of a female, supposed to be that of Mrs Richmond, wife of Jason Richmond, of Exeter, R I, who had been missing since Jun 10th last, was found on Aug 23 under the stump of a tree that had blown over, & that Mr Richmond had been arrested in suspicion of having murdered his wife. One day last week, however, the missing woman came home. She left home on account of a family jar which she & her husband had managed to create. [Copied as written.]

Positive sale of very superior harness & saddle horses, buggies & carriages, harness, & saddles, at auction, Sep 30th, at the stables of Allison Nailor, jr, corner of 13½ & E sts, who is retiring from the business. We will sell his entire stock. –Wall & Barnard, aucts

Richd Sippach, butcher by trade, took a rather wild steer to his slaughter-house, near Davis' saw-mill for the purpose of killing him. Mr Swicke desired the privilege of shooting the animal, & when he did, the ball passed through the door, struck Sippach penetrating the femoral artery, killing him in a few minutes. –Nebraska Republican

On a hunting trip, on Sep 17, Messrs Saml Clifton & Sherwood Denton, of Franklin Co, N C, were hunting rabbits. Mr Clifton accidentally shot & killed Mr Denton.

Orphans Court of Wash Co, D C. In the case of Eliz Wise & Joel Wise, excs of John Wise, deceased, the Court & executors have assigned Oct 25 next, for the final settlement of the personal estate of the deceased, of the assets in hand. -Ed N Roach, Reg/o wills

Mrd: on Sep 20, at **Duncannan**, the residence of the bride's father, near Lexington, Ky, by Rev R J Brank, Col Hart Gibson, of Woodford, to Miss Mary Duncan, eldest daughter of Henry T Duncan.

Died: on Sep 25, in Wash City, after a long & painful illness, Priscilla Eliz Lansdale, wife of Henry N Lansdale. Her funeral is today at 3 o'clock, from her late residence, corner of M & 8th sts.

Died: on Sep 24, in Wash City, Jas Patterson, aged 37 years, a native of the county Craven, Ireland, but for the last 10 years a resident of Wash City. His funeral will be this evening at 2 o'clock, from his late residence, 4½ st, near Md ave.

TUE SEP 27, 1859
Francis J Stone, of St Mary's Co, Md, has had on his farm for several years a vineyard, & expects to realize over a 100 gallons of wine from this year's vintage. The grape he plants is of the Catawba variety.

Lesson, the murderer of Daybens, in Wash Co, anticipated justice by hanging himself in his cell, at Hillsboro, on the night before the day appointed for his execution.

Va Military Warrants 8,573, for 1,185 acres, issued Jun 6, 1838, in favor of Danl Laws, Mr Larry Laws, & Asiana Ritch, & 8,596, for 296 acres, issued Jun 20, 1838, in favor of James, Fanny, & Betsey Viney, heirs at law in part of Timothy Laws, a midshipman in the Va State Navy, have been lost or mislaid. Application will be made to the Com'r of the Gen Land Ofc for the issue of scrip on duplicate warrants of them within 6 months from this date. –Wm D Bell, Atty for heirs

Died: on Sep 21, at Schenectady, N Y, Harriet Augusta, daughter of Dr C H & A C Van Patten, formerly of Wash, aged 2 years.

Latest from Europe. 1-Sir Wm Eyre, late cmder of the forces in Canada, died on Thu. 2-The Florence correspondent of the London Times says it is reported that Pope Pius had received extreme unction or sacrament administered to the dying.

St Louis, Sep 26. The *Fort Smith Times* [Ark] says that Indian Agent Neighbors has been killed by McKnett; also, that Col Leiper, the agent for the Camanches, has been killed by Indians.

WED SEP 28, 1759
Household & kitchen furniture at auction on Oct 3, at the residence of Mrs Gueble, on H, between 21st & 22nd sts. -A Green auct

Household & kitchen furniture at auction on Oct 3, at the residence of the late Chas St John Chubb, on north I st, between 15th & 16th st- the entire furniture & effects. -Jas C McGuire & Co, aucts

The Navy Dept has ordered the following ofcrs to repair to Pensacola, Fla, & to investigate the circumstances attending the loss of the steamer **Fulton**: Cmder McIntosh, Com Farrand, & Lt Kell; Capt J D Simms judge advocate.

Mrd: on Sep 27, by Rev John C Smith, John T Hancock to Dorcas G Dudley, both of Balt.

Died: on Sep 27, in Wash City, after a long & painful illness, Margaret Robbins, wife of Thos Robbins, aged 58 years. Her funeral is this evening at 3 o'clock, from her residence, corner of 12th st & Mass ave.

Obit-tribute to the memory of Margaret, wife of Wm Greenwell, of the U S Coast Survey, who died in Calif. Prayers for her life were poured to Heaven in vain. I can fancy I saw the young Margaret dying, dead, & in the shroud; at her side her agonized & devoted husband. -A

Three days from Europe. 1-The steamship **Great Eastern** will be delayed from sailing til Oct 20th. Mr Brunel, her designer, has died from paralysis. [Sep 30th newspaper: Mr Isambard Kingdom Brunel was of French descent; his father, Mark Isambard Brunel, came from the vicinity of Rouen. In 1793 he fled for political reasons from France to N Y. The Britannia Tubular Bridge, the Suspension Bridge at Hungerford, London, the Box Tunnel on the Great Western Railway, the board gauge system of railways in England, & the ocean steamer **Great Western**, steamer **Great Britian**, & the steamer **Great Eastern**, are the noble products of the mechanical genius of the late Isambard Kindgon Brunel. –N Y Post]

THU SEP 29, 1859
The U S steam sloop-of-war **Brooklyn**, Capt D G Farragut commanding, arrived at N Y on Sunday from a trial trip, having been absent nearly 8 months. List of her ofcrs: Capt D G Farragut; 1st Lt & Exec Ofcr, Jas A Doyle; Lts, Albert N Smith, Wm N Jeffers, Wm Mitchell; Lt & Acting Master, Henry A Adams, jr; Surgeon, Lewis W Minor; Assist Surgeon, T W Leach; Purser, Thos W Looker; Marine Ofcr, Geo R Graham; Chief Engineer, Joshua Follansbie; 1st Assist Engineers, E S De Luce & W B Brooks; 2nd do, M P Jordan; 3rd do, F E Brown, G H White, & J W Whittaker; Sailmaker, Francis Boon; Gunner, Wm Allen; Master's Mates, Chas F Ellmore, Francis H Bacon, G R Haswell; Capt's Clerk, Byrd Dallas; Purser's Clerk, Forbes Parker.

Fatal shooting on Sep 19 in the Ruby Coffee-house, on Common st, during which Dr Graham, a well known physician of New Orleans, was almost instantaneously killed by Mr Ernest Toledano, also well known in the city, & at present the nominee of the American party for the ofc of Clerk of the 3rd District Court. –New Orleans Bulletin

N Y, Sep 27. Marmaduke Reeves, alias John McAlpine, the young lady music teacher swindler, was yesterday sentenced to the State prison for a term of 5 years.

The barque **Ocean Eagle** sailed from N Y on Tue for the Liberian coast. She takes out as passengers the family of Mr Thos Cooper, a Liberian merchant, who has been visiting the U S, & returns with several thousand dollars' worth of goods purchased with cash. Several missionaries are also passengers. Rev Walter Clark, of Milburn, N Y, & Rev M L St John & wife, of Marietta, Ohio, are destined to strengthen the mission at Gaboon under the care of the American Board. Miss Marion Melville, of Wash, DC, Miss H C Rolf, of Lexington, Mo, & Miss L L K Spaulding, of Laurence, Miss, are to be connected with the Protestant Episcopal mission under Bishop Payne. Rev C Loomis & wife will proceed to Corisco under the charge of the Presbyterian Board.

Inquest held yesterday on the body of a young colored man, Aloysius Bronaugh, [Dr Hezekiah Magruder, of Gtwn, his master,] who was poisoned by a colored boy, Alfred Jones, in Gtwn, some days since. Jones was arrested last evening in Gtwn by ofcr Daw. Jones is a slave, his victim a free boy.

Norfolk, Sep 28. Maj Chapman, of the U S army, stationed at Old Point, committed suicide on Tuesday by cutting his throat.

Rock Hill for sale or rent: about 30 acres on the banks of the Potomac river, Va side, immediately opposite & within gunshot of Gtwn, D C: with a gardener's house of 3 rooms, & inexhaustible stone quarry on the river. Terms made known by calling on the properietor R B Lloyd, at the ofc of Lloyd & Co, Claim, Pension, & Bounty Land Agents, 15th st.

FRI SEP 30, 1859
Auction by order of the Orphans Court of D C, of coffins, tools, & lumber, on Oct 4, at the late residence & warehouse of John Connelly, deceased, on the west side of 7th st, between G & H sts north. -A Green auct

Allow me to put the Old Soldier & Old Sailor to rights. 1-Resolution of Congress for War with Tripoli, Mar 3, 1805. Master & Cmder Chas Stewart, brig **Syren**, of all the gallant spirits of Cmdor Preble's squadron now alone survives. 2-Resolutions of Congress War of 1812. Ships **Constitution & Guerriere**, Aug 19, 1812, Capt Hull. Commo Geo C Read, then a lt, now retired. Commo Wm D Salter, then midshipman, now retired.
Ships **United States & Macedonian**, Oct 25, 1812, Cmdor Decatur. Commo Geo C Read, then lt, now retired. Commo J D Sloat, then sailingmaster, now retired. Commo P F Voorhees, then lt, now retired. Capt Wm Jamesson, then midshipman, now retired.
Ships **Wasp & Frolic**, Oct 18, 1812. Capt Jacob Jones. Commo W J McCluney, then midshipman, now commanding home squadron. Surgeon Thos Harris.
Ships **Constitution & Java**, Dec 29, 1812, Commo Bainbridge. Commo John C Long, then midshipman, active list.
Lake Erie, Sep 10, 1812. Master Com O H Perry. Capt Saml Champlin, then sailing master, retired. Commo John B Montgomery, then midshipman, now commanding Pacific squadron. Capt Hugh N Page, then midshipman, retired. Lt Thos Brownell, then sailing master, retired.
Ships **Enterprise & Boxer**, Sep 4, 1813, Lt Com Burrows. Commo John H Aulick, then midshipman, active list.
Ships **Hornet & Peacock**, Feb 24, 1813, Mas Com Lawrence. Commo French Forrest, then midshipman, active list.
Lake Champlain, Sep 11, 1814, Mas Com Macdonough. Commo Jos Smith, then lt, Chief of Bureau of Yards & Docks, active list.
Commo E A F Lavalette, then sailingmaster, commanding N Y Navy Yard, active list.
Comm Hiram Paulding, then midshipman, active list.
Commo T A Connover, then midshipman, active lits.
Capt John H Graham, then midshipman, retired.
Cmder Chas T Platt, then midshipman, retired.
Lt Frank Ellery, then midshipman, retired.
Ships **Peacock & Epervier**, Apr 29, 1814, Master Cmder Warrington. Commo P F Voorhees, then lt, retired. Capt John Percival, then sailingmaster, retired.
Ships **Wasp & Reindeer**, Jun 28, 18184, Master Cmder Blakely. Commo David Geisinger, then midshipman, retired.
Ships **Constitution, Cyane, & Levant**, Feb 20, 1815, Capt Chas Stewart.
Senior Flag Ofcr on the Active list, Chas Stewart.
Commo Wm B Shubrick, then lt, Chairman Lighthouse Board, active list.
Capt Horace B Sawyer, then midshipman, retired.
Ships **Hornet & Penguin**, Mar 23, 1815, Master Cmder Biddle. Commo Isaac Mayo, then lt, active list. Sep 20, 1859. -Another Sailor

Circuit Court of D C. John W Thompson & Wm Thompson against Margaret F Lindsey, Beverly G Lindsey, Walter Lindsey, Margaret J Lindsey & Ann Lindsey, widow, admx, & heirs at law of Geo F Lindsey. Statement of account of the personal estate of said Geo F Lindsey, on Oct 10 next, at my ofc in the City Hall, Wash. –W Redin, auditor

The Acting Com'r of Indian Affairs has received a letter from Indian Agent Leiper, who was reported dead by a recent telegraphic despatch from St Louis. Mr Leiper reports that on Sep 6, whilst returning from the settlements on the False Washita in company with Indian Superintendent Robt S Neighbors, they were attacked & wounded by a band of hostile Indians. They escaped, & some days afterwards arrived at Belknap, Texas, & were detained there. While at Belknap Maj Neighbors was shot & so wounded that he survived but 20 minutes. It was reported that the difficulty in which he lost his life grew out of his severe animadversion upon the murder of a reserve Indian which occurred recently.

By intelligence from Old Point Comfort we learn that Maj W W Chapman, of the U S army & connected with the artillery stationed at **Fortress Monroe**, committed suicide on Tue at the fort, by cutting his throat with a razor. It appears he was subject to attacks of mental depression, & during the forenoon he sent for Dr Cuyler, the surgeon, & consulted with him concerning his health. He then appeared on parade & review, on the occasion of the visit of Gov Floyd, Sec of War. Nothing indicative of the contemplation of the act that was soon to startle the community. Maj Chapman made up a package of valuables, his watch, etc, & took the package to the ofc of Capt Carlisle, where he left it. He took leave of a lady friend, bid her an affectionate farewell, & declined accompanying her to the boat. He returned to his rooms at the quarters, inflicted 2 dreadful gashes upon his throat with a razor, laid down upon his bed, & was found in that position. He was a native of Mass, & entered the army about 1837, & was made major by brevet in 1847. –Sun

Telegraphic despatch from Watertown, N Y, announcing the continued want of any information of the balloonists, Messrs La Mountain & Haddock, missing since their ascension on Sep 22, from Watertown. –N Y Sun

On Sep 23 fire broke out in the ship **Hellos**, Capt Mason, loading for Liverpool with cotton, & was destroyed. She was owned by Jos Titcomb, of Kennebunk, Maine, & was worth about $70,000, & we believe, insured in Boston & N Y. –New Orleans Bulletin

Mrd: on Sep 27, by Rev A Holmead, Pastor of Grace Church, Mr G R Thompson to Miss E V Robey, eldest daughter of John E Robey, all of Wash City.

Died: on Sep 15, in the vicinity of Piscataway, PG Co, Md, of typhoid fever, Dr Wm H Gwynn, in his 25th year. He was an exemplary son, an affectionate & devoted brother, & generous almost to a fault.

Albion, N Y, Sep 28. Main st canal bridge, in this village, fell this afternoon with an immense crowd of people who were attending the County Fair. Killed as far as learned: Adelbert Wilcox, of West Kendall; Mr Stilson, of South Butler; Thos Cady, of Albion; Jas L Avery, of Albion; Sarah Thomas, Augusta Martier, Mr Henry, & Ransom Murdock, of Carlton; Mrs Ann Niele, of Barre; Thos Handy, of Yates; Sophia Pratt, of Toledo; Perry Cole, of Barre; Sophia Harris, of Albion; & Mr Cornell, of South Barre.

SAT OCT 1, 1859

Mr John Head, 17, only son of Sir Edmund Head, was drowned on Sunday last, while bathing in the river St Maurice, at La Grand Mere. He had arrived from England by the Anglo-Saxon about a fortnight ago from Europe, whither he had gone for educational purposes. A Canada paper of Sep 26: His Excellency the Govn'r Gen, Lady Head, Miss Head, & Mr John Head, with a distinguished party, left Three Rivers on Tue last to visit the River St Maurice as far as the Piles Falls. Hon J Browne, son of the Earl of Kenmair, with Mr John Head, left the camp to take their usual morning bath. Mr Head took to the water, struggled, & disappeared. His body was recovered.

Fire of the Chinese was directed with fatal skill; British Admiral Hope leading in one of the gunboats, was badly injured. I went with my Flag Lt, Mr Trenchard, in my barge to visit him. Within a few feet of the Cormorant a round shot struck the boat, killed my coxswain, & slightly bruised my flag-lt. Letter from Josiah Tattnall, Flag Ofcr Commanding East India Squardon, to Hon Isaac Toucey, Sec of the Navy, Wash. Mr Coxswain, John Hart, whose death I have to lament, was the son of John & Mary Hart, now living at Jamaica, Long Island. He was a widower, but has left a young daughter 8 years old. I shall communicate the said event to his parents, & as his child whom he supported will be entitled to a pension, may I beg the favor of you, as soon as the proper papers shall be filed at the Dept, to direct that pension be issued without unnecessary delay? Hart had been a long time in the navy, having served under me 15 years ago.

Treasury Dept, Ofc Lighthouse Board, Wash, Sep 19, 1859. Notice to Mariners. Official information has been received from Capt W H C Whiting, Corps of Engineers U S Army, that the new lighthouse at **Cape Lookout** has been completed. The tower is the frustum of a cone. It is built of brick, & is surrounded by an iron lantern painted black. The color of the tower is red, & and focal plane is 156 feet above the level of the sea. The keeper's dwelling, which is a part of the old tower, is painted red & white horizontal stripes.
-W B Franklin, Sec

At a military encampment at Lewistown, Pa, an affray occurred between Henry J Platt, one of the soldiers belonging to the Jackson Artl, of Stone Valley, & a sentinel, Edw Mills, of Juniata Co, which resulted in the death of Platt. Platt had attempted to get into camp in defiance of the sentinels; a scuffle ensued, & Mills musket was discharged & the unfortunate man fell dead.

The Pres has appointed Wm G Jones district judge of the U S District Court for the northern & southern districts of Alabama, vice John Gayle, deceased.

Wm Graves, an elderly & quiet citizen of Richmond, Va, died on Sep 28, from the effects of a pistol wound inflicted by John L Taylor. The quarrel seems to have been about the ill usage of a horse hired by Taylor from Graves.

Public sale of land at the Court-house door, in Rockville, Montg Co, Md, on Oct 11, the farm of the late Thos W Wakius, containing 300 acres, lying on both sides of Cabin John Run, near the River road, 9 miles west of Gtwn. Also, the unsold portions of the lands belonging to the estate of the late Zachariah Gatton, deceased, containing about 200 acres; lies on **Watt's Branch**, near the River road. –G M Wakius, trustee

Mrd: on Sep 29, at the Methodist Episcopal Church South, [Rev J C Granberry,] by Rev Thos B Sargent, D D, Wm H Smith, of Balt, Md, to Sophie Sargent, daughter of Enoch Tucker, of Wash City.

Died: on Thu, in Wash City, Dr Chas W Handy, late of the Eastern Shore of Md, in his 49th year. His funeral is today at 2 o'clock, from his late residence, 377 13th st.

Culpeper Court-house, Va, Sep 30. The colored girl Angelina, who, some months ago, set fire to the dwlg of Henry Shackleford, thus endangering the lives of his family, was hanged here today.

Orphans Court of Wash Co, D C. Letters of administration on the personal estate of Christoph Kloppinger, late of Wash Co, deceased. –Frederika Kloppinger, admx

MON OCT 3, 1859
Died: in Buffalo, on Sep 19, where he had resided since 1815, Hon Albert H Tracy, a man of rare abilities, & worth. He represented his district in Congress from 1819 to 1825; served on the bench several years, & was a State Senator from 1830 to 1837. He was offered a seat in Pres Polk's Cabinet, but the exalted office had not sufficient charm to induce him to give up the pleasure of domestic retirement.

Letter from Stockholm of Sep 6 says: By permission of the King, & on the demand of M Fryxell, the historian, the tomb of Charles XII, in the church of Riddarholm has been opened in order to ascertain exactly in what manner the Swedish hero died. The King, Prince Oscar, the Ministers, Prof Fryxwell, 3 physicians, & some other personages were present. The medical men arrived that the King must have been struck by the fragment of a projectile in the left temple, & that it came out the right on. As at the moment he was killed the King had his left side turned away from the fortress of Fredericksteen, there is some reason to suppose that he was fired at by one of his own men & assassinated.

Dr N Myer, Botanic Physician, of Richmond, Va, was bitten by a rattlesnake yesterday morning & died in a few hours.

On Sat a violent & unprovoked assault was committed by Jas R Gates, one of the City Watchmen, & a large & powerful man, upon the person of Mr Andrew Duffy, a master coppersmith employed at the Capitol. Gates was much intoxicated at the time & gave a great deal of trouble to Ofcrs Martin & Harrover, & County Constable Kelly, by whom he was arrested & conducted to the ofc of Justice Donn. The first assault was committed near the Tiber Bridge, on Pa ave, in passing from which westward Gates overtook Duffy, & again dealt him a severe blow. When sober Gates was a protector & guardian of the public peace & order; when intoxicated, a violent breaker of both.

A man registered his name at a public house in Princeton, N J, on Thu last, as C Porter. He went out gunning on Fri with Mr Wm Ledwitch. Hearing the report of a gun, Ledwitch went to see what game his comrade had shot, when he found him dead, the entire back of his head being blown off. From papers found on his person, his name is believed to be John B Thayer.

Obit-died: on Sep 19, of malignant carbuncle, at his residence on the Bay of St Louis, Hon Robt N Ogden, in his 56th year. He died in the bosom of his family, attended by his 2 brothers & surroundered by kindred & friends. This evening, in a secluded spot selected by himself, his remains were committed to the grave by Rev Dr Leacock. Judge Ogden was a native of N C, of the best Revolutionary stock; his mother a daughter of that ardent patriot, Govn'r Abner Nash, & niece of Gen Francis Nash, who fell at the battle of Germantown, while his father's family, of N J, were among the foremost in their country's service in the war of independence. Since 1823 he has resided in Louisiana. He later removed to New Orleans, where he soon took position among the most eminent of her advocates. He was a kind & devoted husband, father, & friend. His sudden demise will afflict many people. -Bay St Louis, Sep 20, 1859. -J F H C

On Friday the boiler used for heating & cooking puposes in the Girard House, N Y, exploded, killing John O'Conner, a plumber, & injuring the fireman, John Collins, to such an extent that his recovery is considered impossible.

Died: on Sep 30, at Middleburg, Va, after a lingering illness, Mrs M Louisa Noland, wife of R W N Noland, of Albemarle, in her 37th year.

Died: on Oct 1, Michl Troutmann, aged 65 years, a native of Germany, but for the last 27 years a resident of Wash City. His funeral is today at 3½ o'clock, from his late residence, 589 N J ave, Capitol Hill.

Four days later from Europe. 1-Sir Jas Stephens, Prof of Modern History at Cambridge, & formerly under secretary of the colonies, is dead.

TUE OCT 4, 1859

On Friday at Jersey City, an explosion of a newly invented apparatus for making gaslight out of a certain description of patent oil, ignited Thos Carswell, & he died the next day.

A man named Burekhart Schafer was killed on Sep 29, by a bull on the premises of Mr John Culver, of Brighton. The animal had been to the County Fair Ground for exhibition, Schafer being in charge of him. Schafer put him in the barn, but the bull escaped. Schafer's body was found, with severe wounds, the bull having attacked him. –Rochester Democrat

On Friday a young lady, Maria Gartland, residing in N Y, was accidentally shot by her brother [age 14] whilst on a yatchting excursion up the Hudson. The rifle he was carrying accidentally discharged. She lies in a precarious condition.

Jas McKenzie, one of our most worthy & estimatable citizens, a native of this place, died on Friday last. His health had been infirm for some time. At the time of his death he was an ofcr in the Exchange Bank. –Alex Gaz

In the late English papers is a report of the sale by auction of a portion of the Westbury & Henbury estates of the late Hon W M Noel. They are within 3 miles of the port of Bristol. The Westbury land, 22½ acres, brought $530 an acre; the Henbury land, 40 acres, $415 an acre; & some lands near Thornbury $800 an acre.

I hope that <u>Another Sailor</u>, if he should favor us with an additional list, will not fail to give the name of Mr Fudge, which he will find in page 198 of Force's Register for 1830, the book heretofore referred to as authority. –An Old Soldier

Mrd: on Thu last, in Wash City, by Rev Stephen P Hill, Isaac Entwisle to Phebe J Sanderson, all of Wash City.

WED OCT 5, 1859

Henry M McGill has been appointed by the Pres to be Sec of the Territory of Wash.

A verdict of $20,000 damages rendered at Detroit in favor of Mrs Jas B Corey, in the suit of herself & husband against the City Corp, as recompense for injuries received by falling into a open sewer. The lady's limbs were paralyzed in consequence of the injury received. The jury held the city gov't responsible to the full amount of damages claimed for having neglected to place the necessary safeguards around the sewer.

Child lost. At noon yesterday a little child of 4 years, John Welch, the son of parents living on 20th st, near F, strayed from home, & up to 9 o'clock last night had not been heard of by his agonized father & mother. He was last seen in the neighborhood of his home following a wandering organ grinder.

Washington's first love. A correspondent of the Century, tells of the old country seat called *The Cottage*, in Hanover Co, Va, where Gen Washington proposed for the hand of Mary Cary, & his rejection by her father. Her father was Wilson Cary, of *Celeys*, in Eliz Co City, descended from the noble family of Hunsdon, in England. His relative, Col Archibald Cary, of Ampthith, in Chesterfield, was, at his death, the heir apparent to the Earldom. His beautiful daughter was a great heiress, & had many suitors. The one here alluded to was a young man of very high character, a relative of Geo Wm Fairfax, who lived in Belvoir, on the Potomac; & here he met with Miss Cary, who came to visit Mrs Fairfax, her eldest sister. He at once proceeded to fall in love. When Miss Cary went back home to *Celeys*, on the James river, he followed her & laid open siege to the fair fortress. In the good old times the youth duly asked a private interview with the old lord of the manor. When the lover had finished this interview, Mr Cary rose, made him a low bow, & said that if this was young Mr Washington's errand at *Celey*'s, his visit had better terminate-his daughter had been accustomed to ride in her own chariot. Young Washington bowed & turned away, & in due time married the young widow, Martha Dandridge Custis, who resembled Miss Cary, as much as one sister ever did another. Mary Cary was unable to return this affection of the youth-that was all. She married him who won her heart, Edw Ambler. He was descended through his mother from the great Huguenot house of La Roche Jaqueline, in Vendee, & inherited the honest instincts of his race. At 12 years of age he had been sent for his education to England. He graduated at Cambridge, made the grand tour of Europe, returning to Va when he was 21. He was married to Miss Cary soon afterward; & became collector of York. He died at age 35. His beautiful widow moved away from the scene of her grief, & took refuge in the *Cottage* far up in Hanover. [*Belvoir*, the seat of the Fairfaxs spoken of above, was on the bank of the Potomac, 3, 4, or 5 miles below *Mount Vernon*. The only remains now of that fine residence is a low mound of broken mouldering bricks, covered over with wild vines.]

About 1793 Danl Rowell & Henry Neal started on a hunting expedition up the Little Kanawa, to what is now Elizabethtown, when they were fired on by the Indians. Neal was killed & fell overboard, his body recovered a few days after. Rowell swam to the other shore, carrying his gun. He hid this gun under a red oak log, in a drain known as *Burning Spring* run. Rowell frequently in his lifetime, [he having died in Alabama, at his son's, Dr Neal Rowell, in 1854, aged 93,] to gratify a curiosity, looked for his gun. It was found in a most wonderful state of preservation, in a barrel 4 feet long, with a brass box with the words Liberty or Death engraved on it. The muzzle of the gun had grown fast to a dogwood bush, & had been carried up by its growth about 6 inches from the ground.

Mrd: on Sep 27, in Shepherdstown, Va, by Rev Henry Edwards, Rector of the Episcopal Church Hagerstown, Md, Dr Chas G W Macgill, of the latter place, to Louisa T, eldest daughter of John H McEndree.

On Sunday Dr Nathan Myer, a medical herbalist, residing in Richmond, Va, was bitten by a rattlesnake, & all medical attendance proving unavailing, he died 4 hours later. He was 54 years of age, of the Hebrew persuasion, & a native of Freudenstadt or Friedenthal, in the Kingdon of Wertemburg, in South Germany, where he has a wife & family. He came to Amercia some 7 years ago; resided some time in Ohio, & moved to Richmond about 3 years since from Cincinnati, where he has property. –Enquirer

The subscriber offers for sale her land, in Wash Co, D C, on the road leading from the Navy Yard bridge, by Good Hope, to T B. It contains 250 acres, more or less, with a neat frame dwlg, & out-bldgs. Mr Beavens, residing on the place, will show it. Reference may be had to Col H Naylor, at the City Hall, Wash. For terms apply by mail to Saml Cox, near Port Tobacco, Chas Co, Md. –Lucy B Walker.

Mrd: on Oct 3, by Rev T F Carson, Mr Fred'k Saxty, of Bridgeport, Conn, to Miss Mattie C Simonds, of Wash City.

Mrd: on Sep 29, in Balt Co, Md, by Rev T W Simpson, Wm M Isaac, of Wash City, to Ella, daughter of the late Thos Phillips, of the former county.

Mrd: on Sep 29, by Rt Rev Bishop Williams, at Bridgeport, Conn, Wm G Waller, of Baton Rouge, La, to Harriet S, only daughter of Surgeon D S Edwards, U S Navy.

Died: on Oct 3, Catherine, wife of Louis G Thomas, in her 30th year. Her funeral is on Thu at 3 o'clock, from her late residence, 330 5th st north.

Died: on Oct 4, in Wash City, Duncan Flood, son of Geo W & Mary J Flood, aged 7 months & 17 days. His funeral will take place on Oct 6 at 12 o'clock, from the residence of his parents, 467 13th st, between E & F sts.

THU OCT 6, 1859
On Friday last two young men, Basil Mott & Jos Fogle, residing in Woodsboro district, Fred'k Co, were out gunning for squirrels, when Mott was accidentally shot in the head & mortally wounded. By some means, Fogle was also shot in the arm.

Orphans Court of Wash Co, D C. Letters of administration on the personal estate of Jas Patterson, late of Wash Co, deceased. –Mary Ann Patterson, admx

Child found. The child, John Welsh, lost on Tue, happily fell into the hands of Police Ofcr Ginnity, who finally restored the child to his parents.

Mrd: on Sep 29, in Poughkeepsie, N Y, R Sparke Widdicombe, of Wash City, to Alice, 2nd daughter of Cmdor s Bayard Wilson, U S Navy.

Mrd: on Oct 5, at Trinity Church, by Rev Dr Butler, Dr Jos S Smith to Lizzie, daughter of Jonathan Prout, all of Wash City.

A married man, wishing to settle permanently as a Teacher in a pleasant town in Southern Va, can do so by purchasing the very desirable residence now occupied by the subscriber. Said lot contains 2 acres; excellent dwlg, all necessary out-houses, & in first rate repair. Address the subscriber, at Clarksville, Mecklenburg Co, Va. –Wm T Bailey

FRI OCT 7, 1859
Late advices from Europe announce the death of Sir Jas Stephen, a distinguished essayist & historian. He was about 70 years of age; studied at Cambridge; was admitted to the bar; appointed Under Sec of State during the existence of the Melbourne Ministry; on his resignation in 1848 he was knighted & appointed a member of the Board of Council of Trade. His death is a great loss to English scholarship & letters.

Valuable lot in Gtwn, on Prospect st, at public auction, Oct 20, part of lot 20, at present having thereon Mr E Shoemaker's carpenter shop. -Barnard & Buckey, aucts, Gtwn

Orphans' Court of PG Co, Md, letters of administration on the personal estate of Zach B Beall, late of PG Co, deceased. –Martha E Beall, Hugh Caperton, adms of Zach B Beall. All comunications upon the above subject must be made to Hugh Caperton, Gtwn, D C.

One day last week Mr John Avent, of Nash Co, N C, living within a mile or two of the Halifax line, was accidentally killed, when his dog reared upon him, & in coming down hit the trigger, causing it to fire killing Mr Avent almost instantly.

Aqueduct Mill, Gtwn, Oct 3, 1859. The copartnership formerly existing under the name of Elms, Taylor & Co, has been this day dissolved by mutual consent, Mr Taylor withdrawing from the firm. The undersigned will assume the liabilities of the late firm & continue to carry on the milling business under the firm of Elms & Bradley.
-Jas Elms, Wm A Bradley, jr

Mrd: on Oct 4, at the Church of the Ascension, by Rev Dr Pinkney, Wm W Macgill to Belle R Contnor, all of Wash City.

Mrd: on Oct 5, by Rev Andrew G Carothers, Mr M J Higgins, formerly of N J, to Miss Dora Rollings, of Wash City.

Mrd: on Thu, in the Fourth Presbyterian Church, by Rev John C Smith, Bernard C Major to Miss Susie L, daughter of G W Fales, all of Wash City.

SAT OCT 8, 1859
Hon Israel T Hatch, of Buffalo, has been appointed by the Gov't to investigate & report upon the practical working of the Reciprocity treaty.

On Oct 3, at Ottawa, Canada, Mr La Mountain & Mr Haddock, who ascended in the balloon Atlantic from Watertown, N Y, on Sep 22nd, safely arrived.

Mr Chas Martin Leupp, committed suicide on Wed, at his residence in N Y. He has exhibited unmistakable symptoms of insanity. He shot himself with a double-barrelled fowling piece in the bathroom. His age was not far from 52 years. He was a Director in the Mechanics' Bank, & formerly Pres of the Mechanics' Society. –N Y papers

Mrd: on Oct 4, by Rev Mr Nadal, Mr John R Hunt, of Wash City, to Miss Sarah V Lowe, daughter of Warren Lowe, of PG Co, Md.

Died: on Oct 7, in Wash City, [the anniversary of her birth,] after a long & painful illness, aged 55 years, Mrs Eliz Mary Fendall, wife of Philip R Fendall. Her funeral will take place on Oct 11 at 11½ o'clock, from the family residence, corner of 4½ st, whence her remains will be taken to Alexandria, Va.

Three days later from Europe-the Fate of Sir John Franklin ascertained. Sackville, Oct 7. The steamship **Canada**, from Liverpool, Sep 24, arrived at Halifax yesterday. The Artic steamer **Fox** has returned to England with intellgence of the fate of Sir John Franklin & his men, & interesting relics of his expedition. At Point William was found a record dated Apr 25, 1848, signed by Capts Crozier & Fitz James, of the ships **Erebus & Terror**, saying that their ships had been abandoned 3 days previously in the ice, & that the 105 survivors were proceeding to the Great Fish& River. Sir John Franklin had died on Jun 11th of the previous year, 1847. The total number of deaths to the date of the record had been 9 ofcrs & 15 men. Many interesting relics were found on the western shore of King Williams's Island, & others were obtained from the ship **Equimaux**, who stated that, after the abandonment of the ships, one of them was crushed by the ice & the other forced ashore. Several skeletons of the men of the expedition were found, & a duplicate record up to the abandonment of the ships was also discovered, as well as quantities of clothing.

MON OCT 10, 1859
Excellent piano forte & household & kitchen furniture at auction on Oct 14, at the residence of Luther R Smoot, 322 north K st, between 13th & 14th sts. -A Green auct

Trustee's sale of frame house & lot at auction, on Oct 21, by deed of trust from Wm S Martaini dated Mar 16, 1857, recorded in Liber J A S No 134, of the land records for Wash Co, D C: sale of parts of lots 43 thru 46 in subdivision of said square beginning at the s e corner of lot 43; with improvements, a good 2 story frame house with other out-bldgs. –T G Clayton, trustee -A Green auct

Austin [Texas] State Gaz of Sep 22. On the 14th ult, while Maj R S Neighbors was crossing from his hotel, at Belknap, to the old garrison, he was intercepted by Messrs Murphy & Cornet. The former asked Maj Neighbors if he had reported that he [Murphy] & certain others had, themselves, stolen certain horses, charged to have been stolen by the Indians. Maj Neighbors said, "No, I never did," & was in the act of explanation when young Cornet shot him. He exclaimed, "Oh Lord!" & fell dead. Cornet, of last dates, was at Murphy's, & not arrested.

Thos Barlow, one of our oldest & most highly esteemed citizens, died on Sat night last. He was found lying near the steps leading from the back yard to the porch of his house, & from the cold & rigid condition of the body it was evident that it had been dead for some hours. Examination revealed he had fallen from the porch, striking his head on the hard ground. He was for many years connected with the American Embassy to France, & we believe to Russia also. For many years past he has living in strict privacy & retirement, in consequence of feeble health. –Wash [Pa] Examiner

Mrs Matilda Klein, wife of Dr Carl Klein, of N Y, died on Thu from a dose of chloroform taken to relieve a toothache. Her daughter heard her moaning as if in pain. The deceased was about 24 years of age & a native of Germany.

On Thu night the jewelry store of Mr Benj L Hood, at Albany, N Y, was robbed of jewelry valued at $20,000.

Notice. Estate of John H Buthmann, deceased. The undersigned gives notice that she has revoked & annulled the power of atty heretofore granted by her to Wm H Campbell. Persons indebted to the said estate will please make payment to the undersigned. -A E Buthmann, admx, 383 Pa ave, south side, between 4½ st & 6th sts.

Died: on May 28 last, at the Bay of Islands, in New Zealand, of a pulmonary disease, Geo R West, American Consul at that place, aged about 40 years. He was a native of N C, but resided in Wash City several years, where, as well as in the State of his nativity, he has left several affectionate relatives & many attached friends to mourn his loss. He was one of the attaches who accompanied to China Mr Cushing, our Minister to that country, & when Mr Cuching returned home Mr West remained 7 years in China, which he spent in traveling as far as he could through the interior of that vast & courious & but little known country.

We are requested to say that the funeral of Mrs Fendall will take place on Tue at 10:45 o'clock, instead of 11:30 o'clock, as first announced.

TUE OCT 11, 1859
Land sale in Kent Co, Md: the farm of H W Carvill, in said county, containing 640 acres, has been purchased by Mr Edw Comegys for $36,000. This farm has remained in the family of its late owner for more than a century & a half, without having been once sold.

The ceremony of laying the corner-stone of the N Y Ave <u>Presbyterian Church</u>, on H st, near 13th was witnessed yesterday by about 3,000 persons; prayer by Rev W D Maley, Chaplain of the Masonic Grandd Lodge of D C; Grand Master Geo C Whiting laid the stone; Rev Dr Gurley, pastor of the church, read a list of the articles deposited in the copper box in the corner stone; & prayer by Dr Septimus Tustin.

Trustee's sale of a valuable farm in Fairfax Co, Va, by two deeds of trust from Aza Gladmon & Ann Gladmon, his wife, recorded in the land records of said county; fronts on Middle Turnpike road, 5 miles from Alexandria, known as **Springfield Farm**-209 acres. Improvements are a good dwlg house with numerous out-bldgs.
–Chas H Upton, Lambert Tree, trustees -O G Sage, auct

Mrd: on Oct 9, in Wash City, by Rev Andrew G Carothers, Mr Wm T Jones to Miss Lucy A Cox, both of Va.

Died: on Sep 25, at Newark, Ohio, Horatio J Harris, U S Atty of the southern district of Mississippi, which ofc was conferred upon him by Pres Taylor, & in which he has continured during each succeeding Administration.

Died: on Aug 31, at St Augustine, East Fla, Col Gad Humphreys, aged 74 years. He was born in Conn; entered the U S Army in 1808, as Lt; served through the war of 1812; was slightly wounded upon the Erie frontier, promoted to a Lt Colonelcy, & disbanded in 1821; was appointed agent for the Seminole Indians, in Fla, 1822, & served until 1830, when he was removed. In the subsequent Seminole war he lost nearly all his property, & it was not until recently that he was remunerated by the Seminoles. For the last 10 years he was Judge of Probate.

Died: on Oct 9, Mr Wm Blain, aged 45 years. He was a citizen of N Y, but for many years a clerk in the Sixth Auditor's Ofc, Treasury Dept. He was a member of the Episcopal Church, & during his illness bore his sufferings with Christian fortitude. His funeral will be from his late residence on 9th st, between H & I, today at 1 o'clock P M.

Died: on Oct 10, in Wash City, Jas D Kerr, formerly of Alexandria [Va] in his 65th year. He was for several years an efficient clerk in the War Dept. His funeral is tomorrow at 2 o'clock, from St Mary's Church, Alexandria.

Died: on Oct 9, at Staten Island, N Y, aged 88, Frances, relict of Michl Hogan, formerly Consul of the U S at Valparaiso.

Orphans Court of Wash Co, D C, Sep 13, 1859. In the case of Sarah J Somervell, admx of John H Somervell, deceased, the administratrix & Court have appointed Nov 1 next, for the final settlement of the personal estate of said deceased, of the assets in hand.
-Ed N Roach, Reg/o wills

WED OCT 12, 1859
The Carroll [Tenn] Patriot announces the Hon John Bell as the candidate of the United Opposition for the next Presidency.

Hon John B Floyd, Sec of War, returned to Wash City yesterday, & we are gratified to hear, in improved health.

Orphans Court of Wash Co, D C. In the case of Saml McKenney, adm with the will annexed of Wm McHenry Osborne, deceased, the administrator & Court have appointed Oct 22 next, for the final settlement of the personal estate of said deceased, of the assets in hand. -Ed N Roach, Reg/o wills

Orphans Court of Wash Co, D C. Letters of administration on the personal estate of S G Deeth, late of Wash Co, deceased. –Joshua A Ritchie, adm

M W Galt & Bro: wedding presents, ladies' & gentlemen's extra fine watches. Jewellers, 354 Penn ave, 4 doors west of Brown's Hotel. –M W Galt & Bro. [Ad]

THU OCT 13, 1859
Valuable library of the late Chancellor Bibb at public auction, by order of the Orphans Court of Wash Co, D C. Sale on Oct 20, at the auction rooms of A Green, corner of 7th & D sts, of the Law & Literary Library of the late Hon Geo M Bibb, formerly of Ky. -Robt G Thrift, adm -A Green auct

The Pres of the U S returned to Wash City yesterday, in good health, from a brief visit to **Wheatland**, his former residence.

One of the Green Mountain Boys, Asa M Wyman, a Revolutionary veteran, is still living in Windham Co, Vt, at the extraordinary age of 106 years. His mental faculties are sound.

Dr Rutland has been convicted at Clarksville, Tenn, of killing his wife, & sentenced to 3 years in the State prison.

Another murder by a Louisiana vigilance cmte: the cmte in Lafayette parish, La, visited the house of Bernard Lacouture, who had been warned on Sep 30th, & calling him to the door shot him dead. His mother attempted to get a warrant for the arrest of his murderers, but the magistrate refused to receive her statement, & the coroner resigned rather than hold an inquest over the body.

Wash Corp, Oct 10. 1-Ptn from J C Wilson & others for the construction of a bridge across the Tiber Creek at 3rd st west: referred to the Cmte on Improvements. 2-Bill for the relief of Thos R Dyer: passed. 3-Cmte of Claim: bill for the relief of Jas McCarthy: passed.

Anthony Dey, for many years a member of the N Y bar, died on Oct 9, at his residence in Hudson City, [Bergen Hill, N J,] at the advanced age of 83 years.

Sir John Franklin: whenever & wherever the story of Franklin & his comrades is told, the names of Bellot, of Kane, of Grinnell, will be remembered with the names of Ray & Richardson, of Ross, of Maclure, & McClintock.

Dedication of St Aloysius Church, Sunday, Oct 16, 1859. Ceremony of Blessing the Church in Latin & English, with Explanation of the Mass, & proper Mass of the Festival. Little book for the occasion: price only one dime. Sold wholesale or retail by O E Duffy, Bookseller & Stationer, 536 7th st, near the avenue.

For rent: a first class 3 story brick house on E st, between 6th & 7th sts. –Mrs Jane Lawrence, 167 West st, Gtwn, of Dr N Young, 421 Pa ave, between 3rd & 4½ sts.

Mrd: on Oct 11, at Wesley Chapel Parsonage, by Rev D Ball, Mr Geo Thompson to Miss Ruth Ann Reynolds, both of Wash City.

Died: on Oct 3, near Nashville, Tenn, Mrs Andrew Erwin, mother-in-law of Hon John Bell, late Senator from the State of Tenn, in her 91st year.

FRI OCT 14, 1859
Household & kitchen furniture at auction on Oct 20, at the residence of E B Wilson, 190 I st, between 19th & 20th sts. -A Green auct

Trustee's sale of valuable real estate, by deed of trust from Chas H Winder & wife, dated Mar 14, 1855, recorded in Liber J A S, No 103, folios 50, of the land records of Wash Co, D C: sale on Oct 25 of lot 1 in square 170, in Wash City; also, all that part of lot 2 adjoining said lot 1; the same being the whole of said lot 2, except a portion of 10 feet in width cut off for an alley: fronts on 18th st. –W D Davidge, trustee -A Green auct

Another fatal duel in Calif, on Sep 17, near San Andreas. The duel was fought with rifles at 50 paces. The parties were Dr Peterson & Col Wm A Gatewood. The former fell mortally wounded, & died in 2 hours. [Oct 21st newspaper: fatal duel on Sep 16 about 5 miles from San Andreas, Calif, between Dr Preston Goodwin & Col Wm Jeff Gatewood; weapons-rifles; distance-40 yards. At first fire Dr Goodwin was mortally wounded & died about 2 hours afterwards. –Calif paper]

Minor, Heath, & Gallaher, were tried for forgery in Fredericksburg, Va, last week, convicted & sentenced as follows: Minor to 4 years, Heath to 2 years & 6 months, & Gallaher to 1 year's imprisonment in the penitentiary.

Superior Pippin Apples for sale, at $5 per barrel, deliverable at home or at Jackson, Bro & Co's Store in Wash. –Jos R Robert, Rox Mount, near Bladensburg.

At Columbia, S C, on Sat last, John I Crawford, for gaming, was sentenced to 3 years' imprisonment & $1,500 fine; John Brasseur was ordered 50 lashes for stealing a mule; & Henry Shaver for petty larceny, had his back striped.

All persons are hereby cautioned against purchasing the following Bounty Land Warrants, Act 1855, viz: No 18,739, for 120 acres, issued to Clark Wright; No 34,189, for 120 acres, issued to Barney Carteel; & No 7,078, for 80 acres, issued to Jesse Four. Sold warrants were assigned in blank, & owned by Johnson P Willborne, who mailed them to Blairsville, Ga, on Jul 18, 1856, to Hon Howell Cobb, at Wash City, D C, since which time they have not been heard of. A caveat has been filed in the Gen Land Ofc to prevent the issue of a patent, & application will be made to the Com'r of Pensions for the issue of duplicate warrants. —Clifton Hellen, Atty for Johnson P Willborne.

Orphans Court of D C, Oct 11, 1859. In the matter of the ptn of Margaret Buckignani, guardian of the infant children of Margaret Randolph, deceased. The guardian reported that at a public sale made by her on Jun 11, 1859, Caleb Cushing became the purchaser of one undivided sixth of square 135, in Wash City, for $725, & he hath complied with the terms of sale. —Wm F Purcell, Judge of the Orphans' Court. -E N Roach, Reg/o wills

Circuit Court of Wash Co, D C-in Chancery. Danl W Hall & David A Hall vs Wilson McBee. The object of this suit is to procure a decree for the re-conveyance of certain premises in Wash City, D C, which the cmplnts, by mistake, conveyed to the dfndnt on Oct 16, 1858. The bill states that the cmplnts, excs of the late Fred'k Hall, deceased, on Jun 9, 1858, conveyed unto the dfndnt a certain part of lot 3 in square 449, in said city, &, that doubts having afterwards arisen whether the last will & testament of the said Fred'k Hall had been duly executed & proved so as to vest in the said cmplnts the legal title to the real estate of which he died seized, they, [the said cmplnts] procured a conveyance of the same from the heirs at law of the said Fred'k Hall; that, on Oct 16, 1858, the said cmplnts, for the purpose of confirming & perfecting the title of said dfndnt to said part of lot 3 in square 449, executed & delivered another deed to the said dfndnt; but that, by reason of a mistake in the description of said premises, said last mentioned deed purports to convey the whole of said lot 3 in square 449; & that they have repeatedly requested the said dfndnt to execute a reconveyance of that part of said lot which was not included in said first mentioned deed, but that said dfndnt fraudulently refuses to comply with such request. The bill further states that the said dfndnt resides out of D C. Absent dfndnt is to appear in this Court, in person or by solicitor, on or before Feb 15 next. By order of Wm M Merrick, A J -Jno A Smith, clerk

Orphans Court of Wash Co, D C, Oct 13, 1858. In the case of Ellen Morton, admx W A of Jas F Morton, deceased, the administratrix & Court have appointed Nov 5 next, for the final settlement of the personal estate of said deceased, of the assets in hand. -Ed N Roach, Reg/o wills

Mrd: on Oct 9, in Leesburg, Va, by Rev John Lanstreet, Mr John W B Parker, of Leesburg, Va, to Miss Sarah Frances Flowers, of Wash.

Mrd: on Oct 13, at Wesley Chapel, by Rev Dabney Ball, Mr Jos R McNeir to Miss Priscilla Lowe, both of Wash City.

Died: on Oct 5, in the city of Vicksburg, Miss, Robert Brodnax, eldest son of Chas E & M Love Smedes, aged 9 years.

Died: on Oct 7, in New Orleans, Robert Ellis, in his 31st year, 2nd son of the late Robt Ellis, of Wash City.

SAT OCT 15, 1859
Sir John Bowring, the British Govn'r of Hong King, is an apologist for the opium trade. He thinks that the injurious effects of opium have been greatly exaggerated; that the evil produced is nothing in comparison with that resulting from the use of intoxicationg liquors in England & elsewhere; in fact, that this trade is, in a negative sense, productive of incalculable good. He recommends that it should be legalized.

Chancery sale of valuable house & lot on 4½ st, near Pa ave, by decree of the Circuit Court of Wash Co, D C, in Chancery, No 1,310; public sale on Nov 7, on the premises, all the right, title, & interest of Jas Williams, dfndnt in said cause, in & to lot 27, in Reservation 10, fronting 44 feet on 4½ st, with two 2 story dwlg houses.
–Chas S Wallach, trustee -Jas C McGuire & Co, aucts

Will be exposed to public sale on Dec 29, at the Town House, the following lots & parts of lots hereinafter mentioned, in Gtwn, D C, or so many thereof as may be necessary to satisy the Corp of Gtwn, D C, for taxes due on them for the year 1859 with costs & charges, the rate of tax be 87 cents on a hundred dollars. Terms cash.
To whom assessed/valuation/ amount of taxes due:
Alexandria Canal Co-63 feet front, P B T & Deacon's addition, 63 feet front, the south side of Water st/$1,000/taxes $8.70
Bloxham, Jas, front foot tax on lot 280, B & H addition, 100 feet west side Fayette st/ taxes $42.
Blagrove, Mrs, parts of lots 63 & 64, west side of Jefferson st, brick house/val $1,400/ taxes $12.18.
Custards, Jacob's heirs, north part of lot 267, B & H addition, 66 feet front, west side of High st, frame house/val $500/taxes $4.35.
Crawford, Wm jrs' heirs, subdivision lot 5, Holmead's addition, 37 feet front, east side Rock st/ val $185/taxes $1.61.

Cassel, Wm, parts lots 59 & 60, P B T & D addition, 54 feet front on south side First st, brick house/val $1,700/taxes $14.79.
Dunlop, Eliz's heirs, lot 65, Peter's square, 25 feet front on north side of Water st/ val $600/taxes $5.22.
Daily, Richd, parts of lots 29 & 19, Beall's addition, 24 feet front, north side Bridge st, frame house/val $1,500/taxes $13.05.
Ellis, John, part of lot 75, O G T, 25 feet front, north side Water st/val $625/tax $5.44.
Gray, Hyram, lots 168, Beall's addition, & 25, Holmead's addition, 60 feet front, north side Olive st, frame house/val $1,000/taxes $8.70.
Gordon, Chas, part of lot 177, Beall's addition, 21 feet front, north side Bridge st, brick house/val $1,560/taxes $13.05.
Goldsbrough, Mrs, east part of lot 88, Threlkeld's addition, 30 feet front, south side of Second st, brick house/val $1,000/taxes $8.70.
Gensler, Henry, part of lot 14, Holmead's addition, 30 feet front, north side Bridge st, frame house/val $700/taxes $6.09.
Hurst, Margaret, parts of lots 70 & 71, B & H addition, 16 feet front, south side First st, frame house/val $625/taxes $5.44.
Humphreys, Joshua Mrs, lot 145, B & H addition, 70 feet front, south side Third st/ val $850/taxes $7.40.
Johnson, Benedict, part of lot 23, B & H addition, 42 feet front, east side of High st/ val $420/taxes $3.65.
Lee, Nancy, lot 27, B & H addition, 50 feet front, north side of 6th st, frame house/ val $1,000/taxes $8.70.
Ditto, parts of lots 194, 195, 197, Threlkeld's addition, 30 feet front, north side of 6th st, brick house/val $500/taxes $4.35.
Lloyd, R B, parts of lots 99 & 100, in Beall's addition, 72 feet front, north side Beall st/val $750/taxes $6.53.
Ditto, front foot tax on same/taxes $25.75.
Lewis, Vincent, lot 35, D L & C addition, 30 feet front, west side of Green st, frame house/val $700/taxes $6.09.
McCrown, Mr, house & lot 5, of the Twenty Bldgs, 20 feet front, north side Fourth st, brick house/val $300/taxes $2.61.
May, Jos J, part of lot 65, O G T, 24 feet front, north side of Water st/val $700 /taxes $6.09.
Mason, Jos's heirs, part of lot 127, Beall's addition, 15 feet front, north side Dunbarton st, frame house/val $300/taxes $2.61.
Ogle, Mary, front foot tax on part of lot 188, B & H addition, 13 4-12 feet front, on west side of Market st/taxes $6.53.
Queen, Wm, part of lot 66, Holmead's addition, 46 foot front, north side Beall st, old frame/val $300/taxes $2.61.
Ross, Jane, part of lot 53, Threlkeld's addition, 26 1-12 feet front, south side First st, frame house/val $500/taxes $4.35.
Serrin, Danl, lot not numbered, Holmead's addition, 60 feet front, Monroe st, two old tenements/val $700/taxes $6.09.

Sullivan, John, part of lot 88, Threlkeld's addition, 30 feet front, south side of Second st, brick house/val $800/taxes $6.96.
Swartz, Conrad, part lot 261, B & H addition, 130 feet eash side of High st/val $324 /taxes $2.91.
Ditto, lot 262, same addition, east side High st/val $250/taxes $2.18.
Ditto, lot 274, same addition, 104 feet front, east side of Fayette st, & 104 feet front on west side same st/val $150/taxes $1.31.
Ditto, front foot tax on same/$87.36.
Thompson, Gen Jas, part of lot 151, Beall's addition, 30 feet front, north side of Gay st/val $300/taxes $2.61.
Thorne, Jos O, part of lot 188, B & H addition, 13 4-12 feet front, west side of Market st, brick house/val $270/taxes $3.
Ditto, front foot tax on same/$6.53.
Waters, Bazil & Ignatius, part of lot 221, B & H addition, 59 6-12 feet front on west side of Market st/val $295/taxes $2.57.
Walker, Elijah's heirs, part of lot 22, Beall's addition, 20 feet front, west side of Wash st, brick house/val $400/taxes $3.48.
Waters, J H, parts of lots 74 & 75, O G T, 42 2-12 feet front, north side Water st/val $1,200/taxes $10.44. –Chas D Welch, Collector, Gtwn, Oct 15, 1859

Mrd: on Oct 4, by Rev Alfred Holmead, John B Abell, of St Mary's Co, Md, to Violet A Williams, of Wash City.

Died: on Sep 3, 1859, at the residence of her nephew, Mr John S Skinner, Miss Anna Skinner, aged 79 years & 9 months. She was the eldest sister of the late Mr John S Skinner, long known as the editor of the American Farmer, & as one who took an active & untiring interest in agriculture, horticulture, & in all things pertaining to domestic comfort & economy.

Died: on Oct 2, in Washington, Pa, Thos Barlow, in his 66th year. He was a favorite nephew of Joel Barlow, the poet, savan, & diplomatist. He was a graduate of Yale College, & his diploma bore the signature of the great name of Dwight. Mr Thos Barlow acted as Sec of Legation to his uncle, Minister to the French Court by Pres Madison in 1811. He went with him to Wilna, where the Emperor Napoleon held his court on his march to Russia. On his journey back to Paris Mr Joel Barlow, overcome by the excessive cold & other hardships of the journey, died at Tarnovil, near Cracow, in Poland. His nephew then returned to the U S. He again visited France in 1817, & married Miss Anica Preble, an accomplished niece of Cmdor Preble, of the Revolution. -R H L, Wash, Pa.

Detroit, Oct 14. The Supreme Court of this State rendered a decision denying the jurisdiction of the U S Court in the noted case of Marshal Tyler, charged with killing Capt Jones, of the brig **Concord**. Mr Tyler has been remanded for trial in the State court.

MON OCT 17, 1859

Guerrilla attack on Brownsville [Texas] under date of Oct 1st & 5th. On Wed last from 60 to 100 armed men on horseback, all Mexicans by nativity, but most of them outlaws from Mexico whom we on the American side have foolishly given asylum, rode into our city, posted their sentinels, & picked out the men most disagreeable to them. Geo Morris, Wm P Neale R L Johnson, Clemente Reyes, & Viviano Garcia were killed by them. Alejos Vela, belonging to Cortinas' gang was killed by Johnson. They had no animosity against Johnson & Garcia, but Mr Johnson was the jailor, & they demanded the keys of him, & he refused to deliver them. Mr Garcia's sole offence was the shelter he afforded to Johnson. He was a good, inoffensive, quiet, industrious man, a Mexican like themselves. Mr Neale was killed in his bed. Mr Morris was hunted down.

The dedication of St Aloysius Catholic Church, at the n w corner of North Capitol & I sts, took place yesterday, a beautiful day. Blessing of the new church was conducted by Rev Mr Villager, of the Society of Jesus, assisted by Rev Messrs Maguire & Fulton, S J. Very Rev Archishop John Hughes, of N Y peached the sermon-[40 minutes.] The church is 160 feet in length by about 80 feet in breadth; the height of the interior from the floor to the ceiling is 57 feet. The tabernacle of white marble was designed, worked, and polished in the highest style by Mr Jacob Veighmeyer. Over the main altar is a painting representing the first Communion of the Saint to whom the Church is dedicated, executed by Mr Brimidi, well known as the artist by whom so much of the decoration of the U S Capitol had been performed. The church is capable of seating say 1,200 people. The organ cost $3,000. This whole building was planned by and executed under the personal supervision of Rev B Sestini, of the Society of Jesus. In round figures the cost of the church will be $50,000. It will be heated by a large furnace in the basement. St Aloysius was born in Mar, 1568, in the Castle of Castiglione, in Lombardy, a few miles s w of Peschiera, on the Lago Garda; the son of Ferdinand Gonzaga, a prince of the Holy Roman Empire, and seems to have been greatly indebted to his mother for his early attention to religious subjects and duties. He entered the Society of Jesus at about 18 years of age, against the wishes of his father, who died soon after. He himself died in Rome on Jun 12, 1591, of an epidemic which prevailed there, and was buried in the Jesuit Church of the Ascension. He was beatified by Pope Gregory XV in 1621, & canonized by Pope Benedict XIII in 1726.

Died: on Oct 15, very suddenly, Cephas Simmons, about 70 years of age, formerly of Md, but during the last 8 or 9 years a resident of Wash City. The early portion of his life was passed in Balt in commercial pursuits. On leaving that city he took up his abode in Anne Arundel Co, & was soon selected to represent his fellow citizens in the Legislature. To his conception & exertion the Annapolis Branch Railroad owes its existence. His funeral is this morning at 10 o'clock, from Mrs Taylor's boarding-house, 411 3rd st. between Pa ave & C st.

Mrd: on Oct 11, at *Clay Hill*, by Rev W B Dutton, D D, Dr Wm Wallace, of Fredericksburg, Va, to Miss Jeannie Allen, youngest daughter of Wm Hurst, of Jefferson Co, Va.

Died: on Sunday, after a long & severe illness, Mary, wife of John H Wallis, in her 30th year. Her funeral is on Tuesday at 2 o'clock, from 419 8th st, between G & H sts.

Died: on Oct 15, in Wash City, Saml Lee, aged 66 years. His funeral is tomorrow at 10 o'clock, from his residence on 6th st, between F & G sts.

Obit-died: on Oct 5, at the residence of her brother-in-law, Mr John Bowie, near Bladensburg, PG Co, Md, Mrs Eliza Sprigg, widow of Wm O Sprigg, of Wash Co, in her 80th year. She had long adorned her Christian profession by a consistent Christian life. She lived & died in the communion of the Catholic Church. -C

TUE OCT 18, 1859
Hon John Y Mason, our esteemed Minister at the Court of France, died suddenly in Paris on Oct 3. [Oct 24th newspaper: Hon John Y Mason never recovered completely from his first attack of apoplexy which occurred 4 years ago; an incomplete paralysis of the left side remained as a result of the first attack, but his health of mind & body was restored in other respects. On the morning of his death, Mrs Mason heard an unusual noise in her husband's room, & approaching his bedside, found him in convulsions & unconscious. He remained in this condition until he died 8 hours later. The body of the deceased was embalmed, & will be taken home. It was in the vault of the American Chapel in the Rue de Berri. Mr Anderson, of Va, who married a month ago one of the Misses Mason, is happily still in Paris, & will take charge of the family. Mr Mason leaves a widow & 10 children. Of the latter four are married. A married & unmarried son & 2 married daughters live in Va. Mrs Anderson, 3 unmarried daughters between the ages of 16 & 20, & 2 sons under 15 are in Paris. Rev Mr Seely preached the funeral sermon.]

On Sunday last a crowd of not less tham 1,000 negroes assembled on the basin [at Lynchburg, Va] to take leave of the negroes belonging to the estate of the late Mrs Frances B Shackelford, of Amherst Co, who, in accordance with the will of the deceased, were about to depart, by way of the canal, for a free State. The whole number set free was 45, men, women, & children, but only 37 left-the rest preferring to remain in servitude in Old Va rather than enjoy their freedom elsewhere. Some of those who did leave were thrown on the boat by main force, so much opposed were they to leaving, & many expressed their determination of returning to Va as soon as an opportunity offered. Then the boats stated from their wharves the freed negroes struck up, Carry me back to Old Virginney." The negroes have for several years past been under the charge of Mr H H Lewis, the executor, who superintended their removal out of the State.
–Lynchburg Rep

A new post ofc is established at Agricultural College, PG Co, Md, & John O Wharton appointed postmaster. It will be specially supplied from the railroad.

Mr Wm L Morris, of N Y C, was killed on Tue, near Cambridge, Miss, by the accidental discharge of his own gun while hunting. He was near a lake, his comrade walking in front of him.

The estate of Saml Gibbons, in Page Co, Va, has been sold to Saml Moore, of Shenandoah, for $40,000. The **Lionberger Farm**, belonging to the estate of Wm B Yancy, deceased, in Rockingham, Co, was purchased at public auction by Col E S Yancey, for $12,500, last week. At the same time the **Mountain Farm** was purchased by Hiram Kite for upwards of $8,000.

Fatal affray in Arizona on Sep 20, over a gambling table at Tucson, between Col P Robinson & Col R A Johnson, which resulted in the death of Johnson. The deceased served with Gen Wm Walker throughout his Nicaraguan career, & held the position of Assist Adj Gen. He was a lawyer by profession, & has lived in Calif for several years.

Jas Vaughn killed John R Charles at Mound City, Ill, on Monday. The citizens took the murderer & hung him to a tree. Charles was from Pittsburg.

Rev Saml Willard, D D, well kown in Massachusetts as the blind preacher, died at Deerfield, Oct 8, in his 83rd year. For about 40 years he was totally blind. He graduated at Harvard College in 1803, & was the class-mate of the famous Dr Payson.

Trustee's sale of valuable coal land, & mining equipment, by decree of the Circuit Court of Alleghany Co, Md, passed in the cause of Newman vs Franks & others: sale on Dec 20, 1859, on the premises, 557+ acres, known as the **Alleghany Mining Co**, adjoining the town of Frostburg, Alleghany Co, Md. Property will be shown by Mr E K Huntley, Frostburg, Md. –Geo W Dobbin, trustee, Balt, Md.

Orphans Court of Wash Co, D C. Letters of administration on the personal estate of Eliza J Ferguson, late of Wash Co, deceased. –J Hall Moore, adm

Mrd: on Oct 13, at Cedar Ridge, Montg Co, Md, by Rev Mr Suter, Jas H Davidson, M D, to Sarah Slater, daughter of Henry Bradley, all of said county.

Died: on Oct 16, at the residence of her mother, in Wash City, Mrs Jennie Massie Granbery, consort of Rev John C Granberry, & youngest daughter of the late Thos J Massie. Her funeral is this afternoon at 2½ o'clock at the Methodist Episcopal Church.

Died: on Oct 15, at Harper's Ferry, Va, A Eugenia, 4th daughter of Rev Norval Wilson, in her 22nd year.

Spiced oysters! Just received from the depot of Henry Fitzgerald, Norfolk, Va. C Gautier, 252 Pa ave, between 12th & 13th sts.

WED OCT 19, 1859
Insurrection at Harper's FerryError! Bookmark not defined.. Mr Andrew J Phelps, conductor, Mr Jacob Cromwell, baggage-master, & Mr Wm Wooley, engineer, reached a point near the bridge at Harper's Ferry this morning when it was stopped. The ringleader is said to be Anderson. Fred'k: Oct 17: F Beckham, railroad agent was shot twice. The watchman at the railroad depot was found dead. Gen Steuart, commanding the First Light Division Md Volunteers tendered the services of his command. Harper's Ferry, Oct 18. Mr Beckham, agent of Railroad Co, was shot through, & his murderer fell almost at the same instant, pinned by a rifle ball from a friend of Beckham. Capt Aaron Stephens, of Norwich, Conn, is now dying of his wounds. Among the insurgents are Kagg, of Ohio; Todd, of Maine; Wm Seaman & Brown, of Ohio. The insurgents threaten to sacrifice the lives of Lewis Washington & Col Dangerfield, whom they now hold as prisoners. Allen Evans, one of the insurgents, a white man, is lying here dying. He is from Conn, but has been in Kansas. Col Shriver, of Fred'k has just had an interview with Capt Brown in the Armory. He avowed to defend himself to the last. Fountain Beckham, the railroad agent, was shot dead from the Armory windows. Col Lee arrives, & thinks that there are abundant troops here to capture the rioters. Capt John Brown is barricaded in the Armory with his men. Harper's Ferry, Oct 18. The freight conductor Evan Dorsey was killed, & two other conductors, Bowman & Holbert, were seriously wounded. The rioters still have the following persons prisoners: Armistead Ball, chief draughtsman of the armory, Benj J Mills, master armorer, John P Daingerfield, paymaster's clerk, Lewis Washington, farmer & a prominent citizen, John Allstadt, farmer, & son age 16. The three last were seized on farms several miles from this place. Geo W Turner, a graduate of West Point, & one of the most distinguished citizens in this vicinity, was shot yesterday while coming into town, & died during the night. The killed among the citizens, as far as ascertained, are Fountain Beckham, Mr Haywood, a negro porter at the railroad station, Jos Burnley, of Harper's Ferry, Evan Dorsey, & Conductor Geo Richardson, of Martinsburg. Another rioter, negro, Lewis Leary, has just died. He confessed to the particulars of the plot, which he says were concocted by Brown at a fair held in Ohio some months ago. The rioters have just sent out a flag of truce; but if not protected by the soldiers the bearers will be captured & hung. Col Shutt approached with a flag of truce & demanded an immediate & unconditional surrender. The insurgents refused the demand. The door to the armory was broken down & the insurgents were brought out. Capt Ossawatomie Brown & his son were both shot. The latter is dead, & the former is dying. He lies in the arsenal enclosure, talking freely. He says his whole object was to free the slaves. J C Anderson was also shot down in the assault. He was from Conn. Two insurrectionists were unwounded, Edwin Coppish, white, from Iowa, & Shields Green, black, also from Iowa. Balt: we are awaiting further dispatches from Harper's Ferry. At latest accounts Brown was not dead. He may yet live to be hung. He is not seriously wounded as first supposed.

Posthumous malignity frustrated. The will of Jos Minor, deceased, leaving a property of $80,000 to three sons, & cutting off 4 children with five to one hundred dollars each has been set aside in the Fayette Circuit Court, Indiana.

Patrick Maude, who murdered his sister, Mrs Mary Turbett, in Newark, N J, on May 28th last, was found guilty at Newark last Saturday.

San Francisco papers of Sep 20: duel between Hon David C Broderick, Senator for Calif, & Hon David S Terry, Chief Justice of the Supreme Court of Calif. The difficulty has been long pending. Mr Broderick received a ball in the breast & fell, & Judge Terry left the ground with his friends. Mr Broderick was conveyed to the house of Mr Leonidas Haskell, at Black Point. The ball was extracted. On Sep 16th he expired. The last rites of the church were administered by Rev Fr Maraschi, who had been with the Senator from the time he was wounded. The deceased was born in the District of Columbia, & was 40 years of age. He came to his death from a wound inflicted by a pistol ball fired from a pistol intentionally, by David S Terry, on Sep 13, 1859.

Mrd: on Oct 11, at the *Vineyard*, near Millwood, Clarke Co, Va, by Rev Mr Jones, Andrew E Kennedy, of Jefferson Co, to Marie Pendleton, 2nd daughter of the late Philip P Cooke.

Died: on Oct 17, Mary A Stevenson, in her 61st year. Her funeral is this morning at 11 o'clock, from the residence of the late Philip Otterback, near the Navy Yard, from whence her remains will be conveyed to Alexandria.

Died: on Oct 18, at the residence of her daughter, Mrs Mary A Davis, in Wash City, Mrs Sarah Sletor, aged 73 years. Her remains will be taken to Easton, Pa, for interment in the family burying ground.

Died: on Oct 9, at the Rectory of All Saints' Parish, Calvert Co, Md, William Warwick Christian, the only child of Rev William & Eliz M Christian. Requiescat in Pace!

St Louis, Oct 17. John Calhoun, ex-Surveyor Gen of Kansas & Nebraska, & Pres of the Lecompton Constitutional Convention, died at St Joseph's on Oct 13.

THU OCT 20, 1859
Household & kitchen furniture at auction on Oct 24, at Mrs Robinson's Boarding House, 563 north side of Pa ave, between 1st & 2nd sts. -Barnard & Buckey, aucts,

Rosewood piano forte & household & kitchen furniture at auction on Oct 27, at the residence of Hon John Appleton, F st, between 13th & 14th sts: all his effects.
-J C McGuire & Co, aucts

Harper's Ferry: 1-Also wounded the son of Dr Murphy, of Harper's Ferry. 2-Capt Brown's chief aid was John E Cook, a comparatively young man, who has resided in & near Harper's Ferry for some years. He was first employed in tending a lock on the canal. He afterwards taught school on the Md side, & after a brief residence in Kansas, returned to the Ferry, & married there. 3-Lt J E B Stuart, of the 1st cavalry, acting as aid for Col Lee, advanced to parley with the besieged, Saml Strider, an old & respectable citizen, bearing a flag of truce. They were received at the door by Capt Cook. Lt Stuart demanded an unconditional surrender, only promising them protection from immediate violence & trial by law. Capt Brown refused all terms. Finally Lt Stuart walked slowly from the door. Immediately the signal for attack was given, & the marines, headed by Col Harris & Lt Green advanced in 2 lines on each side the door; the door gave way; the marines advanced to the breach, Maj Russell & Lt Green leading. 4-One of the dead was Capt Brown's son Ottowa, the wounded man his son Watson, whilst the father laid upon the grass a gory spectacle, his face & hair clotted with blood & a severe bayonet wound in his side. 5- About the middle of the stream of the broad Potomac lies the body of one of the insurgents named Wm H Leeman, who was shot on Monday, while attempting to make his escape from the town. His black hair may just be seen floating upon the surface of the water. The visitors, upon discovering the body today, saluted it with a shower of balls, but the action was one of very questionable taste & propriety. In the attack one of the soldiers was about 10 feet behind him as he tried to escape; the man turned round, threw up his hands, & said, "Don't shoot." The soldier fired, the man fell, his face blown away. His coat skirts were cut from his person, & in his pockets was found a capt's commission to Capt W H Leeman from the Provisional Gov't. The commission was dated Oct 15, 1850, & signed by John Brown, Cmder-in-Chief. 6-Aaron D Stevens, a capt of the rioters, shot at the bridge, was taken into the Carroll Hotel, where his dreadful wounds were dressed by Dr McGarrity. He is expected to die before morning, & wanted somebody to telegraph to his father, at Norwich, Conn, to say that his son died at Harper's Ferry, in an attempt at high treason against the State of Va. He was alive at 4 o'clock Tue morning. 7-Insurgents killed: Stewart Taylor, & Albert Hazlitt, both killed instantly. 8-Killed: Fountain Beckham, railroad agent, on Sun, by a single shot; Hayard Sheppard, colored porter at the railroad station, killed Sunday night in working at the train; Thos Boorly, grocer, of Harper's Ferry, killed in Monday's assault; Wm Richardson, of Martinsburg, killed in same assault; Geo W Turner, of Charlestown military, killed on Monday also; Wm Brown, son of Old Brown; Stewart Taylor, insurgent; J C Anderson, insurgent; W H Leeman, insurgent; Albert Haslitt, insurgent. Wounded: Ossawotomie [old] Brown; Watson Brown, a 2nd son; Evans Dorsey, mortally; Allen Evans, mortally; Pvt Quinn, U S Marines, mortally; Alex'r Kelly; Geo Murphy, State's atty, of Martinsburg. Taken prisoners: Edwin Coppee, of Iowa; Shields Green, colored of Harrisburg; Watson Brown, a son of old Brown. 9-Prisoners held by the rioters & released unhurt: Mr Lewis Washington; Mr Dangerfield, paymaster's clerk; Mr Ball, master machinist; Mr Mills, master armorer; Dr Murphy, paymaster; Mr Kilzmeiller, superintendent's clerk; & Mr Donohue, R R Clerk.
+

Brown says he made one mistake in either not detaining the train on Sunday night or permitting it to go on unmolested. The mistake, he seemed to infer, exposed his doings too soon, & prevent his reinforcements from coming in. Names of his party at the Ferry on Sunday, except 3 that he sent away on an errand, with their titles under the Provisional Gov't: Whites-Gen John Brown, Cmder-in-Chief, will recover; Capt Oliver Brown, dead; Capt Watson Brown, dead; Capt Aaron C Stephens, of Conn, badly wounded with 3 balls in him-cannot live; Lt Edwin Coppee, of Iowa, dead; Lt Wm Leman, of Maine, dead; Capt John E Cook, of Conn, escaped; Stewart Taylor, of Canada, dead; Chas P Tidd, of Maine, dead; Wm Thompson, of N Y, dead; Capt John Kagi, of Ohio, but raised in Va, dead; Lt Jeremiah Anderson, of Indiana, dead. [One name was not readable.] Negroes: Daingerfield, of Ohio, but raised in Va, dead; Emperor, of N Y, but raised in S C, unhurt & a prisoner; Lewis Leary, of Ohio, raised in Va, dead; Copeland, of Ohio, raised in Va, unhurt & a prisoner. Gen Brown has 9 wounds, none of which are fatal.

Trustee's sale of superior iron safe, desks, & ofc furniture, on Oct 22nd, at the banking house of Chubb Brothers. -Jas C McGuire & Co, aucts

Died: on Oct 17, in Wash City, Mrs Eliza Hamilton Holly, daughter of the late Gen Alex'r Hamilton.

Died: on Oct 18, in Wash City, after a lingering & painful illness, Josephine Mary, youngest daughter of Jas & Sarah R Townley, in her 19th year.

Circuit Court of Wash Co, D C, No 1,488, in Equity. John C Roemmele against Margaret Foley & John & Martin Foley, jr, admx & heirs of Martin Foley. The above & the creditors of the said Martin Foley, are to appear on Nov 12 next, at the Court-house for the distribution of the trust fund. –W Redin, auditor

Circuit Court of Wash Co, D C-in Equity, No 1,4_8. John C Roemmele et al vs Martin Foley's heirs. John F Ennis, trustee, reported that on Jul 18, 1859, he sold the north half of lot 28 in square 105, in Wash City, to Wm H Forrest, for $1,025, & the purchaser has complied with the terms of sale. –Jno A Smith, clerk

FRI OCT 21, 1859
Cmder G G Williamson, late in command of the U S steam frig **Fulton**, died at Pensacola on Oct 16.

Fatal duel on Sep 16 about 5 miles from San Andreas, Calif, between Dr Preston Goodwin & Col Wm Jeff Gatewood.

Died: on Oct 20, in Wash City, after a long & painful illness, Henry L Harvey, aged 56 years. His funeral is on Oct 22 at half past 3 o'clock, from E st, between 3rd & 4th sts.

Harper's Ferry, Oct 20. Despatches tonight from Hagerstown declare that Cook's wife certainly went to Harrisburg on Tue & took board in the same house with old Brown's daughter-in-law.

Moneka, K T, Mar 29, 1853. Letters: 1-From Gerrit Smith to Capt John Brown; Petersboro, Jun 4, 1859. Dear Friend: Mr Sanborn said your address would be your son's home, West Andover. I have done what I could thus far for Kansas. My wife joins me in affectionate regard to you, dear John, whom we both hold in very high esteem. I suppose you put the Whitman note into Mr Kearney's hands. It will be a great shame if Whitman does not pay. What a noble man is Mr Kearney. How liberally he has contributed to keep you in your Kansas work. –Gerrit Smith. 2-A Wattles to Capt John Brown: we are all well; send all the abolitionists you can; I am a member of the Historical Society of Kansas. Dr Weaver killed himself, I presume you have heard, while bringing in guns from Missouri to murder his neighbors with. It was a Providential interference for our protection, I have no doubt. 3-From O S to Capt Brown, jr; Chambersburg, Pa, Sep 9, 1859. Dear Brother, Sister, & others: All is well with us. Tidd is here. God speed you. Your brother, O S. 4-Letter from Fred Douglas: Mr Dear Capt Brown: I am very busy at home; will you please come up with my son Fred, & take a mouthful with me? In haste, yours truly, Fred Douglas 5-Letter from M R Delaney to J H Kagi: among the papers was found a paper at Chatham, Canada, Aug 16. Delaney says: I have been expecting to see something of uncle's movements, but as yet have seen nothing. The letter fell into the hands of Tidd, who opened it & appended to it: Friend Kagi: seeing a letter for you from Canada, & knowing that a letter from there would relate to business, I took the liberty to peruse it. I know you will not think hard. -Tidd

SAT OCT 22, 1859
Mrd: on Oct 19, at Bladensburg, Md, by Rev Mr Chew, Geo Williamson Smith to Sue Duvall.

G M Follett, a justice of the peace, charged with forging pension papers, was tried at Albany, N Y, on Oct 19th, before the U S District Court, & found guilty.

Serious accident occurred on board the steamboat **Alice Fox**, plying between Alexandria & the Md shore, on Monday. Miss Thorn, of PG Co, Md, went on board the boat, & entered the engine room for the purpose of warming herself, when her dress was caught in the machinery & she was carried over the shaft once or twice, & would have been killed had not Capt Griffin heard her shrieks & at once stopped the engine. She is seriously injured, & fears are entertained that she will not recover. -Gaz

Fire in Gtwn yesterday broke out in the brick dwlg-house of Mr Henry King, on 3rd st, Gtwn, from either a defective flue or in falling sparks from the chimney upon the roof. The bldg, which was the roomy & handsome one for so many years the residence of the late O M Linthicum, was rendered quite untenantable. Mr King is the Sec of the Potomac Fire Ins Co, & it is presumed he was fully insured.

Alexandria Gaz: the body of Mr Jos Burley, who was killed at Harper's Ferry by the insurrectionists, was brought to this city & interred in the St Mary's burial ground on Wed. Mr Burley was the brother of Mr Wm Burley, of this city.

Circuit Court of D C-in Equity, No 1,366. Geo & Thos Parker & others against Jas Kennedy, Mary Kennedy, & John Magee. Statement of the trustee's account on Nov 14, at the court-house, & debts due from said Patrick Magee. –W Redin, auditor

MON OCT 24, 1859
Circuit Court of D C-in Equity, No 1,368. Robt A Cassin against Stephen J Cassin, Jos M Cassin, John Williams & L M Williams his wife, J Johnson Smith & Virginia Smith his wife, Mary E Dyer, Sophia Cassin, Olivia Cassin, John Cassin, Margaret Cassin, Roberta Cassin, John Cassin, Stephen C Spalding, & Edw D Spalding, heirs-at-law of Cmdor Stephen Cassin. Statement of the trustee's account, & distribution of the trust fund, on Nov 15 at the court-house, Wash. -Wm E Woodward, special auditor

Circuit Court of Wash Co, D C-in Equity. Julia Davis & Azelie Davis, by her next friend Julia Davis, vs John R Condon, Rufus Prentice, et al. John C Kennedy, trustee, reported that on Oct 11, at public auction, [without prejudice to any existing right of dower which Julia Davis, one of the cmplnts in said cause, may have in said property] all of the north half of lot 12 in square 42 in Wash City, with all the bldgs, improvements, & appurtenances to the same, & that Thos Cogan, of said city, became the purchaser for $665. –Jno A Smith, clerk

Bailiff's sale: by an order of distrain against the goods & chattels of John D Chanor, for rent due & in arrears, I have seized & taken sundry articles of furniture, & shall, on Nov 1 next, proceed to sell said goods to satisfy said rent due & in arrears. -J M Busher, bailiff -A Green auct

Executor's sale of negroes, farm, farming utensils, & horse, at auction, on Nov 9 next, on the premises, the farm known as ***Conjuror Defeated***, belonging to the estate of Susan Evans, deceased, about 2 miles from Anacostia or Navy Yard Bridge, adjoining the farm of Thos Jenkins, containing about 100 acres, with a good 2 story dwlg, & other necessary out-houses. –Francis S Walsh, exc -A Green auct

Ex-Govn'r Robt P Dunlap, of Maine, died at his residence in Brunswick on Thu last. In 1833 he was elected Govn'r of the State; in 1843 elected a Rep in Congress, in which capacity he served 4 years; in 1848-49 he was appointed collector of Portland, & held the ofc of postmaster of Brunswick from 1853 to 1857. He has been for many years Pres of the Board of Overseers of Bowdoin College. He was nearly 70 years of age.

Obit-died: on Oct 1, 1859, at her residence, in Wash Co, Md, Mrs Ann Talbott Kehler, wife of Rev John H Kehler, in her 58th year. As a wife she was most affectionate & devoted, as a mother tender & kind, as a mistress considerate & reasonable.

Died: yesterday, in Wash City, Geo Venable, aged 58 years. He was a good citizen & deservedly esteemed. His funeral is on Tue afternoon, at 2 o'clock, from his late residence, E st north, between 9th & 10th sts.

Richmond, Va, Oct 23. Rev Henry C Lay, D D, of Alabama, was today consecrated missionary Bishop of the Southwest.

Orphans Court of Wash Co, D C., Oct 2, 1859. In the case of John Hoit, exc of Eliz Talburt, deceased, the executor & Court have appointed Nov 15 next, for the final settlement of the personal estate of said deceased, of the assets in hand.
-Ed N Roach, Reg/o wills

TUE OCT 25, 1859
Excellent household & kitchen furniture at auction on Oct 28, at the residence of J F Bollmeyer, 11th st, between G & H sts, all his effects. -Jas C McGuire & Co, aucts

Excellent household & kitchen furniture at auction on Oct 31, at the residence of B F De Bow, 297 F st, between 12th & 13th sts. –C W Boteler, auct

On Sunday at Newark, N J, in the house of Mr Danl Horton, Mr & Mrs Horton were at table, when she playfully accused her husband of having been drinking. He appealed to Geekie to support his denial & playfully pointed a revolver at Geekie. It went off with fatal effect. The circumstances seem to have been accidental.

Valuable farm for sale: by order of the Orphans' Court of PG Co, Md, the subscriber, as administrator c t a of Thos P Ryon, late of said county, deceased, will sell at public auction, on the premises, on Nov 16 next, the farm on which the said deceased lately resided, containing about 140 acres; adjoins the farm of the late Thos B Crawford; with a comfortable dwlg house & out bldgs. Apply to Richd J Ryon, at Wash, D C, Adm C T A of Thos P Ryon.

Mt Washington College for Young Ladies, 6 miles from Balt, has just entered upon its 4th year. –Rev Gro Lewis Staley, Mt Washington, Balt Co, Md. [Ad]

Gtwn, Oct 24, 1859. Partnership existing between Elias Rohr & Aaron Newberger, by the name of E Rohr & Newberger, is this day dissolved by mutual consent. Henry Rohr will continue to act as the agent of A Newberger in the same business.

Died: on Sunday, in Wash City, Geo W Venable, aged 58 years. He leaves a wife & 3 children to mourn his loss. His funeral is this afternoon at 2 o'clock, from his late residence, 400 E st, between 9th & 10th sts.

WED OCT 26, 1859
A man named Fred'k Deisch, residing in Coxtown, met with a shocking death at Barto's Hotel, in Reading, Pa, on Thu. During the night he opened the front window & fell 5 stories, & was killed instantly. He was sober when he went to bed.

A suit was lately tried at Rochester between Mrs Perkins & the Central railroad, for the death of Mr Perkins, while traveling on the railroad on a free pass. Mrs Perkins claimed $5,000. The jury awarded Mrs Perkins $5,000.

Outbreak at the State Prison yesterday, while employed in loading the schnr **Bolinas** with bricks. They seized the man guarding them, carried him on board, imprisoned the captain & mate in the hold, made all sail in haste; but they forgot that the **Bolinas** was moored to the buoy, & as soon as she run out the length of her fast it swung her round & brought her into the wind. The guard on shore immediately commenced a cannonade on the schnr. Names of the following persons who were either killed or wounded: 1-John Dixon, sent from San Francisco for grand larceny, 4 years, died half an hour after being brought to the hospital; shot in the breast. He bore an assumed name. Said to be of a good family in Wash City. Shot dead on the spot. 2-A R Winchell, sent from Sacramento for grand larceny, 5 years, shot dead on the spot; riddled by rifle & grape shot. 3-Wm Burke, sent from Sacramento for robbery, 14 years, shot through the belly & must die. 4-J H McKenny, sent from Sacramento for grand larceny, 5 years, severely wounded in the hip. 5-John Hart, from Contra Costa, for robbery, 3 years; shot through the foot, not serious. 6-Alex'r McClure, from Sierra Co, murder in the 2nd degree, 15 years, shot through hand & wrist badly shattered. 7-Geo Johnson, from Siskyou, grand larceny, 3 years; arm broken by rifle ball, & could not be extracted. 8-Jas Mullins, from Sacramento, for burglary, 10 years; shot through the hand, injury not serious. 9-Mr A D Moore, the acting lt, was shot through the upper portion of the left arm, & the bone broken. There are hopes that amputation will not be necessary.

Telegram from Carson Valley news is received of the death of Hon Jas M Crane, delegate to Congress last year from Nevada Territory, & who was lately re-elected to the same position. He died on Sep 26, at Gold Hill, Carson Valley, in an apoplectic fit. His remains were to be buried at Carson City.

Accident at Scranton, Pa, on Monday, when the boiler of a locomotive belonging to the Delaware & Western railroad exploded, killing Robt Starrett, engineer, John Brown, fireman, Mr Swartz, formerly of Moscow, Pa, Patrick Welsh, & Wm Allen.

Excellent household & kitchen furniture at auction on Oct 26, at the residence of Theo Wheeler, E st, between 10th & 11th sts. -J C McGuire & Co, aucts

Dentistry, B M Gildea, D D S, corner of 7th & E sts. [Ad]

Marshal's Court. Yesterday a jury was empanelled to sit before the Marshal & try an inquisition under a writ from the Circuit Court de lunatico inquirendo, into the mental state of Robt A Hawke, now an inmate of the Insane Asylum of D C, in which he has lived since Jan, 1855. Dr C H Nichols, in charge of the asylum, testified to Hawke's continued insanity, which wears the form of religious melancholy. Mr Patrick Sweeney testified to the particulars of the property of the patient, & the jury made up their verdict according to the testimony of both witnesses. Mr Hawke is the person who in one of his paroxysms, took his wife's life. The next was a case of the same character relative to the mental state of Henry Emmert, for many years a tinner & resident of the First Ward. Dr Lieberman was examined as to the mental state of the party, & stated him to be laboring under monomania at the time he first saw him, last July. Mr Wm Emmert, brother of the patient, gave evidence touching his property, & also as to his mental condition for the year past. The jury found accordingly.

The Art Gallery Bldg, which is under erection by Mr Corcoran at Pa ave & 17th st, has got up as far as the completion of the brick & stone work of the basement story. The bldg will cost nearly $150,000.

Circuit Court of D C-in Equity, No 1,363. Stephen P Franklin against Sarah Foy, Stanislaus Murray, John C Hamilton, & Saml Hamilton. I shall state the trustee's account, the debts due from said Foy, & the distribution of the fund, on Nov 17, at the Court-house. –W Redin, auditor

Mrd: on Oct 25, by Rev C M Butler, Benj U Keyser, formerly of Phil, to Miss Esther A, daughter of Wm B Todd, of Wash City.

Died: on Oct 20, at Phil, Chas Leon, son of Geo & Richilde Benkert, aged 2 years & 5 months.

Circuit Court of D C-in Equity, No 1,459. S B Blanchard vs Mary Holmead, widow & admx, & Christopher C Callan & Susan Callan his wife, Ada Holmead, Cordelia Holmead, & Wm Holmead, heirs of Wm Holmead, deceased. The trustee has sold part of the land of which Wm Holmead died seized, containing 20 acres, 2 roods & 39 perches, to Hiram Walbridge for $2,074.37, & he hath complied with the terms of the sale. -Jno A Smith, clerk

THU OCT 27, 1859
Robt Stephenson, the celebrated engineer, died in London on Oct 14, at the age of 56 years. Glowing eulogies on the deceased are published. [Oct 28th newspaper: Robt Stephenson was the son of a celebrated engineer Geo Stephenson. He was born at Wilmington, England, in 1803, & was in his 56th year.]

Died: on Sep 24, in London, suddenly, Geo Krehmer, Russian Consul Gen. Mr Krehmer resided in Wash several years, from about 1828, as first Sec of the Russian Legation.

Elegant furniture, handsome china dinner set, cut glass ware, chandelier, & ornaments, at public sale on Nov 3, at the Auction Rooms, the effects of Mrs M H Conrad. -J C McGuire & Co, aucts

People of <u>Dacotah</u> have organized a provisional Territorial gov't, preliminary to the action of Congress, & by the death of Gov Masters, Jas M Allen, Territorial Sec, becomes the acting Govn'r. Govn'r Allen of Dacotah, is the son of Hon John W Allen, of Ohio. —Cleveland Herald

Examination of the Harper's Ferry conspirators; Charlestown, Va, Oct 23, 1859. Magistrates on the bench: Col Davenport, Presiding Justice; Dr Alexander, John J Lock, John F Smith, Thos H Willis, Geo W Eichelberger, Chas H Lewis, & Moses W Burr. Chas B Harding, atty for the county, assisted by Andrew Hunter, counsel for the Commonwealth. The prisoners, Capt Brown & Edwin Coppee were manacled together. John Copeland is a bright mulatto, about 25 years of age. Green is a dark negro, about 30 years of age. Sheriff Campbell read the commitment of the prisoners on the charge of treason & murder. The Court assigned Messrs Chas J Faulkner & Lawson Botts as counsel for the prisoners. Col Washington was the first witness examined; he tells of his being taken & conveyed, with his negroes, to the Armory. Mr Kittzmiller gave the particulars of his being taken prisoner & locked up. Armistead Ball stated the particulars of his arrest by the insurgents. Mr John Allstadt, who was brought into the Armory with his slaves, detailed the particulars of battering down his doors & his seizure by 6 armed men. Alex'r Kelly detailed particulars of collision with insurgents. Wm Johnson testified to the arrest of Copeland, the yellow man, who was attempting to escape across the river. Andrew Kennedy was at the jail when Copeland was brought in. Jos A Brua was one of the prisoners in the engine-house. The Court remanded the prisoners for trial before the Circuit Court.

Mrd: on Oct 25, at the parsonage of Christ's Church, by Rev Mr Morsell, Mr Wm H Keilhultz, formerly of Balt, to Mrs Mary Ann W Harrington, of Wash City.

Circuit Court of D C-in Equity, No 1,459. S B Blanchard & others against Mary Holmead, widow, & Ada, Cordelia, & Wm Holmead, & Christopher C Callan & Susan his wife, heirs of Wm Holmead. On Nov 21 the trustee's account, debts due from said Holmead, & distribution of the trust fund, at the Court-house, Wash. —W Redin, auditor

Circuit Court of D C-in Equity, No 1,023. John Hazle vs Horatio R Maryman, exc & trustee, & John H, Richd A, Almira E, & Zachariah A Maryman. The trustee reported he sold lot 15 in square 867, in Wash City, for $604, to Casper Wagner, & he hath complied with the terms of sale. —Jno A Smith, clerk

FRI OCT 28, 1859
Obit-died: on Tue, Mr Geo W Turner, of Wheatland, Jefferson Co, a valued & respected citizen. His friendship was of no ordinary kind. He will long be missed. —Clarke Co, Va

Fire on Monday at Weymouth, Mass, in a small bldg near the Almshouse, was found to be wholly in flames. It was occupied as a place of confinement for two poor crazy persons, Falvius Hayden, & ___ Tirrell, who for several years have been kept in it in cages. They had torn their clothes to shreds & it appeared pieces lodged upon the stove in the bldg & were set on fire, which communicated to the bldg.

Harper's Ferry insurrection: Circuit Court, Jefferson Co, Va, Judge Parker on the bench, Oct 26, 1859. The indictments against each prisoner were read: First, for conspiring with negroes to create an insurrection; second, for treason against the Commonwealth of Va; third, for murder. Dr Mason was sworn-thought Brown was able to go on with his trial, that his wounds were not such as to affect his mind or recollection. Mr Cockrill, one of the guards of the jail, said that Brown had always been ready to converse freely. Mr Avis, jailor, sworn: would not like to give any opinion as to his ability to stand his trial. [At this point the telegraph gave out between Harper's Ferry & Charlestown.]

A few days since, Mr Richd Gardener, of Fallsburgh, Sullivan Co, N Y, was accidentally shot by his son, James. James had risen early & did not think anyone else had risen, took aim at a knot in the smoke-house, & fired. His father came from behind the smoke-house & exclaimed, "James, what have I done that you should shoot me?" He was alive when last heard from, but it is feared that he cannot recover. Young Gardener is an only son, & managed his father's farm, his parents living with him. This occurrence has rendered him nearly insane.

Wm B Dayton, son of the late A Ogden Dayton, for many years the estimable Fourth Auditor of the Treas Dept, has been admitted to the Bar in our city, & has opened an ofc on Louisiana ave, near the City Hall, Wash.

SAT OCT 29, 1859
Harper's Ferry insurrection: Circuit Court, Jefferson Co, Va, Oct 27, 1859. 1-John Copeland, the mulatto prisoner from Oberlin, Ohio, has made a full confession. 2-Letter: Tribune Ofc, Apr 30, 1859. Mr J H Kagi-Sir: Yours is received, & we enclose our check for $41 dollars for 7 letters from Kansas & two from Ohio. Yours, etc, Horace Greeley & Co. [Kagi, one of the killed, was formerly a correspondent of the Tribune.
+
Capt John E Cook, one of the conspirators who escaped unhurt, was arrested on Tue near Chambersburg, Pa. He has been lodged in jail at Charlestown.

Household & kitchen furniture at auction on Nov 4, at the residence of the late Mrs E Hamilton Holley, on I st, near Conn ave, all the effects, comprising a portion of the furniture of Gen Alex'r Hamilton. -Jas C McGuire & Co, aucts

Mrs Saloma Schneider, the wife of an engineer, yesterday died when the blood in the heart accumulated in the sac which invests the heart, & this ruptured. –St Louis Rep

Reading Adler: Mr Saml Troutman, at Host, in Tulpehoccon township, recently, was looking over a book with his son Israel. They rose to retire to bed, when his elder brother, not knowing that a gun he found was loaded, pulled the trigger in sport. The poor little fellow called twice for his mother & fell down dead. He was 6 years & 9 months old.

Mrd: on Oct 18, in Winchester, Va, by Rev Dr A H Boyd, C De Witt Smith, of Wash, to Lizzie H, daughter of Jas Meredith.

Died: on Oct 26, near Phil, Mrs Sophonisba Sellers, daughter of the late Chas Willson Peale, of that city.

Harper's Ferry trial; Charlestown, Oct 28. Capt Cook arrived today & was lodged in jail. Gov Willard, of Indiana, a brother-in-law of Cook's, accompanied by J E McDonald, Atty Gen of Indiana, D M Voorhees, & M M Randolph, also arrived, & had an interview with Cook at jail. Geo H Hoyt, of Boston, arrived as counsel for Brown, but stated that he would not take any part in the trial at present. Witnesses examined: Armistead Ball, John Allstadt, Alex'r Kelly, & Albert Grits.

MON OCT 31, 1859
Harper's Ferry trial; Charlestown, Oct 28. 1-Conductor Phelps recalled; Lewis Washington recalled. 2-Alex'r Kelly sworn: witness described the manner of Thos Burley's being killed on Monday. Brown's party fired at witness & witness returned the fire; Mr Burley was with witness & armed with a gun; saw him soon after he was shot; he lived about 2 hours. 3-Albert Grist sworn: On Sunday night he had been to meeting with his son; on coming home across the Shenandoah bridge was seized by 2 men with rifles; got to the end of the bridge was stopped by a man with a spear; was told the town was under martial law; asked me if there were many slave holders about Harper's Ferry; I told them no; Brown came up; we were taken to the armory; Brown said the object was to free slaves. Mr Kelly recalled he saw Geo W Turner killed on High st; he was shot while in the act of levelling his gun. 4-Henry Hunter sworn: went to the Ferry with the Charlestown Guards; saw Beckham fall when he was shot; the shot that killed Beckham came from the engine-house at a tank. 5-Col Gibson sworn: helped a portion of the militia of Jefferson Co to suppress the insurrection. 6-Benj F Beall sworn: went to Harper's Ferry armed; did not join the military, but was at the Galt House in Capt Bott's company; saw Mr Beckham shot; Mr Young, one of the Jefferson Guards, was wounded while making a charge against the insurgents; McCabe was wounded. 7-Lewis Starry sworn: testified respecting the killing of Mr Turner. 8-Jas Beller sworn: Stevens was shot before Capt Botts' company reached the Galt House. 9-Henry Hunter: I am related to Mr Beckham, who was my grand uncle; when he was shot I was much exasperated, & started with Mr Chambers to the room where the prisoner Thompson was confined, with the purpose of shooting him; leveled our guns at him, when Mr Foulk's sister threw herself before him, & begged us to leave him to the laws; we then took hold of him & dragged him out by the throat; carried him to the bridge, & two of us leveled our guns, & before

he fell, a dozen more balls were buried in him; we then threw his body off of the trestle-work of the bridge, & returned to bring out Stevens, intending to serve him in the same way. We found him probably dying.

Luther Preston, late postmaster at Fillmore, Minn, was convicted 2 weeks ago, & sentenced to 15 years imprisonment in the penitentiary at Stillwater by the U S Court. He was tried for robbing the mail.

The boiler of the steam saw-mill owned by Messrs Walston & Payne, of Edgecomb Co, N C, about 3 miles from Sparta, exploded on Monday last, killing Richd Gilliam & Nathan Payne, of Va, Chas Oast, of Wilson, N Y, & Geo, a slave belonging to the estate of Harman Ward, of Edgecombe Co.

Mr Edw Jas Thayer, lately the director general of the post ofc in France, died recently. He was a son of the late Jas Thayer, a native of Rhode Island, & a lineal descendant of Roger Williams, the founder of Rhode Island.

Mrd: Oct 25, by Rev J H Lemon, Geo E Alderslade, of Fla, to Miss Jane M Lloyd, of Va.

Mrd: on Oct 25, in Wash City, at the McKendree Chapell, by Rev Mr Hamilton, C Edwin Green to Miranda, eldest daughter of the late Geo Lambright, all of Wash City.

Died: on Oct 3, at Sacramento, Calif, Mrs Mary Ferguson Lee, wife of Harvey Lee, & daughter of John Ferguson, formerly of Wash City, aged 27 years. She died in the triumphs of the Christian faith. The loss to parents, husband, & children is eternal gain to her.

Richmond, Oct 30. The funeral of Hon J Y Mason today was very large & imposing. His remains were deposited in **Hollywood Cemetery**, near the grave of Mr Monroe.

Memphis, Oct 29. Ex-Govn't Jas C Jones died here today.

Circuit Court of D C-in Equity, No 1,442. Lyndall vs Barry et al. Richd Barry, trustee, reported that on Jun 11, 1859, he sold the south part of lot 1 in square 879 to Wm Boyd for $528.75; & the residue of the lot to John Jolly, for $1,038.15; & purchasers have complied with terms of sale. –John A Smith, clerk

TUE NOV 1, 1859
Mrd: on Oct 25, at the residence of Mr Wm Newman, by Rev S A H Marks, Mr John S Carter to Miss Mary J Fountain, both of Dumfries, Va.

Mrd: on Oct 13, at Raymond, Miss, by Rev T D Ozanne, Geo Latimer, M D, formerly of Wash City, to Miss Emma H, daughter of Wm Hal Smith, of that place.

Mrd: on Sep 25, in Wash City, at the McKendre Chapel, by Rev Mr Hamilton, C Edwin Green to Miranda, eldest daughter of the late Geo Lambright, all of Wash City.

Harper's Ferry trial; Charlestown, Oct 29. 1-Arrival of H Griswold, from Cleveland, Ohio, to take part with Geo H Hoyt, of Boston, in the defence, has increased the excitement. 2-Saml Chilton, of Wash, arrived & will join the defence. 2-John E P Dangerfield called; was a prisoner in the hands of Capt Brown at the engine-house. 2-Mr Mills, master armorer was sworn: was a hostage confined in the engine-house. 3-Saml Sunder sworn: detailed all the circumstances of the two days, what he saw, & what he heard.

At Balt on Sat, Wm McPhail, the Mayor of Balt ex officio, during the sickness of Mr Swan, was dangerously wounded by a pistol shot. He was shot by Marshall J Hanna, a reporter of the Sun, at the ofc of the Central Station of the City Police & Fire Alarm Telegraph. Cause unknown.

Circuit Court-Wash-Mon. 1-Saml Strong vs Robt W Brooke, a suit of debt; judgment non pors. 2-Mary E Bronaugh vs Thos S Robinson, which is a suit for the recovery of a family of negroes claimed by dfndnt as his under a bill of sale from the plntf, but contested by the latter. Case goes on today.

Circuit Court of D C-in Equity, No 1,442. Mary Lyndall against Jos Buffington, Wm B Lyndall, & others, devisees of Thos Lyndall, deceased. Meeting at City Hall on Nov 29 for report of the balance of the purchase money of lot 1 in square 879, sold under the decree, for investment, pursuant to the will of said Thos Lyndall. –W Redin, auditor

Mrd: on Oct 25, at the residence of Mr Wm Newman, by Rev S A H Marks, Mr John S Carter to Miss Mary J Fountain, both of Dumfries, Va.

Mrd: on Oct 13, at Raymond, Miss, by Rev T D Ozanne, Geo Latimer, M D, formerly of Wash City, to Miss Emma H, daughter of Wm Hal Smith, of that place.

Mrd: on Sep 25, in Wash City, at the McKendre Chapel, by Rev Mr Hamilton, C Edwin Green to Miranda, eldest daughter of the late Geo Lambright, all of Wash City.

Died: on Oct 13, at Paris, France, suddenly, Geo May, a native of Wash City, & for many years a resident of New Orleans.

Died: on Oct 12, after a brief illness, at the residence of Mrs Ogden, in Madison Co, La, Rev Wm Latta McCalla, in his 71st year. The deceased was by birth & education a Kentuckian, & was widely known as a minister of the Gospel in the communion of the Old School Presbyterian Church. To his widow & adopted daughter, [her niece,] as well as to his surviving brother & his family & other kindred, his loss will be irreparable.

Sale of real estate in Alleghany Co & PG Co, Md; by the last will & testament of Saml Hamilton, late of PG Co: public sale on Nov 23, in Alleghany Co: part of *Treasure Amended*, 1,169¾ acres; *Resurvey, on Horse Lick*, 302¼ acres; *Hamilton's Choice*, 148-7/8th acres; *Sugar Tree Bottom*, 32¼ acres. Real estate of the deceased in PG Co: lot 1 contains 276¾ acres, more or less, with a small dwlg, barn & other out-bldgs. Lot 2 contains 162 acres. Lot 3 contains 146¾ acres, more or less. These lots have no improvements. Mr Morsell, one of the executors will show the same. For further information address W H Tuck, Annapolis, or B K Morsell, Beltsville.
–W H Tuck, B K Morsell, excs

WED NOV 2, 1859
Harper's Ferry trial; Charlestown, Oct 31. 1-Brown looks better, his health is evidently improving. He laid on his bed, as usual. 2-Mr Chilton spoke of the embarrassment with which he undertook the case. He intended to do his duty faithfully, & had come to deal with the prisoner, not as Capt Brown, the leader of this foray, but simply as a prisoner under the charge of violating the law. His birth & residence until a few years past had been in Va. He is now a resident of D C.

Adm's sale of stocks, valuable books, & surveyor's compass, at the auction rooms, on Nov 7, by order of the Orphans Court of D C; a portion of the personal property of the late Wm Ingle. –Jos Ingle, adm -J C McGuire & Co, aucts

Superior Cabinet furniture, Brocatelle curtains, Velvet & Brussels carpets, & China ware, at public auction, on Nov 10, at the residence of J Bartram North, on Indiana ave, between 3rd & 4½ sts [Blagden's row.] -Jas C McGuire & Co, aucts

F H Burns, agent for Langton & Co's Express, Downieville, was yesterday arrested in this city on board the steamer **Golden Gate**, by the detectives Johnson & Lees. On Tue the Chief of Police received a telegraphic dispatch from Mr Langton stating that the express had been robbed of some $8,000, & demanding the arrest of F H Burns. Burns confessed the robbery. He still had $3,700 in his possession.

Drowning of 6 persons in Lake Minnetouka, Minn: Mr M B Stone, formerly of N Y, with his wife & 2 children, Nathl Butterfield, & Loring Loveling, both formerly of Vt. Mr Stone, who had been living at the northern part of the lake, was removing the family & household effects 12 miles down the lake in a sail boat, & Butterfield & Loveling were assisting him. A sudden gale of wind upset the boat, Mr Stone, his wife, & children perished. The boat turned bottom upwards, & Messrs Butterfield & Loveling clung to the boat; becoming chilled & exhausted, sank to the bottom, leaving Mr John McKinzie, a passenger, alone clinging to the boat. He is recovering. Mrs Stone was an English lady, & had but a few weeks ago received intelligence of a fortune left her by a wealthy relative in England.

Alexandria Academy, teachers: Delaware Kemper, Kosciusko Kemper, J G Clark, W W Randolph, & A Zappone. Sessions begin Sep 15 & close Jun 30.
–W S Kemper, Alexandria, Va.

Mrd: Nov 1, at the Assembly's Church, by Rev A G Carothers, Geo C B Mitchell, Atty at Law, of Wash City, [formerly of Va,] to Miss H Sophie Fowler, of Calvert Co, Md.

Chicago, Nov 1. An excursion train from Fond du Lac ran off the track at Johnson's Creek. Among the 8 killed are A B Bonesteel, Indian Agent, & Judge Flint, of Fond du Lac.

THU NOV 3, 1859
Lt Govn'r Trask has recovered from the Hartford & New Haven Railroad Co a verdict of $6,500 damages for the loss of bldgs in Springfield, directly alongside of the railroad, which were destroyed by fire in April last.

Members of St Aloysius & other Choirs of Washington:
Miss Kate Anderson
Miss Alexander
Mr Ball
Mr Balluff
Miss Clare
Miss Kate Cain
Mr Clarke
Miss De Boye
Mr Dawson
Miss Angela Dorsey
Dr Draper
Miss Emily Elliot
Miss Mary Elliot
Frhr F W von Egloffstein
Mr Maedel
The Misses Maedel
Mr French
Miss French
Mr Kretschmar
Miss Gurley
Miss Neall
Mr Flannery
Mr Guillot
Mr Jones
Mr James
Miss Murray
Mr Ketchan
Miss Ketcham
Mr A W King
Miss Lucas
Mr Pelling
Miss Scott
Mr Arthur Scott
Mr Thompson
Miss Callan
Miss Julia Stumpf
Mr Whyte
Mr A De Witzleben
Miss Ward
Esquire Walter
Mr Noyes
Mrs Newton
Miss Johanna Major
Miss M Major
Miss Mary McLaughlin
Miss Mason
Mr Morgan
Mr Paton
& many others.

Mrd: on Oct 25, at Decatur, Ill, at the residence of Col J W Berry, by Rev Mr Oviat, N O Williams, of Chicago, Ill, to Mrs M Lizzie Berry, of the former place.

Circuit Court-Wash-Wed. 1-Mary E Bronaugh against Thos S Robinson concluded by a compromise between the parties. This comprised a verdict by the jury for plntf by consent, thus surrendering to her the negroes in suit, & a reference of the accounts between the 2 parties to the Auditor of the Court, Wm Redin, for examination & settlement. 2-John Moore vs Richd F Jackson, a suit of debt, in which verdict was for plntf. 3-John Purdy & Mahlon W Richey, verdict for plntf.

Dissolution of co-partnership by mutual consent. S Prentiss takes the whole stock & assumes the debt. Mr Holmead will remain at the place of business to close up the old business, & will have charge of the new business as clerk.
–Anthony Holmead, S Prentiss

Capt Montgomery C Meigs, of the Corps of Engineers, was yesterday relieved by the War Dept from the charge of the Capitol Extension, the Continuation of the Gen Post Ofc Bldg, & the New Dome of the Capitol, & the superintendency of these great public works was transferred to Capt Wm B Franklin, of the Corps of Topographical Engineers. We are not cognizant of the causes which led to this change, but we are sure that all who have witnessed the manner in which Capt Miegs had discharged his duties in the prosecution of these works will testify to his capacity, integrity, industry, & energy.

Chicago, Nov 1. An excursion train from Fond du Lac ran off the track at Johnson's Creek. Among the killed are M J Thomas, U S Marshal, Milwaukie; Mr Boardman, Geo F Emerson, Jerome Mason, telegraph operator, Fond du Lac; T L Gillet, J Snow, Jos Lund, C Peterailia, L Sherwood, Dr T Miner. Badly injured: A B Bonersted, Indian Agent; T L Gillett, Judge Flint, Mrs Bedford, E H Sykes, both legs off; Mrs Lewis, leg broken; Mrs Jas Kenney, leg broken; Mrs Calwin, of Oshkosh, both legs broken; Mr Van Buren Smead, editor of the Fond du Lac Press, skull fractured & not expected to recover. The accident was caused by the train running into an ox. [Nov 7th newspaper: Mr Geo B Edwards, of Shawano, Wisc, was on the train, & survived. Also killed: J Boardman, J L Gillet, Fond du Lac; John Lunt, G E Emerson, C Peters, E H Sickles, L Sherwood, Oshkosh; Dr S Miner, Watertown. Injured-new list: B Smead, editor of the Press, Fond du Lac, skull badly fractured, not expected to recover; E H Sykes, Fond du Lac, both legs off; A D Bonesteel, Fond du Lac, one leg broken; Robt Flint, Fond du Lac, one leg broken; Mrs J Radford, Fond du Lac, badly cut up; R M Lewis, Fond du Lac, one leg broken; Mrs Baldwin, Oshkosh, both legs broken; Mrs Jas Kinney, Fond du Lac, one leg broken; Amos Page, Fond du Lac, injured in legs & shoulders; A A Hobart, conductor, ribs broken & head injured; Jas Page, baggage master, badly hurt; J Q Griffiths, Fond du Lac; Mr Bixby, clerk of the Matteson House in this city, badly injured; T F Craig, Chicago, badly hurt in the groin; Miss Foreman, Miss Jenkins, Mrs Jewell, Mrs Page, Mrs Cartwright, Mrs A P Knapp, Mr Coles Bashford, Mrs Parker P Sawyer, Jas Partridge, C C L Gould.]

Horatio Stone, the sculptor, has matured & modeled his design of a statue of the late Thos Hart Benson, as he often appeared before the American Senate. We are informed it has been produced for the adornment of some appropriate place in the city of St Louis.

FRI NOV 4, 1859
Died: on Nov 1, at her late residence, near Trenton, N J, Mrs Mary H Welling, relict of the late John Welling, in her 99th year. She remained none the less an attentive & interested observer of contemporary events until the closing days of her life. A professed Christian for more than three-quarters of a century.

Horrible massacre by the Indians 25 miles west of **Fort Hall**, on Lander's Cut-off, on Sep 2, on a party of 6 men, 3 women, & 10 children, part from Michigan & part from Buchanan Co, Iowa. The emigrants were surrounded as they were about camping, & shot down before they had time for defence. Some who escaped fell in soon after with a company of dragoons under command of Lt Livingston. The dead were horribly mangled & scalped. Murdered: El Miltimore, Sen Jas Miltimore, jr, Wm Miltimore, Mary Ellen Miltimore, & Myron Cline. Missing: Mrs Miltimore & child 3 months old, & Albert Miltimore. Escaped, Milton H Harrington, wife & child, A Hill, wife & child, Geo Alonzo, Nelson Miltimore, Frank Hubbard, Nathan Titus & Wm Marsh.

Household & kitchen furniture at auction on Nov 8, at the residence of Capt Chas Steadman, U S N, corner of F & 20th sts. –J C McGuire & Co, aucts

Harper's Ferry trial; Charlestown, Nov 2. 1-Coppee guilty on all counts. 2-John Copeland, a negro conspirator, made a confession. He confessed to being the John Copeland, of Oberlin, who was indicted last year at Cleveland for rescuing the slave John. His parents reside in Oberlin; induced to enter into the Harper's Ferry movement by letters written by J H Kagi & John Brown, jr, to Leary, at Oberlin; Ralph & Saml Plumb gave me $15 to bear my expenses; Leary was killed in the river near the rifle works; stopped at Isaac Sturtevant's, on Walnut st, Cleveland, until Tue; Mrs Sturtevant knew I was going to Va; Mr Sturtevant probably knew also; Ralph Plumb gave me the money, Saml Plumb & Leary were present. There was an attempt to raise a movement of that kind in Ky about the same time.

Judge Danl Cady died Oct 31 at his residence in Johnstown; verging upon his 88th year. He was one of the oldest, if not the oldest lawyer in the State. –Albany Journal, 1st

Died: Nov 3, in Wash City, Cara A, only daughter of the late Jas R McAlister, of Wash, in her 8th year. Her funeral is today at 3 o'clock, from the residence of her mother, No 2 4½ st.

Balt, Nov 3. Funeral arrangements are being made for Adam Barlie Kyle, jr, who was murdered at the polls in the 15th ward. He was a respected & excellent fellow citizen. [Death date not given-current item.]

SAT NOV 5, 1859

Trustee's sale of valuable business location on 8th st, near D st, on Dec 10, on the premises, by deed of trust from T H Phillips, dated Nov 3, 1854, recorded in Liber J A S No 90, folios 61 thru 64, of the land records of Wash Co, D C: sale of part of lot 1 in square 407, with a brick coach & blacksmith shop. Terms cash. –Benj O Shekell, trustee -Jas C McGuire & Co, aucts

Memphis Enquirer: Hon Jas C Jones died on Oct 29, at his residence, near this city. He was born in Wilson Co, Tenn, on Jun 8, 1809; in 1850 elected to the U S Senate for a term of 6 years. He was a devoted friend of Henry Clay. His family will mourn the loss of a loving husband & a kind & gentle father.

John & Jesse Lewis, brothers, convicted in the Circuit Court of Anderson Co, Tenn, of the murder of the Sheriff & Deputy Sheriff of Campbell Co, have been sentenced to be hung at Jacksonborough on the 3rd Fri in Dec.

Estray small cow came to the subscriber, on 7th st Plank Road, on Nov 1. Owner can prove property, pay charges, & take her away. –Harriet White

Mrd: on Nov 1, in Grace Church, Balt, by Rev A C Coxe, N H Hutton, of Wash, to Meta M, daughter of Col E Van Ness, U S Army.

Died: on Nov 3, of consumption, Wm Howell Bangs, in his 31st year. His funeral is tomorrow at 2 o'clock, from the residence of his father-in-law, Mr Willard Drake, 9th st.

MON NOV 7, 1859

Among the victims of the recent outrages at Harper's Ferry, stands the name of Geo W Turner, an eminent citizen of Jefferson Co, Va. Mr Turner was in his 48th year; trained to the profession of arms at West Point, where his rank was amongst the highest in his class; entered the army; served with constancy in the them pending Florida war; contracting the slow fever, he sought restoration as a civil engineer; at length he retired from public service, resigned his commission in the army, & took possession of the paternal estate of **Wheatland**, devoting himself to the noble pursuits of husbandry & the cultivation & improvement of this beautiful farm, his patrimonial inheritance. Mr Turner leaves an only brother & 4 sisters, & a numerous family connexion to mourn his untimely & tragic death. –Wash, Nov 4, 1859

Died: on Nov 4, Miss Hester J Ridgely, in her 24th year.

Norfolk, Nov 5. The barque **Wm D Platinus**, Capt Bennet, from City Point, James river, has anchored in Hampton Roads with her crew in a state of mutiny. The mate, S Gorham, was dangerously stabbed in the lungs & has been placed in the hospital. Ofcrs have been sent to the barque to arrest the mutineers.

Circuit Court of D C. Antonie Buchignani & Margaret his wife, & Saml Chilton, trustee of said Margaret, vs John B Randolph, Geo C Randolph, Mary G Randolph, Emily C Randolph, Wm H Pendleton & Henrietta his wife, Beverly Randolph & Mary C his wife, & Antonie Sampayo & Virginia his wife. The plntf, Saml Chilton, as trustee of the said Margaret Buchignani, holds the legal title for her sole & separate use to one undivided third & two-ninths part of a certain piece or parcel of ground now vacant & unimproved in Wash City, & designated on the plat of the said city as square 135; that the residue of said square is held & owned as follows: one undivided sixth part by Antonie Sampayo & Virginia his wife, who resides beyond the limits of the U S; another undivided sixth part by John Randolph, Geo C Randolph, Emily C Randolph, & Mary G Randolph, minor children of Margaret Randolph, deceased; & the remaining one-ninth part is claimed by Wm H Pendleton & Henrietta his wife, & Beverly Randolph & Mary C His wife, who reside in the State of Va; that the said Virginia Sampayo & the said minors are entitled, in virtue of their grandfather, & their great grandfather, Wm O'Neale, deceased, & the said Henrietta Pendleton & Mary C Randolph, as heirs at law of their uncle, John H O'Neale, who died intestate & without issue; that the cmplnts desire a partition of said square aforesaid, in order that the portion of said square to which the female plntf is entitled may be set off by metes & bounds, & held by said trustee to her separate use in severalty under the decree & direction of the Court. Absent dfndnts to appear in person or by solicitor, on first Monday in Apr next, at this Court, Wash. –Jno A Smith, clerk

Mrd: on Nov 3, at Wesley Chapel, by Rev Dabney Ball, Thos Hagerty to Elbertine H, eldest daughter of Wm Phillips, all of Wash City.

TUE NOV 8, 1859
On Thu Mr Chas Lambert, a German butcher, at Clifton, Staten Island, was burnt to death & his wife almost lost her life, when a camphene lamp exploded. His wife lies terribly disfigured.

Miss Thompson, in Tenn, has recently recovered $15,000 in a suit for breach of promise against a man named Patterson.

Mrd: on Oct 25, at the parsonage of Christ's Church, by Rev Mr Morsell, Mr Wm H Keilholtz, formerly of Balt, to Mrs Mary A W Harrington, of Wash City.

Died: on Nov 6, in Wash City, Thomas Gideon, son of John S & Amelia J Williams, aged 14 years & 8 months. His funeral is today at 3 o'clock, from the Church of the Ascension, Rev Dr Pinckney, on H st, between 9th & 10th sts.

WED NOV 9, 1859
Norfolk, Nov 5. The barque **Wm D Platinus**, Capt Bennet, from City Point, James river, has anchored in Hampton Roads with her crew in a state of mutiny. The mate, S Gorham, was dangerously stabbed in the lungs & has been placed in the hospital. Ofcrs have been sent to the barque to arrest the mutineers.

Died: on Nov 4, Miss Hester J Ridgely, in her 24th year.

Howard Co Tribune: the divorce of Mr Wm Hoffman, of N Y C, Jun, 5, 1857, from his wife Emma, was annulled on Oct 23, 1858, on the ground that it had been fraudulently procured, her husband not being a resident of Howard Co, but of N Y C. Now the law requires the applicant to be a resident for a year, before he can begin a suit at all.
–Indianapolis Journal

Vacant lots wanted in the States of Va, Tenn, Mo, & Ga. Address Alfred H Reip, Balt.

Orphans Court of Wash Co, D C, Nov 8, 1859. In the case of Absalom A Hall, adm of Jacob Hall, deceased, the administrator & Court have appointed Dec 3 next, for the final settlement of the personal estate of the said deceased, of the assets in hand.
-Ed N Roach, Reg/o wills

Mrd: on Nov 2, at Wesley Chapel, by Rev L F Morgan, John B Wheeler to Mary E, daughter of Jas D Chedal.

Memphis, Tenn, Nov 8. W N Palmer, one of the alleged Harper's Ferry insurgents, has been arrested here on the requisition of Gov Wise.

THU NOV 10, 1859
Capt Thos Paine, U S Navy, died last evening at Brown's Hotel, [Wash] after a short illness of pneumonia. He was severely wounded during the war of 1812 in repulsing an attack upon the American gunboats near Savannah by the boats from a British squadron, by which he was permanently disabled for active service. He was a native of Georgia, but has resided for many years in Charleston, S C.

Harper's Ferry trial; Charlestown, Nov 7. 1-A D Stevens was brought into court & placed on a mattress, looking pale & haggard. 2-Gov Willard & a Mr Crowley, brothers-in-law, will be present during the trial.

Died: yesterday, in Wash City, after a brief illness, Mary Eliz Peyton Grymes, wife of Dr Jas M Grymes, & eldest child of Jas M Robut, of Wash City, aged 22 years. Her pure spirit, beckoned away by her new-born babe, has followed it to that rest where the pure in heart behold their God. Her funeral is today at 2:30 P M from Trinity Church.

Died: on Nov 8, in Wash City, Charlotte Le Compte Nevitt, daughter of Capt Chas L & Susan G Nevitt. Her funeral is this evening at 2:30 P M, from her late residence on 7th st, between L & M sts south.

Died: on Nov 8, at Bladensburg, John A Hunnicutt, of Va.

Died: on Nov 9, in the glorious resignation of a triumphant Christian faith, after a protracted illness, Annie E McConnell, youngest daughter of Dr Wm P & Eliza McConnell, aged 15 years & 4 months. Her funeral will take place this evening at 2 o'clock, from the residence of her father, Pa ave, near 3rd st.

Died: on Nov 8, at his late residence on 13th st, Vincent Masi. His funeral is this morning at 9:30 o'clock. His remains will be taken from the family residence to St Patrick's Church, where a requiem mass will be celebrated.

Circuit Court of D C-in Equity, No 1,517. Edw Wheeler, Ana M Wheeler, John A Baldwin & Martha R Baldwin, Philip Whilwright & Eleanor Whilwright, Wm Carter & Caroline Carter, Jas E Morgan, against Eliz M Garner, Thos H Garner, & the heirs of Richd McConchie. On Nov 21, at City Hall, Wash, I shall report whether lots 19 thru 22, in square 117, are susceptible of specific partition between the parties; 2, if not, whether it will be to their advantage that the same should be sold; 3, the proportions of the respective parties in the estate of Barbara McConchie, deceased. –W Redin, auditor

$1,000 reward for runaway negro men & 2 negro boys: Joe Gurry, aged about 30; Isaac King, aged about 28; Ben King, aged about 25; Henry, aged 19; Wm, aged about 19. -Jos K Roberts, residing near Bladensburg, PG Co, Md.

FRI NOV 11, 1859
Trustee's sale of valuable real estate, by deed of trust from Chas H Winder & wife, dated Mar 14, 1855, recorded in Liber J A S, No 103, folios 5, et seq; public sale on Nov 23, all that part of lot 2, in Davidson's subdivision of square 170, in Wash City, on 18th st west. –W D Davidge, trustee -A Green auct

Chancery sale of beautiful & valuable bldg lots in Wash City, situated in square 167, fronting on Lafayette Square, & in sight of the Pres' House. The undersigned, Trustees appointed by a decree of the Circuit Court of D C, passed on Oct 26, 1859, in a cause therein depending between Augusta McClair, Julia Ten Eyck, & others, cmplnts, & Wm Gadsby & others, devisees, & heirs at law of the late John Gadsby, dfndnts, [No 1,445 in Equity.] Public auction on Dec 15, 1859 of lot 27 in square 167, on Jackson Pl; lot 38 with the same front; lot 37, fronting on Jackson Pl; lot 35 fronting on north H st; lot 34 fronting on north H st; lots 33 & 32 of the same front; & lot 31, corner lot, fronts on H st. –Saml Chilton, A B Magruder, trustees -C W Boteler, auct

Died: on Nov 10, in Wash City, Dr Geo P Todsen, a native of Denmark, but for many years a citizen of the U S, formerly in the medical service of the U S, & subsequently agent of the American Colonization Society at Liberia, where he rendered valuable services to the Society. His funeral is this afternoon at 4 o'clock, from his late residence at Mr Norr's, corner of E & 11th sts.

Howard Co [Mo] Banner. Mrs Frances A Digges, of this county, furnishes the Banner with the following letter from Mrs Bettie Shepherd, [her daughter,] who was one of the party of Howard emigrants that suffered from an attack by the Indians between this & Calif. The entire party was from Howard, & well known. Ione City, Sep 12, 1859. After a long & tedious journey we arrived in Ione City the 10th of Sep; on Jul 26, we arrived at Cold Spring; when we arrived a train was encamped there, & we were informed by then that the Indians had made an attack upon them, killing one man & wounding another, & carried off cattle; on Jul 27 we prepared to start; about 2 miles some of our men looked back & saw that the Indians had attacked the train again, wounding one man, & taking more cattle; our captain thought it best to go on; after a few miles one of Wm Shepherd's horses was taken sick & fell; we stopped a few minutes; the men were standing looking at the horse, when we were suddenly fired upon, killing our captain, Ferguson Shepherd. The war-whoop was then given, followed by shots from each side of the rocky, bushy canon, killing Wm Shepherd, Wm Diggs, Claborn Rain, & wounding 2 men, 1 woman & a child. Mr Wright was mortally wounded; he lived 9 days. I M Smith slightly wounded; Mrs Wright was wounded, but not fatally; her baby's thigh was broken by being whirled against a rock by a savage monster; afterwards 6 men & one woman were shot. Geo Avery & Jas Ward fled, saying that they would be killed if they remained there another moment. In a few moments Geo Parson & McGuire left; the Indians were still firing upon us. I was standing in the road with my baby in my arms, exposed to the bullets that came whirling around me. I looked around & I saw Mr Shepherd; I called for him; I told him I thought we had better try & make our escape; he said well. We started; myself, I M Smith, Mrs Annie Shepherd, & Mrs Wright's little son; Mrs Annie Shepherd's little babe was also with us. Mr Shepherd followed. The Indians shot at us a good many times as we were going off. Mrs Annie Shepherd, being a very delicate woman, became weak, & could proceed not further, so she secreted herself in some bushes; I M Smith, one of the wounded men, had her babe; but he became so weak from loss of blood that he was compelled to hide in some bush. We journeyed on. After 2½ miles Townsend Wright overtook us, riding one of our mules; he said he was in the wagon attending to his wounded brother, & he cut the mule from the wagon & made his escape. I walked between 10 & 12 miles bareheaded, barearmed, & barenecked, & carried my baby part of the way. We reached camp exhausted. Mrs Annie Shepherd came in camp. She was almost like an insane woman. Next morning we started on our journey again. There were about 60 wagons & 250 men; we arrived at the place where the massacre was commited. Mr Wright, Mrs Wright, her son Joe, & her babe were found to be still living. Capt G Pierce had a wagon prepared for the dead, in which they were placed, & the wounded properly cared for. Mrs Annie Shepherd's babe was also found; it was very much sunburnt & bruised by the bush. We traveled on, stopped to bury the dead. Dr A W Trader attended to the wounded. The fight lasted about three-fourths of an hour. There were about 50 Indians.

Receiver's sale. Drane vs Ingle, adm, etc. Circuit Court of Wash Co, D C, in Equity, No 1,557. Sale, at the County Jail, on Nov 14, 43 head of cattle, 52 hogs, & 10 sheep. -G W Phillips, receiver

The Pres appointed Rev D X Junkin, D D, to be a Chaplain in the U S Navy. This enables him to complete his history of that good old Commonwealth, Pa, in the relief it will afford from the cares of parochial duty. Dr Junkin was for some years pastor of the F st Presbyterian Church in this city.

Public sale of valuable bldg lots on the Island, on 6th st west; by the last will & testament of Hanson Barnes, deceased, by order of the Orphans Court of Wash Co, D C: sale on Dec 4, of lot 19, in Wm B Todd & Wm H Gunnell's subdivision of square 465. Title indisputable. –Alex'r Lee, Adm, C T A -A Green auct

J Crockett Harrison has sold 7,000 acres of land, in Tazewell Co, Va, to Mr Sheppardson, of N Y C, for $110,000. John M Norvell has sold his tract of land in Albemarle Co, Va, near the Nelson Co line, containing 520 acres, for $50,000. The purchasers are Northern gentlemen, who will work the place for its supposed mineral wealth.

Pistols. Colt's, Adams' & Smith & Wesson's Revolvers. We call particular attention to the latter, being the smallest & most pocketable arm now in use. –M W Galt & Bro, Jewellers, 354 Penn ave, 4 doors west of Brown's Hotel.

Died: on Nov 9, at Brown's Hotel, Wash City, Capt Thos Paine, of the U S Navy, in his 74th year, a citizen of S C, & for the last 20 years a resident of Charleston. The ofcrs of the Navy & Army & citizens of S C are requested to attend the funeral of the late Capt Paine from Brown's Hotel, at 12 o'clock A M, this day, Friday, the 11th.

Died: on Oct 19, at Defiance, Ohio, William, son of John W & Margaretta F McKim, aged 4 years, 1 month & 21 days.
+
Died: on Nov 3, at Defiance, Ohio, Edward, son of John W & Margaretta F McKim, aged 1 year, 9 months & 16 days.

SAT NOV 12, 1859
Mr Gerrit Smith, the erratic pilanthropist, became on Monday last an inmate of the N Y State Lunatic Asylum, where it has been found necessary to place him on account of marked insanity. We learn that he is very violent & exhibited a disposition to commit suicide. Mr Smith is said to have an hereditary predisposition to insanity. His father, Peter Smith, though the possessor of an immense estate, was subject to fits of profound despondency. The late Peter Sken Smith, the brother of Gerrit, was for some time an inmate of a lunatic asylum, though when he died he was generally regarded as in possession of his reason. Gerrit Smith has lost all his children except one, the wife of Col Miller, of Peterboro. A nephew of Mrs Smith, Col Fitzhugh, was the captor of the fugitive Cook, a fact which greatly disturbed the mind of Mr Smith, N Y Post

Trial of Capt Cook, Charleston, Nov 9, 1859; his confession, conviction, & sentence. 1-Cook met Capt Brown some 2 years ago in Kansas; he had courted & married Miss Kennedy, of South Bolivar; Mrs Kennedy, his mother-in-law, entered the court room, she seemed in great distress of mind & wept considerable during the testimony. Young Kennedy, brother of Cook's wife, was also present. 2-Col L W Washington was first witness sworn; met Cook in South Bolivar. 2-Terrance Byrne, sworn, lives in Wash Co, Md. 3-Jas Byrne sworn: saw Cook & his party in the road; told his sister to come out & see the men. 4-Linn Curry sworn: resides in Jefferson Co, Va, but teaches school in Wash Co, Md. 5-Mr Kennedy, the father-in-law of Cook was sworn; stated that Cook had ordered him from his own house shortly after having married his daughter. Intimated that he would not object to seeing him hung. 6-Dr Starry, Col Barbour, & B F Beall testified, but they did not throw any additional light on the case. 7-Affidavit from Mrs Almira L Steptoe, of this county, testifes that several years ago she spent the winter in Phil, & stopped at the Congress Hall Hotel, & John E Cook, the prisoner, & she became well acquainted ; saw him frequently playing with his children. Affidavit of Miss Lucy Thompson, a grand-daughter of Mrs Steptoe, who said she was also at the hotel at the same time. 8-Gov Willard, of Indiana, sworn: became acquainted with Cook in 1847, when he married Cook's sister.
+
Charlestown, *Oct 10. The Court refused the motion for an arrest of judgment in the case of Cook & the negroes Copeland & Green, for sentence. They were all sentencd to be hung on Dec 16. Capt Brown had been previously sentenced to be hung on Dec 2, but it is thought the Govn'r will respite him until the 16th, & hang them all together. The Court then adjourned for the term. [*Copied as written.] [Nov 14th newspaper: John E Cook, Edwin Coppie, Shields Green, & John Copeland, found guilty. All to be hung by the neck until dead on Dec 16, Green & Copeland between the hours of 8 in the forenoon & 12 of that day; Cook & Coppie, between the hours of 12 & 5 of the same day.]

Circuit Court-Wash, Friday. Mary O'Donnell is plntf & the administrators of the late Matthew Trimble are dfndnts. Damages are laid at $4,875, being for unremunerated services of plntf to the deceased, Mr Trimble, as housekeeper, nurse, etc, for a series of years. [Nov 15th newspaper: on Sat the jury gave a verdict for plntf for $1,500.]

Mrd: on Nov 8, at St Patrick's Church, by Rev Fr O'Toole, Lewis Johnson to Mrs Susan H Strahan, both of Wash City.

Mrd: on Nov 9, in Cumberland, Md, by Rev E R Lippitt, Dr W F Lippitt, of Wash, D C, to M Louisa, daughter of Hon Thos Perry.

Died: on Oct 27, at Indianola, Texas, of yellow fever, Jas L Gray, formerly of Wash City.

Hon John Dennis, a distinguished citizen of Somerset Co, Md, died on Nov 1st. He was in his 52nd year of his age. [Nov 19th newspaper: The late Hon John Dennis was buried on Thursday in the Episcopal burying ground. –Somerset [Md] Union]

MON NOV 14, 1859
For sale, 20 to 30 acres of land, near Wash City boundary. For terms apply to R C Brooke, 558 7th st, or on the premises, west of the Anacostia bridge.

Mrd: on Nov 8, at **Cedar Grove**, King Geo Co, Va, by Rev Kinsey Stewart, Mr S T Stuart, of Fairfax Co, to Rosalie Eugenia, eldest daughter of Dr R H Stuart.

Foreign news. 1-Lord Brougham has been elected Chancellor of the Univ of Edinburgh. 2-The widow of Sir Robt Peel is dead.

TUE NOV 15, 1859
New Book: History of the Life & Times of Jas Madison, by Wm C Rives. Vol 1: Boston: Messrs Little, Brown & Co, 1859. Washington: Taylor & Maury. Jas Madison was born on Mar 16, 1851, at the house of his maternal grandmother, Mrs Conway, on the northern bank of the Rappahannock, King Geo Co, Va. The residence of his parents was in Orange Co, 50 or 60 miles distant, but his birth took place during a visit of his mother to an ancestral home in the Northern Neck. The ancestry of Mr Madison can be traced through 4 generations of Va planters to John Madison, his grandfather's grandfather, who in 1653 obtained a patent for a tract of land on the shore of the Chesapeake bay, in the vicinity of York River. There was indeed in the colony, as early as 1622, the date of the Indian massacre so nearly fatal to the infant settlement, a Capt Isaac Madison, who distinguished himself in the Indian war that followed. He may have been the founder of the Va family of Madisons, but its genealogy cannot be traced beyond the John Madison above mentioned. Ambrose Madison, grandson of this John & grandfather of Jas Madison, emigrated to what was then the extreme Western frontier, now Orange Co, Va, settling on that same estate of **Montpelier** which, after having been occupied by Mr Madison's father, descended eventually to him. His father, who also bore the name of James, was a leading man in the affairs of his county, & held during the Revolutionary war the ofc of County Lt.

Madame Urdard, a native of the State of Ohio, 60 years of age, who has resided a number of years in New Orleans, a fortune-teller, was found murdered & robbed in her apt there on Monday. She was a shrewd well educated woman. Her throat had been cut.
–New Orleans Bee

Circuit Court of D C-in Equity, No 1,557. Patrick Sweeny & others against Robt A Hawke & Michl P Callan, his cmte. Statement of the account of said Hawke, at my ofc, City Hall, Wash, Dec 8th next. –W Redin, auditor

WED NOV 16, 1859
On Friday last, at Rectortown Station, Manassas Gap railroad, Mr C R Ayres, was shot & instantly killed by Mr Jas Philips. The difficulty was about the location of a road.
-Alexandria Gaz

Henry E Hyams, a clerk in Messrs G N Morrison & Co's drug store, was murdered by Matthew Hughes, a policeman, who was not on duty last night. The deceased & 2 friends were accosted by Hughes, who asked which of them shouted for Parker. They disclaimed having done so. As Hyams started to move away, Hughes shot him in the back. He staggered & dropped dead. Hughes got away. New Orleans Bulletin, Nov 9.

Jos W Thornton, who assassinated Jos Charles, in the streets of St Louis on Jun 3, was hung in that city on Friday last. He was about 38 years of age.

Circuit Court of D C-in Chancery, Oct Term, 1859. Ernest Loeffler vs Adam Raab, [adm] Thos Blagden, [trustee,] Jos Fugett, & the heirs of Ferdinand Greentrup. This suit is to procure a decree for the sale of certain real estate in Wash City, D C, to satisfy certain indebtedness in favor of cmplnt. The bill states that the said Greentrup, deceased, was in his lifetime indebted to cmplnt in a certain sum of money particularly stated in said bill & account filed; that the said Greentrup being the owner of certain real estate in said city, viz. a portion of the west half of lot 1 in square 516, fronting on I st north, did, on Sep 10, 1845, convey the same to Thos Blagden in trust to secure the payment of certain notes in favor of Jos Fugett; but cmplnt is informed that said indebtedness has been satisfied; that, being so indebted to cmplnt, the said Greentrup, in 1858, died intestate, leaving the aforesaid real estate with the legal title outstanding & some personal estate, & leaving heirs to cmplnt unknown; that administration of his personal estate was granted by the Orphans Court of D C. to Adam Raab; that by virtue of the order of said Court, the said Raab sold the same; but that cmplnt is informed that said personal estate has been exhausted, & that a sale of said real estate is necessary to satisfy the claim of cmplnt. Unknown heirs to appear in Court, in person or by solicitor, on or before Mar 20th next. –Jno A Smith, clerk

Beautiful country residence for sale: the subscriber, desirous of moving nearer his place of business, offers the place in which he now resides, on North Boundary st, at 3rd st, outside of the city limits, combining the advantages of a city & country residence. The house is large, 17 rooms, with 11 acres of ground attached. Inquire of Z D Gilman, Druggist, 350 Pa ave.

Died: on Nov 15, suddenly, of paralysis, Josiah F Caldwell, in his 86th year, a native of Elizabethtown, N J, & for the last 40 years a resident of Wash City. His funeral will take place at 12M, on Thursday.

Died: on Oct 30, Lizzie, daughter of Edw & Eliz Waller, aged 7 years & 19 days.

TUE NOV 17, 1859
Sale by order of the Orphans Court of Wash Co, D C., of liquors, cigars, tobacco & household & kitchen furniture at auction on: Nov 24, at the store & residence of the late Jas Patterson, on 4½ st, between Md ave & C st. –Mary Ann Patterson, admx
-Jas C McGuire & Co, aucts

Public sale of fine saddle, harness horses, colts, cows, buggy, wagons, & harness, on Nov 23, at the store of Mr L L Brunett, at 7th st & Piney Branch road, the property of a gentleman who has no further use for them. -A Green auct

Twelve Years of a Soldier's Life in India, being extracts from the letters of the late Major W S R Hobso, B A, including a Personal Narrative of the Seige of Delhi & Capture of the King & Prince, 1 vol; price $1. For sale by Blanchard & Mohun, Pa ave.

Mrd: on Nov 15, at the Methodist Episcopal Church South, by Rev Mr Scrivener, Mr Thos J Steele to Miss Eliza Ellen Turner, both of Wash City.

Mrd: on Nov 15, at Kellyville, Culpeper Co, Va, by Rev C George, John S Berry, of Gtwn, D C, to Fanny F, daughter of John P Kelly, of the former place.

Died: on Nov 6, suddenly at the residence of her son, Robt M English, in Jefferson Co, Va, having nearly completed her 77th year, Mrs Lydia H English, relict of David English, sr, late of Gtwn, D C.

FRI NOV 18, 1859
Rev Dr Abel Barnes, of Phil, states that all his published works on the Scriptures, amounting to 16 volumes, have been written before 9 o'clock in the morning. His custom was to rise at 4 o'clock.

Mrd: Thu, by Rev John C Smith, Mr Jacob Bowers to Miss Martha A Carr, both of Va.

Mrd: on Nov 1, at Chantilly, Hanover Co, Va, by Rev C C Bitting, Mr W LeRoy Broun, of Albemarle Co, to Miss Sallie J Fleming, daughter of Dr Geo Fleming, of Hanover.

Desirable residence on the Heights of Gtwn for rent: that commodious dwlg, with surrounding grounds, known as the **Carter Place**. The house is partially furnished with excellent furniture, which can be purchased if early application is made. Apply to Jas C McGuire & Co.

SAT NOV 19, 1859
Mr Frank Lewis, an estimable citizen of Phil, who was to have been married on Wed to a daughter of Cmdor Stockton, died after an illness of a few days on Monday. The invitations had been issued & preparations had all been made for the wedding ceremony.

Capt McClintock has been notified by the Lords of the Admiralty that Queen Victoria, in consideration of the brilliant success by which his late expedition to the Arctic regions was attended, has been pleased to order that, from Apr, 1857, to Sep, 1859, during which time he was in command of the yacht **Fox**, shall count to him as sea time. This favor can only be granted by the Sovereign, & is rarely exercised.

Rev J R Downey, a Missionary of the Methodist Episcopal Church, died at Lucknow, India, on Sep 16. He was one of 5 Missionaries who sailed from Boston for Calcutta a few months ago, & had but recently arrived at Lucknow.

Ex-Govn'r Gilmer, of Georgia, died at Lexington, in that State, on Wed. He had been ill for about 4 weeks.

Died: on Nov 17, at her residence, in Gtwn, D C, Mrs Margaret Dick, in her 84th year. She was a most devoted mother to an equally devoted & affectionate son. Her funeral will take place on Nov 19 at 10 o'clock.

Nashville, Nov 18. Allen A Hall, editor of the News, killed G G Poindexter, editor of the Union & American, in a street rencontre, by shooting him. This fatal act was the result of an editorial quarrel.

MON NOV 21, 1859
Counterfeiters caught on Mon in the act by Jacob Rehm & his ofcrs, at Cordova, in Rock Island Co, on the Miss river. They were Timothy L Bigelow, age 66, who has a family, a wife & several children; Chester C Clark, aged 25 or 26; Jas Smith, aged 26 or 28. -Chicago Tribune of Nov 16

Sailing of missionaries: Rev Geo B Claflin, a graduate of the Bangor Theological Seminary; Rev J H Dodge, of Andover Theological Seminarry; & Mr Richd Miles, of Ohio, with their wives, will sail today from Bangor, direct for Sherbro Island, West Africa. The lumber & other materials for 2 houses for these missionaries [to be erected in Africa,] have been prepared & put on board the vessel. –Portland Adv of Wed

First class bldg site on H st, between Conn ave & 17th st & 3 desirable lots at K & 19th st, at public sale, on Nov 28, on the premises. We shall offer parts of lot 1, 19, & 20, in square 165, adjoining the residence of Com Shubrick. On the H st front is a very fine stone foundation laid in cement, for a first class house, 36 x 58, designed to be built by Chas H Haswell, late Chief Engineer, U S N. The owner, B I Semmes, has permanently removed from the city & is determined to sell. We shall also sell lots 9 thru 11 in square 107, fronting on K st. -Jas C McGuire & Co, aucts

Orphans Court of Wash Co, D C. Letters of administration de bonis non, with the will annexed, on the personal estate of Francisco Masi, late of Wash Co, deceased. –Mary Brien, admx D B N, W A

Orphans Court of Wash Co, D C. Letters of administration with the will annexed on the personal estate of Vincent Masi, late of Wash Co, deceased. –Mary Brien, admx, w a

Orphans Court of Wash Co, D C. Letters of administration on the personal estate of Wm Lewis, late of Wash Co, deceased. –Jane Lewis, admx

Mrd: on Nov 2, by Rev Fr O'Toole, Thos K Davis to Miss Josephine A Plummer, both of Wash City.

Mrd: on Nov 5, at St John's Church, N Y, by Rev Mr Berryman, A H Jackson, of Tenn, to Miss F J Blake, of N Y C.

Died: on Nov 19, Eliz Ford, relict of the late Wm Ford, in her 59th year. Her funeral will be this afternoon at 2 ½ o'clock, from her late residence, corner of F & 19th sts.

Died: on Nov 20, suddenly, in Wash City, Anna Grace, infant daughter of John & Augusta M Robinson, aged 5 days. Her funeral is this afternoon at 3 o'clock, from her parents' residence, 98 F st south.

Died: on Nov 20, in Wash City, Mary A, 2nd daughter of Robt H & Ann Sophia Graham, aged 3 year & 3 months. Her funeral is this afternoon at 3 o'clock, from 300 Va ave, between 9th & 10th sts, Island.

Charlestown, Nov 19. The military force is augmenting. The barns, stacks in the yards, & agricultural implements, amounting to several thousand dollars, belonging to John Burns, Geo H Tate, & Mr Shirley, have been burnt. These gentlemen were jurors in the recent conspiracy trials. Hon Andrew Hunter professes to be convinced that an attempt will be made to rescue the prisoners.
+
Harper's Ferry, Nov 19. Lt John Birrell, who went as volunteer with the Mount Vernon Guards, reached this city this evening. He was informed by his Capt, W H Smith, that Mr C M Castleman had come in & reported that there had been a fight at Underwood's farm, in Clark Co, between some of the citizens & a party there. Smith Crane said he heard that a body of 500 men was organized to march for Brown's rescue. There is great excitement both at Harper's Ferry & Charlestown. The soldiers will be retained until after the execution.

TUE NOV 22, 1859
Orphans Court of Wash Co, D C-Nov 19, 1859. In the case of Chas Mades, exc of Bonaventure Schad, the executor & Court appointed Dec 10 next, for the final settlement of the personal estate of the deceased, of the assets in hand. -Ed N Roach, Reg/o wills

Four men sentenced to be hung, by Judge Yerger, on Dec 9, at the late term of the Bolivar Co [Miss] Court: Saml Moore, convicted of the murder of D C Dunbar, on a steamboat; John, a slave, property of Deeson, & Joe, property of Gowan, for the murder of Jos Cleary; Geo, property of Lafayette Jones, for poisoning.

Vernon House, Wash, D C. Aaron Gage has taken the new House, on the corner of Missouri ave & 3rd st, & will open it on Dec 1: 40 rooms completed & furnished.

Homicide in Fairfax Co, Va: Mr Wm Wesley Phillips accidentally met Mr Ayres in the road, on foot, in company with Mr Nelson Gibson. As Mr Phillips started to ride off, he turned & said to Mr Ayres, You are a damned son of a ____. Mr Ayres then followed him & struck him once over with shoulders with a small horse whip. Mr Phillips rode on saying you shall pay for this. Mr Phillips went home & armed himself with a rifle & large 6 barrelled revolver, & his son, Saml C Phillips, with a double-barrelled shot gun; & rode back to Rector Town, & found Ayres in a small shoemaker's shop. Ayres drew a small Colt's revolver; Mr W W Phillips first shot him through the heart with his rifle, & then drew his revolver. The son discharged one of his barrels into the lungs & heart of Mr Ayres. Mr Phillips & his family were raised in Ohio, & have within some 2 or 3 years settled in this country. –Fauquier Co, Va, Nov 18, 1859.
–A Disinterested Observer

Mrd: on Thu last, in St Paul's Church, Richmond, by Rev Wm H Kinckle, Mr Jas McDonald, former editor of the Lynchburg Virginian, & now associate editor of the Richmond Whig, to Mrs Carrie M Saunders, daughter of the late Lewis Ludlam, of Richmond.

Mrd: on Nov 16, by Rev Wm Hamilton, D D, Minor Bawsel & Helen Lindsay, both of Wash City.

Orphans Court of Wash Co, D C. In Re. The ptn of Alex'r Lee, Adm C T A of Hanson Barnes, deceased. Alex'r Lee, adm, reported, in pursuance of the last will & testament of said Hanson Barnes, deceased, that on Jul 27, 1859, he sold lot 18, in the subdivision made by Wm B Todd & Wm H Gunnell, of square 465, to Woodford Stone & Saml C Magruder, for $454.40, & the purchasers have since complied with the terms of sale. -Wm F Purcell, Judge of the Orphans' Court -Ed N Roach, Reg/o wills

WED NOV 23, 1859
Died: on Nov 22, in Wash City, Wm W Stuart, M D, late of Sussex Co, Delaware. His funeral will take place from the Infirmary today at 2 o'clock P M.

Died: on Nov 21, at Urbana, Md, Mr Jos Stretch, long a sufferer from epileptic fits, but who endured his suffering with patientce & Christian fortitude.

Died: on Nov 22, Philip T Ellicott, a much esteemed & well known resident of Wash City. His very numerous friends will deeply lament his loss.

Orphans Court of Wash Co, D C-Nov 22, 1859. In the case of Geo F Barrett, adm of Isaac Holland, deceased, the administrator & Court appointed Dec 17th next, for the final settlement of the personal estate of deceased, of assets in hand. -Ed N Roach, Reg/o wills

Surviving women of the Revolution [out of about 5,000 admitted] who were pensioned under the first act that was passed by Congress, viz Jul 4, 1836, for the services their husbands in the Revolutionary war. To entitle them to a pension the act required that the marriage should have taken place prior to the completion of their husbands' services in that war. It is remarkable they should be living 84 years after their marriage, & have enjoyed their country's bounty for 38 years.

State-pensioner-present age-year of marriage:
Conn: Mary, widow of Nathan Beers; 96; 1781.
Conn: Lucy, widow of Saml Davis; 94; 1782
Conn: Susannah, widow of Jos Harvey; 99, 1778
Ky: Ann, widow of Wm Davis; 92; 1780
Maine: Ann, widow of Jos Winch; 98; 1779
Mass: S Bonney, widow Clem Drake; 104; 1774
Mass: Hannah, widow of Giles Curtiss; 92, 1782
Mass: Asenath, widow of Elisha Cole; 95, 1783
N H: Amy, widow of Ebenezer Spaulding, 100; 1777
N Y: Ruth, widow of Alex'r Brush; 96; 1780
N Y: Margaret, widow of J M Charlesworth; 94; 1783
N Y: Mary, widow of Enoch Leonard; 94; 1783
N Y: Thankful, widow of Jos Enos; 95; 1780
N Y: Thankful, widow of Ephraim Miner; 97; 1781
N Y: Mary, widow of Phineas Rugg; 92; 1782
N Y: Jane, widow of Isaac Slaughter; 93; blank
N Y: Wintie, widow of J D Van Patten; 102; 1782
N J: Eliz, widow of John H Post; 100; 1780
N C: Martha, widow of Joshua Elkins; 102; 1780
N C: Ann, widow of Jas Hutchines; 99; 1781
N C: Winnifred, widow of Jacob Holly; 104; 1778
N C: Eliz, widow of Wm Lane; 98; 1781
N C: Susannah, widow of Wm West; 100; 1775
Penn: Sarah Benjamin, widow of A Osborn; 103; 1780
Penn: Eliz, widow of Robt Keller; 103; 1776
Penn: Martha, widow of John Lee: 91; sp'l act
Penn: Ruth, widow of Geo Mathiot; age blank; sp'l act
Penn: Nancy, widow of Jos Serena: age blank; sp'l act
Penn: Martha, widow of Mich Young; 103; 1776
Tenn: Sarah, widow of John Fitzpatrick; 105; 1781
Vt: Anna, widow of Abner Perry; 96; year blank
Vt: Rebecca, widow of Pierson Freeman; 93; sp'l act
Va: Sally, widow of John Goodall; 105; 1775
Va: Sally, widow of Furbush Stewart; 100; 1776
Va: Anna, widow of Wm Taylor; 102; 1780

Circuit Court of Wash Co, D C-in Chancery. Murray & Semmes vs Susannah Defalco & others. The object of this suit is to procure a discovery & sale of the real estate of which the late Pasquale Defalco, deceased, was seized or possessed at the time of his death for the payments of the debts due by said Pasquale Defalco to the cmplnts & others in his lifetime. The bill states that the said Pasquale Defalco, being indebted to the cmplnts in the sum of *$297.42, & to other persons in large sums of money, died intestate in Oct, *1856, leaving the dfndnt, Susannah Defalco, his widow, & the dfndnts, Pasquale Defalco, Geudon Defalco, & Mary Defalco, [all of whom are infants under the age of 21 years,] his children & heirs-at-law; that the said Susannah Defalco took our letters of administration upon the personal estate of the said Pasquale Defalco, deceased, & possessed herself of said personal estate, but that it was not sufficient for the payment of the aforesaid debts. The bill futher states that the said Pasquale Defalco, deceased, was at the time of his death the owner of lot 6 in square 1,113, with the appurtenances, in Wash City, & also had an equitable interest in lots 9 thru 11 & part of lot 13, in square 949, in Wash City; that in 1848, Geo B McKnight & Martha H McKnight, his wife, leased the said parcels of ground in square 949 to the decedent, Pasquale Defalco, for the term of 99 years, with the privilege of purchasing the fee-simple at any time during said term; but that the said Pasquale Defalco, designing to delay, hinder, & defraud the cmplnts & his other creditors, did not cause the said lease or leases to be recorded. Susannh Defalco, Pasquale Defalco, Geudon Defalco, & Mary Defalco, reside out of D C, & the jurisdiction of this Court. They are to appear in this Court on or before the first Monday of Apr, 1860. –Jno A Smith, clerk [*The numbers underlined are what they appear to be-the ink partially missing.]

THU NOV 24, 1859
Ex-Govn'r Gilmer, of Ga, who died a few days ago was at one time a Lt in the U S army, & took an active part in the Creek war. He had been frequently a member of the Ga Legislature, 3 times elected to Congress, & twice Govn'r. In 1855 he published a historical work called the Georgians. For 30 years he acted as a trustee of the College of Georgia.

The St Louis News tells of what happened in Illinois, opposite that city, on Monday last. Mrs Greenlief left her 2 girls, 4 & 8 years of age, locked up in the house while visiting at Illinoistown, & during her absence the wooden bldg caught fire, killing the children.

Ben F French's 10 annual sale of Books & Stationery at auction, at the store of W F Bayly, 278 Pa ave, near the Kirkwood House. –H Kempshott, agent
-Ben F French, salesman

Mrs Wilson died the other day at Wilson's Mills, Maine, at age 104. She was born a subject of George II, & was nearly 5 years old when the monarch left his earthly crown for a heavenly one. She was almost a woman when Napoleon was born, was in her 21st year when Independence was declared.

Mrd: on Nov 21, by Rev Mr O'Toole, Mr Edwin Jones to Miss Mary Ann McGowan.

Mrd: on Nov 22, in Wesley Chapel, by Rev Littleton F Morgan, Jas Emery Hibbs & Marion Frances Warder, all of Wash.

Nashville, Nov 23. Mr Eastman, senior editor of the Union & American, died this morning of apoplexy. [Mr Eastman left Wash only a few weeks ago in improved health. His numerous friends here will receive this announcement of his sudden death with surprise & regret. –Reporter]

SAT NOV 26, 1859
For rent, a furnished house, 459 12th st, between G & H sts, containing 10 rooms besides bathroom & cellar. Inquire of Dr Lester Noble, at his ofc, 278½ Pa ave, between 11th & 12th sts.

Died: on Nov 25, Miss Mary Ann Ingle, daughter of Jos Ingle, deceased, formerly of Alexandria, Va. Her funeral is on Sunday at 3 o'clock, from the residence of her brother, 455 D st, between 2nd & 3rd sts.

Died: on Nov 25, Mary Olivia Edelin, wife of T F Semmes, of Wash City, in her 52nd year. Her funeral will be tomorrow at 2:30 P M, from the residence of her husband, on H st, between 6th & 7th sts.

A handsome & valuable real property for sale, by the power contained in a trust deed, dated Nov 10, 1858, recorded among the land records of Chas Co, in Liber J H C, No 1, folio 40, from the late John H Digges to the undersigned, he will sell at public sale, on the premises, on Dec 19, the estate on which the said John H Digges lately resided, in said county, at the junction of the Wicomico & Potomac rivers; contains 500 acres of land, more or less. The house is commodious with numerous out-bldgs. Mr H Lucket, manager, will show it. –John H Mitchell

Circuit Court of Wash Co, D C-in Chancery. Thos Welsh vs Edw Semmes, adm, & the heirs of Thos Barnes, deceased. The bill in this cause states that Thos Barnes died in 1857, unmarried & intestate, indebted to the cmplnt in the sum of $575, for which he obtained judgment against the administrator of said Thos Barnes, at the May term of 1859 of said Court, on the law side thereof, & $58.38 costs. That letters of administration on the personal estate of said Thos Barnes were granted by the Orphans Court of D C. to said Edw Semmes; that said personal estate was but of little value, & totally inadequate for the payment of said debt; that said Thos Barnes died seized in fee of lot 31 in square 517, in Wash City, a sale of which is absolutely necessary for the payment of deceased debts, & that his heirs at law & next of kin are unknown to cmplnt. The object of this bill is to obtain a decree for the sale of said lot, or a sufficiency thereof, to pay the debt of deceased. Notice to unknown heirs to appear in person or by solicitor in the Court on or before the first Monday of Apr next. –Jno A Smith, clerk

MON NOV 28, 1859
Balt Patriot of Sat. Hon Z Collins Lee, Judge of the Superior Court of Balt, whose illness was noticed, died this morning.

Trustee's sale of valuable improved property, by deed of trust, dated Aug 11, 1858, recorded in Liber J A S, 159, folios 361, of the land records of Wash Co, D C: public auction on Dec 24, of part of lot 5 in square 380, as surveyed & marked for Mrs Julia Keep, by Wm Forsyth, City Surveyor, on the plat of Wash City; improved by a 2 story brick dwlg house. –H C Spalding, trustee -Jas C McGuire & Co, aucts

Circuit Court of D C-in Equity, No 1,436. Jas F Slater & Jas E Morgan against Chas Slater & Saml A Peugh, heir & administrator of Eliz Slater. Statement of the account of Eliz Slater, & of the debts due by her, & if it is necessary to sell, & what part of lot 22 in square 411, & part of lot 5 in square 346, in Wash City, of which she died seized, for the payment of her debts. Claims to be filed with me on or before Dec 20 next at my of in the City Hall. –W Redin, auditor

Circuit Court of Wash Co, D C-in Chancery, No 1,160. Henry Walker & others vs Eliz J Walker, Danl R Walker, & Elijah M Walker, & others. The bill in states that Elijah Walker died in 1852, intestate, seized of part of lot 22, in Thos Beall's of Geo addition to Gtwn, D C, leaving surviving him his widow, Eliz Walker, since dead, & his 5 children, to wit: Henry Walker, Sarah A Gaither, [formerly Sarah Walker, now a widow,] Danl Walker, Geo Walker, & Singleton Walker; that Danl Walker is dead, intestate, leaving Sarah Walker, [since intermarried with P W Morris,] & 4 children, to wit, Robt M, Eliz J, Danl R Walker, & Elijah M Walker; that the said Geo Walker hath died intestate, leaving his widow, Mary Walker, & his *7 children, to wit, Eliz, Margaret, [since intermarried with Jas Selden,] Julia, Sarah Augusta, Geo, & Redfern Walker, the last 3 of whom are minors; that the said Eliz J, Danl R, & Elijah M Walker, children of the said Danl Walker, minors at the filing of said bill, but since become of full age, are absent dfndnts, & reside in the State of N C; that the said property is of little value & not susceptible of partition in specie; that the improvements thereon are greatly out of repair, & that it would be to the benefit of all parties to have the same sold, for the purpose of division among the heirs of said Elijah Walker; & the object of the bill is for a decree of sale for the purpose of divison among the said heirs. Absent dfndnts are to appear in this court, in person or by solicitor, on or before the first Monday in Apr next. –Jno A Smith, clerk [*There are 6 children listed; could Sarah Augusta, which does not have a comma, be Sarah, Augusta? None of the others have double names.]

Miss Anne Nicholson, a daughter of Mr L Nicholson, residing in 12th st, Phil, died on Wed from the effects of 6 grains of sulphate of morphia administered by mistake for sulphate of quinine.

Oliver Wilson, convicted of the murder of Mr Krantz, has been sentenced to be hung by Judge Crain, of the Circuit Court of PG Co, Md. The Judge, grand jury, & jurors who tried the case joined in a recommendation of mercy to the Govn'r, asking a commutation of the sentence.

A T Stewart, of N Y, has made a donation of $500 to Wm & Mary College.

Senator & Mrs Douglas have so far recovered from their recent illness as to be able on Sat last to take an airing in their carriage.

Orphans Court of Wash Co, D C. Letters testamentary on the personal estate of Geo W Venable, late of Wash Co, deceased. –Catharine Venable, excx

Orphans Court of Wash Co, D C. Letters testamentary on the personal estate of Eliza H Holly, late of Wash Co, deceased. –Philip Hamilton, exc

Mrd: on Nov 26, in Trinity Church, by Rev Dr Butler, Maj E S Sibley, U S Army, to Mrs E M Churchill.

The funeral of Judge Z Collins will proceed from the cars at quarter past ten Monday morning. The hacks will leave Mrs Washington's, on 6th st, at 9¼ o'clock.

TUE NOV 29, 1859
Letter to the Sun, dated Nov 26, gives the names of the military companies then on duty at Charlestown, as follows: the Richmond Greys, 1st Lt Bossieux; Co F, Capt Carey; Va Rifles, Capt Miller; Young Guard, Capt Rady, & Richmond Howitzers. The foregoing constitute a large portion of the 1st Regt of Va volunteer. The Alexandria Riflemen, Capt Mayres; Mount Vernon Guards, Capt Smith, & the Alexandria Artl, Maj Duffey; the Morgan Continentals, Capt Washington; the Petersburg Artl, Capt Nichols; the Jefferson Guards, Capt Rowan, & Executive Guards, Capt Hunter; the Upper Fauquier Cavalry, Capt Scott; the Lower Fauquier Cavalry, Capt Ashley, & the Newtown Cavalry, Capt Drake. The entire command now under arms is but little short of 1,000 men.

Hon John J Pettus was last week inaugurated Govn'r of the State of Mississippi.

Methodist Church South: appointments for Wash District: W G Cross, P E-Wash City Station, J A Proctor; Winchester Station, E M Peterson; Alexandria Station, W C Blount; Rock Creek, J M Anderson; Fairfax, H C Cheatham; Potomac, W G Hammond; Leesburg, J H Riddick; Loudoun, R S Watts; Warrenton, W M Ward; Springfield, W F Bain; Patterson Creek, J E McSparrow; Clark, J S Reise & L H Crenshaw; Prince Wm, J S Porter; Berlin, J P Brock.

Rosewood piano forte, & household & kitchen furniture at auction on Dec 2, at 138 G st, between 21st & 22nd sts, the effects of the late W W Young. -Jas C McGuire & Co, aucts

Steamboat Express rioters arrested at Cambridge, Md, in Aug last, have all been convicted & sentenced. John Skinner to confinement in the Dorchester Co jail until Dec 2, then to imprisonment in the penitentiary till Aug 21, 1862. Jerry Donnelly, John Dorsey, & Geo Robinson, have each been sentenced to confinement in jail till Aug 21, 1860.

Rosewood piano forte, & household & kitchen furniture at auction on Dec 1, at the residence of Mrs Kirtland, at the **Carter Place**, on the Heights of Gtwn, opposite the entrance to Oak Hill Cemetery. -Jas C McGuire & Co, aucts

Mr John A Washington has sent to Mr Geo W Riggs, the treasurer of the **Ladies' Mount Vernon Association**, an order for $1,228 as his contribution to the **Mount Vernon** fund, being the proceeds of the **Mount Vernon** steamboat trips for the past year, which, though payable to Mr Washington, he has generously caused to be made over to the association.

The Cumberland Alleganian announces the demise of Meshach Browning, one of the early settlers of Alleghany Co, Md. He published a book of reminiscences of his eventful life, titled Forty-four Years of the Life of a Hunter. [No death date given-current item.]

Emmanuel Myers, of Carroll Co, Md, has been convicted in the Court of Quarter Sessions of Cumberland Co, at Carlisle, Pa, of kidnapping. Myers had gone into Pa to arrest 3 runaway slaves. He with others captured the negroes, &, without appeal to the courts under the fugitive slave law, carried them back to Md.

The wife of Lt Godfrey Weitzer, of West Point, died on Nov 24 from burns. She was married on Nov 3. On Nov 22, being alone at the time, & feeling faint & dizzy, she rose to go to her bedroom. Leaning a moment against the mantel, her skirts caught fire & she was terribly burnt.

Don Ramon Luis Irarrazaval, Minister from Chile to Peru, was shot on Oct 15 & died on Oct 25. He was only able before he died to say that 4 robbers in masks entered his residence at Chorrillos, shot him & robbed him of 1,000 doubloons, which he had received that day from Lima.

In virtue of a warrant issued by Nicholas Callan, a Justice of the Peace in & for Wash Co, D C, to me directed, reciting that whereas it has been made appear to me that the Levy Court of said county intended to open a new county road near to & along the northern line of the tract of land claimed by the heirs & reps of the late Chas J Queen, lying in said county; which part, so surveyed & laid out, extends from the eastern line of Mrs Ann McDaniel & the west end of the road left by will for the congregation of Queen's Chapel, & is part of a tract of land known as **Haddock's Hill** & enclosures. On Jan 9, 1860, a jury of 12 good men of said county, to appear on said land for the purpose of assessing the damage the owner or owners will sustain by reason of the opening of a road through said land. —W Selden, U S Marshal, for D C

Geo Nelson, one of the 3 men suspected of a purpose to break into the Penitentiary at *Greenleaf's Point* last Sat, & who were anticipated by the guard, died on Sunday in jail. He had concluded a term in the Penitentiary, & came out of it only last Tue. It is not certain by which of the guards he was killed. Verdict: the guards who shot Nelson were justified & acted in self-defence.

Marble Mantels for sale at prices that cannot fail to please. –Alex'r Rutherford, Marble Yard, Pa ave, corner of 12th st.

Mr E French, with the charges against whom for fraudulent practices in refernce to the accounts of the Treasury Extension, was yesterday surrendered by his bail & committed to jail by Capt Goddard, acting as a Magistrate.

WED NOV 30, 1859
Chancery sale of valuable property, under a decree of the Circuit Court of Wash Co, D C, in Equity, duly passed on Nov 25, 1859, in a cause pending in said court wherein Wm Higgins & Isabella Higging are cmplnts, & Fred'k Cudlip & Eliza Cudlip et al dfndnts, [No 1,532 chancery docket,] public auction on Dec 11, 1859, of part of lot 2 in square 246 in Wash City, adjoining the lot conveyed by C L Coltman to M E Gray, by deed recorded in Liber W B, No 120, folio 240, with the improvements thereon.

St John's, [N B] Nov 27. The steamer **Indian**, Capt Smith, of the Canadian line, left Liverpool on Nov 9 for Portland, Me, & was totally wrecked on Nov 21 at Marie Joseph, a fishing village, about 70 miles from Halifax. The passengers were mostly of the laboring class, many of them Germans & Hungarians. Cabin passengers saved: Hon Mr Botsford, Mr Meldrum, Mrs Meldrun, Mr Patterson, Mrs Patterson, Mrs Street, Mr Street, & Mr Elliott. Steerage passengers saved: A G Howland, Irving Kulstar, wife & 4 children, Wm Eickmann, Richd Brown, G Croman, Wm Cross, Jos Mann, Anton Borgresson, Wm Masin, & Mr Pierson. Drowned: Lewis J Moses, wife & 2 children, Mrs Eickmann & child, Alex'r Deane, Jas Dixon, Thos Chanonhouse, Wm Johnston, & Thos M Cleveland. Crew lost: Jas Lang, the joiner; John Herron, Henry Carroll, seamen; W Ross, 3rd engineer; Robt Ritchie, 4th engineer; John Milland, fireman; Jas Standwell, steward; & Thos L Loud, chief cook.

Two deaths from burning fluid: Mrs Merritt, of Dutchess Co, N Y, was burnt to death on Wed last from the explosion of a fluid lamp. On the same day a young girl named Mohan, of Hudson, Columbia Co, N Y, died on the following day by the same cause.

Orphans Court of Wash Co, D C. In the case of Caleb Dulaney, adm of Adam Dulaney, the administrator & Court have appointed Dec 24 next, for the final settlement of the personal estate of said deceased, of the assets in hand. -Ed N Roach, Reg/o wills

Mrd: on Nov 25, in Chicago, Ill, at the residence of the bride's father, by Rev Dr Clarkson, of St James Church, Lambert Tree, of Chicago, to Miss Anna J Magie, daughter of H H Magie.

Obit-died: on Nov 29, in Wash City, Professor Wm W Turner, Librarian of the U S Patent Ofc, aged 45 years. He was a loving husband, a devoted brother, a faithful friend, & a useful citizen. Mr Turner was a native of England, & having settled in N Y, he became connected with the Union Theological Seminary in that city. [Dec 5th newspaper: Prof Turner was born in London in 1810, his father an Englishman of moderate fortune, which being in some way lost, caused his emigration to America about the time this subject was 5 years old.]

N Y, Nov 29. The announcement of the death of Washington Irving, the eminent American writer, will carry a feeling of sadness to the hearts of thousands abroad as well as at home. He breathed his last at *Irvington*, his country residence, last evening.

THU DEC 1, 1859
The Utah mail has arrived at St Louis with dates to Nov 3. They contain accounts of the execution of Thos H Ferguson, for the murder of Alex'r Ferguson, being the first judicial execution that has ever taken place in the Territory.

Washington Irving died at his residence on the Hudson; by a peaceful & painless death; unwell for several months past. Sunny Side, Nov 29. He retired to his room complaining of pain in his side. Just as he reached his room, & while his niece was near him, he suddenly fell, & in a moment was gone. A physician was soon with him, but no mortal aid could avail to bring him back. Mr Irving was born in this city on Apr 13, 1783; at 16 began the study of law, but he was even then a dabbler in literature. To the Morning Chronicle, of which his brother, Peter Irving, was editor, he contributed a series of papers under the signature of Jonathan Oldstyle. In 1804, in consequence of ill health, he made his first trip to Europe where he resided for 2 years, journeying through the south of France to Italy. When he returned he took part in a series of whimsical papers under the name of Salmagundi. His coadjutors were Jas K Paulding, & a brother, we believe, Wm Irving. This serial continued during the whole of 1807. –N Y Post

On Nov 9th the Prince of Wales attained his 18th year, & in the event of a demise of the Crown would rule in his right as Albert the First.

A quack doctor's career ended. Dr W H M Howard, of Bradford, Vt, who has so long managed to elude justice, met his reward, he having been sentencd to 2 years in the State prison at Windsor on Sat last. His real name is Drew. While at Bradford he attended a man who died, & whose widow he married, taking possession of all her property which he got hold of. She died last summer, broken-hearted. –Boston Traveller

Charlestown, Nov 23, 1859. As the day fixed for the execution of John Brown approaches the excitement grows; the morning train from Winchester brought down the Valley Guards, Capt Gibbons, 82 men, from Harrisonburg, Va. Amongst the members of the company were John D Pennybacker, State Senator, & Lt Saml T Walker, member elect to the Va House of Delegates. The evening train of cars brought the Portsmouth Nat'l Greys, 61; Woodis Riflemen, 68; West Augusta Guards, 60; Monticello Guards, 60; & Mountain Guards, 45. About 100 troops from Norfolk at Harper's Ferry to be brought up today. No less than 2,000 troops by Friday. [Part of the proclamation issued by the ofcrs in command:] Instructions from the Govn'r of Va. From now until Dec 2, strangers found within Jefferson Co & counties adjacent, having no known proper business here, & no satisfactory account of themselves, will be at once arrested. No women or children will be allowed to come near the place of execution. –Wm B Taliaferro, Maj Gen Com Troops; S Bassett French, Military Sec; Thos C Green, Major; Andrew Hunter, Assist Pros Atty; Jas W Campbell, Sheriff. Nov 28, 1859. At the reading of the general orders yesterday Col L W Washington, of Jefferson, & Col W H Browne, of Stafford, were appointed aids to Gen Taliaferro. There are now more staff ofcrs here than participated in the battle of Buena Vista.

Mr Allen Page, of Conecuh Co, Ala, was murdered a few days since for considerable money about him, & the thirst for gold. The murderers were 2 brothers named Ward, who confessed the deed, & who were hung by the people without judge or jury.

Mr Richd T Waters, of Snow Hill, Md, & his son Thos, met with very serious injuries on Sat of last week, from the premature discharge of a gun. Both were disabled by their wounds.

On Sat as the express train was passing North Bridgewater, Mass, Mrs Barrett, about 60 years old, thinking her grandchild in danger, rushed towards the train, & in attempting to cross the track, was struck by the engine & instantly killed.

Orphans Court of Wash Co, D C. Letters of administration on the personal estate of Geo P Todson, late of Wash Co, deceased. –Richd Smith, adm

Died: on Nov 20, at Norfolk, Va, Newton Calvert King, in his 47th year.

Died: on Nov 29, in Wash City, Prof Wm W Turner, Librarian of the U S Patent Ofc, aged 45 years. His funeral is today at 2 o'clock from his late residence on South B St.

From Europe. Earl de Grey is dead. He was 78 years old. In the administration of Sir Robt Peel he held high offices. [No death date given-current news item.] [Dec 3rd newspaper: The Earl Grey, whose death was reported a day or two ago, was the son of an eminent British statesman. He was early known as Lord Howick. In 1841 he succeeded his father in the House of Peers. His age was 57 years.]

Information wanted by the undersigned of his brother, Henry O'Neill, a native of Wash City, who, if living, is now aged about 30 years. When last heard from he was engineer on board of a steamer running between Panama & San Francisco. By the death of a brother, Hugh O'Neill, in Columbus, Ohio, in 1856, a small sum of money is coming to us as his surviving brothers & heirs. Any information touching his present residence or fate will be thankfully received if addressed to me or the Probate Clerk, Columbus, Ohio -Jas O'Neill, Wash City, Nov 30, 1859.

FRI DEC 2, 1859
A golden wedding party was held at Easton, Mass, on Nov 16, the occasion was the 83rd birthday of Moses C Dunbar, & the 59th anniversary of his wedding day. His 2 sons, with their wives, sons & daughters, & so on in the line of relationship to great great grandsons & daughters, to the number of about 60, surprised the aged couple by approaching their dwelling, which is several miles from any depot, in companies of about 10 each, from different directions & at different periods of time, each group loaded with good things. A grand merry-making was had, to the great enjoyment of all.

On Friday last the wife of Patrick Fahay, residing in Greenfield, Mass, locked her 3 little daughters in while she went to the village to make some purchases. On her return, in less than an hour, she found the house on fire, & 3 children burnt to death.

Mrd: on Nov 29, by Rev Mr Ball, Mr Julius Keck to Miss Mary Miranda Godfrey, all of Wash City.

Died: on Nov 30, Rufus Dawes, in his 57th year. His funeral is today at 2 o'clock, from his late residence, D st south & 2nd st east. [Dec 3rd newspaper: Mr Dawes has for many years worthily held a high place among the poets of America. Mr Dawes was a member by ties of blood & marriage of the family of the late lamented Judge Cranch, & died at the family residence in Wash City.]

Died: on Nov 30, after a brief illness, Michl Buckey, in his 77th year. He died in the triumphs of the Christian faith. His funeral will be this morning at 10 o'clock, from the residence of his son, M V Buckey, on Bridge st, Gtwn.

Died: on Dec 1, in Wash, at the residence of her son-in-law, R D Cutts, Harriet Hackley, aged 76 years, widow of the late Col R S Hackley, of Richmond, Va. Her funeral will be from the Church of the Epiphany this afternoon at 3½ o'clock.

Louisiana improved land for sale: I will offer my plantation at public sale on Jan 3 next; it is in the island of False River, parish of Pointe Coupee; the land has 600 acres, more or less, with a new & well built dwlg house, & other out-bldgs. The slaves, stock, cattle, & other movables will be sold the same day. –J F Lapice, Waterloo, P O

Milledgeville, Nov 29. Choice, the murderer of Webb, was pardoned today by the Legislature, but the Govn'r vetoed the bill.

SAT DEC 3, 1859
A young gentleman by the name of McCrabb, formerly of Wash, but more recently of Columbus, Ga, was shot & killed by some unknown person on the corner of Market & Perry sts lat night. No one has been arrested. –Montg [Ala] Adv of Nov 18.
+
The deceased was the son of the late Capt J W McCrabb, of the U S Army, a mere youth at the time of his murder, not being 21 years of age. All efforts to discover his assassin have as yet proved unsuccessful.

Seaborn Williams, of Tuskegee, Ala, for many years a member of the Legislature from Macon Co, was killed near Rome, Talapoosa Co, on Nov 27th. His horse had become frightened & threw him. He died in a few hours.

Mrd: on Nov 29, in Alexandria, Va, by Rev John L Pascoe, Mr Wm E Grubb, of Phil, to Miss Mary R Pascoe, of the former city.

Mrd: on Nov 9, by Rev Chas H Stonestreet, Nicholas Stonestreet to Miss Amelia D Thompson, daughter of Col Francis Thompson, all of Chas Co, Md.

Mrd: on Nov 30, at Trenton, N J, by Rev John Hall, D D, Louis Watkins, of Wash City, to Emily H, youngest daughter of Saml Evans, of the former city.

Letter to John Brown. Shattangoga, Tenn, Nov 20, 1859. Sir: Although vengeance is not mine, I confess that I do feel grateful to hear that you were stopped in your fiendish career at Harper's Ferry. With the loss of your two sons you can now appreciate the distress in Kansas when you, then & there, entered my house at midnight & arrested my husband & 2 boys, & took them out of the yard & in cold blood shot them dead in my hearing. You can't say you did it to free our slaves. We had none & never expected to own one. It has only made me a poor disconsolate widow, with helpless children. While I feel for your folly, I do hope & trust that you will meet your just reward. Oh! how it pained my heart to hear the dying groans of my husband & children. If this scrawl gives you any consolation you are welcome to it. –Mahaly Doyle
N B: My son, John Doyle, whose life I begged of you is now grown up, & is very desirous to be in Charlestown on the day of your execution, & would certainly be there if his means would permit it.

Charlestown, Va, Dec 1. By permission of the State authorities the wife of John Brown arrived here this afternoon in a carriage from **Harper's Ferry**, escorted by mounted troops. The interview of the husband & wife took place in presence of the sheriff. An embrace, a kiss, but no tear was shed. She will await the reception of the body of her husband tomorrow.

Charlestown, Va, Dec 2. Capt John Brown was hung at 11:15 o'clock; brought out of the jail accompanied by Sheriff Campbell & his assistants & Capt Avis, the jailer; he was not accompanied by any minister, desiring to hav no religious ceremonies either in the jail or on the scaffold; at 11:30 the trap was pulled away, & with a few slight struggles John Brown yielded up his life. His body was placed in the coffin as soon as life was extinct, & is now on its way to Harper's Ferry, to be delivered to his wife, accompanied by a strong military escort.

MON DEC 5, 1859

Died: on Dec 3, suddenly, of hemorrhage of the bowels, George C, son of C & Sarah P Woodward, aged 26 years, 4 months & 2 days. His funeral will be from the residence of his father, 443 11th st, between G & H, on Dec 5 at 2 o'clock.

Died: on Nov 20, at Alexandria, Va, Lydia Syphax, wife of the late Wm Syphax, in her 99th year. She originally belonged to the **Mount Vernon** estate, but had resided at Alexandria for the last 60 years. Her life was one of unsullied honor & Christian purity, & she died in full & honored membership of the Methodist Episcopal Church.

St Louis, Dec 3. Overland mail arrived with San Francisco dates to Nov 11th. Jas Jamison, the deputy clerk of Sacramento, absconded on the steamer of the 5th ult, being a defaulter in the sum of $30,000.

The funeral of Washington Irving took place at Tarrytown, N Y, on Thu. Business was suspended in the town & the stores were closed. The bells of the churches tolled for some hours. A procession, more than a mile in length, followed the remains of the deceased to the grave. Most of the distinguished men of the city were nearly all the Episcopal clergy.

TUE DEC 6, 1859
Criminal Court-Wash: Grand Jury:

Geo W Riggs
Thos H Parsons
Jos Bryan, of Ala
Wm F Bayly
Wm G Freeman
Geo Parker
Jas C McGuire
Aaron W Miller
Thos Lumpkin
Jonathan T Walker
Robt Beale
Jos C Willard
Judson Mitchell
Saml Cropley
Jacob Gideon
Esau Pickrell
Richd Wallach
Jos Bryan
Jehiel Brooks
Thos Blagden
Saml Pumphrey
Hamilton Loughborough
Jas Towles
Allen P Dodge

List of the Petit Jury:

John W Martin	Valentine Connor
Fred'k A Klopfer	Leoanrd Harbaugh
Edw Tolson	John W Easby
Wm H Perkins	Geo R Hall
Robt Wright	Edmund Barry
John McCullom	John R Minor
Jonathan Schafer	Edw L Harbaugh
Wm M Belt	Abner C P Shoemaker
Anthony Addison	Michl Green
Columbus Alexander	John W Shiles
Geo W Stroud	Edmund G Duley
John G Robinson	Michl Nash
Jos C Reynolds	Jas L Davis
Thos Lewis	John W Burns
Jos Follansbee	Edw Krouse

Criminal Court-Wash-Mon. Edw Miller was found guilty for renting a house for disorderly purposes.

Mrd: in Wash City, at St Matthew's Church, by Rev Fr White, D D, John T Fenwick, of Wash City, to Louisa Sterrett, eldest daughter of R M Carter, late of New Orleans. [No marriage date given-current item.]

Columbia, S C, Dec 5. Edmund Bellinger, an eminent lawyer, died in this city on Saturday last.

WED DEC 7, 1859
Mrs W Hazlewood, of Franklinton, N C, was shot dead a few days ago by the accidental discharge of a gun in the hands of her husband.

Criminal Court-Wash-Tue. 1-U S against Thos O'Donnell, charged with a violent assault against ofcr Benj Suit, committed in the ofc of Justice Henry G Murray, at the Navy Yard-the jury found him guilty.

The proprietors of the New Orleans Crescent in Jul, 1857, refused to pay a tax of $75 on property invested in their newspaper establishment, on the ground that it was exempt from taxation under the article 106 of the State constitution, the first clause of which reads, "the press shall be free." Supreme Court: the dfndnts should pay one per cent a month interest as damages to the aggrieved city, from the time of the refusal to pay the tax.

THU DEC 8, 1859
Died: Dec 5, in Phil, Mary, daughter of Dr Richd H Stuart, of King Geo Co, Va, in her 20th year.

Richmond, Va, Nov 26, 1859. To Mrs Mary A Brown, now in Phil. Enclosed is an order to Maj Gen Wm R Taliaferro, in command at Charlestown, Va, to deliver to your order the mortal remains of your husband, when all shall be over, to be delivered to your agent at Harper's Ferry, & if you attend the reception in person, to guard you sacredly in your solemn mission. With tenderness & truth, I am, very respectfully your humble servant. -Henry A Wise

Yesterday at the bar of the Golden Age coffee house, among whom were Wm H Evington, a police ofcr, & W G Coupland, an ex-policeman. The latter drew forth his revolver & gave it to Evington, telling him only one chamber was loaded, & told him to aim & fire. Coupeland was shot through his heart, & instantly died. It would seem that Coupland had deliberately planned his own death. -New Orleans Bee, Dec 1.

Clement Marsh, a son of Jos W Marsh, of Greenland, N H, has expended $10,000 in paying the debts of his father, who died 15 years ago. This is a shining example of filial respect: the Portsmouth Journal.

Asa A Gore, of Preston, Conn, died in that town on Dec 1, at age 81 years & 5 months. He was the last survivor of the Wyoming massacre, having been carried away, when a child, in his mother's arms. His father & all his relations but his mother were killed.

No Ex-Pres has ever lived in more studied retirement than Martin Van Buren. He is seldom away from his home, & never seems to covet attentions of any kind. On Dec 5 he passed his 77th year. He is said to be writing a memoir of his times.
-Albany Journal

Gov Hicks appointed Arthur W Machen to the Judgeship of the Superior Court of Balt, made vacant by the death of Judge Lee. That gentleman declined to accept, & the appointment has been tendered by the Govn'r to Hon Robt N Martin.

Criminal Court-Wash-Wed. 1-Deborah Wise guilty of petty larceny for stealing carpeting & bed clothes. Motion for a new trial was entered by her counsel, Mr Swann. 2-Geo Word, Stanislaus Taylor, & Geo T Langley were found guilty for assault & battery: sentenced to pay $6 each & costs. 3-Mr Innes Jas Randolph was, on motion, admitted to practice at the bar of this Court.

The <u>Convalescent</u> is the title of a painting on exhibition at Messrs Galt's jewelry store, on Pa ave. It is by Mr Turner, a young & promising artist of Va birth, & was painted at Dusseldorf, whence it has just arrived. The subject of it is the Chevalier Bayard, during his recovery from wounds received at the siege of Brescia, in Italy, when he was so fortunate as to have for attendants two lovely daughters of his noble host. In his drapery Mr Turner is particularly successful, & he manages his lights & shades with good effect.

Obit: The Florence [Tuscany] correspondent of the Newark Daily Advertiser, under date of Nov 6, 1859: Mr Wm Henry Beck, of Phil, died rather suddenly, after a brief illness, on Tue, in his 36th year. The funeral solemnities were performed on Thu by Rev Mr O'Neill, Chaplain of the British Legation, & he was interred in the rural Protestant Cemetery, situated in the immediate vicinity of the city. He leaves a little son of 9 years & a widow, who is just now on a visit at her father's house, Hon Richd H Bayard, of Phil.

FRI DEC 9, 1859
Senate: 1-Ptn from Thos Brown, asking payment of a balance claimed to be due him as Sec of the Senate of Fla when a Territory. 2-Ptn from Lt David Porter, U S Navy, asking that his accounts for certain secret services performed in the Island of St Domingo in 1846, by order of Sec Bancroft, may be settled upon principles of equity & justice..

The Duke of Cambridge, Cmder-in-Chief of the British army, has just issued an order which is virtually an abolition of the punishment of flogging heretofore much practiced in the service.

Criminal Court-Wash-Thu. 1-Otho T Vermilion convicted in two cases for assault & battery on Danl Whalen & Francis Edelin: sentenced to 4 months' imprisonment in the county jail & pay $15 costs. 2-John Stahl, Jacob Feig, & Antoine Daum were several tried on charges of larceny & acquitted.

Mrd: on Dec 7, at the First Baptist Church, 13th st, by Rev S P Hill, D D, Augustus H Martin, of King & Queen Co, Va, to Miss Kate J, daughter of Dr R J Powell, of Wash City.

Died: on Nov 17, in Montg, Ala, Alfred P McCrabb, son of the late Capt John W McCrabb, of the U S Army, in his 21st year. His remains were interred in the **Congressional Burial Ground** on Dec 7.

Died: on Dec 8, in Brooklyn, N Y, Frances Rebecca, wife of P H Sims, aged 24 years.

SAT DEC 10, 1859
Maj B B French, of Washington, is not the Maj French mentioned in the public papers as a defaulter. The name of the person alluded to is Edmund French; & it is further proper to say, to prevent another error, that it is not Edmund F French, of the Treasury Dept.

Francis Daniels was found dead yesterday by his bedside in a wretched habitation on Wash st. He had been long living a very dissipated life, had probably fallen from the bed in a fit, & died from exposure to the cold. He was aged 58 years.

Mrd: on Dec 7, in Raleigh, N C, by Rev Dr Mason, Mr S Griffith Davis, of Harford Co, Md, to Miss Annie E G Hollister, of that city.

Norfolk, Dec 9. Virginius, a promising son of A F Leonard, editor of the Argus, aged 11 years, was found murderd this evening in a room at the Nat'l Hotel. A deep stab had been inflicted in his neck. There is great excitement among the citizens in consequence of this horrid deed. No arrest has been made.

Rockbridge, Mass, Dec 9. Theodore Sedgwick, District Atty of the U S for the southern district of N Y, died here last night.

N Y, Dec 9. Mrs Wood, wife of Hon Fernando Wood, Mayor elect of N Y, died here this morning.

Circuit Court of D C-in Equity, No 1,531. Marshall Brown against Jesse B Haw, adm & heir of John S Haw. The creditors of the late John S Haw, are to appear at my ofc in the City Hall, Wash, this afternoon, for statement of the account of the respective claims of the cmplnt & said John S Haw. -W Redin, auditor

MON DEC 12, 1859
Mr John Maupin, brother of the editor of the Berkeley American, & formerly editor of the Cumberland Civilian, died in Moorefield on Dec 5. He was accidentally shot on Nov 25 by his brother, editor of the Hardy Whig, & his death was the result of that accident.

John Barry, the Catholic Bishop of the Diocese of Georgia, died at Paris. Dr Barry was born in Parish Olgate, Wexford Co, Ireland, in Jul, 1799, & emigrated to the U S about 1822. He was ordained to the priesthood in 1825, & consecrated as Bishop of the Diocese of Ga in Aug, 1857. –Augusta Constitutionalist [No death date given-current item.]

Orphans Court of Wash Co, D C. Letters of administration, with the will annexed, on the personal estate of Jas Connor, late of Wash Co, deceased. –Denis Connor, adm, w a

Criminal Court-Wash-Fri. 1-Thos Keenan was convicted of stealing clothing: sentenced to 4 months in jail & fined $5. 2-Moses Lowenstein was found guilty of keeping a disorderly house. 3-Edw Bresnehan, for assault & battery on a watchman, was sent to jail for 2 months. 4-Allison Naylor was put to trial for renting a house for disorderly purposes. 5-Deborah Wise was sentenced to 4 months in jail, her counsel having withdrawn his motion for a new trial.

Died: on Sat, of consumption, Mrs Cathrian Worthen, wife of Chas Worthen, in her 38th year. Her funeral is this morning at 9 o'clock, from her late residence on 10th st, between N & O sts.

Died: on Dec 8, in Wash City, Miss Mary Brashears, aged about 72 years. Her illness was severe & protracted. –J O W

Died: on Nov 10, at Dayton, Ohio, Horatio G Phillips, aged 76 years.

Norfolk, Dec 9. A F Leonard, a promising son of Va, & for the last 11 years editor of the Southern Argus, was found murdered in a room at the Nat'l Hotel this evening, with a deep stab in his neck. No arrest has been made. [Dec 13th newspaper: we learn that a loaded gun had been left in the room, which he got hold of & accidentally discharged, the whole load entering his neck.]

TUE DEC 13, 1859
Senate: 1-Ptn from Raymond Reynolds, a citizen of Wisc & soldier of the war of 1812, asking a pension.

Circuit Court of D C-in Chanery, No 1,514. Antonio Fegaro against Wm & Mary E McGinnis & Edw, Wm A, & Robt Stewart, adms, & heirs of Wm E Stewart. I am directed to ascertain & report whether the debts of the cmplnt & of Middleton & Beall are just; whether the deceased, Wm E Stewart, left any personal estate applicable to said debts, & how much; what real estate was left by him, & of what value, & whether it will be necessary to sell any part thereof for the payment of said debts. Notice is given to the above parties & to Wm H McGinnis, the guardian ad litem of the minor dfndnts, to attend at my ofc on Jan 17 next, City Hall, Wash. –W Redin, auditor

Circuit Court of D C-in Chancery, No 1,227. John R Wood et al vs Richd G Briscoe's heirs & Jos S Clarke et al. Wm R Woodward, trustee, reported that at the sale made by him, T M Johnson & R M Sutton became the purchasers of part of lot 11 in square, with two brick bldgs thereon, at the price of $5,100; Allison Nailor of the north 39 feet of lot 14 in square 255, for $805; & Wm Redin of the east half of lot 2 in square 643, for $1,137.50; & the purchasers have complied with the terms of the sale.
–John A Smith, clerk

Circuit Court of D C-in Equity, No 1,541. Geo Parker, Thos Parker, & Jos B Bryan against John Niel, Barbara Niel, & Sophia M, Henry, Lewis, Jos, & Georgia Kleindienst, widow & heirs of John P Kliendienst. Statement of the account of said John P Kliendienst on Jan 17 next, at my ofc, in the City Hall, Wash. –W Redin, auditor

The second son of Govn'r Lethcer, an interesting youth of 10 years, died of lockjaw on Dec 5, at his father residence in Lexington. –Richmond Enquirer

Harper's Ferry Convicts. Friday next, Dec 16, is the day appointed for the execution of the other insurgents associated with Brown, & convicted at Charlestown, Va. Gov Wise is assembling another strong military force. The Wythe Grays, from Wytheville, Va, have arrived at Charlestown. This is a new company, & have traveled 600 miles from their homes. The Fincastle Rifles have arrived at Charlestown. The Chesterfield [Va] Guards, Capt Cox, left for Charlestown yesterday morning.

John Brown's funeral took place on Thu last at North Elba, NY. Short addresses were made by Wendell Phillips, of Boston, & J M McKim, or Phil.

WED DEC 14, 1859
Senate: 1-Ptn from Wm Brenton Boggs, a purser in the navy, asking to be allowed additional pay during the time he was attached to the expedition for the exploration & survey of the China seas & Behring's straits. 2-Ptn from Allen Gaylord & other citizens of N C, asking that land may be granted to the heirs of those who served in the Indian wars & in that of 1812 with Great Britian.

On Friday week near Buckland, Prince Wm Co, a young man, Enos Coram, was found dead on the ground. It is thought that his gun accidently discharged.

Criminal Court-Wash-Tue. 1-Thos E Kirkley guilty of perjury in having induced a youth named Peters to testify falsely on a trial in which Kirkley was dfndnt, for cruel usage to a negro. Mr Norris entered a motion for arrest of judgment. 2-Jos B Stewart charged with assault & battery on John Fill & his son John C Fill, on Feb 7 last. The cmplnts had gone to collect a debt, & not getting paid the elder made some remarks which exasperated the dfndnt, & induced his striking him. The son went to his father's assistance, & was also struck. Jury returned a verdict of guilty as indicted as respected Mr Fill, sr, but not guilty as respected his son. 3-Danl Barry & Hugh Reagan, both connected with the Soldiers' Home, were arraigned for the highway robbery of an old infirm old soldier, Francis Carver, much afflicted wth palsy, belonging to the Soldiers' Home, on Sep 13 last. [Dec 17th newspaper: Barry & Reagan found not guilty.]

Mrd: on Tue, in the Fourth Presbyterian Church, by Rev John C Smith, Geo C Patterson to Miss Julia B Belt, both of Montg Co, Md.

Died: on Nov 12, at Lancaster, Mass, Mrs Abby Shaler Stillwell, aged 72, only sister of the late Wm Shaler, former Consul-Gen at Algiers, & of Capt Nathl Shaler, the brave privateer cmder in the war of 1812-15.

Orphans Court of Wash Co, D C. Letters of administration on the personal estate of David C Broderick, late of Calif, deceased. –Geo Wilkes, adm

Orphans Court of Wash Co, D C. Letters of administration on the personal estate of Eliz Ford, late of Wash Co, deceased. –Asbury Lloyd, adm

THU DEC 15, 1859
Household & kitchen furniture at auction on Dec 20, at the residence of T F Semmes, 531 H st, between 6th & 7th sts. -A Green auct

About 1,500 bottles of choice old wines, belonging to the estate of the late A de Bodisco, Russian Minister, at Public Auction on Dec 22, in the large room in the 2nd story of Sibley & Guy's bldg. —Brooke B Williams, adm -Jas C McGuire & Co, aucts

Trustee's sale of very valuable real estate on K st, opposite Franklin Square; by decree of the Circuit Court of D C, passed in a cause in which John W Thompson & others are cmplnts, & Margaret E Lindsay & others are dfndnts, the undersigned will sell at public auction, on Jan 6, 1860, lot 7 & part of lot 8 in square 248 in Wash City, with a 2 story brick dwlg-house. –C Ingle, trustee -Jas C McGuire & Co, aucts

Trustee's sale of valuable improved real estate on D st, between 13th & 14th sts west, by decree of the Circuit Court of D C, passed in a cause in which Otis J Preston & David G Day are cmplnts & Martha Winter & others are dfndnts: public auction on Feb 23, 1850, of the west half of lot 2 in square 256 in Wash City, fronting on D st south, between 13 & 13½ sts; with a two story frame dwlg house with back bldg. -C Ingle, trustee -Jas C McGuire & Co, aucts

Trustee's sale of valuable improved real estate, by decree of the Circuit Court of D C, passed in a cause in which Otis J Preston & others ar cmplnts & Thos Welch is dfndnt: public auction on Jan 19, 1860, of the west part of lot 29 in square 517, in Wash City, fronting 24 feet on Mass ave, with a frame dwlg house thereon. –C Ingle, trustee -Jas C McGuire & Co, aucts

Trustee's sale of improved real estate in Wash City, by decree of the Circuit Court of D C, passed in a cause in which Eliza J Burke & others are cmplnts & Walter L Burke & Eliza L Burke, the younger, are dfndnts: public auction, on Jan 9, 1860, of the south part of lot 3 in square 11, in Wash City, fronting on 26th st; with a frame dwlg house. –C Ingle, trustee -Jas C McGuire & Co, aucts

On Sat week, as John Warner & Saml Kessler were gunning in the vicinity of the White Horse tavern, Berks Co, Pa, the former was shot & killed by the accidental discharge of Kessler's gun.

The Rome Sentinel has an account of the burning of the dwlg-house of David H Green, near Constableville, Lewis Co. Two boys, sons of Mr Green, aged 11 & 9 years, perished in the flames.

In Nantucket, Mass, on Dec 4, Mr Geo H Coleman, about 25 years of age, son of Capt Eben Coleman, had a pair of pistols he was cleaning. His sister retired for a few minutes, & during her absence, heard the report of a pistol. She found her brother shot through the heart. It is presumed that his death was the result of accident.

Died: on Dec 13, Willie T Ford, eldest child of Jas H & Sarah J Ford, in his 8th year. His funeral is this afternoon at 2 o'clock, from the residence of his grandfather, John N Ford, corner of Va ave & 11th st.

The Forrest divorce case has been finally determined by the courts of N Y. Mrs Forrest shall receive $4,000 a year as alimony from Mr Forrest, from Nov 19, 1850, & that Mr Forrest shall place the mortgage on his *Fonthill* property in the hands of the U S Trust Co as security for the payment of the allowance.

Died: on Dec 14, Charlotte Essellerugge, daughter of the late Herman & Louise, Essellerugge, in her 17th year. Her funeral will take place this afternoon at 2 o'clock, from the residence of her uncle, C H Munck, 478 9th st.

Trustee's sale of real estate, by deed of trust, dated Oct 7, 1857, recorded in Liber C S M, No 2, folio 64, of the land records of PG Co, Md: public auction on Mar 15, 1860, of parts of tracts of land, [except that part sold by Judson C Pumphrey to Mary Allen, lying on the south side of Alexandria road, supposed to contain 5 acres, more or less,] called *Poor Man's Industry*, *Edmond's Frolick*, *Slip*, & *Pumphrey's Little Addition*, containing altogether 130 acres more or less, in fee simple, being the property conveyed by the said John S James & his wife, C A James, by deed bearing even date herewith, to the said Horatio N Gilbert. –Horatio N Gilbert, trustee

$600 reward for 3 runaway negro men: Sandy Green, 24; Wm Brent, 21; & Daniel, 20. -Wm J Berry, living near Upper Marlboro, PG Co, Md.

FRI DEC 16, 1859
Senate: 1-Ptn from Lt S R Franklin, of the navy, asking to be allowed the difference between his pay & that of purser for the time he performed said duties on board the U S ship **Falmouth**. 2-Ptn from Chas F Anderson, asking remuneration for his plan of the Capitol. 3-Ptn from J H Wheeler & others, asking construction of a passenger railway from the navy yard to Gtwn. 4-Ptn from Richd Young & others, asking the incorporation of the Wash & Gtwn railway company. Also, from J L Williams & others, to the like effect. 5-Additional papers in relation to the invention of Jno Sample for the protection of tiller ropes from fire.

Rev Dr P D Gurley, of Wash City, was elected Chaplain of the Senate during the present session.

In Executive session on Wed the Senate confirmed Amasa J Parker as U S District Atty for the southern district of N Y, vice Theodore Sedgwick, deceased. Also, John Heart as Superintendent of Public Printing, vice G W Bowman, resigned. –States.

A fire broke out in the city of Wmsburg, Va, on Sat night, Dec 10th, which consumed the old Raleigh tavern. It is the place where Richd Henry Lee & others met; & famous as the place where Patrick Henry stopped when he made his debut in the House of Burgesses.

Chancery sale, by decree of the Circuit Court of Wash Co, D C, made in the cause of Patrick Sweeny & al vs Robt A Hawke, No, 1,557, equity: auction on Jan 10 next, of part of lot 2 in square 424; & all of lot 3 in square 556. –Walter S Coxe, trustee
-Jas C McGuire & Co, aucts

Rev Saml L Southard died in Missouri on Nov 24. He was for many years the pastor of Calvary Church, in N Y. He was the son of Hon Saml L Southard, who filled several terms as U S Senator from N J, & afterwards acted as Sec of the Navy under John Quincy Adams.

A sister-in-law of Mr Laight, who resides near Sing-Sing, lost her life on Friday when her clothes took fire from the grate.

Tribute: Horaitio Gates Phillips died in Dayton on Dec 10, aged 76 years. He was born in N J on Dec 21, 1783, the son of Capt Jonathan Phillips, of the regular army of the American Revolution, who entered the service as a lt, commissioned by John Hancock, Pres of Congress, in 1775. As captain he participated in the capture of Burgoyne at Saratoga, Oct 17, 1777, & served with distinction throughout the war. The deceased has descended from one of the best stocks of the Revolution. Mr Phillips settled at Dayton in 1805, & was among the earliest merchants located in the town. To his children & grandchildren his loss is irreparable. To his noble daughters, Mrs Worthington & Mrs Lowe, the full meed of merit is due for their nursing, care, & labors, by night & day, at the couch of their devoted father. He was in age, my junior by 8 years. His funeral was last Sat, & his remains were interred in ***Woodland Cemetery***. –John Johnston, near Dayton, Nov 18, 1859.

$5 reward for return of a setter dog, Taylor, stolen on Nov 10. –John Bonini, Navy Yard

In Chancery, No 1,350. Smith Pettit vs Anne G V McKinstry, Wm B Webb, Calisca, Ann & Wm McKinstry. Wm B Webb, trustee, sold lots 6 thru 8 in square 260, to Wm M Ellis & Jonas B Ellis, of Wash City, for $19,000, & the purchasers have complied with the terms of sale. –Jno A Smith, clerk

Circuit Court of D C-in Equity. Agnes M Easby vs Horatio N & John W Easby, Henry King et al. Wm B Webb, Richd H Clarke, & Jos H Bradley, trustees, sold lots 4 & 26 in square 5 to John Marbury for $164.75. –Jno A Smith, clerk

Orphans Court of Wash Co, D C. Letters of administration, with the will annexed, on the personal estate of Thos G Clinton, late of Wash Co, deceased.
–John Carroll Brent, adm, w a

Orphans Court of Wash Co, D C. Letters of administration on the personal estate of Jas Barnes, late of Wash Co, deceased. –Martha E Barnes, admx

Mrd: on Dec 15, in Wash City, by Rev P D Gurley, Mr W H H Barclay to Miss Katie Ridgely, daughter of the late David Ridgely, all of Wash City.

SAT DEC 17, 1859
Gov Magoffin, of Ky, recommends the Legislature of that State to prohibit by law, under severe penalties, the marriage of cousins. He says that imbecile, insane, deaf mutes, & blind in the different asylums of the State who are the offspring of cousins is from 16% to 20% of the whole number.

Mrs Haselwood, of Franklin Co, N C, was instantly killed on Friday last by the accidental discharge of a shot gun in the hands of her husband. Mr H is almost insane from mental distress. He is one of the best citizens of the county, & much sympathy is felt for him. -Raleigh Register

Criminal Court-Wash-Fri. 1-Jas W Kelly guilty of stealing a watch & $25: sentenced to 1½ years in the penitentiary. 2-Two men, Litchfield & Summers, guilty for stealing clothes: each sent to the county jail for 10 months. 3-Patrick McKenny, found guilty of stealing a hat from Mr Saml Cropley, in Gtwn. Recommended to the mercy of the Court, & sentenced to 4 months in jail. 4-Andrew Chase found guilty of petty larceny in stealing a coat & pantaloons. He was not sentenced, as there is a charge of grand larceny against him yet to be tried.

Died: on Dec 27, at Pensacola, Fla, Mr Isaac S Middleton, a native of Va, aged 75 years, formerly a resident of Wash City.

Dr J B Tuft, 450 6th st, Wash, gives notice that he has removed to Wash City, & offers his professional services.

MON DEC 19, 1859
The U S steam frig **Wabash** returned to N Y on Friday from a cruise of nearly 20 months in the Mediterranean. Her ofcrs are: F A F Lavalette, Flag-ofcr Com Mediteranean squadron. Capt of Fleet J A Dornin. Capt, Saml Barrow. Lts, C P Rodgers, Silas Bent, T G Corbin, Watson Smith, John H Russell, R W Henry, J Taylor Wood. Master, C S Norton. Midshipmen, J A Howell, H L Howison, Geo Dewey, Jas Bishop, E G Furber, G S Storrs. Acting Boarswain, A Pomeroy. Gunner, John Caulk. Carpenter, John Rainbow. Sailmaker, Jacob Stephens. Purser, J Geo Harris. Fleet Surgeon, Wm Johnson. Brevet Maj of Marines, J Zellin. Chaplain, J Lee Watson. 1st Lt of Marines, J Wiley. Passed Asst Surgeon, [blank] Rudenstein. Asst Surgeon, J H Kitchen. Chief Engineer, B Garvin. Flag-ofcr's Sec, W K Falls. 1st Assit Engineers, N P Patterson, M Fletcher; 2nd do, E W Manning, J B Kimball; 3rd do, J W Thompson, G B N Powers, M English, J Butler. Capt's Clerk, C McCollier. Purser's Clerk, John Ferguson.

Crowds of Jesuits were seeking refuge in Sardinia on account of the suppression of their order in Romagna.

Died: on Dec 18, Wm Johnson, aged 88 years. His funeral will take place today at 2 o'clock, from his late residence on 7th st, between Q & R sts.

Died: on Dec 17, William V, youngest child of the late John H Trenholm, aged 22 months. His funeral will take place today at 10½ o'clock, from the residence of its mother, 356 D st, between 9th & 10th sts.

Harper's Ferry, Dec 16-P M. The four criminals Cook & Coppie, & the negroes Green & Copeland, were hanged today. A prayer was offered by Rev Green North. Their bodies were placed in coffins.

Dr Robt E Martin, the universally popular Clerk of the Supreme Court of Ga, lost his life in the night of Monday last, when he lost his balance, & fell down a flight of stairs, with such force as to cause a concussion. He lingered for a few hours in an insensible state & then breathed his last.

John J Bowen, convicted at New Castle, Del, of the murder of John W Doolin, has been sentenced to be hung on Feb 10, 1860. This is the same day on which Robinson & Turner are to be executed.

Criminal Court-Wash-Sat. 1-Wilson DeKraft, a young white man about 22 years old, was found guilty for an assault & battery, with intent to kill, wholly unprovoked except by intoxication, on ofcr Wm T Craig, of Gtwn. He was sentenced to 4 months in the county jail.

TUE DEC 20, 1859
Senate: 1-Hon Benj Fitzpatrick President pro tem of the Senate in the absence of the Vice President.

Pot & Bouquet Flowers: the subscriber has at his Green Houses, N Y & N J ave, a variety of good flowers & window plants. –John Howlett

Criminal Court-Wash-Mon. 1-On motion of John E Norris, were admitted to the bar of this Court, Nicholas Vedder & Jabez H Norton. Also, on motion of Robt Ould, District Atty, Christopher C Callan was similarly admitted. 2-Thos Maloney & Martin Crenan were acquitted of the charge of grand larceny in stealing silver spoons & other jewelry from Mr Saml Samstag. 3-Eli Legg was found guilty of stealing a large quantity of clothing from Mr Openheimer. He was sentenced to 2 years in the penitentiary.

Mrd: on Dec 15, at the Cathedral, N Y, by Most Rev Archbishop Hughes, Richd H Laskey, of Wash City, to Miss Julia Fay Hunt, of N Y C.

Died: on Dec 19 in Wash City, Thos J Dawson, in his 29th year. His funeral will take place from his late residence, 514 Mass ave, on Wed, at 3 o'clock.

Died: on Dec 18, of consumption, after an illness of 18 months of constant suffering, Mary G, the beloved wife of J J Mulloy, in her 40th year. Her funeral is this morning at 9½ o'clock, from the residence of her husband, 507 north C st, Capitol Hill.

Orphans Court of Wash Co, D C. Letters of administration on the personal estate of Sarah A Schureman, late of Wash Co, deceased. —Wm Schureman, adm

WED DEC 21, 1859
Chronometers & fine watches repaired & adjusted by Jno Kulinski & Co, 302 Pa ave, between 9th & 10th sts, Wash.

Orphans Court of Wash Co, D C. In the case of Stanislaus Murray, exc of Martin Murphy, the executor & Court have appointed Jan 31st next, for the final settlement of the personal estate of the said deceased, of the assets in hand. -Ed N Roach, Reg/o wills

Criminal Court-Wash-Tue. 1-Emmanuel Dodson, colored, was indicted in 3 cases for stealing several quantities of corn & cornmeat from Alfred Jones: guilty in all 3 cases. 2-Jas Welsh & Chas Dant, found not guilty of larceny on Mr Saml Samstag. 3-Wm Moody, Chas Blue, & John Brogden, all colored, were acquitted on a charge of stealing a horse from Mr Alonzo Fowler, & a wagon from Mr John W Tucker. 4-Geo W Mahoney, colored, was found guilty of stealing a bale of hay, valued at $1.50, from Alfred Lee: sentenced to 9 months in jail. The Court said the sentence was made heavier on account of the larceny being accompanied by a breach of trust.

Died: on Dec 10, at Camden, N J, Isabella, youngest daughter of Dr Richd S James, formerly of Wash City, aged 6 years, 2 months & 4 days.

THU DEC 22, 1859
Messrs Warner, Miskey & Merrill, of Phil, have lately finished a life-like bust of Patrick Henry, copied from the only authentic portrait bust of him in existence. Capt P M Henry, of Wash City, grandson of the patriot, certifies to this cast being a faithful copy of the original terra cotta bust, & bears testimony to the fidelity of the likeness.

Criminal Court-Wash-Wed. 1-Jas P Allston found not guilty of stealing a violin from Chas W Turner. 2-Philip Reagan & John McCauly found guilty of stealing a piece of salt beef valued at thirty-four cents. They were sentenced to 6 months in the county jail. 2-Em Emmanuel, Silas Lewis, Geo Jones, & Geo W Yates, acquitted on a charge of riot.

Cincinnati, Dec 21. The Commercial of this morning published a dispatch announcing the death of Hon Linn Boyd, of Ky.

Senate: 1-Ptn from Ann R Allen, widow of an ofcr of the militia of N Y in the war of 1812, asking to be allowed a pension. 2-Ptn from Theodore J Eckerson, military storekeeper of ordnance at Benicia, Calif, asking an increase of compensation. 3-Ptn from W L S Dearing, asking the reimbursement of money expended by him in raising a company of volunteers in Florida. 4-Ptn from John Peebles, asking remuneration for surveying for the U S in the southern district of Alabama, & asking an examination of the report of the Court of Claims, with the testimony thereon. 5-Ptn from S Eastman, asking a restoration of the copyright of his pictures used in illustrating the Gov'n't work on the history of Indians. 6-Ptn from S S Wood & W P Kirkland, asking the passage of a joint resolution authorizing the Executive to appoint a commission to investigate the cause which led to the destruction of Greytown, in Central America, by Cmder Geo N Hollins, of the U S sloop-of-war **Cyane**, in Jul, 1854. 7-Ptn from Geo Squier, asking to be allowed an outfit as charge d'affaires to each of the Gov'ts of Guatemala, San Salvador, Costa Rica, & Honduras, & also a balance of salary claimed to be due.

Died: on Dec 21, after a painful illness of 6 days, from the effects of being scalded, Ella, aged 2 years, 10 months & 9 days, daughter of John W & Eliza E Dick. Her funeral will be today at 2 o'clock, from the residence of her parents, 206 N Y ave, between 4th & 5th sts.

Phil, Dec 21. Fire & loss of life in the store at No 54 Broad st last eveving. Policeman Stewart was fatally injured; Mr Eley, a wine merchant, was killed.

Detroit, Dec 20. The body of J Barney Campau, a prominent citizen, whose disappearance 3 weeks ago caused great excitement from the supposition that he had been foully dealt with, was found in the river yesterday. His watch & valuables were undisturbed, & there were no marks of violence on his person.

FRI DEC 23, 1859
Senate: 1-Ptn from the widow of Brig Gen Thos Childs, asking to be allowed a pension: referred. 2-Ptn from Haym M Salomon, asking indemnity for money advanced & losses sustained by his father during the war of the Revolution: referred. 3-Ptn from Mrs Eliz Lansdale & M Fox, sole heirs of gen Stephen Maylan, of the army of the Revolution, asking that his accounts may be settled on the basis indicated by the late Mr Hagner, Third Auditor of the Treasury: referred. 4-Ptn from Thos Crown, asking relief in Consequence of the arbitrary abrogation of a contract made by him with the U S Gov't. 5-Ptn from Catharine McLeod, asking relief on account of losses & sufferings of her father in aiding the cause of the American Revolution: referred. 6-Ptn from David H Burr, late Surveyor Gen of Utah, asking to be allowed the salary appertaining to that office until he was relieved by the transfer of Govn'r Cummings: referred. 7-Ptn from John H Wickizer, asking compensation for taking the census of the counties of Monterey & Santa Cruz, in Calif: referred. 8-Ptn from L W Boggs, asking an appropriation for his salary as Alcalde & Judge under the military gov't of Calif: referred.

Mrd: on Dec 20, in Wash City, by Rev Dr Hill, Mr Edwin W W Griffin to Miss Carrie C McCutchen, all of Wash City.

The remains of John E Cook, one of the executed Harper's Ferry conspirators, were taken to Wmsburg, N Y, for interment. The Lee Avenue Church was first applied for, & it is said unconditionally refused. Some 4 years since the misguided man was a leading member of this society, & Superintendent of the Sabbath School. The Dutch Reformed Church in 4th st, Rev E D Porter pastor, our of Christian sympathy with the stricken relatives, consented to the use of their bldg. The Consistory notified that the funeral will have to take place somewhere else. The funeral ceremonies took place on Tue at a private dwlg in Wmsburg.

Col Isaac Munroe, extensively known as the proprietor & conductor, up to a recent period, of the Balt Patriot, which he originated in 1813, died suddenly in Balt yesterday. He was in his 75th year. As a husband, brother & friend no man had a higher title to excellence.

Hartford [Ct] papers of Tue: this morning the Patent Safety Fuse Factory of Toy, Bickford & Co, near the center of Simsbury, blew up. Killed: Kate Brissey, Mary Jane Bacon, Hannah Head, Harriet Head, & Mrs Chas E *Lamson, of Simsbury. Jos Toy, jr, son of the proprietor, was badly burnt. Mr Edwin Griswold was seriously injured. His daughter, Martha J Griswold, was also among the killed. Mrs *Lampson leaped out of the burning bldg & ran, all burnt as she was, 20 rods before she fell a corpse. She had inhaled the flame. [*Could be 2 spellings for the same person.]

Circuit Court of D C-in Chancery, No 1,574. David Bassett vs Geo Atkinson & Wm Atkinson. This suit is to procure the conveyance of the legal title to part of lot 9 of square 370, in Wash City. The bill of cmplnt states that said dfndnts, Geo & Wm Atkinson, claiming to be the owners in fee simple as tenants in common of lot 9 in square 370, Wash City, by an instrument of writing under seal duly made & executed on Feb 8, 1836, authorized & empowered one David A Hall to sell certain property in said city, including lot 9, at public or private sale, for cash or on credit, & to give full receipts & discharges for the purchase money, & to convey the same to the purchaser thereof by a good & sufficient deed, with covenants of warranty of title. That said Hall, acting at atty for & in the name of said Geo & Wm Atkinson, on May 26, 1843, sold that part of said lot 9, to one Jas Pilling, jr, for a full consideration in money & its market value at that time, & on the same day executed & delivered a deed to said Pilling for the same, containing a covenant of general warranty; & said purchase money was duly paid said Hall, acting as atty a foresaid; & that said Pilling subsequently, to wit, on Oct 14, 1847, by a deed, duly executed & recorded, conveyed said premises to your orator. And it appearing to the satisfaction of the Court that said Geo & Wm Atkinson do not reside in this District of Columbia. Absent dfndnts are to appear in the ofc of the Clerk of said Court on the first Monday of May 1860. –Jno A Smith, clerk

Rev Matthew B Hope, D D, Prof of Belles Lettres, etc, in the College of N J, died suddenly on Sat at Princeton. He had been afflicted for several years with neuralgia & sudden fainting. It was in one of these fainting spells, on Sat, that he died.

Valuable farm for sale; lies directly on the Potomac River, in Md; contains 608 acres; improvements are 3 large barns as good as new, a large double granary built in 1856, a new overseer's house, & quarters sufficient for a large number of servants. Apply to Dr P R Edelen, Piscataway, PG Co, Md.

Agnes Robinson, a colored woman, who was arrested in Wash City last June, & taken to Wash Co, Md, where she was claimed as a slave, has been declared, after a jury trial in that county, to be a free woman under a deed of manumission from John Witmer, sr, dated in 1847.

Died: on Dec 22, in Gtwn, of heart disease, Mrs Mary J, wife of Alfred Curtis, in her 56th year. Her funeral will take place from her late residence, 129 Beall st, Gtwn, this afternoon at 2 o'clock.

Died: on Dec 22, in Wash City, Virginia, daughter of Rev Dabney & Mary D Ball, aged 5 years. Her funeral will take place at the residence of her parents, on F st, between 6th & 7th sts, this afternoon at 1:30 P M.

SAT DEC 24, 1859
Miss Cunningham, the Regent of the *Mount Vernon Association*, states that the whole amount paid over to Mr Washington, including principal & interest, was $199,924.

Criminal Court-Wash-Fri. Jos Goldsmith was put to trial on a charge of stealing 2 watches & a sum of money from E Kaufman, in Gtwn, to whom he was clerk. The case will be continued.

Mrd: on Dec 20, in Wash City, by Rev Dr Hill, Mr Edwin W W Griffin to Miss Carrie C McCutchen, all of Wash City.

Died: on Dec 22, in Gtwn, of heart disease, Mrs Mary J, wife of Alfred Curtis, in her 56th year. Her funeral will take place from her late residence, 129 Beall st, Gtwn, this afternoon at 2 o'clock.

Died: on Nov 22, in Wash City, Virginia, daughter of Rev Dabney & Mary D Ball, aged 5 years. Her funeral will take place this afternoon at half past one o'clock, at the residence of her parents, on F st, between 6th & 7th sts.

MON DEC 26, 1859
Jas J Roosevelt appointed by the Pres & confirmed by the Senate as District Atty for the southern district of N Y, made vacant by the death of Theodore Sedgewick.

The plantation boat of Mrs Harriet Pinkney, of *Pinkney Island*, while crossing over to the city of Savannah, on Monday night, came in contact with a steamboat, was upset, & 13 persons drowned. Amongst them was Mr Winningham, overseer for Mrs Pinkney. All the rest were blacks.

Hon Edmund Deberry, formerly a Rep in Congress from N C, died at his residence in Montg Co, N C, on Dec 12.

Lt Julian May, of the U S Army, died in New Mexico, after a few hours' illness. He was a gallant ofcr & as a man beloved by all who knew him. The regt to which he was attached was the Mounted Rifles, to which corps he was appointed at the date of its formation, in 1848. –Balt Exchange [No death date given-current item.]

On Friday last Robt Ould, District Atty of the U S for the District of Columbia, sent in his resignation to the City Councils of Gtwn as Recorder of that town, an ofc he has held for several years. His resignation was consequent on his change of residence lately made from Gtwn to Washington.

Coroner's inquest was held on Sat at the Infirmary on the body of Chas W Raborg, aged about 36 years, who died at the Infirmary on Friday night. On Thu Raborg & Mr John Bligh were at the Salutation House on Pa ave, Raborg being much in liquor. It is possible that John Essex, [the same who killed Owen Quigley in Jun, 1856, & was acquitted by a jury,] knocked Raborg down, & then stamped upon his face. Essex decamped.

Criminal Court-Wash-Fri. 1-Augustus Ridgely, Wm Tucker, jr, & Geo Jones were put on trial for riot at a tavern on 7th st: verdict guilty-fined $10 each & costs by the Court. 2-Michl Doyle, charged with an assault on battery on Ann Quigley & on ofcr Davis, submitted his cases to the Court, & was sentenced to $15 & costs. 3-Marion Ward, put on trial for an attempt to break into the house of Patrick McKenna: verdict not guilty. 4-Bartlett Lipscomb convicted with steaming various articles of clothing worth $21.50: sentenced to 1½ years in the penitentiary. 5-Lawrence Keeley was convicted of assault & battery on his wife, Margaret Keeley, when asleep: sentenced to jail 1 month. 6-Wm H White guilty of stealing jewelry valued at $9: sentenced to 1 year in the penitentiary. 7-Saml Rouzzee found not guilty of passing a counterfeit $10 note on John O Meara knowing it to be counterfeit.

Mrd: on Dec 22, at Alexandria, at the residence of Rev D F Sprigg, Addison W Deahl, of Wash, to Lizzie C, daughter of the late Jno L Proctor, of the former place.

Mrd: on Dec 7, at Idlwald, near Port Gibson, Miss, by Rev Dr Butler, Mrs Ann E Railey to Mr Wilson Benson, of Madison Co, Miss.

Died: on Dec 24, in Wash City, at the residence of his son-in-law, S C Wailes, Mr Thos Stanford, formerly of Balt, in his 56th year.

WED DEC 28, 1859
Mrd: at *Allenwick*, PG Co, Md, by Rev Dr Young, Robt A Parrish, of Phil, to Fanny *Elliott, daughter of Wm Tyson. [No marriage date given-current item.] [Dec 29th newspaper: Mrd-at *Alnwick*, PG Co, Md, by Rev Dr Young, Robt A Parrish, of Phil, to Fanny *Ellicott, daughter of Wm Tyson.]
*Note: Elliott/Ellicott

Senate: 1-Ptn from Eliza J Vandeventer, widow of the late Maj E Vandeventer, asking Congress to provide for back pension due her husband while holding a commission in the army: referred. 2-Ptn from S Calvert Ford, complaining of a decision of the Court of Claims, & asking a revision of said decision, with the argument of his counsel thereunto annexed: referred. 3-Ptn from J W Deeble, representing that the Court of Claims have decided adversely on his claim, & asking a re-examination of the same when it shall be reported to Congress.

Died: on Dec 26, Mrs Eliza R, the beloved wife of John M Jameson. Her funeral will be from the residence of her husband, 451 2nd st, East Capitol Hill, Wed at 2½ o'clock.

Died: on Dec 20, at the residence of his mother, in Chas Co, Md, Magruder D Tubman, son of the late Geo M Tubman, of Wash City, aged 24 years.

Criminal Court-Wash-Wed. 1-John Boyle & Danl Carroll convicted of assault against John Lynch: fined $5 each & costs. 2-Motion for a new trial in the case of Sonny Jackson was withdrawn.

The marriage licenses issued during 1859 at the Clerk's Ofc in the City Hall amounted to 920, the highest number-94 for any one month were issued in Sept; the fewest-55, during the present month. Average is about 76 per month.

Louisville, Dec 27. The steamer **Vixen**, from Pittsburg for St Louis, was burnt yesterday. Geo Mott, a school teacher, of Lynchburg, Va, was burnt to death.

THU DEC 29, 1859
Hon Timothy Jenkins, a prominent lawyer of Central N Y, & formerly a Rep in Congress, died on Sat at Martinsburg, N Y, where he was attending court.

W B Hopkins shot himself through the heart at the St Chas Hotel, New Orleans, on Dec 9. A few moments after his body was discovered in his room, John E Musgrove, of St Louis, Mo, threw himself from the portico of the hotel & was instantly killed.

The Jury in the case of the State of Ohio vs Wm H Gibson, late Treasurer of Ohio, returned a verdict of guilty on Dec 21. He is charged with embezzling $132,128. John G Breslin, who was a brother-in-law of Mr Gibson, was a principal defaulter, & that he had misapplied the means of the State some time before the expiration of his term. Mr Breslin escaped from the country.

On Wed Jas Stewart, a young man, printer by trade, put an end to his life by hanging himself in a stable at the rear of his mother's residence, on Missouri ave. He had difficulty finding regular employment.

Mrd: on Dec 25, at Westminster, Md, by Rev Theodore Gallaudet, Henry M Scon, of St Geo, Bermuda, to Julia H Gallaudet, the 2nd daughter of the officiating minister.

Criminal Court-Wash-Wed: 1-Wm Ford, colored was found guilty for assaulting & beating his wife, Susan Ford: sentenced to 2 weeks in jail & fined $10 & costs. 2-Constantine Edwards, Harry Smith, alias English Harry, Saml Spalding, & Thos McNany, were found guilty of a riot at a house in the First Ward.

Died: on Wed, Alex'r Lee, in his 53rd year, formerly of Lynchburg, Va, but for the last 28 years a resident of Wash City. His funeral will take place on Dec 30, at 2 o'clock, from his late residence, 475 6th st west.

Died: on Dec 26, in Wash City, of consumption, Hannah Jones, eldest daughter of Frances A & A Bradley Waller.

Circuit Court of D C-in Chancery, No 1,537. Peter F Brown, cmplnt, vs Edw Swann, Wm H C Ellis, Jos C C Ellis, DeWitt C Ellis, & Vespasian Ellis, dfndnts. This suit is to procure the appointment of a trustee in the place of Vespasian Ellis, deceased. The dfndnt Swann was indebted unto the complnt for $1,180, evidenced by his promissory note for that sum, dated Aug 25, 1854, & payable one year after date, with interest, to cmplnt's order; that the dfndnt Swann & Maria L Swann, his wife, did, on Aug 25, grant & convey to the late Vespasian Ellis & his heirs part of lot 14 in square 490, to secure the payment of the said indebtment. That since the happening of the aforegoing the said Vaspasian Ellis hath departed this life, leaving the said ofc of trustee vacant; that a large portion of the said debt is still unpaid & owing, but that payment of the same cannot be enforced by proceedings under the said deed on account of the said trustee's decease; that the heirs at law of the said Vespasian Ellis are Wm H C Ellis, Jos C C Ellis, & DeWitt C Ellis, & Vespasian Ellis, who are non-residents, living beyond the jurisdiction of this Court. The non-residents are to appear in this Court on the first Monday of May, 1860. -Jno A Smith, clerk

FRI DEC 30, 1859
Explosion at Martinville, Va, on Wed last. The son of Mr Fritz was killed. The father & mother, & a little girl, were slightly injured. They obtained a livelihood by mining coal.

In the Supreme Court of N Y, Edw Hughes has recovered $3,000 from Michl Green for the loss of his little daughter, who was killed by the falling of rock through the roof of his house. Green was blasting rocks in the neighborhood, & the rock fell upon the roof & descended to the basement, striking the child upon the head.

On Sunday a promising young man, Jacob S Souder, was drowned, while skating on the Schuylkill, some distance above the city. He was a student at Yale College, in his 21st year, was spending time at the residence of his realtives in Montg Co, for the holydays. The ice broke while he was skating. –Phil Bulletin

A daughter of Wm Harvey, of Swanville, aged 14, was found frozen to death, about a mile from her father's house, on Sat last. She left home to visit her elder sister, Mrs Mardin, about 3 miles distant, & on Thu attempted to return home. She appeared to have lost her way.

In Balt, on Tue, Mr Sahrland, a medical student, accidentally killed himself, whilst handling a loaded pistol. On Monday night, Franklin, alias Petty Naff, was shot, & probably fatally wounded, in Lovely Lane, near Calvert st. There were several street fights on Monday, & numerous accidents from the use of powder are reported.

Criminal Court-Wash-Thu. 1-Jas & Ellen Dunn were fined $5 each for an assault on Eleanor Keefe.

SAT DEC 31, 1859
Extensive sale of fine groceries, on Jan 4, at the store of Geo Pearson, on Pa ave. -Jas C McGuire & Co, aucts

Senate: 1-Memorial of Wm Collicott: referred to the Cmte on Public Lands. 2-Court of Claims: in the case of Susan Decatur, widow of Cmdor Stephen Decatur, & the memorial of Jos K Boyd, for remuneration for aiding in the capture of the frig **Philadelphia**, which were referred to the Cmte of Claims; & the memorials of John Frost & Eliza A Johnson, & of Chas J Sweet: referred to the Cmte on Naval Affairs.

The Globe of yesterday announces the death of Hon Saml Casey, Treasurer of the U S, on Dec 22, at Caseyville, Ky, where it appears he retired in the beginning of last month on account of sickness. His age was about 71 years. He was a gentleman of unblemished character, & was appointed to the office of Treasurer of the U S in the early part of the administration of Mr Pierce.

Sir Jas Macaulay, the first Chief Justice of the Court of Common Pleas of Upper Canada, is no more. He died a short time after complaining of severe pain in the chest. He was a Canadian by birth, & was 67 years of age. His death was caused by disease of the heart.

Died: on Dec 30, in Wash City, Saml Wilson, son of Annie E & S W K Handy, & grandson of the late Saml W Handy, of Wash City. His funeral will take place from the residence of his parents, 632 south 11 st, [Island,] this day. [No time given.]

Obit-died: on Dec 27, after a lingering illness, Harrison Perry Lewis, aged 46 years, 2 months & 21 days. He was the last surviving son of Saml & Thomazine Lewis, deceased-the last, save one, [his sister,] of a numerous family; each deceased early in life, & all victims of that fell disease, consumption, which, as we look back down the vista of years, has set up the whitened monuments, at almost regular intervals making its destructive march. An honest, upright, amiable man, a kind husband, an indulgent father, the deceased had many friends & few enemies. His last hour was calm & peaceful.

A

Abbot, 191
Abbott, 20, 168
Abell, 153, 306
Abercrombie, 151
Abernethy, 234
Abert, 57, 94, 189
Abott, 161
Ackroyd, 168
Acutt, 147
Adam, 230
Adams, 14, 15, 24, 28, 29, 37, 43, 59, 62, 64, 67, 68, 81, 87, 114, 164, 189, 214, 227, 230, 235, 282, 288, 333, 361
Adamson, 16, 58
Addison, 28, 43, 89, 164, 353
Adler, 3
adulteress, 145
Agassiz, 219
Ager, 150
Agnew, 10
Aiken, 127
Ailier, 197
Airley, 169
Alba, 190
Albert, 115, 261
Albertsen, 11
Albertson, 77, 255
Alburtis, 131
Alburtson, 16
Alden, 7, 150
Alderslade, 322
Aldrich, 43
Aler, 176
Alexander, 43, 65, 105, 112, 173, 203, 213, 241, 284, 319, 325, 353
Alexandria Gazette, 4
Aliery, 106
Alig, 87
Allan, 200, 230
Alldredge, 92
Allegany Mining Co, 41

Alleghany Mining Co, 309
Allen, 13, 32, 43, 53, 62, 73, 97, 101, 122, 163, 218, 239, 247, 252, 254, 255, 269, 273, 288, 308, 317, 319, 360, 365
Allenwick, 369
Allison, 87
Allstadt, 310, 319, 321
Allston, 364
Almon, 79, 85
Almy, 152
Alnutt, 237
Alnwick, 369
Alnwick Female Seminary, 221
Alonzo, 327
Ambler, 30, 295
Amy, 283
Anderson, 79, 91, 100, 198, 211, 223, 265, 277, 308, 310, 312, 313, 325, 345, 360
Andrew, 97
Andrews, 112, 143, 145, 280
Andrus, 43, 91
Andry, 215
Angell, 272
Angermann, 243
Angus, 42, 129
Ann Smith College, 192
Anthan, 31
Antisell, 101
Appleby, 43, 225
Appleman, 284
Appleton, 126, 311
Appo, 197
Archer, 26
Arden, 43
Arguello, 73
Arguillo, 279
Armistead, 46, 254
Armitage, 43, 168
Armstrong, 75, 222, 261
Arnett, 144

Arnold, 36, 43, 59, 99, 129, 130, 198, 211, 223, 235, 250
Arrington, 192
Arthur, 216
Artot, 19
Ash, 59
Ashby, 196
Ashford, 43
Ashley, 32, 345
Askins, 192
Astor, 196
Atherton, 151
Atkins, 262
Atkinson, 17, 35, 206, 366
Atlantic cable, 195
AtLee, 58
Atwell, 95
Atwoods, 226
Atz, 69
Aulick, 280, 289
Austin, 12, 153, 194
Avaya, 279
Avent, 297
Averett, 192
Avery, 43, 291, 332
Avis, 320, 352
Ayer, 282
Ayres, 203, 211, 335, 340
Ayton, 177

B

B_ggs, 207
Babbington, 210
Bache, 67, 94
Backus, 112
Bacon, 13, 93, 99, 135, 141, 217, 248, 257, **288**, 366
Baden, 35, 129, 259
Baese, 272
Baggerly, 206
Bagioli, 108
Bagley, 103
Bagman, 44
Bailey, 105, 153, 179, 205, 214, 234, 252, 297
Bain, 44, 345
Bainbridge, 93, 239, 289
Baker, 26, 44, 167, 192, 198, 222
Balcom, 257
Baldwin, 44, 128, 165, 176, 195, 196, 201, 208, 226, 233, 326, 331
Baley, 39, 72
Ball, 10, 16, 44, 73, 103, 115, 144, 177, 203, 207, 272, 279, 302, 304, 310, 312, 319, 321, 325, 329, 350, 367
Ballard, 233
Ballenger, 43, 170
Balluff, 325
Baltimore Cemetery, 132
Balzer, 226
Bancroft, 355
Bangs, 89, 254, 328
Bankes, 271
Bankhead, 21, 234
Banks, 266
Bannister, 90, 97, 106
Baptist, 105
Barbaour, 114
Barbee, 72
Barber, 145
Barbot, 261
Barbour, 128, 129, 334
Barclay, 35, 99, 118, 124, 272, 362
Bareley, 149
Barksdale, 184
Barlow, 299, 306
Barnard, 17, 107, 112, 128, 205, 236
Barnes, 10, 14, 44, 59, 167, 168, 173, 188, 204, 333, 337, 340, 343, 362
Barnetson, 124
Barney, 35
Barnitz, 62
barque **Austria**, 203
barque **Jane Black**, 96
barque **Ocean Eagle**, 288
barque **Race Horse**, 197
barque **Rawlins**, 265

barque **Release**, 203
barque **Resolute**, 19, 21, 67
barque **Wm D Platinus**, 328, 329
Barr, 44, 58
Barrett, 10, 44, 128, 340, 349
Barringer, 169, 230
Barrington, 161
Barron, 44
Barrow, 362
Barrows, 183, 186
Barry, 14, 30, 43, 44, 56, 74, 103, 147, 166, 322, 353, 356, 358
Bartholow, 129
Bartlett, 5, 191, 235, 368
Barto, 317
Bartol, 229
Barton, 13, 27, 70, 78, 128, 129, 133, 263, 285
Bascom, 222
Bashford, 326
Bass, 203
Bassett, 177, 211, 223, 349, 366
Bassford, 59
Batchelder, 100
Batchelor, 95
Bateman, 30, 44, 202
Batemen, 270
Bates, 24, 184, 225, 242
Baum, 129
Baume, 119
Bawner, 33
Bawsel, 340
Baxter, 24, 29, 97, 106
Bayard, 354, 355
Bayley, 5
Baylis, 115
Bayliss, 43, 58
Bayly, 13, 44, 189, 342, 352
Bayne, 90
Beach, 44
Beale, 35, 99, 102, 105, 352
Bealer, 44

Beall, 41, 43, 44, 51, 63, 64, 202, 208, 229, 231, 235, 283, 297, 321, 334, 344, 357
Beall's & Edmonsion's Discovery, 206
Bean, 43, 58, 177, 192, 230
Beard, 167, 228
Beardsley, 88
Beasley, 44
Beatty, 80
Beaubian, 115
Beauchamp, 223
Beauharmais, 191
Beavens, 296
Beck, 215, 247, 266, 355
Becket, 44
Beckett, 63, 178
Beckham, 198, 222, 310, 312, 321
Bedford, 326
Beebe, 131
Beers, 44, 341
Beeson, 21
Beetham, 120, 127
Begg, 5
Beiser, 231
Beitzell, 59
Belknap, 199
Bell, 32, 44, 79, 97, 105, 106, 112, 153, 159, 182, 286, 301, 302
Beller, 321
Bellinger, 353
Bellot, 302
Belser, 30
Belt, 59, 353, 358
Belvoir, 295
Bender, 132
Benedeck, 194
Benedict, 132
Benedict XIII, 307
Benefield, 68
Benham, 261
Benkert, 318
Bennet, 77, 85, 328, 329
Bennett, 30, 43, 211, 222, 269, 284
Benson, 327, 368

375

Bent, 362
Bentley, 26, 126, 192, 273
Benton, 27, 43, 44, 96, 209
Beresford, 141
Bergershausen, 174
Bergmann, 268
Berkeley, 108
Berkeley Springs, 6
Berker, 213
Berkley, 153, 231, 251, 269
Bernadotte, 229
Bernard, 208
Bernhard, 44
Berret, 10, 94, 116, 142, 189
Berry, 34, 55, 58, 82, 89, 202, 256, 326, 337, 360
Berryman, 67, 239, 339
Berthelon, 241
Berthelong, 242
Bertoletto, 31
Bestor, 1, 99, 202, 246
Bethell, 163
Better, 100
Betts, 84, 125
Betz, 14
Bevan, 44
Beyer, 58
Bias, 44
Bibb, 136, 138, 167, 263, 301
Bicksler, 44
Biddle, 155, 278, 289
Bigelow, 218, 243, 273, 338
Biggs, 79
Bigley, 44
Binckley, 280
Bingey, 37
Bingham, 125
Binnicks, 184
Binnix, 225, 226
Birch, 44, 208
Bird, 8, 44, 58, 98, 173, 176, 238
Birrell, 339
birth-place, 66
Birthplace of Gen Jackson, 148

Biscoe, 247, 272
Bishop, 29, 175, 362
Bissell, 203
Bitting, 337
Bittinger, 124, 144, 235
Bivan, 149
Bivens, 42
Bixby, 326
Black, 78, 102, 134, 142, 267
Blackford, 87, 232
Blackwell, 7
Blagden, 15, 78, 82, 99, 324, 336, 352
Blagden's Row, 169
Blagrove, 304
Blain, 300
Blair, 43, 70, 209
Blake, 2, 64, 161, 190, 268, 339
Blakely, 239, 289
Blakeman, 43
Blanchard, 42, 82, 88, 318, 319, 337
Blanco, 22
Blandford, 91
Blanding, 119
Blaney, 62
Blattenberger, 13, 69
Bleecker, 73
Blew, 5
Bligh, 368
Blincoe, 167
Blint, 284
Bliss, 77, 186
Block, 79, 163, 165
Blodget, 161, 218, 227
Blodgett, 273
Blondin, 260
Bloom, 233
Blount, 345
Bloxham, 304
Blue, 364
Bo_ling, 225
Board, 210
Boardman, 87, 326
boat **Blue Bird**, 253
boat **Contra Costa**, 149

Boat No 158, 239
boat **Sea Gull**, 239
Bodell, 19
Body, 94
Boerum, 239
Boggs, 216, 358, 365
Bogue, 230
Bohn, 43
Bohrer, 9, 43, 57, 202
Boice, 284
Boilleau, 96
Boisseau, 189
Boland, 127
Bollmeyer, 316
Bond, 42, 44, 66, 99, 105, 130, 147
Bonersted, 326
Bonesteel, 325, 326
Bonilla, 279
Bonini, 361
Bontz, 44
Boon, 288
Boone, 8, 44, 107, 224, 231, 232
Boorly, 312
Bootes, 14
Booth, 236, 239
Boots, 160
Borchert, 192
Bordley, 262
Borgresson, 347
Borland, 43
Borreman, 44
Borrows, 58, 190
Boss, 44, 270
Bosse, 44
Bossier, 146
Bossiere, 163
Bossieux, 345
Boston, 208
Bostwick, 247
Boteler, 44, 87, 105, 146, 169, 193, 316, 331
Botentint, 229
Botetourt, 70
Botsford, 347

Bott, 321
Botts, 177, 251, 319, 321
Boucher, 128, 165
Bouck, 143
Boudouin, 155
Bourgeois, 106
Bourne, 257
Boutwell, 19, 182
Bowden, 73, 93
Bowder, 275
Bowe, 97
Bowen, 44, 45, 66, 74, 91, 99, 177, 184, 225, 363
Bowers, 7, 145, 337
Bowie, 28, 30, 42, 151, 172, 308
Bowlin, 31
Bowling, 31, 90
Bowman, 24, 39, 122, 133, 160, 255, 310, 360
Bowring, 304
Bowyer, 165, 285
Box Hill, 254
Boyce, 32, 97, 106, 210, 264
Boyd, 9, 96, 135, 321, 322, 364, 371
Boyer, 114, 237
Boyle, 37, 44, 73, 93, 196, 198, 252, 264, 272, 369
Boylston, 138
Boynton, 44, 262, 281
Brackenridge, 44
Braden, 169
Bradford, 136, 249, 273
Bradin, 85
Bradley, 45, 86, 102, 152, 187, 191, 202, 203, 265, 272, 297, 309, 361
Brady, 44, 137, 265
Bragg, 159
Braid, 114
Braiden, 2, 3
Brainard, 236
Bramwell, 119
Brandon, 97, 106
Brandt, 55, 58, 74, 82
Brank, 215, 286

Brannan, 64
Brashears, 67, 356
Brasseur, 303
Bratt, 87
Braun, 87
Brayer, 170
Brayton, 95
Breckenridge, 44
Breckinridge, 105
Bredd, 124
Breedlove, 184
Breeze, 280
Brehany, 255
Brennan, 180
Brent, 5, 44, 84, 154, 161, 229, 242, 360, 361
Brentville, 242
Brereton, 44, 276
Breslin, 370
Bresnehan, 356
Brest, 14
Brewer, 97, 106, 222, 236, 243
Brewers, 97
Brewerton, 190
Briceland, 178, 179
Bridget, 128, 237
Bridgett, 44
Bridwell, 220, 225
Brien, 133, 338
brig **Bainbridge**, 175, 223
brig **Boxer**, 238
brig **Chippewa**, 239
brig **Concord**, 132, 306
brig **Dolphin**, 175
brig **Etna**, 239
brig **General Armstrong**, 12, 13
brig **Hornet**, 239
brig **Nautilus**, 239
brig **Pickering**, 239
brig **Rattlesnake**, 239
brig **Siren**, 239
brig **Syren**, 289
brig **Truxton**, 239
brig **Tyrant**, 114

brig **Vengeance**, 240
brig **Vesavius**, 240
brig **Viper**, 240
brig **Vixen**, 240
Bright, 86
Brightwell, 99
Brimidi, 307
Brinley, 18, 62
Brisbane, 8
Brisco, 173
Briscoe, 44, 45, 180, 357
Brissey, 366
Briton, 227
Brittain, 14
Broaddus, 7
Brobst, 21
Brock, 345
Brockett, 78
Broderick, 311, 358
Brodhead, 99, 131, 143, 144
Brodnax, 304
Brogden, 364
Bronaugh, 13, 66, 71, 77, 88, 115, 235, 288, 323, 326
Brook, 128
Brooke, 43, 102, 130, 150, 175, 180, 193, 211, 212, 217, 231, 237, 323, 335
Brooke Hill, 102
Brookridge, 28
Brooks, 12, 43, 44, 84, 99, 110, 202, 220, 244, 247, 256, 282, 288, 352
Broome, 73
Brou, 64, 93
Brougham, 135, 335
Broun, 337
Brounstein, 63
Brower, 269
Browers, 60
Brown, 5, 8, 12, 14, 28, 31, 36, 39, 41, 43, 44, 56, 58, 65, 73, 80, 98, 100, 101, 103, 105, 110, 113, 135, 137, 139, 163, 164, 174, 183, 186, 187, 188, 193, 202, 215, 220, 223, 226, 235, 243, 251, 262, 269, 272, 273,

288, 301, 310, 312, 313, 314, 317,
319, 320, 321, 323, 324, 327, 334,
335, 339, 347, 349, 351, 352, 354,
355, 356, 357, 358, 370
Browne, 156, 291, 349
Brownell, 289
Browning, 31, 44, 125, 157, 213, 260, 346
Brua, 319
Bruff, 48
Brumidi, 189
Brunel, 287
Brunet, 44
Brunett, 34, 337
Brush, 73, 341
Bryan, 44, 53, 55, 65, 79, 99, 135, 157, 172, 173, 178, 180, 202, 256, 257, 352, 357
Bryant, 14, 36, 43, 114
Buchanan, 30, 61, 78, 98, 111
Buchignani, 329
Buchley, 44
Buck, 24, 95, 272
Bucke, 2
Buckey, 17, 205, 350
Buckignani, 194, 303
Buckley, 10, 137
Buckner, 161
Buffington, 323
Buford, 222
Bullock, 81
Bully, 129
Bunker, 4
Burch, 10, 44, 46, 58, 165, 256
Burche, 43, 44
Burchell, 44
Burdell, 160
Burdine, 44
Burford, 43
Burgess, 103, 121
Burk, 97, 159
Burke, 39, 104, 120, 221, 317, 359
Burkett, 181
Burkhead, 27

Burks, 122
Burley, 315, 321
Burnap, 272
Burnett, 31, 39, 43, 260
Burning Spring, 295
Burnley, 310
Burns, 5, 122, 129, 211, 324, 339, 353
Burnside, 219
Burr, 21, 101, 188, 236, 251, 319, 365
Burress, 83, 106
Burroughs, 90, 101, 215, 256
Burrow, 283
Burrows, 67, 152, 289
Burt, 257
Burton, 124
Busch, 120
Busey, 193
Bush, 43, 44, 198, 223, 285
Bushby, 115
Busher, 315
Bushnell, 26, 164
Bussard, 201
Butcher, 44
Buthmann, 74, 78, 106, 299
Butler, 12, 13, 20, 21, 41, 43, 44, 61, 79, 99, 101, 102, 127, 134, 151, 154, 164, 169, 202, 210, 280, 297, 318, 345, 362, 368
Butt, 134, 193
Butterfield, 16, 324
Butterworth, 19, 39, 108, 142
Butts, 125, 251
Byas, 220
Byers, 186
Bynn, 193
Byram, 44
Byrne, 44, 130, 212, 235, 334
Byron, 105, 277

C

Cabot, 16, 45, 151
Cadey, 149
Cady, 143, 291, 327
Caffey, 206

Caffrey, 67
Cagger, 138
Cahill, 242
Cahoe, 45
Cain, 325
Cair, 143
Caldwell, 61, 118, 336
Calhoun, 90, 97, 106, 311
Callaghan, 45, 248
Callahan, 45, 55, 229
Callan, 42, 44, 45, 56, 264, 318, 319, 325, 335, 346, 363
Callanan, 45
Calloway, 13, 80
Cally, 239
Calvert, 5, 205
Calwin, 326
Camees, 190
Cameron, 270
Camp Floyd, 167, 177
Camp Radziminski, 181
Campau, 365
Campbell, 16, 19, 29, 34, 45, 46, 66, 93, 95, 101, 113, 142, 152, 175, 192, 198, 213, 231, 256, 262, 264, 275, 278, 283, 299, 319, 349, 352
Cancemi, 4
Canfield, 136
Cannon, 81, 93
Canonge, 106
Cantine, 38
Cape Lookout, 291
Caperton, 244, 297
Carber, 93
Carberry, 146
Carbery, 99, 107, 183, 229, 230
Cardoni, 25
Carey, 5, 112, 219, 345
Cargill, 4
Cariene, 250
Carlin, 103
Carling, 198, 223
Carlisle, 45, 55, 186, 290
Carlton, 198, 223

Carlyle, 183
Carnahan, 95
Carothers, 4, 61, 75, 77, 91, 103, 104, 123, 124, 131, 152, 153, 170, 249, 279, 297, 300, 325
Carpenter, 239, 261
Carper, 211
Carr, 97, 106, 190, 337
Carrey, 106
Carrico, 43, 45, 230, 256
Carrier, 235
Carrigan, 143
Carrington, 39, 63, 139, 215, 272
Carroll, 16, 45, 103, 143, 230, 252, 254, 267, 347, 369
Carson, 36, 102, 103, 115, 296
Carstang, 185, 276
Carswell, 294
Carteel, 303
Carter, 12, 32, 39, 59, 89, 121, 128, 147, 157, 195, 207, 322, 323, 331, 353
Carter Place, 337, 346
Cartin, 262
Cartwright, 326
Carusi, 45
Carver, 81, 133, 358
Carvill, 299
Cary, 167, 295
Carztang, 212
Casaduco, 9
Case, 5
Casey, 168, 371
Casilear, 119
Caslo, 91, 93
Casparis, 135, 163, 214
Casparis House, 266
Cass, 10, 90, 97, 118, 167
Cassel, 305
Cassell, 131, 144, 158, 177, 189
Cassidy, 20, 45, 103, 105
Cassin, 160, 245, 315
Castel, 186
Castell, 176
Castleman, 57, 99, 125, 339

Cathcart, 241
Catlett's Station, 169
Caton, 45, 234
Catron, 100
Caulk, 362
Causer, 45
Causten, 67, 78
Cavenaugh, 45
Cawthon, 150
Cazenave, 33
Cazenove, 31
Cedar Grove, 335
Celeys, 295
Cellar, 45
Cenas, 192
Centre, 185
Chabert, 267
Chadbourne, 213
Chadwick, 275
Chafee, 45
Chaffee, 66
Chamberlain, 84
Chambers, 45, 112, 321
Champayne, 203
Champion, 103
Champlin, 280, 289
Chandler, 45, 89, 156
Chanonhouse, 347
Chanor, 315
Chapel Grave yard, 233
Chapin, 26, 57, 99, 176
Chaplain, 80
Chaplin, 93, 240
Chapman, 10, 45, 112, 168, 179, 204, 233, 243, 283, 288, 290
Chapman's farm, 32
Chapmen, 19
Charles, 185, 309, 336
Charles XII, 292
Charless, 185, 221
Charlesworth, 341
Charnley, 168
Chase, 362
Cheatem, 97

Cheatham, 345
Cheathath, 106
Chedal, 330
Cheney, 20, 213
Cheshire, 45
Chester, 249
Chester's Gap, 269
Chetwynd, 116
Chever, 45
Chew, 88, 102, 214, 314
Childress, 131
Childs, 21, 81, 176, 217, 365
Chillon Castle Manor, 252
Chillum Castle Manor, 195
Chilton, 45, 60, 130, 178, 212, 323, 324, 329, 331
Chinese flag, 261
Chipchase, 91
Chipley, 59
Chiswell, 193
Chittenden, 45
Chitty, 244
Choate, 224, 264
Choice, 1, 8, 351
Cholmondeley, 110
Choteau, 41, 78
Chrisman, 190
Christian, 31, 311
Christie, 101, 215
Christopher, 147
Chubb, 45, 274, 287, 313
Chulp, 210
Church, 45, 119, 128
Church of St Aloysius Gonzaga, 169
Churchill, 345
Cinnamond, 125
Cissel, 24, 165, 283
Citz, 190
Claflin, 338
Clagett, 55, 99, 110, 164, 285
Claiborne, 192, 266
Clampitt, 210
Clara, 22
Clare, 325

Clark, 15, 16, 18, 36, 45, 59, 78, 93, 97, 106, 111, 125, 129, 144, 152, 158, 162, 184, 189, 245, 257, 272, 273, 277, 283, 288, 325, 338
Clarke, 23, 30, 38, 43, 45, 46, 55, 56, 62, 99, 107, 128, 129, 159, 166, 197, 229, 231, 232, 252, 254, 263, 272, 325, 357, 361
Clarkson, 7, 348
Clary, 3, 168
Claude, 243
Clauzel, 110
Clay, 80, 105, 328
Clay Hill, 308
Clayton, 243, 285, 298
Cleary, 55, 101, 215, 339
Clemens, 4, 196
Clements, 45, 154
Clemments, 33
Cleveland, 16, 347
Cliffe, 259
Clifford, 100, 273
Clifton, 286
Cline, 327
Clingman, 165
Clinton, 115, 143, 361
Clinton Academy, 235
Clitz, 112
Clive, 200
Closman, 180
Clowser, 103
Cluskey, 45
Coakley, 45, 110
Coates, 211
Cobb, 247, 303
Cochran, 11, 45, 54, 224, 277
Cochrane, 279
Cock, 45, 72
Cockburn, 97, 135
Cockburne, 106
Cocke, 216
Cockerill, 255
Cockrell, 43
Cockrill, 320

Coddington, 45
Coe, 103
Coffee, 106
Coffey, 97
Cofran, 280
Cogan, 164, 315
Coggin, 244
Cohen, 129
Colclazer, 45, 74
Colcord, 260
Cole, 39, 67, 84, 115, 119, 182, 188, 291, 341
Coleman, 17, 73, 219, 229, 359
Colison, 177
Colley, 128
Collicott, 38, 76, 371
Collier, 21, 91, 93, 156
Collingwood, 117
Collins, 10, 16, 29, 45, 59, 78, 79, 83, 110, 124, 198, 222, 256, 293, 344, 345
Colston, 94, 192
Colt, 340
Colt's Armory, 266
Coltman, 347
Columbian College, 95, 213
Combs, 72, 215, 277
Comeaus, 97
Comegys, 299
Comeygs, 14
Comonfort, 7
Compton, 180
Comstock, 16, 84
Concklin, 127
Condict, 86
Condon, 315
Cone, 131, 181
Congress Burial Ground, 214
Congressional Burial Ground, 355
Congressional Cemetery, 100
Conio, 198
Conjurer Detected, 193
Conjuror Defeated, 315
Conklin, 239
Conkling, 260

Conn, 157, 172
Connell, 109, 137, 160
Connelly, 45, 242, 266, 284, 289
Conner, 22, 45, 223, 243, 293
Connolly, 14, 230, 241
Connor, 353, 356
Connors, 180
Connover, 289
Conover, 280
Conrad, 319
Contnor, 297
<u>Convalescent</u>, 354
Conway, 335
Cook, 23, 42, 45, 61, 66, 72, 78, 114, 273, 284, 312, 313, 314, 320, 321, 334, 363, 366
Cooke, 35, 218, 311
Cooley, 241, 242
Coolidge, 108, 130, 256
Coombe, 45
Coombs, 44, 45, 59, 103, 124, 128, 129, 277
Cooney, 141, 170
Cooper, 7, 15, 36, 68, 80, 129, 202, 218, 288
Copeland, 313, 319, 320, 327, 334, 363
Copley, 276
Coppee, 312, 313, 319, 327
Coppie, 334, 363
Coppish, 310
Coram, 358
Corbet, 180
Corbin, 101, 215, 362
Corcoran, 5, 22, 34, 45, 51, 131, 193, 209, 318
Corey, 294
Corneau, 106
Cornelius, 24, 103
Cornell, 291
Cornet, 299
Cornwallis, 148
Correll, 36
Corrie, 19, 36, 109, 122, 132
Corrigan, 4, 27

Corse, 272
Cortinas, 307
Cosby, 188
Cosgrove, 176
Costello, 10, 45
Costen, 45
Coster, 57, 129
Costigan, 45
Costin, 45
Cottage, 295
Cottrell, 45
Coumbe, 45
Countess de Chateaubriand, 110
Countess of Sandwich, 110
Couper, 23
Coupland, 354
Courtney, 271
Covey, 233
Cowan, 186
Cowell, 186
Cowsat, 148
Cox, 10, 20, 46, 84, 150, 156, 164, 176, 178, 245, 296, 300, 357
Coxe, 45, 93, 145, 156, 328, 361
Coxen, 24
Coxswain, 291
Coyle, 13, 129, 202, 229, 246, 278
Cragg, 262
Cragin, 31, 227
Craig, 15, 43, 62, 94, 112, 128, 186, 326, 363
Craige, 11, 32
Craighill, 222
Crain, 345
Cranch, 42, 43, 46, 66, 350
Crandall, 282
Crane, 5, 151, 178, 239, 317, 339
Crapin, 16
Craven, 32, 213, 261
Crawford, 45, 75, 89, 115, 148, 218, 303, 304, 316
Creed, 250
Crenan, 363
Crenshaw, 88, 345

Crews, 101
Crilley, 198
Crilly, 223
Crittenden, 190, 222
Croggon, 179
Croman, 347
Crome, 224, 228
Cromwell, 60, 261, 310
Crone, 79
Crooks, 196
Cropley, 18, 20, 352, 362
Cropps, 19, 42, 122
Crops, 109, 132
Crosby, 69, 149, 229
Cross, 28, 44, 45, 62, 170, 345, 347
Crouse, 4, 160
Crow, 95, 148
Crowley, 221, 330
Crown, 45, 62, 107, 365
Crozier, 20, 298
Cruger, 104
Crutchett, 20, 45
Cruvelli, 19
Cuddy, 151
Cudlip, 347
Cugnot, 104
Cuil, 210
Cull, 59, 210
Cullenane, 45
Cullinaine, 45
Cullinan, 10
Culver, 294
Cumberland, 58
Cumming, 245
Cummings, 69, 175, 365
Cummins, 86, 266
Cunningham, 48, 147, 160, 175, 187, 189, 255, 367
Cupit, 101
Curly, 101
Curran, 12, 152, 211
Curry, 189, 334
Curson, 10, 45
Curtain, 59

Curtis, 41, 160, 219, 367
Curtises, 226
Curtiss, 341
Cushing, 45, 232, 299, 303
Cushley, 45
Custards, 304
Custis, 295
cutter **Harriet Lane**, 251
Cutts, 119, 159, 166, 194, 350
Cuyler, 290
Cyphus, 109, 122, 132

D

Da Ponte, 137
Dabney, 187, 367
<u>Dacotah</u>, 319
Dacy, 79
Daggett, 238
Daggy, 50
Dahlgren, 82, 223
Daily, 250, 305
Dainese, 46
Dainesse, 92
Daingerfield, 84, 310, 313
Dale, 56, 238
Daley, 46, 85, 229
Dallas, 175, 288
Dalton, 46, 220
Daly, 79
Dana, 161, 263
Dandridge, 295
Danforth, 167
Dangerfield, 195, 310, 312, 323
Daniel, 46, 103, 233, 360
Daniels, 355
Dankworth, 142
Dant, 230, 364
Darden, 61, 266
Dardenne, 23
Dargan, 198
Darling, 120, 163
Darnell, 128
Darrell, 175, 180, 196
Dart, 13

Dashiell, 194, 268
Dashiels, 234
Daum, 355
Davenport, 32, 106, 186, 319
Davidge, 19, 45, 46, 73, 93, 155, 210, 302, 331
Davids, 262
Davidson, 3, 25, 46, 175, 309
Davis, 14, 20, 23, 26, 28, 29, 32, 46, 55, 56, 66, 72, 87, 88, 91, 93, 94, 99, 105, 129, 130, 158, 176, 190, 206, 245, 250, 258, 261, 268, 270, 284, 286, 311, 315, 339, 341, 353, 355, 368
Daw, 27, 59, 142, 288
Dawes, 350
Dawson, 46, 82, 99, 167, 171, 237, 325, 364
Day, 131, 151, 359
Daybens, 286
Dayton, 149, 320
de Arguello, 73
De Bevoise, 113
de Bodisco, 359
De Bow, 316
De Boye, 325
De Burgheim, 38
De Camp, 33
de Celis, 41
De Celis, 19
de Galvez, 283
de Grey, 349
de Klyn, 80
De Krafft, 25
De Kraft, 46, 152
de La Reintrie, 71
De Lave, 266
De Luce, 288
De Marbais, 254, 263
De Menou, 108, 133
De Metz, 119
De Neckere, 199
De Neven, 5
De Selding, 40, 46, 85
De Tocqueville, 147

De Witzleben, 325
Deacon, 239
Deahl, 368
Deakens, 30
Deale, 129
Deaman, 32
Dean, 14, 175
Deane, 210, 347
Deans, 210
Dearing, 365
Deas, 208
Dease, 83
Deasey, 46
Deberry, 368
Debold, 128
Decamp, 46
Decatur, 239, 289, 371
Dedication of St Aloysius Church, 302
Deeble, 369
Deeson, 339
Deeth, 301
Defalco, 46, 264, 342
Defore, 95
Degges, 10
DeHart, 112
Deisch, 317
DeKraft, 284, 363
Delafield, 108, 131, 143, 198
Delamere, 110
Delaney, 97, 106, 314
Delano, 25, 133
Delaplace, 180
Delee, 106
DeLee, 97
Delins, 262
Dellaway, 46, 135
Delphy, 265
Dement, 46, 180, 217
Denby, 283
Deneale, 40
Denham, 21, 46
Dennis, 129, 216, 334
Denny, 26
Dent, 34, 206, 221, 243

Denton, 226, 286
Derrick, 76
DeSoto, 22
Desser, 114
Devan, 249
Devine, 7, 58
Devoe, 270
Dew, 70
Dewees, 46, 187
Dewey, 46, 362
Dewhurst, 83
DeWitt, 102, 268
Dey, 302
Dick, 244, 261, 338, 365
Dickens, 39, 227
Dickerson, 284
Dickey, 95, 122
Dickins, 46, 133, 134
Dickinson, 119
Dicks, 132
Dickson, 103
Dietz, 146
Digges, 27, 35, 87, 88, 99, 124, 230, 245, 256, 332, 343
Diggs, 206, 272, 332
Dillard, 252
Dillaye, 270
Dillon, 73, 130, 184, 225, 226
Dimitry, 215
Dimmock, 139
Dinwiddie, 226
Disasters to our Navy, 238
Discovery, 206
Disharoon, 23
Divine, 168
Dix, 195
Dixon, 46, 123, 175, 251, 269, 283, 317, 347
Doak, 183
Doane, 149
Dobbin, 309
Dobbyn, 256
Dobson, 46
Dod, 213

Dodds, 158
Dodge, 1, 38, 165, 338, 352
Dods, 24
Dodson, 6, 46, 128, 364
Dogan, 250
Doggett, 250, 271
Doghty, 264
Dogue Creek, 232
Dogue Run Farm, 232
Dohna, 110
Dolk, 29
Donaghe, 236
Donaldson, 18, 160, 164, 278
Donelan, 46, 132
Donelson, 23, 265
Donn, 37, 46, 47, 49, 59, 214, 293
Donnelly, 129, 250, 346
Donoho, 55, 56, 189, 208, 230
Donohoo, 46, 172
Donohue, 271, 312
Donophon, 46
Dooley, 215
Doolin, 363
Dornin, 362
Dorrance, 83, 213
Dorry, 128
Dorsay, 26
Dorsey, 29, 46, 284, 310, 312, 325, 346
Dorsheimer, 229
Dort, 246
Doubleday, 168
Dougan, 244
Dougherty, 46, 47, 131
Doughty, 246, 254, 260
Douglas, 24, 26, 27, 46, 159, 314, 345
Douglass, 58, 157, 270
Dove, 46, 56, 94, 204, 229
Dowdall, 122
Dowling, 31, 34, 128
Downer, 108, 130, 131
Downes, 269
Downey, 46, 138, 338
Downie, 128
Downing, 259

Downs, 46, 73, 93, 239, 248, 272
Doyle, 108, 130, 131, 184, 225, 226, 227, 288, 351, 368
Drake, 95, 262, 328, 341, 345
Drane, 276, 332
Draper, 325
Drew, 348
Driver, 262
Drumright, 103
Drury, 16, 38, 46, 58, 59
Duane, 46
Dubant, 120, 132
Dubessey, 110
Dubois, 236
Dubuis, 214
Ducachet, 132
Ducket, 215
Duckett, 51, 70
Dudley, 60, 224, 287
Dudrow, 108, 130, 143
Duer, 202
Duffey, 46, 134, 345
Duffoo, 172
Duffy, 134, 293, 302
Dugan, 37
Duhamel, 189, 229
Duke of Abrantes, 242
Duke of Cambridge, 355
Duke of Leeds, 171
Dulaney, 46, 347
Duley, 46, 353
Dulin, 46
Dumb, 105
Dunbar, 74, 339, 350
Duncan, 93, 286
Duncannan, 286
Duncanson, 160, 162, 196, 206
Dunlap, 188, 198, 315
Dunlop, 89, 195, 237, 244, 284, 305
Dunn, 250, 371
Dunnawin, 55
Dunnican, 147
Dunnington, 56
Dupece, 2

Dupont, 33
Durbin, 84
Durr, 46
Dusenberry, 72
Dusenbury, 93
Dutton, 46, 236, 308
Duval, 152, 274
Duvall, 126, 128, 129, 153, 164, 245, 314
Duxbury Hall, 117
Dwight, 236, 306
Dwyer, 214, 280
Dyer, 46, 99, 107, 128, 158, 166, 168, 256, 271, 301, 315
Dykes, 72
Dyson, 229

E

Eakle, 46
Earl of Shrewsbury, 116
Earle, 78
Earls, 232
Early, 101, 257
Easby, 46, 200, 233, 353, 361
Eastman, 218, 267, 273, 343, 365
Eastwood School, 150
Eaton, 159, 194, 207, 221
Echorn, 230
Eckel, 46
Eckerson, 365
Eckloff, 27, 46, 59
Edelen, 60, 367
Edelin, 14, 46, 58, 59, 82, 343, 355
Edes, 32, 160
Edge Hill, 76
Edmond's Frolick, 360
Edmonds, 7
Edmonston, 57, 59, 129, 189
Edmundson, 168
Edrington, 274
Edwards, 23, 29, 46, 59, 74, 77, 91, 93, 103, 160, 202, 234, 276, 278, 280, 295, 296, 326, 370
Egbertson, 69

Eggleston, 121, 175, 189
Egleston, 73
Eichelberger, 319
Eichhorn, 245
Eickmann, 347
Eitlemann, 29
Ela, 8
Elder, 46
Elding, 31
Eldred, 205
Eldridge, 167
Eley, 365
Eliason, 232
Eliot, 101, 160, 285
Elkins, 341
Ellaville, 205
Ellery, 289
Ellet, 43
Elley, 91
Ellicott, 340, 369
Elliot, 46, 325
Elliott, 190, 347, 369
Ellis, 27, 46, 107, 112, 123, 128, 217, 220, 229, 304, 305, 361, 370
Ellmore, 288
Ellory, 280
Ellsworth, 1, 6
Elmore, 244
Elms, 297
Elvans, 214
Elwood, 267
Emerick, 46
Emerson, 58, 141, 229, 265, 326
Emich, 206
Emmanuel, 364
Emmert, 272, 318
Emmett, 168
Emory, 86
Emperor of Austria, 247
Emperor of Japan, 9
Emperor of Russia, 195
Emperor of the French, 247
Emperors of France, 39
Empie, 70

Empress of Brazil, 191
England, 284
Englehart, 87
Engles, 175
English, 46, 99, 337, 362
Ennis, 14, 46, 70, 110, 160, 164, 165, 204, 229, 235, 313
Enos, 341
Entwisle, 294
Entwistle, 251
Episcopal burying ground, 334
Ernest, 188
Erskine, 22, 171
Erwin, 302
Eslin, 10
Espey, 38
Espy, 257
Essellerugge, 360
Essex, 368
Estlin, 120
Etcherson, 103
Eustis, 131
Evans, 46, 50, 60, 97, 106, 161, 172, 208, 218, 222, 237, 259, 273, 284, 310, 312, 315, 351
Everett, 46, 120, 214, 219
Evington, 354
Ewbank, 247
Ewell, 35, 70
Ewing, 5
Exchange Hotel, 87
Eyre, 46, 287

F

Faber, 47
Fagan, 47
Fahay, 350
Faherty, 47
Fairbank, 72
Fairbanks, 42
Fairchild, 244
Fairchilds, 13, 81, 93, 155
Fairfax, 261, 295
Falconer, 47, 238

Fales, 297
Faley, 116
Falls, 362
Falls Plantation, 249
Fann, 122
Fanning, 59, 80
Fant, 213
Farley, 28, 114, 140
Farmer, 120
Farnham, 169, 257
Faron, 152
Farquahar, 192
Farquhar, 17
Farra, 106
Farragut, 288
Farrand, 287
Farrar, 47, 97, 161
Farrell, 47
Farrish, 161
Farrow, 169
Faulkner, 147, 148, 319
Fauntleroy, 268
Fauquier White Sulphur Springs, 212
Favier, 47
Fay, 282
Fearson, 47, 114, 160, 196, 202
Featherstone, 69
Feeney, 216
Fegaro, 357
Feig, 355
Fejee Islands, 61
Fellows, 73
Felsom, 47
Felt, 258
Felton, 219
Fendall, 15, 163, 298, 299
Fenelon, 271
Fennell, 95
Fenno, 47
Fenwick, 95, 118, 135, 165, 182, 353
Feortney, 70
Feran, 47
Ferguson, 47, 92, 149, 275, 309, 322, 348, 362

Ferris, 47
Ferry, 32, 124
Feutchwanger, 30
Fewkes, 168
Field, 86, 91, 111, 213
Fill, 358
Fillebrown, 62
Finch, 47, 208
Finkman, 47
Finley, 164
Finney, 261
Fire King, 267
First Things, 104
Fischer, 47, 63, 169, 174, 181, 186
Fish, 23, 73
Fisher, 13, 17, 44, 47, 56, 65, 80, 107, 126, 158, 159, 166, 168, 178, 220, 229, 238, 247, 252, 271
Fisk, 47
Fisler, 275
Fitch, 100, 119, 136, 218, 262, 273
Fitzgerald, 47, 49, 107, 168, 261, 310
Fitzgerld, 59
Fitzhugh, 13, 47, 182, 191, 333
Fitzpatrick, 77, 127, 229, 284, 341, 363
Fitzwilliam, 116
Flagg, 18
Flaherty, 59, 142, 229
Flannerty, 241
Flannery, 47, 211, 325
Flannigan, 70
Flashell, 230
Fleckinger, 210
Fleckner, 71
Fleetwood, 220
Fleming, 94, 99, 337
Fletcher, 10, 47, 80, 239, 282, 362
Flint, 47, 325, 326
Flood, 296
Flower Hill, 272
Flowers, 265, 304
Floyd, 100, 213, 290, 301
Flynn, 47
Foer-tsigo, 9

Fogle, 296
Foley, 124, 132, 157, 204, 218, 263, 313
Folk, 36
Follansbee, 353
Follansbie, 288
Foller, 63
Follett, 30, 314
Fonthill, 360
Foote, 215
Forbes, 36
Force, 47, 56, 76, 283, 294
Ford, 129, 177, 339, 358, 360, 369, 370
Fore, 73, 78, 93
Foreign Protestant Cemetery, 223
Foreman, 326
Forest, 227
Forest Hill, 245
Forney, 151, 188
Forrest, 9, 21, 47, 121, 129, 161, 202, 267, 280, 289, 313, 360
Forsyth, 55, 98, 344
Fort, 171
Fort Adams, 268
Fort Arbuckle, 151
Fort Atkinson, 190
Fort Belknap, 134, 181
Fort Bliss, 92
Fort Brown, 34
Fort Erie, 234
Fort Hall, 327
Fort Independence, 268
Fort John, 41
Fort Kearny, 190
Fort Leavenworth, 267
Fort Monroe, 203
Fort Puebla, 203
Fort Randall, 26
Fort Ripley, 220
Fort Smith, 151, 287
Fort Washington, 184, 275
Fort Wayne, 171
Fortress Monroe, 290
Foster, 46, 138, 259, 267
Foulk, 321

Foulkes, 47
Fountain, 310, 312, 322, 323
Four, 303
Fowble, 47, 92
Fowke, 47
Fowle, 211, 272
Fowler, 24, 47, 237, 325, 364
Fowlkes, 158
Fox, 18, 47, 80, 314, 365
Foy, 47, 318
Fraley, 114
Francher, 188
Francisco, 211
Frank, 112
Franklin, 99, 291, 298, 302, 318, 326, 360, 371
Franklin Row, 94
Franks, 41, 309
Frasch, 161
Frazee, 13
Frazer, 26, 131
Frazier, 47, 131
Fredinberger, 47
Freeland, 122
Freeman, 8, 137, 341, 352
Freiz, 154
Fremont, 13, 19, 41, 209
French, 1, 47, 133, 189, 203, 204, 249, 255, 281, 325, 342, 347, 355
Frezzolini, 19
Friend, 52
Friendship, 242
frig **Chesapeake**, 239
frig **Essex**, 239
frig **Fulton**, 313
frig **Niagara**, 91
frig **Philadelphia**, 371
frig **Powhatan**, 125, 282
frig **President**, 239
frig **Roanoke**, 208
frig **St Lawrence**, 161
frig **Wabash**, 362
Fristoe, 97
Fritz, 370

Frononberger, 11
Frost, 227, 371
Frothingham, 168, 219
Froude, 110
Fry, 127, 183, 186
Frye, 54
Fryxell, 292
Fudge, 294
Fugett, 336
Fulce, 192
Fullalove, 99
Fuller, 122, 123, 162, 255
Fullerton, 229
Fulmer, 257
Fulton, 31, 121, 307
Funk, 250
Furber, 362
Furguson, 177
Furnace Farm, 27

G

Gachet, 192
Gadsby, 47, 179, 331
Gage, 22, 339
Gaines, 78, 93, 101
Gaither, 23, 66, 344
Gale, 17, 106
Gallagher, 47, 239
Gallaher, 244, 250, 302
Gallant, 47, 58, 229
Gallaudet, 370
Galligan, 47
Galloway, 145
Gallup, 26
Galt, 128, 161, 167, 259, 301, 321, 333, 354
Gamble, 154, 240
Gambrill, 109, 122, 132
Gammon, 81, 93
Gantt, 156, 172
Gantz, 253
Garcia, 193, 307
Gardener, 95, 153, 320

Gardiner, 21, 47, 56, 95, 144, 215, 220, 256
Gardner, 27, 47, 151, 210, 224, 273
Garland, 217, 261, 268
Garman, 26
Garner, 47, 195, 331
Garnett, 85, 159, 226
Garrett, 5, 47, 128
Garrison, 197, 199, 273
Gartland, 294
Garvin, 362
Gasenheimer, 4, 27
Gaskins, 175
Gassaway, 243
Gassawy, 79
Gasynski, 163
Gatch, 250
Gates, 58, 59, 230, 293
Gatewood, 302, 313
Gatton, 292
Gault, 59
Gautier, 229, 310
Gaw, 8
Gawler, 128
Gay, 44
Gay Mont, 208
Gayle, 232, 292
Gaylord, 358
Geary, 61
Gedney, 74
Geekie, 316
Geisinger, 280, 289
Gelston, 16
Gensler, 305
George, 337
George II, 143, 342
Gerhardt, 19, 61
Gerry, 238
Gevasco, 198
Geyer, 96, 172
Gholson, 268
Gibbes, 193
Gibbons, 23, 33, 242, 309, 349
Gibbs, 31, 62, 196, 246

Gibson, 35, 47, 54, 99, 124, 208, 245, 266, 272, 286, 321, 340, 370
Gideon, 45, 152, 329, 352
Gifford, 171, 177
Gignoux, 119
Gilbert, 360
Gildea, 317
Giles, 164, 168, 224
Gill, 59, 68
Gillespie, 213
Gillet, 210, 326
Gillett, 209, 326
Gilley, 231
Gilliam, 322
Gillis, 47
Gilliss, 154
Gilllingham, 232
Gilman, 128, 183, 198, 336
Gilmer, 146, 338, 342
Gilmore, 275
Gingle, 86
Ginnaty, 59
Ginnity, 139, 296
Giustiniani, 117
Given, 128, 189
Givenny, 49
Givens, 119, 222
Glading, 261
Gladman, 47
Gladmon, 64, 300
Glanding, 93
Glasco, 218
Glass, 221
Glavecke, 12
Glaze, 173
Gleesen, 115
Glenn, 13, 80, 93, 152, 156
Gline, 147
Glover, 97, 106, 194
Gobright, 204
Goddard, 47, 59, 60, 128, 134, 165, 229, 347
Godey, 29
Godfrey, 47, 164, 350

Goff, 38, 93, 156
Golden, 277
Golding, 164
Goldsborough, 50
Goldsbrough, 305
Goldschmidt, 241
Goldsmith, 367
Gonzaga, 307
Goodall, 129, 341
Goode, 214
Gooding, 191, 222
Goodnow, 257
Goodwin, 107, 243, 302, 313
Goodyear, 60
Gorden, 272
Gordon, 18, 47, 119, 280, 305
Gore, 354
Gorham, 328, 329
Gorman, 7
Gormley, 223, 246, 276
Gormly, 59
Gough, 123
Gould, 326
Gouverneur, 47
Gowan, 339
Gowen, 5
Grady, 250
Graham, 18, 38, 74, 168, 270, 280, 283, 288, 289, 339
Grammer, 47
Granberry, 292
Granbery, 309
Grandin, 103
Grant, 7, 33, 167
Granwell, 263
Gratiot, 35
Grattan, 243
Graves, 68, 79, 292
Gray, 60, 65, 139, 141, 173, 219, 276, 305, 334, 347
Grayson, 12, 82
Greeley, 320
Green, 14, 22, 27, 47, 65, 89, 129, 130, 133, 135, 147, 152, 172, 197, 212,

216, 219, 246, 261, 271, 273, 310, 312, 322, 323, 334, 349, 353, 359, 360, 363, 371
Greene, 26, 192, 218, 252
Greenleaf, 47, 83, 142
Greenleaf's Point, 96, 135, 136, 347
Greenlief, 342
Greenough, 194, 229
Greentrup, 47, 147, 336
Greenwell, 10, 129, 287
Greenwood, 161, 163
Greenwood Cemetery, 109
Greer, 47, 261
Gregg, 1, 47, 118
Gregory, 84
Gregory XV, 307
Grenan, 47
Gresam, 200
Grey, 270
Grier, 62, 152
Griffen, 242
Griffin, 99, 124, 145, 161, 210, 314, 366, 367
Griffith, 45, 103, 170, 171, 180, 355
Griffiths, 326
Grigsby, 85
Grimes, 164, 211
Grinder, 129
Grinnell, 302
Grist, 321
Griswold, 89, 323, 366
Grits, 321
Gritzner, 47
Groenveldt, 47
Groff, 47
Groom, 124
Grooms, 23
Groot, 47
Gross, 47
Grosse, 119
Groux, 68, 216
Groves, 12, 196, 236
Grubb, 36, 351
Grymes, 56, 330

Gtwn College, 215
Gueble, 287
Guenther, 198, 223
Guiees, 2
Guillory, 39, 85
Guillot, 325
Guise, 200
Gulliver, 257
Gunnell, 47, 204, 284, 333, 340
Gunnells', 173
Gunton, 37, 47, 169, 181, 186, 202, 224
Gurley, 60, 95, 136, 231, 235, 243, 300, 325, 360, 362
Gurry, 211, 331
Guthrie, 261
Guy, 128, 359
Guys, 2
Gwinn, 47
Gwinne, 108
Gwynn, 290

H

Habicht, 64, 93, 155
Hackett, 193
Hackley, 350
Haddock, 290, 298
Haddock's Hill, 346
Hagan, 77, 106, 127, 242
Hager, 48
Hagerty, 329
Hagner, 365
Haight, 253
Haines, 94, 167, 269
Haislip, 48
Haldemar, 143, 144
Hale, 26, 33, 75
Haley, 20
Hall, 13, 15, 19, 23, 33, 48, 69, 87, 89, 93, 101, 105, 109, 115, 147, 154, 162, 188, 192, 198, 206, 208, 223, 236, 240, 251, 281, 303, 330, 338, 351, 353, 366
Hallam, 81
Halliday, 55

Hallonquist, 222
Halloway, 5
Hallowell, 91, 254
Halpin, 146
Halse, 284
Halsey, 84
Hambleton, 64, 72
Hamer, 73
Hamersley, 179
Hames, 244
Hamilton, 41, 47, 48, 62, 84, 103, 115, 133, 134, 143, 158, 166, 236, 262, 276, 313, 318, 320, 322, 323, 324, 340, 345
Hamilton's Choice, 324
Hammersley, 164
Hammett, 177
Hammitt, 95
Hammond, 5, 26, 48, 165, 244, 345
Hancock, 10, 238, 287, 361
Hand, 227
Handly, 142
Handy, 48, 59, 134, 217, 243, 291, 292, 372
Hanna, 323
Hannegan, 89
Hanover, 124
Hanretty, 250
Hanscom, 84
Hansell, 32
Hanson, 7, 48, 84, 259
Harbaugh, 56, 58, 99, 110, 353
Harbour, 97, 106
Harcourt, 184
Harden, 125, 223
Hardin, 198
Harding, 77, 110, 319
Hardwick, 226
Hardy, 13, 48, 93, 154
Hare, 68
Hargate, 71
Harkness, 39, 48, 61, 129, 244
Harkreder, 26
Harlan, 95

Harper, 48, 128, 130, 160, 164, 230
Harper's Ferry, 309, 310, 312, 314, 315, 319, 320, 321, 323, 324, 327, 328, 330, 339, 349, 351, 352, 354, 357, 363, 366
Harper's Grove, 259
Harrington, 319, 327, 329
Harriott, 236
Harris, 11, 14, 15, 16, 19, 23, 26, 39, 41, 48, 82, 90, 92, 94, 161, 187, 210, 218, 221, 273, 280, 283, 284, 289, 291, 300, 312, 362
Harrison, 48, 59, 90, 93, 110, 129, 210, 261, 333
Harrover, 59, 128, 265, 293
Harry, 27, 370
Hart, 48, 76, 119, 141, 170, 209, 223, 291, 317, 327
Harte, 5, 216
Hartly, 190
Hartnett, 233
Hartstene, 19, 21, 67
Hartung, 69, 122, 150
Hartwell, 210
Harvard Univ, 229
Harvey, 62, 95, 229, 313, 341, 371
Harwood, 73
Haselwood, 362
Haskell, 48, 59, 73, 111, 311
Hasker, 175
Haskin, 131, 139
Haslitt, 312
Haslup, 48
Hass, 115, 118
Hassler, 45, 210
Hasson, 150
Hastings, 39
Haswell, 288, 338
Hatch, 298
Hatfield, 218, 261, 273
Hatton, 48
Haughton, 213
Hauptman, 128, 218
Havenner, 48

Haw, 28, 48, 137, 269, 356
Hawk, 209
Hawke, 318, 335, 361
Hawkes, 136
Hawkins, 97, 250
Hawks, 211
Hawley, 48, 151
Hawn, 188
Haxton, 261
Hay, 156
Hayden, 118, 320
Hayes, 131, 143, 221
Hays, 48, 119
Hayward, 66, 188
Haywood, 310
Hazard, 85, 216, 259
Hazel, 249
Hazeltine, 125
Hazle, 319
Hazlewood, 353
Hazlitt, 41, 277, 312
Hazzard, 94
Head, 23, 291, 366
Health Report, 76
Heaney, 201
Heard, 167
Hearsey, 106
Heart, 33, 160, 360
Heath, 48, 221, 302
Hedgman, 153
Hedgpeth, 18
Heider, 241
Heiner, 164
Heitmiller, 48
Hellen, 303
Helm, 84
Hemphill, 69
Henbury, 294
Henderson, 11, 15, 31, 66, 67, 77, 82, 186
Hendrick, 37
Hendricks, 121, 269
Henessy, 103
Hening, 23, 194

Heningsen, 102
Henke, 48
Henlein, 48
Henley, 240
Hennessy, 161
Henning, 11, 48, 52, 59, 74, 136
Hennis, 285
Henry, 70, 141, 173, 183, 186, 222, 250, 275, 291, 361, 362, 364
Henskin, 11
Hensley, 62, 64, 210
Hepburn, 48, 99, 129, 130, 162
Herbert, 28, 48, 71, 101, 215
Hermitage, 11
Herndon, 207
Herring, 272
Herron, 125, 347
Herty, 48
Hetzel, 48, 126, 136
Heuskin, 23, 94
Hewitt, 48
Heydon, 204
Heyn, 168
Hibben, 167
Hibbs, 343
Hickey, 48, 229
Hickling, 40
Hickman, 48, 113
Hicks, 12, 354
Higbee, 48
Higdon, 236
Higgins, 67, 297, 347
Hildreth, 11, 23
Hill, 5, 10, 11, 12, 16, 48, 86, 87, 101, 150, 153, 167, 199, 215, 235, 236, 253, 262, 277, 294, 327, 355, 366, 367
Hillandale, 94
Hillar, 239
Hillmacher, 119
Hillyer, 24
Hilt, 244
Hilton, 39, 64, 167
Hinckley, 119
Hincks, 143

Hine, 84
Hines, 48, 95
Hinton, 48, 129, 184
Hiriart, 110
Hisch, 22
Hitz, 48, 58, 218, 266, 268
Hoag, 100
Hobart, 161, 326
Hobso, 337
Hodes, 106
Hodge, 64
Hodges, 90, 97, 113, 144, 234
Hodgson, 96, 142
Hoester, 61
Hoffa, 204
Hoffman, 2, 48, 258, 330
Hogan, 48, 121, 125, 300
Hogg, 22, 195
Hoit, 316
Holbert, 310
Holbrook, 5, 62
Holden, 60, 282
Holfield, 119
Holgate, 32
Holker, 86
Holladay, 182
Holland, 48, 340
Holley, 320
Holliday, 213
Hollingshead, 210
Hollins, 95, 365
Hollister, 355
Holly, 313, 341, 345
Hollywood Cemetery, 322
Holman, 273
Holmead, 7, 42, 44, 82, 223, 241, 290, 305, 306, 318, 319, 326
Holmes, 5, 23, 28, 93, 151, 251, 256, 275
Holmes' Run, 64
Holsey, 132
Holston, 95
Holt, 60, 207
Holtzclaw, 48

Holtzman, 48
Hood, 299
Hooe, 128
Hooker, 62
Hooper, 8, 98, 173, 176, 220
Hoover, 18, 19, 48, 68, 128, 130, 134, 183, 253, 279
Hope, 82, 291, 367
Hopfar, 19
Hopkins, 48, 61, 99, 130, 137, 237, 243, 369
Hopper, 41
Horner, 135
Horseman, 176
Horton, 316
Hosmer, 278
Hotchkiss, 225
Hough, 84
Houry, 110
Houser, 161
Houston, 48, 128, 152, 283
Houzam, 48
Howard, 48, 73, 90, 96, 101, 116, 142, 145, 215, 227, 348
Howe, 184, 200, 284
Howell, 48, 81, 83, 99, 104, 200, 328, 362
Howick, 349
Howison, 239, 362
Howitt, 233
Howland, 168, 347
Howle, 33, 172
Howlett, 363
Howlin, 163
Howser, 284
Hoyt, 321, 323
Huarck, 97
Huard, 106
Hubbard, 64, 93, 155, 282, 327
Hudry, 7
Hudson, 31, 36, 91, 106, 195, 239
Huertas, 81
Huff, 188

Hughes, 48, 56, 129, 271, 307, 336, 363, 371
Hull, 161
Hulse, 152
Humboldt, 170
Hume, 60
Humphreys, 35, 37, 100, 156, 283, 300, 305
Humphries, 48
Hungerford, 140
Hunnicutt, 330
Hunsdon, 295
Hunt, 48, 222, 275, 277, 298, 363
Hunter, 85, 121, 154, 157, 167, 211, 260, 319, 321, 339, 345, 346, 349
Huntley, 161, 309
Hurd, 226, 247
Hurdle, 99, 124, 220
Hurley, 124, 208, 274
Hurst, 305, 308
Huston, 25
Hutchines, 341
Hutchings, 70
Hutchins, 48, 59, 67, 110, 160, 164, 165, 216, 235
Hutchinson, 24, 48, 59, 78, 136, 148, 208, 249, 276
Huthmann, 29
Huttman, 32, 87
Hutton, 270, 328
Hyams, 336
Hyatt, 28, 48, 134, 199, 212
Hyde, 24, 37, 48, 89, 108, 117, 128, 200, 220, 223, 225
Hyle, 85
Hynes, 187

I

I'on, 228
Iardella, 99
Iddins, 48
Imlay, 69
Indermauer, 48
Indian Headquarters, 168
Indiana divorces, 257
Ingersoll, 33, 64, 93, 105, 156
Ingle, 48, 55, 99, 235, 324, 332, 343, 359
Ingraham, 15, 31
Insurrection at Harper's Ferry, 310
Irarrazaval, 346
Irby, 243
Ironside, 57, 174
Irvine, 22
Irving, 160, 348, 352
Irvington, 348
Irwin, 48, 76, 164
Isaac, 296
Isbell, 101
Iseman, 48
Ives, 107
Ized, 97
Izod, 106

J

Jackson, 1, 5, 48, 66, 67, 80, 97, 106, 113, 124, 128, 138, 147, 148, 165, 168, 194, 211, 214, 215, 222, 252, 260, 284, 302, 326, 339, 369
Jacobi, 49, 172
Jacobs, 13, 49, 200, 209, 241
James, 37, 81, 95, 106, 197, 246, 298, 325, 360, 364
James' creek, 264
Jameson, 256, 369
Jamesson, 289
Jamieson, 84, 193, 195
Jamison, 352
Janney, 127
Jannings, 49
Jansen, 213
Jaqueline, 295
Jarvis, 119
Jasper, 107
Jeffers, 49, 288
Jefferson, 70, 236
Jeffrey, 135
Jeffries, 221

Jenkins, 49, 67, 96, 128, 147, 315, 326, 369
Jennett, 143
Jennings, 127, 164, 169, 187
Jennings' Estate, 187
Jennison, 266
Jensenney, 244
Jerome, 73
Jesuits, 363
Jesup, 222
Jesus, 40
Jewell, 49, 237, 326
Jillard, 128
Johns, 142, 145
Johnson, 21, 32, 37, 39, 49, 58, 59, 61, 95, 99, 100, 102, 109, 118, 119, 128, 143, 152, 157, 165, 169, 170, 176, 230, 236, 240, 243, 247, 252, 253, 255, 282, 305, 307, 309, 317, 319, 324, 334, 357, 362, 363, 371
Johnston, 55, 95, 167, 173, 230, 251, 347, 361
Johnstone, 22
Joiner, 271
Jolly, 49, 322
Jomard, 241
Jonathan Oldstyle, 348
Jones, 9, 10, 12, 18, 22, 23, 32, 39, 49, 57, 58, 61, 69, 70, 82, 89, 101, 107, 110, 132, 141, 160, 162, 164, 165, 174, 178, 189, 208, 209, 213, 220, 229, 235, 236, 240, 241, 250, 261, 275, 288, 289, 292, 300, 306, 311, 322, 325, 328, 339, 343, 364, 368, 370
Jordan, 49, 63, 168, 229, 284, 288
Joslin, 231
Joyce, 163, 229
Joynes, 85
Judd, 138
Judsons, 226
Juertas, 93
Jumpertz, 69, 122, 260
Junkin, 333
Junot, 242

K

Kaehler, 176
Kagg, 310
Kagi, 313, 314, 320, 327
Kaiser, 14, 49
Kall, 49
Kalorama, 165
Kammerhueber, 49
Kanalley, 61
Kane, 12, 73, 99, 177, 192, 230, 278, 302
Kapps, 147
Kaufman, 367
Kay, 81
Kean, 77
Kearney, 141, 239, 314
Keating, 49, 258, 284
Keck, 350
Keech, 29, 36, 71, 230
Keefe, 371
Keefer, 54
Keegan, 68
Keehlan, 49
Keeler, 236
Keeley, 368
Keen, 49
Keenan, 184, 225, 227, 230, 356
Keene, 168
Keep, 344
Keese, 49
Kegan, 107
Kehew, 100
Kehler, 315
Keiler, 135
Keilholtz, 176, 329
Keilhultz, 319
Keilsey, 32
Keister, 6
Keith, 84, 130, 152, 205, 212, 215, 285
Keitt, 172, 176
Kelcher, 256
Kell, 287
Keller, 49, 58, 196, 258, 341
Kelley, 168

Kelly, 23, 49, 59, 64, 74, 85, 92, 115, 128, 130, 168, 257, 279, 293, 312, 319, 321, 337, 362
Kelsey, 37
Kelton, 122, 190
Kemper, 325
Kempshott, 342
Kenallly, 85
Kendall, 49, 111
Kendrick, 49
Kenevane, 190
Kennaugh, 276
Kennedy, 5, 21, 26, 39, 49, 57, 80, 88, 105, 127, 147, 150, 157, 200, 230, 257, 311, 315, 319, 334
Kenney, 43, 326
Kennicutt, 5
Kennon, 120, 239
Kenrick, 170, 240
Kent, 145, 243
Kerfoot, 258
Kern, 188, 198
Kerowltin, 26
Kerr, 167, 260, 300
Kersey, 25
Kessler, 359
ketch **Brothers**, 22
ketch **Intrepid**, 240
ketch **Spitfire**, 240
Ketchan, 325
Kettle, 204
Key, 13, 17, 33, 49, 70, 89, 100, 108, 111, 130, 135, 137, 138, 139, 142, 147, 154, 170
Keyes, 112
Keyser, 318
Kibbey, 48, 49
Kidd, 200
Kidder, 49
Kidwell, 19, 49, 59, 230, 245
Kieckhoefer, 33
Kiernan, 49
Kieth, 14
Kilburn, 22

Kilgour, 193, 194
killed, 321
Killman, 49
Kilzmeiller, 312
Kimball, 258, 362
Kinckle, 340
King, 31, 49, 59, 71, 77, 79, 81, 89, 93, 95, 115, 124, 129, 142, 150, 155, 175, 182, 192, 213, 220, 230, 253, 265, 314, 325, 331, 349, 361
King of Sweden, 229
Kingdon, 244
Kingford, 257
Kingman, 5
Kingsford, 226, 234, 235
Kingsland, 131
Kingston, 106
Kinkhead, 236
Kinney, 326
Kinsey, 129
Kinsley, 43
Kinsolving, 224, 250
Kinston, 97
Kinzer, 234
Kipp, 201
Kirby, 186, 216
Kirk, 79, 99, 166, 184, 209
Kirkland, 365
Kirkley, 206, 358
Kirkwood, 208, 342
Kirtland, 346
Kitchen, 362
Kite, 309
Kittzmiller, 319
Kleiber, 56, 70, 85
Klein, 299
Kleindenst, 49
Kleindienst, 357
Kling, 265
Klitman, 76
Klopfer, 49, 55, 136, 353
Kloppinger, 292
Knapp, 210, 326
Knick, 22

Knight, 21, 49, 128, 130, 158, 172, 189
Knoblock, 108
Knooks, 169
Knott, 270
Knox, 49
Koch, 127
Kokouski, 72
Koons, 135
Korrel, 11
Koscialouski, 41
Koscio_ski, 179
Kraft, 49, 59
Kramer, 103
Krantz, 345
Kreamer, 32, 153
Krehmer, 318
Kretschmar, 325
Kroft, 49
Kronk, 262
Krouse, 353
Kuhland, 24
Kuhn, 49
Kulinski, 364
Kulstar, 347
Kurtz, 49
Kyle, 327

L

La Mountain, 96, 290, 298
Lacey, 49, 60
Lackey, 229
Laclere, 248
Lacouel, 106
Lacouture, 301
Lacy, 14, 192
Ladies' Mount Vernon Association, 346
Lafar, 176
Lafayette, 64
Lafontaine, 50
Laight, 361
Laird, 211
Lakemeyer, 114
Lamar, 236

Lamb, 49, 89, 202, 231
Lambert, 119, 189, 208, 329
Lambright, 322, 323
Lammond, 50
Lampson, 366
Lamson, 366
Lanahan, 88, 103, 126, 165
Lanard, 25
Lancaster, 50, 215, 256
Land, 219
Lander, 42
Landry, 64
Landsdale, 152
Landstreet, 103
Landy, 93
Lane, 6, 74, 163, 180, 210, 213, 341
Laney, 148
Lang, 237, 347
Langdon, 103
Langenbech, 265
Langhorn, 147
Langley, 92, 354
Langton, 324
Lansdale, 286, 365
Lanstreet, 304
Lanthall, 126
Lapice, 350
Larcombe, 184, 225
Lardner, 171
Larned, 15
Larrabie, 159
Laskey, 20, 49, 50, 229, 363
Lathan, 148, 204
Latimer, 222, 322, 323
Latta, 236, 323
Laub, 97
Lauck, 60, 235
Laurant, 155
Laurens, 94, 108
Laurenson, 57
Laurent, 13, 32, 39, 93
Lauri, 208
Lavalette, 289, 362
Lavellette, 280

Laville, 106
Law, 50
Lawrence, 19, 49, 208, 239, 246, 260, 289, 302
Laws, 286
Lawson, 15, 49
Lawton, 5, 152
Lay, 183, 222, 316
Layman, 13, 93
Lazella, 92
Lazenby, 49, 89
Le Compte, 330
Leach, 31, 50, 129, 170, 236, 262, 288
Leacock, 104, 293
Leak, 80
Leake, 21, 152
Lear, 50, 143, 165
Leary, 223, 310, 313, 327
Leas, 31
Leavitt, 217
Lebanon, 10
Lecaze, 8, 38
Leddy, 184, 225
Ledwitch, 293
Lee, 26, 27, 31, 34, 41, 49, 50, 81, 93, 107, 111, 112, 121, 127, 167, 173, 181, 184, 185, 190, 204, 209, 216, 222, 268, 280, 305, 308, 310, 312, 322, 333, 340, 341, 344, 354, 361, 364, 370
Leech, 88
Leef, 33
Leeman, 312
Lees, 168, 324
Lefevre, 108
Legett, 232
Legg, 363
Leggett, 49, 232
Lehman, 152
Lehne, 232
Leidy, 129
Leighton, 161
Leiper, 287, 290
Leite, 128

Leith, 110
Leman, 313
Lemist, 249
Lemon, 103, 322
Lendrum, 112
Lennie, 128
Lenox, 27
Leonard, 194, 213, 341, 356, 357
Lephard, 49
Lepine, 100
LeRoy, 261
Leslie, 148, 174, 184, 283
Lesson, 286
Lester, 176
Letcher, 146
Lethcer, 357
Letherman, 150
Leupp, 298
Leutze, 88
Lever, 103, 264
Leverett, 190
Leveritt, 2
Levy, 36, 239, 284
Lewis, 5, 10, 17, 34, 49, 50, 60, 62, 64, 72, 84, 93, 123, 143, 152, 155, 178, 209, 213, 219, 223, 232, 305, 308, 319, 326, 328, 337, 338, 353, 364, 372
Libbey, 24, 31, 120, 144, 245
Lieberman, 318
Liebermann, 101
Lightell, 50
Ligon, 26
Limantour, 71
Limbeck, 147
Lincoln, 150, 210, 229
Lind, 114, 241
Linden, 195
Linden Farm, 32
Linderman, 265
Lindsay, 115, 340, 359
Lindsey, 118, 290
Lindsley, 202
Ling, 19
Lingan, 30, 66, 205

Lining, 31
Linkins, 10, 50, 58
Linthicum, 99, 103, 314
Linton, 224
Lintz, 21
Lionberger Farm, 309
Lippard, 49, 99
Lippitt, 334
Lipscomb, 64, 368
Litch, 261
Litchfield, 362
Little, 13, 20, 50, 335
Little Hunting Creek, 232
Littleton, 343
Livingston, 18, 31, 32, 327
Lloyd, 50, 57, 61, 63, 92, 100, 102, 137, 140, 173, 218, 256, 288, 305, 322, 358
<u>Loch Willow School</u>, 225
Lochett, 171
Lock, 319
Locke, 55, 57, 178, 284
Lockerey, 143
Lockett, 198, 222
Lockridge, 6
Lockwood, 124, 227
Locquet, 110
Locust Grove Farm, 30
Loeffler, 59, 100, 336
Loefler, 92
Logan, 35, 131
Loker, 243
Lommond, 129
Long, 13, 25, 93, 126, 154, 168, 187, 289
Long Old Fields, 269
Longfellow, 229
Looker, 288
Loomis, 81, 93, 249, 288
Looney, 10, 168, 225, 227
Lopp, 273
Lord, 7, 84
Loring, 139, 190
Loud, 347
Loughborough, 49, 352

Loughlin, 269
Loury, 167
Love, 196, 208
Lovejoy, 49, 56
Lovelace, 215
Loveling, 324
Lovete, 142
Lovett, 28
Lowe, 49, 92, 99, 298, 304, 361
Lowenstein, 356
Lowndes, 165
Lownds, 96, 257
Lowry, 50
Loyd, 59
Luber, 17
Lucas, 27, 37, 325
Luce, 115
<u>Lucifer matches</u>, 176
Lucket, 343
Luckett, 49, 73, 230
Ludlam, 340
Ludwig, 192, 223
Lumpkin, 50, 269, 352
Lumsden, 103
Lund, 326
Lunt, 50, 326
Lurget, 106
Lurty, 97, 106
Lutz, 9
Lycurgus, 145
Lyddane, 194
Lyle, 168
Lynch, 45, 143, 152, 163, 369
Lyndall, 166, 322, 323
Lyndhurst, 276
Lyon, 247
Lyons, 3, 58, 85, 130, 147, 212
Lytle, 119

M

Maack, 51
Macabee, 63, 64
Macalester, 119
Macaulay, 371

Maccour, 31
Macdonough, 289
Macgill, 295, 297
Machen, 354
Macintosh, 129
Mack, 59
Mackall, 51
MacKenzie, 192
Mackey, 102, 205
MacLeod, 246
Maclure, 302
Macmurdo, 65
Macnamara, 50, 184
Macomb, 50, 62, 134
Macomber, 82
Macon, 245
Macrae, 152, 221
Macy, 210
Maddam's Neglect, 63
Madden, 69
Maddox, 7, 19, 50, 104
Mades, 177, 339
Madison, 50, 70, 101, 119, 236, 239, 245, 306, 335
Maedel, 325
Maffit, 94, 261
Maffitt, 108
Magee, 7, 31, 157, 315
Magher, 230
Magie, 348
Magoffin, 362
Magrath, 22, 24
Magruder, 31, 60, 65, 82, 89, 102, 103, 129, 151, 172, 189, 242, 245, 288, 331, 340
Magruder's Plains Enlarged, 282
Maguire, 10, 22, 31, 167, 307
Mahan, 192
Mahar, 24
Maher, 51, 138, 153, 158, 166, 168, 271
Mahoney, 364
Mahorney, 229
Major, 215, 297, 325
Majors, 84

Malesherbes, 147
Maley, 300
Malierino, 236
Malihan, 32
Mallet, 8, 38
Malone, 59
Maloney, 363
Malvina, 263
Mandeville, 31
Manhart, 281
Mann, 5, 134, 139, 142, 219, 238, 246, 277, 347
Mannery, 214
Manning, 200, 263, 362
Mansfield, 61, 79, 259
Mansion House Farm, 232
Maraschi, 311
Marbury, 89, 125, 126, 164, 361
Marcellus, 194
Marceron, 158
March, 14, 73, 103
Marcy, 194, 262
Mardin, 371
Marine Corps, 82
Marion, 215
Marix, 90
Markoe, 83
Markriter, 144
Marks, 97, 106, 135, 151, 322, 323
Marlow, 50, 129, 245
Marquis of Waterford, 138, 141
marriage licenses, 369
Marron, 94, 98, 101
Marryman, 50
Marsh, 38, 229, 327, 354
Marshal de Saxe, 104
Marshall, 51, 161, 182, 215, 245, 247, 263
Marston, 239
Martaini, 298
Martier, 291
Martin, 13, 51, 58, 77, 95, 108, 127, 130, 131, 189, 215, 221, 280, 282, 284, 285, 293, 313, 353, 354, 355, 363

Marvell, 139
Marvin, 84
Marx, 249
Maryman, 319
Masi, 331, 338
Masin, 347
Mason, 26, 50, 121, 134, 166, 207, 224, 232, 248, 254, 265, 270, 290, 305, 308, 320, 322, 325, 326, 355
Massey, 25, 91, 148
Massie, 107, 122, 309
Masters, 186, 234, 319
Mather, 104
Mathews, 209
Mathieu, 31
Mathiot, 53, 216, 341
Mathis, 95
Matlock, 127, 253, 282
Matschack, 153
Matterson, 234
Matteson, 26, 326
Matthews, 99, 145, 155, 209, 230, 231
Matthewson, 104
Mattingly, 52, 58, 129, 153, 160, 202, 217, 256
Maude, 311
Maulsby, 71, 142, 282
Maupertuis, 35
Maupin, 187, 356
Maury, 12, 13, 67, 94, 100, 102, 105, 111, 115, 147, 154, 157, 335
Maxcy, 217
Maxwell, 4, 50, 51, 67, 85, 92, 151, 281
May, 75, 127, 208, 265, 305, 323, 368
Mayer, 262
Mayers, 206
Mayes, 37
Mayfield, 128
Maygart, 41
Maylan, 365
Mayo, 278, 289
Mayor, 152
Mayres, 345
Mays, 268

McAfee, 165
McAlister, 327
McAllister, 153
McAlpine, 288
McArery, 79
McAvery, 69
McAvoy, 50
McBee, 303
McBlair, 142, 146, 175, 179
McBride, 22, 50, 186
McCabe, 321
McCalla, 50, 163, 323
McCallough, 66
McCamie, 66, 148
McCarick, 216
McCarrick, 241
McCarthy, 50, 51, 301
McCartney, 248
McCarty, 50, 122, 250
McCauley, 15, 75, 92, 93, 103, 141, 155
McCauly, 364
McCay, 148
McCeny, 99
McClair, 331
McCleary, 51, 162
McClelland, 85
McClery, 106, 144, 197, 235, 283
McClintock, 302, 337
McClosky, 141
McCluney, 280, 289
McClung, 236, 263
McClure, 317
McCoffrey, 168
McColgan, 61
McCollier, 362
McCollum, 3, 10, 50, 51, 79, 168
McConchie, 195, 331
McConkie, 50
McConnell, 331
McCook, 112, 192
McCord, 73
McCorkle, 50, 105, 144
McCormack, 168

McCormick, 33, 42, 50, 84, 91, 130, 131, 179, 239
McCown, 83
McCoy, 55, 108
McCrabb, 116, 351, 355
McCrown, 305
McCulloch, 69
McCullock, 148
McCulloh, 25
McCullom, 353
McCullough, 210
McCutchen, 50, 366, 367
McCutcheon, 72
McDaniel, 88, 126, 245, 346
McDermot, 229
McDermott, 14, 59, 129, 130
McDonald, 50, 141, 162, 186, 244, 321, 340
McDonough, 115
McDougal, 273
McDougall, 62, 218
McDowell, 22, 149, 243
McDuel, 81
McDuell, 81
McDuffie, 121
McElfresh, 50, 272
McElhone, 134, 141, 143
McElroy, 127
McEndree, 295
McFall, 124
McFalls, 204
McFarlan, 250
McFerran, 64
McGaffey, 141
McGarrity, 312
McGee, 50, 51, 103, 122, 178, 185, 236, 246, 270
McGill, 51, 153, 263, 269, 294
McGinnis, 50, 357
McGinniss, 50
McGlone, 243
McGlue, 50, 107, 207
McGonigal, 226
McGowan, 93, 343

McGrann, 199
McGraw, 50, 165
McGregor, 106, 147
McGuire, 10, 36, 50, 166, 252, 332, 352
McHenry, 59, 230
McIlvaine, 99
McIlvillis, 168
McIngle, 147
McIntire, 50
McIntosh, 88, 287
McKee, 6, 21, 33, 149
McKelden, 50, 205, 285
McKenna, 51, 59, 368
McKenney, 1, 97, 202, 301
McKenny, 317, 362
McKensie, 44
McKenzie, 69, 294
McKeon, 50
McKim, 333, 358
McKinley, 165
McKinstry, 50, 51, 361
McKinzie, 324
McKnett, 287
McKnew, 51, 128
McKnight, 50, 51, 147, 342
McLain, 235, 252
McLaine, 284
McLane, 59, 98, 157
McLaughlin, 115, 178, 215, 229, 258, 325
McLean, 79, 256
McLeod, 365
McMahon, 21
McManus, 151
McMeehan, 51
McMellon, 223
McMicken, 87, 143
McMillan, 78
McMillion, 244
McMinn, 51
McMullen, 147
McMurtrie, 261
McNairy, 148
McNamara, 59

McNamee, 50, 122, 162
McNancy, 51, 113
McNaney, 10, 272
McNany, 370
McNaughton, 140, 223
McNeill, 278
McNeir, 304
McNerhany, 189, 218, 230
McPhail, 323
McPherson, 39, 112, 194
McPiers, 51
McQueen, 232
McQuillan, 51
McQuinn, 149
McRee, 5
McReynolds, 7
McSherry, 86
McSparrow, 345
McWhorter, 148
Mead, 38, 78, 264
Meade, 189
Meader, 34
Meador, 9
Meadow Farm, 152
Meadows, 265
Meara, 368
Mechlin, 55, 169
Mecklin, 5
Medley, 118, 184
Meech, 198
Meehan, 168
Meeker, 20
Megowan, 61
Meigs, 50, 326
Mela, 118, 138
Melchoir, 40
Meldrum, 347
Mellen, 102, 146, 203
Melville, 288
Mendina, 279
Mercer, 18, 95, 213
Meredith, 136, 321
Merman, 50
Merrick, 3, 17, 201, 205, 206, 209, 303

Merrihew, 168
Merrill, 198, 222, 364
Merritt, 347
Merry, 84
Mervine, 62, 78
Metternich, 209
Mewze, 61
Meyer, 241
Michel, 280
Micken, 143
Mickum, 58
Middleton, 50, 51, 56, 60, 101, 129, 212, 357, 362
Mignot, 119
Milburn, 50, 51, 128, 205, 237
Mildeberger, 73
Miles, 112, 272, 338
Milland, 347
Millar, 168
Miller, 2, 8, 12, 19, 49, 50, 51, 56, 57, 58, 61, 73, 104, 105, 107, 125, 126, 127, 128, 129, 134, 142, 147, 154, 168, 169, 210, 216, 226, 248, 254, 255, 256, 258, 262, 270, 333, 345, 352, 353
Milles, 168
Mills, 13, 24, 28, 50, 51, 81, 87, 139, 153, 224, 236, 291, 310, 312, 323
Millson, 154
Milnes, 114
Milstead, 50, 57
Miltimore, 327
Milton, 24, 27
Minard, 93
Miner, 100, 326, 341
Minifie, 128
Minis, 73, 93, 155
Minnegerode, 65
Minnix, 140
Minor, 49, 94, 238, 268, 284, 288, 302, 311, 353
Minors, 226
Minturn, 72
Miramon, 81

Mishaw, 210
Miskey, 364
Missimer, 124
Mitchell, 13, 16, 39, 50, 51, 63, 129, 189, 213, 244, 270, 284, 288, 325, 343, 352
Mix, 50
Mockabee, 51
Moeller, 6
Mohan, 347
Mohler, 50
Mohun, 51, 55, 56, 57, 134, 162, 189, 202, 229, 337
Mohuns, 88
Molesworth, 200
Monahgan, 77
Moncure, 140
Money, 7
Monroe, 71, 322
Montgomery, 7, 50, 134, 280, 289
Montpelier, 335
Moody, 364
Moone, 105
Moore, 9, 56, 65, 78, 80, 88, 101, 127, 128, 129, 130, 161, 179, 184, 190, 211, 222, 226, 243, 264, 270, 273, 309, 317, 326, 339
Moors, 7
Mora, 279
Morales, 215
Moreau, 169
Moreland, 38, 216
Moreno, 114
Morfit, 50
Morgan, 50, 55, 58, 60, 61, 71, 101, 103, 114, 165, 180, 189, 191, 195, 204, 206, 235, 257, 325, 330, 331, 343, 344
Moriarty, 168
Mormon, 278
Mormons, 267
Morrell, 5
Morris, 25, 29, 84, 183, 200, 205, 240, 284, 307, 309, 344
Morrison, 125, 126, 128, 236, 336

Morrow, 279
Morse, 33, 259
Morsell, 3, 15, 75, 83, 196, 259, 319, 324, 329
Mortimer, 154
Morton, 51, 167, 303
Moseley, 218, 273
Mosely, 116
Moses, 37, 72, 347
Mosher, 129, 195
Motley, 67
Mott, 296, 369
Motze_, 250
Mount Calvert, 28, 102
Mount Olivet Cemetery, 144
Mount Pleasant, 120
Mount Prospect, 122
Mount Vernon, 14, 189, 295, 346, 352
Mount Vernon Association, 14, 188, 367
Mount Vernon Estate, 232
Mount Vernon Hotel, 255
Mount Vernon Ladies' Association, 119
Mountain Farm, 309
Mously, 38
Moye, 95
Moylan, 20
Mozante, 198
Mt Washington College, 316
Muddy Hole Farm, 232
Muirhead, 157
Mullen, 243
Muller, 119
Mulley, 57
Mullikin, 199
Mullins, 168, 317
Mullowny, 102
Mulloy, 50, 57, 183, 364
Muncaster, 272
Munck, 360
Munroe, 30, 50, 79, 251, 366
Munson, 95, 182
Muntz, 135

Murad, 149
Murdoch, 104
Murdock, 291
Murphey, 97
Murphy, 50, 59, 90, 103, 106, 125, 160, 161, 168, 184, 236, 243, 250, 299, 312, 364
Murray, 95, 103, 135, 202, 217, 226, 318, 325, 342, 353, 364
Musgrove, 369
Musser, 136
Muter, 200
Mutter, 112
Myer, 106, 259, 293, 296
Myerle, 32
Myers, 12, 50, 190, 211, 227, 276, 346
Mystic Hall Seminary, 84

N

Nadal, 74, 103, 159, 214, 298
Naff, 371
Nailor, 51, 286, 357
Nairn, 128, 166
Nally, 92, 100, 176
Nance, 119
Napier, 112, 118, 119
Napoleon, 73, 191, 306, 342
Napoleon III, 247
Narracott, 200
Nash, 59, 228, 268, 293, 353
Nason, 7
national flag, 191
Naval Ofcrs, 280
Naval Ofcrs of 1812, 283
Naylor, 51, 63, 144, 179, 244, 296, 356
Neal, 295
Neale, 58, 59, 99, 104, 130, 215, 247, 307
Neall, 325
Needham, 20
Neighbors, 290, 299
Neill, 33, 75, 262
Neilson, 13, 37, 168, 231
Neitzey, 10, 51

Nelson, 51, 161, 207, 256, 269, 347
Nesbet, 112
Neumeyer, 230
Neville, 156, 200, 271
Nevin, 228
Nevitt, 330
New Orleans Crescent, 353
Newberger, 316
Newell, 152, 283
Newman, 51, 113, 164, 309, 322, 323
Newton, 14, 47, 51, 128, 179, 240, 278, 325
Nicholls, 34, 75
Nichols, 51, 125, 190, 256, 318, 345
Nicholson, 51, 84, 100, 239, 244, 250, 344
Nicodemus, 112
Niel, 357
Nielder, 211
Niele, 291
Noah, 5
Noakes, 129
Noble, 32, 51, 74, 77, 235, 343
Noel, 294
Noerr, 164
Nokes, 223
Noland, 293
Nolston, 179
Nonsuch, 5, 154, 171
Noon, 77
Norfleet, 214
Norman, 168
Norr, 331
Norris, 51, 239, 270, 358, 363
North, 324, 363
Northrop, 22
Northup, 236
Norton, 256, 362, 363
Norvell, 333
Norwood, 59, 151, 191, 225
Nott, 168, 218
Nourse, 19, 51, 166, 182
Noyes, 14, 51, 58, 85, 325
Nuckolls, 250

Nugent, 51

O

O'Brien, 14, 86, 93, 158, 184, 186, 279
O'Bryan, 2
O'Callaghan, 10
O'Conner, 280
O'Connor, 163
O'Day, 12, 83
O'Donnell, 51, 56, 189, 334, 353
O'Donnoghue, 118, 123, 131, 230
O'Donnohue, 51
O'Hare, 51, 57
O'Leary, 7, 51, 99
O'Neale, 51, 58, 193, 329
O'Neill, 22, 168, 350, 355
O'Rieley, 71
O'Rourke, 164
O'Sullivan, 258
O'Toole, 16, 258, 334, 339, 343
Oak Hill, 1
Oak Hill Cemetery, 136, 346
Oaken-Brow, 178
Oakshott, 101
Oast, 322
Ober, 57, 189
ocean steamer **Great Western**, 287
Odenheimer, 178
Offut, 89, 183, 198
Offutt, 73, 128, 183, 198, 199, 285
Ogden, 243, 293, 323
Ogier, 6, 122
Ogle, 231, 305
Ogleton, 167
Olcott, 272
Old Sailor, 288; 289
Old Soldier, 283; 294
Old Soldier's Home, 213
oldest Church, 277
Oldham, 220
Oliver, 71, 165, 188
Olmstead, 253
Olmsted, 166
Olson, 179

Openheimer, 363
opium trade, 304
Order of Redemptionists, 103
Ordromax, 95
Orme, 39, 57, 58, 128, 189, 202, 215, 233, 249
Orr, 51, 62
Osborn, 33, 161, 341
Osborne, 51, 301
Oscar, 229
Osgodby, 51
Osgood, 25, 79
Ostrander, 149
Otero, 5
Otey, 128
Otis, 62, 261
Ott, 128
Otterback, 311
Ottinger, 20, 93, 155
Ould, 363, 368
Ourand, 73, 244
Ouseley, 146
Oviat, 326
Owen, 16, 51, 69, 103, 141
Owens, 57, 161, 230
Owner, 51
Owney, 274
Oyler, 103
Oyster, 51, 58
Ozanne, 322, 323

P

Pacetti, 51
Packard, 90, 213, 279
Packwood, 7
Page, 5, 28, 52, 64, 108, 135, 167, 173, 192, 289, 326, 349
Paige, 167, 222
Paign, 104
Paine, 158, 330, 333
Palmer, 7, 23, 55, 57, 63, 168, 190, 208, 253, 330
Pangburn, 85
Paprenitza, 94

Parish, 22
Parker, 7, 13, 51, 52, 57, 65, 75, 79, 85, 88, 129, 135, 138, 157, 161, 172, 178, 181, 200, 202, 203, 257, 275, 288, 304, 315, 320, 326, 336, 352, 357, 360
Parkinson, 168
Parmelee, 110
Parran, 280
Parrish, 7, 369
Parrott, 193
Parrott's Woods, 193
Parry, 70
Parson, 332
Parsons, 35, 90, 149, 197, 352
Part Piney Point, 177
Partridge, 326
Pascall, 276
Pascoe, 351
<u>Patapsco Female Institute</u>, 26
Patchin, 281
Paton, 325
Patrick, 176
Patten, 261
Patterson, 31, 39, 51, 286, 296, 329, 336, 347, 358, 362
Patti, 7
Paugburn, 18
Paulding, 280, 289, 348
Paxton, 168
Payne, 2, 10, 18, 52, 110, 169, 187, 288, 322
Payson, 309
Peacock, 263
Peale, 89, 321
Pearce, 24, 213
Pearl, 52
Pearson, 36, 51, 56, 61, 64, 80, 238, 269, 371
Pease, 29
Peck, 158, 161, 259
Peddecord, 226
Peebles, 32, 39, 62, 85, 365
Peel, 335, 349
Peeps, 167

Pegram, 190, 223
Peirce, 114
Pellet, 119, 188
Pelling, 325
Pendergrast, 66
Pendleton, 51, 108, 131, 132, 139, 140, 141, 169, 172, 193, 204, 311, 329
Penn, 120, 122, 185, 250
Pennibacker, 147
Pennington, 5, 25
Pennybacker, 349
Pennyfield, 181
Pepper, 202
Pepperell, 119
Percival, 62, 193, 289
Perin, 143
Perkins, 218, 219, 222, 261, 273, 317, 353
Perrigan, 127
Perrin, 248
Perry, 11, 21, 65, 93, 98, 128, 133, 166, 239, 240, 289, 334, 341
Persifor, 39, 80, 93
Peter, 52, 53, 120
Peterailia, 326
Peters, 31, 52, 102, 115, 150, 260, 326, 358
Peterson, 302, 345
Petronella, 96
Pettibone, 35, 129, 202
Pettit, 51, 284, 361
Pettite, 230
Pettus, 345
Petty, 157
Peugh, 51, 52, 191, 344
Peyronnet, 12
Peyton, 130, 150, 169, 176, 212
Pfeil, 52
Pfister, 52
Pfromer, 127
Phagin, 35
Phelds, 261
Phelps, 5, 26, 52, 87, 88, 310, 321
Pheney, 135

Philip, 3, 52
Philips, 52, 175, 335
Phillips, 2, 52, 97, 98, 106, 130, 156, 206, 212, 224, 249, 279, 296, 328, 329, 332, 340, 357, 358, 361
Philps, 88
Phinney, 84
Phoenix, 157
Phythian, 161
Pickell, 91, 93
Pickett, 52, 96
Pickrell, 76, 89, 128, 352
Pico, 275
Pier, 7
Pierce, 5, 6, 31, 52, 114, 165, 220, 224, 250, 255, 263, 264, 267, 332, 371
Pierson, 347
Pike, 229, 276, 278
Pike's Peak, 190, 203
Pilgrims, 1
Pilgrims of Md, 178
Pilling, 366
Pillow, 147, 171, 177, 260
Pinckney, 15, 39, 211, 247, 329
Pindle, 243
Piney Point Pavilion, 195
Pinkard, 195
Pinkins, 19
Pinkney, 297, 368
Pinkney Island, 368
Piser, 211
Pitcher, 52, 112
Pitchlyn, 5
Pitzer, 76, 102
Place, 125
Platt, 52, 280, 289, 291
Playfair, 135
Pleasanton, 52
Plimpton, 241
Plowman, 218
Plumb, 327
Plumer, 194
Plumley, 261
Plummer, 41, 102, 118, 146, 203, 339

Plunket, 261
Plunkett, 152
Plympton, 242
Poe, 99
Poindexter, 338
Poitezin, 284
Polk, 17, 52, 89, 104, 188, 279, 292
Polkinhorn, 11, 22
Pollard, 18, 52, 147, 210
Polton, 51
Pomeroy, 362
Poole, 137
Poor Man's Industry, 360
Poore, 5
Pope, 10
Pope Pius, 287
Porter, 52, 73, 76, 78, 87, 93, 151, 152, 207, 211, 218, 238, 239, 273, 293, 345, 355, 366
Portier, 171
Posey, 13, 51, 128
Post, 114, 121, 341
Potentini, 226
Potter, 73, 119, 128, 132, 164, 165, 284
Potts, 177, 201, 220, 222
Poulton, 89
Powell, 52, 57, 131, 188, 189, 355
Powers, 51, 143, 150, 235, 284, 362
Poyles, 76
Prather, 51
Pratt, 51, 52, 75, 243, 291
Preble, 289, 306
Prentice, 315
Prentiss, 192, 326
Presbyterian Church, 300
Prescott, 40
Preston, 108, 145, 159, 267, 322, 359
Prettyman, 103
Preuss, 52
Price, 42, 58, 144, 189, 216, 234
Pride, 188
Priestley, 278
Primley, 168
Prince Jerome, 39

Prince of Wales, 348
Prince Otho, 110
Princeton College, 213
Printz, 85
Proctor, 197, 234, 345, 368
propellar **Lady of the Lake**, 125
Prospect Hill, 71, 72, 144, 235
Protestant Cemetery, 355
Prout, 52, 297
Pryor, 146
Pugh, 113
Pumphrey, 52, 116, 118, 129, 131, 199, 352, 360
Pumphrey's Little Addition, 360
Purcell, 52, 124, 129, 166, 202, 218, 303, 340
Purcely, 277
Purchase, 67
Purdy, 202, 326
Pyfer, 238
Pyne, 32, 131, 134, 141, 142, 151, 228
Pythian, 218, 273

Q

Queen, 58, 108, 113, 208, 256, 305, 346
Queen of England, 11
Queen of Portugal, 235, 242
Queen Victoria, 337
Queensborough, 237
Quig, 97, 106
Quigley, 61, 117, 368
Quincy, 80, 166
Quinn, 159, 211, 312
Quirke, 52
Quitman, 9

R

Raab, 147, 336
Rabbitt, 32, 59
Raber, 168
Raborg, 368
Radcliff, 256
Radford, 16, 128, 168, 326
Rady, 14, 345

Rafferty, 220
Ragan, 14, 27, 52, 79
Railey, 52, 368
Rain, 332
Rainbow, 362
Rainey, 37
Rains, 104
Raleigh tavern, 361
Raley, 127
Rally, 52
Ramsay, 111
Randall, 7, 35, 38, 140, 143, 154, 168
Randolph, 32, 57, 91, 101, 121, 159, 211, 233, 303, 321, 325, 329, 354
Ratcliffe, 139
Rathbone, 11, 31
Rathbun, 81
Ratley, 135
Rawlings, 52, 57, 243
Ray, 3, 179, 215, 221, 250, 302
Rayner, 258
Reab, 276
Read, 16, 80, 181, 210, 278, 289
Reagan, 61, 358, 364
Reardon, 52
Reaver, 164
Redfern, 52
Redin, 36, 120, 132, 326, 357
Redrick, 164
Ree, 52, 215
Reed, 85, 108, 130, 131, 132, 192, 222, 239, 240, 267
Reeler, 52
Rees, 12
Reese, 198, 222, 273
Reeside, 35, 68
Reeves, 83, 97, 106, 153, 200, 288
Regan, 211
Regester, 75
Register, 51, 103
Rehm, 338
Reid, 12, 103, 147
Reiff, 183
Reilly, 168

Reily, 179, 180
Reinhart, 19, 250
Reinl, 183
Reip, 330
Reise, 345
Remey, 192
Remmely, 52
Rench, 31
Rennigee, 218
Reno, 170
Renshaw, 239
Resurvey, on Horse Lick, 324
Retinger, 248
revenue-cutter **Harriet Lane**, 249
Revolutionary pensions, 247
Revolutionary soldiers, 244, 257
Reyes, 307
Reynolds, 14, 21, 64, 72, 93, 105, 147, 155, 161, 183, 199, 256, 302, 353, 357
Rhae, 67
Rhett, 22
Rhineman, 150
Rhinesmith, 259
Rhodes, 16, 127, 128, 211
Ricar, 52
Rice, 39, 167
Rich, 87, 93, 103, 112, 155
Richards, 97, 106, 127, 184, 200
Richardson, 92, 103, 140, 173, 216, 218, 243, 277, 302, 310, 312
Richeux, 162
Richey, 58, 229, 326
Richmond, 8, 285
Richter, 250
Richy, 129
Ricker, 7
Ricketts, 58
Riddick, 345
Ridgate, 150
Ridgeley, 56
Ridgely, 32, 142, 216, 231, 264, 328, 330, 362, 368
Ridgeway, 52
Ridgley, 134

Ridout, 243
Rieckleman, 215
Rielly, 30
Riely, 258
Rigdon, 19, 36, 42, 188
Riggles, 58
Riggs, 8, 52, 56, 73, 86, 199, 209, 241, 270, 346, 352
Riker, 22
Riley, 29, 52, 95, 128, 173, 253, 254, 274, 280, 284
Rima, 197
Ringgold, 1, 75, 126, 228
Rio, 170
Rising, 26, 257
Ritch, 286
Ritchie, 52, 282, 301, 347
Rittenhouse, 64
River Farm, 232
Rivers, 252
Rives, 65, 185, 223, 335
Roach, 25, 52, 120, 218, 223, 364
Roane, 222
Robb, 69, 279
Robbins, 16, 31, 32, 58, 270, 287
Robert, 75, 155, 302
Roberts, 52, 56, 65, 93, 112, 172, 182, 224, 253, 261, 280, 283, 331
Robertson, 1, 85, 129, 144, 186, 208
Robey, 52, 290
Robidoux, 13
Robins, 12
Robinson, 14, 22, 26, 39, 52, 62, 78, 81, 88, 93, 112, 120, 122, 127, 129, 164, 186, 190, 205, 221, 222, 239, 309, 311, 323, 326, 339, 346, 353, 363, 367
Robison, 207
Robles, 191
Robut, 330
Rochat, 52
Rochelle, 284
Rock Hill, 288
Rockwell, 32, 163
Rockwood Farm, 157

Rodbird, 52
Rodgers, 11, 52, 60, 157, 168, 362
Rodman, 106, 197
Roemmele, 157, 204, 313
Roemmelle, 114
Roger, 73
Rogers, 8, 62, 103, 194, 250
Rohr, 316
Rokman, 31
Rolf, 288
Rolfe, 229
Rolles, 92
Rollings, 297
Rollins, 277
Rollison, 243
Roman, 37
Rooney, 59, 261
Roosevelt, 124, 199, 367
Rosamond, 215
Rose, 79, 211, 234
Rose Hill, 153
Rose Mount, 253
Rosedale, 152
Rosedale Cottage, 216
Ross, 5, 18, 52, 59, 267, 273, 302, 305, 347
Rothwell, 52, 187
Rouson, 190
Rout, 183, 186
Rouzy, 220
Rouzzee, 368
Rowan, 194, 345
Rowell, 295
Rowland, 5, 52, 59, 111, 172, 188, 218, 220
Roy, 204
Rudd, 15, 172, 176
Rudenstein, 362
Ruff, 129
Ruger, 154
Rugg, 341
Ruggles, 52, 95, 210, 236
Ruple, 165
Rupp, 52, 81, 100

Rush, 208, 236, 245
Russ, 20
Russel, 84, 183
Russell, 15, 41, 57, 64, 67, 73, 95, 125, 133, 155, 189, 216, 241, 242, 250, 254, 312, 362
Rutherford, 20, 347
Rutland, 301
Rutledge, 154, 234
Ryan, 22, 103, 163, 230, 271
Rye, 52
Ryland, 222
Ryne, 52
Ryon, 246, 316

S

Sackett, 114
Saddler, 151
Sadler, 184
Sage, 52, 300
Sahrland, 371
Salisbury, 42
Salmagundi, 348
Salomon, 38, 365
Salstonstall, 229
Salter, 229, 280, 289
Salyard, 107
Sammis, 263
Sampayo, 329
Sample, 71, 360
Samples, 183, 186
Samson, 79, 85, 95, 97, 103, 182, 191, 235
Samstag, 363, 364
Samuels, 11
Sanborn, 314
Sanchez, 197
Sanders, 34
Sanderson, 176, 294
Sandidge, 235
<u>Sandy Valley Advocate</u>, 270
Sanford, 13, 53
Sanger, 161
Sardo, 220

Sargent, 292
Sartiges, 136
Sasscer, 256
Saulsbury, 24
Saunders, 3, 53, 112, 340
Saur, 53, 72
Sauter, 60
Savage, 99, 229
Savoy, 24
Sawen, 257
Sawyer, 26, 79, 151, 166, 170, 280, 289, 326
Saxton, 53, 151
Saxty, 296
Sayre, 72, 108
Scaggs, 202
Scaggs' Crossing, 242
Scale, 149
Scanlon, 10, 284
Scarburgh, 86
Scarff, 59
Scattergood, 262
Schad, 177, 339
Schafer, 294, 353
Schaffer, 59, 120
Schaffner, 91
Schaub, 34
Schenig, 113
Schlegel, 243
Schlessinger, 119
Schley, 52, 69
Schlottembeck, 221
Schmidt, 164
Schneider, 10, 320
Schnier, 178
schnr **Alligator**, 238
schnr **Bolinas**, 317
schnr **Caroline**, 240
schnr **E S Rudderow**, 72
schnr **Enterprise**, 21
schnr **Enterprize**, 239
schnr **Ferret**, 239
schnr **Grampus**, 239
schnr **Growler**, 239
schnr **Helen**, 239
schnr **Hornet**, 240
schnr **Julia**, 239
schnr **Lynx**, 239
schnr **Mechanic**, 61
schnr **Ohio**, 239
schnr **Onkahye**, 239
schnr **Porpoise**, 239
schnr **Retaliation**, 239
schnr **Revenge**, 239
schnr **Rudderow**, 28
schnr **Scorpion**, 239
schnr **Sea Horse**, 240
schnr **Shark**, 239
schnr **Somers**, 239
schnr **Sylph**, 239
schnr **Tigress**, 240
schnr **Wasp**, 240
schnr **Wildcat**, 239
schnr **William A Hamill**, 94
schnr **Wm A Hamil**, 23
schnr **Wm A Hamill**, 36
schnr **Worcester**, 16
Scholfield, 53
Schoolcraft, 32, 93
Schoonmaker, 192
Schott, 227
Schroeder, 73
Schrote, 258
Schue, 58
Schureman, 364
Schussler, 53
Schuyler, 241
Schwartz, 53
Schwinghamer, 37, 225
Scon, 370
Scott, 3, 16, 21, 37, 53, 67, 70, 97, 106, 107, 130, 155, 165, 168, 186, 187, 205, 208, 212, 252, 279, 282, 285, 325, 345
Screven, 132, 230
Scrivener, 53, 74, 99, 140, 337
Scudder, 177
Seals, 69

Seaman, 310
Sears, 53, 67, 118, 128, 213, 246
Seaton, 15, 247
Seaver, 5
Secor, 41
Seddon, 168
Sedgewick, 367
Sedgwick, 356, 360
Seeley, 139, 236
Seely, 130, 137, 308
Segar, 203
Segui, 94
Seibold, 11
Selby, 63, 271
Selden, 65, 84, 128, 152, 262, 272, 281, 283, 344, 346
Sellers, 321
Semmes, 108, 129, 176, 268, 285, 338, 342, 343, 358
Sengstack, 52, 147
Senseney, 244
Serena, 341
Serrin, 59, 305
Sestini, 307
Settle, 52
Sewall, 53
Seward, 16, 112
Sewell, 99
Seymore, 261
Seymour, 90, 97, 106, 160, 190
Shackeford, 215
Shackelford, 130, 152, 212, 308
Shackleford, 292
Shade, 246
Shaeffer, 27
Shafer, 154
Shaffer, 9
Shaffner, 30, 71
Shakspeare, 79
Shaler, 358
Shannon, 167, 241
Sharp, 2
Shartuck, 253
Shattuck, 5
Shau-bee-nay, 234
Shaver, 303
Shaw, 42, 65, 153, 168, 212, 230, 276
Sheahan, 227
Sheckell, 53, 215
Sheckells, 58
Sheckels, 159, 189, 197
Sheckles, 139
Sheets, 53
Shekell, 52, 201, 256, 328
Shelley, 277
Shepard, 257
Shephard, 239
Shepherd, 161, 197, 199, 332
Sheppard, 312
Sheppardson, 333
Shepperd, 113
Sherberne, 97
Sherburn, 106
Sheriff, 227
Sherman, 53, 211, 238, 247
Sherrard, 196, 266
Sherwood, 75, 220, 326
Shewell, 277
Shields, 19, 26, 53, 122, 278
Shiles, 77, 213, 353
Shinn, 91
Shinnors, 83
ship *Argue, 240
ship *Boston, 240
ship *Columbia, 240
ship *General Green, 240
ship Africa, 229
ship Alert, 240
ship Arago, 205
ship Asia, 180
ship Bainbridge, 211
ship Boston, 238
ship Charles Wood, 253
ship City of Baltimore, 138
ship Col Crosman, 158
ship Concord, 239
ship Congress, 240
ship Constitution, 15

ship **Cyane**, 15, 208, 240
ship **Eagle**, 239
ship **Eastern Monarch**, 200
ship **Epervier**, 239
ship **Equimaux**, 298
ship **Erie**, 240
ship **Falmouth**, 360
ship **Flora McDonald**, 96
ship **Frolic**, 239
ship **Greenwich**, 240
ship **Guerrier**, 240
ship **Hellos**, 290
ship **Insurgent**, 239
ship **Iowa**, 240
ship **Iriam**, 204
ship **John Adams**, 19, 240
ship **Junior**, 102, 146, 203
ship **Levant**, 15, 67
ship **Louisiana**, 240
ship **Macedonian**, 240
ship **Natchez**, 240
ship **Northern Light**, 236
ship **Oxford**, 62
ship **Peacock**, 239
ship **Persia**, 172
ship **Pomona**, 168
ship **Princeton**, 1
ship **Saratoga**, 83
ship **Southern Star**, 227
ship **Therse**, 275
ship **Washington**, 240
ship **Wasp**, 239
ship **Waverley**, 1
Ships **Constitution & Guerriere**, 289
Ships **Constitution & Java**, 289
Ships **Constitution, Cyane, & Levant**, 289
Ships **Enterprise & Boxer**, 289
ships **Erebus & Terror**, 298
Ships **Hornet & Peacock**, 289
Ships **Hornet & Penguin**, 289
Ships **Peacock & Epervier**, 289
Ships **United States & Macedonian**, 289

Ships **Wasp & Frolic**, 289
Ships **Wasp & Reindeer**, 289
Shirley, 121, 339
Shockley, 7
Shoemaker, 53, 89, 202, 297, 353
Shore, 69, 149
Shorter, 53
Shriver, 310
Shryock, 161, 218
Shryrock, 273
Shubrick, 39, 239, 278, 289, 338
Shucking, 227
Shugert, 110, 123
Shutt, 310
Sibley, 112, 165, 252, 345, 359
Sickels, 81
Sickles, 108, 130, 134, 135, 137, 138, 139, 142, 165, 326
Simmonds, 53
Simmons, 37, 153, 271, 307
Simms, 14, 53, 60, 99, 229, 287
Simonds, 296
Simons, 22
Simpson, 23, 24, 53, 81, 169, 296
Sims, 355
Sinclair, 61
Singleton, 85, 259
Sinon, 121, 272
Sipes, 103
Sippach, 286
Sister Cyprian, 256
Sister of Charity, 256
Skerrett, 196
Skillings, 86
Skinner, 104, 190, 306, 346
Skippen, 99
Skirving, 88, 108, 129
Slade, 29, 181
Slater, 53, 167, 191, 309, 344
Slatford, 60
Slaughter, 25, 341
Sletor, 311
Slick, 147
Slidell, 142

Slip, 360
Sloan, 161
Sloat, 278, 289
Slocumb, 52
sloop **Albany**, 238
sloop **Alligator**, 239
sloop **Growler**, 239
sloop **Heron**, 204
sloop of war **St Mary's**, 208
sloop of war **Vandalia**, 208
sloop **Yorktown**, 239
sloop-of war **Germantown**, 125
sloop-of-war **Argus**, 239
sloop-of-war **Brooklyn**, 288
sloop-of-war **Cyane**, 365
sloop-of-war **Dale**, 175
sloop-of-war **St Louis**, 208
sloop-of-war **St Mary's**, 105
sloop-of-war **Vandalia**, 61
Small, 53
Smallwood, 12, 20, 53, 58, 209, 279
Smead, 326
Smedes, 304
Smethurst, 271
Smit_, 200
Smith, 2, 3, 5, 6, 15, 18, 24, 25, 27, 34, 36, 39, 53, 55, 56, 59, 60, 70, 71, 73, 77, 78, 80, 81, 84, 85, 89, 91, 93, 96, 99, 101, 102, 103, 106, 107, 108, 109, 110, 113, 114, 115, 116, 118, 121, 127, 128, 135, 143, 149, 157, 160, 161, 166, 167, 168, 172, 181, 182, 185, 187, 190, 192, 195, 196, 197, 205, 206, 207, 210, 211, 213, 214, 215, 216, 222, 227, 234, 235, 236, 239, 248, 256, 257, 262, 267, 268, 270, 277, 278, 280, 287, 288, 289, 292, 297, 314, 315, 319, 321, 322, 323, 332, 333, 337, 338, 339, 345, 347, 349, 358, 362, 366, 370
Smith's Island, 260
Smithurst, 266
Smitson, 53
Smoot, 53, 90, 128, 272, 298
Smull, 53
Sneed, 74
Snell, 2
Snelling, 11
Snellwood, 20
Snow, 185, 326
Snyder, 53, 101, 206, 245
Society of Jesus, 307
Somers, 240
Somervell, 300
Sommers, 53
Sothard, 121
Sothoron, 128
Souder, 53, 371
Soule, 165
Southard, 361
Sowers, 95
Spa Spring Woods, 205
Spaet, 53
Spalding, 7, 315, 344, 370
Spangler, 190
Sparks, 101, 172, 176, 215
Sparrow, 250
Spaulding, 84, 163, 288, 341
Speake, 53
Spear, 25, 36
Speddon, 261
Speed, 30, 71
Speelman, 158
Speir, 90
Spelman, 277
Spencer, 58, 193, 224, 251, 276, 278
Spilman, 130, 212
Spinck, 186
Spink, 231, 268
Spotswood, 23
Spotts, 131
Sprague, 28, 64, 83
Sprigg, 78, 308, 368
Springfield Farm, 300
Springman, 81, 126
Squier, 80, 365
Squiers, 21
St Aloysius, 307

St Aloysius Catholic Church, 307
St John, 32, 62, 147, 287, 288
St Mary's burial ground, 315
St Mary's Female Institute, 256
St Peter, 17
St Peter's [Catholic] Church, 269
St Vrain, 115
Stabler, 260, 273
Stachlin, 245
Stacon, 160
Stafford, 253
Stahl, 58, 355
Stake, 89
Stakes, 230
Staley, 316
Stambaugh, 228
Stamford, 249
Stammer, 30
Stampee, 226
Standish, 117
Standwell, 347
Stanford, 129, 169, 251, 369
Stanly, 196, 201
Stanton, 146, 220, 269
Stark, 161
Starnes, 167
Starrett, 317
Starry, 321, 334
Steadman, 175, 327
Stealy, 7
steamboat **Augusta**, 131
steamboat **John G Lawton**, 196
steamboat **Princess**, 90
steamboat **St Nicholas**, 147
steamer **Alma**, 229
steamer **America**, 81
steamer **Anglo-Saxon**, 277
steamer **Col Harney**, 19
steamer **Cyclops**, 229
steamer **Detroit**, 254
steamer **Edith**, 239
steamer **Ethiope**, 204
steamer **Fox**, 298
steamer **Fulton**, 152, 227, 283, 284, 287

steamer **George Page**, 217
steamer **Golden Gate**, 324
steamer **Great Britian**, 287
steamer **Great Eastern**, 287
steamer **Indian**, 347
steamer **Mount Vernon**, 272
steamer **Niagara**, 22
steamer **North Carolina**, 41
steamer **Ocean Spray**, 158
steamer **Princess**, 97, 106, 107
steamer **Princeton**, 146
steamer **St Nicholas**, 164, 171, 177
steamer **Star of the West**, 105
steamer **Vanderbilt**, 13, 205
steamer **Vixen**, 202, 369
steamship **Canada**, 298
steamship **Central America**, 207
steamship **City of Manchester**, 124
steamship **City of Washington**, 121
steamship **Fulton**, 240
steamship **Great Eastern**, 264, 287
steamship **Missouri**, 240
steamship **Princeton**, 240
steamship **Washington**, 208
Stearns, 84
Steele, 122, 337
Steeley, 29, 35
Steers, 53
Stein, 265
Stephanie, 242
Stephen, 185, 242, 270, 297
Stephens, 120, 124, 132, 147, 197, 293, 310, 313, 362
Stephenson, 6, 105, 236, 318
Steptoe, 190, 334
Sterling, 53, 247
Sterrett, 95, 353
Stettinius, 53, 144
Steuart, 310
Stevens, 5, 97, 99, 106, 126, 149, 150, 195, 244, 312, 321, 322, 330
Stevenson, 262, 311
Stevin, 16

Stewart, 7, 10, 15, 19, 26, 27, 31, 33, 53, 58, 72, 81, 94, 106, 108, 140, 141, 152, 180, 189, 208, 223, 225, 255, 261, 278, 280, 283, 289, 335, 341, 345, 357, 358, 365, 370
Stier, 116
Stiff, 193
Stiger, 53
Stille, 143
Stillman, 13
Stillwell, 358
Stilson, 291
Stimers, 31
Stith, 70, 174
Stockbridge, 229
Stockton, 10, 208, 337
Stoddard, 125, 270
Stoddert, 35
Stoessel, 174
Stokely, 75
Stokes, 148
Stone, 22, 23, 24, 53, 55, 59, 82, 95, 97, 106, 108, 126, 130, 132, 171, 198, 200, 215, 223, 257, 286, 324, 327, 340
Stonestreet, 53, 165, 284, 351
Stony Ridge, 12
Stopford, 200
storeship **Supply**, 269
Storrs, 229, 362
Story, 62
Stott, 16, 195
Stoughton, 57, 198, 223
Stover, 252
Stovin, 169
Stowall, 274
Strahan, 334
Straight, 26
Strange, 53
Stratton, 86, 127, 225
Straumal, 259
Strawbridge, 111
Streeks, 183
Street, 213, 347
Stretch, 340

Stribling, 160, 164
Strider, 27, 312
Stringfellow, 161
Strobhart, 196
Strong, 12, 77, 96, 195, 252, 323
Stroop, 13
Strother, 6, 38
Stroud, 353
Stuart, 18, 42, 62, 84, 97, 147, 164, 165, 171, 242, 259, 312, 335, 340, 353
Stumpf, 325
Sturge, 180
Sturges, 127
Sturm, 153
Sturtevant, 327
Stutz, 85
Suckley, 150
Suddards, 32
Sugar Tree Bottom, 324
Sugden, 168
Suit, 12, 53, 59, 63, 142, 353
Sullivan, 53, 82, 85, 92, 100, 163, 168, 176, 220, 250, 306
Sulter, 171
Sumby, 53, 115
Summers, 362
Sumner, 165
Sumter, 275
Sunder, 323
Sunderland, 128, 150, 199, 235
Surget, 97, 106
Surratt, 256
Suter, 53, 309
Sutherland, 88, 98
Sutter, 153
Sutton, 128, 218, 219, 357
Swaile, 265
Swan, 262, 323
Swann, 53, 187, 354, 370
Swartz, 229, 306, 317
Swartze, 53
Swasey, 192
Swayne, 145
Sweeney, 47, 53, 318

Sweeny, 39, 52, 53, 54, 111, 228, 246, 335, 361
Sweet, 371
Sweetser, 13
Sweezy, 186
Sweringen, 95
Swicke, 286
Swift, 16
Swigart, 186
Sykes, 326
Sylvester, 53, 99
Syphax, 53, 352

T

Tabler, 54
Taggart, 35, 127
Taggert, 17
Taggit, 188
Tagnalaneri, 22
Tait, 14
Talbert, 54, 150
Talbot, 116, 161
Talbott, 25, 315
Talburt, 54, 316
Talcott, 13, 72, 93, 156
Taliaferro, 85, 349, 354
Taney, 243
Tansill, 31
Taswell, 168
Tate, 13, 28, 339
Tattersall, 264
Tattnall, 291
Taverns, 53
Tayloe, 49, 54, 99, 142, 255
Taylor, 4, 7, 12, 13, 41, 54, 57, 58, 76, 78, 80, 83, 94, 95, 97, 102, 105, 106, 115, 117, 124, 143, 156, 157, 168, 169, 170, 178, 186, 187, 192, 196, 221, 233, 250, 253, 265, 272, 283, 292, 297, 300, 307, 312, 313, 335, 341, 354, 361
Temple, 255
Templeton, 21, 61
Ten Broeck, 95

Ten Eyck, 179, 331
Teney, 89
Tenido, 22
Tenney, 128, 129
Terry, 311
Tew, 147
Thackam, 22
Thatcher, 25, 219
Thaw, 54, 199
Thayer, 293, 322
The Cottage, 295
the yacht **Fox**, 337
Thecker, 164
Thoburn, 138
Thom, 168, 209
Thoma, 35, 122
Thomas, 10, 28, 53, 54, 59, 68, 90, 103, 112, 161, 183, 187, 199, 205, 246, 265, 291, 296, 326
Thomlinson, 22
Thompson, 8, 12, 16, 20, 22, 48, 53, 54, 59, 75, 91, 100, 114, 115, 141, 152, 158, 168, 182, 187, 207, 210, 213, 214, 215, 236, 241, 243, 254, 257, 262, 284, 290, 302, 306, 313, 321, 325, 329, 334, 351, 359, 362
Thorn, 62, 164, 314
Thornburn, 105
Thorne, 306
Thornhill, 207
Thornley, 99
Thornton, 59, 64, 185, 213, 336
Thorpe, 168
Threlkeld, 305
Thrift, 263, 301
Thruston, 53, 54, 76
Thumb, 225
Thurber, 79
Thurston, 100
Thyson, 197
Tibbett, 253
Tiber Creek, 301
Tidball, 25, 108, 130, 131, 142
Tidd, 313, 314

Tiffany, 64, 75
Tiger Tail, 22
Tilghman, 7, 53, 54, 135
Tillery, 37
Tillinghast, 115, 214
Timms, 53
Tirrell, 320
Tiswold, 211
Titcomb, 210, 290
Titus, 26, 235, 327
Tobin, 54
Todd, 39, 52, 54, 162, 173, 204, 310, 318, 333, 340
Todsen, 54, 331
Todson, 349
Todtschinder, 268
Token of Love, 193
Toledano, 283, 288
Toll, 54
Tolson, 224, 353
Tompkins, 143
Toner, 56, 190
Tonis, 230
Toombe, 138
Tophan, 129
Topping, 177, 243
Torbert, 178
Torney, 263
Torry, 234
Totten, 54, 73, 165
Toucey, 15, 26, 291
Toulmin, 278
Towers, 53, 63, 133
Towles, 54, 152, 162, 352
Townley, 32, 313
Townsend, 11, 20
Toy, 366
Tracy, 215, 283, 292
Trader, 332
Trask, 236, 325
Traub, 239
Trautwein, 128
Travers, 54, 113, 223
Treadway, 238

Treasure Amended, 324
Treck, 54
Tree, 57, 64, 189, 300, 348
Trego, 28
Trenchard, 291
Trenholm, 363
Trevey, 95
Trial of Danl E Sickles, 108, 128, 129, 132, 133, 134, 135, 137, 138, 139, 141, 142, 143, 144, 145, 146
Trimble, 15, 37, 334
Trook, 54, 237
Troutman, 321
Troutmann, 293
Trumbo, 10
Trunnell, 249
Truscott, 204
Tubman, 180, 369
Tuck, 90, 275, 324
Tucker, 10, 38, 54, 59, 79, 82, 85, 94, 128, 129, 135, 152, 215, 292, 364, 368
Tudor Place, 127
Tuel, 58
Tuft, 362
tug **Salvor**, 217
Turbett, 311
Turk, 42
Turkey, 26
Turnbull, 73, 93, 222
Turner, 9, 103, 239, 249, 310, 312, 319, 328, 337, 348, 349, 354, 363, 364
Turton, 57, 73, 189
Tustin, 206, 300
Tutwiler, 7
Twiggs, 190
Twine, 54
Twining, 236
Twish, 143
Twomay, 54
Tyler, 11, 15, 28, 54, 77, 85, 95, 111, 132, 136, 162, 172, 213, 267, 306
Tyson, 8, 221, 369

U

Umbaw, 236
Uncle's Good-Will, 63
Underwood, 30, 32, 64, 94, 260, 339
Union Farm, 232
Unity, 66
Upham, 198, 223
Upperman, 129
Upshur, 1, 75, 108, 130, 131, 142
Upton, 300
Urdard, 335
Usher, 54, 99
Utermuhle, 129
Utley, 12
Uttermuhle, 210

V

Vail, 33
Vale of Benjamin, 208
Valentine, 105
Vallete, 280
Valley View, 159
Van, 201
Van Allen, 3
Van Amburgh, 74
Van Antwerp, 167
Van Buren, 354
Van Buskirk, 7, 84
Van Dorn, 67, 181, 185, 190
Van Dyke, 155
Van Etten, 281
Van Hook, 47
Van Horn, 100
Van McCollom, 152
Van Ness, 2, 54, 69, 328
Van Patten, 54, 125, 287, 341
Van Pelt, 24
Van Rensselaer, 133
Van Reswick, 57, 79, 135, 173, 189
Van Riswick, 28, 177
Van Skiver, 61, 92
Van Wart, 127
Van Wick, 130, 132
Van Wyck, 108, 131

Vance, 38, 275
Vandervoort, 255
Vanderwerken, 54, 62, 176
Vandeventer, 369
Vandyke, 79
Vanfleet, 140
Vansyck, 211
Vanzant, 183, 186
Varden, 226
Varnell, 54, 129
Varnum, 11, 54
Vass, 54
Vaughan, 122
Vaughn, 309
Vedder, 269, 363
Veighmeyer, 307
Veinant, 150
Veitch, 54
Vela, 307
Velter, 92
Venable, 54, 129, 316, 345
Verbeekhooven, 119
Verhoutsraeien, 38
Vermilion, 355
Vermillion, 30, 54
Vernet, 162
Vernon, 54, 106, 146, 163
Verren, 180
Verrill, 276
vessel **Anacosita**, 261
vessel **Atlanta**, 261
vessel **Caledonia**, 261
vessel **Crusader**, 261
vessel **Flora McDonald**, 118
vessel **Jane Black**, 118
vessel **M W Chapin**, 261
vessel **Memphis**, 261
vessel **Metacomet**, 261
vessel **Mohawk**, 261
vessel **Mystic**, 261
vessel **Pulaski**, 261
vessel **Southern Star**, 261
vessel **Sumpter**, 261

vessels **San Jacinto, Portsmouth, & Levant**, 261
Vessey, 54
Vetteir, 100
Vick, 174
Vickers, 196
Vigne, 97
Vignee, 106
Villager, 307
Vincent, 8, 38
Viney, 286
Vineyard, 311
Vinson, 54
Vinzant, 248
Violett, 84
Vollmer, 183
Von Delkin, 244
von Egloffstein, 325
Von Humboldt, 170
von Kammerhueber, 153
von Kammeshueber, 111
Von Schmidt, 107
Vondersmith, 149, 157
Voorhees, 280, 283, 289, 321
Voorhies, 62
Vreeland, 36

W

Wade, 27, 121, 278
Waer, 13
Wagner, 55, 71, 85, 93, 135, 198, 319
Wagoner, 118, 222
Wailes, 369
Wait, 125, 140
Waite, 210, 258
Waits, 97
Wakefield, 38, 40, 67, 71, 93
Wakius, 292
Walbridge, 82, 131, 318
Walcheran, 241
Walden, 30, 41, 77
Waldron, 102, 150, 242
Waldrup, 113
Wales, 30, 217

Walker, 2, 10, 31, 34, 54, 58, 83, 105, 123, 134, 161, 176, 213, 228, 235, 269, 271, 272, 279, 296, 306, 309, 344, 349, 352
Wall, 18, 270
Wallace, 57, 149, 161, 201, 261, 269, 273, 274, 308
Wallach, 28, 135, 140, 177, 185, 223, 226, 304, 352
Waller, 296, 336, 370
Wallingford Place, 282
Wallingsford, 54, 55, 122
Wallis, 308
Walsh, 30, 54, 55, 58, 79, 92, 109, 229, 241, 259, 263, 315
Walston, 199, 322
Walter, 100, 111, 153, 174, 219, 224, 258, 269, 325
Walters, 21, 33, 55, 86, 225
Walton, 95, 232, 278
Walworth, 55, 211
Wan, 22
Wannall, 269, 270
Wappner, 183
Ward, 7, 8, 23, 36, 54, 55, 72, 98, 105, 111, 152, 173, 176, 179, 184, 189, 206, 214, 215, 226, 229, 251, 254, 322, 325, 332, 345, 349, 368
Wardell, 127
Warden, 145
Warder, 343
Ware, 169, 170
Waring, 55, 95, 256
Warner, 65, 112, 154, 247, 359, 364
Warpeton, 211
Warr, 171
Warren, 54, 82, 152, 225
Warring's Lot Enlarged, 63
Warrington, 62, 283, 289
Warwick, 34, 164, 311
Waser, 22
Washburn, 106

Washington, 4, 13, 55, 65, 69, 111, 117, 119, 181, 184, 188, 232, 271, 310, 312, 319, 321, 334, 345, 346, 349, 367
water pipes, 175
Waters, 31, 42, 54, 55, 58, 102, 118, 176, 217, 254, 306, 349
Watkins, 26, 161, 261, 279, 351
Watson, 54, 59, 81, 93, 140, 245, 312, 362
Watt, 157
Watt's Branch, 292
Watterston, 54, 215
Wattles, 84, 314
Watts, 90, 249, 345
Waugh, 138
Way, 95
Wayne, 55
Wayson, 58
Weaver, 55, 314
Webb, 1, 8, 55, 119, 169, 193, 351, 361
Weber, 153
Webster, 55, 168, 284
Weed, 55
Weeks, 32, 67, 222
Weens, 14
Weightman, 45
Weisiger, 191
Weitzer, 346
Welch, 294, 306, 359
Welling, 327
Wells, 26, 225, 236
Welsh, 163, 250, 296, 317, 343, 364
Wemple, 37
Wendell, 133
Wensley, 84
Werner, 29, 69, 260
Wesson, 333
West, 2, 55, 66, 131, 168, 173, 176, 197, 211, 277, 299, 341
West Point, 167
Westbury, 294
Westerfield, 236, 262, 266
Westinghouse, 30, 37
Westward, 103

Westwood, 220
Wever, 192
Whalen, 59, 355
Whaley, 158
Wharton, 137, 309
What's Left, 193
Whealey, 31
Wheat, 96
Wheatland, 301, 328
Wheatley, 10, 55, 83, 213, 251
Wheeler, 54, 55, 128, 129, 195, 198, 214, 222, 247, 277, 317, 330, 331, 360
Whelan, 54
Whemple, 30
Whilwright, 331
Whipple, 192
Whish, 200
White, 6, 8, 33, 35, 51, 54, 55, 65, 72, 74, 99, 104, 128, 161, 163, 192, 210, 272, 288, 328, 353, 368
White children recovered, 188
White Hall, 194
White Sulphur Springs, 130, 212
Whitehead, 81
Whitemore, 58, 183
Whiting, 23, 30, 112, 267, 291, 300
Whitley, 168
Whitlock, 55
Whitman, 202, 314
Whitmore, 55
Whitney, 149
Whiton, 139
Whittaker, 288
Whittingham, 194, 243
Whittington, 26
Whittlesey, 75, 128
Whitwright, 195
Whyte, 58, 126, 325
Wiber, 272
Wickham, 121
Wickizer, 365
Wickliffe, 267
Widdicombe, 297
Widdie, 273

Wife, 218
Wigg, 6, 94, 156
Wiggin, 43
Wight, 128, 129, 130, 236
Wilcox, 97, 106, 291
Wild, 54
Wilder, 5
Wiley, 191, 203, 362
Wilkes, 54, 358
Wilkins, 85
Willard, 13, 20, 35, 92, 165, 309, 321, 330, 334, 352
Willborne, 303
Willett, 54, 56, 58, 101
Williams, 7, 23, 24, 34, 53, 54, 55, 58, 59, 86, 89, 95, 96, 103, 106, 120, 124, 129, 137, 150, 160, 164, 168, 185, 194, 195, 219, 221, 222, 245, 247, 248, 259, 274, 296, 304, 306, 315, 322, 326, 329, 351, 359, 360
Williamsborough, 129
Williamson, 18, 20, 22, 59, 95, 284, 313
Willie, 19, 127
Willis, 99, 157, 188, 319
Willloughby, 233
Willner, 228
Wills, 215
Willson, 135, 145, 157
Wilmer, 70
Wilson, 21, 35, 54, 55, 57, 58, 67, 86, 103, 114, 115, 122, 128, 129, 130, 135, 136, 148, 163, 168, 170, 196, 218, 223, 238, 243, 251, 256, 257, 262, 282, 283, 297, 301, 302, 309, 342, 345
Wilson's Endeavor Enlarged, 63
Wilt, 190
Wiltberger, 54, 55, 129
Wiltse, 193
Wimsatt, 58
Winch, 341
Winchell, 317
Winder, 39, 45, 54, 55, 132, 175, 210, 213, 302, 331

Wingerd, 7, 245
Winkler, 9
Winn, 67, 129
Winningham, 368
Winsor, 166, 184
Winter, 106, 131, 359
Winterhalter, 119
Winthrop, 62
Wirt, 55, 154, 181, 203, 216, 218, 224, 266
Wise, 55, 58, 82, 85, 130, 207, 212, 230, 236, 262, 286, 330, 354, 356, 357
Wisham, 209
Withers, 84, 190, 207, 214
Witmer, 205, 367
Wm & Mary College, 70, 76, 85
Wold, 127
Wolf, 118
Wolley, 267
Wolling, 124
women of the Revolution, 341
Wonters, 43
Wood, 6, 7, 22, 32, 45, 54, 58, 90, 143, 147, 163, 186, 230, 249, 255, 356, 357, 362, 365
Woodbridge, 178
Woodbury, Conn, 226
Woodhull, 175
Woodland Cemetery, 361
Woods, 125, 158, 173
Woodside, 225
Woodward, 8, 54, 98, 130, 132, 173, 315, 352, 357
Woody, 54
Wool, 268
Wooley, 310
Woolford, 194
Woolridge, 135, 141, 142
Woolson, 123
Word, 354
Wordsworth, 77
Wore, 279
Worrell, 55
Worster, 284

Worth, 198, 223
Worthen, 356
Worthington, 29, 54, 99, 130, 361
Wright, 54, 55, 76, 81, 99, 102, 111, 112, 115, 145, 150, 198, 210, 218, 222, 242, 284, 303, 332, 353
Wroe, 10, 55
Wurdemann, 35
Wurtz, 95
Wyatt, 186
Wylie, 11, 124, 134
Wylly, 125, 155
Wyman, 55, 301
Wyvill, 123

Y

Yale, 97
Yale College, 236
Yancy, 309
Yarbrough, 188
Yarrow, 120, 185
Yates, 25, 36, 364
Yaw, 211
Yeager, 117
Yearwood, 32, 76, 93
Yeatman, 59
Yendall, 257
Yerger, 339
Yocum, 233
Young, 5, 11, 20, 24, 36, 43, 55, 59, 101, 129, 150, 154, 165, 166, 169, 171, 196, 219, 265, 278, 302, 321, 341, 345, 360, 369
Younger, 55
Yulee, 80

Z

Zang, 135
Zange, 55
Zantzinger, 280
Zappone, 1, 325
Zealy, 22
Zellin, 362
Zevely, 98
Zimmerman, 59, 86
Zuloaga, 81

Other Heritage Books by Joan M. Dixon:

National Intelligencer *Newspaper Abstracts*
Special Edition: The Civil War Years
Volume 1: January 1, 1861-June 30, 1863

National Intelligencer *Newspaper Abstracts*
Special Edition: The Civil War Years
Volume 2: July 1, 1863-December 31, 1865

National Intelligencer *Newspaper Abstracts*
Volume 1840 - Volume 1860

National Intelligencer *Newspaper Abstracts, 1838-1839*
National Intelligencer *Newspaper Abstracts, 1836-1837*
National Intelligencer *Newspaper Abstracts, 1834-1835*
National Intelligencer *Newspaper Abstracts, 1832-1833*
National Intelligencer *Newspaper Abstracts, 1830-1831*
National Intelligencer *Newspaper Abstracts, 1827-1829*
National Intelligencer *Newspaper Abstracts, 1824-1826*
National Intelligencer *Newspaper Abstracts, 1821-1823*
National Intelligencer *Newspaper Abstracts, 1818-1820*
National Intelligencer *Newspaper Abstracts, 1814-1817*
National Intelligencer *Newspaper Abstracts, 1811-1813*
National Intelligencer *Newspaper Abstracts, 1806-1810*
National Intelligencer *Newspaper Abstracts, 1800-1805*

www.ingramcontent.com/pod-product-compliance
Lightning Source LLC
Chambersburg PA
CBHW050830230426
43667CB00012B/1949